THROUGH THE CHAIRMAN'S EYES

THROUGH
THE CHAIRMAN'S
EYES

VIEWS FROM
COMPANY MEETING REPORTS
PUBLISHED IN

THE TIMES

DURING 1968

LONDON
TIMES NEWSPAPERS LIMITED
PRINTING HOUSE SQUARE
E.C.4

PRINTED FOR, AND PUBLISHED, BY
TIMES NEWSPAPERS LIMITED
PRINTING HOUSE SQUARE, LONDON, E.C.4.
1969

CONTENTS

CONTENTS

*Unless otherwise specified, all statements quoted
in the following chapters were made by the chairmen of the respective companies at the relevant
date. The date given in brackets immediately
after the name of a company is that of its annual
general meeting.*

PREFACE

THE criticism of the Government by company chairmen continued in their statements published in 1968. Even where the objectives of the Administration's actions were in general approved by business men, the measures taken to reach them were too often characterized as being too little, too late. Of no other action, or inaction, was this proved more true than of the Chancellor's delay in taking steps to reduce home consumption after devaluation in November, 1967, till the spring Budget in 1968. This left the way open for the notorious "buyers' spree," which besides its effect in contributing to the high level of imports also led to growing loss of confidence in the real value of paper money, by which it was in turn fed. As the cost of living went ahead, in spite of all that the Treasury could do in the way of controlling price rises, this lack of confidence was communicated to the gilt-edged market, which, declining as it had been for years, plunged to abysmal depths, the yield on War Loan, for example, rising above 8 per cent, a shocking index to the credit of the British Government.

However, the business world, faced by what it felt was a hostile Government, set itself to improve its efficiency and succeeded so well that many companies reporting in 1968 were able to announce higher profits notwithstanding the Government control of prices. All this is a much telescoped version of economic happenings in 1967-68. Chairmen reporting in this period complained of many other things besides price restrictions—the 50 per cent increase in Selective Employment Tax certainly did nothing to reconcile business men to this most hated of all recent impositions—as will be evident from a perusal of this book.

Except that a new chapter on devaluation is included, this, the twentieth annual volume in the series of "Through the Chairman's Eyes" runs on now familiar lines. The excerpts from company chairmen's statements published in 1968 which follow are chosen for their general interest as showing the lines along which the ideas of business were running. Most of the quotations on the leading topics of the day could be multiplied several times by confirmatory statements by other chairmen which there is not sufficient space to include. Thus the volume reflects faithfully the state of business opinion in 1968.

THE ECONOMIC BACKGROUND

IT would be difficult to find a period so full of extraordinary events affecting British companies as the year under review in this volume. MR. D. J. BARRON cited some of them, though by no means all, when he declared that since his last report *Rowntree and Company Limited* (June 14) had passed through a year into which had been concentrated severe prices and incomes control, a devaluation, the removal of resale price maintenance, an investigation by the Prices and Incomes Board and an increase in purchase tax—all these in addition to the routine problems of an international business. He paid a warm tribute to the skill and diligence of the 23,000 employees, on whom such a year inevitably had thrown additional burdens.

Having lost an Empire for the second time, Britain must find a new role, and LORD CLITHEROE in his statement (*The Times*, March 11) for *The Mercantile Investment Trust Limited* had no doubt what it was to be.

"We shall," he declared, "replace our lost Empire by ever-increasing trade and commerce. We must trade with all the world, with the new world as well as with the old. Never has the City of London worked harder than it is doing now. Already some 37 per cent of our overseas earnings come from invisible exports; from our shipping and civil aviation, our banking and insurance, our tourist business and the many services which the City of London renders to the world; these include the receipts from overseas investment in which Investment Trust Companies play so large a part. Only in seven of the last 175 years have our visible exports exceeded our imports: we have lived largely on our wits and must do so more than ever in the future.

"Our earlier empires owed their origin to our trade and commerce and our natural and proper desire to see law and order and good government in the less developed parts of the world in which we traded. Now with our backs to the wall we will extend our trade and commerce, serve the world and put Britain once again in her proper place. This can and must come about. The opportunity is there but can only be realized if there are reasonable incentives and if industry and commerce are not frustrated by ill-designed taxation and excessive interference by Government, which has plenty on its hands without trying to run everything in the country."

The past year had seen the supply of property investments and developments at home dwindle, mainly because of the uncer-

1

tainties caused by legislative measures in recent years, MR. DAVID E. WEBB told members of *The Artizans' & General Properties Company Limited* (June 19); and he went on to assert:

"Whilst we are continuing to obtain industrial developments, it is now extremely difficult in this country to find investments in shops or commercial property which are attractive to the company. Your Board is therefore intensifying its search abroad for worthwhile assets. But in that field too, efforts are hampered by Government restrictions on the free transference of funds. Indeed, successive Governments have browbeaten the populace into accepting the notion that any company showing increased profits is acting against the interests of the country; that senior executives looking for some financial incentive and encouragement to reward their efforts are upsetting the planned economy; and that Trades Union members trying to keep their wage structure at a level which will preserve their living standards are directly responsible for inflation. Meanwhile, those self same Governments, blameless in their own eyes, continue their own mad spending spree at an even higher level and are directly responsible for the inflation they seek to blame on others."

In dealing with the future prospects of *Hick, Hargreaves and Company Limited* (March 6) MR. G. F. DAVIES declared that they could not look for quick benefits from devaluation, nor could the group expect to prosper, however good its product might be, however effective its sales effort, unless the potential buyer had confidence that he too could prosper, not in snatching a short-term gain, but by making a long-term investment on which the return would not be mulcted by ill-advised administrative action. He continued:

"This is a fact of life often ignored by academics and politicians, who, having led sheltered lives themselves, are quite ignorant of how business is actually done. All we can do is to be ready to take advantage of every opportunity that offers, and the necessary preparation and training for this state of readiness is today one of the principal responsibilities of the Management, which we will discharge to the best of our ability.'

Business confidence has been so undermined in the last few years by Government action that signs of its return are sought with some desperation. However, a few chairmen professed to be able to discern something of the kind, among them MR. R. M. PERCIVAL, who informed members of *Hindson & Andrew Reid Limited* (October 17) that towards the end of the year the company began to notice a feeling of confidence which was translated into a growing order book. This had continued for a long enough period to give the board hope that the economic climate was more

favourable. He had to be careful in what he said in this connection as there was still a long way to go.

For *Argentine Southern Land Company Limited* (February 28) MR. KENNETH F. SUGGETT reiterated the criticism of the United Kingdom's fiscal policies as being "biased against this country's profitable investments made abroad in years gone by." He then gave this specific instance of how the United Kingdom Government's policy was throttling the company:

"The Board considered that an irrigation project at one of the company's estancias would increase the productivity of its land and therefore earnings. The cost, and I give approximate figures, would be about £100,000. The Argentine Government appreciates that schemes like this will help that country's economy and as a consequence it will (in addition to other most welcome assistance) allow a reduction of at least £80,000 in the company's liability for Argentine income tax, thus leaving your company to find less than £20,000 for the project. Under current circumstances the whole of the £80,000 would be taken in United Kingdom Corporation Tax. The United Kingdom Government has, under the present tax law, categorically refused our specific application for relief—even concessional or unilateral—despite the fact that if relief is not given and we therefore cannot afford to go ahead with the scheme, the United Kingdom Government will not get the £80,000 referred to above. In short, it costs the United Kingdom Government nothing to give a relief which would increase profits and eventually help the United Kingdom sterling reserves. Surely it is utterly illogical for our Government to give many millions of pounds yearly in aid to developing countries—for 1965 this aid totalled about £200m.—and yet refuse to give on a development project in Argentina the sort of relief for which your board has asked and which would not cost this country one single penny. It is scarcely believable that such crass and dangerous stupidity is possible under a British Government in such contrast to the Argentine Government's farsightedness over the kind of scheme the company has been considering. It is only too evident that more intelligent and less dangerous fiscal policies prevail abroad."

As chairman of *British American and General Trust Limited* (March 13) MR. G. P. S. MACPHERSON expressed his belief that the United States economy was expanding again after a year's sluggish performance, and that in Europe economic growth would also improve. This, he pointed out, was a favourable climate for an export-led revival of the British economy. He qualified this statement by the provisos that operating costs must be contained and that the necessary resources must be available for the export, import substitution and capital investment industries, and asserted:

"The provisos are, however, vital and necessitate both an acceptance that devaluation involves temporarily a reduction in the standard of living until it is redressed by higher productivity, and good economic management; neither of these is yet certain."

In his speech as President of the *Norwich Union Insurance Group* (May 7) MR. DESMOND E. LONGE, referring to an overseas tour, principally to Australia and New Zealand, from which he had recently returned, said:

"I was appalled and depressed beyond measure at the disparaging opinions I heard of this country; the failure to honour its word and to face up to its commitments, the loss of markets resulting so often through political ineptitude, and the lack of confidence in the stability of this country at present existing throughout so much of the world. One can but hope that the damage done to our standing in recent years can be repaired before the great fund of goodwill that exists towards the people of these islands is dissipated for all time."

That that part of the net assets of *Grampian Holdings Limited* represented by stocks and debtors less creditors had increased was stated by MR. ANDREW RINTOUL in his annual review (*The Times*, April 11), but though this was in effect financed by bank overdraft, he showed that it was the result of foresight; the relevant passage from his report is subjoined:

"To a large extent the rise in stocks was caused by some subsidiary companies taking early deliveries at pre-devaluation prices and certain other subsidiaries purchasing goods in advance of normal trading requirements to take advantage of the boom which they had very rightly anticipated would occur in the period before the Budget. The debtors were increased by an exceptionally high level of year-end trading by some subsidiaries and represent on the average 10 weeks of the full year's turnover by the group as against 8 weeks a year ago. I am glad to say that we have the full support of our Bankers, but naturally the improvement of our liquidity now has top priority."

On the other hand, MR. D. BUSSELL told shareholders in *Yatton Furniture Limited* in his statement (*The Times*, September 26) that the "so called pre-Budget buying spree" had very little effect on the subsidiary Avalon's profits as its order book was already full. He was able to report an increase in group profits of almost 25 per cent over the previous record figure of 1966–67.

Qualifying his view that *J. Brockhouse & Co. Limited* (December 20) should be able to show an overall improvement in results, MR. JOHN BROCKHOUSE had one reservation to make, and that was the grave uncertainty of the national position. About this he stated:

"I cannot convince myself that we are about to see an 'economic miracle' and what I fear is that the Government may restrict industrial expansion, in the belief that this will curtail demand on the home market and somehow reduce the burden of imports—needless to say, I believe this is a completely erroneous assumption. I am sure we have to expand our industrial activity by every means possible, if we are to have a hope of balancing our overseas payments. Reductions do not curb appetites, they tend to whet them. Neither do I think we are going to solve our problem by a plethora of committees, commissions and supervisory bodies which achieve little else than providing comfortable salaried positions for the elite and not only detract from the real issue of work and effort, but add substantially to overhead costs."

After referring to the greatly increased burden of taxation and allied charges, and stating that the total estimated net charge for S.E.T. alone in the hotels and licensed premises of *Scottish & Newcastle Breweries Limited* (September 5) would be just over £600,000 a year, SIR WILLIAM MCEWAN YOUNGER went on to complain of the vast amount of paper work thrown on company executives by Government requirements. He declared:

"Another deplorable feature of the past few years is the great, and increasing, amount of, for our purposes, wholly unproductive work which is required of us, and which occupies a substantial amount of the time of senior Directors and Executives. To give but one example: the reference of our industry to the Monopolies Commission has required our Finance Director to spend, in the last two years, the equivalent of fully three months of his time dealing with the innumerable facts and figures required. In this, and other similar references and investigations, all sense of priorities seems to have been lost. It will, no doubt, he argued that the Tied House system has defects, but what is beyond question is, firstly, that largely as a result we have a very high, and still rising, standard of licensed premises of all kinds, and, secondly, if defects do exist, they are wholly peripheral to the very grave economic and financial problems which confront this country to-day.

"There has, in fact, been built up a tremendous new apparatus of bureaucracy, both costly and time-consuming. What, beyond all the fine phrases, the great bulk of its operation achieves of actual benefit to the economy is certainly not apparent. Indeed, it is hard to see how it can be possible to achieve anything approaching an adequate rate of growth in the economy when its private sector, on which everything depends, is subjected to continually increasing burdens, interference, and dislocation."

SIR ERIC CLAYSON wryly observed in his statement for *Birming-*

ham Post & Mail Limited (December 20) that whenever things looked a little brighter it seemed to be necessary for the Government to tighten the screw again. The recent changes in hire purchase arrangements for motor cars, television sets and similar things, if they achieved their purpose, could not fail to affect the trading prospects of many businesses, including their own. Nevertheless, he had every hope that for the current year profits would be maintained.

The next quotation comes from the statement (*The Times*, April 18) by MR. H. J. VENNILS for *The International Investment Trust Limited*:

"There appears little prospect of any really substantial improvement in the private sector of industry in the U.K. when conditions generally are so largely influenced by political expediency. No free economy can function successfully if the rewards of enterprise are kept in check and if business and industrial growth is stultified by excessive legislation and controls. There must be a removal of disincentives and the restoration of positive spurs to increased efficiency and greater enterprise."

Many chairmen emphasized the need for modification of taxation policies in order to give incentives to greater productivity. Among them was MR. J. H. JACOBS of *John I. Jacobs & Company Limited* (May 3), who declared:

"It is a tragedy that in this country we have had and unbelievably still have successive governments and members of Parliament and other prominent public figures from all parties who either cannot or will not see that for an economy that works we must either have full dictatorship with the individual counting for nothing and allowed no freedom of choice which would be abhorrent to us all or the free market place of supply and demand with government interference and spending drastically reduced and taxation radically altered to give the vital incentives to those who wish to take business risks and who wish to work to better themselves, their families and their country. Either system would bring about the discipline and the latter the responsibility that is now missing. Indeed the Government should be striving to reduce taxation and not be working out ways of increasing the burden. It is obviously quite useless to take money out of the pockets of private industry and individuals by higher taxation unless this money is saved. If it is subsequently spent by the Government it is just as inflationary as if it had not been taxed away in the first place. At least during the 'thirteen wasted years' the standard rate of income tax was re-reduced from 9*s*. 6*d*. to 7*s*. 9*d*. in the pound, no mean feat during a period of inflation and one during which money continued its historic role of losing its value.

"The foregoing would, of course, compel the inefficient and

6

lazy to play their part, leaving the community to support only those people unable to help themselves. A kind of half baked, mixed up, in-between solution such as we have had and such as we still have is to my mind always going to be doomed to failure. Above all, I feel governments should be concerned with maintaining confidence. This can only be done with honest and consistent policies enabling new investment decisions to be made with the knowledge that when the plans come to fruition, fresh legislation will not have made nonsense of them."

The Government, said SIR REAY GEDDES of *The Dunlop Company Limited* (May 13), had understandably felt it necessary, as a temporary expedient, to be more than normally selective in new overseas investments and for companies to raise money abroad, wherever this could be done economically. Dunlops, he asserted, had long pursued such a policy, and hitherto had not been able to point to really attractive opportunities which had been missed because of this restraint. He continued:

"But that is no longer true. Furthermore, an active policy for industrial investment in the countries which are growing faster than our own is essential if we are not to lose ground in competitive strength or to miss opportunities which may not recur. The danger is not so much in the short-term expedients as it is in the body of doctrine which is then developed to justify them as a carefully thought out long-term policy. It is hard to reconcile the discouragement of overseas investment with current policy towards Europe, let alone traditional relations with Commonwealth countries, and harder still for a company like Dunlop to feel confident that we will be permitted to back up an investment or a partnership after it has been arranged.

"What are our facts? In the last eight years, £63m. has come from overseas in the form of dividends, technical aid fees, and from exports of machinery and raw materials, compared with net new investment from the U.K. of only £5m. We have therefore contributed some £58m. in foreign exchange in this period of eight years—over £7m. per annum on this account alone. In addition we made direct exports of finished products amounting to £26m. last year.

"The investment dollar premium, the so-called voluntary programme, and the bias in taxation cannot be removed overnight, but one of the first priorities as our balance of payments improves might well be to encourage those companies which need to undertake profitable investment overseas. In this connection the Chancellor could help by enlarging the present overspill tax relief on foreign income so that it is more directly related to current and future income. As a first step this relief, which will otherwise start to taper off, should be made permanent."

7

One serious handicap under which holders of American stocks suffered was mentioned by SIR EDMUND HUDSON of *The Scottish Widows' Fund and Life Assurance Society* (March 12), who was only one of many to draw attention it. This was the provision whereby one-quarter of the dollars received in respect of sales had to be surrendered to the Treasury without receiving the market premium, at that time in the region of 30 per cent. He commented that it was perhaps debatable whether or not this impost was justifiable in the case of outright sales but that there was certainly no justification whatsoever when an American stock was sold and the proceeds used to purchase another American stock. In effect, he pointed out, the regulation in question imposed a tax on investment mobility.

MR. GEORGE FLETCHER of the *Association of Unit Trust Managers* (February 22) said that the total membership of the association had risen to 117 trusts, that 1967 was a very active year for the movement, net new investment of £83·9m. being higher than in any previous year except 1966; between the end of 1959 and of 1967, he added, the total value of funds had risen from less than £200m. to £853·6m. He also pointed out that the industry had been quick to devise and promote new savings facilities; "one of the most rapidly growing developments is the unit-linked insurance policy."

Another chairman who referred to the great growth of unit or open end trusts in the United Kingdom was SIR DENYS LOWSON. Addressing the annual meeting of the *National Group of Unit Trusts* (October 29), he claimed that the total amount invested in these funds was approximately £1,304m., but there was obviously considerable scope for increased unit trust savings in this country. He based this conclusion on the figures of the corresponding movement in the United States, where in the 27 years since 1940 the net assets had increased approximately 100 times and the number of unit holders' accounts 27 times, while the corresponding increases in this country were only just over 11 times and 4 times respectively.

Another chairman who confidently expected to see unit trusts becoming the most popular and widely used form of savings was MR. EDWARD DU CANN, of *Martins Unicorn Limited* (May 16), a majority interest in which had been acquired during the past year by Martins Bank. He hoped the Government would introduce legislation in the next session to implement the recommendations of the Jenkins Committee, and provide, in a new Unit Trust Act, "a satisfactory legal framework for the future." The Government's fiscal policies, too, should give practical encouragement to savings, which would be wiser and happier than "the sterility of ever increasing direct taxation."

That 1967 brought a rise in the value of the investments of the *Second British Assets Trust Limited* (March 7) of approximately

50 per cent, the largest percentage rise in any of the last 20 years of the company's history, was asserted by MR. ALASTAIR C. BLAIR, who went on to claim:

"A rise of this magnitude demonstrates the advantages of investment trusts as investment media for private individuals. It is perhaps instructive to consider how this has been achieved. It has been our consistent policy to look for opportunities of growth throughout the world and in recent years we have had over half our funds invested in North America. This policy has proved of great value to our shareholders who could not easily have invested in North America for themselves. I would emphasize, however, that this policy has also been of great value to the country. The dollars from our American *income* over the last 20 years, which have been sold to the Bank of England at current rates of exchange, have more than paid for the *capital* cost to the country of *all* our dollar investments. The country is, therefore, now receiving our substantial annual dollar income from an investment which had cost the country's dollar reserves nothing. In addition, as the capital value of our dollar investments grows, so do the second line reserves of the country grow. Academic economists advising the government have often attacked portfolio investment overseas but it would be truer to regard investment trusts, and particularly Scottish ones, as among the greatest dollar earners for the country."

For the *British Empire Securities and General Trust Limited* (December 18) MR. V. S. LAURIE pointed out that it would be possible to achieve an immediate increase in income by the sale of low-yielding equities and the purchase of further high-yielding prior charges, but declared that in face of the threat of continued inflation this course was considered to be imprudent. Incidentally, he was among the company chairmen who referred to contributions to political parties; he used these words:

"We have no great faith in commercial benefits from political parties but we have made a small contribution, not large enough to require publication, to the party which we hope will do least harm to your company's affairs."

Reporting that the asset value of the Ordinary shares of *New York and General Trust Limited* (April 3) had risen by 40 per cent on the year, SIR ROBERT ADEANE said:

"Formerly, high share market values would have followed good company trading results and a sharp increase in valuation one year would indicate higher revenue for an investment trust in the following year. This does not altogether follow today for a major factor in the market rise has been the fear of further erosion in the buying power of the pound. This fear was justi-

fied by devaluation last November and the subsequent period of government inaction. The recent Budget Medicine constituted an attempt to rectify the position. It has been said that the medicine should be strong enough to cure the country's financial ills, but the speed of recovery surely depends upon the confidence the doctor can generate and the will of the patient to endure the treatment. Confidence is not generated by the example of unabated government expenditure and substantial price increases by nationalized undertakings. The patient's reactions are awaited with interest and some anxiety."

In common with all industry, *Maynards Limited* (November 21) would incur heavy expense in changing over to the new decimal currency, stated MR. J. DOUGLAS MAYNARD; the board were closely studying all the implications. At present, he added, there was an extensive trade in unit lines costing from a penny to sixpence, and the directors were very concerned at the inflexibility of the new coinage in the range. "The Decimal Currency Board," he commented, "seem completely indifferent to this problem."

As a tailpiece to this chapter there are appended the remarks on inflation made by MR. P. L. FLEMING at the annual meeting of *The Omnium Investment Company Limited* (March 14):

"I suppose there has always been inflation. One has only to look at the price of pigs in the Domesday Book to see that this sort of thing has been happening all along. But what is quite new is how fast inflation is going and the way people seem to be resigned to the probability that it will go faster still. Now if one looks at the seven ages of man one sees that there are ages at which he would be wise to take any opportunity of preserving and increasing his capital and other ages at which he needs all the income he can get. The conventional capitalization of an investment trust, with safe debentures, comfortable preference shares and mildly adventurous ordinary shares, used to offer the necessary range of choice. But inflation has made nonsense of all that; and the basic principles of our capital structure will have to be incorporated into a more subtle and sophisticated design if we are going to function as a modern savings medium. Some companies have already experimented with two-tier capitalization, giving the shareholder a very clear choice between building his capital and increasing his income. There appear to have been some teething troubles, and no doubt there will be legislative difficulties to overcome—if only because all governments which owe their position to electoral bribery are instinctively allergic to the financial independence of the citizens. But I think we shall have to evolve some scheme of this sort if we are to continue as heretofore to receive shareholders' money with the confidence that we can look after it to their satisfaction."

10

DEVALUATION

D EVALUATION of sterling in November, 1967, naturally was one of the subjects to which most chairmen referred as an influence upon their companies' sales and profits. Companies which take a significant part in the country's export effort stood to gain by reason of their greater competitiveness, but many chairmen had to point out that increases in costs over which they had no control were already wiping out part of the selling price advantage which devaluation had produced. Companies with businesses or investments in countries that had not devalued their currencies gained from the increases in sterling value of remittances to the United Kingdom, to say nothing of the higher sterling equivalent of their foreign net assets. On the other hand, companies more or less dependent on raw materials from overseas suffered an immediate increase in costs, quite apart from the higher charges for wages and salaries and for various services which were common to most of British industry or commerce.

SIR DENYS LOWSON in his address for *Cairnton Investment Trust Limited* (January 19) explained the theory of how devaluation should work as follows:

"Basically our present problem is the inability to expand the economy without running the current account into a large deficit. In this connection the only permanent solution is to increase the volume of our exports and here the recent devaluation of Sterling has provided a great opportunity: this should give British industry a price advantage of approximately 8 per cent in world markets, after allowing for the increase in the cost of our imported raw materials which go into exports, the increase in Corporation tax and the removal of S.E.T. payments to manufacturers. In addition to the deflationary measures brought in at the time of devaluation cuts in public expenditure amounting to £716m. over the next two years have already been announced, all this being part of a plan to shift resources from the domestic front to the requirements not only of exports but equally important import substitution and Private Investment.

"The prospects for 1968 therefore depend on whether the latest measures are successful and the ability of British Industry to take advantage of the new situation without any excessive rise in costs."

What MR. ALASTAIR C. BLAIR of *Second British Assets Trust Limited* (March 7) described as the humiliation of devaluation marked, he declared, the end of 20 years of national illusion

"during which as a nation we have all demanded a standard of living which we were not prepared to earn in the competitive world." He continued:

"Successive governments have tried in turn policies of stop and go, and of freeze and squeeze, but have never tackled the fundamental resistance to change which has characterized all sections of the community. 1968 promises to be a hard year for all of us, but we must hope and have faith that it will see a national rebirth springing from a desire to take advantage of the opportunities of the future instead of looking back to the glories of the past."

The period of severe economic restraint had continued, and during the year under review, declared LORD ROTHERMERE of *Associated Newspapers Limited* (July 24), not only had further restraints and controls been imposed, but the country had also had to endure the effects of devaluation—"a punishment inflicted upon it as a result of economic folly."

In the course of a careful analysis of the various ways in which *British-American Tobacco Company Limited* (March 14) would probably be affected by devaluation MR. D. R. N. CLARKE said:

"In respect of the companies which operate in countries whose currencies were not devalued there will in the first place be a substantial capital profit in the Group accounts as a result of the revaluation in sterling of the net current assets of these companies. The profit estimated at a little over £30m. is, of course, in no way related to current trading nor is it available for dividends. It will appear in the consolidated accounts as an addition to Reserves in the Group Balance Sheet, but the addition may be reduced by charges against reserves in the event of overseas currencies being devalued against sterling in the course of the year. These charges against Group reserves have been a regular feature in our accounts in recent years. There has already been a devaluation of the Brazilian cruzeiro since the 18th November."

Devaluation, LORD NELSON OF STAFFORD asserted in his review for *The English Electric Company Limited* (March 27), "does no more than give us an opportunity to restore our credit abroad." To do this, he added, it must be shown that we were prepared to work more effectively and that the Government was prepared to resist claims to improve living standards until they were earned and could be afforded. He went on:

"The country depends on industry for the greater part of its overseas earnings. All our efforts must be directed to improving these earnings. In 1967 English Electric obtained £130m. of export orders, the great majority prior to devaluation. At the same time arms embargoes and vetoes on South Africa and other

countries have lost this country many £m. worth of export orders for military equipment and other capital goods. Many of these orders would have come to English Electric. One must ask whether the country can afford doctrinaire policies with such a serious effect on industry and our economic position.

"The Government measures associated with devaluation including withdrawal of the export rebate, mean that the apparent devaluation price advantage of 14·3% is reduced to a figure of between 6% and 8%. Products sold from stock or with short manufacturing cycles are only a small proportion of our exports, and in this field we shall make as much use as possible of any export price advantage. However, the greater part of our export orders are capital goods with deliveries extending well into 1969. Earnings on these will be affected by the loss of S.E.T. recoveries and by any increases in costs arising from devaluation. It is only after mid-1969 that we shall start deliveries of capital goods ordered since devaluation and by then advantages in volume or price must be offset by increases in the cost of imported materials and by any increases in wages and salaries."

Emphasizing the importance of fostering export trade, MAJOR W. E. GURRY in his statement (*The Times*, March 29) for *Johnson & Slater Limited* declared that devaluation was not the simple remedy that corrected all the problems in export. It was a weapon of many edges. Agents must work harder to secure a larger share of the market for the same reward, or manufacturers must augment their commissions to make up for a devalued pound. Freight rates were increased, he added, and imported raw materials, fuel oil and transport all became more costly and were likely to remain so in the foreseeable future.

LORD RANK forecast higher flour and bread prices in his statement for *Ranks Hovis McDougall Limited* (January 25), as the following excerpt shows:

"Devaluation will bring cost increases throughout the Group, particularly as regards imported grain. We shall endeavour, wherever possible, to absorb these increases by continued progress towards higher levels of productivity. Costs which cannot be absorbed in this way, however, will unfortunately have to be passed on by way of price increases. It follows, therefore, that the price of flour and bread will have to go up."

It appeared to MR. J. A. F. BINNY of *The Law Debenture Corporation Limited* (April 19) that the forced devaluation of sterling had not been sufficiently foreseen and planned for in advance by the Government, and that stock markets were still reflecting the fears of continued inflation. The situation was not a healthy one, he declared, but "at present good Ordinary shares, well spread, seem to offer the best prospects."

13

In the course of an uninhibited attack on Government policies, SIR HALFORD REDDISH of *Rugby Portland Cement Company Limited* (May 24) included this paragraph:

"I find exhortations 'to make devaluation work' or 'to reap the benefits of devaluation' particularly distasteful, since by implication we are showing no sense of shame at having welshed on our creditors. Rather should the appeal be to work hard to re-establish our honour and our good name in the world; but that calls for the type of leadership which is so sadly lacking in this country today."

Another chairman who singled out the slogan "making devaluation work" for comment was MR. D. W. MARTIN, who in his statement (*The Times*, May 23) for *Gill & Duffus Limited* described it as a phrase which seemed to suggest that devaluation was a wise and far-sighted act of policy.

While export potential might be better as a result of devaluation, DR. H. SIMON of *Evode Holdings Limited* (February 27) considered it deplorable that such action became necessary, and he thought that the country as a whole, as well as individuals, would have to pay a heavy price.

Pressure on retail profit margins as a result of devaluation was forecast by MR. F. L. CHAPLIN of *F. W. Woolworth and Co. Limited* (March 8) in this paragraph:

"The main problems in 1968 will arise from the increased cost of goods and services as the result of devaluation which, to some extent, has already taken place and which, in the longer term, is likely to affect almost all forms of expenditure. We anticipate pressure on profit margins which will be countered by a determined policy of sales expansion based on offering attractive merchandise at competitive prices and the most efficient economy in controllable expense."

Devaluation overshadowed all, asserted MR. P. N. M. RUDDER of *Malgavita Limited* (February 13), for the company's principal product lines depended on imported raw materials; in turn, its customers, the bakers, also depended on other imports. "We are endeavouring," he added, " to keep our increases in selling prices to a minimum, but we may well find that the eventual consumer will reduce his total demand."

Another chairman who already had to record increased costs as a result of devaluation was MR. H. J. HEINZ of the *H. J. Heinz Company Limited*, who in his annual review (*The Times*, August 16) stated:

"Already the increased costs arising from devaluation are pressing hard on profit margins beyond the extent that a company can balance with improved efficiency. We have, therefore, been compelled to raise prices on a selective basis. We have

always prided ourselves in being able through operating economies and improved productivity to restrict price increases to an
absolute minimum and the latter have been well below the food
index as a whole. This will continue to be our policy."

Following devaluation *BPB Industries Limited* (July 31) was
affected on the one hand by higher costs and on the other by unexpected increased competition in the home market from overseas
producers. This is made plain in the following excerpt from the
statement of MR. R. S. JUKES:

"The main impact of the devaluation of sterling in November
1967 has not yet been reflected in the results of our United
Kingdom subsidiaries but there are already signs that the so-
called benefits of this step are having unexpected results on
costs—for instance, our paper and paperboard plants which
partly depend upon imported pulp, not only felt the immediate
impact of devaluation by way of higher prices for pulp but also
experienced increased competition in the home market from
finished products from Scandinavia and Canada. These imported
products were not increased in price to cover the full effect of
devaluation."

Devaluation would affect *The British Oxygen Company Limited*
(February 28) in diverse ways, it appeared from MR. J. S. HUT-
CHISON's review. It would increase the value of the company's
share of the overseas companies' profits; on the assumption that
these profits and all other things were to remain unchanged the
improvement, because of the new exchange rates, would be about
£1m. In United Kingdom trading, on the other hand, the group
would have to recover the increased cost of imported raw materials
which it used extensively, such as carbide and copper, along with
many other costs, while absorbing the loss of the greater part of
S.E.T. premium. The overall pattern, he averred, was upsetting
and would bring need for some adjustment of the company's prices.

In his statement (*The Times*, May 30) for *Coats Patons Limited*
MR. CHARLES W. BELL made this pronouncement on devaluation:

"To those of us who spend our working lives in foreign
business, some of the public pronouncements immediately
following devaluation appeared distressingly naive. Every individual company has differing problems. Within an individual
company each market has different characteristics requiring
different treatment. This is a complex operation to be handled
by experts. Rightly or wrongly the Government re-phased or
was forced to re-phase the trading climate with devaluation.
Thereafter it must leave executive action to those most closely
concerned and most knowledgeable. Sufficient in our own case
to say that measures have been taken to secure maximum
advantage from the change in exchange rates."

15

Devaluation of the £ in November, 1967, declared SIR JOHN BROWN in his survey (*The Times*, August 21) for *Metal Traders Limited*, triggered off a whole series of doubts about the ultimate validity of currencies which threatened at one moment to plunge the trading nations into financial chaos. In these conditions it was not surprising, Sir John asserted, that people holding paper money fled for cover, "one of the most popular shelters being the purchase of commodities, particularly those which are non-perishable, such as metals." He then described what the future might hold given no fears of currency changes:

"It does appear that if there were today no fears of currency changes, many of the commodities in which your company trades would almost certainly be priced lower than they actually are. The fact is that political and monetary considerations dominate markets to the exclusion of economic factors and while it may at present seem unrealistic to look to the day when considerations of supply and demand will dominate, there is no doubt that, if it were so, it would render much easier my task of indicating prospects. As it is, at this stage in our financial year it is quite impossible to indicate the likely outcome, although there is an apparent increase in the level of production of manufactured goods and a somewhat steadier tone in sterling, particularly in the forward positions, as compared with the situation only a few weeks ago. It is of prime importance that the position of sterling as a major trading currency should be maintained. It would be impossible for a company such as this to avail itself of trading opportunities on the scale to which it is accustomed and for which its organization is geared, if it were not in a position to rely on an international currency acceptable to the world trading community."

After announcing that exports of *Storey Brothers and Company Limited* with an increase of 4 per cent in 1967 created a new record, the chairman in his annual statement (*The Times*, June 4) declared that devaluation gave the group "the opportunity to be either more competitive or more profitable, according to the circumstances prevailing."

For *S. & W. Berisford Limited* (February 8) MR. A. BERISFORD pinpointed the higher cost of living which must be one of the results of devaluation. He stated:

"In November, 1967, the pound was devalued, and shareholders may ask how this will affect their company. Handling as many commodities as we do, it is impossible to give a general reply. It is certain, however, that any goods imported from those countries who have not similarly devalued their currency will cost more. It is possible that certain countries might find difficulty in competing with countries who have devalued and might

16

be forced to reduce their prices unless other outlets can be found, but as almost all our products are what might be termed basic foodstuffs and not luxury items, it is unlikely to affect your company's trading, dealing as we do with all parts of the world. It is certain, however, that devaluation must increase the overall price of imported foods and thus raise the cost of living."

SIR GEORGE HARVIE-WATT informed members of *The Monotype Corporation Limited* (March 19) that the immediate effect of devaluation on the company, although favourable, was unlikely to be substantial. He went on to cite some of the disadvantages which hindered British exporters in seeking to obtain or increase overseas markets:

"It will be realized that the ability of exporters to benefit fully from the effect of devaluation in those countries which have not devalued has been offset to some extent by the measures announced simultaneously with devaluation, namely the removal of the Export Rebate, the cancellation of the premium element of the Selective Employment Tax refund, an increase of $6\frac{1}{4}\%$ in the amount levied for Corporation Tax, and an 8% Bank Rate. To these must be added the increased costs of our organizations abroad. Nevertheless we have been able to pass on some benefits to customers in lower prices.

"I said last year that in the confused state of our economic affairs, it would be unwise to make any prophecy about the immediate future. What I said then still holds good today and the main considerations are still close control of costs with increased confidence in the economy at home and greater freedom from artificial barriers abroad. I think that with exports running at 73% of production, we have done well in a difficult year. We are broadening our base of activity both in variety of products and development of markets and will take advantage of every opportunity which arises."

Although competition encountered by *General Refractories Group Limited* in the export field was more severe than ever, SIR GEORGE BRIGGS stated in his annual review (*The Times*, March 28) that the group's export sales were of a very similar value to those of the previous year. After devaluation it was found necessary to increase sterling prices, but nevertheless he added that the net effect was that the great majority of the company's products were offered at lower prices in terms of local currencies.

Within days of the devaluation of the £ sterling, declared SIR CHRISTOPHER CHANCELLOR of *The Bowater Paper Corporation Limited* (April 24), the price of woodpulp imported from Scandinavia and Canada was increased by 16·6 per cent. Price increases for United Kingdom paper and board followed later, but only to the extent of 8 to 12 per cent. The price of imported paper was

17

increased only by the same percentages as were applied by the home industry. The result was, he asserted, that the United Kingdom paper industry faced higher imported raw material costs with no relief whatsoever from the competition of imports of the finished product. Bearing in mind the importance of the group's overseas operations, however, he thought devaluation on balance would be beneficial to Bowaters.

The pricing policy after devaluation of *Hoover Limited* (April 2) in export markets is the subject of the following quotation from MR. F. N. MANSAGER'S statement:

"Devaluation of sterling will undoubtedly help us in our efforts to regain a more competitive position, and our pricing policies have been actively reviewed in the light of present and future marketing conditions. However, the advantages of devaluation on the prices of our products destined for overseas markets, will be considerably less than the full amount of the fall in the value of the pound would suggest, in view of the cancellation of the export rebate and the certain increase in the cost of raw materials.

"In considering our pricing policies, therefore, we are adopting varying approaches depending on the intensity of competition, giving the full benefit of devaluation in some countries for price reductions and increased promotion, and less emphasis in other areas in which the price structure is less competitive. We believe that the increase in trade, which we hope will result from these policies, will pave the way to increased sales and greater profitability in the long run."

For *The "Shell" Transport and Trading Company Limited* (May 2) MR. D. H. BARRAN pointed out that one of the effects of devaluation was to produce an increase in group net income expressed in sterling. He explained that an appropriation for additional depreciation was made in 1967, and would continue to be made in future, "in order to correct what would otherwise be a misleading appearance in the level of group profits." He continued:

"After making this appropriation the balance of 1967 net income was £30m. higher than in 1966, approximately £5m. of which was attributable to the higher sterling values of the income of companies operating in countries which did not devalue in November. In 1968, both the appropriation for additional depreciation and the residual effect of devaluation will naturally apply to twelve months' trading and will therefore be proportionately higher."

Although fabrics produced by *John Bright and Brothers Limited* (July 3) were widely exported in the form of finished goods produced by home trade customers, MR. I. M. L. D. FORDE stated, direct exports had hitherto formed only a small proportion of the

company's sales. Devaluation, however, had presented Brights with greater opportunities in this field, "and we have already secured substantial orders."

In his statement (*The Times*, April 1) for *Anglo-International Investment Trust Limited* MR. F. HOCK declared that devaluation of the £ had given British industry a great new opportunity in export markets. With reasonable growth in the United States and the leading European economies, the country should experience an export-led recovery, he forecast.

Devaluation of the £, declared MR. J. M. A. PATERSON, had undoubtedly greatly improved the competitive position abroad of *The Bifurcated and Tubular Rivet Company Limited* (May 9), and he saw encouraging signs that the company's exports during the current year would increase substantially.

BANKERS' FORUM

B ANK chairmen reporting early in 1968 naturally gave prominence in their annual statements to the devaluation of sterling
in November, 1967, which almost without exception they
referred to as a serious defeat for the country that must have un-
pleasant consequences. The bankers also outlined the policies
that should be followed if the opportunities in the export field provided by devaluation were to be secured. Other topics discussed
in their statements included the report of the Prices and Incomes
Board on bank charges and kindred matters, some of the recommendations in which the chairmen were inclined to treat with reserve. The Government restrictions on the freedom of bankers to
extend credit, and even, indirectly, on the location of their head
offices, were mentioned. So were the questions of banking hours
and Saturday opening, of possible competition from the Post
Office Giro, the growing use of cheque cards, the increase—as
much as 76 per cent for one bank—in medium- and longer-term
lending for export sales, the extension of the clearing banks' activities to the merchant banking and overseas banking fields by the
formation of jointly owned companies or the acquisition of existing enterprises. And of more than domestic interest were the
massive bank mergers, of which that between Barclays, Lloyds
and Martins was later negatived by the Government on the finding
of the Monopolies Commission, though Barclays was allowed to
acquire Martins.

CLEARING BANKS

For the reason that the projected merger of Barclays and
Lloyds, with Martins thrown in, was not mooted until after publication of MR. JOHN THOMSON's statement (*The Times*, January
17) for *Barclays Bank Limited*, he did not refer in it to the amalgamation. Apart from matters of mainly domestic interest to the
bank's shareholders, he did comment on a number of topics of
more general concern, of which the following extract is an example:

"The devaluation of the 18th November is no longer news.
Authoritative pronouncements before that date should nonetheless be remembered: devaluation would amount to default
or welshing on our obligations; it would cure nothing; and the
so-called "breathing space" would be an excuse for lack of
urgency. The first assertion remains true but it is vital that we
prove the second and the third to be false. While it is the future

which matters, it is nonetheless neither reassuring to our international creditors nor comforting to those who have suffered grievously to gloss over the fact that devaluation, inevitable though it may have become, involved honourable men in prevarication and inflicted severe trading and personal losses. It is a serious matter when prudent merchants, whose enterprise is vital to our economy, are unable to hedge their risks. It is a matter of opinion whether the pound was overvalued before mid-November last, but we must, by paying our way, contrive that we are spared the hardships and anxieties of a nation whose people have lost faith in their currency. Against such a background it is understandable that there is sometimes criticism that the earnings of the Bank should benefit from the abnormally high interest rates which so often flow from the nation's misfortunes. However, the true gain is now somewhat less than may be popularly imagined; the increasing trend in the proportion of our credit balances on interest-bearing accounts is such that an increase in interest charged is now more closely matched by an increase in interest allowed, whilst we continue to provide export and other special credits on low fixed rates. Higher money market earnings are eaten into by higher provisions in times of stringency and a probable depreciation in the market value of fixed interest investment. It is in fact an appropriate time to endeavour to build up reserves.

"Severe limits have been imposed on our lending. Our first priority must be to honour arrangements which have been negotiated but not yet fully used. This in itself, despite high interest rates, could prove to be no mean task if the economy starts to move forward, since in recent times of uncertainty the margin between limits and lendings has become abnormally wide and is now over 45%. Once again the hope must be expressed that the arbitrary ceiling on advances fixed by a chance figure on a particular day should replaced by some other measure, if one is needed, at the earliest possible moment. The present system is directly hostile to the spirit of competition which we are all urged to promote."

At the annual meeting of *Lloyds Bank Limited* (February 17) MR. HARALD PEAKE remarked that ever since 1918 the banks had been given to understand that the authorities would in no circumstances allow any of the Big Five banks to amalgamate with each other. It was not until November, 1967, that Martins Bank announced it was prepared to consider proposals from other banks to acquire its shares; and on January 25, 1968, Mr. Peake said, Lloyds submitted proposals to acquire Martins' shares. He continued:

"It came as a tremendous surprise to us to hear on the following day that the Bank of England and the Treasury had

approved the amalgamation of the fourth and fifth largest British banks. Not unnaturally this great change in policy on the part of the authorities prompted as we believe by the Report of the Prices and Incomes Board on Bank Charges, caused the Directors of the first and third largest British banks to immediately reconsider their position. On Monday January 29 we were informed that Barclays and ourselves were the only two banks to make proposals for the acquisition of Martins shares. There appeared to be no great difference between the estimated value of the proposals. Both banks had been given until Tuesday, February 6, to revise their proposals if they so wished.

"It was between January 29 and February 6 that Barclays and ourselves considered the new policy of the authorities in regard to the large banks, and reached the conclusion after consultation with our Directors that an amalgamation of our two banks, with the addition of Martins, would be not only in the national interest but also in the interest of our shareholders, our staff and our customers After a series of conferences between representatives of the three banks, and the Bank of England and also with the Treasury, the decision to recommend the shareholders to approve the amalgamation of the three banks was announced at a press conference held at the Stock Exchange on Thursday, February 8."

Simultaneously, the Board of Trade announced that the proposals had been referred to the Monopolies Commission, which, Mr. Peake pointed out, was asked to report on them within six months. In the event, though he obviously could not predict any such outcome, the Commission reported in the negative.

While in broad national affairs 1967 ended in the grave disappointment of devaluation, SIR ARCHIBALD FORBES of the *Midland Bank Limited* (February 16) declared that for the banks as business undertakings it was a period of constructive development, in which the Midland played a leading part.

"We have," he stated, "embarked upon major changes in our organization and structure, changes that are noteworthy because they follow a course distinct from that indicated in the report of the National Board for Prices and Incomes on Bank Charges, published last May. With all appreciation of the efforts of the Board to indicate other paths for development in banking, most of them thoroughly explored in years gone by, I for one have substantial reservations as to the validity of the main assumptions and arguments upon which the Board bases its recommendations. In truth, these doubts are shared over a wide field, but in any event we in the joint stock banks would not feel free to carry forward some of the recommendations without the concurrence of the authorities because of the implications for the whole of Britain's monetary arrangements. Incidentally,

22

it is hard to reconcile the brave call from the Board to the banks to evolve as commercial undertakings, and at the same time the Board's acceptance of the existing cash and liquidity ratios in the interest of monetary regulation, the extension of these to other lending institutions, and possibly the taking of reserve powers to limit deposit rates.

"The views of the banks have been conveyed to the appropriate authorities, and generally I do not propose to develop our arguments here; nor do I consider it proper that I should do so at this stage. However, I must remark that part at least of the Board's analysis as it related to the supposed effects on the clearing banks of the activities of other institutions does not command wide acceptance among those who give these matters continuous study. It is also worthy of note, that in so far as deposit moneys are open to competitive bidding, then the Midland —like other clearing banks—has not been idle. Indeed, at the end of last year, deposits held by our wholly-owned subsidiaries, other than the affiliated banks in Scotland and Ireland, amounted to £154m. while those of Midland and International Banks stood at over £260m., including sums held in foreign currencies. Thus around £420m. had been collected at competitive rates through side-doors, so to speak, or about one-fifth of the total for deposits entering by the front door of the Midland Bank itself.

"As to the aspect of banking operations that was specifically referred to the Board, namely 'the system and level of charging customers', its findings were far from critical. Broadly, said the Board, 'it does not seem that the actual level of charges could be described as unreasonable'. Even this admission is qualified, however, and here again the comments are not altogether consistent."

Reference was made by MR. D. J. ROBARTS in his statement to the removal of *National Provincial Bank Limited* (February 15) to Drapers Gardens.

"As most shareholders will know," he stated, "we had laid careful and imaginative plans for rebuilding our Head Office at 15 Bishopsgate. Surrounding property was acquired at considerable cost and preparations were well advanced to give us what would have been one of the finest office buildings in the City. Just as we were about to start development, restrictions were imposed and we were forced to seek alternative accommodation. Fortunately, this was available in Drapers Gardens but only at a high rent. In the meantime we continue to use the old buildings at 15 Bishopsgate for important, but secondary, purposes.

"I am glad to report that the move from 15 Bishopsgate to Drapers Gardens of most of our executive and administrative

23

departments went extremely smoothly and reflected the greatest credit on all concerned. But, as we look out from our windows on the new building going on all around us, it hardly seems equitable that our own plans were so badly frustrated."

For the *Westminster Bank Limited* (February 14) MR. DUNCAN STIRLING stated that besides devaluation the London clearing banks had also to deal with an unprecedented succession of other events.

"These included," he continued, "the evolving phases of the squeeze and the freeze comprised in the Government's economic policy; the Report of the Prices and Incomes Board on Bank Charges; the new Companies Act; the setting up of the Bank Giro system; completion of plans for automation of the Clearing House; negotiations for financing shipbuilding exports on special terms and renewal of the existing export finance scheme; the attempt to establish a national negotiating system between banks and their staffs; strike action by a section of the staffs in certain places; and protracted discussion of banking hours. "In Westminster Bank, besides being concerned in all the foregoing, we entered the Unit Trust field jointly with Hambros Bank, and launched in London with four large overseas banks the International Commercial Bank, to undertake medium-term finance. We let the contracts for the latest 'third generation' computer equipment which is planned to serve all our branches by 1970/72, and acquired the leasehold of ample premises here in the City where all our computer operations and other administration services will be concentrated. Other major undertakings have been the completion or progress of rebuilding at three of our largest branches, Leeds, Chancery Lane and Lombard Street; the development of staff organization and training, and the decentralization of our metropolitan business under four District Offices, which completes the dispersion of centralized control from Head Office to localities. Lastly, but far from least in this long list, was our decision to commission McKinsey & Co. Inc. to carry out a full study of our whole organization and operational system."

The next quotation comes from the statement by SIR CUTHBERT B. CLEGG for *Martins Bank Limited* (February 13):

"In August, in conformity with our policy to seeking profitable extensions of our normal banking business, to provide for our customers, and indeed others, a more comprehensive financial service, we acquired a 75 per cent interest in Unicorn Securities Limited and Dillon Walker and Company Limited, respectively the managers and the share distributors of the Unicorn Group of Unit Trusts. This Group, now renamed Martins Unicorn, is well established with an excellent reputation, hav-

ing been a pioneer in the post-war development of Unit Trusts, and we are delighted that Mr. Edward du Cann and Mr. A. W. Fowler, both of whom played such a prominent part in the early development of the Unit Trust movement, have agreed to continue their association with it. The Group already has in issue over £50m. worth of trust units, and with the additional expertise which the bank can provide, and with our ability to develop the market through over 700 branches, we confidently look forward to even greater progress in the future. Martins Unicorn has already shown, by its introduction of £20 Bonds and the outstanding response to the new Financial Trust, that it has an active and forward-looking sales policy, and further interesting developments are under consideration."

Dealing with the restrictions on bank advances imposed by the Government, SIR RICHARD SUMMERS of the *District Bank Limited* made the following comments in the course of his statement (*The Times*, January 18):

"At the beginning of the year the credit controls imposed in 1966 were still holding down the level of advances. After these controls were relaxed in April we met a growing demand for new lendings of medium and small amounts. It so happened that a number of large advances to industrial customers were reduced during this period for a number of unrelated reasons, including steel nationalization. The net effect was to keep the average monthly figure for advances slightly below the figure for 1966 although the actual number of advances had grown materially.

"The measures of severe restraint imposed in November at the time of devaluation leave us, therefore, with some difficulty in reconciling the commitments agreed during the period of relaxation with the new limits imposed on total lendings. The priority categories of exports, shipbuilding and import-saving production, which includes agriculture, will of course be given special consideration. In the case of agriculture we have a strong farming connection in areas which have been badly affected by foot and mouth disease. We are ensuring that our managers take a sympathetic view when discussing with farmer customers the problems involved in making a fresh start."

After mentioning in his statement (*The Times*, December 2) for *Williams Deacon's Bank Limited* that the bank's parent company, the Royal Bank of Scotland, during the year had amalgamated with the National Commercial Bank of Scotland to form National and Commercial Banking Group Limited, MR. KENNETH G. HOLDEN made the following comment on the question of Saturday closing of banks:

"One of the most contentious subjects of the year has been

C 25

the decision of the Clearing Banks to close on Saturday mornings from the 1st July next. The difficulty is fundamentally that of obtaining staff of the right calibre, and the widespread acceptance of a five-day week in industry and commerce generally has made it virtually impossible for the Banks to obtain their requirements. Every possibility has been considered and every means explored to avoid taking this step.

"We are extending the provision of automatic banking facilities in the form of night safes and are also installing cash dispensers to make cash available to customers outside the hours when banks are open to the public. The change has already been accomplished in Scotland and it is hoped that the new system, when fully operative in England, will prove acceptable."

SCOTTISH AND IRISH BANKS

In his first annual statement for the new merger bank, *National and Commercial Banking Group Limited* (December 20) MR. J. O. BLAIR-CUNYNGHAME gave this account of the way in which the closing of the Scottish banks on Saturday mornings had been received:

"From June this year the Scottish Banks have been closed on Saturday mornings with late opening on one evening of the week, this step having been taken after discussion between the Banks and the appropriate bodies representing the staff. Despite certain initial anxiety that in the short-term customers might be inconvenienced, in general the change has been running quite smoothly while there has been an increased use made of the cash dispensers and of night safes. In the long run it is already clear that this change will restore the relative attractions of a career in banking to the high quality of staff upon whom we depend to provide our many services to customers."

LORD POLWARTH's statement as Governor of the *Bank of Scotland* (April 16) included the following remarks on the progress of Scottish industry:

"While Scotland has had to contend with the problems that have affected the United Kingdom as a whole, there are clear signs of a greater stability north of the Border in terms of industrial production and employment. Manufacturers have expressed continuing confidence in the amount of work being received and this reflects the much broader range of products which has been introduced into Scotland within the past few years and the wider range of international markets now supplied from Scotland. This general impression is confirmed by the latest available figures. These show that the output of industry in Scotland was only slightly lower than during the very good conditions of 1966. The level of Scottish exports has been steady

during the year, according to the general evidence available. We estimate that Scotland exported goods to the order of £525m. during 1967. The principal sources of industrial growth are the expansion of companies already in Scotland and the arrival of new companies from south of the Border and from North America. The general trend of unemployment during the year has been downward, after an initial increase. Ruling out the effect of seasonal and cyclical factors, the underlying situation in Scotland is encouraging and there is evidence to show that our position, relative to the United Kingdom as a whole, is improving. As Scotland, with the regrettable exception of Edinburgh and Leith, is entirely a development area, it can offer industry distinct advantages by way of finance, availability of labour, and factory space. We can therefore look forward with some confidence to further industrial growth, whether from within Scotland or from outside, to the benefit of the economy and of the business of the Bank."

In his comments on the general economic situation of the United Kingdom included in his statement (*The Times*, October 31) as Governor of *The British Linen Bank* the DUKE OF HAMILTON asserted that after devaluation the scene was set for a significant reduction in home demand. But for some inexplicable reason the necessary steps to curb consumption were not taken until the March Budget. He continued:

"As a result, there was a spending spree of almost unprecedented proportions, and it is not impossible that this high consumer spending has contributed substantially to the resilience of imports since devaluation. The Budget when it came incorporated the heaviest ever increases in taxation in British fiscal history, designed to raise £775m. in 1968/69 and £923m. in a full year; wide ranging changes included increased duties on tobacco, wines, spirits, petrol, motor vehicles, hire purchase and selective employment taxes. . . .

"Notwithstanding the severity of the budgetary measures, the balance of payments problem continued as intractable as ever, not because of an indifferent export performance, but largely because of the sustained high monthly import bill. The composition of this, however, would now appear to be changing for the better, and, recently, there have been some signs that the corrective influences are beginning to work,"

At least for the foreseeable future, following devaluation, the country must be prepared to suffer restraints at home in the interests of export trade, declared LORD MACLAY of *Clydesdale Bank Limited* (January 31) and he went on to outline some of the directions in which the banks helped the export drive:

"The banks, of course, play an important part in the drive for

increased exports and will continue to do so. In addition to the financial assistance they provide in the ordinary course of business they make accommodation available at a fixed rate of interest of $5\frac{1}{2}$ per cent for certain categories of exports covered by the Export Credits Guarantee Department. During the past year the banks agreed to co-operate in extending these advantageous terms in appropriate cases to shipbuilding. Furthermore, through their overseas departments the banks give information on foreign markets, help in establishing connections abroad and advice on documentation and Exchange Control Regulations."

That the Irish economy was developing with commendable vigour was the view expressed by MR. EDMOND M. R. O'DRISCOLL in his statement for *Allied Irish Banks Limited* (Dublin, February 27).

"Perhaps the most significant event of 1967 for the Irish economy," he declared, "was the devaluation of the £ sterling in November and the corresponding devaluation here. It is now evident that throughout the preceding months of 1967 the Irish Economy had been developing with commendable vigour. Despite difficulties in effecting expansion, exports have been reaching record levels and the trade gap has been reduced to tolerable proportions. Great credit is due to exporters for the efforts which are producing this result and to those organizations entrusted by the Government with implementation of the policy of providing practical encouragement for export operations. The improvement in the trade situation has been accompanied by capital inflows better than average and, generally, the Balance of Payments position has been brought to a healthy state with promise of further improvement."

FINANCE CORPORATIONS

Addressing the annual meeting of *Finance Corporation for Industry Limited* (June 26), SIR HUMPHREY MYNORS said:

"The 'undoing' of the steel industry—I use the word solely in its F.C.I. context—was satisfactorily organized: outstanding commitments cancelled, a loan due in September 1967 paid off on the due date, the balance to go off evenly during the period to March, 1970. Some progress has been made in obtaining new business: £19m. committed, of which £8½m. advanced by the end of the year."

For *Industrial and Commercial Finance Corporation Limited* LORD SHERFIELD made these general observations in the course of his statement (*The Times*, July 5):

28

"During the year to last March there has been a growing disparity between the investment experience and plans of large and small firms. The year began with widely reported cut-backs in future investment, but, as the year developed, these plans began to be revised upwards. Broadly speaking the largest firms—responsible for a third of the country's output and a half of its capital investment—began to report increases over the past year: but the decline in investment for the small and medium firm persisted. This picture from the C.B.I. and other surveys is in line with our own experience, as our figures show.

"The reasons for this reluctance to invest are not obvious or clear-cut. There has been, of course, a general malaise about the country's economic prospects. There is also great preoccupation among the Directors of smaller firms about the Close Company provisions of recent legislation. Though these may not be quite so serious and harsh in their effects as is generally supposed, some further alleviation of the provisions of the Act would do much to restore confidence that Governmental policy is not hostile to small business.

"The prospects are that the contrast between large and small firms will continue in 1968. The expansion in industrial production which we hope to see will be largely based on exports, a field in which the large firm is dominant. Companies which supply the home consumer market can expect an even more competitive situation than in 1967. The greatest benefit will probably accrue to the smaller firms which are themselves already successful exporters, or which are sub-contractors to such firms."

SAVINGS BANKS

For the past four years *The Devon and Exeter Savings Bank*, LORD LAMBERT claimed in his speech (*The Times*, February 1), had been stressing the necessity of providing the unsophisticated investor with a hedge against inflation. He was therefore delighted that the savings banks now had their own Unit Trust. And MR. EDWARD DU CANN, who also addressed the meeting, said that many factors had led to the important position trustee savings banks commanded as a medium of savings, but the more recent development—the T.S.B. Unit Trust—took them into wholly new fields.

The funds of the *East Anglian Trustee Savings Bank* (January 15) increased on the year by £6m. to a total of almost £84m., according to SIR RICHARD BARRETT-LENNARD, who went on to declare that in six years the funds had doubled, whereas the total funds of all Trustee Savings Banks had increased by some 54 per cent.

The annual meeting of the *Hull Savings Bank* was held on January 3, which MR. JOHN HOWLETT declared was literally the 150th anniversary of the founding of the bank. Now, with 465,000

depositors, the bank could record that for the first time in its long history interest accruing to them had exceeded £2m.

The *Newcastle upon Tyne Trustee Savings Bank* (January 10) was also founded 150 years before to the day, according to MR. H. PETER BELL, following a public meeting called by the then Mayor of Newcastle. Since then there had been a continuing association between the local authority and the bank.

LIEUTENANT-COLONEL SIR JOHN DUNNINGTON-JEFFERSON took the opportunity provided by the annual general meeting of *York County Savings Bank* (January 10) to explain why the trustees of the bank decided, first, that they would not refuse to meet the requirements of those depositors who might wish to buy or dispose of units in the T.S.B. Unit Trust, and, later, that they would not, after all, apply for the necessary consent to undertake this type of business. Referring to the first decision, he said:

"In reaching that decision we had to assume, in spite of our doubts, that this new service could legally be authorized under existing powers, without conflicting with the main purpose of Trustee Savings Banks, as also defined by Statute. Since we took that decision there has been a devaluation of the pound. But devaluation has not been allowed to affect the planned date for the launching of the new unit trust. So it remained for our Bank to decide whether, at this time of exceptional uncertainty, we should apply to the Commissioners for their consent to undertake this particular type of business. Much as we regret taking a decision which may not conform with the independent decisions of other Trustee Savings Banks, we believe that it would be wrong to apply for that consent at the present time, and we shall not do so.

"If, contrary to all our hopes, inflationary tendencies should persist and our next state should be even worse than our last, equity prices may behave as they did for the greater part of last year. If, however, such tendencies are curbed and the dangers of continuing inflation are seen to recede, one might reasonably expect a gradual but fundamental re-appraisal, restoring the normal relationship between securities free from business risks and those exposed to them. To think otherwise, is to regard the 'reverse yield gap', as it is called, as a norm rather than one of the symptoms of a passing economic affliction. We all hope that it is the latter."

MERCHANT BANKS

Every year, declared MR. J. O. HAMBRO of *Hambros Bank Limited* (June 26), the City of London hoped most fervently that it would be allowed to enjoy peaceful and stable economic conditions in which to get on with its traditional job of financing international trade and helping the economy of this country. He continued:

"Year after year, however, we are condemned to see this hope shattered. The present year has certainly proved to be no exception. Not only have we had to face the tragedy of a sterling devaluation which has brought discredit upon the Government of this country, reduced the status of the Sterling Area and of sterling as a world currency and damaged the role of Great Britain as a banking and trading nation, but we have witnessed a series of monetary convulsions which have shaken the financial structure of the whole Western world. In spite of these events, however, the Bank has had a successful year and has emerged in a stronger position than ever before. Our Net Profit shows an increase of 24 per cent over last year and every department of the Bank has contributed to this most satisfactory result."

Among the points made by LORD SHERFIELD in his statement (*The Times*, July 16) for *Hill, Samuel & Co. Limited* were that both profits and dividend had increased substantially; that deposits further increased by £31m. to £198m.; that the surplus resulting from the devaluation of sterling had been transferred to contingencies reserve; that activities overseas had expanded particularly in Europe and North America; and that Lambert Brothers Limited had been acquired since the year-end.

The following paragraph is extracted from MR. GORDON RICHARDSON'S statement (*The Times*, March 2) for *Schroders Limited*:

"The Banking Division was restricted in its domestic credit and lending operations by the continuation of the official ceiling on sterling credit and the new lending restrictions introduced after devaluation. The continued expansion of Euro-currency markets, however, provided an opportunity for us to increase our activities in foreign currency financing and we were able in this way to assist both our domestic customers in their external requirements and also our international customers. This has made a major contribution to the overall expansion of our banking business in London."

For *Kleinwort, Benson, Lonsdale Limited* MR. ERNEST G. KLEINWORT reported (*The Times*, February 21) that the group had had a prosperous year and had further extended its activities. MR. CYRIL H. KLEINWORT gave figures reflecting another extremely busy year for the banking division in spite of the maintenance of the credit restrictions and the uncertain economic conditions. He went on to state:

"As a leading operator in the Euro-currency field, we were able not only to extend our activities in our traditional areas overseas, but also to meet United Kingdom customers' requirements in the field of exports. It is very satisfactory to note that

31

the direct financing of exports has now been removed from the credit squeeze limits. It is gratifying to be able to report an increase in the figure of acceptances on behalf of customers from £28m. to £36 m."

In October, 1967, the Midland Bank Limited acquired a one-third interest in *Montagu Trust Limited* (July 29), stated the chairman of the latter concern, MR. LOUIS FRANCK; and he claimed that this was the first direct link between a clearing bank and an established merchant bank. A close and very effective relationship had already been established between the two banks, which promised to be "most advantageous."

For *Singer & Friedlander Holdings Limited* SIR GEORGE RENDEL asserted (*The Times*, March 11) that although 1967 was a year beset by many uncertainties it created a situation where the services of merchant bankers were in great demand. The company's activities, in both the domestic and international fields, had been at "an extraordinarily high level throughout the year, with every part of our business making its contribution."

The next quotation comes from the statement (*The Times*, October 30) by MR. CHARLES M. KEYSER for *Keyser Ullmann Holdings Limited*:

"As a matter of general policy the Board of Keyser Ullmann Holdings have decided that the company's efforts and resources may be most profitably used in the further development of the merchant bank, and have decided over a period to dispose of the major part of the Group's direct industrial interests. This will not apply to the majority shareholding in Westool, where there are unusual opportunities for growth. The experience acquired through investment in industry will be invaluable to the growth of the merchant bank and of Keyser Ullmann Industries, a rapidly developing division of the Group's activities which under the direction of the Rt. Hon. Edward du Cann, is providing an increasing volume and range of specialist financial and industrial advice for companies."

The increase in the disclosed profits of the banking subsidiary of *Guinness Mahon Holdings Limited*, stated MR. JAMES GUINNESS in his annual review (*The Times*, June 28), reflected an active and successful year in all departments. He added that a part of the overall increase was attributable to security dealing, profits on which were bound to fluctuate and might not necessarily be repeated in future years.

In his statement (*The Times*, June 6) for *Brown Shipley Holdings Limited* MR. ION GARNETT-ORME remarked that the restrictions on sterling credit facilities to customers in the private sector "have been with us for three years, and there are no signs at present of any general relaxations of these regulations." He continued:

32

"Since we are at present restricted in our capacity to develop our sterling credit facilities it is necessary to seek expansion in other fields. Accordingly we are concentrating on business transacted in U.S. dollars and other foreign currencies as we see considerable scope for our services in the ever-growing demand for these currencies, from our domestic as well as our overseas customers. It is significant to note that an increasing proportion of our deposits, and similarly our advances and investments, are in currencies other than sterling. While this is a measure of the diminishing importance of sterling as a trading and reserve currency, nevertheless the interest earnings and profits arising from this business form part of the City of London's contribution to our 'invisible exports' and so help towards the task of redressing the national balance of payments deficit."

Associations of *Arbuthnot Latham & Co. Limited* (March 26) with other banks were the subject of comment by MR. J. F. PRIDEAUX in the following excerpt from his statement:

"During the year we welcomed The Chartered Bank as a substantial shareholder. Already there is evidence that this association will give us valuable support, and we record with pleasure this link with an important institution with such extensive trading connections. Our joint business with Philadelphia National Bank and Philadelphia International Investment Corporation continues to grow satisfactorily. It is evident that there are opportunities which we can turn to mutual advantage, and we especially welcome the fact that our association with Philadelphia National Bank and The Chartered Bank enables us on occasions to operate on a larger scale than would otherwise have been possible."

For *Rea Brothers Limited* (April 4) MR. WALTER H. SALOMON remarked that the recent Budget was tough, as was necessary and as should have been long before. However, the Budget had not done away with a completely archaic system of raising taxes; and, while some praiseworthy but long-overdue attempt had been made to cut Government expenditure, it was frightening to think how much was still spent wastefully and unproductively by Government Departments. He added:

"The new investment income levy is a completely unfair and inequitable tax which hits those who have diligently saved in the past and who are now penalized for having done something which was encouraged as being in the best interests of the country. Worse still, the Budget in several instances proposes retrospective legislation. All these matters looked upon together are a continuous attack on the liberty of the individual, for, historically, liberty is very rarely taken away in one step but it is eroded by legislation of this sort, which paves the way for a

totalitarian state. The excuse for introducing measures such as those mentioned—and this includes also the exchange controls on travel—is that they are in the national interest. This is an absolute travesty of the truth for they are harmful both at home and to our image abroad."

From the report (*The Times*, August 29) of the directors of *Gresham Investment Trust Limited* the following account (in part) of the business of the merchant banking subsidiary is taken:

"Gresham Trust was originally incorporated in 1925 and carries on business as an issuing house and as merchant bankers. It is a member of the Issuing Houses Association and has been certified by the Board of Trade as carrying on the business of banking under the Companies Act, 1967.

"For the eighth consecutive year the net profit was in excess of the previous year. Although new issue business has again been restricted, banking business increased substantially and the company was again active in advising on mergers and other reconstructions."

Members of *Inchcape & Co. Limited* (October 30) were informed by the directors' annual review that Gray, Dawes & Company Limited completed its first year operating solely as a bank, having transferred its non-banking functions to other companies in the group. The company showed a satisfactory increase in profits, assisted partly by the additional cash made available to it during the year by an increase in its issued capital from £½m. to £1m. The year was also marked by the successful introduction of a computer for the handling of bank accounts.

Among the growing activities as merchant bankers of *Ionian Bank Limited* (July 24) MR. R. E. BROOK mentioned that it had acted "with considerable success" on behalf of clients in a number of take-over bids, both "defending" and "attacking"—if those terms might be used—but also as a marriage broker where it had become clear that a strong case existed for the merging of activities of different companies operating in the same field.

DISCOUNT HOUSES

At the end of 1966, MR. ERIC O. FAULKNER recalled, he had reported that the *Union Discount Company of London Limited* (February 28) was well poised to take advantage of whatever opportunities for enlarged trading 1967 might offer. He now stated:

"With three falls in Bank Rate in the first five months, the first half of the year brought us good profits both from Bills and Bonds, but when in the last quarter Bank Rate rose in stages from 5½ per cent to 8 per cent—the highest Bank Rate at the end of

any year since 1857—our profit margins were first reduced and then extinguished. It is therefore gratifying to be able to report that we not only ended the year with higher profits than in 1966, but that with our securities standing in our books at less than market value, our inner reserves were quite untouched and our total resources were greater than at the beginning of the year.

"The policy we have consistently followed since 1965 has thus yielded its reward, and the warm thanks of the Board and of the Stockholders are due to the Management for the steadfast manner in which they adhered to this policy during difficult and testing times."

The installation of computers for mechanized accounting by the *National Discount Company Limited* (February 28) was referred to by LORD MCCORQUODALE in these terms:

"Early in the year we decided to install a mechanized accounting system based on two N.C.R. 500 machines. To this end we have transformed the layout of the ground floor and in addition built an excellent mezzanine floor providing a further 1,100 square feet of office accommodation. We hope to be fully operational by April with our new equipment, which should enable us to make further use of our assets and to handle an increasing turnover without an increase in staff. The planning of the new office layout and the programming of the computers have been largely carried out by our own staff."

An entry in the balance-sheet of *Alexanders Discount Company Limited* (February 19) showing a total (expressed in sterling) of £6m. dollar certificates of deposit, MR. J. P. R. GLYN explained, reflected the result of the decision taken to trade in this new form of security. He added that the market in them had grown quickly and to the company's profit.

SIR JOHN MUSKER of *Cater Ryder & Company Limited* (July 17) remarked that the City of London came about by evolution and that undoubtedly the London discount market was now undergoing considerable change. It was important, he added, that companies like Cater Ryder should have the ability to handle all types of short money flowing into and out of London, and he showed that the company was creating such an organization.

The turnover of *Allen Harvey & Ross Limited* (May 29) in dollar certificates of deposit in the last 12 months (adding together certificates bought and sold) had been $598,456,000, MR. J. J. BUCHANAN revealed, and the company's profit had been more satisfactory than had been expected. In the new financial year the company expected to be dealing in two markets new to it.

"The first," he explained, "is that of sterling certificates of deposit. Mention was made of the imminence of the launching of this credit instrument in the Chancellor's Budget Speech and

in the Finance Bill. The second market is that of Bills of Exchange in currencies other than sterling. Until now the Discount Market has not been allowed to deal as principals in such bills, but we are hoping shortly to get permission to do so, Within the bounds of prudence we intend to be active in both these markets, and we believe that our experience in dollar certificates of deposit will be valuable to us in these somewhat related spheres."

During the year *Gerrard & Reid Limited*, MR. K. H. WHITAKER stated in his annual review (*The Times*, June 6), had increased its investment in Long, Till & Colvin and, as in the past, the cost had been debited to inner reserves.

OVERSEAS BANKS

In his address to members of the *Bank of London & South America Limited* (April 4) SIR GEORGE BOLTON said that, as he had feared, devaluation was followed by problems which were still disturbing the Western world. He continued:

"The postponement, until Budget day, of the full implementation of a plan of deflation, created an atmosphere of unreality in this country resulting in a reckless spending spree. The escalation of the war in Vietnam, with its social and financial effects in America, was followed almost at once by the Gold Crisis. Both the dollar and sterling systems tottered on the brink of collapse, and we can only hope that the temporary respite which followed the decisions to introduce a two-tier price for gold, will soon be followed by a fundamental overhaul of our international monetary system."

In the course of his world-wide survey of politico-economic conditions for members of *The Hongkong and Shanghai Banking Corporation* (Hongkong, March 22) MR. J. A. H. SAUNDERS commented on the British withdrawal from the East. He said:

"The economic difficulties into which Britain has fallen are basically a result of allowing domestic consumption and government spending to rise more rapidly than production. As part of its efforts to resolve this situation the British Government has determined to reduce both defence spending and private investment overseas. It has to be recognized that there has long been a school of thought in Britain, represented in all parties, which takes the view that western military commitments in South East Asia are either ineffective or positively disadvantageous. It is argued that they inhibit the development of a stable situation based on local forces. Ironically it has been the great success of British forces in resisting Confrontation that has made it possible now to argue that they can safely be withdrawn from

South East Asia. Several governments in the area itself will clearly regret a complete British withdrawal. It will also, of course, be very unwelcome to Australia, New Zealand and the United States, particularly at the present stage of the Vietnam conflict. Whether the arguments for withdrawal are valid for the long term or not, the rapid abandonment of the bases, withdrawal of troops and dismissal of tens of thousands of local employees must impose an economic strain, especially on Singapore, and to that extent will endanger political stability."

Apart from the problems caused by devaluation, *The Chartered Bank* (April 3) group throughout the year pursued its policy of steady expansion.

"In addition to opening further branches in existing operational areas," MR. W. G. PULLEN stated, "we obtained permission to start our operations in Korea, where we shall be the only British, in fact the only European, bank. A change for the better in the political scene in Indonesia also enabled us to make progress there and we have reached a satisfactory settlement with the Indonesian authorities regarding our erstwhile business and have received permission to open a branch in Djakarta as soon as the new banking legislation there becomes clarified. Burma still has not honoured its obligation to pay fair and adequate compensation for the nationalization of our business, but even in Rangoon the situation is slightly more hopeful and we await the result of an appeal to the High Court there in connection with our claim.

"During the year we also continued our policy of spreading our interests and in this country we took a share participation in the merchant banking firm of Arbuthnot Latham and Company Limited, which has led to much closer working with that company, and we also acquired over twenty per cent of the capital of Financings Limited, a small but progressive hire-purchase company. We also brought into operation in Hong Kong one of the first on-line computers to be used in banking anywhere in the world."

LORD ALDINGTON summarized the year's performance of *National and Grindlays Bank Limited* (April 23) as follows:

"First in the high taxation countries: in India a good result in line with the expansion of deposits at branches; Pakistan a less good year for us; in Ceylon satisfactory results in prevailing circumstances; of the other overseas countries the profits of Kenya were lower than in 1966 principally because of the loss of the Central Government's accounts, but also because of the cost of fast expansion; in Uganda profitability recovered in the second part of the year but the business there was also expanding and new branches are not always immediately profitable;

37

in Zambia the growth of business and profits continues; in Rhodesia there is no change; in Aden results were satisfactory in all the circumstances. In London our business is growing and widening and the profits of the Bank's business in London taken separately from subsidiaries show an increase of over 25% on the previous year. But in considering the year's profits it is misleading to omit the subsidiaries and associated companies in which we have invested something over £4½m. in the last three years. 1967 saw a substantial improvement in earnings from this large investment to an amount already giving a return of over 10% and shows promise of an appropriate further increase."

That devaluation offered British industrialists and manufacturers considerable opportunities in the Middle East was reported by MR. C. E. LOOMBE in his statement for *The British Bank of the Middle East* (March 18). He went on to explain:

"The production of crude oil in the areas in which we and our associate banks operate has increased during 1967 and the estimated total oil revenue was about the equivalent of £1,000m. Due to this increasing oil revenue, the demand for both capital and consumer goods is expanding rapidly and the Middle East is undoubtedly a market where British exporters could play a more active role. Some United Kingdom firms already have valuable trading links but it is to be hoped that the attractions of the market will appeal to many United Kingdom manufacturers who have hitherto ignored this area. Our competitors appear to be fully alive to this expanding market and it is to be hoped that more and more United Kingdom exporters will find it worthy of attention. The Bank can make available much information and background knowledge both in London and through its network of branches abroad to the exporter; I must emphasize that worthwhile results will only be achieved by on-the-spot investigations by competent representatives of the firms concerned. The Bank welcomes enquiries and will readily place its services and facilities at the disposal of anyone who is interested in these markets."

Two main events occurred during the year under review which were of the utmost significance to the *Ottoman Bank* (May 8)—the hostilities in the Middle East in June and devaluation of the £ sterling in November. Having made these points LORD LATYMER continued:

"The war in the Middle East, and its subsequent effects, are unfortunately a matter which causes your Committee the utmost concern. Until it is possible for the countries involved to come to a fair and lasting settlement, the business of your Bank cannot fail to be adversely affected. It is greatly to be hoped that

the major powers in the world will realize the appalling danger inherent in the present situation and will bring their influence to bear so that a just peace may be restored.

"At the present time, the West Bank of the Jordan is in occupied territory, and the five Branches of your Bank, two in Jerusalem and one each in Bethlehem, Nablus and Ramallah, have been closed since 5th June by order of the Jordan Government. It has not yet proved possible to reopen these Branches despite the hardship the closures have inflicted on our numerous depositors. It seems extremely unlikely that arrangements acceptable to the two Governments concerned will be possible in the near future to permit the reopening of these Branches, until a general peace treaty has been concluded. Your Committee has this problem constantly before it.

"When sterling was devalued last November, nearly all the countries in the Sterling Area in which the Bank operates maintained their pre-devaluation parities. I am glad to say, however, that no heavy loss was caused by this devaluation of sterling since the possibility of such an event had been foreseen by your Committee and measures had been taken to lessen any harmful effects to your Bank."

In his address for *Bank Leumi le-Israel B.M.* (Tel-Aviv, March 24) DR. Y. FOERDER said that 1967 had been marked by an economic recession, then mobilization and war, and then the devaluation of the Israel Pound following upon the devaluation of sterling. The Israel economy had stood the test extremely well. In this connection he paid tribute to the exemplary behaviour of the public who had made no increased withdrawals during the war, and he also placed on record that all the Banks abroad, without exception, had shown the greatest confidence and loyalty during those difficult days.

After commenting on the complete change in outlook in Israel resulting from military victory, from pessimism to renewed optimism in the prospect for the country's economy, SIR HENRY D'AVIGDOR-GOLDSMID in his statement (*The Times*, February 16) for *Anglo-Israel Bank Limited* declared that by the end of 1967 unemployment had shown a steady monthly fall, production was rising, and there were clear signs that the economy was entering a period of new investment, expansion and growth. The trade deficit he added, was estimated to have declined by nearly £40m. in 1967.

The report (*The Times*, March 6) of the *Arab Bank Limited*, (Amman) records the cessation of activities at the branches on the West Bank of Jordan and Gaza "since the Israeli aggression on June 5." On the other hand, the main Beirut branch was stated to be moving early in 1968 to its premises in the new building, which had all the necessary modern equipment; and it was hoped the

branch's activities would be doubled and that it would better serve the Lebanese economy in particular and the Arab economy in general.

The already strong position of the *Australia and New Zealand Bank Limited*, LORD CARRINGTON asserted in his annual statement (*The Times*, December 13) had been strengthened further in 1968 not only in its figures but also in the broadening of its activities and organization. "We are," he declared, "well poised to take full advantage of the further opportunities which the future will bring in the Pacific area." He mentioned the formation with Hambros Bank of A.N.Z. Hambros Investment Services Limited to provide portfolio investment and management services in Australia, and he stated that the newly opened New York representative office would provide an important link with the American financial and commercial community.

LORD HAMPDEN of the *English, Scottish and Australian Bank Limited* (November 13) stated that, in an endeavour to dispel lingering doubts concerning maintenance of the new parity of sterling following devaluation, substantial credits had subsequently been made available to the United Kingdom.

"Of particular importance," he declared, "was the U.S. $2,000m. stand-by credit provided in September, 1968. Its aim is to enable the United Kingdom to finance withdrawals of balances by official holders in the sterling area, but to minimize this risk; at the same time the British Government has provided the countries concerned with an undertaking to maintain the U.S. dollar value of the bulk of their sterling reserves.

The jolt to international confidence provided by sterling devaluation, and the continuing American deficit situation, rendered the United States dollar suspect. The fear that it might be depreciated in value by an increase in the gold price, accentuated the drain of the metal from U.S.A. monetary reserves. This situation was combated by the establishment in March 1968 of a two-tier price system, comprising an official market in which gold continues to be transferred between monetary authorities at the existing price of U.S.$35 an ounce, and a private market where the price is dictated by factors of supply and demand."

Like other youthful, growing nations Australia was hungry for capital to use for many different purposes. Thus spoke SIR JAMES FORREST in his address (*The Times*, December 12) for *The National Bank of Australasia Limited*. He asserted that Australians were making a great effort to help themselves in this respect, as they were devoting a higher proportion of their income to capital investment for the future than other comparable nations with the exception of Japan. He also said that overseas capital was also making a vital contribution to Australia's development.

"It is helping," he continued, "to expand and modernize our manufacturing and other industries, including the great, new mineral enterprises. With this inflow comes overseas 'know-how' and technical advances which are aiding productive efficiency, and the training of Australians in modern techniques developed abroad. We must continue to welcome overseas capital, for we shall be looking for a large inflow until the end of the century, if our country's development is not to be prejudiced.

"Having in mind the excellent prospects of our country, I believe that where practicable it would be wise for overseas concerns to provide for an appropriate local sharing of interest. I would not for a moment suggest any form of compulsion, but it would be a clear-sighted policy and something which we, as Australians, might legitimately expect."

The next quotation comes from the statement by the late MR. MICHAEL G. H. BROWN for *The National Bank of New Zealand* (January 24):

"The new situation arising from the devaluation of sterling, followed by the greater reduction in the value of the New Zealand dollar to parity with the unchanged Australian dollar, emphasizes the continued importance of New Zealand's special relationship with the United Kingdom, gives scope for increased mutual trade and enhances New Zealand's competitive position in the Pacific area.

"In the economic conditions of the past eighteen months the Banks' total deposits have shown a tendency to fall and lending has been much circumscribed by Government policy. The Banks have been forced at time to borrow heavily from the Reserve Bank at the penal Reserve Bank Discount Rate of 7%. So far, the Authorities have not accepted the Banks' proposals that interest rates should be used in a more flexible manner. To single the Banks out for vigorous and arbitrary methods of control is not in the national interest. Until a more sophisticated system of financial adjustment is attained, the Banks will not be able to contribute as effectively as they might to the realization of the country's economic aspirations."

The management of *Barclays Bank D.C.O.* was conscious that in the rapidly changing environment in which the bank operated strict adherence to a traditional role was liable to mean stagnation or worse. This view was expressed by MR. FREDERIC SEEBOHM in his statement (*The Times*, December 9), and he maintained that flexibility to meet new needs as they arose or before they were seen to arise and to diversify into new fields of activity, was essential to the progress of the business. He cited the formation of a number of new finance companies dotted about the world as one example of this diversification:

D   41

"Almost twelve years ago, together with other important financial organizations, we sponsored the formation of Bahamas International Trust Company Limited which provides trustee, company management and international financial services on a broad basis. Over the years BITCO has shown very satisfactory progress and provided a useful service to many of our customers. A sister company has now been formed in the Cayman Islands.

"In South Africa, we have recently established the National Bank Development and Investment Corporation Limited, as a wholly owned subsidiary of our Bank, to engage in all types of medium term finance and underwriting. A good start has been made in the face of difficult conditions. In Jamaica, in Trinidad and in the Bahamas, three separate finance companies have been formed in conjunction with the Bank of London & Montreal, while in Cyprus and Malta wholly owned subsidiary companies of a similar type have been started up. All these organizations are geared to undertake long term and other financial business which lies outside the usual function of a commercial bank. In Malta, we are forming a merchant bank in conjunction with Hambros Bank Ltd., while in South Africa, we have interests in a hire purchase company, a merchant bank and in a leasing company."

The role of the overseas banks in Africa was outlined by SIR CYRIL HAWKER in his statement for *The Standard Bank Limited* (July 31), in which he also disposed of some fallacies apparently held by Africans:

"It is still apparently widely believed that the overseas banks drain resources from the African countries for employment in London. In fact increasingly in recent years the reverse has been true. In very few cases have local deposits been enough to support the level of local lending. Funds from London have been brought in to assist with crop financing, the discounting of trade bills, and other demands of developing economies. Sterling is made available through central banks in exchange for local currency to support local lending. On these sterling sums the Bank could earn a substantially higher return in London or other international markets, but chooses not to do so in order to further longer-term objectives. The resources provided are partly seasonal in nature, depending on the need for financing producers until crops are sold, but more and more they are developing a 'hard core' of outstanding lending in what are now in many instances virtually foreign currencies, no longer pegged to sterling. These funds are mostly uncovered for exchange risk and in the event of a local devaluation we could incur a loss.

"I am not saying that we should not invest in Africa. On the

contrary, we believe in the future of the continent and we cannot expect to continue banking in these countries unless we are prepared to have a stake in them and a real identification of interests. In many areas we have already made sizeable property and other capital investments. As regards the crop finance and so forth of which I have been speaking we are prepared to shoulder the credit risks that may arise therefrom—this is part of banking. But we feel that it is one of the functions of central banks to provide a forward market in which importers and exporters can cover their exchange risks on a short-term basis, and that the new central banks of Africa should be prepared to assist business operations in this way. We also feel that it should be recognized that the British overseas banks are in a real sense continuously putting capital resources into Africa.

"As I have said in earlier years. I believe that British overseas banks bring benefits to developing countries, and that the countries themselves will increasingly come to recognize both their local value and the importance of the links with international money and capital markets that they provide. My earnest hope is that co-operation for mutual advantage will continue and be strengthened. Changes will be needed—certainly areas of co-operation already in existence such as assistance to locally formed banks must be developed and Africanization of our staff proceeded with as rapidly as is consistent with efficiency. British institutions are able to adapt themselves to changing conditions, and the overseas banks are no exception."

In his address for the *Bank of Montreal* (Montreal, December 2) MR. G. ARNOLD HART said that from time to time in recent years, in reviewing the state of the Canadian economy, speakers had commented on the fact that Canada was achieving successive records for uninterrupted growth. Now, he declared, the country was approaching the end of yet another year of expansion, the eighth since the current upswing began. He went on to say:

"The balance among the various sources of growth has, of course, shifted over time, but it is notable that taking the period as a whole the export sector, which has always played such an important role in Canada's economic development, has displayed remarkable strength. In view of this record of success the speculative attack that was mounted against the Canadian dollar last winter certainly seemed irrational at the time and in retrospect seems even more unwarranted in the light of what we have since learned about the continuing buoyancy of our exports."

MR. A. C. BUTLER told members of *Butlers Bank Limited* (Nassau) in the course of his statement (*The Times*, June 14) that the devaluation crisis pointed to the need for the Bahamas to move closer to the dollar area. "We note," he stated, "an energetic

43

move by Government, with the knowledge and cooperation of the Bank of England, towards the establishment of a central monetary authority in the Bahamas."

The report (*The Times*, July 9) of the board of directors of the *Société Générale* included the following passages on the continuation of banking reforms in France:

"Following the reforms introduced in January and July of 1966, a Decree of 6th September, 1967, permits deposit banks to the extent of their own resources, to take holdings in industrial and commercial undertakings. Merchant banks are already authorized to accept deposits for less than two years and while, in principle, there remains a distinction between the two types of institutions, the border lines between them are now less rigid.

"Savings banks have been given powers to sell shares in their own unit trusts, to encash pensions and allowances, to give receipts on behalf of various public services on the settlement of accounts and to grant loans on property. The 'Caisse Nationale de Crédit Agricole' has become more independent of the Treasury and is authorized to intervene on the money market as are other institutions, such as insurance companies, which, by their nature, have liquid funds. The money market itself has been the subject of modifications to enlarge its scope and regulate its functioning. Since the withdrawal of certain facilities by the Bank of France, banks having recourse to the market are finding conditions more competitive.

"Credit interest on current accounts may no longer be paid, but rates on deposits in excess of F.250,000 for more than two years may now be freely negotiated. These and other changes have been made in order to stimulate and consolidate savings. Banks are no longer required to obtain approval prior to opening new branches and are thus enabled to organize their networks in accordance with changes in the economy on population.

"In general, it now seems to be accepted that prudent and reasonable reforms should be introduced in the banking industry at a time when changes in the structure of companies are giving rise to substantial financial requirements which fall outside the usual short-term range."

In spite of the economic difficulties and credit squeeze in Britain, it was stated in the annual report (*The Times*, July 23) of *Crédit Lyonnais*, increased results were achieved by the bank's branches in the City and West End of London. These stemmed mainly from further expansion of their activities in financing international trade and facilitating commercial investment abroad in foreign currencies.

In France, the *Société Centrale de Banque* (Paris, May 21) continued to carry out its programme of reorganization and expansion, according to the annual report of the directors. The bank

opened two new branches in Paris and also in Puteaux and Neuilly, and set up new offices in Nice and Villeurbanne. In the next few months, the report continued, new branches would be inaugurated in Pau, Valence and Aix-en-Provence.

At the annual meeting of stockholders of the *Banque de Paris et des Pays-Bas* (Paris, May 30) authority was given to the board of directors to proceed with a major transformation of the bank's structure. On the completion of the reorganization scheme approved by the stockholders the bank was to become a holding company with the name Compagnie Financière de Paris at des Pays-Bas. It would thus control a deposit bank, an industrial holding company and an international holding company which would group the bank's foreign interests, including the holdings in its foreign subsidiaries arising out of the transformation of its Belgian, Moroccan, Dutch and Swiss branches into companies incorporated under the laws of their host countries.

The annual report of *Banque Française du Commerce Extérieur* (Paris, March 27) showed an increase on the year in the total of the balance-sheet of 22 per cent, the result mainly of the continued expansion of foreign trade transactions.

The *Société Générale de Banque* (April 23), it was stated in the annual report, had been operating for several years in the Euro-currency market, and its dealings in Euro-currency capital issues had been increasing substantially. It was in keeping with these developments that the bank participated, together with a group of European banks, in the formation in Brussels of the European Bank for Medium Term Credit, established under Belgian laws to provide medium term facilities for periods ranging from 3 to 7 years to firms seeking finance for their international investments. Among the banks participating in the new institution were the Midland Bank and Samuel Montagu and Co.

In the course of its comments on the major holdings of *Compagnie Lambert pour l'Industrie et la Finance* (Brussels, April 25) the board's annual report stated that the stockholders' equity of Banque Lambert increased by B.F.200m. during the fiscal year; the consolidated profit of the bank and its subsidiaries amounted to B.F.72½m.

At the annual meeting of the *Deutsche Bank* (May 16) it was resolved to increase the capital. The report stated:

"With the new capital increase, the bank will finance a number of important investments, amongst them the participation in the new European Bank in New York (European-American Banking Corporation and European-American Bank & Trust Company). This institution was founded by the Deutsche Bank together with the Amsterdam-Rotterdam Bank, the Midland Bank, London, and the Société Générale de Banque, Brussels, and was opened on May 1, 1968."

45

A steady expansion of foreign business was recorded in the annual report (*The Times*, June 24) of the *Dresdner Bank*, which stated:

"The Bank took part in forming Société Financière Euro-péenne (SFE) at Paris and Luxembourg. Our newly established subsidiary, the Compagnie Luxemborgeoise de Banque S.A., commenced operations in July, 1967, thus contributing to the extension of the Bank's international business. With the new Representative Office in London the number of offices abroad increased to 18. In Latin America these are operated jointly with our affiliate, the Deutsch-Südamerikanische Bank. Money and Foreign Exchange operations expanded considerably and a large amount of funds was employed abroad."

DR. HANNS DEUSS in his statement (*The Times*, May 16) as chairman of the Supervisory Board of *Commerzbank AG.* advocated greater concentration in the German economy.

"The 'multinational concern'", he declared, "had come to mean something. Whilst formerly companies with a worldwide character were almost exclusively American, European concerns were today working in that direction. By building up a world organization with its own production units abroad, they were creating the basis for their participation in the expansion of promising markets all over the world. They were ahead of the exporter who only produced at home, not only by being more knowledgeable about the foreign market but also because they had the advantage of being safe from unexpected import restrictions and currency changes. Thus they were in a position to secure a larger share of the world market and accordingly a higher turnover. A higher turnover, however, in its turn reduced the cost per unit of research and development expenditure. The large company in such growth sectors as chemicals and electrical engineering was therefore by nature of a multinational character."

Dr. Deuss noted with satisfaction that all the likely companies in the Federal Republic were advancing along this path. An additional reason he found for aiming at concentration was the need for an efficient sales organization. In this connection he pleaded particularly for mergers and co-operation in mechanical engineering as well as in the textile and brewing industries.

In his comments on the 1967 balance-sheet of *Österreichische Länderbank* (February 21) Dr. FRANZ OCKERMÜLLER stated that total deposits increased by Sch. 1,400m., but that this was slightly below expectations; savings deposits in particular failed to equal the previous year's rate of growth.

General progress by the *Banco di Roma* (Rome, April 20) was reported by the board, evidenced in particular by an increase of

18.2 per cent in the funds deposited and one of 17.2 per cent in investments.

The growing foreign business of the *Banca d'America e d'Italia* (Milan, April 4) was outlined in the board's annual report, and it mentioned particularly the fruitful relations with the affiliated Bank of America, "whose position in the principal markets of the world continued to gain strength."

After referring to the "substantial growth" in the operations of *Moscow Narodny Bank Limited* the chairman's statement (*The Times*, April 26) included these remarks on the outlook for the bank:

> "In planning the development of the Bank in the year ahead, one is, of course, extremely conscious of the apparent instability in the international payments system, of the obvious upward pressures on international interest rates and of the tendency of world trade growth to slow down. Indeed, as a Bank which is based very heavily on the finance of international trade and which obtains its funds to a very important extent from the international market, the period ahead is outwardly one which is not conducive to the expansion of the Bank's business. However, in view of our experience over the past year, I am confident that the Moscow Narodny Bank is capable of further expansion in the year ahead. East-West trade, which is the main area of our operations, has revealed its ability to sustain a high rate of growth at a time when other areas of trade have shown a tendency to contract. As a specialist East-West trade Bank, our intention is to participate in this trade as fully as possible, to the mutual benefit and advantage of all concerned."

47

HIRE PURCHASE FINANCE

AFTER the devaluation of sterling in November, 1967, further restrictions were imposed on finance houses, reported MR. IAN W. MACDONALD to members of *Lloyds & Scottish Limited* in his annual survey (*The Times*, December 11). These he enumerated in the following extract:

"The aggregate of advances to the private end of the economy was not to exceed the level prevailing at 31st October 1967, although (until May 1968) finance for export transactions was excluded from the restrictions. The hire purchase controls on passenger cars—already severe—were further tightened. As anticipated, an immediate down-turn in instalment business resulted but, due to delay in the application of the restraints, an unexpected upsurge in consumer spending in early 1968 caused many finance houses temporarily to exceed the permitted ceiling. Since then the level of total instalment debt has followed a steady but unspectacular downward trend. The hire purchase restrictions recently announced are intended to accelerate this trend."

To make up for the necessary curtailment of activity the company has been pursuing more actively a policy of diversification by new acquisitions, Mr. Macdonald explained.

In his report (*The Times*, September 5) for *United Dominions Trust Group* MR. ALEXANDER ROSS declared that it was of the utmost importance that there should be a clear and acceptable definition of consumer credit. Official practice, he added, was to include all the business of finance houses as falling within this category. He believed that it was time a sensible attempt was made to recognize and distinguish between the consumer and industrial fields in which finance houses employed their funds. He went on to make this point:

"It is not a difficult task to curtail the volume of direct personal lending to individuals, but, in the sphere of finance for companies and industry, that task becomes invidious. Upon our ability to maintain a steady course with funds for industrial development, production, distribution and sales depends to a large extent the efficient and successful trading of borrowing companies in these industries."

The Lombank subsidiary of *Lombard Banking Limited*, stated the joint chairmen, MR. ERIC J. P. C. L. KNIGHT and MR. MAXWELL JOSEPH, in their annual review (*The Times*, April 26),

had combined quality and volume of new business with low levels of default, and produced the most profitable year's operation in the history of Lombank. But difficulties that might lie ahead were added to by the Bank of England restriction on aggregate balances outstanding from customers to the figure prevailing on October 31, 1967; in addition, of course, there were Board of Trade Orders regulating initial deposit and repayment periods on instalment credit transactions.

Dealing with the solid progress of *Bowmaker Limited* (February 12) over the five years from 1962 to 1967, SIR JOHN COWLEY stated:

"Business on the books has been directed away from individual small units (furniture and domestic appliances), which we no longer handle, towards commercial vehicles, plant, computers and machine tools. Our profit from the car business, where we deal with first-class motor dealers, represents just under half our total outlay but over half our total income, as the rates on the heavier end of the business are finer."

Commenting on the climate in which the *Astley Industrial Trust Limited* (February 6) was required to operate under Government decree, particularly in motor car financing, SIR STANLEY BELL asserted:

"In order to offset the impact of these restrictions your company is using every endeavour to diversify its activities. It continues to develop the leasing and deferred-purchase of Plant and Equipment and is meeting with reasonable success in this field. The capacity of manufacturers and others to extend their capital equipment must however be governed by their own ability to expand the volume of their business and, with the high price of money, their willingness to pay current rates. Nonetheless, we provide a useful service in helping industry particularly when capital resources are often committed. Another field of operation has been the provision of short term bridging finance where finance houses are able to give a quick and acceptable service and this has also made a worthwhile contribution to our earnings."

The next quotation comes from the statement (*The Times*, January 4) by SIR MARK TURNER for *Mercantile Credit Company Limited*:

"Once again we are in an era of high money costs and very tight monetary control. That our margins will suffer immediately is inevitable, as will the flow of business until national and international confidence is restored. I hope that Bank Rate and money costs generally are soon reduced, for not only is the private individual discouraged from buying, but many im-

49

portant commercial and industrial concerns are less anxious to proceed with their plans in times of such high money costs."

On October 31, 1967, the issued share capital of the merchant banking company, Julian S. Hodge & Company Limited, was acquired by *Anglo Auto Finance Company Limited*, MR. JULIAN S. HODGE remarked in his annual review (*The Times*, April 4) for the latter company. He declared that the merging of the two companies was already proving advantageous to both. The new group was now in a position to offer a complete range of credit facilities from any office. "This," he added, "undoubtedly strengthens our competitive position, and should lead in future to an increasing share of the available total national credit cake. A return to normal and stable conditions in the economy will see the tangible results of the merger."

The chairman of *Western Credit Limited* (October 29) was able to report that the accounts showed a welcome improvement over the disappointing results in the previous year, and he made these remarks on the outlook:

"The profits before tax for Western Credit Ltd., and its Finance Subsidiaries for the three months to 30th September, are in line with those for the same period last year. It is anticipated however, that provided there are no further credit restrictions and that there is no increase in present money costs, the profits for the group in the current financial year will show a worthwhile increase over those achieved to 30th June, 1968."

After recording that the profit before tax was a record since the company was incorporated 10 years ago, the chairman of *F. C. Finance Limited* stated in his review (*The Times*, September 19) that they had made a promising start in the current year in that draft accounts to June 30 showed an improvement over the past year's figures.

An extract from SIR LEONARD DYER'S statement for *Goulston Discount Company Limited* (February 28) follows:

"The amount advanced by way of hire purchase and credit sale agreements in October and November, the first two months of the current financial period, was nearly three times the advances for the corresponding two months of 1966. Following the devaluation crisis and the fresh restrictive measures taken by the authorities, turnover in December 1967 and January 1968 was 107 per cent and 132 per cent respectively of the corresponding months in the previous year. Trading in the current month of February indicates turnover of 140 per cent of the corresponding month last year."

The transformation in the nature of the business of *Walker and Martin Limited* (July 19) over the 10 years that had elapsed since

the Bentinck industrial banking group was acquired is the subject of this quotation from MR. H. GREENHALGH's survey:

"Meanwhile, it is now 10 years since the acquisition of Bentinck, and in that period, notwithstanding a succession of squeezes, freezes and other controls, this Division has been developed to become the dominant profit factor of the Group and should continue to be so. In other words, the character of your Group has changed over the years from being primarily leather to that of industrial bankers, with additional investments in leather and footwear repairing, and it is in this context your investment should be viewed."

SIR WILLIAM WATSON attempted to put into perspective the effect on the finances of *Standard Life Assurance Company* (March 5) of the "much-publicized misfortunes," as he described them, of Capital Finance Company Limited. He said that Standard took a substantial interest in Capital Finance in January, 1966, and during 1967 had advanced additional sums to enable it to carry on its normal hire purchase business.

"No effort is being spared," he went on, "to improve Capital Finance's position—its Board has been almost entirely re-constituted and the senior management changed and strength-ened. As its Chairman indicated in his recent statement, the company's troubles have arisen almost entirely from investments outside its own hire purchase field which were made some years ago and have subsequently proved to be unprofitable. It is encouraging that its hire purchase organization has continued to produce excellent results and has indeed secured a record amount of new business during its last financial year, which ended on 31st January 1968—a fine achievement in very difficult and discouraging conditions.

"As a precautionary measure, we have made a provision in these accounts of the whole of our original investment. It is too early yet to forecast the eventual outcome but the effect on our finances cannot be other than marginal because the Balance Sheet value of our assets exceeds £620m. and, even after making the provision to which I have referred, the margin by which the aggregate market value of these assets exceeded the figure in the Balance Sheet has never been greater."

The recovery in the turnover of *Kundenkreditbank K.G.a.A.* (Düsseldorf, May 16) from the setback of 1966 is shown in the next quotation, from the report of the general partners, DRS. WALTER and STEFAN KAMINSKY:

"KKB is satisfied with the general trend of 1967. The re-duction in turnover, which during 1966 amounted to 15 per cent due to restrictions introduced by the Bank, continued during the

first few months of the year only. Since April 1967 arrears have been made up step by step and at the end of the year a level approaching the one for the previous year has been reached. During 1967 KKB granted new instalment credits amounting to DM 635·3m., compared to DM 651·6m. in the previous year. This represents a reduction of 2 per cent. Due to a continued increase in demands for Personal Loans the actual number of credits granted increased. The total number of 455,786 credits granted during the previous year was exceeded this year by more than 4,000 credits.

"The slow improvement in the general economic situation, and thus in our volume of business, is, however, regarded favourably by us, since we firmly believe that a slow improvement represents a better basis for a permanent economic recovery. Quick or excessive increase would only endanger the stability of price structure or put a strain on the labour market."

INSURANCE

THE improved underwriting experience which marked 1966 for a number of British insurance companies went further in 1967, the year covered by most chairmen's statements issued in 1968. This was particularly true of fire and accident (notably motor) insurance, on which losses were materially reduced and in some instances transformed into modest profits, thanks to more selective underwriting and adjustments of premium rates. Incidentally, the collapse of the tariff premium-fixing system came too late in the year 1968 for comment to be included in statements published in that year. For marine underwriters the 1965 account that was closed in 1967 showed losses, sometimes heavy, but such indications as were then apparent of the results of the 1966 and 1967 accounts suggested that similar remedial measures had led to improvement. In the various forms of life assurance most offices reported increased business and larger premium incomes, some achieving fresh records. A number of life and composite companies increased their dividends moderately. One thing which nearly every insurance chairman protested against was selective employment tax, increased as it was by 50 per cent, the main ground for their complaints being that even if insurance was only a service industry its service to the country was vital in fostering savings and channelling them to industry, national and local government, &c.—a service which the tax could only make more expensive.

Asserting that the affairs of the *Sun Alliance and London Insurance Limited* (June 5) had shown "an appreciable improvement" upon the poor results of the previous two years, MR. T. D. BARCLAY pointed out that this had been achieved in spite of a very heavy loss in the marine department and a number of catastrophic losses in various parts of the world. There was, he conceded, still a long way to go, but the underlying trend was more favourable. On the subject of expense ratios, he had this to say:

"The year has seen the final amalgamation of our head office administration. Both at home and abroad our branch integration has been completed. The accomplishment of all this in little more than two years is a notable achievement bringing benefits by way of economy in operating costs. Our expense ratio in the fire and accident departments (including commission) was reduced from 38·0% to 37·1%. Increased efficiency is being made possible by the greater use of computers and new techniques of management and control. Unhappily much of the

53

benefit will be dissipated by the heavy additional U.K. taxation. Last year the full cost of the selective employment tax was £470,000. We shall now have the burden of the greatly increased rate of this iniquitous tax as well as higher costs in many directions. We estimate that our expenses will have to bear an additional £600,000 in a full year."

Better results for 1967 of *Phoenix Assurance Company Limited* were partly attributed by LORD DE L'ISLE, V.C., in his annual review (*The Times*, May 10) to its programme of expanding business while achieving more economical methods of working, as well as to a general improvement in premium rates. He hoped this would continue, and pointed out that growing industrialization and a greater concentration of risks—for example, in larger aircraft—demanded a corresponding increase in the capacity of the insurance market. Maintaining that reserves must not merely be maintained but further enlarged to meet heavier burdens, while the return on existing risk bearing capital must be adequate if the further capital that would undoubtedly be needed by the wide field of insurance was to be attracted, he went on to make this declaration:

"The British insurance market as a whole can better devote its energies to the means of enlarging its collective ability to carry the greater liabilities required by industrial and technical developments than to the mutual cutting of throats. Nowhere has the process of economic growth and the expansion of insurable risks gone faster than in the United States, the world's most rapidly expanding economy. Your company has been operating in that country since 1804. Despite some intervals of stringency, our operations there have, over the years, proved very remunerative, although the past ten years or so have shown themselves to be a period of particular difficulty. An insurance company such as ours cannot, without injury to its power and reputation, hastily renounce long established and well proven connections. For this reason, despite the difficulties, we have not only maintained, but expanded our United States business rather than retreat from that market. Our financial strength has shown itself adequate for this burden. The rise in the capital value of our investments in the United States and the annual income derived therefrom have outweighed the losses incurred on our underwriting.

"But we have never remained content to rely on our investment income alone. It has been our firm intention to make an underwriting profit as well. During 1967 we were able to reach an agreement with our American associates, the Continental Insurance Company, of New York, which offers us a very good prospect of achieving this aim. It was agreed that on the 1st January 1968 the Continental would take over the direction of

all our insurance operations in the United States and that at the same time the Phoenix would enter the pool into which the business of the Continental group of companies is placed. Through participation in this larger insurance group we look to a significant reduction in our cost ratio and have greatly improved our chances of operating profitably in America.

"It is an important aspect of this association that we retain a 100% ownership of our subsidiary, the Phoenix Assurance Company of New York, and with this of the valuable investment portfolio of that company. There has been no change in our agreement with the Continental whereby that company's interest in the Phoenix will be limited to a maximum of 25%, the basis upon which our understanding and mutual dealings rest."

Disappointing underwriting results of the *Royal Insurance Company Limited* (May 29), stated the late MR. F. LESLIE ORME, should be seen against the background of a year when catastrophe claims had been exceptionally severe. He continued:

"Some windstorm losses are to be expected every year but the incidence of such storms in 1967 was particularly heavy—the most notable being hurricane Beulah—and our losses of some £2m. were well above what one might expect in a normal year. What was particularly disquieting about catastrophe experience in 1967 was the severity and widespread nature of civil disturbances. Insurers in America have been accustomed to including cover for riot in their policies for a very modest premium, as countrywide losses from this cause have in the past been small. In 1967, however, our Group alone paid out some £1m. in riot claims and the cost of such claims to the whole of the American insurance market is reported to have been in the region of £25m. It is impossible to predict the scale of possible future disorders and this question is one of grave concern, not merely to the insurance industry but to the whole American nation. A special committee, appointed by President Johnson last autumn, presented a report early this year which largely endorsed the urgent and forceful representations of the American Insurance Association; this had stressed the fact that the problem was essentially a political one for which the Government had responsibility and should therefore bear some of the financial risk. Legislation has already been introduced in Congress, which we can only hope will shortly be enacted, providing that losses exceeding a given percentage of premiums will be borne by the Federal or State authorities."

Even when British insurance companies suffer an underwriting deficit, of course, this is almost invariably more than wiped out by their investment income. For investment forecasting 1967 proved

55

an unusually difficult year, SIR JOHN MELLOR declared in his statement (*The Times*, April 24) for *The Prudential Assurance Company Limited*. In the early part of the year, he recalled, a concerted attempt to reduce interest rates in the Western world met with some success. However, he continued, events in the Middle East and the escalation of the American war effort in Vietnam reversed this trend in both the United Kingdom and the United States.

"The economic position in the United Kingdom," he added, "deteriorated rapidly, resulting in the devaluation of sterling in November, and once again interest levels at the end of the year were higher than at the beginning. Whilst high rates of interest are usually beneficial to life assurance funds, instability is not, and in this respect the current year is likely to prove no less difficult than 1967. The recent international monetary crisis has underlined the seriousness of the economic problems facing the world and until it becomes clearer how these are going to be tackled, it will be most difficult to formulate any reliable view as to the future course of Western economies generally."

In a reference to the investment policy of *The Scottish Widows' Fund and Life Assurance Society* (March 12) SIR EDMUND HUDSON said that British Government securities were sometimes regarded as unsuitable investments at any price, an attitude he asserted to be tantamount to writing off sterling as a major currency and Great Britain as a financial centre. He continued:

"Notwithstanding the failure of successive governments to tackle the problem of inflation, we regard any such point of view as irresponsible. At present prices, fixed interest stocks provide a suitable medium for a considerable part of the Society's funds. With yields of more than 7 per cent on British Government securities and 8 per cent or more on mortgages and debentures, the rolling up effect of compound interest is extremely powerful and provides a built-in growth factor to set against the growth in dividends which one expects to obtain from ordinary shares. There are, of course, ordinary shares which will show a very high rate of growth far outweighing the deficiency in the return in the early years, but the selection of the right shares is more difficult when the equity market as a whole is at a high level."

As regards investments in property, MR. LEWIS G. WHYTE in his review (*The Times*, March 26) for *London and Manchester Assurance Company Limited* stated that the company had not as a matter of practice participated in the development of new office or new residential property, but had been engaged in the ownership, management and improvement of a number of residential estates. He went on to say:

56

"The most important is the Packington Estate in Islington, which was acquired in 1945. During the last two decades the company has invested substantially here in modernization, conversion and general improvement. We have also been ready to sell by mutual agreement to sitting tenants, or if we get an empty house, to a prospective occupier who wants to make it his home. The company has a twofold aim: to be a good landlord and to obtain a satisfactory return on the money invested. Our experience has been that these two aims are both attainable and need not be in conflict with each other. In recent years other estates have been bought in Battersea, Southwark and elsewhere. We intend to continue this policy as and when suitable opportunities arise."

During 1967 *Britannic Assurance Company Limited* (April 5) made reasonable progress in all branches, MR. JOHN F. JEFFERSON asserted, but while the growth of income from all sources continued it was nevertheless disappointing to see expenses also rising as a result of increases imposed upon the company. He declared:

"It is the constant preoccupation of the management of a business like ours to keep strict control on expenses by improving efficiency and to do so without detriment to our staff's earnings. It is frustrating to have successes in this field wiped out by extra charges for national insurance contributions, redundancy pay contributions, graduated state pensions and selective employment tax."

Speaking at the annual general court of the *Royal Exchange Assurance* (June 19) the Governor, LORD KINDERSLEY said that on the whole he was satisfied with the then current year's progress to date, and the management were making every effort to improve their performance. It was because they saw the possibilities of significant savings in expenses as well as potential for expansion that they had entered into the negotiations with the Guardian for the merging of their interests.

Dealing with the installation of a computer by *Provincial Insurance Company Limited* (June 12) MR. PETER F. SCOTT said that in January of 1968 the whole of the head office records, previously on a punched card basis operated through mechanical tabulating and sorting equipment, were converted to magnetic tape and the computer became fully operational in March in respect of renewals, accounts and all processes formerly carried out by mechanical equipment. He added:

"What we have seen so far is only a beginning. Our machine is capable of undertaking a much wider range of clerical operations, but this will involve long preparation in the shape of systems analysis and programming. Moreover, while our existing management and staff forge steadily ahead with the

programme of additional usage which we already envisage, we shall also conduct research into the possibilities of even more sophisticated usage in the long term."

In his review (*The Times*, April 24) for *The Prudential Assurance Company Limited* SIR JOHN MELLOR asserted that the uncertainty of the application of the Finance Act, 1965, to the availability of franked investment income of the life branches for Schedule F purposes had been resolved by the Finance Act, 1967: this provided that Schedule F tax in respect of dividends paid to shareholders by a proprietary life assurance company could only be offset by income tax on the shareholders' proportion of its franked investment income. He explained that the policy of acquiring franked investment income for the general branch, where there was no restriction in its use, as in the life branches, had resulted in the dividend payable for the past year being fully covered by franked investment income, with the result that there was no charge for Schedule F tax in the general branch.

LIFE, INDUSTRIAL LIFE AND PENSIONS

Commenting on the "contribution of prime importance to the future of the country" which institutions like the *Royal London Mutual Insurance Society Limited* (April 30) made by encouraging saving, MR. E. H. HAYNES said:

"Saving through the Royal London is not only remunerative to the policyholder, it helps to solve another of the Chancellor's problems. Sterile savings may help to solve the problem of the moment but are of no help to the future. Savings through the Royal London and similar institutions are not sterile; they are dynamic. We act as a channel through which the savings of the many are converted into the capital needed by industry for modernization and expansion; capital which could be found in no other way. Thus in expanding our business we are making an important contribution to the future well-being of the country."

After defining the primary purposes of life assurance and annuity business, SIR GEOFFREY KITCHEN of *Pearl Assurance Company Limited* (May 22) declared that some people had sought to effect, or had persuaded others to effect, life assurance contracts the real object of which was nothing to do with these primary purposes but was simply to extract the maximum financial advantages out of the combined effects of tax laws and life policies. He went on:

"The outcome is, not for the first time, that the Government has decided to introduce restrictive measures to deal with the situation that has developed. At the time this statement is being

prepared, these restrictive measures seem likely to have disadvantageous effects on people who wish to arrange their affairs within the true spirit of the primary purposes of life assurance, including even people taking out quite normally industrial assurance policies as well as a variety of eminently reasonable ordinary branch contracts. It will also be regrettable if, as seems likely, the life offices have to shoulder a substantial administrative burden in order to enable the Inland Revenue to operate these new restrictions."

That life assurance was the largest source of consistent voluntary saving in this country was claimed by MR. C. G. RANDOLPH of *Sun Life Assurance Society Limited* (April 24): it must be manifest to individuals and Government alike that such a vital element in the national well-being needed to be safeguarded and encouraged, he asserted, and he continued:

"I must therefore deplore the failure of the Government to safeguard the value of the £ sterling. Apprehension as to the future of money values is a disincentive to saving and an encouragement to the public to seek more speculative media. Whilst equity-linked life assurance policies continue to receive much publicity in the press, and cause us constantly to study developments in this field, it is still my view that the with-profits endowment assurance is a most satisfactory method of preserving security of capital and providing at the same time a useful hedge against inflation."

SIR JOHN DENN of the *United Kingdom Provident Institution* (April 24) emphasized the immense importance of the life assurance business to the nation in fostering self-reliance and independence and building up resources necessary for economic stability now and in the future; and he recalled that Sir Winston Churchill more than 50 years ago said: "Had I the powers of a dictator, I would cause the word insure to be inscribed on the lintel of every home in the land."

The next quotation comes from the address of MR. JAMES KENNEDY for *The Scottish Provident Institution* (March 26):

"It is regrettable that the estate duty advantages which were hitherto obtainable in respect of certain types of policies which created separate and non-aggregable estates are to cease. I believe these advantages were a very real incentive to save and, in my opinion, it is unfair that such advantages which were given statutory authority in the Finance Acts of 1954 and 1959 should now apparently be withdrawn in such a way that people who made dispositions in good faith on the basis of recent legislation may now find themselves in a worse position than if they had done nothing."

At the meeting of *National Mutual Life Assurance Society* (May 7) MR. KENNETH A. E. MOORE reported that, although new business had been buoyant in the first quarter of the current year, there were now signs that it was being adversely affected by the budget proposals and the attendant uncertainties. However, on the brighter side the market value of the Society's holdings of equities had advanced very substantially so far this year.

After stating that death claims on the *Marine and General Mutual Life Assurance Society* (July 3) showed no significant increase, MR. C. E. WRANGHAM mentioned that once again there was a rise in payments against policies surrendered, and more policy loans were granted. To some extent, he thought, these tendencies might reflect the economic and financial conditions prevailing, but manifestly they were also related to the rise in the volume of business.

In his survey (*The Times*, June 13) for *Noble Lowndes Holdings Limited* MR. ROY L. LOWNDES referred to the tragic loss at sea in January and early February of three North Sea trawlers, resulting in the death of many brave men. He stated:

> "It would be an intolerable assumption to suggest that any form of monetary payment could compensate the bereaved families for the loss of their menfolk. Nevertheless, it was a source of some satisfaction to us to know that by means of the life assurance and pension scheme which we designed and operate for the British Trawlers' Federation the sum of £25,000 was made available to their dependants."

SIR ALEX ABEL SMITH, of *Provident Mutual Life Assurance Association* (March 29), was one of several insurance chairman who pointed out that under the Companies Act, 1967, life offices must now make statutory valuations at intervals not exceeding three years, instead of five as hitherto. He continued:

> "We shall therefore be making such a valuation at the end of this year; this will be followed by a declaration of bonus and distribution on the lines traditional to the Association. We view this change with mixed feelings, for this operation, under which, according to past experience, about 80,000 cash payments may have to be made, imposes a heavy burden on the organization as a whole and . . . inevitably gives rise to increased overheads. On the other hand, a bonus distribution has the effect of stimulating and encouraging new business from satisfied policy-holders."

The *Clerical, Medical and General Life Assurance Society* (April 24) was facing increasing competition from unit trusts linked with life assurance, stated LORD GEDDES, who went on to declare:

> "It is good for the old-established life assurance industry to face such competition. The Society welcomes it and meets it in

60

full confidence. The Society's participating policyholders have the benefits, which do not normally accrue to those who invest in unit trusts, of strong reserves, and profits arising from other classes of business. This is supported by investment management which is not only conscious of the merits of investment in equities and real property but is also flexible enough to invest in British Government and other fixed interest securities when, in times of high interest rates, this may be more profitable."

For *Standard Life Assurance Company* SIR WILLIAM WATSON said that the board had decided to stop writing new business in Uruguay from February 15, 1968; they did so reluctantly after a long and happy association with the country over nearly 80 years, but having regard to the continued and increasingly rapid depreciation of the Uruguayan currency it did not seem desirable to enter into long-term contracts such as life assurance policies in that currency.

In 1967 the outstanding feature of the life department of the *Commercial Union Assurance Company Limited*, according to MR. RONALD C. BROOKS, was the merger of the life funds of the Commercial Union and the North British, about which he stated:

"Rates of premium for new life policies had been the same for both Funds for some years, and the same rates of bonus were declared in respect of North British and Commercial Union With Profit policies (except for a few minor classes) at the declarations made at the end of 1963 and again at the end of 1966. It had been apparent to us for some time that the bonus prospects of these policies were unlikely to diverge in the future and accordingly a scheme of merger of the Life Funds on the basis of equality of bonus rates in the future was prepared, sanctioned by the High Court as required by law, and became effective from 1st January 1967. The administrative savings which will emerge will benefit the With Profit policyholders and shareholders. The merged U.K. Life Fund at the end of 1967 amounted to £210·3m., whilst the rate of interest earned thereon during the year was £7.2s.9d. per cent. The Annuity Account of the North British, which by that Company's Constitution is an entirely separate account from the Life Fund, was not affected by the merger and continues its separate existence."

In his reference to the dollar investments held by *The Scottish Life Assurance Company Limited* (March 26) MR. C. R. MUNRO spoke on similar lines to many other insurance chairmen. He said:

"Our oversea investments have been maintained but—at the request of the authorities—our operations (chiefly in the dollar area) are confined to switching existing holdings. Assessment of these switches must take account of the incidence of Capital Gains Tax and Income Tax but the investment criteria are

further complicated by the requirement to surrender 25 per cent of the dollar premium on the sale proceeds. This restrictive measure, introduced in the short-term interests of the balance of payments must in the longer-run operate to the disadvantage of the economy and as the balance of payments position strengthens and opens the way to a desirable relaxation of exchange control restrictions it is to be hoped the Government will take early action to relieve U.K. investors of this hampering regulation."

The average premium per new policy in the industrial life branch of *The Prudential Assurance Company Limited* continued to increase, stated SIR JOHN MELLOR in his annual survey (*The Times*, April 24), and now exceeded 15s. a month compared with about 10s. five years ago. He went on:

"This is in contrast with the very small premiums being paid under large numbers of policies taken out many years ago and still on our books. These policies for small premiums which will have no precise equivalent in decimal currency will present problems when the new currency is introduced in three years' time, and we are engaged in preparations for the change."

Sir John also referred to the Government's intentions on national pensions, under which it was thought likely that both benefits and contributions would be related to earnings, and that benefits would be enlarged to provide eventually about half pay on retirement for those whose earnings were at the national average level. He then made this comment (in part):

"If this in fact proves to be the future shape of national pensions, then clearly the impact on occupational schemes will be considerable. Assuming that the state scheme continues to be financed on a 'pay-as-you-go' principle and that improvements in pensions would take effect gradually over a period of years, the present generation would not pay contributions commensurate with the cost of the improved pensions promised to them. The cost of these higher pensions would have to be met by considerably higher contributions or by increased taxation from subsequent generations."

MARINE AND AVIATION

The *Royal Insurance Company Limited* (May 29), stated the late MR. F. LESLIE ORME, had now closed the 1965 marine underwriting account, which, in line with market experience, showed a loss, though in view of the very strong marine fund it was not necessary to make any transfer from profit and loss account. However, he went on to make this more encouraging forecast:

"The high incidence of total and partial losses in the past few

years has resulted in a marked hardening of both hull and cargo insurance rates, which provides at least some hope of a return to profitability. The gross tonnage of ships totally lost last year, although still higher than the average of the past few years, was less than the exceptionally high figure of 1966 and the number of partial losses was also lower. While it is too early to forecast the eventual outcome of the 1966 and 1967 accounts they seem likely to show some improvement on 1965."

The advent of specialized ships and new methods like containerization called forth these comments from LORD KINDERSLEY, Governor of the *Royal Exchange Assurance* (June 19):

"The rating of specialized tonnage such as liquid-gas carriers, container ships and drilling rigs continues to exercise underwriters' minds and, while there is increasing application of automation and other sophisticated equipment, ship owners' problems of manning remain a source of concern. There is much topical interest in the use of containers for the shipment of general merchandise. Container operators are apt to argue that this form of transport will produce a better out-turn at destination, but our experience to date both here and overseas is that claims for shortages and breakages still arise, and from an underwriting point of view it is vital that we obtain the right level of rating for this particular type of risk."

The detention of vessels in the Suez Canal had given rise to many cargo claims and had added a further burden to the marine account of the *Phoenix Assurance Company Limited*, declared LORD DE L'ISLE, V.C., in his review (*The Times*, May 10). He also made this statement on aviation risks:

"In the aviation department strenuous efforts are being made to obtain increases for hull risks, thus reversing the past expensive trend towards a reduction in rates. Provided adequate rates can be obtained insurance cover should be available for the larger aircraft and higher liabilities in the future. Our aviation business is progressing well."

The expected profit on the 1964 aviation account of *Orion Insurance Company Limited* (June 5) had materialized, stated MR. P. B. GILBERT. Heavy claims had been settled against the 1965 account, and it appeared that the result would be marginal. The 1966 account was, however, showing considerable improvement, and to date the 1967 account could be considered very satisfactory.

Another company which found that the years 1965 and 1966 were unprofitable in the marine and aviation department was the *Cornhill Insurance Company Limited* (May 2), according to MR. DONALD C. CANN, who added that it had been necessary to transfer £100,000 from profit and loss account to maintain the strength of

63

the marine and aviation fund. However, he also stated that in 1967 the London Marine market pursued a firm policy designed to secure realistic rates of premium to meet the high incidence of claims which had been the feature of recent years, and this was reflected in increased premiums.

FIRE AND ACCIDENT

While the late MR. F. LESLIE ORME considered it encouraging to be able to report an underwriting profit on the United Kingdom fire operations of *Royal Insurance Company Limited* (May 29), he none the less went on to sound a cautionary note in these terms:

"The estimate for direct damage from fire for the country as a whole rose by a further 10 per cent to £90m. This huge amount, largely the result of carelessness, is an unnecessary burden which the nation cannot afford. The campaign to make industry more aware of the seriousness of this situation continues. Much still needs to be done to lessen the susceptibility of premises to fire. We have increased the number of our fire surveyors who, whilst assessing the risk for us, advise insured on all aspects of life protection—not least the desirability of sprinklers.

"Fire premium rates are constantly under surveillance with a view to each class of risk making its proper contribution; consequently some rates have been increased but others have been reduced."

The prevalence of widespread under-insurance was mentioned by a number of insurance chairmen, among them MR. T. D. BARCLAY of *Sun Alliance and London Insurance Limited* (June 5), who stated that during 1967 steps were introduced to counteract the disadvantage under which insurers were placed by this practice.

According to MR. JOHN F. JEFFERSON, *Britannic Assurance Company Limited* (April 5) set up its own organization to take over the running of the fire and accident business from January 1, 1968; it had appointed the key personnel required and recruited 160 extra staff. Thanking the Commercial Union for the help given to Britannic in creating its own system, he also stated:

"It must also be pleasing for them, as it is for us, to see that during the last year of our association we had record progress and only just fell short of £2m. premium income, a fitting landmark to end an association which began with the British General Insurance Company 43 years ago."

In his first year as chairman of *Guardian Assurance Group* LIEUTENANT-COLONEL C. P. DAWNAY was able to report a record profit. In his survey (*The Times*, May 22) he referred to 1967 as the cross-roads because the company had come through difficult years,

it had now seen two years with improving trends, and, "if un-justified competition is not allowed to affect the analytical way in which we underwrite, there are signs that these trends will con-tinue." He added:

"Last year the results of our operations in Home Fire showed an improvement and there are indications that the revisions in rates and in sums insured have now brought premiums to a level where they are more closely compatible with the risks under-taken. In 1967 our income from direct business increased by 11·2 per cent and, with losses showing a welcome reduction in spite of the still rising National fire loss figures, a satisfactory margin of profit resulted.

Motor business for the *Eagle Star Insurance Group*, it appeared from SIR BRIAN MOUNTAIN'S statement (*The Times*, May 8), pro-duced a reasonable profit, and the company's competitive rating structure, coupled with high "no claims bonuses", had justified itself. Measures to improve standards of driving and road safety he welcomed, but the repair costs on vehicles and judicial awards for personal injuries were rising, and he feared, if these trends continued, higher premiums for the motorist would be inevitable.

A satisfactory profit was reported by SIR STANLEY NORIE-MILLER in the fire department of the *General Accident Fire and Life Assur-ance Corporation Limited* (May 29), even though he noted a sharp increase in windstorm and other catastrophe claims in the United States. The company was also involved in the Tasmanian bush fires claims. He was concerned with the unsatisfactory results still resulting from large industrial risks in the United Kingdom, but was gratified to observe indications that greater emphasis on discipline in factories and workshops was being shown by manage-ments in industry. It was, he remarked, long overdue.

For *Cornhill Insurance Company Limited* (May 2) MR. DONALD C. CANN mentioned that as a result of past lack of this discipline insurers had been obliged to introduce tougher criteria for selection and rating designed to penalize the heavy risk and to offer financial inducements for adequate fire protection and good management.

LORD HARCOURT observed that the good results in the fire branch of *Legal and General Assurance Society Limited* (May 15) in part reflected the steps taken in the last few years by the industry to establish more equitable and adequate premium rates. As regards accident business, he stated that burglary insurance in particular had been unsatisfactory in certain areas.

The next quotation, from MR. I. MURASE'S statement (*The Times*, July 19) for *Taisho Marine & Fire Insurance Company Limited*, is of interest as recording the experience of a leading Japanese office in fire business:

"During the year under review, we have continued, as one of

our most important policies, to make intensive efforts to strengthen our position in the market of non-industrial risks, which is considered to be the basis for the steady growth towards the future. In order to attain this target, we have endeavoured to expand and to develop our agency network.

"Benefiting from the above mentioned policy, and also being greatly assisted by the remarkable increase of business volume from the industrial side, which has resulted from vigorous capital investment activities throughout a wide range of industries, the premium income amounted to Yen 9,602m. compared with Yen 8,347m. in the previous year. Claims paid and outstanding, however, have risen to Yen 3,541m. as against Yen 2,490m. in the previous year. This rise is basically accounted for by an unusually large number of heavy claims raised, which somewhat reduced our underwriting surplus."

One direction in which there had been a marked deterioration of the year's results, SIR GEOFFREY KITCHEN informed members of *Pearl Assurance Company Limited* (May 22) was employers' liability in the United Kingdom. In view of the rising cost of settlements a reassessment of the liabilities outstanding for 1967 and prior years had been made, and he stated that inflationary trends rendered it prudent to transfer an additional reserve from profit and loss.

The unprecedented epidemic of foot and mouth disease gave rise to large numbers of claims under farmers' policies for consequential loss, declared the late MR. F. LESLIE ORME of *Royal Insurance Company Limited* (May 29).

Referring to a number of failures among companies specializing in cut-rate motor insurance, MR. G. J. STEWART informed members of *London & Edinburgh Insurance Company Limited* (July 31) that the management could have augmented premium volume "very appreciably" had it accepted much of the business that came on to the market from that source, but had preferred not to do so.

The effects of the breathalyser and other Government measures to reduce motor accidents were mentioned by several chairmen. SIR GEOFFREY KITCHEN of *Pearl Assurance Company Limited* (May 22) stated:

"It is too early to assess the recent introduction of legislative regulations designed to promote road safety, but the initial effect has been significant and whilst any restrictions which are imposed on the freedom of the individual must be kept to the minimum, if the result proves to be a reduction in the hitherto ever-rising carnage on the roads then this must surely be a reasonable price to pay."

MR. M. WILCOCK HOLGATE of *Refuge Assurance Company Limited* (April 25), too, said that the measures introduced by the

Minister of Transport relating to "drink and driving" appeared to have had an initial beneficial effect, and the reduced number of accidents had been reflected in the company's figures.

In regard to the inspection of damage to cars before settling claims, MR. DONALD C. CANN made this statement to members of *Cornhill Insurance Company Limited* (May 2):

"Cornhill has for a number of years employed experienced staff motor engineers to provide the best possible claims service to policyholders and control payments to repairers. This policy has been continued by the appointment of additional staff engineers who are usually able to make an immediate inspection and authorize the repair of damage to vehicles. We do not favour asking our policyholders to obtain alternative estimates from repairers because our engineers are qualified men who know what the repair should cost and rarely have difficulty in agreeing a price with the repairer. We find the majority of motor traders to be fair and reasonable in their approach, and it is very seldom necessary to move a vehicle elsewhere. Our procedures save time and tedious enquiry by the policyholder, and considerably reduce the period during which he is deprived of the use of his car."

REINSURANCE

After an association going back over 50 years, stated MR. H K. GOSCHEN, the Swiss Reinsurance Company of Zurich decided to sell its holding in *The Mercantile and General Reinsurance Company* and this was acquired by the Prudential Assurance Company. In his survey (*The Times*, July 9) Mr. Goschen declared that the British insurance industry today needed a powerful professional reinsurance market operating internationally, and the above-mentioned development would "certainly be of assistance in this direction." He then made the following statement:

"In the situation of today's underwriting problems and pressures it is important that those engaged in this complex and constantly changing business should be ready to co-operate and work together for the improvements in technical conditions that all concerned quite clearly need. We know that we will continue to exchange information about the technical side of the business with the Swiss Reinsurance Company and indeed continue to co-operate with them in many ways.

"Generally speaking, the climate in which international professional reinsurance operates remains difficult and increasingly we see our role involving a much closer association with direct business than we have ever considered necessary before. Allied to this is the necessity for us to be better informed about the business we receive under automatic treaties, both pro rata and

non-proportional. There is an irreducible minimum of information without which we cannot do our job properly, and we are campaigning to rectify this situation.

"Reinsurers have no one to blame but themselves for the technical condition of the General branch business. Certainly we do not blame our ceding companies. However, to remedy many of the underlying troubles we shall require their help and collaboration and this will sometimes involve innovations and require concessions on their part. We are confident, however, of obtaining the co-operation needed to achieve this."

Foreshadowing an issue of new shares in *The Reinsurance Corporation Limited* (June 28) to shareholders to raise approximately £½m., MR. JONATHAN BACKHOUSE pointed out that insurance had for several years been passing through a period of unprofitable underwriting, and continued:

"The adverse underwriting results of the direct-writing offices have had an even more adverse effect on reinsurers generally and this has been reflected in the results of your company in recent years. Because of this, we have been engaged in a revision of the whole of our Fire, Accident and Marine portfolios with the objective of reducing peak exposures and eliminating business which had become unprofitable or where the prospects seemed unattractive. This special exercise has resulted in a progressive reduction in overall premium volume as shown in the Accounts for 1965, 1966 and 1967. It is considered that with the completion of the review of our 1968 portfolio undertaken last year the necessary pruning has been accomplished.

"Your Directors now feel that, with the improvements which have taken place in the direct market, a profitable trading position should be attainable and that it is desirable for the company to proceed with a careful and selective build-up of portfolio through the acquisition of new business which conforms with current underwriting standards. To cover adequately the financial requirements of the anticipated growth of the business, your Directors are proposing to increase the authorized share capital of the company."

INSURANCE BROKERS

On future trends in the marketing of insurance, asserted MR. ROGER F. MARTIN, chairman of the Council of the *Corporation of Insurance Brokers* (May 28), it was inevitable that the recent spate of mergers among the larger insurance company groups would mean that the public would be served by fewer branch offices throughout the country. He went on to state:

"The need therefore for the public to receive advice from qualified *bona fide* insurance brokers who have the full con-

fidence of insurers is likely to increase over the next year or two.

"Another trend which is inevitable is that on both the company and the broker sides administrative costs are increasing due largely to legislative measures. We may not agree with the legislation which has been introduced but, if one thing is absolutely clear, surely it is that duplicated administrative costs as between companies and brokers must be reduced and as far as possible eliminated."

Marked progress in turnover and profits was made by the insurance broking subsidiaries and sub-subsidiaries of *C. T. Bowring & Co. Limited* (June 27), MR. IAN SKIMMING showed in the course of his annual statement. The London based broking companies in particular had continued to move ahead since the reorganization in 1966. Some of the increase in profit, he conceded, was the result of devaluation, a significant part of their earnings being derived from overseas, but even discounting this factor, he declared, the pure increase in profits was encouraging. During the year a number of other insurance broking firms, operating in the United Kingdom, Eire, South Africa, and other places, had been acquired.

New high levels in brokerage figures were also reported by MR. D. H. ERLEBACH for *C. E. Heath & Co. Limited* (June 20), as will be seen from the following extract from his statement:

"In 1967 the Group achieved an all-time record in its brokerage income, the total of £2,356,000 being an increase of 24 per cent on 1966. Devaluation played a part in this increase with a benefit in 1967 of £83,000, and in a full year it is estimated that the benefit will be in excess of £200,000. Apart from devaluation, and further benefits obtained by a reduction in the time taken to process insurances, the general level of brokerage income shows a considerable improvement over last year."

Another group of insurance brokers to record a "very satisfactory" increase in earnings was *Minet Holdings Limited*, group profit having increased by 18 per cent, following a 25 per cent growth in 1966. MR. L. H. CLARKE, whose statement was published in *The Times* of May 29, was the more pleased with this showing because of higher costs, including S.E.T., and "the continuing difficulties encountered in placing business with Lloyd's underwriters and insurance companies following recent unsatisfactory underwriting experience."

In 1967, MR. ROY L. LOWNDES disclosed in his review (*The Times*, June 13) for *Noble Lowndes Holdings Limited*, the company's total new business completed under pension schemes and by way of individual life assurance contracts was distributed among 85 life offices. Less than 1 per cent of the total was placed with Noble Lowndes Annuities, which specialized exclusively in annuity and life assurance business. He continued:

"This entirely objective selection of underwriters on the merit of their many and varied contracts is the raison d'etre of the qualified broker. It is naturally to the advantage of the client, large or small, to whom the insurance market, in which more than 100 Life Offices compete, necessarily presents an otherwise insoluble problem of selection."

The increase in the pre-tax profits of *L. Hammond & Co. Limited* (September 23) had resulted not only from the expansion of the business and higher rates of premium after the adverse experience of the insurance market over the past few years but also from the devaluation of sterling. Stating that business for the current year was progressing satisfactorily, MR. GORDON BIGGS commented that future profits should be enhanced by further economies through increased integration within the group and the more effective and wider use of the computer.

The brokerage earnings of *Price, Forbes (Holdings) Limited* were of world-wide origin, and in his annual survey (*The Times*, March 5) MR. I. H. F. FINDLAY stated that over 70 per cent of them arose from sources outside the United Kingdom, very largely in countries which had not followed the devaluation of sterling: the income of the group would benefit accordingly in the future.

Devaluation had helped towards a 10 per cent overall increase in consolidated profits of *Staplegreen Insurance Holdings Limited* (October 15) which MR. E. S. HOGG considered satisfactory since very poor results in the underwriting market resulted in only a minimal commission being earned from this source. He pointed out that the annual report covered the first financial year of the integrated brokerage businesses forming Hogg, Robinson & Gardner Mountain Limited. It was the opinion of the board, he added, that the commission from the underwriting agencies would improve, and that the company's brokerage business would continue to have the benefit of devaluation. Shareholders could therefore look forward to profits in the current year broadly in line with those of the year under review.

As regards credit insurance, the following excerpt is taken from the statement of MR. F. E. P. SANDILANDS for *Trade Indemnity Company Limited* (May 9):

"During the calendar year 1967 we earned gross premium of £3,108,387, which is the highest figure we have so far reached in the history of the company and is 11·27 per cent more than in 1966. Net of brokerages and reinsurances, premiums amounted to £1,097,341, an increase of 14·28 per cent over the previous year. It will, however, also be seen from the Underwriting Accounts that the figure for claim payments at £1,551,970 (£414,250 net after reinsurance) is much increased and that the balance transferred to Profit and Loss Account at £39,686 from the closed 1965 Account compares unfavourably with the

corresponding balance available a year ago. This is a direct reflection of economic conditions during 1967 and of the high incidence of business failures which, apart from a brief respite in the latter part of last year, have prevailed since the beginning of 1965. This trend is by no means over and a persistently high volume of claim payments is a continuing feature of the two open Underwriting Accounts of 1966 and 1967."

BURDEN OF TAXATION

F AR from there being any reduction in the crushing burden of taxation in 1967–68 fresh increases were piled up by the Chancellor of the Exchequer. Nor did the Government do much to simplify the needlessly complicated tax structure. MR. G. S. PITT of *The City Offices Company Limited* (April 4) attacked what he termed "the ridiculous complexity and vicious unfairness" of much of the corporation tax, close company and capital gains tax legislation. This, he asserted, had had the result that even professional advisers and the Inland Revenue were unable to advise the business community with confidence about their taxation affairs, and had led to a drain of confidence and a flight of capital. He added:

> "What is required is the repeal of much of the existing legislation and a return to sanity so that the taxes can be seen to be simple and just, and not hurriedly conceived pieces of theoretical socialism."

After showing that the effective rate of tax charged on *The British Oxygen Company Limited* (February 28) now totalled about 60 per cent of profits, against a really comparable figure of about 35 per cent before the 1965 Budget, MR. J. S. HUTCHISON implied that excessive personal taxation was one of the main causes of the brain drain. He stated:

> "Nor has there been any relief from the handicap imposed by excessive taxation on personal enterprise and initiative in this country. This makes it difficult, or impossible, to reward adequately and encouragingly those who really get for us the productive improvement the country so urgently needs. Surely in present circumstances it is madness to cling to a tax system that penalizes merit by grabbing for the Inland Revenue more money—and often very much more—than goes to the person who has achieved success and brought general benefit to the community. The best in management and in development expertise will, if this system continues, soon be centred outside this country with the most serious consequences for us all for the future. Already it is practically impossible to attract, as we must, experts from abroad who may be of great value; at the same time, as we all know, far too many of this country's experts are leaving, attracted by the greater opportunities elsewhere or driven away by taxation penalties."

In the course of his statement (*The Times*, April 25) to members of the *Institute of Chartered Accountants* the President, MR. W. E. PARKER recalled to their memory the letter he had sent to the Chancellor of the Exchequer on behalf of the Council of the Institute in February, 1968. In this he had urged a radical simplification of "the whole accumulated hotch-potch of fiscal legislation," and suggested machinery by which this massive task might be undertaken. He now declared:

"We are convinced that the essential first step is to fix the overall responsibility for examining feasibility, in relation both to new and to existing fiscal legislation. We believe that the right body for this continuing purpose is Parliament itself, acting through one or more Select Committees."

MR. W. R. B. FOSTER vividly illustrated the crushing burden of taxation on *John Foster & Son Limited* by showing in his statement (*The Times*, May 29) that if the company had not existed the Government would have lost over £410,000 of revenue in a year when the shareholders received only £102,802. He went on to assert:

"Few of the problems which were with us in the early part of 1967 have been resolved. For example, though the attempt to enter the E.E.C. has failed for the time being, we continue to knock on the door, which so obstinately remains closed. The Government has failed utterly to produce an economic climate in which business confidence can flourish and as a result the country's difficulties have shown no sign of diminishing. In recent years the country has been in an almost continual state of crisis. The tax burden on individuals and companies is excessive, the incentive to save has been almost destroyed, and the incentive to work and take risks has been considerably reduced. Finally, high taxation, contrary to current economic thinking, is the cause of inflation, not the cure for it. So we in this country will continue to lurch from crisis to crisis and there is no chance of any improvement until we have a Government which has the courage to stop the rackets connected with the welfare state and immigration, and to reduce taxation to such a level that it pays to work, to save and invest. Meanwhile, the brain and capital drain continues."

With an increase of 7 per cent in world sales of *Boots Pure Drug Company Limited* (July 11) a further improvement in productivity saw pre-tax profits up by 13 per cent, or by £1,936,431. But MR. W. R. NORMAN showed that after tax profits increased by only £340,847 because of higher taxes and reduced allowances. As he said, "What would the Government do for taxation without private enterprise!" The ridiculous nature of some of the decisions by the Treasury on dividend restraint is aptly suggested by the following paragraph from Mr. Norman's statement:

"Shareholders will remember that because of the good half year figures the interim dividend last November was raised from 6 per cent to 6½ per cent. This increase in itself is fractionally more than allowed by the dividend freeze later imposed by the Government in March. We therefore have no alternative but to reduce the final dividend to 7·99 per cent even though to repeat a final of 8 per cent would only have meant paying out an extra £3,840 out of a distribution of more than £5½m. Representations were made to H.M. Treasury but in vain. Comment is superfluous. In normal course because of the improved profit we would have recommended a final dividend of 9½ per cent making a total of 16 per cent for the year. This is now the second year that freedom of action over dividend policy has been restricted. With an interim dividend of 6½ per cent and a final of 7·99 per cent the total for the year is therefore 14·49 per cent, exactly the permitted 3½ per cent more than the total of 14 per cent last year, the dividend being covered 1·65 times."

As the income from the American investments of *The English and New York Trust Company Limited* (April 2) was subjected to foreign corporation tax, British corporation tax and, finally, to British income-tax when passed on to the shareholders by way of dividends, MR. I. M. L. D. FORDE declared that this was double taxation without relief.

"It is strange," he continued, "that the Investment Trusts, who have made a major contribution to invisible exports in the form of profits and dividends from their foreign investments, should be penalized in this way. I hope the new committee which has been formed to examine all questions in connection with invisible exports will succeed in persuading the Government and the public that the contributors to this vital element of our overseas trade should be encouraged rather than penalized."

Among much that he saw fit to condemn in the British taxation system, SIR HALFORD REDDISH of *Rugby Portland Cement Company Limited* (May 24) apparently was most hurt by the description "unearned income" applied to dividends paid on the investment of savings. His attack on current taxation policies read (in part) as follows:

"Hard work and thrift are the twin virtues which should animate our economic life. The recent Budget contained nothing to reward hard work, nothing to encourage thrift, yet the Chancellor cast a benevolent eye on untaxed receipts from lotteries—a seeming paradox which critics abroad were not slow to observe. We have a heavy tax on earnings, and if a man does save and invests his savings in industry his dividends are taxed as 'unearned' income. There is neither moral nor economic justification for any tax on income—the tax should be on expen-

diture: but if income is to continue to be taxed it would make more sense to encourage savings and investment in our industries by having a lower rate of tax on dividends. As it is, the man who invests his savings in non-income-producing assets not only escapes income tax and sur-tax but would also have avoided the confiscatory 'levy' this year. A leading Canadian newspaper recently said of U.K. taxation, 'the inequities are heavy, contradictory, damaging and fathomless'. (It might just as well have said 'iniquities'.)"

From the details in the accounts of the remuneration of directors of the *National Mutual Life Assurance Society* (May 7), MR. KENNETH A. E. MOORE stated, members would be correct in assuming that the "take-home" of each of the seven non-executive directors, including the chairman, after deducting income-tax and surtax, was undoubtedly less than that of the average junior. He then made this comment:

"The incidence of taxation on the earnings of persons of broad experience and heavy business responsibilities in a variety of activities has now reached the point of *reductio ad absurdum*. I only mention it because it is likely to make it more difficult in future to recruit directors of the right calibre."

MR. GEOFFREY SALMON mentioned that *J. Lyons & Company Limited* (July 16), having already had to modify its plans in accordance with the Government measures which had accompanied devaluation in November, 1967, found it necessary to re-shape them once again to allow for the Budget changes in March, 1968.

"We estimate," he continued, "that for the group as a whole the Budget measures will add £650,000 to costs in a full year, including £238,000 for extra selective employment tax. In addition the extra purchase tax on ice cream, soft drinks and chocolate biscuits, which could amount to a further £500,000 per annum, is certain to have a depressing effect on sales if past experience is any guide. The extra costs and purchase tax represent only part of the Budget's effect upon us."

For the *Institute of Taxation* (May 14) the President, MR. GEORGE WHILLANS, made it clear that he did not object to the anti-avoidance provisions introduced in the 1968 Finance Bill as such, but he condemned "legislation which is retrospective in effect," and declared that "this retrospective legislation is a highly important and almost alarming feature of this year's Finance Bill."

The income-tax liability of *The British Petroleum Company Limited* on dividends payable for 1967 was £27·6m., and it appeared from SIR MAURICE BRIDGEMAN's statement (*The Times*, April 17) that this had been mainly offset by transitional reliefs of £26·2m.

75

Like many other company chairmen, he was worried about the extent of tax liabilities when transitional reliefs run off. He stated:

"These transitional reliefs should go far to offset withholding tax liabilities for 1968 and possibly for 1969 also, but they will then taper off, to be extinguished in 1972, leaving the company to bear the full burden on dividend payments. We now pay overseas taxation amounting to upwards of 65 per cent of our net income before tax, and the increasing double taxation which will occur from 1969 onwards will become a serious burden. In this international industry we must compete with foreign oil companies whose tax arrangements are more favourable, and it must be hoped that some means will be found of avoiding the competitive disadvantage which will soon begin to affect us."

The serious effect of the advent of corporation tax and Schedule F on shipping companies was the subject of comment by MR. JOHN M. HOULDER of *Houlder Line Limited* (April 17). Previously, he stated, shipping companies were virtually exempt from all taxation during periods of adversity since their capital allowances more than offset the reduced trading profits.

"This, in effect," he went on, "meant that they paid their taxes only in periods of boom. Now they pay all the time. This is a factor which is bound to have an important long-term effect on the industry, on its structure and on its organization. We have shown the Schedule F taxes clearly in our accounts because it is often said that the Schedule F is a tax on the shareholders and not on the company. It is, of course, nothing of the kind (except indirectly); if the company maintains the same rate of dividend as before it is the company which pays the taxes, and it is these taxes which appear, at the present time, to be making inroads into our very substantial reserves. In fact, however, as mentioned by me last year, the Schedule F tax, shown in the accounts, is probably recoverable as a three year surplus, but this is the last year in which such a recovery can be made."

Addressing members of *Imperial Continental Gas Association* (July 1) LORD TANGLEY made some caustic remarks about the new taxation system, which he stated was designed to penalize foreign investment. I. C. Gas, he pointed out, earned well over £1¾m. worth of foreign currency annually without any corresponding foreign expenditure, a contribution to the balance of payments which, if it took the form of the export of goods, would merit consideration for the Queen's Award. "Being only an 'invisible' earning," he declared, "it is on the contrary something to be penalized. One wonders how long we have to wait before this nonsense is swept away."

The adverse effect of the loss of overseas trade corporation status was referred to by SIR JOHN D. BARLOW in his address for the

Muar River Rubber Company Limited (December 4). He said:

"The average rate of tax during the last three years since the introduction of corporation tax has been 66 per cent. The average rate of tax in the previous four years was 48 per cent, which shows the effect of losing overseas trade corporation status.

"The main conclusion in Mr. W. B. Reddaway's recent report to the Confederation of British Industry was that capital invested overseas yields a higher return to the national income than it would have done if the funds had been put to any likely alternative use. In Muar River's case the capital was invested in plantations over 50 years ago and the estates have been modernized out of profits. As the return from this investment is higher than from any likely alternative, is it wise for the British Government to tax U.K. companies operating in Malaysia so severely, when the locally registered companies there pay only 45 per cent of their profits in tax? Why not restore to British plantation companies the rates of tax provided under overseas trade corporation legislation?"

Another direction in which taxation was increased in the 1968 Budget was purchase tax. In his statement (*The Times*, May 25) for *Gala Cosmetic Group Limited* MR. S. H. PICKER mentioned the uncertainties created by the Budget which in this case had almost doubled purchase tax, from 27½ per cent to 50 per cent. However, he added that with four brands selling at different price levels the Group was well placed to stand up to any effect which increased prices might have on consumer purchasing power.

To make an overall assessment of prospects it was necessary to estimate Government payments of one kind or another which were now the counterpart of inordinately high rates of taxation, MR. P. T. STEPHENS declared in his annual statement (*The Times*, July 1) for *Saunders Valve Company Limited*. Thus export rebates were now to cease altogether. This was said to be a result of devaluation, but it seemed to Mr. Stephens more like "the desire of Central Government to take an immediate 2 per cent profit on our existing export turnover because it expected future export turnover and its profitability to increase as a result of devaluation." The difference of a mile or two in the geographical position of a factory made all the difference in one important aspect of Government aid, as he showed in the following extract:

"In the past year we received, as did all manufacturers, a substantial sum in Selective Employment Tax premium. This also now disappears. Yet if our main factory were situated not more than two miles to the north using the identical labour force we should receive regional employment premiums which would exceed £120,000 in a full year. Any comment on the economic

or social logic of the payment and withdrawal of such sums, which have no relevance to this company's actual trading conditions would be superfluous."

Because of the revised taxation agreement with the Republic of South Africa it was no longer of any advantage to *The Ever Ready Trust Company Limited* (June 17) to hold shares in any company there in which the Trust does not own at least 10 per cent, MR E. N. ROWBOTHAM asserted. Consequently a major portion of the holding in Eveready South Africa Limited was sold during the year, resulting in a capital profit of £249,171 which had been credited to capital reserve account. He then criticized Government policy in the following paragraph:

"Our income from South Africa will, as a consequence, be reduced substantially this year. The British Government is steadily but inexorably driving investment managers out of foreign investments either by the weapon of taxation or confiscation by means of surrender of Dollar premiums. Hence, no longer are we free to carry out investment based upon merit."

MR. D. F. McCURRACH compiled a closely reasoned case, in his statement for *The Alliance Trust Company Limited* (May 3), buttressed with figures from the Trust's own experience, against "the restraints and taxes put on by the present Government" on its United States investment operations, including the jungle of capital gains tax. Here there is space only for the concluding paragraph of a long argument:

"This company was formed, starting nearly a century ago, specifically to invest in the United States and has done so continuously since. We, like many other overseas institutional investors, have been able to contribute substantially to the country's Dollar war chest twice in two generations. But we cannot conduct our business in our own or the country's interests without from time to time exchanging our capital assets for others. This is the very essence of whatever success we may have. When we do so we are now severely taxed on a purely notional paper profit which we have not realized, which we have no desire to realize, and which even if we did realize we are prohibited by the very Inland Revenue Regulations which govern our tax status from distributing to our stockholders. This is pure confiscation, and represents a sacrifice of a major national interest to an imagined short term advantage of tiny proportions and to political appeasement. The recent Clarke Committee Report has shown the vital contribution to the country's balance of payments made by invisible exports of which our overseas business forms a part. It seems a form of lunacy to have devised, all within the last three years, this new system of taxes, of the 'surrender' and of the 'gentleman's agreement' restricting

overseas investment, at once so damaging to both national and private pecuniary interests as well as to confidence both at home and abroad."

For *Benn Brothers Limited* (September 20) MR. GLANVILL BENN reminded shareholders of the roles which companies played as unpaid tax collectors for the Government and cited figures from Benn's own experience which caused him to declare that "it is not taxation; it is extortion!"

In recent years the British public had been spending some £1,500m. a year on tobacco products, said MR. JOHN PARTRIDGE of *The Imperial Tobacco Company* (*of Great Britain and Ireland*) *Limited* (March 18). Of this, over £1,000m. represented duty collection by Customs and Excise.

"Since the end of the second world war," he declared, "we have added 5d. to the price of a 20s packet of medium-size cigarettes in order to meet increases in costs. Over the same period Governments have added, by Duty increases, approximately 2s. 8d. per 20. Here is the reason why both tobacco revenue and public spending on tobacco have been swollen to gargantuan proportions; and since tobacco is a near-necessity for over 20m. people and since the Tobacco Duty is a highly regressive tax, here in my judgment is one of the reasons for the inflationary pressure for higher incomes that has characterized our post war situation."

Small wonder that Mr. Partridge thought the whole tax structure had been crying out for reform for a long time past and came down in favour of "a broadly-based tax on spending—by way either of a general sales tax or a tax on value added."

But probably the most hated tax, at least as far as the service industries are concerned, is the selective employment tax, about which many chairmen complained. MR. E. H. HAYNES was fully representative of insurance chairmen in general when he told members of *Royal London Mutual Insurance Society Limited* (April 30) that a life assurance company was in no position to vary the premiums charged to its existing policyholders, and in consequence this tax must be found from surplus which would otherwise be available to provide bonuses for policyholders. He showed that the society's bill for this tax alone, which in 1966 was £86,000, had risen to nearly £260,000 in 1967, and now a further 50 per cent (*i.e.*, a sum of £130,000) was to be added.

It seemed unfair and illogical to MR. JOHN W. WAUDBY that S.E.T. was repaid to the factories of *The British Steam Specialties Limited* (July 25) but had to be borne in full by the distributive units selling the very goods which those factories produced.

MR. J. DOUGLAS MAYNARD of *Maynards Limited* (November 21) again protested at what he described as "the iniquity of the

pernicious Selective Employment Tax," and he asserted that even though the Government had set up a committee to investigate the whole subject of S.E.T., they had in the interim increased the charge by 50 per cent and had also withdrawn the premium which was allowed to the company's manufacturing operations.

Chairmen of a number of tea companies complained of high export and excise duties in India, quite apart from the loss of overseas trade corporation status in this country. The following quotation from MR. J. R. VERNÈDE's statement for *Western Dooars Tea Holdings Limited* (October 29) is typical of many other chairmen's reactions:

> "The sums paid out last year by this company's subsidiaries in excise duty amounted to no less than the equivalent of £223,000 and in export duty of £207,000. When it is remembered that on whatever profit may be left Central and State Government taxes take some 60 per cent and there is still Schedule F income tax to pay on any dividends paid in the United Kingdom, the case for all-round taxation relief seems strong indeed."

In his statement (*The Times*, May 22) for *Estate Duties Investment Trust Limited* LORD SHERFIELD listed some of the tax burdens which had lately been imposed on family businesses:

> "Verbal recognition is given in official statements from time to time, though often it seems rather grudgingly, to the contribution made by the family business to the national economy. But the actions of the Government nullify these kind words and steadily increase the difficulties with which private companies are beset. The 1968 Finance Bill is the latest example. It will bear with particular hardship on the successful family business, which is usually a close company.
>
> "The Special Charge on investment income for the year 1967/68, by which income may be taxed at a top rate of 27s. 3d. in the £, does not merely affect those with inherited wealth, but will seriously hurt the major shareholders in a private company. Under the provisions of the 1965 Finance Act they may be compelled to distribute 60 per cent of their profits after tax, and the Special Charge on this distribution will be a capital levy which it is only possible to meet by the sale of shares in the company. The statement that in 1969/70 the income of children's trusts is to be aggregated with that of the parent, will largely nullify the Estate Duty advantages of transferring shares to children while still maintaining effective control of the business. Finally, the extension of the gifts *inter vivos* period from five to seven years with no Estate Duty relief during the first four years can only create another obstacle to a business which is steadily growing, but is not yet large enough to obtain a market quotation for its shares.

"These are further burdens for the shareholders in a family business. The purpose of the Trust is to mitigate such burdens, now much more onerous than they were when it was first establlished. The need to make timely provision for Estate Duty, therefore, is becoming more pressing, and the Trust has the resources and the experience to give every assistance to the family which wishes to take advantage of them."

One of the points made by MR. DAVID POWELL in his annual review (*The Times*, May 16) for *Booker McConnell Limited* was his suggestion that it was in Britain's longer-term interest to modify existing company taxation arrangements "so as to encourage, and not discourage, more trade and investment in developing countries."

Referring to current prospects in his statement for *J. Coral Limited* (December 9) MR. JOSEPH CORAL declared that it was apparent that the doubled Betting Duty was inhibiting turnover throughout the industry. However, he hoped, by continuing the policy of sensible expansion whenever suitable opportunities arose, to maintain the group's prominent position in the betting industry.

WAGES, COSTS AND PRICES

As a rule, British industry and commerce again suffered increased costs during 1967–68, some arising from devaluation, others from price increases by the nationalized industries, others from heavier taxation, and still others from higher wages. Most of these increases in the costs of supplies were quite beyond the control of directors. On the other hand, official policy was to discourage the raising of selling prices to offset these augmented costs, and a number of proposed price increases were referred to the Prices and Incomes Board, together with many wage increases which had been agreed between employers and employees but appeared to go beyond the Government's maximum. All this resulted in pressure on profit margins, and great was the drive for economies in outgoings in other directions. Some companies, particularly those that benefited from the spending spree and were able to spread their costs over a large turnover, still managed to report increased profits, but others, especially in the capital goods industries, found it more difficult.

The dislike of employers for wage controls, hardly less than for price regulation, is illustrated in the following extract from COLONEL W. H. WHITBREAD'S statement for *Whitbread and Company Limited* (September 6):

"It has always been the object and endeavour of your Board to inspire good human relations between us all. This is an important ideal which runs through the history of this great company. Those who have recently joined the Group must realize that we look upon members of our staff and employees as individuals and have created an atmosphere that we are all in this together for the good of everyone concerned.

"However, the present Government squeeze on wages and salaries creates an unhappy state of affairs, and we hope that our staff and employees fully realize that we dislike this situation and wish to shake off the shackles of Government control as soon as possible. In was indeed fortunate that just before the squeeze your Board put up the salaries of all in the Group by 10 per cent.

"It must be obvious to all of us in this Group that, although we realize the Government must somehow slow down the inflationary tendencies, their present regulations on prices, salaries and wages are very rough justice to some of us and the sooner your Board can deal with those who work for us without

reference to the Ministry the sooner everyone will be happier."

Though he was able to report that *Tollemache & Cobbold Breweries Limited* (March 18) had been able to make a modest increase in the price of certain beers in the London area only from July 1, 1967, the late SIR THOMAS BLAND indicated one of the difficulties inherent in the price regulation policy as worked by the Government in this extract from his statement:

"Required to work, as we are, within the confines of a narrow price control structure, it is impossible for us to make the price adjustments between different qualities of beer which commercial considerations would indicate to be appropriate."

Signs that changes were taking place in the marketing, distribution and retailing of shoes, following the abolition of retail price maintenance, were noted by MR. W. J. JOBSON of *George Ward Holdings Limited* (November 7). A particularly noticeable feature, he stated, had been immediate price cutting in certain directions; while it was not possible reliably to forecast its effect, the situation was being kept under close review by the board. Meanwhile, the company's factories were working to capacity, the forward order position was satisfactory and branded sales were being well maintained.

Turnover of *J. Lyons & Company Limited* (July 16) had lacked buoyancy, especially in catering, although the company had succeeded in maintaining its position in the various markets it served, declared MR. GEOFFREY SALMON. He then referred to the advancing trend of costs in these terms:

"Costs continued their upward pressure. The official period of severe restraint on incomes came to an end last June, and since then there has been the expected rise in labour costs, which we have counteracted whenever possible by economies and higher productivity. Because of devaluation and other factors, many of our vital raw commodities have gone up significantly in price—notably flour, tea, coffee, meat and packaging materials. Increased costs cannot always be absorbed through greater efficiency, nor is it always commercially practicable to increase prices. A further complication is the Government's prices policy, compliance with which has delayed or prevented price increases we should normally have made."

How *Rowntree and Company Limited* (June 14) was affected by the rise in costs and the Government's price controls is vividly illustrated in the following quotation from MR. D. J. BARRON'S survey:

"The year 1967 was marked by substantial rises in costs. Many of the Group's important raw materials, particularly cocoa beans, were significantly higher in price and labour, and

overhead costs also moved sharply upwards in many countries. Interest rates—a significant factor in an operation which involves the holding of considerable stocks of expensive materials —were of course at an exceptionally high level. The benefit of holding long stocks—and the eventual advantage to the consumer—was underlined by the devaluation of Sterling in November, for the greater part of the Group's raw materials come from countries which have not devalued.

"It was possible by virtue of higher volume of sales and by improving productivity to offset some of the increases in cost but some rise in selling prices was inevitable. Competitive conditions in all the countries in which we operate effectively control the extent to which higher costs may be passed to the consumer. In the United Kingdom—our largest market—the operation of the prices and incomes policy was an additional influence on the level of earnings. The negotiations with the Government resulted not only in the absorption by the company of a considerable amount of higher costs but also imposed a costly delay in the implementation of approved price increases. The present method of applying price control causing, as it does, some wastage—for example, of packaging materials—and some loss of efficiency, also introduces uncertainty and inflexibility and makes for difficulty in long-term planning."

Mr. Barron also noted that resale price maintenance on confectionery ceased in July, 1967, after a lengthy court hearing, but stated that the effects of that decision on sales and profitability would become apparent only in the longer term, and that it was too early then to make any meaningful comment.

MR. JOHN PARTRIDGE told members of *The Imperial Tobacco Company* (*of Great Britain and Ireland*) *Limited* (March 18) that prices for its tobacco products had last been increased in August, 1964, since when many costs had risen substantially. In particular, the company had had to replace Rhodesian tobacco by additional purchases in other markets, mainly in the dollar area and at significantly greater cost. He went on to give an estimate of the combined cost of the Rhodesian substitution and of devaluation, the relevant passage in his address being subjoined:

"We have been able so far to hold our prices steady by greater operating efficiency, by various economies in manufacture, by careful husbandry of our Rhodesian leaf stocks in this country, and in general by lower overheads per unit sold. But now our Rhodesian stocks are nearing exhaustion, and on top of this we have to face the severe effect of the devaluation of sterling on the great bulk of our leaf imports. The full additional cost to the U.K. tobacco industry of these two factors— on the one hand the loss of Rhodesia as a source of supply, and on the other hand devaluation—will rapidly build up to

nearly £30m. per annum; and the cost to us nearly £20m. per annum.

"These circumstances inevitably foreshadow an increase in the prices of our tobacco products; but as and when such an increase has to be made we shall keep it to the minimum necessary to meet the needs of the situation."

In spite of strict Government control of prices and incomes, the experience of *Coast Lines Limited* (September 26) had been that the wage restrictions had not halted the rise in operating costs, and increased taxation had also added considerably to expenses, particularly in road transport. This was said by SIR ARNET ROBINSON, who added that where a sound case could be made for an uplift in charges traders generally had been understanding, but the blessing of the appropriate Government Department to an increase was often delayed for months at a time. The resultant loss in much-needed revenue, he asserted, could not be recouped.

The next quotation comes from SIR GEOFFREY KITCHEN'S statement for *Pearl Assurance Company Limited* (May 22), and gives the background to the wage increase for the staff which was referred by the Ministry of Labour to the Prices and Incomes Board:

"Good staff relations are a prerequisite to the sustained growth of any large organization and we have for many years recognized and negotiated with trade unions representing the three main groupings of our staff in the United Kingdom. This aspect of our affairs is being further developed at present by means of working parties, on which the Field Staff unions are represented together with Chief Office personnel, which have been set up to deal with various practical matters. Among the objects of these developments is the furtherance of our continued efforts to achieve more economical working. Apart from the long-term pressure of competition to do our best to give good value to our policyholders, the upward trend of costs outside our control is also an incentive towards seeking more efficient methods. This incentive is especially strong in the case of a life office servicing existing contracts the premiums under which cannot be increased to meet subsequent rises in costs, so that there is but a limited margin available for expenditure of all kinds. In this context we have been able to show very useful economies from our electronic data processing machinery and arrangements are being made for replacement of some of our existing machines with faster machines of greater capacity to enable us to benefit further from the use of computers.

"It is for these reasons that we were surprised when the Ministry of Labour decided to refer to the National Board for Prices and Incomes an agreement we had reached with the staffs'

representatives for modest uplifts in the salary scales affecting about 20 per cent of our employees. Much valuable time of senior Civil Servants and senior Pearl personnel will now have to be diverted to the Board's examination of this agreement. It seems evident that there is inadequate recognition of the constant pressure, to which I have referred, exerted upon us by the limited resources out of which we have to meet our expenses."

For *The "Shell" Transport and Trading Company Limited* (May 2) MR. D. H. BARRAN declared that one of the most encouraging aspects of group results in 1967 was the reduction in operating costs in some major sectors of the business. This, he said, was perhaps most marked in tanker operations, where, if it had not been necessary to charter additional ships because of the closure of the Suez Canal, unit costs would have been between 8 and 9 per cent lower than in 1966.

"Further good progress in this direction," he continued, "is expected in 1968 with the entry into Group service of vessels with a deadweight of 200,000 tons or more: by the end of the year we expect to have 14 ships of this capacity in service. Although we have had some teething troubles (which were to be expected as we are virtually the first to operate this entirely new class of ship), we are confident that these new ships will behave well and perform fully up to expectation, thus contributing to continuing reductions in our shipping costs."

In common with industry generally, asserted MR. JOHN RAYMOND, *Fluidrive Engineering Company Limited* (March 28) was suffering from the pressure of rising costs and higher taxation, both of which, with selling prices limited by competition, were inevitably eating into its profit margins.

SIR ARCHIBALD FORBES informed members of *Spillers Limited* (June 7) that devaluation would have a significant effect on the company's raw material and certain other costs in 1968–69, and the authorities had approved increases in the prices of flour, bread, animal feeds and certain pet foods. These came into operation early in the current financial year, and should cover most of the impact of devaluation. However, as will be seen from the following extract, he remained critical of the ability of Government agencies to give a prompt and fair decision in matters of pricing policy:

"Other increases in costs, both direct and indirect, will stem from the Budget and the new regulations about transport, and it would be unwise to assume that there will not be other upwards movements of a more general nature. It has always been and will continue to be our policy to try to achieve the greatest practicable absorption of costs through increased operating efficiency and expansion of sales. But it has to be accepted that

the maximum of effort may not succeed in containing costs and there comes a stage when prices ought to be increased to preserve that level of profit margin which shows a reasonable return for effort and investment. We live in times when these decisions are no longer left to the judgment of those in industry but are made by Government Departments and official bodies set up for the purpose. It is difficult for such institutions to deal quickly and fairly with a mass of applications which descend upon them and this is an added risk to which we, in company with many others, are exposed. Apart from expanding the business in general, our major preoccupation in 1968–69 is the securing of better earnings in the bakery and animal feed activities."

Considerable savings in overhead costs of *Charrington, Gardner, Locket & Co. Limited* (July 18), Mr. K. M. Stobart declared, had contributed to the improved results. However, he went on to complain:

"It is naturally frustrating that the profits accruing from all our efforts to improve efficiency and reduce costs are continually being eroded by additional burdens imposed by the Government, most of which appear to be directed with special emphasis against the distributive and service industries in which we are mainly engaged."

Commenting on the menace of increasing costs, Mr. Harry Smith of *British Ropes Limited* (May 30) stated:

"Our efforts to reduce costs and improve efficiency are continuing and further operating economies were achieved in 1967. It is always difficult to reduce costs and it is disheartening for those concerned when their success is offset by increases in the costs of supplies and services. During the last few years we have suffered very steep rises in these costs, most of which are now directly under Government control. The recently announced increases in the costs of gas, telephones and postal charges are not very encouraging signs for the future, as it is extremely important that we now have a long period of stability in this whole area if we are to maintain our competitive positions in world markets. Given this stability, and further progress in our own efforts of cost reduction, we can look forward to a healthy development of our overseas trade."

On a comparable basis pre-tax profits of the British Industrial Sand Limited subsidiary of *General Refractories Group Limited* fell by 18 per cent. Sir George Briggs reported in his statement (*The Times*, March 28). The reasons behind this decrease he gave as follows:

"Costs again mounted sharply and whereas in previous years

it was possible to match increases by additional sales we found ourselves for the first time in many years, having to contend with some reduction in demand. Quarrying makes heavy calls on capital for the acquisition of mineral reserves and the provision of plant to meet even tighter specifications. Regretfully we may have to increase prices to offset these various factors."

Overshadowing other increases in costs *Birmid Qualcast Limited* (December 20) had had to meet in the year under review had been those which arose directly or indirectly from sterling devaluation; raw materials and general supplies originating abroad were all affected. After making this statement, LORD EXETER went on to enumerate the other cost increases affecting profit margins as follows:

"Other heavy burdens placed on our margins during the year by Government action have been increased National Insurance contributions, an unfavourable change in the incidence of Selective Employment Tax and the withdrawal of export rebates, while as I forecast last year, National Boards have contributed to the problem by substantially increasing the prices of electricity and foundry coke and reducing the levels of Industrial Training Grants. Not all of these increased costs have been capable of immediate reflection in our selling prices and our margins therefore have inevitably suffered."

Among the points made by MR. WILLIAM P. CAPPER in his review (*The Times*, May 30) for *Capper-Neill Limited* was that profit margins generally were tending to shrink, and for the process plant industry the political as well as economic outlook was somewhat obscure. For 1968–69, however, the board were encouraged by the volume of work recently booked from overseas markets which the company had not previously penetrated. Sales activities to increase the group's share of business from these areas were being vigorously expanded.

F. W. Thorpe Limited (December 12), MR. K. C. BRANGWIN asserted, had again been faced with increased competition in a severely reduced market. Manufacturing costs, he added, increased by reason of the devaluation of the pound, but "we could not raise our selling prices." However, he declared that in the first three months of the current year confidence appeared to be returning to industry: the company's sales and orders showed a marked improvement over the same period of the past year.

Another company chairman to report that devaluation had increased a substantial portion of raw material costs was the late MR. R. P. CHESTER of *Donald Macpherson & Co. Limited* (March 27), who added "that these increases will be absorbed as far as possible, but some price rises are inevitable."

Competitive pressure for all work offering *The Harland Engineer-*

ing Company, Limited, whether at home or abroad, was such that margins were frequently slender, it was said in the chairman's statement (*The Times,* May 30). Special steps had been taken in 1967 to curtail expenses, and efforts were being continued to contain costs and improve productivity; and, in the absence of unforeseen circumstances, it seemed likely that 1968 profits would be no less than the 1967 figures.

Some of the credit for the improvement in profits of *J. H. Fenner & Co.* (*Holdings*) *Limited,* stated MR. S. B. HAINSWORTH in his annual review (*The Times,* January 4), must be given to "our tough but fair management team," who had made it possible to increase production and turnover and, in some instances, to reduce production costs.

The increase in group profit and turnover for the *Ozalid Company Limited* (August 22) were considered satisfactory by MR. C. A. G. HEWSON in view of the adverse factors with which the company had had to contend. These included a further rise in costs, combined with price competition in certain products both in the office equipment sphere and the drawing office trade, as well as dock strikes, the closure of the Suez Canal, sanctions in Rhodesia, civil war in Nigeria, and sterling devaluation, which created problems in relation to imported materials, but produced advantages in some directions, although he considered the last-named might probably be short-term.

The next quotation comes from the statement by MR. JAMES ANDERSON for *Anderson Mavor Limited* (July 17):

"During the year continuing efforts have been made to reduce manufacturing and other costs through improved methods, and I am glad to report that these to some extent have minimized the effects of rising costs of material and labour. It is the Board's policy that these efforts should be continued, as only by so doing can we maintain our competitive position at home and abroad."

During the year the board of the *Exchange Telegraph Company* (*Holdings*) *Limited* (July 25), in conjunction with management consultants, stated MR. T. F. WATSON, had brought into operation a programme of reorganization which it was hoped would result in increased profitability throughout the group. Rising costs, particularly wages, would undoubtedly absorb some of the benefits for which they were planning, but nevertheless the board looked to the future with optimism.

The marked improvement in profits of *BTR Industries Limited* (June 5) on about the same level of sales, declared the late SIR WALTER WORBOYS, reflected in part the great efforts to improve efficiencies and reduce costs in all groups and in part the reduction in central administrative and service expenses. He also stated that great emphasis continued to be placed on the importance of cost reduction in all activities, and he added:

G   89

"During 1967 there was improvement in production planning and control, and much effort was spent on the introduction of work-study-based incentive schemes for operatives in the production and maintenance departments. These are now beginning to bear fruit."

With sales only 3 per cent higher than in 1966–67, *The De La Rue Company Limited* increased its pre-tax profits by no less than 41 per cent, MR. A. G. NORMAN reported in his preliminary statement (*The Times*, May 16), and he continued:

"There was a significant gain of 2.3 per cent in overall margins of profit on sales to a figure of 8.6 per cent and almost all companies in the Group contributed to this improvement. As has been indicated in quarterly reports, most of the gains have been registered in the last half of the year and heavy consumer buying in the U.K. market in this period has increased the volume and profitability in Formica Ltd. and Thomas Potterton."

A large part of SIR RONALD STEWART's statement for *London Brick Company Limited* (May 30) was devoted to the subject of brick prices, including the report of the Prices and Incomes Board. Here there is only space for the following paragraph of his report:

"Although the necessity of having to apply two price changes in a period of a few months was regretted, the overall infliction on the customer was a moderate one. As the Prices and Incomes Board Report on the brick industry pointed out, the advances increased the price of a house built in our products by only a third of one per cent, and their overall effect on building costs was therefore negligible. The Report further recognized that this company had for many years been the effective price leader in the brick industry and that, as such, it had played an important part in holding down the overall level of brick prices. It was for this reason that the recommendations on prices were limited to ourselves."

Commenting on the report of the Prices and Incomes Board upon the television rental and relay industry, MR. JOHN SPENCER WILLS included this paragraph in his statement for *Rediffusion Limited* (July 31):

"The National Board commented upon the very modest average rate of return on the heavy capital cost of relay networks of the HF type. Since the end of the financial year our companies have reluctantly made small increases in their charges for the relay input. For the most part those charges had remained unaltered for $4\frac{1}{2}$ years, during which we had absorbed the general increase in costs and heavy expenses in re-equipping our networks to cater for new developments in

broadcasting. The increases which we are now making go only part of the way to offset entirely new and unexpected increases in cost, resulting from recently increased taxes, devaluation and the higher charges for public utility services. Prior notification of the increases was given to the Government, in the spirit of its prices and incomes policy, although this notification was not obligatory, and no objection was raised.

For *Associated Biscuit Manufacturers Limited* (May 21) MR. RUPERT E. CARR reported that an increase in selling prices agreed in November, 1967, was followed by devaluation. This resulted in a further increase in costs; and the purchase tax on chocolate biscuits was also raised in the recent Budget. The board therefore sought and obtained permission for a further price increase. As the company's selling prices had been very stable over the last few years, the directors had very little experience to go on in estimating the effect upon sales of what amounted to a spate of unavoidable price increases.

LORD ABERCONWAY informed shareholders of *English China Clays Limited* (March 18) that the decision to increase prices of china clay as from July, 1966, could not, because of the "freeze" then starting, be applied to the home market. But when the standstill ended the board reluctantly decided to apply for permission, which the Government granted, to make modest increases in home prices, which during the previous 10 years had been increased on an average by only 7 per cent. He also gave this account of the directors' policy on export prices after devaluation.

"When sterling was devalued last November, we immediately adjusted our sterling export prices by the full proportionate amount of the devaluation. We did this in the conviction that it was in the interests of the country that we should earn the greatest possible amount of foreign currency, and in the knowledge that customers, in those countries which did not also devalue, would have to pay no more for their clay than before in terms of their own currency."

The uninhibited attitude towards prices and costs adopted by the board of *William Briggs & Sons Limited* (March 28), who reported the seventh record year in succession, is well brought out in the following quotation from the statement of MR. N. W. BRIGGS:

"In the event we have this further record-breaking year, and in the light of present-day comment on this country's decreasing standards and inflationary tendencies, it is clear beyond all doubt that in the industries we serve there is no chance whatever of increasing profits on the basis of increased prices. To quote real prices in order to obtain a sufficient share of the available business, and then to turn the orders and contracts

into profitable trade, is only possible on the basis of good management and efficiency which must be made to increase as competition and costs increase. These results do not reflect particularly lucrative contracts or orders, or some outstandingly profitable aspect of our trade, but are brought about by a steady quality and value for money policy."

MR. M. A. T. JOHNSON listed for members of *Richard Johnson & Nephew Limited* (July 19) the many cost increases which faced the company; the relevant paragraph in his speech follows:

"During the current year we will have to forgo Selective Employment Tax premiums, and Export Rebates. We will have to bear the full impact of advances in Wages and Salaries, and other cost increases which were only partially effective last year. Notable amongst these were Electricity charges, National Health Insurance, and Rates. We have even had to pay considerably more for Water, which still falls copiously from the heavens, presumably at no extra cost. Since the New Year there have been further increases in Wages and Salaries, National Health Insurance, and Rates; carriage charges are higher, in addition to which we will have to pay the increased Road Tax on our Transport vehicles. In total, I estimate that the higher charges over the last fifteen months, for which Government action is largely responsible, will cost the Group something between £400,000 and £500,000."

If there is no extra cost attending the rainfall, however, the expense of converting it into water available in the tap generally tends to rise, as MR. RANDAL F. LOWE showed in his speech for the *East Surrey Water Company* (June 21). He said:

"For some years past now stockholders have been told that a steadily rising trend in the company's charges must be expected due mainly to the expenditure that would have to be incurred to develop the Bough Beech source of supply. The impact of the interest on the new capital required for this scheme was much aggravated by the provisions of the Finance Act 1965 which imposed a severe additional tax liability on the company. We are now entering the period when consumers will be sharply affected by the cost of these measures as, in the current year and in the year following nearly £3m. will be spent on the Bough Beech scheme. In addition working expenditure will continue to increase as a consequence of the rising trend of labour, materials and power.

"The water rate for this current year has been increased from 1s. 2d. to 1s. 3d. in the £ on the net annual value of the property supplied, with a corresponding increase in the charge for metered supplies. These higher charges, however, which are approaching the maximum authorized by the company's 1963

Order, will not be sufficient for the reasons already mentioned to prevent a substantial deficit on the year's working having to be met out of the accumulated surplus brought forward on Revenue Account.

"Application is therefore being made to the Ministry of Housing and Local Government under section 40 of the Water Act 1945 for new powers authorising a maximum water rate of 2s. in the £ and a maximum meter charge of 6s. 6d per 1,000 gallons. It is not expected that these maximum charges will come into effect for at least five years, but a rate of about 1s. 6d. in the £ is likely to be required for the year 1969-70."

However, some water companies found their financial results satisfactory enough for them to be able to reduce water charges. MR. H. F. RENNOLDSON sounded a cautionary note about the increase in income from metered supplies by *Sunderland and South Shields Water* Company (March 20), which for the year under review was nearly £500,000. Although this level might not be maintained, the directors had thought it most desirable, in the national interest, to reduce both the water rate poundage and the charges for measured supplies. These reductions were of the order of 4 per cent. The company's aim, he declared, was to stabilize charges for as long a period as possible.

SIR WILLIAM CARR gave an assessment for members of *The News of the World Organisation Limited* (June 12) of the impact of the price increase on the circulation of the *News of the World,* which at the end of May, 1968, was 6,167,000 copies a week. This, he asserted, represented a loss of less than 1 per cent and was better than they had hoped for.

During the latter part of the year *F. J. Parsons Limited* (March 12) increased prices of its newspapers, said MR. F. J. PARSONS, but only about one-quarter of the benefits of this extra revenue had accrued at the year end. He made these remarks on the outlook:

"Profits for the current year to date are in advance of those of the same period for last year, but it has to be borne in mind that we have to face an increase of £7 a ton in the price of newsprint, as well as a rise in journalists' salaries for the remainder of the year. Nevertheless, I am hopeful that we shall show improved results when next we meet."

In view of the further heavy increase in the Selective Employment Tax due later in the year MR. R. J. PRITCHARD revealed in his statement that the board regretfully would be forced to make further increases in the charges of *Pritchard Cleaners (Holdings) Limited.*

A warning note about the impact of sharp wage increases on the Canadian economy was sounded by MR. N. R. CRUMP at the annual meeting of the *Canadian Pacific Railway Company* (Montreal, May 1). He said:

"Last year was not an overly happy one either for the Canadian economy or for the international economy. Particularly threatening to economic stability is the combination of large wage increases and unsatisfactory productivity performance. The real income of our Country is limited to the amount we produce. There is simply no other source of income available to us, and it is illusory to think that we can make ourselves richer by paying ourselves higher money incomes."

In his presidential speech for the *Grängesberg Company* MR. ERLAND WALDENSTRÖM said that the prices trend for the group's chief products could be described without exaggeration as exceptionally unfavourable. "We have not," he asserted, "been able to find any year in the history of the Grängesberg Company in which the overall price declines were so severe as in 1967." Over the past 10 years, he showed, ore prices had fallen 31 per cent, plate prices 21 per cent and the freight rates on the Narvik–Rotterdam trade by no less than 57 per cent. However, in spite of the adverse price and wage trends and the considerably reduced profit margins, the company had been able roughly to maintain the trading results over the years. The foremost two reasons for this, Mr. Waldenström declared, had been the company's ability to operate at full capacity in all fields and the heavy increases in production volume.

INCREASING PRODUCTIVITY
AND EFFICIENCY

IT has been one of the main objectives of management for years past to increase manufacturing efficiency and workers' productivity, for success in this direction offers perhaps the best way of counteracting the effect of the continual inflation of wages and other costs on profits. But since the Prices and Incomes Board really got to work, and the easy way out of raising prices became difficult, managements have increasingly sought, by suitable incentives, to eliminate restrictive practices and generally to raise output without a corresponding expansion in the work force.

A thoughtful analysis of the position was made by MR. C. E. SUTTON in his presidential address to members of the *Institute of Cost and Works Accountants* (May 25), in which he stressed the need for a new approach to incentives and subsidies and their effect on the productivity of workers, managers and companies. In general, he thought, higher productivity was likely to be achieved only if there were incentives to labour, to management and to companies themselves. Frequently, however, particular incentives failed to achieve or only partially achieved their objectives. "Do we not," he asked, "provide subsidies or benefits which may possibly conflict with our efforts to stimulate greater productivity?" It was likely that on occasion they might be confusing the two and might offer incentives which turned out to be only subsidies! Many productivity agreements in the past had failed because one side had not fulfilled its obligation and no penalty had been provided. He continued:

"Society must come to its senses in this matter and in any industrial agreements ensure that no longer can benefits be paid without the provision of good and proper consideration, with sanctions for breach.

"Incentives to higher productivity must be so designed that they have not merely a once for all but a continuing effect. Furthermore, they should provide for sanctions against failure. Benefits and subsidies, too, must be carefully designed to minimize any disincentive effects. Work flow should be designed so that high productivity is a natural outcome and not just a product of hard and tiresome labour. Organization must be such that the potential manager is identified early in his career and given increasing opportunities with definite responsibilities as well as rewards.

"Productivity, however, is not just a matter of bribery and

95

threats; it stems mainly from an attitude of mind and it can only result from the more efficient organization of human behaviour; this can only be achieved by a much better understanding of human nature."

MR. F. N. MANSAGER of *Hoover Limited* (April 2), too, devoted considerable attention to the need for greater productivity in British industry, which became even more essential if the opportunities provided by devaluation to increase exports were not to be frittered away. He stated:

"The management of your company has always been alive to the vital necessity to maximize the use of available resources and manpower. The task has been made doubly difficult by the fluctuating demand caused by the imposition of credit controls at varying levels of intensity, which has bedevilled the industry over the past decade. This lack of a reasonably stable demand has made considerably more difficult the task of improving our productivity which is so essential in order to meet world competition. Thus, we have found it necessary not only to concentrate our energies on the efficient utilization of resources, but at the same time to continue to maintain a high degree of flexibility in our production units to minimize the effects of major changes in demand brought about by these measures.

"Although we have had some success in overcoming the problems of fluctuations in demand induced by variations in credit restrictions there can be no doubt that stability in credit controls would permit major improvements in production efficiency and investment planning. It is particularly disturbing that the fiscal measures which cause the damage which we and other parts of the consumer durables industry have suffered in both home and export markets for over 20 years have repeatedly failed in their avowed purpose. That they reduce domestic sales of consumer durables is evident. It is equally evident that consumer expenditure as a whole is not reduced but is instead diverted to the purchase of other goods and services, many of which have a far higher import content. The repeated dislocation of the consumer durables industry has damaged over a long period the export potential of precisely that type of goods incorporating sophisticated engineering and style on which hopes of improved British export performance must rely."

Referring to the Central Productivity Services Department of *British Insulated Callender's Cables Limited* (May 9), LORD MCFADZEAN declared that its task was to assist in closing the gap between actual and technically attainable performance. And he asserted that one of the most encouraging features in a year of intense activity in this field "has been the way in which, as more and more areas of activity are examined, acceptance grows among

our employees of the basic concept that greater productivity can, in fact, be attained to the mutual advantage of the group and its employees."

"In the light of the labour problems which now confront us in the United Kingdom," he went on to state, "the major step we took two years ago in strengthening and extending our personnel function has proved to be well timed. Increasing attention has been given to the development of senior executives by deliberately planned widening of experience and responsibility. On the shop floor steps have been and are being taken to reorganize the supervisory structure in Divisions, reinforcing the management status of supervisors, providing a clear definition of duties and responsibilities and introducing a trainee foreman scheme open to all hourly paid employees. For both work people and staff we have long established an extremely effective consultative machinery, for it is only through a spirit of full co-operation that the Group can take full advantage of the ever-growing range of management techniques needed to maintain any large company at the peak of efficiency.

"The field of negotiations with the Trade Unions is increasingly influenced by Government policies and by our national efforts to find a workable incomes policy. Waste of vital manpower must be avoided and those employed be fairly rewarded one in relation to another so that they benefit from increasing efficiency. We have during the year concluded a number of productivity deals and I believe our faith in this approach will be fully justified as these are effectively implemented in the future."

That *Harland and Wolff Limited* (Belfast, May 15) had sought throughout its negotiations with the unions to ensure that any advance in rates was accompanied by an increase in productivity was claimed by SIR JOHN MALLABAR. At present, he stated, the company had in operation flexibility agreements covering 89 per cent of skilled workpeople and 50 per cent semi-skilled and unskilled employed in the shipbuilding department; and agreements of a similar nature operated in other departments. These agreements, he asserted, should prove to be of considerable worth in future contracts. He believed they were ahead of anything agreed elsewhere in British shipbuilding, though "it will take some little time before the benefits for which we hope are reflected fully in terms of improved profitability."

For *The Metal Box Company Limited* (July 25) MR. DAVID DUCAT referred in the following terms to the success which had attended efforts to increase productivity:

"By the greater application of management to the advances made in our technology and the improved efficiency in the utilization of our equipment and its attendant labour we have

been able to show substantial improvements in our productivity. As a further step in our plans for rationalization, we decided, with regret, to close our Newcastle-upon-Tyne factory. The work currently undertaken there is to be transferred to the Carlisle branch where capacity exists to absorb the production under conditions which lend themselves to more efficient manufacturing methods."

Dealing with the labour relations of *Williams Hudson Limited* (July 31) MR. L. A. SIMPSON stated that the new productivity agreement was working well. Since the introduction of the scheme, he claimed, the majority of the group's output records had been broken even though piecework was no longer paid.

The conclusion of a number of productivity agreements by *Ranks Hovis McDougall Limited* (January 25) led to these comments by LORD RANK:

"I referred last year to the productivity agreements for individual flour mills which we were then starting to negotiate with the unions. This policy has been extended and I am glad to report the successful completion of five such agreements. Others are currently under discussion. These agreements are making an important contribution to containing production costs and thus increasing our industrial efficiency. They reflect great credit on those concerned—both management and union officials at national and regional levels. Room remains, however, for much further progress in this direction."

Further productivity increases enabled *Black & Decker Limited* to reduce prices in the United Kingdom and overseas, it was stated in the annual report (*The Times*, February 15). Sales per employee rose to a new record of £4,647, or 62 per cent ahead of 1962.

The first productivity agreement which *W. H. Paul Limited* (November 1) had negotiated was referred to by MR. W. H. PAUL in these terms:

"For the first time in its history the company has been able to negotiate a productivity agreement with a large part of its labour force which exchanges increases of pay for improvements in working practices. This agreement, given good will and honest application, could bring considerable benefits to the company's employees and customers and to the company itself."

For *Broom and Wade Limited* (January 31) MR. C. BROOM SMITH stated that the increase in invoiced sales in the parent company had been brought about by improved efficiency in the works, leading to shorter delivery time.

The steady growth of turnover in the optical division of *Augustine Investments Limited* (June 12), MR. R. E. BROOK reported, was maintained throughout the year, and the more fluctuating growth

of profit was resumed. Inescapable overheads did not fail to rise, "but were contained by increased productivity due in the main to the co-operation of the staff." Incidentally, he noted that an instalment of the long-overdue increase in National Health Service fees was at last accorded towards the end of the year—a step which should be "of appreciable benefit" in the current year.

Higher productivity and lower production costs are recorded in the following quotation from LORD BRECON's statement (*The Times*, October 28) for *A.B. Electronic Components Limited*:

"Increased expenditure on methods engineering and on product development has raised productivity. A higher level of sales, particularly during the last six months, has resulted in greater benefits arising from our new plant investments. Growing customer co-operation in standardization is reducing production costs.

For some time the board of *The Leyland & Birmingham Rubber Company Limited* (October 23) had been far from content with the financial return for the capital and personal effort employed in the United Kingdom, MR. H. JACKSON declared. Much was now being done and more was being planned to achieve a marked improvement in efficiency and profitability. He continued:

"None of us can see in the immediate future any change of general conditions which could quickly and substantially alter the economic climate for the better. Indeed, loss of Selective Employment Tax Premiums and to a lesser degree Export Rebates, render improved viability more difficult for us. On the other hand, the fact of our improvement in the U.K. in the second half of this year, due in part to slightly better trading conditions, encourages us to believe that this can carry on into the current year, so that avoiding unforeseen setbacks we might hope for better results next time.

"I am convinced however, that the more tangible prospects of greater achievement in the future lie in the success of our own efforts. I am confident the programme of reorganization and development . . . will in due course lead us through higher levels of efficiency, better utilization of assets, and more rational planning of production to a more satisfying reward for capital and effort. This can only be a gradual attainment and it would be unreasonable to expect immediate and spectacular results. In South Africa, recovery to the extent of surpassing the peak of a few years ago will only be made by continued efficient effort, the results emerging gradually and in step with the economic growth of that developing country."

The management of *Peter Brotherhood Limited* (November 12), MR. G. W. WILKS averred, had continued its efforts to improve productivity and efficiency in all departments; this was essential if

it were to obtain orders in the highly competitive world markets.

In spite of the adverse conditions in the motor trade, the *United Spring Company Limited* (February 22) had had a successful year, improved productivity enabling it to increase both turnover and profit. After making this statement, MR. S. WESTWOOD declared that the company was "in a good position to take advantage of any upsurge in demand."

The next quotation comes from SIR WILLIAM WALKER'S address for *Jute Industries (Holdings) Limited* (February 12):

"A revised wages structure, a general wage and salary increase and shorter day and nightshift working hours took effect in July, 1967. To minimize the ever-increasing cost of materials and labour, management are striving to make the most efficient use of the manpower available, increase productivity and introduce improved methods. This and other problems are tackled energetically, and our thanks are due to management and all our employees on whom the success of the Group is so dependent."

John Bolding & Sons Limited (March 27) started 1968 with a good order book, MR. J. F. BOLDING reported, and he had every hope that the steps which were being taken to increase productivity and sales of the company's own manufactured goods, both at home and abroad, would result in further improvement during the present year.

After stating that one of the objectives of nationalization had been to rationalize the major portion of the steel producing industry, MR. JOHN ANNETTS in his review for *The National Association of Iron & Steel Stockholders* (May 23) went on to make this comment on the growth of rationalization in the stockholding business:

"The Steel Stockholders have, of their own volition, been rationalizing in recent years and there is increasing interest among members in mergers, take-overs and co-operation. There is every indication that at the present time those persons in authority in the Corporation realize that in the interests of productivity and efficiency, the smaller orders must be dealt with by the Stockholders, and it is also believed that the concept of the smaller order involves very useful tonnages. The Stockholding industry is fully geared to deal with the increased tonnages which would result from such a policy.

"In spite of the growth in size of many Steel Stockholders, I am confident that there is also a great future for the medium sized and smaller firms. However, what we must have is efficiency—irrespective of size—giving the Steel User the service he wants at the lowest price which will give the User satisfaction and the Stockholder a reasonable profit.

"If the next twenty years can show the same degree of pro-

gress for the Stockholder as has been enjoyed in the last twenty, then we shall have all done well."

In his statement (*The Times*, June 17) for *Klinger Manufacturing Company Limited* MR. W. G. CASTELL claimed that British machine builders had led the field in advanced designs for textured yarn machinery. In days when higher productivity was so essential, he added, it was interesting to note the large strides made in this direction in yarn processing: a modern machine would do the work of 50 machines 15 years ago, with man hours reduced to less than one-tenth, "and there are still new ideas waiting to be introduced."

From MR. K. J. DEAR's review for *R. & A. G. Crossland Limited* (June 14) the following extract is taken:

"The increase of £11,080 in the pre-tax profit adds a further year of unbroken advance in our company's profits. The trend of rising costs was more than offset during the first nine months by improved productivity and higher turnover. The last three months bore the brunt of the recent economic and political events, and led to a sharp re-alignment of orders from our customers. Margins were under severe pressure and work schedules upset."

Nevertheless, given a reasonable chance, he thought the company would succeed in showing in 1968 yet another advance in profits.

Dealing with short-term prospects at home for *BPB Industries Limited* (July 31), MR. R. S. JUKES declared that the costs of all their United Kingdom operations were bound to rise when the full effects were felt of devaluation, of the Transport Bill and of the various taxation measures introduced by the Government. A part of these extra costs would have to be passed on to the consumer but, to offset much of their effect, "we are further increasing our investment in modern equipment and using the latest techniques in order to raise productivity." He hoped that profitability could be maintained.

With pre-tax profit 50 per cent up in 1967 over 1966, the return on capital employed by *J. Bibby & Sons Limited* had risen by almost 3 per cent, reported MR. H. MASON BIBBY (*The Times*, February 19)—an improvement which had been achieved in the traditional activities of the parent company through increased efficiency.

In the United Kingdom, where over 70 per cent of their new life business was written, productivity per member of the field staff of the *Norwich Union Insurance Group* (May 7) had increased by no less than 23 per cent over the year, which the President, MR. DESMOND E. LONGE, declared was an indication of the calibre of the field staff.

Showing the growth of staff productivity in a different manner, MR. FREDERIC SEEBOHM included the following paragraph in his statement for *Friends' Provident and Century Life Office* (May 8):

"It has been our aim for some years to improve both the efficiency of the service which we offer to Policyholders and also the ratio of expenses incurred in handling our steadily increasing volume of business in all departments. Over the last ten years at Home the premium income, in all departments, has more than doubled and New Life Sums Assured have increased fourfold, whereas the number of staff handling the business, thanks in part to our computer, has increased by only 9%."

With a 23 per cent increase in turnover and an even larger increase relatively in profits before taxation, MR. K. M. WOOD reported to members of *Concrete Limited* (August 2) that higher productivity from the factories had restored the 1968 percentage of profit both to capital employed at 34·6 per cent and to turnover at 8·5 per cent to the 1966 level—the previous best.

Shortage of skilled staff again proved a handicap to productivity for *Anglo-Swiss Holdings Limited* (April 26); and MR. P. R. BRIERLEY said it was felt that the capital expenditure of £35,000 on plant for operator training, sponsored by the Engineering Industry Training Board, was a step towards remedying this situation.

In his speech (*The Times*, July 30) as President of the *Grängesberg Company* MR. ERLAND WALDENSTRÖM declared that the company had enjoyed an extremely favourable productivity trend for a great many years—a trend which he illustrated for the past five-year period by "fairly reliable" statistics. Measured in production per working-hour, he said, the average rise in productivity had been between 8 and 10 per cent for the iron mining, steel and shipping sectors, with even higher figures in stainless steel manufacture at Nyby. These increases were largely the result of increased investments aimed at improving efficiency and raising volume, and also of constant rationalization of technological and administrative procedures.

The report of the board of *Société Internationale Pirelli S.A.* (Basle, September 25) stated that the results of Pirelli S.p.A., Milan, were better than those of the preceding financial period because of lower costs and the higher overall productivity of the company, and the dividend was raised.

The average price for all products of *Stora Kopparberg* (Falun, Sweden, May 10) was 0·6 per cent lower than in the previous year, according to the directors' annual report, which also stated that production costs for most products were reduced thanks to improved productivity and lower raw material prices. Gross profit increased by 20 per cent.

EXPANDING EXPORTS

D URING 1967–68 British exports expanded notably, and many chairmen were able to cite figures showing significantly increased shipments abroad. While devaluation was naturally helpful to British companies seeking to increase their exports, a number of chairmen were inclined to deprecate too sanguine expectations based on this factor, stating that the long continued tendency for costs to rise had been accentuated by Government and quasi-Governmental agencies alike. Several company chiefs, especially in the insurance world, laid emphasis on the importance of invisible exports, which they claimed were not sufficiently appreciated by the general public or, sometimes, by the Government.

A notable point was made by SIR PETER ALLEN when he said that sales overseas by *Imperial Chemical Industries Limited* (March 28) for the first time in one calendar year exceeded sales in the home market. He went on to say:

"This trend of overseas sales should rise faster than home sales and would lessen the company's dependence on the British economy. Of the total sales overseas of £493m., £166m. came from exports from the United Kingdom, compared with £156m. in the previous year. The 1967 figures included just over £7m. for exports from Ilford Ltd. On a true comparison, the 1967 figures would show only a small increase in value, notwithstanding the fact that the volume of exports made a good showing with a rise of 7½ per cent. The small increase in value was accounted for by a fall in export prices, notably those of synthetic fibres and polymers where competition was fierce."

As much as 80 per cent of the total production of *Fairbairn Lawson Limited* (November 27) had been exported during the year, SIR JOHN LAWSON declared. This is an achievement all the more gratifying in view of the difficult trading conditions of which he gave the following account:

"The exporting of capital goods requires highly accurate planning and strategy. Contracts generally take many months to finalize and it must be realized that withdrawal of incentives, increases in charges by Nationalized Industries and in National Insurance Contributions, dock and rail strikes, and other such events, invariably taking place at short notice, make the task of salesmen and manufacturers far more complicated and frustrat-

103

ing than is necessary, and the effects of these are inevitably felt by the customer."

The overseas business of *Joseph Lucas (Industries) Limited* (December 16) continued to expand and prosper, SIR BERTRAM WARING asserted. The company's direct exports increased substantially during the year to a new record of nearly £30m. Including the sales of group factories abroad total overseas business amounted to £56m. Taking account of the very substantial volume of group equipment fitted in the United Kingdom to vehicles, aircraft and aero-engines sold abroad, he estimated the overall value of Lucas overseas business from one source or another at approximately £100m. for the year—equal to the total sales of the group only 10 years ago.

With an additional stimulus from devaluation, companies in the *Birmid Qualcast Limited* (December 20) group, declared LORD EXETER, had spared no energies to expand their export markets, and with some success. Thus sales value of direct exports for the year was some 9 per cent higher than that credited in the previous year's accounts even though the latter included more than a full year's trading for both the Qualcast and Wright Rain groups.

Exports by *Quinton Hazell (Holdings) Limited* (September 19) had continued to expand, stated MR. E. QUINTON HAZELL, and they went to no fewer than 142 countries overseas.

Overseas operations of *Johnson, Matthey & Co. Limited*, MR. L. C. MONTAGUE disclosed in his statement (*The Times*, August 1), expanded and accounted for over 40 per cent of group profits. Direct exports from the United Kingdom were £30m. out of total group sales of £113m., excluding the operations of Johnson Matthey (Bankers) Limited.

The next quotation reveals the high level of export orders received by *British Insulated Callender's Cables Limited* (May 9) and comes from LORD MCFADZEAN's statement:

"Export orders received in 1967 achieved a new record of over £48m. This excludes our indirect exports in the form of goods we supply to other British companies for incorporation in the electrical equipment they export—a figure incapable of accurate assessment but undoubtedly substantial.

"Even allowing for lower metal prices, shipments were, however, slightly down as compared with 1966 due to such factors as the war in the Middle East and the unrest in Africa causing postponement of schemes, and to the self-inflicted wounds of the dock strikes in London and Liverpool. If one of the challenges in Britain today is to win back confidence in ourselves a challenge of at least equal importance in the export field is to win back and build up the confidence people overseas repose in us. In the business sphere few, if any, actions can defeat this latter essential objective more than the breaking of delivery

promises. Price is, of course, also a vital factor and devaluation will undoubtedly help, although in our case only to a limited extent as important constituents in many of our products are metals which have to be imported. In addition, we shall suffer the loss of export rebates.

"We are, both in the national and in our own interests, firmly committed to an ever-expanding effort in the export field and I am delighted to report a further substantial increase in incoming orders this year to date."

In his annual review (*The Times*, June 24) for *Rolls-Royce Limited* LORD KINDERSLEY asserted that the international nature of the company's business in gas turbines, motor cars and diesel engines and the extent to which it was dependent on the export of its products was borne out by the fact that during 1967 nearly 40 per cent of sales were exported.

Direct exports from the United Kingdom of goods manufactured by *The Metal Box Company Limited* (July 25) and its subsidiaries, the directors stated in their report, amounted to £7·9m. Included in this figure were the exports of the machinery building group, which were 14 per cent higher than in the preceding year; the orders from overseas had increased significantly since devaluation. MR. DAVID DUCAT in his statement referred specially to two new developments in export business:

"During the year we have exhibited our products and services in Poznan, Berlin, Gothenburg and Cologne and in April we staged a private exhibition in Warsaw and participated in a trade fair in Katowice. The interest which has been shown in these exhibitions has been most encouraging and during the next twelve months similar activities are planned in a number of Eastern European countries.

"The company has also assisted some of its leading customers in furthering their own export efforts. On two occasions, within the past year, with the backing of the British National Export Council, we have organized export missions to five major European cities with a view to promoting the sales of certain of our customers' products packed in containers of our manufacture."

Exports by *The George Cohen* 600 *Group Limited* were a record at £9,247,000, reported MR. JACK A. WELLINGS in his review (*The Times*, July 9).

Although none of the sales of *British Home Stores Limited* arose from exports, the next quotation, which comes from SIR MARK TURNER's statement (*The Times*, May 31), indicates that the company was by no means indifferent to the country's need for expanded exports:

"In considering our own and the national interest we concluded

H

that it would be better to conduct no direct export business, but rather to introduce all foreign buyers who became interested in Prova merchandise direct to our suppliers, giving them permission and encouragement to conduct a direct export business in which we had no financial interest. I am glad to report that a number of our suppliers are securing substantial export trade from these introductions."

Group exports by the *Rugby Portland Cement Company Limited* (May 24) amounted to a mere £1,066,750, declared SIR HALFORD REDDISH, who went on to give this explanation:

"The cement industry's export trade from the U.K. was virtually killed by the imposition of the fuel oil tax in 1961. At one time in the early post-war years over two million tons of cement were being exported annually. Under the umbrella of the fuel oil tax coal prices were kept up to a level in excess of those charged by the National Coal Board to cement companies on the Continent: and as kiln fuel is by far the largest item in our cost of production we lost our proud boast that British cement was the cheapest in the world. The industry's exports were thus substantially reduced."

The volume of overseas turnover of *The Cementation Company Limited* (September 30), which in the year reached almost £19m., made this concern one of the largest British contractors working overseas, MR. H. A. LONGDEN claimed. He was particularly pleased to mention the contract for the grouting work on the Tarbela Dam in West Pakistan; this contract, worth almost £3m., was the largest of its kind in the world, he asserted.

The Capsula Pneumatics subsidiary of *Metropole Industries Limited* (December 5), MR. G. G. E. MONEY, the managing director revealed, had just secured a firm export foothold in the United States: orders worth $16½m. (approximately £6,875,000) over the next five years were scheduled.

During the year a vigorous marketing operation was mounted abroad by *Kirkstall Forge Engineering Limited* (November 14), particularly in Europe, including Scandinavia. This was stated by MR. R. F. BUTLER, who added that in consequence orders in excess of £1m. were received during the year, with actual shipments rising from £300,000 to £360,000.

The following paragraph from MR. GEORGE V. KEELING'S survey for *Keelavite Hydraulics Limited* (November 5) shows how the company is tackling the German market for its products:

"Arrangements have been made with Schwelm Hydraulik K.G. Neuss, to market Keelavite equipment in Germany. The specialist products of this hydraulic firm are complementary to Keelavite, and we are pleased to report that we have recently acquired the sole selling rights for Schwelm Hydraulik products in

106

the United Kingdom and the Benelux countries. These arrangements, together with the technical advances previously referred to, should lead to a more rapid penetration of overseas markets."

In the export field, stated SIR ALFRED NICHOLAS, the output of *Aberdare Holdings Limited* (May 15) for 1967 was maintained, but because of the intensification of effort made in the overseas markets he was able to advise that in the first five months of the current year incoming export business had increased by over 50 per cent. "A large part of this increase," he explained, "is the result of the new development work carried out in 1967."

For *Fluidrive Engineering Company Limited* (March 28) MR. JOHN RAYMOND declared that both export dispatches and orders received were the highest achieved in the company's history. While unable then to forecast the full consequences of devaluation, he assured shareholders that "we will take all opportunities to increase our business overseas."

The export performance of *Klinger Manufacturing Company Limited*, according to MR. W. G. CASTELL's statement (*The Times*, June 17), had increased steadily year by year, especially over the past six years, when it had doubled almost each year. With the current order book an export turnover in the current year approaching £6m. was expected to be achieved.

Group turnover for *Decca Limited* (October 22), SIR EDWARD LEWIS stated, increased by £7m. to £47m. Including direct exports, overseas turnover was £27,700,000. Total exports at £14,900,000 increased by 25 per cent on the year; exports represented 44 per cent of the turnover of the United Kingdom companies, compared with 40 per cent in the previous year. Incidentally, Sir Edward referred to the increase in purchase tax on records in these condemnatory terms:

"The increase in purchase tax on records from $27\frac{1}{2}\%$ to the penal rate of 50% came as a shock to the industry. The arbitrary way in which records are now classed as luxuries, in the same category as jewellery and fur coats, is in marked contrast to the treatment of books and periodicals on which no tax is levied."

Sales of *BSR Limited* (June 27) were lower than in 1966, but MR. J. N. FERGUSON declared that the decrease was the result of economic measures in major markets, and he added that export earnings still represented more than 80 per cent of sales volume.

During 1967 exports by *Advance Electronics Limited*, SIR EDWARD HOWARD stated in his annual review (*The Times*, April 29), increased by 50 per cent to a new record. Devaluation came only in the last month, he added, and this gave the company an opportunity, particularly with the products of the Volstat division, which previously had been uncompetitive against products of local manufacture overseas.

107

Although the export turnover of *Hoover Limited* (April 2) fell from £11,300,000 to £10,600,000, MR. F. N. MANSAGER remarked that the rate of fall which had been evident since 1964 was reduced. In any case, the turnover, he declared, must be viewed in the light of the slowing down of economic growth in Europe, the most pronounced of which was the marked recession in Germany, where appliance markets were severely affected.

While direct exports of the group controlled by *Dorman Smith Holdings Limited* (September 11), stated MR. T. ATHERTON, were approximately 8 per cent up on the previous year, he had especially mentioned the word "direct" because some companies incorporated the group's goods in their own exports and sent its goods unaltered to other countries.

The next quotation comes from the statement by MR. W. E. WRIGHTON for *F. Wrighton & Sons (Associated Companies) Limited* (August 28):

"The Division operating at the Broxbourne factory and producing the so attractive reproduction furniture has turned in an increased profit and the exports by this company, although yet small, increased three-fold."

The annual report (*The Times*, April 3) of *The British United Shoe Machinery Company Limited* showed that exports by United Kingdom companies in the group reached a record figure with an increase of £234,000 to £6,488,000. A contract had been recently signed with the Soviet Union for the shipment during 1968 and 1969 of about 2,100 machines with a selling value of £2·3m., including £400,000 of complementary machinery from other suppliers. Even before this, the parent company already exported about 45 per cent of its machinery production.

SIR CHRISTOPHER CHANCELLOR stressed the import-saving character of *The Bowater Paper Corporation Limited* (April 24) in this paragraph:

"The new Companies Act requires us to show a figure for direct exports and for 1967 this was £3·9m. This provision reflects the Government's almost obsessive, and in my view much too narrowly defined, emphasis on the word 'export'. Basically the Bowater Organisation is, like British agriculture, an 'import saver' in the United Kingdom—but also by virtue of assets built up over the years in North America it is an important dollar earner. We do not appear to shine as direct exporters by virtue of the nature of our business; but it is worth noting that the products of our packaging companies, although not direct exports in the accepted sense, carry to many overseas destinations a wide variety of British goods. We believe that in 1967 the non-recorded exports of our packaging plants reached a figure of £5m. And in our role as 'import savers' we estimate

that our United Kingdom production of newsprint and other papers in 1967 made the substantial contribution to the country's balance of payments of no less than £38m."

Although *The Thomson Organisation Limited* was not normally considered to be a major exporting company, LORD THOMSON OF FLEET pointed out in his statement (*The Times*, May 1) that during 1967 its total revenue from the export of newspapers, books and periodicals, and from services provided for overseas customers, amounted to no less than £4,087,639.

The importance attached to the export trade by the board of *Berisfords Limited* (April 3) is reflected in this excerpt from the annual review by MR. CHARLES BERISFORD SEBIRE:

"Our export trade as a whole shows a steady increase both as regards direct export and items supplied to other manufacturers to be used on garments which were being exported by them. The increase in exports is due mainly to the fact that my fellow directors have personally taken on the responsibility for this department, and have travelled far and wide to increase our sales; they have considered that customers and agents overseas were entitled to service at the highest level and the results have justified their contentions. Our trade with South Africa is severely handicapped by government policy which is causing our customers in that country to turn to German and Japanese suppliers."

As much as 73 per cent of leather sold by the group controlled by *Strong & Fisher (Holdings) Limited*, MR. J. P. STRONG mentioned in his statement (*The Times*, October 29), was for export; while the majority of these export sales were made to both E.F.T.A. and Common Market countries in Europe, some difficulty had been experienced in holding the group's trade with the latter.

After giving details of the export performances of some of the subsidiaries of *The Guthrie Corporation Limited* (July 31) SIR ERIC GRIFFITH-JONES went on to declare:

"I cannot over-emphasize the importance which I place in building export markets, not only in the national interest but also to reduce dependence on the vagaries of the home market resulting from the vacillation of the Government's economic and fiscal policies."

Another chairman who gave information about the exports of his company was MR. T. HARCOURT POWELL of *Revertex Holdings Limited* (March 28)—he mentioned *inter alia* that about 90 per cent of its natural latex concentrates was still being delivered overseas—and he also made the following general comment about exports:

"As we increase the manufacture of our products overseas in

109

subsidiary or affiliated companies, so our direct exports will decrease. If however, we had not built up these overseas companies, we should have lost a very great deal of overseas business."

A very large proportion of the sales of *English China Clays Limited* (March 15) went overseas, as will be seen from the following quotation from LORD ABERCONWAY's review:

"Throughout the year the home market for china clay was disappointingly quiet, but exports, despite recession in Germany and France, compensated for this. Shipments overall showed a modest increase over the previous year in tonnage, and a bigger increase in value, as the trend continued towards higher quality clays. The proportion exported once again rose, and reached 77 per cent by volume and, because of the emphasis upon the higher quality clays, even more by value. Further progress was made in Eastern Europe where there are good prospects of developing a market for a wide range of qualities of china clay. Export sales of calcined china clay, Molochite, increased by more than 30 per cent. The network of warehouses overseas has been extended to Sweden, while the relatively new Italian and Belgian warehouses are in full operation: the ability to give to customers daily deliveries from these facilities is a powerful marketing weapon and a service appreciated by customers, who are thereby rendered less vulnerable to the hazards otherwise inherent in receiving from overseas materials essential to continuous processes."

The export percentage on the total sales of *Wolstenholme Bronze Powders Limited* (May 6), according to MR. P. L. M. RINK, had been higher than ever before, exceeding 65 per cent. With this large export business, he added, devaluation might be expected to have some favourable influence on results.

MR. P. W. SELIGMAN noted that one-third of the export orders of *A.P.V. Holdings Limited* (April 25) came from the E.E.C., which he considered an excellent result in view of the tariff barrier.

After pointing out that, while the *Hudson's Bay Company* (May 24) itself did not export from the United Kingdom, purchases of British goods by the company's stores, together with its own brand of Scotch whisky marketed in North America, amounted to about £2m., LORD AMORY, the Governor, referred to a project for promoting British goods in Canada in which the company would be co-operating. The relevant passage in his speech follows:

"This coming Fall our company will be participating actively and enthusiastically in a Modern Britain Promotion project to be arranged under the sponsorship of the British National Export Council and the United Kingdom Board of Trade, in Winnipeg, Calgary, Edmonton, Saskatoon and Regina. I would

like to make the point that we are sure there are greater opportunities than are yet being exploited for British products of enterprising design and sound value in Canadian Stores if British manufacturers will go all out to get the business. I can give assurances that when our buyers find such products in Britain they are only too keen to avail themselves of them."

In his statement (*The Times*, January 17) for *The Charter Trust & Agency Limited* MR. G. P. S. MACPHERSON expressed the opinion that the climate for international trade showed signs of improvement; in particular, after their recent brief hesitations, the all important economies of the United States and Germany should provide expanding markets for the world's goods. Thus conditions were favourable for an export-led recovery by the United Kingdom subject to the provisos that strikes and go-slows did not disrupt deliveries and destroy the confidence of purchasers and that resources were available at competitive cost.

The notable expansion of the exports of *British Sidac Limited* (August 2) in the recent past, together with a hope for the future based on improved competitiveness resulting from devaluation, were the subjects of this quotation from MR. S. H. MARECHAL'S statement:

"The immediate effect of the devaluation of sterling was to create exceptional profits of some £100,000 and the longer term effect will be to make our products more competitive in world markets. An increase in exports of 21% by volume and 32% by value was achieved in the year under review. Exports amounted to £2,173,000. Over the last four years the group has exported 155% more by volume and 142% more by value. There undoubtedly remains scope for further expansion."

In furtherance of the export drive—the company's exports from the United Kingdom during the year exceeded £2m.—*L. M. Van Moppes & Sons Limited* (August 8) had purchased and equipped a mobile demonstration unit, stated MR. L. E. VAN MOPPES. Its first assignment was at the International Machine Tool Exhibition at Olympia, and it would shortly leave on a comprehensive tour of Central Europe.

The value of group exports by *The Distillers Company Limited* (September 19) for the year was £71,400,000, MR. ALEX MCDONALD revealed. He stated that devaluation was not expected to have a significant effect upon the volume of exports of Scotch whisky: the imposition in most export markets of relatively heavy import duties meant that the price in sterling was not a major factor in determining local consumer prices.

MR. CHARLES RIDING found it depressing to explain that in the export field covered by *Carrington and Dewhurst Group Limited* (July 18) the apparent advantages of sterling devaluation soon ran

111

off. At the start the group was deprived of the export rebate, and it was soon called upon to bear increased yarn costs. However, it was able to achieve direct exports of £4,331,750, and, allowing for indirect exports, he estimated conservatively that the group's total export achievement was well over £6m.

Another chairman who found that the beneficial effects of devaluation on export prices for the company's cloths had been nullified by a 20 per cent increase in wool values and rising overhead costs was MR. ROBERT WAGSTAFF of *George Mallinson & Sons Limited* (July 3). But he did expect worthwhile results from an extensive tour of the Far East which had recently been made by the Sales Director.

Having stated that exports by *British Ropes Limited* (May 30) to customers overseas showed a useful increase on the year, MR. HARRY SMITH went on to make the following comment on the group's export effort:

"The export trade becomes of even greater importance in our affairs as a result of both devaluation and the lack of demand at home. We are making the greatest efforts to increase exports wherever possible. We have already felt some benefit from the price adjustments we have been able to make following devaluation but this does not apply, by any means, to all products. Our export trade is always greatly influenced by the general economic conditions in the various markets, and economic conditions in many of these markets are not, at present, very favourable."

Not only had exports of the *Ditchburn Organisation Limited* shown a big improvement in the year under review, but the group was also looking, stated MR. G. N. DITCHBURN in his review (*The Times*, August 1), for a "really big" expansion in the current financial year. Their object, he added, was to have exports representing at least one-third of their total turnover within the next five years.

Once again SIR JOHN BENN of the *United Kingdom Provident Institution* (April 24) took up the case for greater publicity for the vital role played by invisible exports in the country's balance of payments. He stated (in part):

"Frequent visits to America on investment business had convinced me that we British are our own worst enemies. Twelve times a year we publicise the monthly deficits on merchandise trade, which have in fact been a regular feature for nearly 200 years, and only quarterly do we issue the invisible earnings which normally more than cover the deficit. It was therefore with some sense of personal satisfaction that I learned from Mr. William Clarke that this topic would be developed in detail by the Committee on Invisible Exports, of which he was the Director of

study, when its report appeared last October. I was even more pleased when, in the same month, Mr. Clarke accepted an invitation to join our Board, and his unrivalled knowledge of the practical work of the City is proving of great value to the Institution.

"The press release on merchandise trade issued by the Board of Trade in March included, for the first time, a reference to the invisible earnings 'averaging some £150m. a year or £13m. a month,' an important step towards the reform of the trade figures, and a real triumph for Mr. Clarke and his colleagues.

"It is now up to the newspapers to play down the monthly gaps and to give the invisibles their proper emphasis by presenting the total picture. Few people outside the City realise that the balance of payments deficit is mainly attributable to government expenditure overseas, and that Britain's merchandise and invisible trade taken together are still well in the black."

MODERNIZATION, EXPANSION
AND RATIONALIZATION

MANY chairman in their annual statements issued in 1968 referred to expenditure on the modernization and re-equipment of their companies' plant and machinery. While capital spending by most of the larger companies continued to rise, it seemed that for the smaller undertakings on the whole the amount of capital devoted to expansion of productive facilities was less than in other recent years; this was the result partly of lack of confidence in the economic and political outlook, partly of high interest rates on borrowed money, and partly of the continuing rise in costs accompanied by difficulties in the way of compensating for higher expenses by raising prices. The last-named factor, however, was responsible for proliferation of steps towards rationalization of production.

Thanks to a substantial improvement for the second successive year in the group cash flow of *Thomas Tilling Limited*, SIR GEOFFREY ELEY asserted in his annual statement (*The Times*, April 9), the company was able to finance capital expenditure and acquisitions amounting to £10½m. almost wholly from internal sources. He defined the expansion policy of the Tilling group in the following terms:

"Apart from expansion by entering new fields, Tillings has aimed for many years to increase the scale of activities of its existing interests; and in 1967 no fewer than nine of our principal companies earned more than £500,000 before tax. The method of securing our objective has been twofold. First, by supporting expansion plans initiated by the operating companies—an example is the development of our glassware group which is currently engaged on a seven year programme involving expenditure of £8m. Second, by external growth through the purchase of companies that have approached us with businesses complementary to those of our existing subsidiaries—an example is our building material and merchanting interests which have been enlarged substantially along these lines.

"Today a more direct approach to acquisition may be desirable, not only in our existing fields but also in promising new areas. Previously we tended to wait for new entrants to the Group to come to us, and of course we continue to welcome men of ability who invite us to consider taking a stake in their businesses—our recent press advertisements are an example of this approach; but we also now initiate, as do our subsidiaries,

talks with the managements of concerns whose association with the Group could be of mutual benefit.

"Our policy of allowing businesses to be run without unnecessary interference remains unchanged. We believe the key to success to lie in first class management in the field. Our Headquarters administration at Crewe House is small. With a Tilling executive as chairman or a director of each main operating company guidance is given to the companies on matters of policy and finance, specialized services are made available, and strong financial support is provided."

For *Imperial Chemical Industries Limited* (March 28) SIR PETER ALLEN said that 1967 was a year of consolidation in which the company brought into effective production several plants which were completed in 1966 and 1967. Another aspect of consolidation had been the reduction of capital expenditure and also of capital sanctioning in 1967 to more normal proportions, which he illustrated in the following excerpt from his address:

"In 1964 we sanctioned £132m. of capital expenditure in the U.K. and spent £81m. In 1965 the sanctioning had risen to £157m. and expenditure to £132m. By 1966 the amount we sanctioned was back to £85m. but the expenditure 'bulge' still continued, with £145m. spent in that year. Only in 1967 has this 'bulge' been absorbed with sanctioning and expenditure levels both at £81m. With this major period of reconstruction and expansion behind us we can plan for some years ahead a steadier level of capital expenditure here in the U.K. of the order of £95 to £105m. a year with fair confidence; this more even load will also help the chemical plant manufacturers and contractors."

In 1968, MR. D. H. BARRAN told members of *The "Shell" Transport and Trading Company Limited* (May 2), total group capital expenditure was expected to rise. In sterling terms this would result in part from the devaluation of the £; on estimates then current, it was likely to be well in excess of £600m. Most of the increase, he said, would be in the Western hemisphere; in the rest of the world the largest rise would be in capital expenditure for tankers, partly a consequence of the low level of 1967 outlays thereon. Mr. Barran went on to make these remarks on the group's investment programmes:

"Capital investment programmes in future years are expected to be maintained at a high level. Group companies are engaged in industries which have strong growth prospects and which are at the same time increasingly capital-intensive. In 1967, for example, the capital employed in Group companies averaged £23,000 per employee, compared with less than £10,000 ten years ago, and this is a figure which will almost certainly con-

115

tinue to rise steadily in the years ahead. In addition to participating in the growth of demand, the aim of Group companies is to improve their profitability by reducing the unit costs of their operations. The Group rate of return is still too low, but, as a result of the receipt of income from investment often made many years earlier, and as a result of the reduction in unit operating expenses, the rate of return is improving. Progress in this direction will, nevertheless, not continue automatically; it will be the product of planning, of investment to put the planning into effect, and of hard work by everyone within Group companies to ensure that the investment operates efficiently. People, we recognize, are our most important resource, and it is essential to the achievement of our aims that we pay the most careful attention to the selection of staff and to their training and development."

In spite of present national and international difficulties *British Insulated Callender's Cables Limited* (May 9), stated LORD MC-FADZEAN, had continued, in pursuit of its search for greater and greater efficiency and its belief in the future, to spend considerable sums on new plant, equipment and the like; gross expenditure during 1967 at home was some £10m. and overseas some £6m. Capital employed in the business had further increased to £160m. at the end of 1967.

SIR REAY GEDDES gave this information about the capital expenditure of *The Dunlop Company Limited* (May 13) in his annual address:

"Of last year's capital expenditure, about £13m. was spent overseas, largely for expansion, while the greater part of £11m. for the United Kingdom was spent on replacement and modernization to improve our products and efficiency. Our policy was and remains to continue long-term programmes which can be justified, even if the economic situation of any one country lengthens the time to complete them."

From MR. F. L. CHAPLIN's statement for *F. W. Woolworth and Co.* (March 8) there is extracted the following paragraph about the progress of the store development plan in 1967:

"The development programme completed during the year comprised nine new stores (including the Woolco Department Store at Oadby), eight relocated stores which were substantially enlarged, fourteen major extensions and the modernization of thirty-one new stores. The larger relocated or extended stores are at Glasgow, Harlow, Huddersfield, Norwich, Scunthorpe, Stroud and Swansea. The total sales area of the new and extended stores is 430,000 square feet. The relocated store at Harlow includes many new features which we intend to incorporate in other large stores now in course of construction.

Particular attention has been given to customer comfort in regard to lighting, decor and catering, and the public response to these improvements has been most gratifying."

In the building of the business of *United Drapery Stores Limited* MR. J. A. SAMPSON asserted in his annual review (*The Times*, July 10) that the board had always directed expansion towards the retail selling area of consumer goods. This policy, he explained, gave, within itself, opportunity for diversification sufficiently extensive to avoid undue dependence on any single source of revenue, while being sufficiently interrelated to enable management to be provided from existing resources. He added:

"It has been our experience in recent years that new businesses have not always brought in immediate profits commensurate with the cost of investment. Our record shows nevertheless that in the longer term our policy of acquisition has provided the company with expansion and stability which has been ultimately reflected in profit growth, a situation we confidently expect to continue.

Reporting an increase of 33.7 per cent in pre-tax profit of *Tower Manufacturing Company Limited*, MR. G. HENRY PROBERT in his statement (*The Times*, December 20) declared that the heavy capital expenditure of recent years was now showing results and was making some contribution towards neutralizing the ever increasing costs which were constantly arising and were a matter of considerable concern. The company, he went on, would continue the policy of investing in additional plant and machinery, "the financing of which presents no problem in view of the strong liquid position as shown in the balance-sheet."

During the year *The Ever Ready Company* (*Great Britain*) *Limited* spent on capital account £3,700,000 in developing and expanding group operations, and at the year end the board's approvals on this account amounted to no less than £7,872,000. This was made known in the course of MR. L. W. ORCHARD'S statement (*The Times*, June 17).

MR. T. E. PEPPERCORN told members of *Triplex Holdings Limited* (July 3) that the ability of the safety glass company to achieve a high level of output was the result of the board's continuing policy of expansion and modernization. He went on to give the following example of the policy in action:

"At the Eccleston factory a new type of toughening furnace was successfully commissioned during the year. Known as the horizontal gas hearth, it represents a major break-through in toughening technology and has been developed with the help of Pilkington Brothers. This furnace can produce nearly 7 million sq. ft. of toughened glass per annum at no more than half the initial capital cost of the older type of furnace capacity which it

117

replaces. For the same output it requires only one-third of the labour, and the glass produced is of better quality."

As LORD ABERCONWAY remarked in his statement for *English China Clays Limited* (March 18), no business operating in this country in 1967 could have found conditions other than difficult. Thus he was entitled to attribute the company's repeat performance of the previous year in again increasing profits before tax by more than £500,000 to a new record to "good management, wise planning, and progressive technology." He gave this explanation of the policy which has led to such results:

"A policy has been followed for many years of spending heavily upon capital account to ensure that the plant used in china clay production is modern, efficient, and capable of producing a finished product which is clean, is uniform, and is closely controlled within prescribed limits of physical properties. This policy has been fully vindicated. It has been applied to the other divisions of the Group with equally happy results."

Capital expenditure in 1967 of *Albright & Wilson Limited* (April 25) exceeded £16m., over £3m. more than the previous record of the year before, according to the annual report. Projects in the United Kingdom accounted for a little less than half the total expenditure (compared with about five-sixths in 1966), reflecting the large sums being spent by Electric Reduction Company of Canada Limited, mainly on the Newfoundland phosphorus plant. In 1968, too, capital expenditure would continue at a high level.

For *Newton Chambers & Company Limited* SIR PETER ROBERTS stated in his annual survey (*The Times*, April 25) that capital expenditure on plant and buildings totalled £764,189 in the year under review; in the next year it was planned to spend approximately £900,000, of which the company was actually committed to £586,955 at the year end.

Group capital expenditure by *Philblack Limited* (September 24) stated MR. P. G. WALKER, was again high during the year, and in fact over the past three years it had reached a figure of just under £2m. The company, he added, had been able to finance this without recourse to any long-term borrowing, and on present plans he hoped it would be possible to continue in this way.

That *Coalite and Chemical Products Limited* (July 24) was now deriving real benefit from its considerable expenditure on expansion during recent years, COMMANDER COLIN BUIST stated. He mentioned that after deducting the value of investment grants, £1,109,008 was spent during the year under review on completing the new Coalite Works at Grimethorpe and on complementary extensions at the Central Refinery. Capital expenditure had totalled £9,297,000 during the six-year period ended March 31, 1968.

Considerable sums of money had been spent on development

and research during the year by *Carbon Electric Holdings Limited* (July 8), according to SIR MILES THOMAS, who added that returns for this expenditure would be forthcoming in future years.

The year 1968–69 had started off well for *Transparent Paper Limited* (July 24), MR. J. F. E. SMITH revealed; the order book at that time was excellent, and the programme of modernization was now producing more efficient results. Incidentally, he foresaw increasing sales in the United States market, "where devaluation has been a help."

Large-scale reorganization and concentration of production facilities were outlined by MR. W. M. LINES for *Lines Bros. Limited* (July 12), the relevant passages (in part) of his statement being as follows:

"The company is undertaking a major concentration of its United Kingdom operation. Production at the expensive Hayes factory has been moved into our main Minimodels plant at Havant and the large Hayes premises will be vacated completely by the end of this year. Distribution depots at Nottingham, Market Harborough and in Lancashire have been, or are about to be, closed and facilities provided in remaining depots and at our main plants for servicing customers more economically. The work performed until now at Canterbury has been split between Margate and Belfast, thus giving these two plants considerably more volume.

"During 1968 we are transferring our total United Kingdom doll production from Merton to Canterbury, where, in an entirely specialized unit equipped with the most modern plant, we should be in a position to produce dolls for home and export competitively with any country outside the Far East. A third of the space vacated at Merton will be used for storage, releasing premises at present rented outside. A third will be occupied by the Raphael Lipkin Subsidiary, now to be concentrated in one area, thus freeing for disposal four scattered units throughout London. A final third will be made ready for manufacture of a completely new non-toy product to be announced in January, 1969. These moves will throw up considerable removal and redundancy expenses.

"Additionally the opportunity has been taken to review the whole range of products from the factories involved in the moves. In order to streamline and simplify these ranges the Directors have decided not to transfer or continue production of certain items and this will involve us in probable loss in disposal of stocks. We have therefore thought it prudent to allocate on December 31, 1967, a sum from Reserves to cover all the above costs in 1968 in addition to those already incurred in 1967 by the closure of Hayes and the reestablishment of production at Havant.

119

"These moves which started early last year and will be complete by the end of 1968, may be thought drastic and place a considerable strain on Management while they are being carried out. The Directors are confident, however, that they will result in great operating economies.

"Modern plant and production methods allow us to produce, in less space, considerably more volume than in the past. Not only will this make for production savings but a great deal of space has been released as a result for storage and despatch, enabling us to save expensive rented accommodation."

In his annual report (*The Times*, September 5) for *Powell Duffryn Limited* SIR HENRY WILSON SMITH remarked that trading profits from the group's coal interests were above those for the previous year. Though the improvement was satisfactory, however, he pointed out that it was at a lower rate than had been achieved by other group activities. He continued:

"To rationalize in line with changing conditions, the coal business of Hall & Co. Limited in Sussex has been acquired and absorbed into Corralls. Similarly, the Group's coal business in Scotland has been disposed of."

Subject to certain formalities the whole of the Ordinary shares of *C. A. Parsons & Company Limited* (May 23) would soon be owned by A. Reyrolle and Company Limited, stated SIR HAROLD MULLENS. It was intended that the combined group should be headed by a holding company named Reyrolle Parsons Limited. Sir Harold proceeded to put on record the part played by Parsons and Reyrolle in the rationalization of the electrical engineering industry to meet changing conditions. Jointly Reyrolle and Parsons had the largest shareholding in the Nuclear Power Plant Company Limited, which he claimed was the first nuclear consortium to be formed. He continued:

"They realized early on that because the output of nuclear reactors was going to be much larger than originally expected the number of orders for nuclear power stations would be fewer and insufficient for the number of nuclear consortia as then constituted. They saw the good sense of some rationalization and led the way by joining forces with the A.E.I./John Thompson consortium in 1959, the other consortia remaining independent. This inevitably incurred sacrifices on the part of the individual manufacturing companies, because there were subsequently more of them to share in the work of any power station ordered from the new combined consortium called The Nuclear Power Group. However, the result of this step is that the Group has built or is building six out of twelve nuclear power stations ordered by the Electricity Boards in the U.K. Only two British nuclear power stations have been sold

abroad, one of which was built (in Italy) by our consortium and which is behaving extremely well."

The next step towards further rationalization was made when it became clear that the policy of the Central Electricity Board, the "predominant customer in the home market" was to move towards only two designs of very large turbo-generators which it intended to order in the future. Parsons then bought the turbo-generator business of the General Electric Company. Parsons had orders for seven out of the nine of the current round of orders in the home market for 660 MW machines. Sir Harold then turned to the current operation of merging Parsons and Reyrolle and stated:

"Throughout the history of the two companies, there have been continuous close and friendly but informal ties which have been of value to both. Reyrolle has since 1931 had a large financial interest in Parsons and your Board believes that the complete integration now assured will greatly aid the joint organization to ride successfully through the early 1970's when deliveries to the Central Electricity Generating Board and the Area Electricity Boards will probably be at a low level. It will also bring economies of operation and greater strength to obtain more of the available business at home and abroad than if they were to continue as separate units."

The process of modernization and re-equipment carried out by *Edgar Allen & Co. Limited* (September 5) over the year under review, MR. F. A. ROSS stated, was continuing: the purchase of major items of plant had already been sanctioned, and other proposals were being considered for removal, re-siting and replacement of plant with the object of improving the economics of production. Since March 30, 1968, Armitage Industrial Holdings Limited had been acquired, and, with the engineering companies of that group, Edgar Allen had now a much wider range of engineering interests. He also mentioned the possibility of the acquisition of additional engineering interests.

The next quotation deals with re-equipment and plant modernization by *Birmid Qualcast Limited* (December 20) and comes from LORD EXETER's statement:

"No major expansion scheme was commenced during the year. The Group's gross outlay of £2,392,539 was incurred partly on clearing up several capital projects which were near to completion at the commencement of the year but mainly on re-equipment and plant modernization throughout the Group generally, thus broadly keeping pace with depreciation write-off. In the coming year or so, we plan to continue this policy of replacement but on a more ambitious scale so that we expect our expenditure to be considerably greater than this

I

year's figure. As I have stressed before, this is imperative if we are to keep in the forefront of our trades and expand the markets for our products. In addition to this general programme of re-equipment, we are expanding considerably our iron die casting facilities at Qualcast, Derby, to meet the increasing demand for castings of this type in the production of which we already lead the field. This expansion scheme should be completed well within this next financial year."

After announcing that extensions had been or were being erected at a number of factories of *British Steel Constructions (Birmingham) Limited* (March 20), MR. BERNARD J. OWEN mentioned that capital expenditure on new plant and machinery already incurred or committed at the year-end amounted to approximately £1m., the bulk of it being for new plant to expand production of the engineering division.

For *Jonas Woodhead and Sons Limited* MR. PETER B. HIGGINS in his statement (*The Times*, July 29) mentioned that the benefits from plant modernization and factory reorganization were beginning to appear; and, providing no more adverse problems were created by the Government or by the nationalization of steel, the directors were looking for increased profits.

Head Wrightson and Company Limited (July 11) were continuing to spend money on new equipment for the works, remarked SIR JOHN WRIGHTSON, and already this year the board had authorized £500,000 capital expenditure. He added that the capital expenditure sanctioned during 1967 had included as usual a substantial volume of machine tools and equipment. "It is our policy," he stated, "to concentrate upon the more efficient manufacture of our existing product lines."

MR. E. C. WOODALL reported that the improved results of *C. & W. Walker Holdings Limited* (July 11), in spite of a slightly reduced turnover had been achieved by more economical and therefore more profitable working. He also included in his review the following reference to modernization:

> "The modernization process at Donnington is continuing. We have already completed the transformation of obsolescent buildings into a modern fabrication shop capable of producing the large vessels and tanks which are required by the industries we serve, and many benefits will undoubtedly accrue from this both to C. and W. Walker Ltd. and Samuel Cutler and Sons Ltd."

In reviewing current prospects of *Harris & Sheldon Group Limited* (May 17) MR. J. D. MILLER said that much work had been done in the past three or four years to eliminate areas of unprofitability either by disposing of certain activities or integrating them with others. Considerable reductions in general overhead

expenditure throughout the group had also taken place. Thus, in spite of increased costs, the board hoped that some benefit from their efforts would at last be allowed to show in increased profits.

The following paragraph is taken from the statement by MR, S. P. HIGGIN for *British Sisalkraft Limited* (January 11):

"The expansion programme in our Paper Converting Division, to which I made reference in my last statement, is virtually completed except for the installation of machinery, which has been slower in delivery time than we had anticipated. Start-up of all new equipment should be effected by June of next year. Consequently, it is unlikely that the benefit of capital expenditure of some £300,000 since the beginning of last year will be fully reflected in our results for 1968."

Recalling that in the previous year's statement he had said that *Lead Industries Group Limited* (June 27) was well equipped to take advantage of any improvement in business generally, MR. ROLAND A. COOKSON claimed that this had been borne out by experience in recent months, and went on to state:

"Our policies of continuous modernization of our factories and organization to contain cost increases: of rationalizing our manufacturing and distribution facilities: and of broadening our activities by both horizontal and vertical expansion are all contributing to show encouraging results which we believe will steadily improve as time goes on."

The funding operation arranged by *The British Printing Corporation Limited* in November, 1967, which raised £13,600,000, declared the late SIR WALTER WORBUYS in his statement (*The Times*, May 7), greatly strengthened the corporation's financial resources. It brought a better balance into the relationship of permanent capital and borrowed moneys; and in consequence BPC had been able to plan a major re-equipment programme, the board having budgeted gross capital expenditure in 1968 of approximately £5m.

The Research Department of *West Riding Worsted and Woollen Mills Limited* (February 21), MR. M. W. SHELTON stated, had several new schemes in the pipeline which the board hoped would find an outlet as business conditions in textiles improved. He continued:

"During the past seven years in particular we have installed the most modern productive machinery based on the best systems available from all parts of the world. Fortunately, this heavy capital expenditure has already been met and during the recent difficult trading conditions every opportunity was taken for full plant overhaul and completion of important alterations. Although machinery developments will continue to demand some expenditure, we are in an excellent position to take advantage of any improvement in trading conditions."

Shareholders in *Winn Industries Group* (May 10) were reminded by MR. G. C. HOWARD that the substantial sums which the board had committed to expansion programmes, although currently contributing to profit earnings, needed a healthy and vigorous economic climate before they could prove to be fully effective.

The modernization of the Bermondsey factory of *Associated Biscuit Manufacturers Limited* (May 21) and expansion of production at Aintree were well under way, declared MR. RUPERT E. CARR. He added that the company continued to invest in new production plant at a fairly high rate and was involved in the creation of a modernized distribution service. These expenditures could not be wholly financed out of the company's own resources; it was envisaged that, before allowing for bank facilities, a total of some £4m. additional finance would be required over the next five years; and proposals would be put forward in the near future to fund part of this requirement.

Group capital expenditure by *Rowntree and Company Limited* (June 14) increased by some £2m. in comparable terms over the previous year to a total of just over £5m., declared MR. D. J. BARRON, who went on to give these details:

"The greater part of this increase arose in Canada and South Africa where major capital expenditure programmes are in progress, in Germany where our subsidiary company purchased its land and building which had hitherto been leased, and in the United Kingdom where substantial expenditure took place on the rationalization and expansion of manufacturing facilities and on productivity projects generally. All these schemes will produce benefits during the next few years.

"The heavy capital expenditure programme, combined with the acquisition of the new businesses . . . and the larger working capital requirements brought about by longer stocks at higher prices, is reflected in the substantial increase in borrowings shown in the consolidated balance sheet."

For the *H. J. Heinz Company Limited* MR. H. J. HEINZ in the course of his statement (*The Times*, August 16) gave this information on capital spending:

"Capital Expenditure net of disposals for the year, covering replacements and additions to facilities, amounted to £1,766,000. To this sum must be added £571,000 representing the gross value of building and equipment of The Samor Pure Foods Limited at date of acquisition.

"The more important items of Capital Expenditure during the year included the provision of additional Tomato Ketchup and Pudding facilities, increased sterilizing capacity, equipment for the mechanical handling of finished goods and improved packaging facilities. In addition installation of additional Soup

124

production capacity and the automatic handling of production materials are well advanced."

SIR ARCHIBALD FORBES told members of *Spillers Limited* (June 7) that capital expenditure during the year (including the acquisition of new businesses) and additional requirements for working capital amounted to some £11m. This was met from the cash flow (including investment grants) of about £6½m., by the issue of new shares on a basis equivalent to about £2½m., and by temporary borrowing of some £2m.

One of the advantages to *Blackwood Morton & Sons Limited* (October 28) of having most of its factories in Development Areas was mentioned by MR. KENNETH M. HAMILTON in the following excerpt from his annual review:

"To minimize production costs and to make the best possible use of available manpower, old plant is constantly being replaced by more modern and efficient machinery. In the past five years more than £2¼m. has been spent on new plant and buildings. Additional wide Wilton looms are on order and new wide Axminster looms are being built in our own engineering department. Plans are also under consideration for improvements to our spinning and dyeing plant. This programme of modernization is greatly assisted by the Government Grants which are available to us because most of our factories are in Development Areas. We shall continue to take advantage of this facility and so ensure that we can compete successfully with other carpet manufacturers both in the U.K. and overseas."

Conditions in the home market had been difficult for *The Monotype Corporation Limited* (March 19), Sir GEORGE HARVIE-WATT asserted. The measures introduced by the Government in July, 1966, he claimed, affected industry generally, and the printing trade was no exception. Many firms with plans for the expansion of their plants abandoned these, and others with programmes for the replacement of old machinery postponed them. These factors, together with the general lack of confidence brought about by the worsening of the country's economy, he added, had an adverse effect on the company's home turnover, which fell by approximately 10 per cent.

The next quotation comes from MR. D. S. HARTLEY's statement for *G. H. Downing & Company Limited* (September 18), and shows the quick success of capital expenditure on the Knutton roofing tile works:

"The first stage of the Knutton development, comprising a tunnel kiln and tunnel drier, came into production in March. Within a few weeks, the results were so encouraging that it was decided to start immediately on the next stage, comprising a second kiln and drier and some plant alterations. This work is

now well under way and should be in production before the end of the current financial year."

In his annual review (*The Times*, July 19) for *E. & H. P. Smith Limited* Mr. G. C. Roberts stated that the company's programme of modernization and consolidation was gathering momentum. Several factories were being re-equipped in a systematic manner, "since we are convinced that only by these means can we remain fully competitive and so have solid growth prospects."

In a reference to the telecommunications interests of *The General Electric Company Limited* Lord Aldington made these comments (*The Times*, July 30) on integration with the corresponding businesses of Associated Electric Industries, taken over:

"Complete integration has been achieved of management functions for production, development and sales of the former GEC and AEI divisions. Production is being concentrated at Coventry, Glenrothes, Hartlepool, Newton Aycliffe, Kirkcaldy and Middlesbrough.

"The reasons for the closure of Woolwich are now well known. The most important lesson to be learnt perhaps is that continuing low productivity in any factory deprives management of any room for manoeuvre when demand is less than capacity. The other AEI telecommunications factories are well equipped and we must do our utmost to bring up their efficiency to the level necessary for survival in the face of fierce international competition.

"The Reliance Telephone Company and the AEI Private Telephone business have also been brought together."

Recalling that *Courtaulds Limited* (July 10) had followed in recent years a policy of expansion and acquisition in the textile field, Sir Frank Kearton said that it was the acquisition element which received a fair amount of attention, but it was the re-equipment and internal expansion programme which was the more exciting for the future. He outlined the company's plans as follows:

"In filament weaving, installation of both water jet and air jet looms proceeds apace. But we are also installing in addition the latest types of automatic looms with mechanical weft insertion. By the end of 1970, we shall have about 50 per cent more capacity than today, in efficient and versatile mills.

"In warp knitting, we have participated to the full in the recent growth of output. We are currently spending some millions of pounds in re-equipment and expansion. The expansion element will take us, by the beginning of 1970, some 40 per cent above today's figures.

"In hosiery knitting, we are also expanding and modernizing.

126

We are charging quite considerable re-organization expenses against current profits.

"In the bulking of filament man-made fibre yarns, our plans are ambitious. Our present plants are currently bulking about 350,000 lbs/week of nylon, acetate, triacetate and polyester. Expansion already in train will increase our capacity to 600,000 lbs/week by the end of 1969, the increase being progressive. Further schemes under study could take our capacity to 800,000 lbs/week by the end of 1970.

"In stockings, we are still in the midst of our considerable modernization programme. Current production of all types totals a little more than 200,000 dozen pairs per week, and the newer kinds of legwear are well represented.

"In double jersey knitting, single jersey knitting and Raschel knitting, we are steadily expanding. In percentage terms, the planned increase in double jersey is the most dramatic. We have put work in train to increase end 1967 capacity threefold by the end of 1970.

"In made-up clothing, we are being successful in developing further our business in women's underwear. Both in branded goods and contract business we are now the leaders. We have also a considerable business in children's wear, and are paying particular attention to building it up further."

The rationalization of the many businesses acquired by *Viyella International Limited* (June 12) was the subject of an intensely interesting passage in MR. JOE HYMAN's statement, from which an extract is given below:

"Thirty-six spinning, weaving and finishing plants have been closed and concentrated during the last three to four years; it is significant that our total number of plants is now just half of those in operation in 1964. Our labour force has been reduced in spinning, weaving and finishing by 8,750, from 21,400 to 12,650, over 40%. I must, however, reiterate and re-emphasize what I have said on many occasions, that factories and warehouses closed down have been disposed of as speedily as possible at a fraction of the cost of new buildings and predominantly for non-textile purposes. The resultant employment in many cases exceeds the numbers previously at work and has benefited the national economy. Rationalization on such a scale and over such a short period could normally only have been achieved by incurring overall losses. Fortunately those parts of the Federation which had previously been reorganized and rationalized have continued to advance their profitability year by year. The other £20/25m. of business and miscellaneous non-consolidated investments, surplus properties, etc., in 1967 produced less than the equivalent of the interest charges on their capital employed.

" 'Unscrambling the omelette' has resulted in the depression of trading profits by virtue of the fact that trading losses, stock losses and reorganization by concentration to fewer manufacturing units are costs reflected immediately they are incurred. The benefits generally only follow in succeeding years due to the time required to dispose of capital assets, working capital, etc., released through rationalization.

"The rationalization programme, to all intents and purposes, has now been completed and this is in line with my statement that total reorganization would be phased on a 1, 3, 5 year basis. As 1964 was a year of acquisitions, the rationalization has been effected within three years, the current fourth year is providing the major growth of profitability which was planned and envisaged."

In his statement (*The Times*, May 30) for *Coats Patons Limited* MR. CHARLES W. BELL declared that it had been a most difficult year for the retail division. The cost of amalgamation of Scotch Wool Shops with Bellman had exceeded expectations. The process of rationalization was not yet complete, he added, but the basic plan was beginning to be effective, and the budget forecasts for both turnover and profits were decidedly better for the new year than the results for the last.

Rationalization was among the things mentioned by MR. A. L. LONG, joint chairman of *Winterbotham, Strachan and Playne Limited* (July 25), in his remarks on the outlook:

"Profits during January, February and March of 1968 have been satisfactory due to some extent to the accumulation of wool stocks prior to devaluation. It is now becoming increasingly necessary to replenish these stocks. We are implementing schemes rationalizing the manufacturing processes of the Group and continual efforts are being made to increase production, eliminate waste and surplus capacity and to reduce costs. Our orders on hand are at a higher level than at this stage last year and assuming no increase in the already considerable burdens we are forced to bear, I look forward with cautious optimism to this year's results."

Re-equipment and modernization of the plants of *George Mallinson & Sons Limited* (July 3) were constantly under review, stated MR. ROBERT WAGSTAFF, and in the coming year they would be modernizing part of the spinning and twisting departments at the Kirkburton Mill.

For *Macanie (London) Limited* (May 2) MR. MAX MAIMANN revealed that turnover of Wilkinson & Riddle and S. C. Larkins for the first two months of their current year showed an encouraging increase, and the merging of their activities in Birmingham was proceeding according to schedule, completion being planned for

128

the end of June, 1968. He went on to indicate the probable extent of the resulting savings in the following paragraph:

"Not only will this rationalization produce a highly efficient and competitive organization, geared to demands of to-day, but it should also effect savings in the region of £150,000–£180,000 in a full year."

Much had been achieved in the rationalization programme of *Nairn & Williamson (Holdings) Limited*, declared SIR GEORGE NAIRN in his annual report (*The Times*, May 16). Thus the holding company and floors division and the computer centre were now at Kirkcaldy; the pile fabrics divison was established in its new location at Lancaster; the greater part of the floors division vinyl production was now located at Kirkcaldy, as was the new 6-ft. Cushionflor plant; at the carpet division plant at Batley the substantial investment programme in dyeing, backing, warehousing and development facilities was virtually complete; and the coated products division would have completed, by the end of May, 1968, the installation of the new Kingfisher plant.

An account of the rationalization process under way in *J. Lyons & Company Limited* (July 16) was given by MR. GEOFFREY SALMON, the relevant passage in his statement being as follows:

"A systematic review of all the activities of the Group is now being carried out by the Managing Directors, with a view to concentrating on those where our greatest opportunities for future development lie. Peripheral activities which are unprofitable at present, and are unlikely to show an adequate profit in the reasonably foreseeable future, are being closed down. At the same time an exhaustive examination is being made of all overheads with a view to rationalizing systems and reducing costs. We anticipate that the first benefit of this series of measures will be felt in the current year, but the full benefit will not be felt until next year because the measures themselves give rise to terminal costs and compensation payments in the year in which they are taken. For example, in the year under review these costs amounted to some £250,000 more than last year."

The annual report of the directors of *International Publishing Corporation Limited* (July 23) stated that the rationalization programme of International Printers, which had been in progress since formation in 1964, continued during the year under review. By the end of the year the 24 factories which had been acquired as the result of publishing mergers before IPC was formed had been reduced to 15. It was expected that the staff of the printing division would be reduced by a further 500 men by the end of 1968. The rationalization programme involved redundancy payments and closure costs of £694,000 in 1967–68 and was expected to cost a similar sum in 1968–69. The report continued:

129

"The closure programme for 1967–68 was achieved without industrial disruption—a credit to both unions and staff—and industrial relations in the division now seem to be well established on a sound basis. . . .

"Updating, innovation, and competitive urgency are vital requirements in the printing industry. Alongside the rationalization programme, the division is pursuing major technological advances in its factories, particularly by establishing production information systems designed to achieve the highest level of machine utilization. These are essential to establish a profitable company keeping up to date with advancing technologies."

For *Anderson Mavor Limited* (July 17) MR. JAMES ANDERSON stated that the policy of rationalization of products and manufacturing facilities within the group continued. Rationalization of manufacturing facilities had entailed the decision to close down the iron foundry and also a small manufacturing unit.

The next quotation comes from LORD RANK's review for *Ranks Hovis McDougall Limited* (January 25):

"Higher sales of all bakery products were achieved and these, together with the further benefits of rationalization and modernization, contributed to the improved profits compared with the depressed figures of the previous year. We have extensive plans for further rationalization but the speed with which they can be carried out will depend very much upon the general economic situation and upon our being able to earn a more satisfactory return on the capital invested in bread manufacture and distribution. In this connection and because of higher costs, an early increase in the price of bread is necessary."

External group sales of *Burrell & Co. Limited*, it appeared from MR. PETER GIBSON's statement (*The Times*, June 19), for the full year slightly exceeded the previous record sales in 1965; and, with further progress being made in rationalizing production and a more favourable sales mix, the profits for 1967 created a new record.

One of the points made by MR. R. A. E. GODFREY in his annual review for *Brickhouse Dudley Limited* (*The Times*, July 2) was that rationalization within the group had already produced results and it was expected that this trend would continue.

With the many mergers of brewery companies in recent years a number of resultant combines have been engaged in rationalizing their businesses. Thus COLONEL W. H. WHITBREAD declared that, in a full programme of rationalization, *Whitbread and Company Limited* (September 6) had closed breweries at Birkenhead, Hythe and Yarmouth, bottling factories at Kirkstall, Hythe, Yarmouth, Barrow-in-Furness and Camberwell, distribution depots at Exeter, Newcastle and Nottingham, and a malting at Dereham. Plans

would be put into effect during the current financial year for the closing of breweries, bottling stores and distribution depots at eight other places. All this had meant, as it always did, he added, the resettlement or redundancy of a great many employees who had served the group well. He also stated:

> "During the last three years we have been building two large bottling stores, which I am glad to say are now at last in production, and we have rebuilt Flowers Brewery on a new site at Luton, a large operation which will go into full production this winter. The money invested in this enterprise has not earned us anything during the last three years."

Capital expenditure on licensed premises by *Watney Mann Limited* (January 26) over the last five years had amounted to over £9m., while a further £10m. had been spent on maintenance and repair. This was placed on record by MR. D. P. CROSSMAN, who added that this investment was "now paying dividends." During the year the group had opened 21 new houses and rebuilt or completed major alterations at a further 101.

In his statement (*The Times*, February 7) for *Arthur Guinness Son & Company Limited* LORD IVEAGH mentioned that the year's total capital expenditure was £5¼m., of which some £4¼m. related to the brewing group, the major part again arising from the continuing expansion of the draught trade.

Commenting on capital spending on the properties of *Courage Barclay & Simonds Limited* (June 5) during the year under review, MR. R. H. COURAGE stated:

> "Capital expenditure of more than £1½m. was incurred in building new public houses and major alterations of existing properties. In terms of new houses, nineteen were completed and a further fourteen were in course of construction at the end of the year. Approximately £2m. was incurred on maintenance repairs and redecoration."

It was clear that, so far, 18 months of recession had hit *Staveley Industries Limited* hard, declared MR. DENIS HAVILAND in his statement (*The Times*, February 20); and only the board's policies of acquisition and rationalization had preserved the group from the worst impact of the nation's economic troubles. "These policies," he added, "provide us with a solid base upon which to reap the fruits of an improvement in our trades when it comes."

The *Brooke Tool Manufacturing Company Limited* (March 29), stated MR. A. OWEN, was in the process of reorganizing and rationalizing its small tool business with a view to concentrating on fewer lines. He did not expect the current year to be better for the company than the one just past, but considered prospects for 1969 and beyond definitely brighter.

In the course of his remarks on the outlook for *Cox and Wyman*

131

Limited (August 1) SIR CHRISTOPHER BULLOCK admitted that certain rationalization measures between the two main factories at Reading and Fakenham might cause some minor and short-term dislocation, but the long-term results should undoubtedly be beneficial and increase profitability.

Apart from the political and economic circumstances affecting industry in general, *Whessoe Limited* (July 30) was faced by considerable problems of integration, of rationalization and re-organization within the group in the immediate future, mainly as a result of two important acquistions increasing the scope, financial and operating size of the group. Having made this clear, MR. JOHN H. LORD went on to declare:

"We are confident, your Directors and every employee, that we can take care of this second factor. There is still great scope for rationalization in the Process Plant and Engineering Industry in the near future and, with the support already accorded to us by the Ministry of Technology and the Industrial Reorganization Corporation. I believe Whessoe can make still further contributions. Primarily we must have the support and agreement of our Members and this may soon be needed, particularly in the subscription of further Capital. We have started 1968/69 with a good order book in our established fields such as supplying the Oil and Gas industries, the Chemical and Power Generating Industries. We have more and more diversified products which we believe will increasingly contribute and the coming year should bring results for several of these."

Commenting on an increase of 115 per cent in pre-tax group profits of *Magnet Joinery Limited* (August 19), MR. W. S. EMMOTT remarked that the steeper rise in the profits curve compared with a year previously "owes a lot to buoyant demand, but in large measure reflects the advantages we won for ourselves by planned rationalization and re-equipment, and we reaped the reward of reduced costs and higher productivity."

For *Delta Metal Company Limited* LORD VERULAM in his annual statement (*The Times*, May 7) reported that work had proceeded on many schemes of rationalization started in the previous year. The company was now over the period of greatest dislocation, and the benefits of this very large expenditure were becoming apparent.

The year was a good one for the solid fuel distribution interests of *Hargreaves Group Limited* (July 9), MR. KENNETH HARGREAVES declared: rationalization, aimed at better use of physical assets, continued, and several small businesses were purchased.

In pursuance of the policy of *Lunt, Comley & Pitt Limited* (September 25) in rationalizing fuel distribution the company, stated MR. R. D. PITT, purchased on June 19, 1968, the Birmingham fuel distributing business of A. Brockhurst Limited. He named also companies which the group had acquired in other fields.

Group sales and exports of *Stone-Platt Industries Limited* (May 30) both reached new records, but pre-tax profits suffered a severe setback, stated the retiring chairman, SIR KENNETH PRESTON. However, reorganization of the group to achieve rationalization, concentration and increased profitability was already well in hand, he added; benefits from these plans would begin to show in 1969 and increasingly thereafter, and the whole group should emerge immeasurably strengthened as a result.

Among the features of the annual statement (*The Times*, March 12) by MR. N. M. PEECH for *The Steetley Company Limited* was the following:

"Improved production methods, concentrated efforts to reduce costs and rationalization of production facilities have contributed to the results. The reorganized Group is intensifying new product development and exports and is rapidly widening its horizons."

In his statement (*The Times*, March 18) for *Norcros Limited* MR. JOHN SHEFFIELD devoted a large part of his text to the "radical reorganization" which was going on in the group. From this the following paragraph is extracted:

"Last year I explained the reasons for the radical reorganization which is currently taking place within your Group. We redefined Norcros Limited as an Industrial Group of Companies with the declared aim that in future our energies should be concentrated on those of our activities having the strongest profit potential. To restructure a Group as large as Norcros is a formidable task, and cannot be accomplished overnight. A great deal of time necessarily needs to be spent to bring together a team of high management calibre and then to allow individuals to settle in, and understand the problems, before positive results flow. This task has started and the effort which has already been made during the last few months has been enormous. Norcros Limited is now moving substantially along its planned course of fresh growth."

AUTOMATION AND COMPUTERS

ALTHOUGH the processes of automation were still being applied to many British businesses both in industry and commerce, it did appear that lack of confidence in the immediate economic outlook was in some instances acting as a brake on the introduction of automated plant and machinery. At any rate, the number of such new installations announced by company chairmen during 1968 revealed only moderate growth. However, the big banks with their multitudinous clients' statements, the insurance companies with their many customers' policies and the larger building societies with their numerous depositors', shareholders' and borrowers' accounts continued to computerize their figures.

The manufacture of computers and other adjuncts of mechanization was being increasingly rationalized during the year through a series of mergers. Thus Elliott-Automation was taken over by English Electric, and, later, International Computers and Tabulators Limited (to be renamed International Computers Limited) and English Electric Computers Limited came together in the new International Computers (Holdings) Limited group. As regards the first of these mergers, LORD NELSON OF STAFFORD told members of *The English Electric Company Limited* (March 27) that the additional capabilities of Elliott-Automation meant that the combined group now had a complete range from the very small computers to the very largest system installations. He also stated:

> "Elliott-Automation brings into English Electric additional experience in systems and control engineering and a wide range of products, both to a great extent complementary to ours. In process automation, the company has, amongst other things, the most extensive range of on-and-off-stream analytical instruments in the world. In on-line computer control, a recent American world-wide survey indicated that Elliotts lay fifth in the 'world league' with 114 systems (excluding defence) already installed or on order at the beginning of 1967."

That *Ferranti Limited* had established a leading position in the application of computer control to industrial plant was asserted by MR. SEBASTIAN Z. DE FERRANTI in his annual statement (*The Times*, July 25).

> "Production of Argus microminiature computers and control and display equipment," he continued, "is now well established. Expanded manufacturing facilities will provide for a considerable increase in output during the coming year."

Looking to the future, MR. P. W. SELIGMAN declared in his statement for *A.P.V. Holdings Limited* (April 25), the board believed that automation would become more and more important to the industries which the company served. "Our leading position as automation engineers, particularly in the food and beverage industries," he went on, "should therefore be most helpful to the future growth of our business."

By intensifying its programme of mechanization and automation of production methods and the development of new techniques, *Colvern Limited* (August 20) would be well equipped to penetrate every available market and poised to take the advantages that would arise as the economy improved. This statement was made by MR. RICHARD F. COLLINSON.

Among the salient points from the address by MR. G. R. BROWNE to members of *MTE Control Gear Limited* which appeared in *The Times* of September 16 were the following:

"During the last three or four years, the economic climate of this country, as a whole, has been such as to make it necessary for those of us who are in the automatic control-gear side of the capital goods industry, to seek out and fight for every order that is in the offing, in order to maintain, let alone increase, the level of our business. Only in the last few months has there been any noticeable improvement. It is against this economic background that the results of the company have been achieved. . . . On the home market the company has increased its penetration in the field of highly sophisticated automatic control equipment which is now in increasing demand. We have also consolidated and improved our position as suppliers of electro-mechanical devices to the control gear industry."

MR. W. GIBSON BIGGART stated that a significant proportion of the Walsall chain production of *Wheway Watson Limited* (September 5) was taken up by the National Coal Board for use in armoured face conveyors on mechanized coal faces. He added that the trend continued towards full mechanization in the profitable mines, and although over the years overall requirements would fall there would be a continuing demand for the company's products. "The National Coal Board," he declared, "have led the world in mechanizing mining, and the introduction of long wall mining methods in other countries could improve our export prospects."

After referring to the adverse effect on profits of two major non-recurring factors, the heavy cost of litigation (now concluded) in America and the expense and teething troubles of the new plant which had been installed at one of the factories, MR. A. J. CLOUGH informed members of *Alfred Clough Limited* (May 22) that the directors were firmly of the opinion that more mechanization and automation would be needed to meet world competition. Costly

though they were, the measures already taken, he declared, "should put your company in the forefront of such developments."

A new automated plant for bath enamelling had been built by *Allied Ironfounders Limited* (July 25) and was then being run in at the Bilston works, stated MR. G. S. STEVEN; and the results were sufficiently successful to require duplication of this plant at Greenford.

In his statement (*The Times*, November 18) for *Duport Limited* the chairman mentioned that the installation of an automated machining line for the production of a new range of Daintymaid kitchen equipment was completed during the year.

The policy of the board of *Walker Crosweller & Co. Limited* of installing highly automated equipment had been fully justified when the demand rose in the second half of the year, MR. R. F. WALKER asserted in his annual review (*The Times*, July 5).

Recalling that in February, 1966, *Decca Limited* (October 22) had acquired Setpoint Limited, SIR EDWARD LEWIS said that this had provided a base for the development of ships' automation equipment to meet the growing requirements for advanced electronic systems to provide engine room and cargo space monitoring, alarm scanning and data logging. He continued:

"The equipment is now in production and is being marketed under the name ISIS 300. Orders already placed with us are for installations in both British and foreign vessels. This extension of our marine activity in ships' automation equipment has, we are convinced, a big potential. We feel that we are in a position to secure a substantial share of the new and growing market for ships' automation equipment."

Dealing with technical developments, MR. MARCUS WALLENBERG stated that development work by *Atlas Copco AB.* (Stockholm, April 18) had been concentrated on producing machines and equipment incorporating an increased element of mechanization and automation. As in previous years, noise abatement and allied work had received particular attention.

MR. RALPH PRICE included these paragraphs in his annual survey (*The Times*, February 21) for *Honeywell Controls Limited*:

"While all divisions of the company were buoyant, the outstanding performances came from the Computer Division and the Temperature Controls Group.

"The Computer Division turnover was 42% greater than 1966, shipments increased by 57%, exports more than doubled. Employment in this division was up by 36%.

"The Residential & Commercial Divisions supplying controls for the heating and air conditioning market shared in the continuing rapid growth in the industry. This growth was greatly affected by the increase in the domestic central heating market and particularly the gas sector."

Incidentally, he remarked that devaluation of the pound had a profound effect on the company's 1968 planning, creating export opportunities and encouraging local manufacture of many devices which previously it had been marginally more economical to import.

An ICT computer was commissioned by *M.K. Electric Holdings Limited* (July 25) at the end of January, 1968, and MR. F. D. O'BRIEN NEWMAN stated that it was successfully handling the Edmonton payroll and associated analyses. He added that parallel runs were then being made on sales ledger and sales statistics, and that future plans provided for a steady transfer during the current year of other applications such as production and stock control.

The next quotation comes from MR. F. L. CHAPLIN'S review for *F. W. Woolworth and Co. Limited* (March 8):

"The Castleton warehouse, which opened in 1966, has extended its operations in 1967 and one of the benefits is the overall reduction in stocks, as shown in the accounts. The processing of stock and accounting records at the adjoining computer centre has greatly simplified the merchandising of the stores at present supplied from the warehouse."

For the *H. J. Heinz Company Limited* MR. H. J. HEINZ announced in his statement (*The Times*, August 16) that increasing work on data processing and new applications in the field of planning having made higher capacity essential, a new computer—English Electric System 4.50—was scheduled for delivery in the spring of 1969.

Commenting on an increase to £36,000 in computer costs for the full year as well as a rise in other expenses, MR. R. E. J. MACREADY made this statement to members of *Macready's Metal Company Limited* (June 12):

"The installation of the new computer has proved to be more complex than was originally anticipated. While some of the costs have been non-recurring, there will be further expenditure during the current year. The directors are satisfied that the additional information to be provided by the computer will be of the greatest importance in increasing the efficiency of selling operations, accounting, purchasing and inventory control."

A new lay-out for the income-tax vouchers and cheques sent in payment of dividends and interest by *Teacher* (*Distillers*) *Limited* (July 10), stated MR. R. M. TEACHER, had been made possible in line with modern practice by the use of a computer now handling all such payments through the centre established by the National Commercial Bank of Scotland in Edinburgh. This had speeded up the work and also relieved pressure on the company's registration department.

In his annual review (*The Times*, May 25) for *Gala Cosmetic*

Group Limited MR. S. H. PICKER announced that the new Computer Centre would go into operation within the next few months and should greatly assist planning and control functions.

For *Spooner Industries Limited* (January 26) MR. WALTER BROUGHTON reported that in April, 1967, Asser Engineering Limited was brought into the group as a wholly owned subsidiary, whose products were "essentially complementary" to those of Spooner Food Machinery Company Limited in a sector of the baking industry which offered "considerable potential for further automation."

That a substantial upward curve in profits could be expected from the computer peripheral and sound reproduction division of *Brayhead Limited* was asserted by MR. A. J. RICHARDS in his annual report (*The Times*, July 5). The $3m. $8\frac{1}{2}$ per cent loan recently placed by the subsidiary Mastertape (Magnetic) Limited, he added, was to be utilized for the production, initially, of random access discs and, subsequently, of other peripheral equipment for the computer industry.

The *Sunderland and South Shields Water Company* (March 20) had hitherto rented its computer installation, but, stated MR. H. F. RENNOLDSON, the policy had now been changed. An order had been placed for the purchase of an I.B.M. 360/25 configuration, which it was hoped would be delivered early in 1969.

Early in 1968 *Union Minière S. A.* (Brussels, May 24), in association with BelgoNucléaire, set up a computer centre, the "Centre d'Informatique Générale" (C.I.G.); and according to MR. L. WALLEF the aim was to develop the two companies' facilities "so as to deal with any problem of administrative organization, industrial or commercial management, and scientific research."

The doubling of the capacity of the computer of *Richard Costain Limited* (June 27) was announced by MR. A. P. COSTAIN in the following terms:

"The capacity of our I.C.T. 1904 computer installation has been doubled by the introduction of some of the latest equipment. The resulting increase in the speed of operation and versatility of the computer will enable us to develop management information systems along the most modern lines. There is growing evidence of the benefits being derived from the use of the computer both in its application to the day to day commercial and technical problems of our business and in stimulating that creative thought which is essential if we are to remain in the forefront of the industry."

MR. E. C. BECK informed members of *John Mowlem & Company Limited* in his statement (*The Times*, May 29) that a new company, Mowlem Computer Grid Limited, had recently been formed to take advantage of the knowledge of computers they had acquired over the last three years. "We are offering," he added, "a com-

puter bureau service which has proved successful, and at the present time about 20 per cent of this time is on work for companies outside the group."

The next quotation deals with an ancillary computer service provided by *Lamson Industries Limited* (May 10) and is extracted from MR. B. H. PEARCE'S review:

"In an age in which the computer is playing an ever more important role it is satisfactory to know that we are playing a vital part. We have coined the phrase Computer Optimization to emphasize the fact that while your company does not manufacture or market computers, it furnishes users with means to make their installations more effective and more profitable. I am pleased to say that we enjoy the closest relations with most of the computer companies at home and abroad, who recognize that their sales forces and our own serve a common purpose towards the business community."

Pyramid Group (Publishers) Limited (May 30) had formed, in association with C.M.G. (Business Computer Services) Limited, a new company known as Pyramid Computer Services Limited in which it held the majority shareholding and which began trading in January, 1968. After reporting this, MR. BERNARD LEWIS went on to state:

"This step occurred after three years of intensive investigation and research into designing a computerized system for up-dating membership records for organizations who maintain a Register or Index of members, individuals or companies, so that subscription accounting, mailing, membership listing and other facilities can be produced from one central source. This service is of particular appeal to professional bodies and national organizations and, allied to the other facilities offered by the Group, does provide considerable room for expansion."

Mr. Lewis stated that contracts had already been placed with the new company by the Royal Institution of Chartered Surveyors, the Estate Agents Council and the Institute of Marine Engineers. He did not expect the new company to contribute materially to the group's 1968 profits, but was optimistic that an increasing return from this new activity would be achieved in subsequent years.

In his statement for *Dun & Bradstreet Limited* (February 29) MR. HANNING PHILIPPS declared that a milestone would be reached during 1968 with the introduction of electronic data processing for storing, up-dating and retrieving in many forms the business information in the Dun & Bradstreet Register.

"By May, 1968," he continued, "the London volume of 35,000 listings will have been converted, and the project will continue until the other four volumes have been converted,

bringing the data bank to 200,000 listings of business enterprises. This project can make available to industry and commerce a range of new services based primarily on the speed and wide selectivity of information that the Data Bank will provide automatically."

The Lowndes-Ajax Computer Service Bureau once again made excellent progress during 1967, gross income increasing by 52 per cent over the previous year. This was stated in the annual review (*The Times*, June 13) by MR. ROY L. LOWNDES for *Noble Lowndes Holdings Limited*. He added:

"Our Payroll Service continued its rapid growth, and now handles payrolls to the value of £17m. per annum. In the light of this success, plans are well under way to launch a further specialized service, this time dealing with Sales Ledger and Purchase Ledger problems. A further diversification of interests has led to an examination of industrial applications, particularly in the areas of production control and of scheduling the efficient use of productive capacity."

MERGERS AND TAKE-OVERS

THE number of mergers and take-overs in British commerce and industry increased rapidly during 1967–68. The reasons for the acquisitions varied from one merger to another, but broadly speaking the basic ideas behind them were: the complementary nature of the two businesses, whereby a wider scope was given to the resultant group; overlapping in the two merging businesses, which when joined offered opportunity for rationalization; plain expansionism where one company taking over another had resources to spare; the opportunity of obtaining a first rate management team from the acquisition of an up and coming company; and the intention of putting to better use the assets of a company whose profits were below a certain standard.

For *The General Electric Company Limited*, which acquired, first, Associated Electrical Industries and, later, The English Electric Company, the main object was to rationalize the electrical engineering industry and to build up a large complex which could stand up to the competition of immense foreign groups. The annual statement (*The Times*, July 30) of LORD ALDINGTON for G.E.C. was published well before the first public proposal for taking over English Electric was made known. However, he dealt at some length with the massive reorganization of the combined resources of the newly created G.E.C.-A.E.I. group which had started during the year under review. There is room here for only a part of his comment:

"Effective integration of manufacturing and trading units which have grown up separately and have learned to depend on distinct methods and personalities is well known to be difficult. There are plenty of examples in industry generally where effective integration has taken a long time to achieve, and some where mergers have been effected in name only. The management of your company operates on the basis that it is obliged, regardless of personal considerations and separate traditions and habits, to ensure as quickly as possible the best use of all the resources committed to its charge. Largely because of the high degree of decentralization already achieved in the GEC, the process of integration and reorganization was able to go forward concurrently over the whole of the Group at home and overseas. While much remains to be done, it can already be said that the two companies have been integrated into a single Group and that the combined management is in a position to take and implement the necessary decisions to achieve the desired standards of efficient working.

"There are important human and social considerations which temper the speed with which the process can be carried through. Some personal upsets and disappointments have been unavoidable, but we have done our best to make fair arrangements, always fulfilling our proper obligations. Even with the extra load on central top management, we have found it both possible and wise to keep our headquarters staff to a relatively small number. In this we differ from many other companies, and from the former AEI practice. Part of the reorganization has already been completed with drastic reductions in central and group costs, an annual saving of about £4m. This does not include the further savings in overhead expenditure resulting from integration and rationalisation within the operating units.

"All the operating units are working in the current year to budgetary practice which conforms much more to the GEC requirements of commercial and financial management."

Meanwhile, *The English Electric Company Limited* (March 27) had been making some sizable acquisitions itself. LORD NELSON OF STAFFORD stated:

"During 1967 the company acquired the whole of the share capital of Combined Electrical Manufacturers Ltd. and of Elliott-Automation Ltd. Associated with the latter acquisition the company received a loan from the Industrial Reorganisation Corporation of £15m. and issued to that Corporation £15m. Subordinated Unsecured Loan Stock. The company also acquired the UK switchgear business of Johnson & Phillips Ltd., the whole of the share capital of Johnson & Phillips South Africa Ltd., a 60% shareholding in Johnson & Phillips (Pakistan) Ltd. and an 18·4% shareholding in British India Electric Construction Company Ltd. These acquisitions involved further issues of share capital. The issued share capital is now £86,466,000."

Describing 1967 as "almost certainly the most eventful in the history" of *Telephone Rentals Limited* (June 12), MR. W. STUART PHILCOX explained that at the beginning of the year the board were engaged in warding off a take-over bid from General Electric and at the end they were themselves making an offer to acquire all the issued share capital of Dictograph Telephones Limited. The former bid was withdrawn, while the latter was successful. Mr. Philcox made these remarks on the benefits to be expected from the acquisition of Dictograph Telephones:

"Since the beginning of February, 1968, our representatives in conjunction with the Dictograph management have been investigating how best to effect rationalisation and reorganisation within the enlarged Group to obtain the most beneficial results from the merger. I am glad to say that our investigations,

whilst not yet complete, confirm at this stage the appreciation we prepared during the early stages of the merger discussions as to the benefits likely to accrue. I would add, however, that these benefits are not likely to become apparent to any marked degree during the course of 1968 but will flow increasingly from the beginning of 1969 onwards."

MR. RONALD C. BROOKS, dealing with the proposed merger of *Commercial Union Assurance Company Limited* (April 8) and the Northern & Employers Assurance Company, said:

"The merger, if agreed, will bring together two of the leading British insurance groups transacting all classes of business and both of them already occupying important positions in the insurance markets in the United Kingdom, United States and other overseas territories. The Commercial Union has a bigger business in the United Kingdom and in a number of overseas territories while, with their American associates, the Northern & Employers have a larger business in the U.S.A., so that in many respects the two groups are essentially complementary to each other. We expect substantial economies to come progressively from integration, which should lead to improved profits for shareholders and the maintenance of a high standard of service to our policyholders throughout the world."

Terms of an offer had been agreed to merge the *Guardian Assurance Group* and the Royal Exchange Assurance under a new holding company to be called Guardian Royal Exchange Assurance Limited, LT.-COL. C. P. DAWNAY said in his statement (*The Times*, May 22) for the Guardian. He went on to make these comments:

"The two businesses are complementary giving the Group greater strength in the United Kingdom market and a wider spread and greater volume abroad. On the Life side there will be further outlets for continuing growth and the two operating Companies 'Guardian' and 'Royal Exchange' will continue to serve all their world-wide connections at they have done in the past. Within this framework substantial economies of management should result through computerization, re-allocation of staff and the pooling of the best and most modern methods of management used by both Groups."

For *Royal Exchange Assurance* (June 19) the Governor, LORD KINDERSLEY, also referred to the reduction in expenses which was hoped for as a result of the merger. He declared:

"It is most satisfactory that the business of the two organizations fits so well together. The modernization which both have carried out in recent times and the closeness of our thinking in

relation to future planning should ensure the achievement of greater efficiency within a relatively short time."

The process of integrating the branch operations of *General Accident Fire and Life Assurance Corporation Limited* (May 29) was only one aspect of a memorable year in which the acquisition of the Yorkshire Insurance Company took pride of place as the outstanding achievement in the history of General Accident. In making this comment, SIR STANLEY NORIE-MILLER also referred to the plans to effect substantial economies in administration as a result of the merger.

The *Provident Life Association of London Limited* (May 22), MR. R. J. W. CRABBE showed, had been going ahead in more directions than one. The relevant passages from his statement follow:

"Early in the year we reached agreement with the Winterthur Life and Casualty Companies of Switzerland who were seeking a United Kingdom partner in their international operations, notably in the field of pensions. We are now able, though Winterthur and their American associates, Continental Assurance and Casualty Companies of Chicago, to provide international pension coverage and facilities throughout Western Europe, the United States of America and Canada.

"A further development was the acquisition in August of the share capital of the United Standard Insurance Company Limited which transacts fire, accident, motor and marine insurance business. Originally a reinsurance company, the United Standard has for some years been developing U.K. fire, accident and motor accounts. These accounts are expanding and showing satisfactory underwriting results and the household fire and accident business, in particular, will fit in well with our life business."

In January, 1968, stated SIR JOHN G. BANKS, a merger was completed by *The Dominion Insurance Company Limited* (June 26) acquiring the whole issued capital of Credit and Guarantee Insurance Company Limited—a member company of the Landel Trust group. They would operate as one single company, thereby using the combined capital of the two undertakings to the greatest advantage.

During 1967, MR. JOHN F. JEFFERSON declared, the investment portfolio of *Britannic Assurance Company Limited* (April 5) was considerably affected by steel renationalization and the flood of take-over bids which occurred. After giving figures to show the size of the problem, he went on to assert:

"We much dislike take-over bids or mergers offering a purchase price for equity capital which is not represented wholly or very substantially by equity capital of equivalent value. Our very large holdings of ordinary shares in first class companies

144

have been built up patiently over the years and we object to terms which involve the acceptance of unwelcome loan stock or cash. It is pleasing to notice an increasing awareness of this problem by those concerned with the formulation of takeover schemes. The incorporation into such schemes of a provision for the allotment of equity capital as an alternative to loan stock should be more widely adopted."

The acquisition of Gabriel Wade & English Limited, declared MR. JOHN M. MEYER, was most important for the future of *Montague L. Meyer Limited* (September 10). The two businesses, he added, were complementary, Montague L. Meyer mainly concentrating on the wholesale side of the timber trade and Gabriel Wade & English on the merchanting and retail side, both spread over a wide area of the country. In the short space of time that the two businesses had been associated, considerable progress had been made in merging the interests of the two organizations "with little or no disturbance to personnel." Benefits from the merger were already being shown, as indicated by the following excerpt from Mr. Meyer's statement:

"The benefits which we anticipated are beginning to be achieved. We are now ideally situated to cater for all requirements, from those of the biggest organizations in the country right down to those of an individual, and a further advantage, that is particularly important for the future, is that we are able to give young men entering the business unrivalled opportunities for training and advancement."

Among the acquisitions of *Slater, Walker Securities Limited* mentioned by MR. J. D. SLATER in his annual statement (*The Times*, May 23) were Greengate & Irwell and Constructors Limited. In the following extract the way in which he reorganizes the businesses he acquires is outlined:

"The cost of Greengate & Irwell was approximately £3m. and at the time of acquisition in 1967 pre-tax profits were £300,000. Pre-tax profits in 1968 are budgeted at £500,000 on a reduced capital employed of £1½m. as a result of better liquidity control, the sale of Bramac Limited and hiving off the elasticized thread division. Profits as a percentage on investment therefore have risen from 10% to 33⅓%.

"Since acquiring Constructors Limited in November 1967, loss making activities have been eliminated. Production facilities are also being rationalized with the result that the manufacture of the remaining products of Constructors, previously carried on in six factories, will be concentrated in the two main factories at Birmingham and Putney."

A whole string of mergers and take-overs was referred to by

145

MR. HANNING PHILIPPS in his review for *Schweppes Limited* (May 9). Reporting another year of progress throughout the group, he mentioned particularly a major strengthening of its position by acquisition and merger "which should provide a sound foundation for future growth in the years to come." The most important acquisition was probably that of the Typhoo Tea group, about which he made these remarks:

"For some time we have been conscious of the need to broaden our base here in Britain as a means of underpinning future overseas development. Your Board agreed that the future growth of the Group would be best secured by a major merger with a soundly based British company whose products offered export possibilities and whose U.K. operation would satisfactorily merge with our own.

"The merger with Typhoo Tea (Holdings) Limited exactly fulfils these requirements. We are sure that together we shall be better able to strengthen our marketing position both at home and overseas."

During the year *Whitbread and Company Limited* (September 6), COLONEL W. H. WHITBREAD recalled, arranged mergers with six other companies—namely, Threlfalls Chesters Limited; Fremlins Limited; Isaac Tucker & Co. Limited; Campbell, Hope & King Limited; Evan Evans Bevan Limited; Cobb & Co. (Brewers) Limited. Other acquisitions had been made since the end of the financial year. Obviously, he declared, these mergers must be followed by a great deal of reorganization before the full benefits could be obtained, and this took time.

The next quotation comes from the statement (*The Times*, August 16) by MR. H. J. HEINZ of the *H. J. Heinz Company Limited*:

"At the time of writing, negotiations are in the final stages for the company to acquire a controlling interest in Moss Waltham & Company Limited. This firm is a well established processor and wholesaler of meat for the manufacturing and catering industries. Its acquisition will provide an entry into an area of the economy which is already important to us as large meat users. We are confident that the association will develop to the advantage of both companies."

Last year *Gill & Duffus Limited*, stated MR. D. W. MARTIN in his annual review (*The Times*, May 23), made two acquisitions. The private partnership of Landauer & Co., which had been in business since 1878, became a limited company of which Gill & Duffus now owned 100 per cent; their trade followed parallel lines to the latter concern's produce divisions. Also, the capital of H. Leonard Puckle & Co. Limited, Lloyd's insurance brokers, was acquired, a development in a field separate from G. & D.'s traditional business that he believed would afford opportunities of

expansion as time went on. On the other hand, in agreement with Rowntree and Company Limited, Gill & Duffus had arranged to dispose of its 40 per cent shareholding in Stewart Esplen & Greenough Limited at a price which showed a modest increase on the price paid for the shares in 1963.

LORD McFADZEAN had some realistic things to say about the Monopolies Commission, with which *British Insulated Callender's Cables Limited* (May 9) had a brush in connection with its acquisition of Pyrotenax. The relevant passage in his statement follows:

"Our major objectives remain as I stated last year to expand sales and earnings through higher efficiency to the benefit of our own people, stockholders, customers and the countries in which we operate. Size in itself is, of course, no guarantee of success, but we believe that in this world of today the objectives I have just set out can be achieved most effectively by a large Group provided it is efficiently operated—a view we hold with some authority as we understand we are the largest Group of our kind in the world.

"Our acquisition of the Pyrotenax Company in December 1966 was referred to the Monopolies Commission who after a most exhaustive investigation ruled that the merger was not expected to operate against the public interest. But the preparation and presentation of our case not only absorbed a lot of my time and that of my senior colleagues and kept the whole matter in suspense for some six months, it also frankly inhibited us from taking other steps that we are convinced could have been in our own and the national interest.

"It is unrealistic to have one Ministry urging people to merge in the interests of efficiency and conquering more of world markets, and another Ministry only doing its legal duty in referring some of such moves to a Monopolies Commission. Of course the public interest must be safeguarded, but a much broader basis of defining this must be devised than prevails at present. I therefore greatly welcome the recent statement by the Prime Minister that we have to re-think our national attitude to problems of monopolies and mergers and I hope this will be urgently tackled.

"There is one further point here which I believe is of great relevance. It is that, generally speaking, the young ambitious man of ability for whom we are all competing today internationally, will seek his future in a large expanding Group rather than in one which may remain static."

For *Initial Services Limited* MR. KENNETH E. GARCKE stated (*The Times*, August 5) that the merger with Allied Industrial Services Limited made it probably the largest company of its kind in the world, with some 16,500 employees, and offered encouraging prospects for development and progress. He mentioned a new

departure for the company with which it was experimenting:

"Linen supply and office cleaning continue to be the main business of Initial but we are experimenting with a new domestic laundry service which may be launched on a large scale. Our vending service has now passed the experimental stage and should shortly be making a contribution to profits."

The improved results of *Croda Premier Limited* were fully in accordance with the forecasts made at the time of the merger between Croda and United Premier in the previous summer; and in his statement (*The Times*, May 24) MR. F. A. S. WOOD reported that the integration of the two groups had proceeded smoothly and rapidly.

A disappointing year for *Macarthys Pharmaceuticals Limited* (November 14) was attributed by SIR HUGH LINSTEAD mainly to the exceptional conditions following the amalgamation with Savory & Moore. He stated:

"Looked at in isolation, the financial year 1967/68 has been disappointing. Most of the reasons have been identified and are to be found in the entirely exceptional conditions created by the amalgamation with Messrs. Savory & Moore. Your Directors believe that these conditions will not recur, for they mainly arose out of the closures of unremunerative depots and pharmacies, the transfer of accounting work from Brighton to Romford and the reorganization of certain subsidiary companies all of which is virtually complete. The consequent economies have come too late to be reflected in the current accounts but they will begin to make their contribution in the current and subsequent years. Similarly, capital invested in new premises, new machinery and modernization will bring a progressive return in the future.

"These are the considerations which have led your Directors to conclude that it would be an error to view this one year in isolation. It must be seen in relation to the past performance of the Group, to the substantial economies and investment that have accompanied the amalgamation and to the indications which are already developing of substantial improvement in our trading experience. The current year has started well. The major companies within the Group have all recorded increases in sales. The level of overheads is being well controlled and the prospects for the current year are therefore encouraging."

SIR ROBERT ADEANE told members of *Second Consolidated Trust Limited* (November 21) that a scheme was being prepared for amalgamation with two other investment trusts in the 117 Group— namely, New York and General Trust and International Financial Society. Today's conditions made it desirable to operate as larger units, which would make use of their experience and result in benefits to shareholders. These schemes, he added, involved many

points of detail, but it was hoped to submit proposals early in 1969.

In pursuit of the directors' intention to widen the scope of the activities of *Babcock & Wilcox Limited* (May 30), SIR KENNETH HAGUE recorded that in March, 1968, they took steps to acquire the share capital of Winget Gloucester Limited.

"This company," he continued, "specializes in the manufacture of machinery and plant for building, civil engineering and pre-cast concrete product industries. Their products include concrete mixers of all types, ready-mix concrete plants, fully and semi-automatic plants for large scale production of concrete, ferrous and high duty castings, refrigeration equipment, dumpers for mining, quarrying and contracting industries, power shovels, mechanical handling equipment, contractors' plant hire and food machinery. The main Works are at Rochester and Gloucester, with smaller establishments elsewhere in the United Kingdom, South Africa and Australia, and there are a number of service depots throughout this country.

"We anticipate that, in view of our experience in the field of tower cranes and Marion excavators, we shall make an increasing impact on the market for the foregoing products in the construction industries at home and overseas."

Parkinson Cowan Limited (July 31) was acquiring Fisher-Bendix Limited from British Motor Corporation for the sum of about £3·7m., according to MR. HUGH P. BARKER, who added that F.-B. made Bendix washing machines, Fisholow sinks and central heating equipment; sales were about £7½m. a year. An offer was also being made to acquire G W B Holdings Limited (Dudley), who were well known manufacturers of furnaces and boilers. With sales in the near future at an annual rate of about £25m. a year, Mr. Barker said: "We have grown from being a large small company to a small large one," and if the economy remained reasonably active he expected the group to enjoy another good year.

It was proposed to amalgamate the steel drum and plastic interests of *Blagden & Noakes* (*Holdings*) Limited with those of the United Kingdom subsidiary of Rheem Manufacturing Company of New York, stated MR. R. S. WALDE. He claimed that Rheem were probably the largest producers of steel containers in the world.

Included in MR. K. M. STOBART's statement for *Charrington, Gardner, Locket & Co. Limited* (July 18) was the following paragraph:

"Since the end of the financial year under review we have made a successful offer for the shares of the Rickett Cockerell Group. The merging of our activities should provide substantial economies and active steps are already being taken to achieve these savings as speedily as possible."

That *William Cory & Son Limited* (September 19) at the end of April, 1968, had successfully concluded negotiations for a participation in Hovermarine Limited, a young and progressive company which was manufacturing sidewall hovercraft, was among the points made by LORD LEATHERS in his annual review.

For *James Howden & Godfrey Limited* (October 31) MR. J. HOWDEN HUME reported that the merger with Sir George Godfrey and Partners (Holdings) Limited was declared unconditional on September 5 when Howdens had received over 94 per cent acceptances.

In MR. HERBERT H. NEWMARK's report (*The Times*, October 25) for *Louis Newmark Limited* the following paragraph appeared:

"The whole of the Share Capital of the Vernon Instrument Company Limited and its two Subsidiaries was acquired for cash. This small Group has an excellent name in the inspection equipment industry and your Directors consider that aided by our existing technical facilities and skills it will prove to be a valuable long-term acquisition."

The recent acquisition by *L. M. Van Moppes & Sons Limited* (August 8) of the entire issued capital of Sharratt & Newth Limited, manufacturers of glaziers' diamond tools and automated glass cutting equipment, was reported by MR. L. E. VAN MOPPES. This long-established family business had been a customer of the group for very many years.

In LORD HAYTER's review (*The Times*, June 20) accompanying the preliminary results of *Chubb & Son Limited* he recorded the acquisition of The Pyrene Company Limited; the major reason for this was the high standing enjoyed by Pyrene in the fire field, which Chubb's intended to develop as quickly as possible. Chubb's also, he added, had acquired the well-known Belgian safe-making firm of Laurent-Fraigneux in order to establish a foothold in the Common Market.

Considerable investigations had been carried out by *A D International Limited* (July 1) into suitable acquisitions, MR. W. H. FREER asserted. This had led to the purchase of Diamond Precision Tools Limited and of a majority interest in a retail depot in France. At the meeting the chairman announced the completion of the acquisition of the dental interests of The Dental Manufacturing Company Limited.

MR. VINCENT C. HARRIS informed members of *Wilson Lovatt & Sons Limited* (July 11) that Ford & Carter Limited and Jenks Builders Limited had been assimilated into the group, and were now full partners and had made their expected contribution to the results.

During the period under review, it was stated in the annual report of *Trafalgar House Investments Limited* (July 24), the company's principal acquisitions were Ideal Building Corporation Limited

and Trollope & Colls Limited; subsequently, Eastern International Investment Trust Limited was acquired.

In his first address to the shareholders of *Financial and Provincial Publishing Company Limited* (June 20) MR. R. P. T. GIBSON pointed out that most of them had been until recently shareholders of Financial News, Financial Times, Westminster Press or Longmans. Of these four companies, the first three were brought together at the end of 1967 as wholly owned subsidiaries of FPPC, and within a few months FPPC made an offer for the stock of the Longman group of publishing companies which had been overwhelmingly accepted.

H. & R. Johnson Limited made a successful offer for Richards-Campbell Tiles Limited, as a result of which *H. & R. Johnson-Richards Tiles Limited* (August 28) came into being. MR. DEREK H. JOHNSON stated that the two merging companies were of similar size and engaged in the same fields of activity, and he made the following comment on the mechanics of the merger:

"Following the acceptance of the offer, a good deal of work has been done but much more remains to be done to ensure that rationalization of the work of the two companies is achieved. This includes a considerable degree of reorganization on various factories in the enlarged group and a study and revision of sales, marketing and accountancy, etc., procedures.

"One realises that the impact of a merger such as has now taken place will require a considerable lapse of time before its full benefits can be achieved. Work to this end will of course continue with all speed since quite obviously, the opportunity which will enable the new group to meet present and future international competition at any level must be grasped as quickly as possible."

Referring to the proposed merger of Timothy Whites and Taylors with *Boots Pure Drug Company Limited* (July 11), MR. W. R. NORMAN declared his conviction that this merging of interests would be of great advantage to the shareholders of both companies and to the community generally.

After agreement had been reached with the board and major shareholders of Montague Burton Limited for the sale of their shares to *United Drapery Stores Limited*, MR. J. A. SAMPSON in his statement (*The Times*, July 10) reported that this acquisition was frustrated by the negative decision of the Board of Trade acting on the recommendation of the Monopolies Commission. He then made this comment on the affair:

"The rationalization benefits and increase in efficiency, which are constantly urged upon us by the Government, would have been very considerable. Your Board was deeply disappointed by this decision as it was convinced that the tailoring interests of

151

the two groups would have provided not only benefits for U.D.S. but also a better service and improved economies for the general public."

Since the end of the financial year, SIR MARK TURNER recorded in his annual statement (*The Times*, May 31), *British Home Stores Limited* had acquired the cash department store business of Henry's Stores Limited. He disclosed that the reason behind this acquisition was the very fine store site which Henry's own in Manchester, where BHS had long wanted to have a major representation; this property, he added, could be developed at reasonable conversion cost into a chain store unit.

Negotiations by *Renwick Wilton & Dobson* (*Holdings*) *Limited* (September 30) with the National Coal Board and Amalgamated Anthracite were referred to by MR. F. C. DOBSON in these terms:

"These negotiations culminated in the formation of a partnership ('Western Fuel Company') to combine the fuel distribution and builders' merchants interests of the Renwick Wilton & Dobson Group and the British Fuel Company (in itself a Partnership between Amalgamated Anthracite Partners Limited and the National Coal Board), within one Partnership business. The primary object of the Partnership is to improve on a sound commercial basis the distribution of fuels to consumers in the Partnership area which includes the whole of Cornwall, Devon, Somerset, Dorset and Wiltshire and parts of Gloucestershire, Oxfordshire, Berkshire, Hampshire and Monmouthshire."

MR. G. K. GALLIERS-PRATT informed members of *F. Pratt Engineering Corporation Limited* (April 24) that the merger with the former Arnott & Harrison Group had shown good progress towards integration and added that the long-term benefits might well be more substantial than first evaluation seemed to indicate.

That Liebig's Extract of Meat Company was now a 100 per cent member of the *Brooke Bond Liebig Limited* group was among the points made in the chairman's report (*The Times*, December 6). Only 10 months' profits for most Liebig companies were included in the 1968 group results, and he disclosed that the greater part of Liebig profits was earned in Britain. He added:

"The merger has given the Brooke Bond Liebig group even greater financial strength, expanded its range of nationally known products in the United Kingdom and enlarged its world-wide network of production and selling facilities."

The acquisition by The Midland Tar Distillers of the issued capital of Yorkshire Tar Corporation, reported MR. R. B. ROBINSON, had effected a merger of the two companies; the resultant group is *Midland-Yorkshire Tar Distillers Limited* (November 1), about which he commented:

"Reasons beyond the control of the parties prolonged the merger negotiations and though financially the affairs of the two companies have been consolidated as and from April 1, 1967, it was not until January 1, 1968, that it became possible to take active steps; since then good progress has been made in re-arranging and streamlining the operations of the Group."

The acquisition of Crofts Engineers (Holdings) Limited was by far the most outstanding event in the year for *Renold Limited* (August 1) and perhaps in the long-term development of the group, according to SIR THOMAS ROBSON, who continued:

"The history of Crofts, so closely connected with the city of Bradford on the other side of the Pennines from our head-quarters in Manchester, runs in many ways parallel to that of Renold. The original firm was founded in 1887 and over the years its successors developed a wide range of power trans-mission products. It was the object of our offer to the Crofts shareholders to add to the Renold and Holroyd products Crofts' complementary range so that Renold with its highly developed sales network could then distribute throughout the world a comprehensive range of transmission products. Rapid progress has been made towards this end in the short time since Crofts joined our Group."

Not only had *The Hepworth Iron Company Limited* acquired in October, 1967, the issued share capital of the Ulster Fireclay group (which comprised seven companies operating successfully in Northern Ireland and manufacturing clayware, sewer pipe, conduit and bricks), but also since the end of the year it had effected a merger with Ellistown Pipes Limited by acquiring over 92 per cent of their issued share capital. In placing these facts on record in his statement (*The Times*, August 15), MR. J. F. BOOTH was confident that the rationalization and integration which it was now possible to achieve would be of the utmost benefit to the group.

The most important event in the year for *Amalgamated Roadstone Corporation Limited* (March 29), stated the late MR. JOHN S. ROBERTS, was the merger with Roads Reconstruction Limited. However, later the *Consolidated Gold Fields Limited* (November 19) in turn made a successful offer to acquire all the issued Ordinary capital of Amalgamated Roadstone. With this major addition to its interests, companies engaged in this industry belonging to the Gold Fields group, SIR GEORGE HARVIE-WATT said, were now supplying about 15m. tons of products a year; this represented some 10 per cent of total demand in the United Kingdom for these construction materials.

The following paragraph from the speech (*The Times*, May 17) of SIR VAL DUNCAN for *The Rio Tinto-Zinc Corporation Limited* refers to two new acquisitions by the group:

L 153

"During 1967 Capper Pass joined the RTZ Group, and early this year the Borax Group also became part of RTZ. These companies are very welcome additions to RTZ, constituting—as far as Capper Pass is concerned—one of the most expert organizations in the world dealing with complex tin ores, and as regards Borax a stronger base for your company's operations in the United States, and a lively marketing and manufacturing organization in Europe for a wide range of products."

MR. KENNETH HARGREAVES of *Hargreaves Group Limited* (July 9) mentioned that on April 1, 1968, The Skipton Rock Company Limited was purchased, and "its merger with our quarry interests will make a much stronger business, which is now one of the largest of its kind in the North."

During the year *The Dunning Group* (December 12) acquired Greyhound Concrete Limited, whose business is the supply of ready mixed concrete, and subsequently it acquired the entire share capital of Road Surfacing Company Limited, whose business is the supplying and laying of coated roadstone. MR. W. J. S. DUNNING expected real benefits from these mergers in due course.

Although he had to record an unsuccessful bid for Hall & Ham River Limited in October, 1967, MR. A. F. F. YOUNG pointed to the considerable success which *Redland Limited* (September 17) had achieved in growth by acquisition and merger: 23 successful bids against three failures or withdrawals over the last 13 years he considered "not a bad record."

For *Associated Newspapers Limited* (July 24) LORD ROTHERMERE referred in these terms to the inhibiting effect of the monopolies regulations on acquisitions of newspapers by the company in this country:

"Our expansion to date has been mainly in the acquisition of newspapers in this country. Owing to the new Board of Trade and Monopolies Commission regulations we may be inhibited from proceeding much further in this field. We shall continue to re-invest extensively in our present operations, but are also examining opportunities to acquire businesses which can themselves benefit from our participation, and bring a corresponding benefit to the group. We believe that your company will maintain steady progress throughout the present financial year despite the kind of difficulties that are likely to be met in these times."

Among the highlights of MR. ALEXANDER CRAWFORD'S statement (*The Times*, July 15) for *Ault and Wiborg Limited* was the acquisition of Shuck Maclean & Co. Limited, "a first class printing ink company with an excellent and increasing profit record."

The integration of Clutsom & Kemp Limited and Penn Elastic Holdings Limited under the name *Clutsom-Penn International Limited* had proceeded smoothly and was now complete, it was

stated in SIR DONALD PERROTT's survey (*The Times*, January 24). But subsequently the merger company itself was acquired by *Courtaulds Limited* (July 10), it will be seen from the following paragraph extracted from SIR FRANK KEARTON's speech:

"Our acquisition during the year of Clutsom-Penn International Limited has given us a strong position in the specialized power-net business, both at home and overseas. Our acquisition of Wolsey Limited added considerably to our position in the men's wear field. We are now putting in hand quite substantial expansion plans for Wolsey. Acquisition of Prew-Smith Knitwear, not a large company, brought with it management with an exceptional performance record in a specialized field."

After reporting the successful acquisition of three other businesses by *Macanie (London) Limited* (May 2), MR. MAX MAIMANN reminded shareholders that in August, 1967, Courtaulds Limited obtained a controlling interest in the company. He continued:

"It was anticipated that this agreement would not only provide Macanie with the necessary help in its expansion by acquisition and shareholders with a continuing increase in income, but also open the doors to a considerably wider market for your company's merchandise and give access to the many facilities which a go-ahead organization like Courtaulds can provide.
"I am now happy to state that a pleasant relationship has indeed developed through this association. Whilst this did not have any marked effect on the results for the period under review, I am convinced the beneficial influence on our future profits will already be reflected in the 1968 results."

In July, 1967, *William Pickles & Co. Limited* (July 25) acquired Douglas Warne & Co., who manufactured a wide range of sports and casual wear, and in May, 1968, the company acquired over 99 per cent of the share capital of Richard Davies & Co., an old established family business of high class shirt manufacturers. This was among the information given to shareholders by MR. WILLIAM PICKLES.

The next quotation comes from MR. THOMAS HINDLE's statement (*The Times*, July 16) for *Scapa Group Limited*:

"Mutually satisfactory terms were recently agreed for the merger of Porritts & Spencer, Ltd., with your company, and the necessary formalities have now virtually been completed. The Boards of the two companies believe that their combination will enable the business to be strengthened and its expansion to gain a new impetus."

155

A statement by the board of *Universal Grinding Wheel Group Holdings Limited* which was published in *The Times* of December 18 revealed that the offers for the Preference and Ordinary shares of English Abrasives Corporation Limited had been accepted by holders of more than 95 per cent of the shares. Accordingly, the offer had been declared unconditional.

Adjusted to an annual basis the group profits of *British Industrial Holdings Limited* (December 19) at £1,027,965, stated MR. JOSEPH GREEN, exceeded by £177,965 the forecast of £850,000 made at the time of the merger between Gas Purification and Chemical Company Limited and Bunting Estates Limited. It was, he added, the board's intention to expand the group "both by strengthening its existing resources and by further acquisitions."

Among a number of acquisitions recorded in the chairman's statement (*The Times*, December 18) for *Mitchell Cotts Group Limited* was that of the minority shares in the Uganda Company. He also stated:

"In the course of the current year we are intending to reorganize the capital of the Uganda Company and also its management structure. Both owe their origins to other conditions and to other circumstances which are no longer operative today. There is considerable scope for streamlining and getting nearer the day when we can carry out our intention of inviting Ugandan participation in local enterprises."

DR. WILLY OCHEL gave some details of the savings in labour which had been made by *Hoesch AG.* (Dortmund, May 15) through rationalization following the merger with DHHU; the relevant passage from his address was as follows:

"As a result of the merger with DHHU the Group's labour force stood on October 1, 1966, at 71,629. Concentration and rationalization reduced it by the end of the year under review to 63,795, or by 10·9 per cent. This comprised 50,077 manual workers and 13,718 salaried employees. By the end of February, 1968, the payroll had declined by a further 1,367. The number of foreign workers employed went down by 39·8 per cent to 1,634. The wage and salary bill fell by 9 per cent to DM 792·3m."

At the annual meeting of *Compagnie Générale d'Electricité* in Paris the chairman announced (*The Times*, August 26) the acquisition of "Cableries de Clichy" and "Alcatel," two important French firms in the fields of cables and telecommunications.

Both MR. G. N. GABELL, President of the *Chartered Institute of Secretaries* (December 10), and MR. E. W. RENWICK, President of *The Corporation of Secretaries* (June 8), reported firm progress in the discussions for a merger of the two organizations.

The annual conference of the *Institute of Purchasing and Supply* was held on October 3, The Institute was formed by the merger

of the Purchasing Officers Association and the Institute of Public Supplies, and it was reported that there had been considerable progress in the first 15 months of the new body. This, MR. K. W. VINCENT, the new President, believed, was attributable to the sense of professionalism that was growing rapidly in the Institute.

DIVERSIFICATION

IN the past few years many companies have sought to broaden the base of their operations by diversifying their activities into new trades or industries. During 1968 a number of chairmen referred in their annual statements to steps taken by their companies in this direction, either by the acquisition of existing businesses or by the establishment of new productive facilities arising from promising research work. It has to be admitted that not all such diversification has been successful, but in many instances the result has been a considerable increase in the companies' turnover and earnings that could not have been made if their endeavours had been restricted to their original objects. Some such examples are given in this chapter, together with intimations by other chairmen of the intention to diversify in the future.

One company that has been diversifying its interests, formerly consisting mainly of holdings in goldmining concerns, into participations in financial, industrial and property firms is *Rand Mines Limited* (May 10), for which MR. P. H. ANDERSON made these comments:

"With the anticipated long term reduction in revenue from our gold mining investments, active steps continue to be taken to increase our interests in other sectors of the economy so that satisfactory returns might be maintained and increased in due course. In looking for growth in the value of investments and for suitable cash flows in the form of dividends, we plan to supplement our needs from time to time by disposing of those assets which can be advantageously sold to provide funds for more lucrative investments. A facet of the company's policy is to acquire substantial interests in industrial, commercial and financial undertakings, ensuring that risk is adequately spread and minimized by planned diversification. New gold mining investment has not, however, been neglected. To this end the company sold quite substantially from its gold holdings mainly in Vaal Reefs and West Driefontein, and acquired further shares in Elsburg, St. Helena and Winkelhaak. The portfolio of industrials included the acquisition of shares in Highveld Steel and Vanadium. In addition, the Astra-Nourse Metals Corporation, which was experiencing growth difficulties, was sold to McKechnie Bros. S.A. (Pty.) Ltd. for a 10 per cent interest in the equity of that company. McKechnie Bros. S.A. is owned by Delta Metals and McKechnie Bros. of Britain, and has a good

profit record in the business of copper refining and fabrication in South Africa. This should turn out to be a satisfactory investment and I hope it will be the beginning of a profitable association. We also acquired the Kendal Colliery Company which has a small portfolio of shares as well as a coal trade allocation from the Transvaal Coal Owners Association. The Kendal Colliery has now been closed down and its T.C.O.A. quota made available on a royalty basis to the other Transvaal collieries of the Group. Apart from providing a satisfactory level of income for Rand Mines, this investment is proving advantageous to the Group collieries.

"The extent of the diversification policy in regard to the company's investments can be gauged from the fact that direct mining investments now account for a little over a third of the portfolio as against two-thirds at the end of 1963."

Mr. Anderson, however, said that it would be quite wrong to jump to the conclusion that the company was gradually abandoning its interests in mining; far from it!

De Beers Consolidated Mines Limited (Kimberley, June 4), too, had continued with its policy of diversification, declared MR. H. F. OPPENHEIMER; one example, he remarked, was a new item in the balance-sheet, "Property and development, South West Africa," amounting to R275,000.

"We have felt for some time," he stated, "that it would be right to extend our investments outside the diamond industry to South West Africa, where our diamond activities through Consolidated Diamond Mines are on a very large scale. This invest ment in property development in Windhoek marks, we hope, the beginning of diversified investment in this territory."

For *The Imperial Tobacco Company (of Great Britain and Ireland) Limited* (March 18) MR. JOHN PARTRIDGE mentioned that if account were taken not only of the activities of the paper and board, distributive trade and general trade divisions, but also of the interest in Mardon Packaging International Ltd. (which the board regarded very much as a trading investment), the proportion of the group's trading capital employed in businesses other than tobacco had now risen to some 20 per cent. These businesses, he added, contributed about 10 per cent of total group profits in 1967, but there was good reason to expect that in 1968 the proportion would be significantly higher. He also made this comment:

"It remains our policy actively to expand these other fields of endeavour. This is not because we take a gloomy view of the future potential of our tobacco businesses: if we did we should not be investing so heavily in them, both in terms of equipment and of first-class management. It is because we think it right to spread our interests more widely and because we judge that we

have the resources, both in management and in other ways, to do so."

In his review for *The British Electric Traction Company Limited* (October 17) MR. JOHN SPENCER WILLS dealt with the affairs of the subsidiary Advance Laundries, which he stated had made a recovery of approximately 22 per cent in profit before tax. The loss incurred by the domestic laundry and dry cleaning services in London in 1966 had been largely eliminated in 1967, and since the end of that year had been completely wiped out. He also made this statement:

"In little more than ten years, the business of the Advance group has changed from predominantly domestic trade to commercial services, viz., towel-cabinet, linen and garment hire, office cleaning and allied activities. These now account for some 70 per cent of total turnover and as much as 80 per cent of group profit."

Describing diversification as a word even more enticing than usual in the prevailing conditions for *Davy-Ashmore Limited* (September 24), though the path thereto was hard and stony, SIR MAURICE FIENNES announced:

"In our search for new products, we have decided to enter the field of plastics machinery. It is a field adjacent to our own and one that we believe offers good growth prospects. Davy-United have negotiated some useful licences and we were fortunate in that Loewy Robertson had experience in complementary plant. We have put these developments together in a new company named Davy Plastics Machinery Limited. It is now based on the works at Bournemouth which were included in the Loewy Robertson acquisition and which are very suitable for the purpose. I must warn members, however, that there is no early bonanza around the corner arising from this. On the contrary, a good deal of development expenditure will be necessary in the early years."

During the year under review, *Hoover Limited* (April 2) introduced 10 new products to the market, according to MR. F. N. MANSAGER, who explained:

"For the first time we entered the gas market with a new Hoover developed gas fire. This marks a new and important objective in our policy of product diversification and heralds our increasing interest in the market for gas appliances which is obviously going to benefit, long-term, from the newly-found natural gas deposits. We intend to explore the range of gas appliances which could yield a high future potential."

On the subject of diversification the following quotation comes

from the annual survey (*The Times*, June 17) by MR. L. W. ORCHARD for *The Ever Ready Company (Great Britain) Limited*:

"The company has reached its present position by exploitation of its highly developed skills—technical, production and marketing—in the field of dry batteries and battery using products. While this will continue to be the main activity of the company, an Industrial Division has been formed to use these skills in other directions, either by building up new businesses based on our own research and development, or by the acquisition in whole or in part of companies which can be integrated profitably with our existing operations.

"It is not our intention to diversify for the sake of diversification or buy profits, at a high price, for the sake of growth. The main objective of the Industrial Division will be to make wider use of our existing know-how and achieve a satisfactory return on any capital invested in it.

"A new factory for the manufacture of Sealed Nickel Cadmium batteries is now being built, and during the year we made a small investment in a company engaged in the production of industrial control equipment. After the end of the year we acquired the factory and some assets of Burndept Electronics Limited, best known for their Sarbe beaconry equipment. This business will continue and the facilities available used to expand our activities in the Electronics and Industrial Lighting fields."

SIR ALFRED NICHOLAS considered that difficulties lay ahead for *Aberdare Holdings Limited* (May 15) in the short term, but he was confident that in the long term the growth which the company had achieved in the past would continue. He had felt for some time that the group had been too dependent on the nationalized industries and that in the future it should diversify and establish a stronger industrial base to its business.

"I am," he continued, "pleased to report that one of the growth industries within our organization during 1967 has been in the industrial field and this growth will be very much intensified by the much larger step now taken into this field by the acquisition of The Electric Construction Company Limited and Erskine Heap and Company Limited, both companies having a large industrial manufacturing potential. Furthermore, the acquisition of Yorkshire Electric Transformer Company Limited, makers of large power transformers, which with our own transformer division completes the range of transformers from small to large equipment, means that we can now cater for the full range of business both at home and overseas."

Once again, MR. J. BOWTHORPE declared in his statement (*The Times*, June 19) for *Bowthorpe Holdings Limited*, the company's policy of diversification within the aerospace, telecommunications,

electronics and electrical industries had paid dividends; the group profits, both before and after taxation, had risen substantially. As to 1968 and subsequent years, he made this forecast:

"In general, we have started this year well up to last year's average and, assisted by devaluation, we are continuing to find new overseas markets for our products. Given reasonable circumstances, the Group should be able, this year, to maintain the profit of 1967. On a longer term basis, I am confident that the enthusiasm and energy of the younger members of our management team, plus the experience of those who have grown up with our various subsidiaries, will ensure a continuing expansion in our activities and profits."

The Govan Works of *Wheway Watson Limited* (September 5) was closed during the year, MR. W. GIBSON BIGGART stated, and the heavy chainmaking plant was moved to Bellshill. This was completed by October, 1967, but the new works at Bellshill, which combined the activities of the former Coatbridge Works with those of the Govan Works, was not fully integrated until the closing months of the financial year, resulting in an unsatisfactory year for Bellshill. Efforts were being made, he added, to diversify and introduce new product lines there, associated with lifting tackle markets; and he was able to report that the prospects for the Bellshill Works had improved.

For *Wm. Dolan (Boxes & Cartons) Limited* (November 15) MR. G. DOLAN looked back on a year of considerable achievement during which the company had successfully carried out a form of diversification by channelling its new production capacity into many different industries not previously served. This policy, he claimed, had also had the effect of reducing Wm. Dolan's vulnerability to seasonal factors, helping to spread the burden of rising costs more evenly.

Commenting on the proposal that the name of the *Rubber Plantations Investment Trust Limited* (June 26) should be changed to Harcros Investment Trust Limited, MR. J. F. E. GILCHRIST showed how the company's holdings had been diversified over recent years; the relevant passage from his statement follows:

"Since 1954, the Board's policy has been to reduce dependence on the plantation industry by gradually diversifying, without depleting income too seriously. The significant change that has taken place in the investment classification has been followed by a more gradual redistribution of income. By March 31, 1968, plantation holdings represented 25 per cent of investment valuation and 46 per cent of gross revenue, and the Board feel that the point has been reached when the name should be altered to recognize the company's changed character."

SIR PHILIP WARTER referred to a proposed increase in the capital

of *Associated British Picture Corporation Limited* (September 6). It was considered prudent, he declared, to have available sufficient authorized capital to cover possible issues to be made in connection with the acquisition of other companies or their assets in the future. "We are alert," he stated, "to the possibilities of diversification, and there are still opportunities for growth within our own organization and our own industry."

It was the intention of *British Sidac Limited* (August 2) to broaden its trading base and reduce its dependence on packaging films, MR. S. H. MARECHAL asserted. However, the moves would be in areas where the company's existing managerial, marketing or technical resources could be effectively utilized. He added that new projects had been studied, and one or two of them were likely to lead to an investment by the company during the current financial year. Meanwhile, following its substantial growth in the year under review, the board had budgeted for an increase in sales and pre-tax profits this year.

Although turnover of *Meade-Lonsdale Group Limited* had been affected in some degree by foot and mouth disease restrictions and by the import ban, MR. G. R. LONSDALE in his review (*The Times*, July 29) was able to refer to the eleventh successive increase in group profits in the company's first year as a public company. As for the future, he remarked, "we are determined to expand and, where appropriate, diversify," and as a first step in this direction a firm of bacon specialists had recently been acquired—the company's first venture in fields other than meat. Negotiations were going on for further acquisitions within the general field of meat.

Much of the company's work, MR. O. M. JEAVONS informed members of *O. C. Summers Limited* (June 11), was on period contracts for public authorities such as regional Gas Boards and the General Post Office.

"One of our gas period contracts," he went on, "expired on March 31, 1968, and has been successfully retained for a further three years. In addition, we secured two more contracts from the G.P.O. bringing our total of these contracts to twenty-one. On the trend to date I am confident that 1968 will be another year of progress and expansion. Looking further into the future your directors are always examining ways of expanding this business. We are particularly interested in diversification within the gas industry and are currently paying special attention to the pipe-lining and gas conversion sectors. We are also studying possibilities of expanding overseas."

Not only had group turnover of *Robert M. Douglas* (*Contractors*) *Limited* increased over the previous year's, but the volume of work in hand was also in excess of that at the same time in 1967. After placing these facts on record in his annual statement (*The Times*, September 4), MR. ROBERT M. DOUGLAS stated that the board

were maintaining their policy of steady expansion and diversification whenever favourable opportunities presented themselves.

In order to cushion the effects on the construction industry caused by its use as a regulator during credit squeezes, *W. & C. French Limited* (May 31), stated COLONEL A. C. NEWMAN, V.C., had decided that positive action must be taken to broaden the company's base in the interests of greater stability. Accordingly, the board had decided to build up steadily its present modest overseas interests, and the proposal to acquire Homes Group Ltd. was an indication of the directors' intention to widen the company's scope in the home market by extending into the private development of the industry.

Somewhat similar decisions were announced by MR. RONALD LEINSTER in his review (*The Times*, September 27) for *Thomas Vale and Sons Limited*; the relevant passage follows:

"The company has been principally engaged hitherto in the field of large civil engineering contracts. House construction and industrial work though significant have played a smaller part. Civil engineering is most vulnerable both to the vagaries of the weather and to the unpredictable actions of Government (who this year have increased S.E.T. by 50 per cent with no provision so far for recovery of this impost on fixed price contracts with Government and Municipal bodies). We are now directing our efforts more towards housing and industrial work, which are less vulnerable to these two hazards and can be kept more effectively under our control.

"In view of the long-term nature of the larger civil engineering contracts, which frequently run for two years or more, this change in emphasis can be achieved only over a period. We look forward, however, to a progressive development on these lines, and the cash resources available to the Group are ample for the financing of the increased turnover which will be involved."

That the growth and diversification of *Lonrho Limited* (June 20) had continued both during the financial year under review and in the current year was stated in the directors' annual report. By then the group was active in Europe, Mauritius and Ceylon as well as in east, central and southern Africa. The report gave some details of various recent acquisitions which extended the group's interests to Kenya, Uganda and Tanzania, to Ceylon and Mauritius, to Europe and the Congo.

The next quotation is taken from MR. S. W. LIVESEY's annual review for *Fothergill and Harvey Limited* (May 31):

"Trading conditions have continued uncertain and difficult throughout the year with varying effects on our operating divisions. However, the steady increase in profits fully justifies the persistent efforts that continue to be made to redeploy our

resources and so earn a higher return. Some 70 per cent of the capital employed still relates to our textile interests. With the growth already planned and contemplated by our other divisions and subsidiaries, we would expect this proportion to reduce. This does not necessarily imply a reduction in the textile programme but, basically, an expansion of our other activities. . . .

"We have already taken initial steps to put the Group on a broader basis. Our immediate task is to integrate our recent acquisitions and make sure that our new developments are successful. Notwithstanding the many difficulties and uncertainties which inevitably lie ahead, I can say that your company sees growth and good prospects in the future."

Apart from retaining leadership in the specialized field of electric wiring accessories, *M.K. Electric Holdings Limited* (July 25) was aware of the advisability of being in a position, at an opportune time, to widen and diversify its range. MR. F. D. O'BRIEN NEWMAN made this statement, and added that an extensive design programme was now being followed with the objective of developing ancillary and complementary new products.

MR. ERIC HURST informed shareholders in the *Brook Street Bureau of Mayfair Limited* (June 5) that he expected that by the end of 1968 the company and its subsidiaries would be operating nearly 100 branches, against 71 at the end of 1967. He continued:

"During the latter months of the year final preparations were being made for the opening of two schools, one in London, the other in Boston, Mass., U.S.A., for the teaching of office and administrative skills. This is a new venture and these Margory Hurst Schools, as they are to be called, are thought to be perhaps the most advanced of their kind both here and in the United States. I have little doubt but that this diversification of your company's activities is likely to prove both successful and of growing importance."

The *Grängesberg Company*, said its President, MR. ERLAND WALDENSTRÖM, in his speech (*The Times*, July 30), continued to reduce its dependence on the general price and marketing situation that affected its main field of activities. This was being done, he went on, through diversification into new fields and also by concentrating on technically advanced and specialized products embodying a high degree of innovation.

The following extract comes from the 1967 report of the directors (*The Times*, May 13) of *The Petrofina Group*:

"During the year our research activities, together with expansion and diversification programmes throughout the group, resulted in a wide range of product and other development including paint, iron powder and plastics for furniture, as well as water resources and real estate ventures."

165

Many rubber plantation companies over the past few years have diversified their interests by planting oil palms. *Cicely Rubber Estates Company Limited* (October 29) is among them, and MR. R. S. ROWLAND stated that the diversification into palm oil that started in 1966 had continued as planned, with a further 260 acres to be cleared for replanting with the palms during the current year. He also revealed, however, that a further diversification was in hand. An offer had been received for the company's rubber estate in Malaya; it was proposed to redeem the convertible debenture stock in order to release the estate from charge; and "in the event that the estate is sold the directors intend to pursue their policy of diversification by investing the proceeds in companies both in the United Kingdom and overseas."

RESEARCH AND NEW PRODUCTS

THE volume of research work carried on by British industry has been increasing over the years, and many companies have followed up their research with active development of the new products and processes and generally improved technology to which it has led. What emerged from the research divisions of *Vickers Limited* (June 6), declared SIR LESLIE ROWAN, was of great importance to the continuing vitality of the group. In the past, he explained, it had been a weakness that the group depended too much in the commercial field on manufacturing other people's products. He continued:

"In choosing new fields of expansion we had strongly in mind the importance of having our own products and being masters in our own house. So, too, in our research and development policy we seek to evolve products which are under our own control. It is in the nature of this work that some of it must reach negative conclusions or fail to produce a viable development. That is the price that must be paid if there is to be any innovation at all."

Sir Leslie then gave evidence of a number of valuable results that were being achieved within the group and which there is not space enough to detail here. To pick out one study of the many he mentioned, that of tissue storage may be selected: here a recent outcome was a machine for storage of kidneys and other organs much in advance, he claimed, of any other similar machine yet developed; the problems involved in transplant operations, he asserted, would clearly become very much less if such machines could be brought to the point where general use was possible.

In elaborating on the distinction between short-term development and long-range research LORD McFADZEAN gave the following fascinating glimpse into the policy of *British Insulated Callender's Cables Limited* (May 9):

"In the attainment of our technical objectives our future progress depends on our holding the right balance in the Group between well-aimed short-range development, on which depends our business in the immediate future, and the more speculative long-range research, without which we would soon be in danger of running out of ideas. The proportions vary from time to time and the boundary is not absolute but, generally, the two fields of work occupy our resources in the ratio of about ten to one.

"The benefits we derive from our massive development effort are self-evident in the continual improvements in all of our products and manufacturing methods, in which we set a high standard for both ourselves and our industry. The results of research are less obvious because, as they emerge, they are absorbed into and become part of our development programmes. I would, however, refer to the promising progress which we are making in our studies of superconductivity which we commenced in 1961 and which, late in 1967, reached what may in years to come prove to have been a turning point when we successfully achieved in our laboratories the transmission of high alternating currents in the superconducting state. No one yet knows what will eventually come of this but, in view of the publicity which is now being given to very low temperature engineering, our own pioneering efforts well deserve mention.

"We do not consider it our proper function to do true fundamental research: that is primarily for the university laboratories which, in our view, would do better to concentrate on it. We in BICC, and others like us in British industry, are entirely capable of doing our job—provided only that we are left with enough money to pay for it. In industry, one is rarely seeking purely technical solutions. The answer must be right in a broad economic sense, and all of the complex factors involved cannot possibly be appreciated by those not wholly immersed in industry, whether they be university research schools or Government research establishments. There is a tremendous potential for research in Britain but, if we are going to get the best out of it, we must see to it that our resources are better allocated than they are at present."

In order to maintain its leadership in the technology of packaging, *The Metal Box Company Limited* (July 25), MR. DAVID DUCAT revealed, spent annually some £1½m. on its research and development department. Reference had been made in previous reports to the development work arising from the use of tinplate in coil. In the year under review, he now stated, the company had installed the second flying shear of its own design. There had been some delays in its building, but it was now running and, he claimed, represented "the most sophisticated piece of plant of its kind." A third coil cutting line with somewhat simpler features had also been installed, and this would supplement present facilities.

The research organizations of *Portals Holdings Limited* (June 24) had been centralized, stated SIR FRANCIS PORTAL. This section of the business was extremely active, he added, and a number of projects were being explored in co-operation with the Atomic Energy Research Establishment at Harwell. He went on to make this comment:

"Perhaps the most interesting of these is the application of

reverse osmosis, a process by which dissolved materials can be removed from solution. For example, salts may be removed to purify brackish water. Equipment being developed includes paper structures coated with a membrane through which the liquid is forced at very high pressures. Among its commercial applications could be the products of petro-chemical, brewing and many other industries."

LORD ALDINGTON informed members of *The General Electric Company Limited* in the course of his annual review (*The Times*, July 30) that the research programmes of AEI and GEC had been carefully examined and rationalized. The concentration of the two research organizations at the Hirst Research Centre at Wembley, to which a number of AEI scientists were moving, had led to a greater scientific potential in the group.

The research capability of *The English Electric Company Limited* (March 27), LORD NELSON OF STAFFORD remarked, had been further strengthened by the specialized electronic and electro-mechanized laboratories of Elliott-Automation, "whose work is substantially complementary to that of our central laboratories."

The extension of the research activities of *The Ever Ready Company* (*Great Britain*) *Limited* prompted this comment in MR. L. W. ORCHARD's statement (*The Times*, June 17):

"Our Central Research and Development Establishment, originally devoted to product and process improvement in the Zinc Carbon battery field, is now more broadly based.

"Research into other electrochemical systems, and the engineering of them into reliable practical power sources, will enable the company to keep pace with the growing demand for cordless appliances whose power requirements are outside the scope of the Zinc Carbon battery.

"A further extension of Research and Development facilities is in hand to provide for the needs of the Group."

That the Renold Research and Development Centre at Wythenshawe, Manchester, was nearing completion was stated by SIR THOMAS ROBSON of *Renold Limited* (August 1). The group believed that with these facilities it would be far ahead of the rest of the world in research and development in its field of power transmission products and in the manufacturing processes used in this industry. The Centre, he added, would be used for product research, both basic and applied, for all divisions of the group.

BPB Industries Limited (July 31) were spending increasing amounts each year on research and development, stated MR. R. S. JUKES, and a growing number of the company's new products were the outcome of concepts developed by its own team of scientists.

"We have," he went on, "just completed the erection of an acoustics laboratory—thought to be one of the finest in Europe

—in order to improve our existing products and to assist in the development of new ones."

Because the board of *Triplex Holdings Limited* (July 3) was convinced of the need for real endeavour to advance technically with improved and new products, and towards greater efficiency and better means of production, the company was now spending more money on research and development, reported MR. T. E. PEPPERCORN. It had been decided, he added, to close the research laboratory near Kenilworth which had been occupied since 1957, and to concentrate these activities in a new centre at Kings Norton, where extensive laboratories and workshops would house a staff of scientists, engineers and technicians in immediate proximity to the factory and the centralized management functions of the safety glass company. Costing some £400,000, the centre was expected to open in November, 1968. He gave some idea of the directions in which research could be moving in the following paragraph:

"Tied as the Safety Glass Company is so largely to the motor and aircraft industries, opportunities for increasing the markets for its basic products are limited, and other types of safety glass do not offer spectacular growth. We can however try to influence the amount of glass used in motor vehicles and the trend here is in our favour. One cannot fail to notice how much more glass is used in cars, coaches and even lorries today compared with a few years ago. During the past year, the idea of toughened glass roofs for cars using Spectrafloat, Pilkington's important development of its Float Process, was explored with some of the major motor manufacturers. These roofs afford a sense of motoring in an open car without what most people regard as the disagreeable inconvenience of exposure to wind, rain and draughts. We are working on the inevitable problems such as excessive heat transmission and once these are solved believe that these transparent roofs should have wide appeal. Another interesting development, which offers real advantages at moderate extra cost, is the Hotline electrically heated rear window. This type of window, with visible heating elements, is cheaper than the well established Triplex laminated electrically-heated glass, and is attracting increasing interest for cars in the medium and lower price brackets."

A major contribution by the research and development division of *Whessoe Limited* (July 30), MR. JOHN H. LORD declared, was in development work for the company's nuclear power station activities, including the A.G.R. Reactor Liners and Insulation Systems for H.T.R. Reactors. He added that the ever-increasing size of storage tanks also necessitated considerable and successful programmes of analysis and measurement of stresses and strains in the more critical parts of these very large structures.

170

COMMANDER COLIN BUIST asserted that many of the achievements of *Coalite and Chemical Products Limited* (July 24) had resulted in large measure from intensive efforts in the field of research. The overall cost, always difficult to define, continued to increase, he stated, but "this expenditure is an investment in your future."

Members of *Super Oil Seals & Gaskets Limited* (May 23) were informed by MR. R. W. ROBERTS that, in order to concentrate more on all aspects of product and process development, a specially designed and equipped research centre was to be built at Cardiff.

As regards new products, the following quotation is taken from MR. JOHN RAYMOND'S statement for *Fluidrive Engineering Company Limited* (March 28):

"Three new product ranges now available include fluid couplings in production for the advanced gas cooled reactor power station at Dungeness, the prototype fast reactor at Dounreay, the Oskarshamns nuclear power station in Sweden. These new ranges will assist us in meeting the increased engineering demands encountered in many of our fields of application."

For *Bovril Limited* LORD LUKE stated in his annual review (*The Times*, July 15) that rationalization of the laboratory structure had proceeded, and the new group central laboratories were established in London at Alperton in 1968. He continued:

"In these laboratories we have provided the facilities needed to cover all phases of our work from objective basic and applied research through technological testing to initial new product development. They will also serve as a technical information and advisory centre for the Group."

The many activities of the central laboratory of *George Wimpey & Co. Limited* (May 3) again expanded considerably, SIR GODFREY MITCHELL reported, and the company made an important contribution of data fundamental to the design of many major construction projects throughout the world. Notable success, he claimed, was also achieved in the introduction of new techniques, "especially in marine construction using our seabed anchorage developments."

In his statement (*The Times*, February 13) for *McCorquodale & Co. Limited* MR. ALASTAIR MCCORQUODALE gave this explanation of the company's research policy.

"The relatively small investment that we have made in the past in research and development has yielded an encouraging return and will, I am confident, make a more significant contribution in the next few years. We are expanding these activities and have budgeted for additional expenditure. We do not engage in fundamental research, but look for improvements to our existing

171

processes and attempt to find better methods for supplying the identified requirements of our customers."

Stating that a number of new lines was introduced and met with a good reception, all selling well, MR. F. D. O'BRIEN NEWMAN went on to make the following comments on the research interests of *M.K. Electric Holdings Limited* (July 25):

"The company has always regarded research and the design of its products as of paramount importance. Much of its success is attributable to the many revolutionary changes in design which it has pioneered and also the adoption of the most advanced techniques of production. Some years ago a new Research Laboratory and Design Development Centre was established at Fore Street, Edmonton. This was sited apart from all production and administrative establishments. The Laboratory is equipped with scientific facilities far beyond what is normally required by a manufacturer of electric wiring accessories, and includes a Low Voltage Short Circuit Testing Station. Because of these comprehensive facilities the company has been accepted as an Associate of the Short Circuit Testing Authorities (Inc.)."

The *Sterling Cable Company Limited* (July 11), according to MR. J. D. CLARKE, was constantly developing the use of new materials and techniques. Thus during the latter part of the year an order was placed for plant to manufacture very specialized instrumentation wires for high and low temperature use; at the time of writing his report, this machine was in production and was "working very satisfactorily."

The following paragraph on new machine developments is extracted from MR. C. A. G. HEWSON'S address for the *Ozalid Company Limited* (August 22):

"I mentioned last year the 3020 Electrophotographic Microfilm Enlarger Printer. Orders are being received from overseas for this machine, as well as from the United Kingdom, and when the machine was recently exhibited at the Leipzig Fair a Gold Medal was awarded by reason of the high scientific and technical level achieved, being one of five granted to British Exhibitors generally. Two new machines were introduced in 1967; firstly, the Banda 100 Series Duplicator, and secondly, the SCM/Banda Model 55 Electrostatic Copier. Both these machines should assist to expand the activities of the Group."

For *James Howden & Godfrey Limited* (October 31) MR. J. HOWDEN HUME reported the formation of a new division—Howden Space Heating. Its first product, he stated, was the Howden Dynaflame oil burner for the domestic heating market. This burner had been developed over the last five years and after stringent tests, carried out in conjunction with the boilermakers

and the oil companies, there were now on hand orders for over £900,000, requiring the setting up of an independent factory which would come into production before the end of the year.

New toys, games and nursery products from *Lines Bros. Limited's* (July 12) own design departments were steadily coming on to the market, reported MR. W. M. LINES, who proceeded to pick out one development in particular, in the following words:

> "We would especially note the successful launch of our Mini-Dinky range of small-scale diecast toys, reserved only for North America, so far, where demand is in danger of outstripping capacity to supply."

New equipment in the transport field launched by the Dobson Division of *Dobson Hardwick Limited*, it appeared from SIR GEOFFREY BARNETT'S statement (*The Times*, September 12), included "swop-body" systems, container handling devices and parking legs for trailers; new developments and further adaptations of existing equipment were expected to do well.

For *G. Brady & Co. Limited* (November 12) MR. R. ROSS SEYMOUR announced a new development in the manufacture of roller shutters in that a self-coloured p.v.c. lath had been perfected. Application had been made to register the new lath under the name "Colorastic." Already, he asserted, the demand had proved encouraging.

Besides the purchase of the share capital of the Alton group of companies (which he claimed was the largest manufacturer of glasshouses in the country), MR. DERRICK H. ROBINS mentioned another significant development for *Banbury Buildings Holdings Limited* (September 20) in the following terms:

> "During the past year not only have new ranges of pre-cast buildings been put on the market but a revolutionary design of Sun Room or Home Extension has been created. This product has received the most encouraging response and we can see that it will clearly play a considerable part in the company's future."

The range of writing instruments produced by *Mentmore Manufacturing Company Limited* was expanding considerably, it was evident from MR. A. E. ANDREWS'S report. In particular, he mentioned the introduction of a fibre-tipped pen retailing at 1s. which "will bring very rapid expansion in sales."

The Bentima Company Limited showed in its annual report (*The Times*, May 16) that it had continued its policy of introducing new models into its ranges of watches and clocks, and the first few months of 1968 recorded an increase in sales.

The annual report of *Ing. C. Olivetti & C., S.p.A.* (Ivrea, April 10) for 1967 included this reference to new products:

> "During 1967 Olivetti further extended its production line to

include a number of highly advanced and increasingly complex new products. In the micro-computer field the P 203 electronic office computer took its place alongside the Programma 101 electronic desk-top computer, and in the telecommunications sector the launch of the new '300 Class' teleprinters was accompanied by a powerful campaign promoting the different types of terminals produced by the company. New optical and magnetic character encoders, accounting and billing machines, numerically controlled machine tools and equipment, electrostatic copiers, typewriters and add-listing machines were also introduced."

FUNCTION OF ADVERTISING

THE number of chairmen who dealt in any way adequately with the function of advertising, or indeed of marketing systems in general, remained disappointingly small. In fact, references to advertising were confined for the most part to annual statements of chairmen of newspaper and independent television companies, of those advertising agents that were public companies, and of purveyors of other forms of publicity, such as billposters. Some industrial and commercial company chiefs mentioned successful campaigns that had been carried through, but even these were few in relation to the number that could have done.

Striking evidence of the rapid progress made by *The Times* since the formation of the merger company Times Newspapers Limited was provided by LORD THOMSON OF FLEET in his statement (*The Times*, May 1) for *The Thomson Organisation Limited*. During 1967, he remarked, development investment had been injected into *The Times* to a total of over £1¾m., and 1968 would call for further investment not far short of the same amount; thereafter the position should change fairly dramatically. Already, he was gratified to report, a number of improvements in performance were becoming manifest.

"The most immediate and obvious of these," he went on to point out, "is in the circulation of the paper: whereas at the beginning of 1967 this was rather under 300,000, by the end of the year it was running at the rate of nearly 400,000 copies a day, and is now comfortably above that figure and still rising. An increase of these proportions over so short a time is quite unprecedented, and provides incontestable evidence both of the improvements which it has been possible to introduce and of the size of the audience which *The Times* will progressively be reaching."

LORD THOMSON also gave some figures to illustrate the growth of advertising carried by *The Times*, as in the following excerpt from his survey:

"On the advertising side, administrative reorganization coupled with an intensive recruitment and training effort started to yield extremely encouraging results by the second half of the year, and *The Times* share of the total number of columns of advertising appearing in the quality press rose between 1966 and 1967 from 13% to 15% for display advertising, from 18½% to 20½% for financial advertising, and from 14½% to 16% for

classified advertising. Between 10th April 1967, when the Business News section was started, and the end of the year, *The Times* carried 17% more financial advertising than in the same period of 1966. Our forecasts for an accelerating rate of increase are currently being more than met."

A considerable increase in the trading results of *Manchester Guardian and Evening News Limited* was attributed by MR. LAURENCE P. SCOTT in his annual statement (*The Times*, October 9) partly to an improvement in local advertising in the *Manchester Evening News* from the low level of the winter of 1966–67 and a rise in selling price from 4d. to 5d., and partly to the pruning operation that was undertaken on *Guardian* costs early in 1967. As regards the state of the national newspaper industry he made these comments:

"We are going through a period when trading conditions are difficult and many newspapers are losing money, a period when the Government is straining every nerve to contain inflation, and yet our costs have risen steadily in the past 12 months at much the same average rate as in the preceding two years, including a sharp increase in the price of newsprint as a result of devaluation. We have been told that our industry has room for great increases in efficiency and in productivity, and yet changes in our customary habits proceed at a disappointingly slow pace. Perhaps the best hope for the future lies in the technical advances now being made in printing. These provide, and will continue to provide, considerable opportunity for more efficient production. They will also pose considerable problems for managements and unions. These problems must be faced and overcome, by both sides working together at national and local levels."

Devaluation, asserted LORD ROTHERMERE of *Associated Newspapers Limited* (July 24), had caused a substantial rise in the cost of producing both national and provincial journals; for example, the 12 per cent increase in the price of newsprint as from March 19 would cost the whole group in a full year more than £1m. Incidentally, he gave an apt description of devaluation—"a punishment inflicted upon it [the country] as a result of economic folly." He reported that the provincial newspapers in the group started their year with lower advertising revenue, but they more than recovered the lost ground, and results for the whole year were slightly better than for the previous year. On the condition of the newspaper industry in general he included these remarks in his survey:

"I referred last year to negotiations then taking place with the unions with a view to implementing the findings of the Economist Intelligence Unit's report, in so far as it dealt with productive efficiency. Positive proposals were put forward by the News-

paper Publishers Association and it is regrettable that no progress resulted. I think there is general recognition by all parties concerned that greater productive efficiency is essential not only for the sake of the Industry but of the whole country as well and it is, therefore, tragic that at the time of writing there cannot be a unified approach to the problem."

Vigorous steps were being taken in *International Publishing Corporation Limited* (July 23), and on an industry basis, to reverse the recent trend towards commercial television and to increase press advertising revenue, it was stated in the annual report of the directors.

"IPC newspapers," the report continued, "already provide area test marketing facilities to advertisers, and the *Daily Mirror* and *Sunday Mirror* are printed in full colour for the Irish market. Full colour is being planned for IPC newspapers, and will greatly enhance their appeal to advertisers and readers.

"IPC's leading magazines have introduced a new market-oriented advertisement rate structure, split-run and regional inset facilities are available and increased colour advertising facilities arc being provided.

"Recent cover price increases have gone some way towards the Board's aim of reducing the dependence of IPC's newspapers and periodicals on advertisement revenue for their profitability."

Overall advertisement revenue of *United Newspapers Limited*, MR. W. D. BARNETSON revealed in his annual statement (*The Times*, May 6), declined by less than 1 per cent, which in view of the economic climate at the time he regarded as satisfactory. This downturn, moreover, was more than offset by other factors, and group profit before taxation reached a new record. He mentioned that new procedures for the development of classified advertising had now been established at Blackpool and Northampton and also in the South London series of suburban weeklies. Thus all group centres were now employing these techniques, with, he declared, "most rewarding results."

With the end of the standstill, *Portsmouth and Sunderland Newspapers Limited* (July 26), said LORD BUCKTON, found it necessary not only to increase their advertising charges but also to raise the prices of its evening newspapers to 5d. Thus the group's surplus on trading had been raised slightly above the peak level of 1965–66, and in spite of heavier depreciation and tax charges and reduced investment income the board were able to maintain the dividend.

A moderate reduction in the group profit before tax of *Dorland Advertising Holdings Limited* (May 23) was ascribed by MR. GEORGE FARRAR partly to reductions in some clients' appropriations (a general experience with advertising agencies in 1967) and partly to the impact of the first full year's S.E.T. The group, he

claimed, was now one of the largest organizations in the British advertising agency business, with a billing in 1967 of over £16½m.

The *Benson Advertising Group Limited* (June 7) had a billing for 1967 of £11m., according to MR. J. W. HATCH, and he was able to announce the acquisition of new business in the last few months which in a full year would increase it by over £1m. Mr. Hatch also said that the personnel advertising division, formed in 1967, was attracting new business at an encouraging rate from both existing clients and other sources.

MR. GEORGE A. TODD informed members of *C. J. Lytle (Advertising) Limited* (May 30) that the board was continuing to examine various acquisition possibilities in the light of operational and financial compatibility; it held the view that worthwhile acquisitions could provide a breadth of turnover that could accelerate the overall pace of the company's growth.

The grocery division of *Spillers Limited* (June 7), SIR ARCHIBALD FORBES claimed, had obtained some notable advertising successes, and the characters in some of its campaigns had become household names.

That the increased expenditure on advertising and sales promotion during the year by *George Ward Holdings Limited* (November 7) had been justified, was declared by MR. W. J. JOBSON, and it was proposed to extend this still further during the current year, when new ranges of shoes would be introduced.

The following paragraph is extracted from MR. DOUGLAS NICHOLSON's address at the annual meeting of *Vaux and Associated Breweries Limited* (September 20):

"For many years we have been spending part of our advertising money on the promotion of sport in the North East, and we have awarded Gold Tankards to the big sporting events which came to the North East for the first time as a result of our encouragement. I believe that this has been a valuable form of advertising in two different directions. On the one hand because it has given great benefit to many thousands of people. In the racing world they have seen much better horses come north as a result of the Vaux Gold Tankard race at Redcar. In the pigeon world something like 50,000 people were anxiously awaiting the return of their birds in the Vaux race from France to the North, and in the athletic world there are two probable contenders in the Olympic Games this year who have benefited from the coaching and competitions which we have sponsored. On the other hand the sign of the Gold Tankard has become synonymous with high quality and we are now producing Gold Tankard Beer in kegs as one of our biggest lines of production."

Announcing a sharp setback in earnings for the 12 months to October 31, 1967, the Chairman of *Mills & Allen Limited* in his annual review (*The Times*, February 21) declared that the profits of

the company's main business, the outdoor advertising division, were very sensitive to the climate of the economy of the country as a whole. This division, he pointed out, carried heavy fixed overheads, since advertising sites and structures, whether sold or not, must be fully maintained and rent and rates paid. Moreover, advertising appropriations themselves were among the most sensitive costs of customers' selling organizations. At that time, the full effect of the measures resulting from devaluation was not known, and he was not able to forecast the immediate future. He continued:

"What can be said, however, is that very little has happened which is likely to affect the long term prospects of the business if the economic situation of the nation itself can only be brought into balance. Recovery when it comes could be both substantial and very rapid."

Another company to report a setback in its results was *Frank Mason & Company Limited* (September 30), which, MR. H. J. MASON stated, had received notice to terminate its concession for advertising in telephone call boxes on June 30; the Post Office, it appeared, had decided that the spaces in the boxes were needed for service requirements. He explained that this department had built up a very effective sales force, and that this was immediately deployed to the company's other media, especially such ancillaries as sub post offices, city guides, &c.

"The results," he continued, "have been very gratifying, but the expanding sales have had an adverse effect on immediate profits since most of the costs have to be met at the outset.

"Regarding advertising on buses, our main activity, we have suffered in common with virtually all media controllers as a result of the severe cutting back of spending by the national advertisers, which started with the economic and credit squeeze."

On the subject of Government restrictions upon advertising of cigarettes and on the issue of gift coupons, MR. MARK NORMAN of *Gallaher Limited* (May 22) had this to say:

"We believe that the interests of the smoking public are best served by a competitive and responsible industry subject to the minimum Government interference. However, over the last three years the Minister of Health has deemed it necessary to restrict the promotion of cigarettes by banning television advertising and by announcing his intention to introduce legislation to limit other advertising expenditure and to ban cigarette coupons. We regard legislation to control our industry with dismay and have striven without success to reach voluntary agreements which would satisfy the Minister and be acceptable to the other manufacturers. We greatly regret that we must now

suffer legislation, but if it must be, then the sooner the better. In the meantime the industry is inevitably in a state of suspense, during which forward planning is difficult not only for marketing purposes but also for the future of the many people employed in handling gifts to a value of over £30m. a year."

LABOUR

THIS chapter is divided into the usual five sections, covering in turn labour relations and disputes; shortage and redundancy; training and education; incentives; and changes in management.

RELATIONS AND DISPUTES

SIR WILLIAM MCEWAN YOUNGER made the wry comment that the most strenuous and not wholly unsuccessful efforts of the management of *Scottish & Newcastle Breweries Limited* (September 5) had been able to achieve for the Ordinary stockholder nothing more than the negative advantage of standing still. It was difficult, he added, to see any change from this pattern in the current year: the company had to face increased impositions and charges of many kinds, and it was quite clear that the most strenuous opposition to price increases would continue. He went on to refer to another possible risk in the following terms:

> "And we face a further danger, the risk throughout the country of serious industrial unrest. It may be possible, in an emergency, to impose a rigid system of control of salaries and wages, for a strictly limited period. But it is a crude weapon at the best, introducing many distortions and inequities, and one which an adequate rate of growth would render quite unnecessary. However, when an attempt is made to continue this policy for a much longer, and still in practice undefined, period, and when the Government itself—often in the face of strike action—acts in breach of its own laid-down policy, that policy can no longer be maintained without widespread and damaging industrial unrest."

"Very satisfactory" relations between management and staff at all levels were undoubtedly the greatest single contribution to the success of a business such as that of *Rediffusion Limited* (July 31) which was based largely on personal service, MR. JOHN SPENCER WILLS stated.

> "The prices and incomes freeze in the United Kingdom," he continued, "has been as frustrating to our employees as it has to the company's business which is their livelihood, but it has been faced on all sides with commendable restraint. It has not, however, kept down our labour costs. We have continually to train staff to higher technical standards and we have had to establish,

181

with the approval of the Ministry of Labour, new and more highly-paid technical grades."

For *West Riding Worsted and Woollen Mills Limited* (February 21) MR. M. W. SHELTON declared that labour relations remained good throughout the industry: "we have been fortunate over many years," he asserted, "with the harmonious manner in which the affairs are conducted between the Wool (and Allied) Textile Employers' Council and the Unions."

On behalf of the board of *Spillers Limited* (June 7) SIR ARCHIBALD FORBES warmly acknowledged the "very considerable" contribution made by the management, staff and employees at all levels towards the improved results for the year. He went on to state:

> "The restrictions arising out of the incomes freeze and period of severe restraint have been borne with fortitude and loyalty in the face of increasing competition for staff and workpeople of high calibre."

MR. J. M. CLAY informed members of *Thos. Firth & John Brown Limited* (March 7) that towards the end of the year the Siemens Melting Department of the subsidiary Firth Brown Limited was closed, and this had improved the demand on the Electric Melting Shop. A continuous "21 shift" system was now being worked in this shop, and he remarked on the co-operative attitude of the trades unions affected by the change, which, he asserted, was an important factor in achieving this step towards improved plant utilization and increased productivity.

In his statement dated November 1 for the *R. S. T. Group of Companies* SIR RONALD PRAIN mentioned that there had been no significant labour stoppages since his annual review of the preceding November. Several claims were made by employee organizations and some of these were taken to conciliation, but throughout the year "relations generally with our 22,000 employees on the copperbelt were good." He also made these comments upon the progress of Zambianization of the work force and kindred matters:

> "Zambianization up to the level of shift boss and shift foreman in all production departments continues and much of the semi-skilled engineering work previously done by expatriate artisans is now being performed by local mechanics, nearly 1,000 of whom have been trained by the group. Mine technical training has also been intensified but progress here will depend largely on the number of candidates available with suitable educational qualifications. Under the group's university scheme for Zambians some 40 students are currently studying abroad or at the University of Zambia for degrees and diplomas in all branches of engineering.

"I referred last year to long discussions which had taken place on the principle of a single wage structure for the industry, with special allowances for expatriates. Discussions continued during 1968 and in August an arrangement was made under which the employees remain essentially on their existing conditions, with some improvements in fringe benefits such as education assistance and passage entitlements. Employees recruited in future will be engaged on a new form of contract in which their basic salary scales will be the same as those of Zambian employees, but which will contain expatriate allowances as well as the amended education and travel benefits.

"Turnover of local labour remains low. The expatriate turnover rate averaged about 30 per cent during the financial year and is currently running somewhat higher. Recruiting overseas has been increased to make sure that our needs in certain specialized fields will continue to be met."

Since the construction industry, of which *Roberts Adlard & Company Limited* (August 29) is an integral part, had always suffered fluctuations, many entirely beyond its control, Mr. E. Vivian Dawson considered that the company's results over the years tended to indicate that "we are able to take advantage of good conditions and at the same time hold our own when circumstances are less favourable." And he expressed the opinion that this was the result in no small measure of the close understanding and co-operation which existed at all levels of employment throughout the company.

The efforts of *Joseph Lucas (Industries) Limited* (December 16) to support the prices and incomes policy, Sir Bertram Waring asserted, had involved the company in a share of the 1968 industrial disputes. Over a long period of years relations between management and workpeople had attained a high standard, and it had been a new experience for the management to be confronted, as it had been during recent weeks, with a whole series of unofficial strikes. He also stated (in part):

"Prospects for the current year are overshadowed by the very widespread industrial unrest now prevalent in the country, and particularly in the engineering industry. Following the very damaging experiences of recent months, the threat of further strikes and stoppages is having a most adverse effect on overseas confidence in Britain's ability to maintain delivery promises, and customers who turn away are not easily won back. At the same time any relaxation of a policy of containing prices and incomes, and any general increase in wages and salaries beyond that derived from increased productivity, cannot but add to total costs and reduce competitiveness in overseas markets. These difficulties come at a time when some of the benefits of devaluation are still with us, offering the opportunity of a very

183

substantial increase in export business which alone can restore national prosperity. It would be a national tragedy if this hard-bought opportunity were to be cast away."

The late EARL OF BALFOUR was sad to have to report the first major strike in the history of *Bruntons (Musselburgh) Limited* (May 2), but he hoped the outcome might result in better understanding. He gave this account of the trouble:

"There was a dispute over bonus payments in one of our smaller departments which resulted in a strike lasting four months. Eventually a general strike was called in support of this department, which lasted four weeks. Following a meeting held under the auspices of the Ministry of Labour there was a full return to work by the end of February, 1968—on pre-strike conditions providing that the management and Trade Union representatives would sit down together to examine the possibility of evolving a change in the bonus scheme based on an increase in productivity which would conform with Government policy. I do not wish to make any further comment for fear of prejudicing these negotiations."

A subsidiary of *Wm. Cory & Son Limited* (September 19), the Mercantile Lighterage Company, handling general goods on the Thames, sustained heavy losses from the unofficial and prolonged London dock strike, LORD LEATHERS revealed.

The profit of *British Ropes Limited* (May 30) for the year (before bringing in profits arising from devaluation) exceeded £3m. as forecast, in spite of an unusually difficult last quarter, stated MR. HARRY SMITH. Not only did the Government's economic measures cause the demand for some products to fall during the latter part of the year, he explained, but the company also felt the effect of the dock strike, which led to delays in the shipment of goods overseas and also restricted the imports of sisal. He hazarded the opinion that the longer term effects of the dock strike might, in fact, be more serious, but they were difficult to evaluate.

SHORTAGE AND REDUNDANCY

Both the Economist Intelligence Unit in its report on the press early in 1967 and the Prices and Incomes Board in its more recent report on newspaper costs and revenue rightly said that there was considerable room for improvement in manning standards on all national newspapers, the directors of *International Publishing Corporation Limited* (July 23) stated in their annual report. It went on to give these details of the progress made by IPC in this direction, to which the corporation had given much attention:

"The Corporation is continuously engaged in negotiations with the unions to reduce production manning levels on both

newspapers and in the Printing Division, but reductions are unavoidably slow as they involve the livelihood of loyal employees and can involve substantial changes in the traditional working customs of the industry.

"The problem is accentuated by the rapid advances that IPC is making in its methods of production. Investment in new methods is necessary to increase IPC's publishing leadership and to meet existing and anticipated competition from television, but would be abortive without rational manning standards. To enable reductions in manning levels to be made with the minimum hardship, IPC operates a scheme for redundancy which provides reasonable financial compensation to those who leave. These payments are initially an expensive charge on revenue, but manpower reductions bring long-term savings which justify the initial cost.

"By these means, IPC has had considerable success in achieving more efficient use of manpower. In the past seven years, during which most of the Corporation's newspapers have increased greatly in size and in circulation, the number of staff required each night to produce IPC's daily newspapers in London has been reduced by nearly 800 men. During the four years since its formation, International Printers has reduced its production staff by over 2,000 men."

LORD ROTHERMERE of *Associated Newspapers Limited* (July 24) also referred to the question of productive efficiency, recalling that a year previously negotiations had been taking place with the unions. Positive proposals, he declared, were put forward by the Newspaper Publishers Association, and he thought it regrettable that no progress resulted, going on to make this comment:

"I think there is general recognition by all parties concerned that greater productive efficiency is essential not only for the sake of the Industry but of the whole country as well and it is, therefore, tragic that at the time of writing there cannot be a unified approach to the problem."

After the previous year's recession, stated MR. KENNETH M. HAMILTON for *Blackwood, Morton & Sons Limited* (October 28), the effort to attain the high level of production necessary to keep pace with sales placed a heavy burden on the executives, and it was difficult to recruit and train additional staff as rapidly as they would have wished.

"Every effort," he continued, "is made to provide attractive working conditions and we employ a full-time doctor of medicine and training officers to look after the welfare and training of employees. In addition, all our U.K. carpet factory workers have over 4 weeks holiday per annum, and the normal working week is now reduced to 40 hours."

Another company which wanted to increase its work force was *Barber Textile Corporation Limited* (November 28), for which MR. J. G. BARBER-LOMAX stated that, with order books for cotton and blended yarns longer than ever before, if extra labour could be recruited increased production would stimulate profit recovery.

According to MR. W. J. JOBSON, *George Ward Holdings Limited* (November 7) was also held back by scarcity of skilled labour, as the following quotation implies:

"The Group's factories were fully employed throughout the year, demand for products exceeding supply for some months. Exceptional efforts were made to expand production from existing manufacturing units, the shortage of skilled operatives being the limiting factor in the desired expansion required to give satisfactory service to customers."

Notwithstanding lower demand and also an important merger in which *Renold Limited* (August 1) was involved, no redundancy and no short-time working had occurred, the reasons for which were given by SIR THOMAS ROBSON in the following extract:

"The combination of lower demand and wage restrictions has presented problems for many employees but we have been able to maintain a full and efficient labour force by careful planning and stock utilization and because of the co-operation of all concerned. There has been no redundancy and no short time.

"During the year a large merger has taken place within the Group. Our problem has been simpler than in the case of many mergers because our philosophy is that we merge for expansion and not for contraction; and we rationalize for efficiency and not redundancy. The result is that we have already been able to provide satisfactory service agreements for all senior personnel of the Crofts companies and we believe that everyone in the Group has greater prospects than ever before. . . .

"Great burdens have been placed on many people throughout the whole of the Group and we want them to know that we recognize all the efforts they have made. The enlarged Group provides plenty of material for our training and assessment schemes and we are sure that many new Group employees will be enabled to take advantage of the opportunities the Group offers."

In his annual statements for 1965 and 1966 SIR FRANCIS PORTAL had made it clear that the operation of the new Bank Note paper mill in India would result in a considerable loss of tonnage for the Overton Mill of *Portals Holdings Limited* (June 24). Also in the interim report in November, 1967, it had been stated that the additional loss and postponement of overseas tonnage affecting Portals at that time, resulting almost entirely from economic difficulties in the countries concerned, would continue in 1968.

Accordingly, he now declared, the first three months of 1968 was a difficult period at Overton Mill, and because of the reduced order book 150 employees had to be made redundant in January. However, he was able to report that during the last month there had been a marked improvement in the position.

The results of the Belgian group belonging to *The Fairey Company Limited* (October 4) were disappointing, stated MR. G. C. D'ARCY BISS, the previous year's profit having been transformed into a loss. Delays in the decision taken by the Belgian Government to choose a replacement aircraft for the F-84F Thunderstreak continued throughout the year, he declared, and although negotiations with the French constructors, Dassault, and with the Belgian Government for the eventual production programme on the Mirage 5 and work-sharing agreements in respect of other programmes continued, contracts had not then reached finality. As regards consequent redundancies in Fairey S. A., he made these comments:

> "It was found necessary in January of this year to dispose of the services of some 130 employees, but due to the incidence of the State Social laws in Belgium, the cost of terminating the services of these employees has been serious. The restrictions placed by the Belgian Government on further reductions of this nature, which are inevitable if the work programme is further delayed, are a matter of deepest concern and the strongest representations are being made to redress the situation."

Reporting on the trading of various subsidiaries of *Lake & Elliot Limited* (November 19), MR. C. J. LAKE mentioned that the low level of order intake of Cockburns Limited in the first half of the year resulted in short-time working and a small measure of redundancy; and in John Allen & Sons (Oxford) Limited the Government financial restrictions caused a further reduction in order intake which necessitated short-time working. However, the order intake for both subsidiaries had since improved considerably, and the outlook accordingly was brighter.

TRAINING AND EDUCATION

Training schemes of *The English Electric Company Limited* (March 27), declared LORD NELSON OF STAFFORD, were most important to the long-term welfare of the undertaking, which continued to exploit new techniques and to devise improved methods. "We have," he added, "made encouraging progress in our management development and management succession planning programmes."

In parallel with the high quality of its plant, *H. M. Hobson Limited* (February 23) required a considerable degree of technical and manufacturing skill on the part of its employees, said MR. T. SIMPSON, who continued:

"The company's training schemes have been formulated to provide the steady supply of skilled manpower so necessary to our type of business, and I am pleased to report that the grant received from the Engineering Industry Training Board exceeds the levy which we, in common with other engineering firms, are required to pay. This can be taken as an official acknowledgement of the quality of our training schemes."

MR. S. B. HAINSWORTH informed members of *J. H. Fenner & Co. (Holdings) Limited* in his annual statement (*The Times*, January 4) that progress continued in the training of the staff at all levels.

"For maximum effect in the shortest time," he explained, "the greatest effort is at the level of shop floor supervision. New concepts of skills analysis training are being applied to factory work. Graduate trainees are given projects to complete which present the same mental stimulation and challenge which they experienced at University, whilst giving them an insight into business problems. Our Apprenticeship programme provides a breadth of training which will be difficult to match in the Hull area. This work will ensure that we continue to provide the management skills our company will need."

For *London Brick Company Limited* (May 30) SIR RONALD STEWART recalled the decision he had mentioned a year previously to make a survey of the company's training practices before the Ceramics, Glass and Mineral Products Training Board began its work. The survey, he declared, had proved most useful in assessing London Brick's own training requirements, and had subsequently been made available to other members of the Training Board. He added:

"Following the survey, a full time training officer has been appointed and full advantage will be obtained from our existing schemes and from new methods of improving the technical training of management, staff and employees."

During the year *Reed Paper Group Limited*, MR. S. T. RYDER stated in his annual review (*The Times*, July 5), had continued its programme of education and training of its employees at every level. Where mastery of the technicalities of a craft or trade was important the company had concentrated on improving the quality of its instruction. For managers, he asserted, efforts were being directed towards early identification of talent, and he went on to make these remarks on the subject:

"The task of making the best use of human resources is, by its nature, a long-term one. We think it is best carried out by the direct involvement of top management who must make a point of knowing those who are rated to have potential wherever they may be. Another influence on the development of managers is

the character of the organization in which they work. Here we are constantly striving to improve its structure in order to provide the maximum number of jobs in which individuals can exercise their capabilities to the full."

Another group which had been paying close attention to the improvement of education and training was *McCorquodale & Co. Limited,* for which MR. ALASTAIR MCCORQUODALE in his annual review (*The Times,* February 13) stated that the aim was not only to increase productive efficiency but also to provide the company with the skills and abilities that would enable it to take full advantage of the impressive technological developments which would become increasingly available to the industry. "The advent of the Training Board for the industry," he commented, "is awaited with enthusiasm, and your company is now well placed to avail itself of the benefits that it will bring."

The next quotation comes from MR. JOHN PARTRIDGE'S address for *The Imperial Tobacco Company (of Great Britain and Ireland) Limited* (March 18):

"The Directors' Report briefly notes that we have continued to accord high priority to employee training and development. In these times of rapid technological change—and I see no likelihood of the pace slackening—the task of management education and development is among the first duties of any business group. I obviously cannot and do not claim that we in Imperial perform the task to perfection: what I can claim is that we know we need to perform it as well as we possibly can. But only a minority of employees can be managers; and to my mind an equally important duty of any industrial undertaking lies in helping as many employees as possible to develop their abilities to the full. In this regard I would like both to record and to praise the many training and development schemes that have been devised, especially for young people, in various parts of the Group, and the considerable effort that is being put behind these projects."

According to SIR ARCHIBALD FORBES, *Spillers Limited* (June 7) had always recognized the importance of training and its contribution towards the individual development of employees and to the efficiency and profitability of the company as a whole; and during the year he claimed the management had intensified their efforts in establishing a comprehensive system of manpower development and the training of staff and workpeople. He added:

"Liaison with Schools, Universities and Colleges of Further Education continues to be developed in order to meet the increasing demand for suitable recruits for the staff."

Parallel with training and education runs the dissemination of knowledge, which is one of the functions of *Pergamon Press*

189

Limited (June 7). MR. ROBERT MAXWELL, M.P., declared that the company's traditional business of providing the worldwide scientific, engineering and medical communities with the results of original research in their respective disciplines through the medium of some 150 specialized international research journals and serials was continuing to grow at a rapid pace. He declared that the increase in profitability was therefore the result not only of the recent and earlier acquisitions made by the group (all of which were making good contributions to profits) but also of the expansion of sales of Pergamon's traditional publications.

INCENTIVES

Less was heard in company statements of general incentives, and more of specific wage incentives in return for giving up restrictive practices. However, some companies continued to offer profit-sharing terms to their employees, among them *Portsmouth and Sunderland Newspapers Limited* (July 26), for which LORD BUCKTON said:

> "The Staff's share of profit has risen from £71,934 to £82,647 and they will receive a distribution of 13⅜ per cent of basic salaries. The fact that this increase in the amount distributed is payable in a year when a much larger part of the surplus has been absorbed by the provision for depreciation calls attention to what I think is a mistake in the rules governing the Profit-Sharing Scheme. The staff's share of profit is calculated upon the surplus on trading and no account is taken of the provision needed to maintain or increase the capital employed in earning the surplus. It would, I think, be fairer to the shareholders and not unfair to the staff, if this provision was borne partly by the shareholders and partly by the staff.
> "I think I should add the Board had today decided to have a thorough examination made of the Superannuation Fund and the Profit-Sharing Scheme to ascertain whether they give the company and the staff the most effective reward and benefits from the resources devoted to them."

Bringing pensions schemes up to date was mentioned by a number of chairmen. Thus MR. F. N. HEARNSHAW made this reference to the pensions arrangements of *Henry Wigfall and Son Limited* (October 7):

> "The company's Pension Scheme for employees, which has remained unchanged since its introduction in 1950, has been amended. Employees will now receive a pension based on a final salary basis—a more suitable arrangement than hitherto, particularly with regard to the long-term service employees."

Similarly this comment on the pension scheme of *Peter Brotherhood Limited* (November 12) was made by MR. G. W. WILKS:

"We propose as from 1st November 1968 to improve the benefits under our Works Employees' Pension & Life Assurance Scheme by approximately 25 per cent. Also, arrangements are being made to bring long service female employees into both the Works and Staff Pension Schemes. We attach great importance to offering up-to-date conditions of employment and good training facilities to satisfy your company's present and future needs more especially for highly skilled craftsmen and technicians.

Some companies by their whole paternal (in the best sense of the word) attitude towards their staffs offer an indirect incentive. *Marks and Spencer Limited* is a case in point. In his statement (*The Times*, June 6) MR. J. EDWARD SIEFF thanked the staff and declared that good human relations were the foundation upon which Marks & Spencer was built. M & S had pioneered medical and dental schemes for staff and these were, today, an important part of the company's welfare policy. Interest in staff was maintained after retirement, and pensions were adjusted to relate to the cost of living. A happy spirit animated M & S, based on companionship and the sense of belonging to a large family.

The following paragraph comes from the annual review (*The Times*, January 10) by MR. C. S. BARLOW for *Thos. Barlow & Sons Limited*:

"There are now over 11,050 employees in our group, working in 164 establishments in South Africa, Rhodesia and Great Britain and it is only by developing intelligent and satisfied teams that we have been able to expand. Continual attention to their welfare is one of the major functions of your directors. We are particularly interested in making sure that there are opportunities created for our younger members and our wide diversification assists us in this task."

The board of *Paterson, Zochonis & Company Limited* (December 19), MR. A. H. LOUPOS revealed, had considered ways by which the company might give assistance to senior members of the staff to acquire shares in the company. It had been decided to do this by the provision of loans, through trustees, on reasonable terms, repayable over a number of years. The board, he declared, was satisfied that such a scheme would be for the benefit of all shareholders.

For *Leslie Gold Mines Limited* (Johannesburg, May 24) MR. C. B. ANDERSON described as a significant event during the year the introduction of a monthly pay scheme for all union men, who had as a result benefited from increased rates of pay, higher pensions and more generous leave. In return, he stated, the unions agreed to abandon certain restrictive practices. It was too early,

Mr. Anderson considered, to assess the effect of the agreement on mining costs, but to some extent it had been beneficial.

MANAGEMENT

For shareholders in *The Metal Box Company Limited* (July 25) MR. DAVID DUCAT gave this account of the make-up and scope of the Management Services Department of the group:

"For many years we have employed people suitably qualified in the fields of work study, organization and methods and in the use of mathematical and statistical techniques. Over the last few years we have brought these together, with additional systems analysts, to form a Management Services Department which provides a consultancy service available to all sections of the company at home and abroad. This arrangement enables the appropriate variety of specialist knowledge to be concentrated on particular operational or administrative problems.

"The department works closely with the operating groups to analyse their information requirements and with the Computer Department to determine which systems are best suited to computerization. Our policy is clearly only to put work on to computers which can be done better or more cheaply than by other means and the progress we are making encourages us to believe that some of the very difficult problems of materials procurement, production planning and control in an industry where great flexibility is required, will be capable of solution."

Commenting on current talk about "professional management," COLONEL W. H. WHITBREAD of *Whitbread and Company Limited* (September 6) declared that a man might have wonderful qualifications—several successes in management courses and even a Double First at a university—but there were three things which were necessary to make him effective in management. These he defined as under:

"(1) to appreciate risks and have the judgment to assess the possibilities, and if in his opinion they are viable to have the courage and skill to carry them out.

"(2) the will to win or the intense desire to make a success of the business for which he is responsible.

"(3) the ability to get along with those who work for him, alongside him and for whom he works."

A man might have a collection of technical qualifications and all the technical and human help he needed, but without the above attributes, he asserted, it would be difficult for him to be a success in management.

The appointment by *J. Lyons & Company Limited* (July 16) at the end of 1967 of two managing directors, stated MR. GEOFFREY

SALMON, was the latest important stage in the reorganization which the group had been undergoing during the last few years. He gave the following explanation:

"The evolution of the business has led us to adopt a different, and more conventional, pattern of organization. Hitherto a general manager in charge of each distinct activity has reported direct to the Board, but the breadth and diversity of the Group's activities were making this increasingly cumbersome. In order to deal with this situation, the entire executive management has been made the responsibility of two Managing Directors and all the various activities of the business have now been grouped in Sectors. The role of the Board will thus be different in the future from its role in the past; as a corollary, its composition will be different too, in that it will no longer consist solely of full-time executive Directors."

Some years ago *John Mowlem & Company Limited*, MR. E. C. BECK recalled in his statement (*The Times*, May 29), appointed as directors of its operating subsidiaries senior men who had been in the company's service for many years to give them greater scope for their knowledge and experience in the industry. That policy had since been extended and younger men promoted. As a result the group, he asserted, now had a highly qualified and experienced team of management assisting the main board in the general conduct of the business and in formulating policies for the future, including the training of personnel, the financial requirements of the group, the investment in new plant and the continuous effort required to secure new turnover.

LORD ROTHERMERE drew attention to the policy of management decentralization followed by *Associated Newspapers Limited* (July 24) and marked in 1967 by the formation of Harmsworth Publications Limited; this policy, he asserted, had proved its worth. Co-ordination, he added, was provided by a committee of the board, presided over by the chairman. This committee, apart from keeping the group's present trading operations and investments under surveillance, ensured that new investment opportunities were fully examined. Later in his statement he gave this account of the way in which Harmsworth Publications was operating:

"This has been the first full year that Harmsworth Publications has operated as a separate entity within the group structure and I am very pleased with the results so far. By encouraging Editors to play a part in commercial and managerial policy, a unified approach towards the more successful marketing of these papers has been made possible. Plans are now being laid for their future development, aimed at improving circulation and advertising revenue."

In a reference to management policy in his survey (*The Times*,

January 4) for *J. H. Fenner & Co. (Holdings) Limited* MR. S. B. HAINSWORTH stated that the company was spending money in building up a larger staff of executives and strengthening certain specialist functions, and in improving its accounting to handle a larger turnover, the sales of a wider range of products, and prompt provision of the information by which managers could manage. "We shall," he added, "continue to do this."

The year's activities of *W. W. Chamberlain (Associated Companies) Limited* (July 15), MR. W. R. F. CHAMBERLAIN declared, had been dominated by a considerable reorganization of the group's management structure, as well as by a major drive to increase again export sales and the development of new products and markets at home and abroad on which to base the future expansion of sales.

For *Allied Suppliers Limited* (June 7) MR. MALCOLM E. COOPER reported the creation, in February, 1968, of a new company, Allied Suppliers (Fresh Meat) Limited, to assume total responsibility for the butchery and poultry trade in all the larger units of the group. He explained:

"Until recent months each of the retail companies has been responsible for its own fresh meat trade, and, let there be no mistake, they have been without exception very successful in this. However, just as some years ago I reported to you that the Board had deemed it desirable to establish a central buying organization for groceries and provisions, so now with the expansion of our total group fresh meat trade into a multi-million pound annual business, it has been decided to seek the advantages of central buying for our butchery departments.

"For technical reasons we have gone further than merely centralizing meat buying; the new company is responsible for all aspects of our butchery operations from buying to design of departments, to staffing them and sales."

THE COMMONWEALTH

THAT *Commonwealth Development Finance Company Limited* was now well-known in 23 countries of the Commonwealth as a source of development capital was stated by the new chairman, SIR GEORGE BOLTON, in his annual report (*The Times*, June 4). Referring to the resignation on March 31, 1968, of Lord Godber, who had been chairman since the company's inception, Sir George declared that under Lord Godber's control and guidance the company had built up its present financial position and had established a reputation for expertise in the appraisal of development projects, for judgment and for stability.

After reporting on recent changes in business and industrial activity, in relations between the countries of the Commonwealth, and in development policies, he went on to declare:

"Unfortunately, the prospects for development are clouded by the recent convulsions in the world's monetary system and the restrictive policies that a number of western countries have felt obliged to introduce. Your company is, of course, most directly affected by the British Government's policies which have found expression in high interest costs, high taxation affecting foreign investment and restraints on the export of capital to certain countries. Additionally, political and economic upheavals in a number of Commonwealth countries have interfered with the smooth progress of our business. All these factors have imposed limitations on the number and variety of development activities open to our participation, slowed down our growth and interfered with our attempts to maintain a balanced portfolio.

"At my request, a review involving a full examination of the company's policies and methods has been put in hand. The hallmark of our activities in the past has been the specialized expertise which the company's staff has devoted to the conduct of its business and in particular to the appraisal of the viability of industrial development projects put to us for investment. It is certainly my intention that this quality of care and skill should be retained. It is the most important asset of your company's business, and any changes in direction that may eventuate will be designed so as to build upon it even more advantageously than hitherto."

AUSTRALIA AND NEW ZEALAND

SIR DENYS LOWSON showed how the Australian economy had recovered during 1966–67 from the setback of 1965–66 in his reports for *Nelson Financial Trust Limited* (January 19), *Melbourne and*

General Investment Trust Limited (May 22) and the *Australian Estates Company Limited* (July 8). The following excerpt is taken from his statement for the last-named concern:

"Following the slow-down of the growth rate of the Australian economy in 1965–66 caused by the drought, there was a strong recovery in 1966–67 even though the drought persisted in some areas. Whilst reduced returns are now being received for some rural commodities, the position regarding minerals, oil and natural gas is encouraging. There has also been a good recovery in the volume of private capital inflow, despite some overseas restrictions on their capital outflow, and with this support the balance of payments continues to be strong. The Government's decision to leave the par value of the Australian dollar un-changed when sterling devaluated by one-seventh (14·3 per cent) was generally considered correct for the economy as a whole. However, it created difficulties in some rural industries and these are under consideration by the Government. Although there are likely to be problems of rising costs, mainly as a result of recent wage decisions, we can look forward with confidence to solid economic growth."

The drought was one of the causes of a 22 per cent drop in pre-tax profit for 1967–68 of *Australian, Mercantile, Land and Finance Company Limited* (December 5), as indicated in the next quotation, which comes from the annual review by MR. J. F. PRIDEAUX:

"Three main factors account for this year's setback: firstly, and principally, the dry to drought conditions during the greater part of the period in the Eastern States of Australia, culminating in the worst recorded drought in Victoria and Riverina; secondly, the lower average wool price during the selling season and, thirdly, the continuing upward trend in costs. The dry conditions in Queensland and in New South Wales, apart from Riverina, continued until early in 1968 when widespread rains brought relief. In Victoria and Riverina the acute drought persisted until the end of April, after which good rains fell. However, the severe drought forced many graziers to sell live-stock before they normally would have been marketed and this, coupled with restricted demand, caused prices to fall. Graziers' incomes also suffered from lower wool prices.

"These factors were reflected in the earnings of the company's Australian agency business and were responsible for a net loss on working the Australian Stations, compared with a modest profit for the previous 12 months."

Having announced the transformation of the previous year's loss into a profit for the year under review and the doubling of the dividend to 3 per cent, SIR JOHN E. GILMOUR made the following

guarded prognostication about the outlook for *Australian Pastoral Company Limited* (December 19) in the current year:

"It is probably more difficult in the pastoral industry than in any other to forecast profits for a year's operations. Not only do we suffer from the same disability as other industries of not being able to prejudge the acts of governments but we are exceptionally reliant upon nature to give us weather conditions suited to our activities in animal husbandry. However, our present expectation is that, in the absence of any adverse circumstances between now and mid-1969, our profits for the current year should exceed those of last year and if, in achieving such a result, we can further increase our stock numbers, then, in the absence of crippling drought, we may surely look forward to a rising level of profits. It is the ever-present fear of drought that makes it improper to be an optimist in this industry."

Like other investment trust chairmen, LORD TANGLEY referred in his speech for *The Trustees Corporation Limited* (July 30) to capital gains tax and the obligation to surrender 25 per cent of the proceeds of sale of foreign investments at the nominal rate of exchange as serious impediments on the management of portfolios at home and abroad. But he also commented on another limitation in these terms:

"There is another restriction imposed on Investment Trusts which makes it impossible to add to our investments in Australia. When one considers the great opportunities there, I cannot believe that it is in the national interest that these opportunities should be denied to Britain while American, Japanese and other interests are free to share fully in the growth of that great country."

Recalling that in its accounts for the year ended August 31, 1960, investments of *C.L.R.P. Investment Trust Limited* in Australasia accounted for 7·5 per cent of the portfolio, MR. H. D. CURRY in his statement (*The Times*, December 23) asserted that at that time it was the exception to find investors or their advisers who were attracted to Australia. Today, he declared, it was rare to meet anyone who was not financially interested in that continent; and in the intervening years there had been a remarkable change in the outlook. He continued:

"The intense interest recently shown by investors in and outside Australia is attributable to the almost fabulous discoveries of minerals and oil across the continent. Imagination responded to the aura of excitement that the discoveries created with the inevitable boom and recession in the mining share markets. Australia now faces a challenge—that of the development of its newly-found extensive natural resources.

"Last year Australian farmers experienced one of the worst droughts in recent memory. The pastoral conditions were indeed black and naturally this had its effect upon consumer spending powers, so that trade in general showed little growth. By contrast prospects this season now look good.

"The great appreciation in the Australian investments is reflected in the increase in the geographical classification since 31st August, 1967, namely, 11·6 per cent to 16·1 per cent. No new money was provided from this country during this period. I am sure Australia still offers outstanding opportunities for long-term investment."

A number of chairmen remarked on the progress of Australian subsidiaries and associated companies, among them MR. S. T. RYDER of *Reed Paper Group Limited*, who included this paragraph in his statement (*The Times*, July 5):

"The progress of the Australian group of companies has been extremely gratifying with profits of over £1m. being some one-third higher than for 1966. These results reflect expanded capacities and improved productivity in packaging and stationery as well as increased sales in all divisions. To fund some of the consequently increased bank overdraft and to finance further intended developments a Debenture issue of A$3m. was made in Australia by Reed Consolidated Industries during April 1968."

The annual review of *Inchcape & Co. Limited* (October 30) reported that the profit earned in Western Australia by Douglas Jones Pty. Limited was "well in excess of that for the previous year," and the outlook for the company's activities in the area remained encouraging. However, the report mentioned that in one direction tree disease was a handicap, as the following extract shows:

"With the completion of a new saw-mill early in the current year, incorporating the most advanced equipment in this field, this company should be well placed to take advantage of any opportunities for expanding its timber operations. Milling operations are, however, still being hampered by a disease, which is affecting the timber extracted from the hardwood forests. Some progress is being made to combat this but, until the quality of available timber improves, the milling operations will not show the return which could otherwise be achieved."

In Western Australia, also, SIR HALFORD REDDISH informed members of *Rugby Portland Cement Company Limited* (May 24), the extension of the plant of the subsidiary, Cockburn Cement Limited, was on schedule. He continued:

"The new kiln, with an annual productive capacity of 300,000

tons should be in production by September. In June last Cockburn Cement Ltd. became a public company and issued
1,800,000 Ordinary shares of 50 cents each (15 per cent of its
share capital) to the Australian public at $A1·60 a share. The
issue was an immediate success and the shares have since
changed hands at over $A4·00. The company made a record
pre-tax profit of $A2,788,213 for the year ended 31st December
1967. The parent company retains its holding of 85 per cent of
the capital. The State of Western Australia continues to flourish,
expanding both its industrialization and its primary industries.
It is immensely rich in natural resources. I view the future of the
State, and within it that of Cockburn Cement Ltd., with considerable optimism."

Satisfactory results, which should be maintained, were reported
for Coles Cranes Limited in Australia by MR. A. G. HOWE of *The
Steel Group Limited* (September 20). Trading conditions there, he
stated, remained much the same as in the year 1966–67—"a
buoyant economy coupled with severe competition in the industry."

The next quotation comes from MR. T. D. BARCLAY's survey for
Sun Alliance and London Insurance Limited (June 5):

"Our business in Australia again increased in volume, principally in the Accidents Department, but our results suffered a
setback. The year started badly with the extensive bush fires in
Tasmania. This catastrophe was followed by other major fires
and we finished the year with a substantial loss on the Fire
account. There was also a marginal loss in the Accident Department. The economy of New Zealand faced a difficult year
despite which we had a modest increase in premium income and
a satisfactory profit, although less than that of 1966."

For *Dalgety and New Zealand Loan Limited* (December 5)
LT.-COL. C. P. DAWNAY stated that in Australia (where severe
drought adversely affected some of the group's interests) and New
Zealand tight control over operating costs, an aggressive exploration of new markets and measures of reorganization helped to
counteract the effect of an exceptionally difficult year and "promise
well for the future."

In New Zealand in spite of the problems of the economy, MR.
B. N. RECKITT of *Reckitt & Colman Holdings Limited* (June 7)
asserted, record sales and profits were achieved. It was hoped, he
added, that the devaluation of the New Zealand dollar to parity
with the Australian dollar would lead to freer supply of imported
materials and a return to easier trading, though of course the
sterling proceeds would be lower.

MR. J. F. E. GILCHRIST of *Harrisons & Crosfield Limited*
(December 10) stated that New Zealand was expected to move

gradually towards the elimination of import licences and, in substitution, to control imports by tariffs. This, he declared, should
be to the company's advantage.

At a meeting of *National Mortgage and Agency Company of
New Zealand Limited* (December 20) shareholders unanimously
passed a resolution effecting the transfer of the company and the
centre of control from the United Kingdom to New Zealand with
effect from and including February 4, 1969.

INDIA AND CEYLON

The business of the *Anglo-Thai Corporation Limited* (December 4)
in India showed some improvement in keeping with the rather
better economic climate in the latter half of the year, SIR DENYS
LOWSON declared, but, he added, "we still suffer from the inordinately high rate of taxation."

"If there is any truth in the saying that 'one swallow does not
make a summer,' " he remarked, "it is equally true that one good
harvest should not be regarded as the end of all India's economic
problems. Nevertheless, the bumper harvest of 1967/68 should
ensure that there is no immediate repetition of the chronic food
shortage which occurred, particularly in certain States, during
mid-1967, and should enable the Government to reduce the
heavy expenditure of recent years on import of foodstuffs, thus
releasing foreign exchange for import of much needed equipment and raw materials. The improvement in the crops can also
be regarded as an indication that the Government's agricultural
policy is beginning to produce results.

"Except for the improved food situation, the same problems
of over-population, massive foreign debts, rising cost of living
and a swollen bureaucracy remain; as also the absence of any
marked improvement in India's relationship with her near
neighbours, although there are signs that the level of tension
between India and Pakistan has been lowered slightly in recent
months."

Having a year previously expressed some caution about prospects in India, MR. P. A. GODFREY PHILLIPS was all the more
delighted to report that the subsidiary there of *Godfrey Phillips
Limited* (June 28) achieved record sales and profits, and that this
trend was continuing during the current year. He also said (in
part):

"Additional production facilities have been obtained in a new
factory just outside Delhi and this plant is now coming into full
operation and should ensure increasing supplies during the
remainder of this year and thereafter. We have a great interest
in the Indian economy and view with admiration the efforts of

200

both Government and people there to overcome the natural difficulties which they face and establish their economy on a sound basis. Subject to our ability to maintain our overworked plant and production facilities in good order and to a continued increase in sales sufficient to absorb ever rising costs, the future for our Indian subsidiary looks better than for some while past, and we can, I think, remain confident that it will continue to make a substantial contribution to total Group profits."

Though 1967–68 was a difficult year for India, a recession in activity following the previous year's bad harvests, LORD ALDING-TON informed members of *The General Electric Company Limited* that G.E.C. India had had another good year in spite of highly competitive conditions and was well poised to take advantage of the improvement in demand that was following the recent good harvest. His statement appeared in *The Times* of July 30.

In the course of a comprehensive review (*The Times*, February 22) of the manifold activities in India of *Voltas Limited* MR. R. F. S. TALYARKHAN referred to agriculture and exports in these terms:

"In keeping with the needs of the nation, the company is paying special attention to agriculture and exports. A new agro-industrial products division will bring mechanized aids, diesel power, hydraulic equipment, chemicals, fertilizers and scientific know-how to farmers. A specially constituted Export Cell has commenced surveys of neighbouring countries in East and West Asia with the intention of exporting the company's products and engineering skills abroad."

Trading conditions in India, it was reported in the annual review of *Inchcape & Co. Limited* (October 30), remained difficult throughout 1967. However, as a result of more efficient agricultural methods and satisfactory rainfall during the monsoon season, harvests were good and food prospects were better than they had been for some years; and the review expressed the opinion that trading conditions should improve, although the effects of the recession would be felt for some time.

After referring to the political instability and the economic recession in India which were in part at any rate directly attributable to the failure of the monsoon in 1965 and 1966, MR. I. A. MAC-PHERSON of *The Calcutta Electric Supply Corporation Limited* (October 31) showed the dramatic effect of the favourable monsoon in 1967 on the crops:

"By contrast it is heartening to report that the Monsoon in 1967 was plentiful and that in the crop year ended 30th June, 1968, a total of 95/100m. tons of food-grains has been harvested —an increase of some 20 per cent on the previous year. The lesson of the last two or three years is that agriculture is still the

o   201

bedrock of the Indian economy and that it is to be given top priority."

The business of *Harrisons & Crosfield Limited* (December 10) in Ceylon had had a disappointing year, and tea trading operations in particular were hampered by the many strikes the causes and settlements of which were completely outside the company's control. Thus stated MR. J. F. E. GILCHRIST.

In the course of his presidential review for the *Ceylon Association in London* (May 2) MR. M. D. C. WATSON referred to a recent attempt to obtain Ceylon Government approval of an unusual procedure for the release of exchange which would enable sterling companies to be bid for and purchased cheaply in what was conceived to be the national interest. The Association had taken the view that it was quite wrong for advantage to be taken in this way of the depressed market prices and Mr. Watson said that he was glad that the Ceylon Government, on representations made, had so far withheld its approval of the proposal.

MALAYSIA, SINGAPORE AND HONGKONG

The tenth anniversary of Malaysia's independence occurred in 1967, and the country, SIR DENYS LOWSON declared in his statement for *Anglo-Thai Corporation Limited* (December 4), could look back with some satisfaction over the achievements of the 10 years, much of the credit for which "must undoubtedly be given" to the leadership of the country's Prime Minister, Tengku Abdul Rahman, as the bestowal on him in June, 1968, of the freedom of the City of London recognized.

However, while the effect of the withdrawal of British forces from the Far East had been felt more severely in Singapore, Malaysia had been not without its problems in the past year, as the following excerpt from Sir Denys's review indicates:

"The price of Rubber continued its downward trend, in spite of buying by the Government, and touched a low point of 45 cents per lb. in March of this year. I am glad to say that there has since been an appreciable recovery and the price now stands at around 58 cents per lb. The price of Tin was supported in the region of £1,300 per ton through purchases by the Buffer Stock Manager, and with stocks in his hands now reaching a dangerously high figure, it was decided at a recent Meeting of the International Tin Council to restrict exports over the next three months in order to prevent the price from falling further. Palm Oil prices also declined slightly."

During the year the Malaysian and Singapore trading companies belonging to the *Inchcape & Co. Limited* group (October 30), it was stated in the annual report, were grouped under a Singapore hold-

202

ing company, Borneo Berhad. Since the end of the year 25 per cent of the equity in this company had been sold to the local public, and the shares of Borneo Berhad were now quoted on the Stock Exchange of Malaysia and Singapore.

A merger in which the Malaysian interests of *The Associated Portland Cement Manufacturers Limited* (July 4) were concerned is the subject of the following paragraph taken from SIR JOHN REISS's statement:

"In Malaysia, Malayan Cement Limited merged with our competitors, Pan-Malaysia Cement Works Limited in April and the co-operation between the two companies since that date under Blue Circle management has been most encouraging. There had been a satisfactory growth in local cement consumption and, following improvements to the technical efficiency of the Pan-Malaysian works, its capacity is to be raised by the installation of additional plant. Further plans for expansion of the company's interests are under consideration."

Some idea of the scale of the employment and other problems resulting from the acceleration of the withdrawal of British forces facing the Singapore Government may be gathered from the next quotation, which comes from SIR DENYS LOWSON's statement for *Anglo-Thai Corporation Limited* (December 4):

"The problems created by the British Government's decision to accelerate by several years the planned withdrawal of British Forces from the Island were accepted by the country's stoic leader, Lee Kuan Yew, and his able colleagues in Government, as a challenge which the country has the ability and will to meet. Nevertheless, the size of this problem should not be underestimated. Apart from the loss of income from the presence of British Forces, Singapore will be involved in increased defence expenditure and have to find jobs for upwards of 30,000 persons at present either directly or indirectly employed in the bases. This is in addition to some 25,000 young people entering the labour market for the first time each year. The significance of these figures can be readily appreciated when measured against a total labour force of approximately 600,000 and about 50,000 persons already unemployed.

"There is no doubt that this small Island Republic well deserves any support which the British Government and industry alike can give to it in the difficult years ahead."

MR. A. R. YOUNG-HERRIES of *Jardine, Matheson & Co. Limited* (Hongkong, June 7) was pleased to be able to report that in spite of troubled local conditions Hongkong continued to prosper: overall trade figures for 1967 increased by comparison with 1966, he added, domestic exports being larger by 17 per cent. These results were the more satisfactory since they were achieved in a

year when Hongkong was affected by civil disturbances, the closure of the Suez Canal and devaluation of the £ sterling.

The reaction of the Colony to devaluation is shown in the following paragraph from MR. S. J. COOKE's statement for *Gilman* (*Holdings*) *Limited* (Hongkong, June 26):

"The second matter affecting the Colony, and particularly the banking and trading community, was the devaluation of Sterling in mid-November last year. For many years the Hongkong Dollar maintained a fixed relationship with the Pound Sterling. Upon Sterling devaluation Government's first decision was to follow United Kingdom action and devalue to the same extent. Very shortly after, however, more complete information being available, a decision was made to re-value the Hongkong Dollar upward by 10%. The consensus regarding this decision was generally favourable having regard to the overall effect on the community of the increase in raw material costs, and particularly food, had devaluation been followed to the full."

The acquisition of a controlling interest in Gilman (Holdings) Limited by *Inchcape & Co. Limited* (October 30) was reported by LORD INCHCAPE. Gilmans, he stated, first started operations in 1841 and was one of the leading concerns in Hongkong.

In his statement (*The Times*, November 8) for *Wheelock Marden & Company Limited* MR. J. L. MARDEN regretted that the negotiations with the British Government for finance for the proposed vehicular tunnel under the harbour had to be broken off because of unduly onerous security terms. Negotiations with other parties were continuing, he added, but meanwhile provision had been made for the expenditure to date of HK $6m. (£412,500).

COLONEL J. D. CLAGUE of *Hutchison International Limited* (Hongkong, October 31) gave as the reason why negotiations in connection with the cross harbour tunnel were in abeyance that the requests by E.C.G.D. for unconditional joint and several guarantees proved unacceptable to the parties concerned.

AFRICA

In Rhodesia, reported MR. H. F. OPPENHEIMER to members of *Anglo American Corporation of South Africa Limited* (Johannesburg, June 14), the group was establishing another nickel mine at Madziwa, in the Shamva district; this was in addition to the expansion of operations at the Trojan nickel mine, in which he had announced a year previously that companies of the group had acquired a controlling interest. He gave these details:

"A new company, Bindura Smelting and Refining Company Limited, will smelt and refine concentrates from both these mines. A holding company, Rhodesian Nickel Corporation

Limited, was recently formed to acquire the entire share capital of the two mining companies and of the smelting and refining company. About 85 per cent of the capital of Rhodesian Nickel Corporation is held by companies of our Group. The whole cost of these projects, amounting to about £10m. (Rhodesian), is being financed from sources within Rhodesia."

For political reasons the Rhodesian operations of *Godfrey Phillips Limited* (June 28), stated MR. P. A. GODFREY PHILLIPS, remained at a complete standstill. Although some of the company's investment there continued income producing, restrictions on remittances, he declared, rendered this income of no immediate value to Godfrey Phillips. He went on to assert:

"An acceptable solution of the Rhodesian problem should not be beyond the powers of Statesmanship, but unfortunately Statesmanship is a commodity of which today there seems to be a strange dearth throughout the world."

MR. H. A. LONGDEN told members of *The Cementation Company Limited* (September 30) that they must hope for an equitable solution of the Rhodesian political problem, which continued to isolate their Rhodesian company from them and restricted its opportunities for expansion. Rhodesians, he averred, had had to turn for the supply of goods and services to non-British sources, with the consequent loss of valuable trade.

Widespread changes in Zambian economic policy were announced by President Kaunda in an important speech at Malungushi on April 19, 1968, and these included a limitation on the amount of profits which could be remitted to shareholders abroad. MR. H. F. OPPENHEIMER referred to this speech in his statements for *Nchanga Consolidated Copper Mines Limited* (Lusaka, September 26) and for *Anglo American Corporation of South Africa Limited* (Johannesburg, June 14), and in the course of a reasoned answer made these points (among others) in his review for the latter company:

"The President in his speech expressed disappointment that the mining industry had not grown more rapidly since the time of independence and he reproached the mining companies for having distributed 80 per cent of their profits each year in dividends. The mining companies have always prided themselves on conducting their affairs with a high sense of the public interest and I feel it right therefore to comment briefly on the dividend policy they have followed in recent years. Of the gross mining profits of the companies of our Group since independence, no less than 64·8 per cent has been paid to the Government by way of royalties and taxation. Last year, when the incidence of the export tax was for the first time felt in full, the Government's proportion of gross mining profits actually amounted to

69·1 per cent. Perhaps in these circumstances the companies might have been forgiven if, having made a direct contribution of this magnitude to the Government they had, in fact, distributed to their shareholders 80 per cent of what remained to them but this by no means represents the full facts of the case. It has been our practice to charge to working costs each year the capital expenditure required to maintain production at established levels. In fact, massive investment has been required in recent years to make it possible to sustain the established rate of production from greater depths and lower-grade ores. We are concerned here not just with maintenance expenditure but with the financing of huge projects for the purpose of opening up new orebodies and treating the production from them. Since independence the mines of our Group have invested no less than K36·4m. in this way, a sum equal to 41 per cent of the dividends paid during the same period. In addition, the sum of K12·6m. which was retained out of net profits was all used for capital expenditure purposes in Zambia so that since independence the mining companies of our Group have applied to capital purposes profits equal to 55·3 per cent of the amount paid out in dividends during that period. For last year alone the figures are even more striking: capital expenditure of K21·2m., a sum equal to 83·3 per cent of the dividends for the year, was financed out of current profits."

MR. D. LLOYD JONES of *United Transport Company Limited* (August 29) gave this explanation of how the overseas group came to make a loss in Zambia:

"In November, 1965, following the declaration of independence by Rhodesia we were called upon by the Zambian Government to undertake the organization and execution of a massive fuel lift by road transport until the Government could set up its own organization. We responded to this call and our fleet of vehicles increased from 400 to 1,000 units. This resulted in a very rapid expansion of our workshops and organization and led to the recruitment of a large number of expatriate staff. As a result the profit of our Zambian Group of companies in 1966 was an all time record, but this was reversed in 1967 when a loss was incurred. Due to the excessive strain under which our staff in Zambia were working our position did not become apparent until the last quarter of the year, since when vigorous steps have been taken to correct the position by sending more assistance from this country. Audited accounts for the year to December 31, 1967, are not available as their preparation would have caused undue delay both in the production of the annual accounts of the Group and in negotiations with the Zambian Government whereby they are to become partners in our interests in that country. Audited accounts are now being pre-

pared for the period to June 30, 1968, the date on which the acquisition of the interest in the Zambian companies by the Government becomes effective."

For *Harrisons & Crosfield Limited* (December 10) MR. J. F. E. GILCHRIST revealed that the branch office opened a year previously at Blantyre in Malawi was now firmly established. He added that an increasing export business in tea was being done with overseas clients.

The East African Common Services Organization was dissolved during the year, and the East African Economic Community came into being with its headquarters at Arusha. This was stated in the annual review of *Inchcape & Co. Limited* (October 30), which added that the Treaty for East African Co-operation was being implemented, and that all restrictions on imports within Kenya, Uganda and Tanzania were to be removed, while certain safeguards for local industry would be provided. The devaluation of sterling in November, 1967, was not followed by the East African countries, according to the review, which reported that some concern had been expressed about the effect on exports of agricultural products as a result.

Dealing with long-term planning, MR. V. A. MADDISON of *East African Power and Lighting Company Limited* (Nairobi, May 24) stated that the National Power Development Plan 1966–86, commissioned jointly by the Kenya Government and the company, was received in May, 1967, and contained a complete forecast and analysis of the technical and financial requirements of the Kenya electricity industry over the next 20 years. After summarizing the chief recommendations of the plan, he went on to say that talks had already been initiated on the potential advantages to both Uganda and Kenya of arrangements which might include co-ordinated and phased development of the two countries' respective hydro-electric resources and the use of the existing Kenya–Uganda transmission line for supply in either direction as the supply situation might, from time to time, require.

In spite of an unprecedented deterioration of the vital public services in Nigeria, *Nigerian Electricity Supply Corporation Limited* (October 23), SIR MILES CLIFFORD claimed, maintained an uninterrupted and reliable service throughout the year. As to the future, he declared that there was certainly little room for optimism while the civil war—"so costly in life, so costly to the Nigerian economy"—continued. Operations over the period March to August, he stated, showed a fall in revenue of approximately 17 per cent compared with the same period of the year under review.

The next quotation reveals the serious effects of the civil war on *John Holt & Company (Liverpool) Limited*; it is extracted from the preliminary statement published in *The Times* of January 20 and covering the year to August 31, 1967:

"The company's results have been seriously affected by the disturbed conditions in Nigeria which have prevailed throughout the year covered by the accounts. In October there was the massacre and flight of the Ibos from the North. This removed most of the company's technically trained staff from those areas. This was followed by a period of tension then at the start of the season, by the complete interruption of traffic on the Niger River, followed by fighting and the blockade of the East by Federal forces and, finally by the occupation by the East of the Mid-West. All these events damaged the company's trade.

"Although the dispute is unsettled, the blockade of the East continues and the company remains out of touch with its interests there, improvements in the situation have taken place. The Mid-West has been re-occupied by the Federal Authorities, and the company is trading again there. It is once more in possession of the port of Warri and is making good the damage. The port is open and operating, though the increased prosperity which the company expects from its investments in the port and the river fleet will now be postponed until the river is freed and the fleet can operate without restriction.

"Since last September careful consideration has been continually given to the effects upon the company, so far as assessable, of these matters. Hopes of an early settlement have slowly faded. It has therefore been decided to provide not only for losses which have already been quantified but also against unascertained losses, including the full value of all the company's assets in those areas which are still outside its control, though the company has no intention of abandoning these assets. In addition provision has been made for the effects of the devaluation of the Ghana cedi in July.

"Trading results coming in so far this year are encouraging both in West Africa and in the Wine Trade, and the Directors believe that unless further major misfortunes outside their control occur the company will move into profit again this year."

MR. JOHN SPENCER WILLS informed shareholders in *Rediffusion Limited* (July 31) that the group's operations in Nigeria had been seriously affected by the political troubles of recent years, and most particularly by the civil war. The Nigerian subsidiary, therefore, had been for some time running at a loss, and he added that it was impossible then to forecast when it would return to profitability. However, it was still making a cash surplus, and, he declared, "we count ourselves very lucky that an extremely loyal staff has held together, through thick and thin, a business which will prosper once again if normal conditions return."

Addressing members of *Consolidated African Selection Trust Limited* (December 10), MR. A. CHESTER BEATTY said that the past 12 months of peaceful administration under the Ghana National

Liberation Council had seen further steps taken or planned towards the return to civilian rule and a strengthening of the economy.

Referring to the importance which *Ashanti Goldfields Corporation Limited* (April 4) attached to Africanization, MAJOR-GENERAL SIR EDWARD L. SPEARS said:

> "It is a matter of great pride and satisfaction to me to see the astonishing speed at which we are bringing out African talent. We have, by using commonsense and refusing to be panicked, made great progress in training Ghanaians for what were previously expatriate posts underground. We now have a larger number of Ghanaian shift-bosses than expatriate and a Ghanaian Acting Mine Captain exercising authority over Europeans.
>
> "This has in the main been achieved by applying two proverbs and one rule. These are 'You must not try to run before you can walk' and the Spanish one 'You must give time to time'. And the rule is: no man at A.G.C. is either given a job or deprived of occupying one because of his nationality or origin."

In a comment on the political instability in Sierra Leone MR. A. CHESTER BEATTY said that the two forcible changes in Government had meant a lapse of several months in each instance before the new Government felt able to tackle the allied problems of the "strangers" (*i.e.*, those who were unlawfully in the area) and the prevention of illicit diamond mining in the licence areas of the subsidiary of *Consolidated African Selection Trust Limited* (December 10).

CANADA

The Canadian economy, SIR DENYS LOWSON told members of *First Re-Investment Trust Limited* (January 17), continued to be subject to considerable pressures, which he categorized as follows:

> "These included considerable increases in prices, a large increase in Government expenditure at both Federal and Provincial levels, a substantial decline in bond prices, a high degree of credit expansion, uncertainties caused by the Carter Commission on taxation and the devaluation of sterling towards the end of the year. Recently, however, the Minister of Finance has indicated that he does not intend to implement the main proposals of the Carter Commission."

The Governor of the *Hudson's Bay Company* (May 24), LORD AMORY, also referred to inflationary pressures in Canada, as will be seen from this extract from his statement:

> "The strong growth pattern in the Canadian economy which had been in evidence for the last six years levelled off in 1967.

Although Gross National Product rose by 7 per cent, the improvement in real terms was less than $2\frac{1}{2}$ per cent. Industrial production advanced by about 2 per cent compared with a gain last year of close to 8 per cent. Capital spending by business was only slightly higher than a year ago.

"Inflationary pressures which had resulted in price increases of 1 per cent to 2 per cent per annum for some years, began to build up significantly in the latter part of 1966. In 1967 prices in Canada accelerated at a pace which afforded anxiety both as to the internal stability of the economy and the ability of the country to compete in world markets as effectively as in recent years. The consumer price index advanced by $3\frac{1}{2}$ per cent in 1967 and there is no sign in the early months of 1968 of any abatement of this trend."

For *Rowntree and Company Limited* (June 14) MR. D. J. BARRON stated that their Canadian company increased its sales, but earnings were below the record level of the previous year. Rapid increases in costs, particularly of salaries and wages, took place, but adjustments in consumer values in a highly competitive market tended to lag behind. However, the programme of investment in buildings and plant then proceeding, he asserted, would increase production capacity and improve productivity.

In his statement for *United Transport Company Limited* (August 29) MR. D. LLOYD JONES stated that Canadian Motorways achieved a record profit in 1967, and that results to date in 1968 showed a further improvement. C.M., however, was not paying a dividend as the profit was being retained to reduce the long-term liabilities of the company.

MR. R. S. JUKES gave this account of the progress of the Canadian interests of *BPB Industries Limited* (July 31):

"Our largest operation overseas is in Canada, where Western Gypsum Limited has plaster and plasterboard plants in Toronto, Winnipeg, Calgary and Vancouver. Housing starts in Canada increased in 1967 by 30,000 units to 164,000, and our subsidiary, benefiting by the higher demand, has shown a considerably improved contribution to the Group's profits. The plants at Toronto and Vancouver were extended during the year and a further extension at Toronto is planned to come into operation during the early months of 1969."

CARIBBEAN

The recent formation of the Caribbean Free Trade Association was being studied with great interest, it was stated in the annual review by *Inchcape & Co. Limited* (October 30), which added:

"If our production plants for vehicles and appliances could look to the whole of the Caribbean for their markets instead of

210

being restricted to Trinidad their future prospects would be better."

While 1968 held good promise for the *Caribbean Cement Company Limited* (Rockfort, Kingston, Jamaica, April 30), SIR NEVILLE ASHENHEIM warned that careful account must be taken of the effects of the devaluation of the Jamaica £. He recalled that in November, 1967, it was decided to devalue the Jamaica £ to parity with the £ sterling after full consideration had been given to the advantages and disadvantages of such action. He continued:

"The effects of devaluation on our company's operations, though not devastating, will place a substantial burden on its production costs as certain supplies and equipment basic to our operation such as fuel oil, paper for sacks, grinding media, refractories and spare parts must be imported from non-devalued currency sources or from devalued currency areas where prices have been increased to meet their increased cost of raw materials. A very careful analysis of these increased prices is currently being made with an aim to determine the most appropriate action that must be taken by our company to alleviate the major portion of these increases."

A wage award, the result of arbitration, to workers for the Jamaica Omnibus Services, an associated company of *The British Electric Traction Company Limited* (October 17), added close on £100,000 to operating costs for 10 months of the year and brought about a substantial reduction in the net profit for 1967, stated MR. JOHN SPENCER WILLS, who went on to make this reference to the Jamaica company's consequent claim for higher fares:

"During the whole of the fifteen years of its existence, the level of the Jamaica company's fares has remained unchanged, but this latest award has so raised costs that the company can no longer maintain adequate and efficient services and provide stockholders with a fair return on their investment. Accordingly, an application for an increase in fares was lodged with the Public Passenger Transport Board of Control in April last but, after five months, a decision on the application is still awaited."

The *Rugby Portland Cement Company Limited* (May 24) had decided to increase its investment in its Trinidad subsidiary, Trinidad Cement Limited, in order to raise the annual capacity of the plant to about 300,000 tons. Placing this fact on record, SIR HALFORD REDDISH reiterated his confidence in the future of the Trinidad company.

In his statement (*The Times*, December 5) for *Amalgamated Securities Limited* MR. J. MORRISON mentioned that a new subsidiary had been formed in association with the Commonwealth Development Finance Company for developments in the Bahamas.

211

EUROPE

WITH the veto by France in 1967 of the United Kingdom Government's request for the inclusion of this country in the European Common Market, British company chairmen apparently considered the matter dead for the time being. At all events, few of them thought it worth any more than a passing reference in their 1968 statements. In 1967, it may be recalled, the overwhelming majority had been in favour of entry. One chairman with a double interest in the question was MR. F. HERBERT of the *Danish Bacon Company Limited* (May 15), who declared that the failure of the British and Danish application to join the Common Market was particularly disappointing to Denmark's very European-minded farmers. However, he drew attention to what he considered to be one result of this failure—namely, an increase in Danish purchases from the United Kingdom. The relevant passage from his statement was as follows:

"Proof of this can be seen from the U.K.'s Overseas Trade Accounts for 1967. Denmark, which is the eleventh largest market for British goods in the world and number two inside E.F.T.A., increased her imports from Britain proportionately more than any other substantial export market for British goods. I hope that British exporters will make the fullest use of this opportunity to gain further ground in a country where British goods enjoy an undoubted built-in goodwill.

"There is, in fact, cheering news this morning. For the first time since 1953 Britain has become Denmark's biggest supplier of cars. This country has exported, during the first three months, 10,135 cars, or 34·7 per cent, against West Germany's 9,620 cars, 33 per cent."

Another chairman who regretted the lack of progress in the negotiations to take Britain into membership of E.E.C. was MR. P. T. STEPHENS, who in his annual review (*The Times*, July 1) declared that the European business of *Saunders Valve Company Limited* remained "a very important factor" in its affairs; overall, it had been on a rising trend since the end of the year. "We hope to gain some advantage in competitiveness," he added, "from the tariff reductions as a consequence of the Kennedy Round."

A number of companies had formed Continental subsidiaries in the past few years, partly as a hedge against Britain's inability to join the market. *Rowntree and Company Limited* (June 14) was one that ran a European division, about which MR. D. J. BARRON made this statement:

"The long-term policy of building a business in Rowntree staple lines was continued in 1967. In spite of the recession in some countries of the European Economic Community, satisfactory growth was achieved particularly with Smarties and After Eight Mints. The establishment of a firmly-based marketing operation in Europe requires considerable expenditure on development costs. At present these are in excess of trading profits but, over the next few years, we will move steadily towards a break-even position and the progress to date encourages us to believe that a profitable operation can be created in Europe.

"We have arranged long-term finance through two German banks which will provide the funds over the next few years for the heavy investment—both in advertising and in plant—which the creation of a European business involves."

The Federal Republic of Germany in particular last year went through its heaviest business recession since it came into existence, said HERR GUNTER VOGELSANG, chairman of the Executive Board of *Fried. Krupp G.m.b.H.* (June 22). He continued:

"The number of people employed in industry dropped by more than half a million. Capital investments—the decisive criterion for the growth of a country's economy—decreased by 10 per cent. The shrinking domestic demand would have had even more serious consequences had it not been partially offset by the export of industrial goods.

"We are witnessing now an appreciable upward turn. Whether this is the prelude to a lasting and stable recovery does not depend on economic factors alone, but there is no doubt that, once the Federal Government has discontinued its stimulating measures, the rates of productivity and profit will more than ever before determine the extent and the speed of future economic development; these rates must be substantially raised and maintained—and general conditions are fairly favourable in this respect; otherwise no impulses with lasting effect on capital investments and employment can be expected."

LORD KINDERSLEY, Governor of the *Royal Exchange Assurance* (June 19), commented on an important step which the company had taken in order to extend its operations in the Common Market. Having had no organization of its own operating in the Federal German Republic for many years, Royal Exchange welcomed the opportunity to acquire, through friendly negotiations, the controlling interest in a German general insurance company with headquarters in Hamburg, the Transatlantische Versicherungs AG., established in 1860. He warmly welcomed this new association and was confident that, given reasonable economic conditions, this company would contribute to the profit of the group in future years.

The next quotation comes from MR. A. F. F. YOUNG's statement for *Redland Limited* (September 17):

"The instantaneous success which attended the introduction of Redland tiles into Western Germany in 1953 is now being repeated in other European countries. At the time of writing there are five works in production, in Holland, France, Italy, Sweden and Switzerland, with a second works in Italy, one in Belgium due to commence operations shortly, and more in prospect."

In his additional remarks at the annual meeting, Mr. Young said that the expansion of the roofing tile business continued unabated in Europe "and in some cases is surpassing our most optimistic forecasts."

MR. A. G. HOWE informed members of *The Steel Group Limited* (September 20) that measures taken by the German Government to improve the country's economy had not been reflected in the handling plant industry, and the company's German subsidiary suffered a substantial loss. After explaining that approximately one-third of this deficit was attributable to development expenditure which should benefit future trading, he went on to state:

"Steps have been taken to restore its position as a significant contributor to group profits but success in doing so is dependent upon the state of the economy of Western Germany and particularly an improvement in the handling plant industry there. The container handling equipment developed by this subsidiary went successfully into operation in Hamburg Port and further business in other areas is in course of negotiation."

In the absence through ill-health of the President, Sir Ian Lyle, the chairman, MR. JOHN LYLE, addressed shareholders in *Tate & Lyle Limited* (March 20) and mentioned the company's new investment in France, amounting to an indirect interest in the Say Sugar Company at a cost of about £3m.; in this venture Tate and Lyle were joined with three European partners. He continued:

"We have, for a number of years, had close and frequent contacts in Europe, notably with Tirlemont in Belgium, but also with a number of French sugar companies and we have kept the sugar situation in the Community under continuous examination. It is clear that Europe is going to produce and consume increasing quantities of sugar and that the French sugar industry should be among the most efficient and prosperous in the Community. The steps we have taken have given us a vital foothold in Europe and we have secured what we believe will be a profitable investment in its own right. Those of us who are directly involved have received a warm welcome from the management of Say, in whom we have every confidence."

The European Division of the overseas company of *Reckitt & Colman Holdings Limited* (June 7), MR. B. N. RECKITT pointed out, had to contend with a decrease in the rate of economic growth particularly in the E.E.C. This had had some effect on the pattern of consumer spending and on the buoyancy of trade. Nevertheless, in that highly competitive area, they had continued to increase their sales, and they believed they had now reached a point at which they would begin to reap the reward of the heavy investment of recent years. He went on to make these points:

"France is still our most profitable market but 1967 was a difficult year for us as for most other companies operating in that country. The French economy is in the process of great change especially with the State-inspired rationalization of industry to make it competitive against the day when the E.E.C. internal tariffs disappear on 1st July 1968. For this purpose the price freeze was substantially maintained yet many costs have risen. Basically, however, our interests are well placed and we expect growth in the future.

"In Germany we believe it is imperative for us to develop strongly in what is the largest market of Europe and we have rationalized and expanded our business there. After an expensive period of development we can now see profits ahead after the end of 1968."

Among other obstacles to profit making in France SIR FRANK KEARTON of *Courtaulds Limited* (July 10) mentioned the strikes and other disturbances there. He said:

"In France, we did well until the half year, after which conditions became very difficult due to a sudden and major deterioration in the conditions in the French textile market. Losses in the second half year wiped out the profits of the first half of the year, leaving a small deficit overall. In 1968, a most determined management effort, and slowly improving market conditions, led to a progressive elimination of losses, so that by May a profit was being made again, with excellent prospects of a good second half year. The recent troubles have changed all this. The cost of the strikes and associated plant shutdowns will be expensive to us, certainly some hundreds of thousands of pounds. And the changed cost structure will delay by many months the return to profitability of what is now a large and complex enterprise. But our managers are young and good, and we are far from despondent for the longer term. One product which became a casualty as a result of the stoppage and the new conditions was viscose industrial yarn. This particular installation at Calais became too small to be viable, and we did not see our way clear to expand it."

Another chairman who referred to the strikes in France was MR.

R. S. JUKES, who gave this information to members of *BPB Industries Limited* (July 31):

"In France, the number of dwelling units completed in 1967 totalled 422,000, which was an increase of 2 per cent on the previous year. The group's subsidiary, Platrières Modernes de Grozon S.A., benefited from this increase in activity and showed improved results, but our associate company, Placoplâtre S.A., which produces plasterboard at Vaujours, near Paris, and at its new plant at Chambéry, had to contend with the cost of launching the latter plant and a certain number of problems due to a more difficult market. Over recent months, until interrupted by the general strike, much better results were achieved."

OTHER FOREIGN COUNTRIES

THE UNITED STATES

THE United States economy during 1967 had continued to be dominated by the pressures of the Vietnam war, SIR DENYS LOWSON told members of *First Re-Investment Trust Limited* (January 17). Pending action on the then President Johnson's proposal of a 10 per cent surcharge on income taxes, which Congress refused to approve unless it was accompanied by simultaneous reductions in Government spending (action on the two proposals was delayed until well into 1968), other measures had been announced, he said, to cut back United States expenditure overseas; this should help to reduce the balance of payments deficit.

"In this connection," he explained, "the U.S. problem is just the opposite to ours in this country. They have showed a surplus on current trading account averaging each year over $3,000m. during the period 1960–66 and were it not for non-monetary investment of all kinds, including Government Grants averaging $5,000m. per annum, the dollar would have been in a more comfortable position. In other words where the cause of U.K. balance of payments difficulties is the Current Account, it is the Capital Account which is the root of the American problem."

Sir Denys went on to examine the extent to which the increase in the Gross National Product reflected higher prices, saying:

"After a slower pace in the earlier part of the year, the economy gathered momentum during the second half. While the Gross National Product amounted to $743,300m. in 1966, by the third quarter of 1967 this was running at an annual rate of $791,200m.; but a somewhat disturbing factor is that nearly half the increase in the third quarter reflected rising prices, rather than growth in real terms. Increased prices were being reflected in higher wage contracts of long term duration and establishing precedents for the large number of important wage negotiations scheduled to arise in 1968. The general consensus of opinion is that during 1968 Gross National Product should rise by $7\frac{1}{2}$ per cent in money terms but only by 4 per cent in real terms."

The United States was the largest newsprint consumer in the world, but after several years of steady annual growth newsprint

consumption there flattened out in the latter part of 1967 and ended the year at approximately the same level as in 1966. Thus wrote SIR CHRISTOPHER CHANCELLOR in his statement for *The Bowater Paper Corporation Limited* (April 24). As the leading newsprint supplier to the United States, the Canadian newsprint industry found 1967 a difficult year with production curtailments and lower profits. Bowaters in Canada had their own special problems resulting from the serious power shortage in Newfoundland, he declared, and went on to give this account of the corporation's interests in the United States:

"In the United States our great newsprint mill at Calhoun, Tennessee, was less affected by market conditions than our Canadian mills and production was only marginally lower than the record figure of 1966. At our Catawba paper mill in South Carolina production of blade coated paper for quality magazines reached a new record figure. The pulp mill at Catawba also ran at full production, despite the sharp deterioration of the pulp market in the United States."

Recalling that a year previously he had referred to operations in the U.S.A., including the setting up of a marketing company in New York, MR. DEREK H. JOHNSON informed members of *H. & R. Johnson-Richards Tiles Limited* (August 28) that the promising start made by that company had continued and its sales had reached very considerable proportions.

"It is true to say," he continued, "that the only limiting factor to sales in this market has been our limit of production from our factories in the United Kingdom. You can be assured that every tile it has been possible to produce has been produced, but despite this, delivery promises have had to be lengthened. However, I can report that the merger with Messrs. Richards-Campbell has given us access to increased production which will assist in enabling us to revert to normal delivery schedules to that country and to other markets in the near future."

For *Dowty Group Limited* (October 7) SIR GEORGE DOWTY stated that Dowty Rotol Inc., of Washington, D.C., which was responsible for the distribution of spares and after-sales service for over 700 aircraft using Dowty equipment in North America, had acquired an additional factory for repair and overhaul of the group's equipment; this had previously been handled in the United States by companies not under control by Dowty. The move, he added, would ensure good service to airline customers and provide an increased and profitable turnover.

This information about the interests of *Lines Bros. Limited* (July 12) in the United States was given by MR. W. M. LINES:

"Our associate company in the United States strengthened its

218

position during the year, greatly reduced its indebtedness to the banks and is now in a strong position to go forward profitably. As we hold a minority interest in this company these improvements are not reflected in our accounts although, of course, the investment costs us over £30,000 per annum in interest charges."

In the United States the R. T. French Company subsidiary of *Reckitt & Colman Holdings Limited* (June 7), stated MR. B. N. RECKITT, achieved satisfactorily increased sales in the highly competitive grocery trade and maintained its Number One market position in its products. Although profits continued under the pressures referred to in his report a year previously, and were also affected by heavy introductory expenses for "Country Style" mashed potatoes, dollar profits were somewhat above those of 1966, and, he declared, devaluation brought notable improvement in terms of sterling.

In his statement (*The Times*, June 17) for *Klinger Manufacturing Company Limited* MR. W. G. CASTELL reported an expansion in the plant in Virginia, U.S.A., which previously had been used exclusively for development work on Pinlon equipment and performing on-the-spot servicing for the company's American machinery users. Now yarn processing was carried out there, and the venture was becoming self-supporting as a result.

SOUTH AMERICA

In Argentina, said SIR DENYS LOWSON in his capacity as chairman of *New Zealand and River Plate Land Mortgage Company Limited* (April 9), inflation continued to be a major problem, but nevertheless the country still enjoyed a favourable balance of payments on external account. He then gave these details:

"In the first nine months of 1967 exports reached a total of U.S. $1,230m. and imports amounted to U.S. $823m. This favourable balance is slightly below that for the corresponding period in 1966, but whereas in the first nine months of that year there was a capital outflow of U.S. $230m., the first nine months of 1967 saw an inflow of capital of U.S. $119m. Furthermore with Argentina's exchange reserves rising to U.S. $926m. (the highest level since the early post-war years), a very suitable background was provided for the visit of Argentina's Minister of Economy and Labour, Dr. Krieger Vasena, to Europe last October and November [1967]. This visit was highly successful and considerable foreign aid was obtained to finance Argentina's large scale development programme."

MR. J. F. PRIDEAUX informed members of *Australian, Mercantile, Land and Finance Company Limited* (December 5) that owing to the diminishing number of absentee estancia owners of British

origin in recent years and the difficulties of conducting an agency business, it was decided that in future years it would be beneficial to concentrate solely upon operating the company's own estancias. Consequently, steps were taken to terminate the small agency business as from June 30, 1968.

Among other information about Argentine Estates of Bovril Limited which LORD LUKE gave to shareholders in *Bovril Limited* in the course of his statement (*The Times*, July 15) was the following:

> "We are continuing to rationalize the structure of the company in the Argentine so as to meet the cost of modernizing plant and equipment from local resources. In this way a more economically viable unit of the group will be built up, and our policy is that it should continue to supply the necessary raw materials for Bovril at the same time as developing independently the other forms of meat processing for which there is a demand in world markets."

After referring to the "continued devaluations" of the Uruguayan peso, MR. R. F. DOUBLET pointed out that when he joined the board of *Montevideo Gas & Dry Dock Company Limited* (November 21) 13 years ago the rate of exchange was not quite seven pesos to the £ sterling, whereas it was now about 600. He continued:

> "We have managed, largely due to the skill and efficiency of our resident engineers, to maintain our out-of-date plant in efficient working order. However, time is fast running out when we can continue to manufacture gas by our present antiquated methods.
> "This has been brought home to the National Government who, having admitted that for the foreseeable future they cannot do without our manufacture of gas, have set up a small commission to investigate and report on the situation of your company. Here, I may add, Government commissions are as numerous and popular in Uruguay as they are in this country and have perhaps as much or as little positive effect. However, one thing emerges from our negotiations with the Commission, and that is the Government is at last convinced that not only are we not interested in continuing to produce gas in a country which allows us no profit margin, but that we have no intention of investing in any modern plant in a country where public utilities are the playthings of, and bones of contention between, political parties."

AFRICA

Addressing members of *Rand Mines Limited* (Johannesburg, May 10), MR. P. H. ANDERSON made these remarks (in part) about

what he described as the "remarkable" performance of the South African economy in 1967:

"The achievement of a real growth rate of 6·9 per cent per annum combined with a reduction in the annual rates of increase of consumer prices from 4·0 per cent to 1·8 per cent and, more important, of wholesale prices from 4·6 per cent to 0·8 per cent reflects great credit on the efforts of the authorities towards the maintenance of growth at the same time as the curbing of inflation. But, as the Minister of Finance has indicated by his budget policies, these are no grounds for complacency. The country's vulnerability to inflation continues and has been accentuated by the substantial inflow of capital during the first four months of this year."

At a time of political disturbances in many parts of the world, asserted MR. H. F. OPPENHEIMER of *Anglo American Corporation of South Africa Limited* (Johannesburg, June 14), it was satisfactory that in South Africa conditions remained stable, that the confidence of overseas investors had improved and that the hostility felt in many countries towards South Africa had sensibly diminished.

"This improvement," he went on, "does not reflect approval of the South African policy of racial separation. It is rather a reaction to racial disturbances in the United States, tensions over non-white immigration in Britain, and continued evidence of instability in some of the African states. There is also a belief in some quarters—which some will think is based on wishful thinking—that the South African Government's racial policy has become more flexible and relaxed. At home, however, these indications of relaxation seem to be contradicted by the Government's expressed intention of intensifying and tightening its policy of removing large numbers of Africans from the urban areas. For businessmen this policy must be a cause of uncertainty and concern. It is difficult to know how seriously it should be taken. If it were implemented fully the effects on industrial development would undoubtedly be adverse and far-reaching. So far all available statistics indicate that development within the Bantu homelands is negligible while that in the border areas adjoining the homelands is not very great and, in any case, is taking place chiefly in the immediate neighbourhood of existing cities. It is by now clearly understood that the Government wishes the political development of the different racial groups to take place along separate lines, but surely it should still be possible to find an acceptable formula which recognizes that a substantial, permanently urbanized African population exists and must continue to exist. This recognition is necessary not only for the sake of our economic development, but also because

221

it would be seen both here and abroad as a realistic acceptance of the actual situation and a practical step forward in race relations.

"It seems to me that a new emphasis in South African policy could combine with the change in the climate of world opinion so as to diminish to a considerable extent the estrangement between South Africa and the great western democracies."

COLONEL W. H. WHITBREAD, who had reported a year previously that *Whitbread and Company Limited* (September 6) had just begun trading from its brewery in South Africa with two products, stated that they had launched two new lines during the year and its trade was 40 per cent up. However, because of the extra duty of 5d. a pint which was "slapped on by the South African Government practically the day we opened," this would be an uphill battle, as the total beer trade in South Africa, which was buoyant before that duty, had now stabilized. "It does not look," he concluded, "as if we shall make profits for some time yet," but, with the growing prosperity in South Africa this "must surely be a good investment for the future."

The board of *Metal Closures Group Limited* (June 26), according to MR. KEITH D. ERSKINE, had been aware for some time of the friendly local interest in the progress of the company's South African enterprise, and during the year it was decided to give investors in the Republic an opportunity to participate in its fortunes and thus increase the local goodwill. Accordingly, 555,000 shares were issued to South African investors at 78 cents a share, thereby, as Mr. Erskine put it, "providing new funds for expansion." He added:

> "A further 45,000 shares have been made available under an option scheme to local staff at the same price. When these options have been fully exercised the Group will hold a 77 per cent interest in the equity of Metal Closures Group South Africa Limited. This business, which follows broadly the product ranges of the United Kingdom organization, is taking vigorous advantage of the expanding South African economy."

In April, 1968, *Inchcape & Co. Limited* (October 30) acquired a majority holding in the Motor & Engineering Company of Ethiopia Limited, a small trading company in Ethiopia, stated LORD INCHCAPE, who added that the group had not operated in that country before. However, the board believed that the possibilities of expansion there were good.

MIDDLE EAST

The unfortunate repercussions of the Arab/Israeli conflict in June, 1967, it was recorded in the annual report of *Inchcape & Co, Limited* (October 30), were reflected in the Gulf in a temporary

upset of the general pattern of trading. However, the position was soon stabilized, and the group continued to enjoy good relationships with the Arab states. Trading results improved, and the outlook was described as encouraging. Among other territories in the Middle East the following reports were made:

"In Iran, trading conditions also improved and revenue from shipping and tanker agency activities increased. The establishment of Bandar Mah Shahr in place of Abadan as the export terminal for refined products is now complete. A new port has been constructed at Bandar Abbas, which will facilitate developments in that area.

"In Bahrein, Gray, Mackenzie & Co. Ltd. improved its trading position and the Bahrein Slipway Co. Ltd. continued to work to capacity throughout the year.

"In Dubai, development continues apace and the calls on the company's resources for marine craft have been heavy, and will be maintained. The export of oil is expected to commence towards the end of 1969 and will bring added prosperity to this progressive State.

"In Abu Dhabi, development is making rapid strides and the company has ordered new craft to meet present and future requirements here and elsewhere on the Trucial Coast.

"In Sharjah, the new deep water pier is expected to be in operation in the latter part of 1968."

The Cyprus Cement Company Limited, in which *The Tunnel Portland Cement Company Limited* (September 12) has an important interest, was stated by Mr. C. HAGERUP to have worked to full capacity through the year, and demand continued on a high level. Profits had been well maintained, but the company was now feeling the effect of cost increases brought about by devaluation of the Cyprus currency and the closure of the Suez Canal.

FAR EAST

In Japan, MR. MALCOLM E. COOPER of *Allied Suppliers Limited* (June 7) reported, imports of tea were liberalized, and the company, with the assistance of its Japanese associates, considerably increased its shipments to that country. Incidentally, he recorded a further remarkable increase in the sale of tea bags, and the figure was running at the rate of 400m. tea bags a year.

Thailand's exports for 1967 again fell below imports, stated SIR DENYS LOWSON of the *Anglo-Thai Corporation Limited* (December 4), but, as in previous years, the deficit had been offset by money coming into the country from the tourist industry and for maintenance of United States bases. At the end of the year Thailand's foreign exchange reserves stood at U.S.\$876m., an increase of about 20 per cent on the year. He added:

"The United Kingdom's share of Thailand's import trade was fractionally lower; but the Group improved slightly its proportion of these imports from the United Kingdom, due primarily to the high demand for tractor and automotive products."

Included in the same statement by SIR DENYS LOWSON was the following reference to Indonesia:

"Experience over a period of 18 months indicated that the chances of covering the heavy cost of maintaining a separate organization in Djakarta would be slight for some time to come, and in May of this year we decided to withdraw our Representative. However, we still maintain the nucleus of an organization and are ready to add to this immediately prospects appear to justify such a step."

A number of chairmen reported the return to their companies of properties which had been taken over by the Indonesian authorities. The next quotation, from MR. J. F. E. GILCHRIST's statement for *Harrisons & Crosfield Limited* (December 10), applies equally to several other companies:

"During the first half of 1968 agreements were signed with the Indonesian Government in Djakarta providing for the return to us of all our properties in Indonesia. Offices and godowns are now under our control, but we have not yet secured vacant possession of some of the houses which we own.

"After an interval of four years estates under our agency have also been restored to their owners and comprise nearly 100,000 acres planted mainly with rubber and oil palms. Although insufficient funds were available during our absence for upkeep and essential fertilizers, our representatives were able to satisfy themselves that the estates were in a viable state. Since reoccupation substantial progress has been made and rehabilitation is proceeding smoothly.

"Prospects for general trading are being studied. Meantime a start has been made in certain specific lines."

Similarly, MR. D. R. N. CLARKE told members of the *British-American Tobacco Company Limited* (March 14) that a satisfactory agreement was reached with the Indonesian Government (which he had mentioned a year previously had offered to return the Indonesian subsidiary it had taken under control in 1964 to British-American). "We re-assumed control in May last [1967]," he added; "considerable rehabilitation will be required before the business can be expected to contribute significantly to group profits, but progress to date is satisfactory."

AGRICULTURE

THE high level of activity of the *Agricultural Mortgage Corporation Limited* (June 12) recorded in the preceding year was continued throughout the 12 months ended March 31, 1968, stated MR. J. P. R. GLYN. Having completed loans of £21,300,000 during this period, A.M.C. was overdrawn with its bankers to the extent of £15,600,000, and in addition there were loans awaiting completion amounting to £8,300,000. The need for a further issue of debentures was therefore obvious, he declared. As regards the high level of interest rates, he made this statement:

"The decrease in long term interest rates which allowed the lending rate to be reduced to $7\frac{1}{2}$ per cent in April, 1967, did not last long and it was necessary to increase the rate on August 22 by $\frac{1}{4}$ per cent to $7\frac{3}{4}$ per cent, by $\frac{1}{4}$ per cent to 8 per cent on November 17 and by $\frac{1}{2}$ per cent to $8\frac{1}{2}$ per cent on December 8; this rate of $8\frac{1}{2}$ per cent remained current for the rest of the year. Interest charges of this order present a considerable problem to the farming industry."

Incidentally, an increase of £34,569 in instalments in arrear (£156,668) Mr. Glyn attributed almost entirely to "efforts which have been made to assist any borrower whose business has been affected by the disastrous foot and mouth disease epidemic."

Group profits and the dividend of *Smithfield & Zwanenberg Group Limited* were alike higher, but MR. J. G. CLARFELT in his statement (*The Times*, August 1) reported that the year had seen the worst epidemic of foot and mouth disease in the history of this country. This outbreak, he asserted, had been largely responsible for the abnormally difficult conditions under which many of the group companies had had to operate—difficulties which were heightened by the dock strikes.

It is a far cry from foodstuffs to betting, but *Mark Lane (Turf Accountant) Limited* was also affected by the foot and mouth epidemic, the report of the directors (*The Times*, June 12) pointing out that the prevalence of the disease eventually resulted in all horseracing being banned throughout December and January.

In his annual review for *Ranks Hovis McDougall Limited* (January 25) LORD RANK summed up the state of British agriculture in these terms:

"The past year has been an extremely difficult one for British agriculture because of its heavy dependence on credit facilities and because livestock and poultry producers have been faced for some time with diminished returns. It is to be hoped, however,

that the more favourable Annual Price Review last year was an indication that encouragement is to be given by the Government to reverse these trends."

Incidentally, he mentioned, as an important event for the company during the year, the successful launch in June of high-quality cereal seeds under the RHM brand.

Although the contribution from non-malting operations to earnings of *Associated British Maltsters Limited*, it appeared from MR. DAVID L. NICOLSON's statement (*The Times*, December 17), was double that of the previous year, the malting division still contributed by far the largest part of profits. Difficulties facing the industry still persisted, he stated, and "the appalling weather this summer has resulted in a difficult and expensive harvest with a most considerable drop in yield."

The following comments on the Australian beef and veal industry are taken from SIR DENYS LOWSON's review for the *Australian Estates Company Limited* (July 8):

"The beef and veal industry makes a substantial contribution to Australian export income and was listed as the third biggest export earner after wool and wheat for 1966–67, earning some $A198 million. Of the 246,000 tons of beef and veal which were exported the American market took some 76 per cent or 178,000 tons, which compared with only 40,000 tons going to the United Kingdom.

"The significant features of the year were the continuing strong market in the U.S.A., the drop in exports to the United Kingdom and Europe, and a steady market in Japan as well as other Asian countries. Australia herself consumed some 447,000 tons of beef during the year, averaging about 86lb. per head, so that the local market requires some two-thirds of the total production. We calculate that within the foreseeable future there will only be a very limited amount available for export, most of what is produced at the time being required for home consumption—a phenomenon which is already being seen in the Argentine."

SIR RICHARD TREHANE, addressing the annual meeting of the *Milk Marketing Board* (July 25), regretted that formal restrictions upon the board's ability to assist producers whose herds fell victim to the prolonged outbreak of foot and mouth had so far been insuperable. That it was possible to maintain the flow of milk to the consumer, he declared, was no more than would be expected of an experienced milk marketing organization. The size of the United Kingdom milk market is apparent from the figures cited in this extract from Sir Richard's address:

"During the past financial year nearly 1,500 of the 2,100 million gallons of milk coming from farms in England and Wales were used for liquid consumption. The liquid market thus

absorbs about 70 per cent of the milk supply. In Scotland and Northern Ireland it plays a less dominant part but, taking the United Kingdom as a whole, it still accounts for around two-thirds of the total output. It happens that these figures are almost exactly the same as in the year immediately before the war.

"The liquid market has been paramount in our industry for nearly a century. The production and marketing arrangements for milk which is to be consumed as such have to observe exacting standards and it is fair to say that the service which the British consumer now receives is the best in the world. Liquid milk is the milk producer's most remunerative outlet; at least during the twentieth century it has commanded a higher market realization than milk used for manufacture into milk products, and this was no doubt largely due to the absence of direct competition from imports of fresh milk—in contrast to the growing pressure of world supplies of dairy produce which found their way to the United Kingdom market."

The characteristic of the United Kingdom bacon market during 1967, asserted MR. F. HERBERT of the *Danish Bacon Company Limited* (May 15), was its great stability. Thus the total quantity of bacon supplied to the market, just over 600,000 tons from all sources, was virtually the same as in the preceding year; and, with no more than nine changes in price at first-hand level, 1967 proved to be one of the most stable years on record; the price of Danish "A" Selection averaged £320 a ton for the year, or within 1 per cent of the previous year's average. Danish shipments, he showed, were slightly up and accounted for half of the United Kingdom consumption and three-quarters of the total importation. But the effect of devaluation on the incomes of Danish producers was adverse, as the following extract from Mr. Herbert's review suggests:

"However, the hopes of what promised to be a reasonably satisfactory year from a producer's point of view were dashed by the devaluation of sterling in November. This was a severe blow to Danish producers and, although its impact was somewhat softened by the devaluation of the Danish kroner by 7·9 per cent, Danish producers suffered a significant reduction in earnings."

That *Spillers Limited* (June 7) would continue to play its significant part in the marketing of the United Kingdom cereal harvest was asserted by SIR ARCHIBALD FORBES, who added that, when deciding its purchasing policy for flour and feed mills, the company always had regard to the importance of utilizing the maximum quantity of home-grown grain.

In his report for *Midland Shires Farmers Limited* (February 24) MR. C. P. NORBURY disclosed that the sales of M.S.F. feeds in the year were 101,500 tons, up by 11½ per cent. During the year some

55,000 tons of grain were purchased from members and used in M.S.F. feeds. He continued:

"In the past five years no grains other than maize had been imported, and the grain content of the feeds had all come from members. Imports saved are exports gained—a theme very germane to our present national economic problems.

"The feed manufacturing activity was a logical development of the farm mixing approach, i.e. a large number of farmers combining to convert their grain crops into precision based feeds for their varied stock requirements. These are sold to them at competitive prices and the profits returned in proportion to the feed bought. The important feature was that farmers ran their own business, successfully operated three mills and secured the benefits of their co-operation."

In just six years, claimed MR. F. W. GRANT in a statement (*The Times*, May 14), *Golden Wonder Limited* had bitten off the lion's share of the potato crisp market. In 1967, he asserted, the company's volume share was 43 per cent of a market which had doubled during the last seven years. As showing the technical know-how of the company, he gave this account of an important development which had come through research into new methods of long-term potato storage:

"Although Golden Wonder are not potato growers, they have made themselves largely immune to potato price fluctuations by means of techniques which more than double the length of time potatoes can be kept in storage. Controlled storage methods ensure a constant supply of finest quality 'Record' potatoes and also provide protection against potato price increases which have caused the failure of many crisp manufacturers over the years. Golden Wonder have the largest potato stores in the U.K. Almost 70,000 tons can be stored at the company's three factories. The size of these stores vary from 50 ton Dutch bins to 8,000 ton bulk stores, and they all have full insulation, ventilation and temperature control."

Another instance of assistance to a branch of agriculture— sugar beet production this time—afforded through scientific research was mentioned by SIR EDMUND BACON in his valedictory statement for *British Sugar Corporation Limited* (February 27); the relevant passage is as follows:

"With regard to disease control, it has been calculated that virus yellows was responsible for a loss equivalent to one million tons of beet in 1957, and there is every reason to believe that similar heavy losses were incurred in earlier seasons. Thanks to the untiring efforts over the years of Dr. Raymond Hull and his staff, of Broom's Barn Experimental Station, systemic insecti-

cides are most effectively used to kill aphids which transmit the disease. As a result based upon daily inspection by our field staff, growers are now advised when to spray their crops, and the ready adoption of this service has provided effective control of the disease. This is an outstanding example of the aid of science to agriculture and losses from this source are now negligible when proper control measures are taken."

Announcing a strong recovery in profits of *David Miln & Co. (Seedsmen) Limited* (December 30), MR. GEORGE E. P. POLLITZER declared that it had been a satisfactory year for the company in spite of the effect of the epidemic of foot and mouth disease in this country. The parent company and its subsidiaries had enjoyed a keen demand for their products, and group sales had been at a record level in the face of strong price competition. Cereals and grasses and clovers had sold well, and a new genetic monogerm sugar beet seed made a successful debut on the commercial market.

At the annual meeting of the *British Egg Marketing Board* (December 3) MR. G. T. KIDNER regretted that the members of the board were not then in a position to know the Government's decisions on the future of the egg industry in the light of the report of the Reorganization Commission for Eggs. The board itself, he averred, was anxious to see changes, and he continued:

"A major difference between our policy and those of certain other organizations is that we feel that the effect of some of the changes proposed has been underestimated. In our view, it will be far better to make those changes that seem to be universally accepted and then pause to assess their effects, rather than be committed to all the changes at once.

"The one matter upon which all seem to be agreed is the need —the urgent need—for the obligation to stamp eggs to be removed. If, in order to facilitate this, it were necessary to change the egg subsidy, which is at present related to the number of first quality eggs handled by the Board, to a block grant, we would be prepared to accept this. Looking rather further ahead to the time when Government attitude towards methods of agricultural support might be changed, we feel that there should also be provision for the Board (or central organization) to raise a levy within the industry."

After examining the constitution and duties of the board, Mr. Kidner said that in preparing their proposals for the future the board had tried to consider the needs of the industry as a whole and to ignore sectional interests. They believed that the majority of egg producers, consumers and indeed the distributive trade would be best served by the continuance of a system of organized marketing of eggs. "This does not mean," he went on, "that we wish to perpetuate it in its existing form. . . . But it does mean that

we see in a free market a very real danger for all except the few who are foremost in clamouring for it."

In his statement for *Allied Farm Foods Limited* (October 9) MR. ERIC REED, after referring to higher profits and an increased dividend, gave this account of the year's trading experience of the company:

"Prices for finished chicken continued at low levels to April, 1968, but increases in volume and efficiency made the maintenance of adequate margins possible. A number of factors interact with chicken prices, but an unusually large rate of industry growth during 1967 is undoubtedly the dominant feature. The indications are that 1968 will see a compensating reduction in growth rate and an associated improvement in margins. The output of our various products continues to expand in all departments including chickens, turkeys, pigs and feeding stuffs."

In his additional remarks at the annual meeting Mr. Reed said that chicken prices to date had not recovered from the large expansion of national production during 1967. Margins continued to be adequate, however, and he hoped for an improvement towards the end of the year. In spite of low prices, he added, the first half year's figures would be at least as good as for the same period of the past year, and he expected "a satisfactory outcome for the year as a whole."

The board of *Grossmith Agricultural Industries Limited* (October 31), MR. N. GROSSMITH remarked in the annual report, would be disappointed if there were not a further increase in group profit in the current year. He also stated:

"The Foods Company and our poultry processing and broiler unit at St. Ives both produced higher profits and an expansion programme is under way. There was a slight reduction in the profits of the farming companies because of lower egg prices. Without anticipating the Government's decisions on the Report of the Reorganisation Commission for Eggs, we believe that the prospects for efficient, low cost producers are favourable and our future development plans include an expansion of egg production."

BUILDING AND PROPERTY

THE development of non-residential property was still hampered and frustrated by controls, asserted MR. GERALD GLOVER of *The City of London Real Property Company Limited* (July 2). He continued:

"The Control of Office and Industrial Development Act, 1965, inhibits the necessary replacement of worn-out buildings and so long as this Act remains in force the construction of the new offices so badly needed in the City of London will be much curtailed. However, your company will continue to seek licences for the improvement of the buildings on its estate to ensure that it continues to provide as high a standard of accommodation as is possible."

Regional Properties Limited (October 3), MR. BERNARD SUTTON stated, had had about 2½ years' experience of the 1965 Rent Act (now consolidated by the 1968 Rent Act with earlier rent control legislation which dated back to the First World War). The level of the company's rents registered under the "fair rent" formula continued to be generally satisfactory and had further confirmed the view he had previously expressed that the rents of the group's residential flats were reasonable. He added:

"In addition to the restraints imposed by the Prices and Incomes policy as stated in various White Papers, new powers have been included in the recently enacted Prices and Incomes Act enabling the Government in certain circumstances to make Regulations to phase increases in residential rents which are already subject to the Rent Act controls. We do not anticipate that these Regulations will adversely affect our income."

In his statement (*The Times*, October 28) for *Alliance Property Holdings Limited* MAJOR G. L. WEBB reported that rent officers' decisions under the 1965 Rent Act had been favourable to the group, demonstrating its fair and reasonable attitude as landlords. Considerable increases, he asserted, could be expected when the second part of the Act, covering older controlled properties, was implemented.

The directors of *J. Lyons & Company Limited* (July 16) believed the current market value of the group's freehold and leasehold properties to be approximately £54m., or 2¼ times the value at which they stood in the balance-sheet, according to MR. GEOFFREY SALMON, who added that about a fifth of all the properties were at

that time let to tenants outside the group. In the following extract (in part) he explained the company's policy on properties:

"There are three basic considerations underling our property policy: first, it affords the advantages inherent in owning the freeholds of properties in which we trade, secondly it adds to the company's financial stability, and thirdly it is profitable. The value of our properties appreciates year by year (though not necessarily at an even rate) and in course of time this growth has added very substantially to the net worth of the Group. Only part of the benefit is reflected in the profit and loss account, and this feature of property investment will always affect the overall rate of return earned by a company like ours with a large proportion of its assets in property."

The board of *London County Freehold and Leasehold Properties Limited* (July 22), MR. C. W. SHELFORD stated, had decided to offer to its tenants the opportunity to buy long leases of their flats wherever the demand would justify this. The substantial sums which under this policy would become available to the company would be invested in suitable commercial retail and industrial properties and developments with the object of increasing the revenue of the company and of improving the character and balance of the property portfolio as a whole.

Another company which is disposing of its residential properties is *Rodwell Group Limited*. This had already been achieved in respect of a minor portion of the residential portfolio, which realized nearly £½m., MR. JOHN S. COHEN revealed in his annual review (*The Times*, December 4), and the board hoped to realize a further £1½m. from the remaining residential properties; they also intended to dispose of a number of small shop and commercial properties. He commented:

"When these disposals have been completed the company will be left with a portfolio consisting chiefly of (a) large office blocks (b) parades of shops with upper parts (c) substantial commercial units and (d) sites for future development. The properties to be retained are broadly spread across the country but with more than 80% in value in the London and Home Counties area. At the end of our current development programme coupled with the re-shaping of your company's property holdings and the completion of developments now in the pipeline, the Group's portfolio will be of the highest calibre with undoubted growth prospects for the years ahead."

At the end of the financial year, MR. C. E. M. HARDIE recalled to members of *Metropolitan Estate and Property Corporation Limited* (December 19), an old-established property company, The Metropolitan Railway Surplus Lands Company, had been acquired. Its main assets consisted of investment properties similar

to those of Metropolitan Estate, together with a number of developments.

MR. A. W. RICHARDSON gave an account of the circumstances in which the Aston Road factory site was lost to *Rippingilles Limited* (January 31); the paragraph in question follows:

"The major part of the Aston Road factory site was acquired for the development of the Aston Expressway by Birmingham Corporation in October, 1967, at a price of £275,000. However, the factory will continue to function on the site for some time and compensation for trading and other losses incurred in any re-siting will be the subject of future claims. This is almost the end of a story which began with the publication of the plans for the building of a road through the middle of our then newly built and equipped press shop and toolroom! I have already referred to the damage that knowledge of the proposed development has done to labour recruitment. In addition, we have lost nearly two-thirds of our older staff in the last two years, most of whom were employed on oil heater production. Yet again, contractors have not unreasonably sought assurances that we would be able to fulfil our subcontracting orders, and it may well be that we have been refused long-term contracts. Is it any wonder that we have come to refer to the building of the Aston Expressway as our 'development blight'? Fortunately, we have made contingency plans for re-siting the factory and now the purchase price has been received these are being re studied in the light of present trading conditions. I hope I may be allowed to defer detailed comment on this matter although it is a vital factor as regards the company's future. It will be the subject of a special report to be made to shareholders as soon as possible."

To *The Artizans' & General Properties Company Limited* (June 19) Pembroke House, Croydon, had been a source of concern, said MR. DAVID E. WEBB, but since the turn of the year, he was able to report, 11 out of 19 floors had been let and further floors were under negotiation.

"We believe this property," he declared, "to have been an outstanding example of the malaise which affected the country last year. It is a good building on a first-class site and until recently, the only thing wrong was a complete absence of prospective occupiers. Apart from Pembroke, voids are currently running at 2 per cent of the total rent roll."

In his statement (*The Times*, August 21) for *Greenhaven Securities Limited* MR. R. H. MACWILLIAM drew attention to "a significant change in the property market during the past year." He stated:

"The increasing desire of institutions, particularly 'gross funds', to purchase first class properties has meant that demand has exceeded supply in this field and prices have risen to a degree where the property company, which suffers tax, can no longer compete in this investment market. Your Group through the expansion of its house building activities and through a new subsidiary, Greenhaven Management Services Ltd., which provides technical and management services to a number of institutions and pension funds, is endeavouring to adjust itself to these changed circumstances."

Reminding members of *Capital & Counties Property Company Limited* (July 29) that a year previously he had stated that it would be difficult to imagine a more frustrating year for property companies than that from which they had then emerged, MR. LESLIE MARLER now declared that he had then been guilty of some lack of imagination! "There is little doubt," he declared, "that in the minds of our Socialist masters the private landlord is Public Enemy No. 1."

Eastrail Property Company, which was managed by City of London Real Property and in which *Edger Investments Limited* (July 19) would hold a 49 per cent interest, was negotiating terms of the lease and ground rent with British Railways for the development of Southend (Victoria). MR. DESMOND A. REID told Edger shareholders that the work was expected to start in late 1969, subject to a revised outline planning consent being obtained.

An interesting point in MR. SYDNEY MASON's statement (*The Times*, June 18) for *The Hammerson Property & Investment Trust Limited* was that during 1967 the company had taken a further step forward in the overseas field by the formation of an association with a Dutch development company to undertake joint developments on the Continent; the first project, an office development in Amsterdam, was then being formulated.

The prevailing lack of confidence among business men led MR. R. W. DIGGENS of *Allnatt London Properties Limited* (September 12) to declare:

"I had to refer last year to the fact that business confidence was lacking, and that trade conditions were worsening. The country has since faced devaluation and a Budget exacting record sums. Perhaps inevitably, these drastic remedies seem to have added in these first months to the uncertainties of the present situation, and to have done little in a general way to revive confidence and to encourage effort. Pressure on the company's resources has as a result eased to some extent, and, taking everything into account, the company's rate of progress in the immediate future, whilst expected to be good, may be disappointing by comparison with the past.

"Valuable contracts in hand will certainly produce substantial

additions to rental income spread over the next 18 months. Other important developments are in the balance."

That *Oddenino's Property and Investment Company Limited* was finalizing plans in Brussels for an office building costing just over £1m. sterling was stated by the chairman in his annual review (*The Times*, October 18). This transaction would be fully financed locally.

Since the Leasehold Reform Act, 1967, took effect on January 1, 1968, only 121 claims for freeholds had been presented to the agents in Cardiff of *Western Ground Rents Limited* (June 24), MR. A. H. CARNWATH announced.

Future policy of *Cornwall Property Holdings Limited* (October 21) is the subject of the following quotation from MR. E. C. MARSLAND's statement:

"Looking to the future we hope to become more interested and involved in development and your company has been engaged for some considerable time in negotiations for the construction of a purpose-built equipment and office building for the Post Office, to be erected in the air space over the canal adjoining Newhall Street. This development will be carried out in conjunction with a prominent insurance company."

Continuing the policy of reducing the proportion of residential investment by *The Berkeley Property and Investment Company Limited*, MR. H. N. SPORBORG in his statement (*The Times*, December 17) asserted that only commercial developments were now being undertaken in this country. He added that earnings in North America increased during the year, and that a new development in Florida was expected to have an impact on future earnings.

Among the points made in his statement (*The Times*, December 9) for *Estates Property Investment Company Limited* MR. A. R. PERRY included the following:

"During the year, further sales of property have been effected and the residential content of the company's investments is now negligible; the remaining properties in this category will be disposed of as rapidly as possible in accordance with the Board's declared intention. I have no doubt that, although over the past year or two, this action has somewhat restrained the company's growth, it has given a much stronger foundation which should be beneficial in future years."

Rental income on all the estates of *Slough Estates Limited* (May 22) in the United Kingdom had continued to increase, mainly from renewal of leases and new construction, stated LT.-COL. W. H. KINGSMILL. The purchase of 17 acres of freehold land on the Monkton Road Industrial Estate, Wakefield, Yorkshire, had

been completed, but because of delays in obtaining approval under the building regulations construction did not start during the year as envisaged. The company's interests overseas continued to progress.

Among developments that were completed by *St. Martins Property Corporation Limited* during the year MR. J. E. LLOYD in his review (*The Times*, August 27) singled out as the principal one that of the second phase of Winchester House. He claimed that this property was a notable addition to the new buildings in the City of London, and stated that it was now fully let, but while it would increase earnings of the company in 1968–69 its full benefit would not be felt until the following year.

Net rental revenue, trading profits, net profits both before and after tax, and the dividend of *Haslemere Estates Limited* were all higher on the year, and MR. F. E. CLEARY in his review (*The Times*, July 9) forecast that net rental revenue for 1968–69 would increase substantially, and that trading profits should at least be maintained. He was confident that with the current demand for offices in the City and Central London the profitable expansion of the group would continue.

A definition of the policy of *Canal-Randolph Corporation* (New York, March 13) was included in the statement by MR. WALTER H. SALOMON, chairman of the board, and MR. RAYMOND FRENCH, president, and is subjoined:

> "Canal-Randolph owns and operates a diversified group of real estate properties located throughout the United States. These investments include residential property, office buildings, industrial parks, parking garages as well as $3,528,000 of undeveloped land at book cost. The policy of your company has been to acquire and operate prime properties for long term investment in the fastest growing metropolitan areas of the United States. Demand for space in Canal-Randolph's buildings continued to be strong in 1967. As a result, your company's real estate properties were operated at very close to full capacity."

CONSTRUCTION

The value of work executed by *George Wimpey & Co. Limited* (May 3) was a record £190m., compared with £180m. in the previous year, but to get that done SIR GODFREY MITCHELL declared that "we were almost washed away by the flood of paperwork which resulted from recent legislation and regulations." The group completed a total of 30,916 homes in the United Kingdom, the highest number it had ever achieved.

The total turnover of *Richard Costain Limited* (June 27) and its subsidiaries for 1967 was £68m., and in addition the group pro-

portion of the turnover of associated companies was another £4m. Profits were substantially higher before tax and less substantially higher after tax. But MR. A. P. COSTAIN stated:

"At home the volume of work available in the private sector continued to be adversely affected by lack of confidence and uncertainty in the economy. Margins remained narrow and although increased site efficiency and reduced overheads resulted in better trading results than last year, further improvement is necessary."

In a difficult year MR. FRANK TAYLOR considered an increase of 13·8 per cent to £74m. in group turnover of *Taylor Woodrow Limited* (June 10), excluding associated companies, together with higher profits, to be "not unsatisfactory." The promptitude with which the group completed an important contract led him to make the following comment:

"Our constant attention to the importance to our clients of construction speed was typified by the handing-over in December of the £2¼m. Daventry Parts Depot to the Ford Motor Company Limited. Commissioned to design and to construct this building with all its services in 52 weeks, we completed two weeks ahead of schedule."

Mr. Taylor also declared that it was essential that more areas of land should be released in suitable districts to allow for the erection of houses by private enterprise at economic prices in sufficient numbers to meet the demand.

Confidence in the future of the group controlled by *Bovls Holdings Limited*, after a year in which profits were greatly increased, is clearly shown in the following quotation from MR. H. VINCENT'S statement (*The Times*, May 27):

"I have spoken about our various activities during the year 1967. The Industry will bear considerably increased costs, notably from the swingeing increase in the Selective Employment Tax. Nevertheless, the services we provide are in demand from the community and our growth in the past has been achieved as a result of providing good value for money. Your Board is confident that the results for the year ending December 31, 1968, will show a marked improvement on those for the year under review and believes that the momentum towards higher profits will be maintained in future years."

Progress in overcoming the effects of Government restrictions was reported by COLONEL A. C. NEWMAN, V.C., for *W. & C. French Limited* (May 31). He said:

"A general review of our trading operations shows that to a great extent they have been influenced by the effects of Govern-

ment legislation. Restriction on office development in the London area, although of itself not having a direct impact on the Constructional Industries, was accompanied in the event by a drastic curtailment of all types of industrial development. Furthermore, there appeared to be an attempt to halt the population drift to the South East as a result of which an area that had been this company's main sphere of operations for many years, then became one of intense competition. As a result of this and other factors there became an urgent need to enlarge our sphere of contracting geographically, whilst at the same time instituting a comprehensive programme of rationalization. This considerable readjustment has needed time to take effect due to the phasing out of contract commitments, but I am pleased to tell you that last autumn saw a check in the downward trend of profitability and our order book is now much more healthy and infinitely better balanced than it has been for several years. Profit margins in the future are unlikely to match those prevailing some years ago, but a steady increase in turnover, to which we can now look forward, should also be accompanied by a corresponding increase in overall profits and with work already in hand this situation should prevail throughout this current trading year and well into next."

The rate of turnover of *Tilbury Contracting Group Limited* had been well maintained in spite of continuing difficult conditions in the construction industry, MR. H. R. TAYLOR declared in his annual review (*The Times*, May 21). Orders in hand in most sectors were higher than those of a year before, he added, and while it was not expected that serious delays or cancellations would be experienced in respect of those orders, in the current uncertain economic situation it could not be foreseen how far the flow of future work would be affected.

In his additional remarks to shareholders in *Erith & Company Limited* (May 23) MR. E. J. ERITH referred to the problems inherent in giving credit to builders in current difficult circumstances. He said:

"Credit still gives us much cause for concern. It is perhaps not generally realized that much private house building is carried out by builders working on contract prices for developers. Because of high land prices and the desire to keep house prices low enough to ensure quick sales, developers are offering contracts to builders on terms which only enable the most efficient to make a profit. The less efficient, almost invariably working on borrowed money at high interest rates, too easily run into difficulties to the disadvantage of their creditors. In addition, the practice of many Local Authorities in accepting the lowest tenders submitted at impossible prices frequently leads to failures which benefit nobody."

238

Thomas Warrington & Sons Limited (May 23) were successful in obtaining many contracts from local authorities and industrial concerns during the year under review, and in his statement MR. VINCENT WARRINGTON announced that at the end of 1967 the value of contracts in hand, together with private enterprise building, exceeded £10m. At the meeting he added:

"Since my statement was published the company has been successful in securing further contracts, mainly with local authorities, to the value of over £1m. The company's work in hand is at its highest ever level and the prospects of obtaining further work are quite good."

For *The Cementation Company Limited* (September 30) the year to March, 1968, was a period of further growth which, MR. H. A. LONGDEN claimed, "confirmed our position as the largest specialist contractor in the United Kingdom and saw us on the way to achieving that status in Europe as a whole." He continued:

"We have always followed a policy of specialization and the addition of the special skills of The Cleveland Bridge & Engineering Company Limited, which became a Group subsidiary in October, 1967, will complement those of the rest of the Group. Cleveland undertake heavy steel fabrication and erection for such structures as power stations, steelworks, and viaducts. An example is the recently completed £4m. Tinsley Viaduct at Sheffield."

Including the appropriate share of associated companies' turnover, group turnover of *John Mowlem & Company Limited* had increased by 26 per cent to £33½m. This was stated by MR. E. C. BECK in his annual review (*The Times*, May 29), and he added that the total value of projects now in hand in Mowlem (Building) Limited was approximately £29m.

Record profits and an increased dividend marked the year for *E. Fletcher Builders Limited* (September 12), according to MR. EDWARD FLETCHER, who added:

"The expansion to which I referred last year will continue to produce increased benefits. We completed more than 1,200 houses during the year under review, a proportion of which were for municipal and other agencies. The demand for our products shows steady improvement and sales forward indicate that the expansion we have programmed will be needed to meet demand."

Truscon Limited (April 29) returned to profitability in 1967, and MR. ROBIN BROOK stated that the remedial action taken by the board had resulted in improved trading in all divisions. As

regards the cash flow, he asserted that retained profits and depreciation together with tighter cost control had made possible a reduction in short-term borrowings of approximately £1m.

Chansom Limited, MR. H. J. T. CHANNING recalled in his review (*The Times*, August 26), obtained a Stock Exchange quotation in February, 1968, and he was pleased to report group profits before taxation for the year ended March, 1968, of £235,731, compared with the forecast of "not less than £215,000." The company, by vigorous action, had maintained its land bank at a high level, he added.

In his statement (*The Times*, January 11) for *Page-Johnson Builders Limited* MR. V. H. JOHNSON included these paragraphs:

"It is a pity that British Governments have not done more to help house purchasers. The pride of owning one's own home does much to stiffen a man's sturdy independence—it is a goal worth working and saving for. It is unbelievable that any Government should continue a vast scheme of Council housing which is such a load around the tax-payer's neck and results in such unloved and monotonous acres of rubber-stamped dullness.

"Every set of accounts since the flotation of the company in 1960 has shown a new peak in profits."

The volume of work carried out by *Drury Holdings Limited* (October 25) reached a record for the group, MR. R. A. GROCOCK reported, and there was a further increase in profit. In the local authority sector, he added, the volume of work in hand was larger than a year before, and the demand for houses on the group's own private estates remained high. While the mortgage situation was causing some difficulty, this was largely being overcome thanks to the company's "excellent association with the leading building societies."

The year under review had seen a marked increase in the scale of activities of the building companies belonging to *North British Properties Limited* (January 9), stated MR. JOHN BELL, who also reported that substantial stocks of land were held levy free, and that the current year had started well.

Record pre-tax profits were announced by MR. R. T. WARDLE in his review (*The Times*, March 29) for *The Arthur Wardle Group Limited*; and already 75 per cent of the 1968 housing output had been sold.

A large proportion of the profits (substantially increased on the year) of *The Greaves Organisation Limited* (October 1), MR. E. I. WHEATLEY averred, was still earned from building lower-priced private houses for sale. He also stated that land had been acquired in the London commuter belt and in the Southampton area in order to expand the company's activities in this direction.

Dealing with the need of *C. S. Wiggins & Sons Limited* (Novem-

ber 16) to extend the area of the group's activities, MR. C. C. WIGGINS commented:

"Within the group itself we have acquired substantial additional land in East Anglia, where we are expecting to build extensively in the future. We have now agreed terms for the acquisition of the whole of the issued share capital of F. C. Fairhead Limited, building contractors and estate developers, of Alresford, Hampshire. This acquisition will give us not only an efficiently run business which will make a valuable contribution to the Group profit, but it will also provide a basis for the further expansion of the Group's activities in one of the fastest developing areas of the South of England. The Group will now be capable of covering an area from Dorset to the Wash and we have every reason to be confident of the future."

LORD STRADBROKE did not expect that any recent legislation would have an adverse effect on the activities of *Daejan Holdings Limited* (November 27), although the Prices and Incomes Act would slow down the expected increase in investment income. On the other hand, the White Paper on old houses, if implemented, should help the group to improve and maintain in much better order than had hitherto been practicable properties whose controlled rents were held at quite uneconomic levels.

INDUSTRIALIZED BUILDING

Included in the remarks by LORD ABERCONWAY on the building division of *English China Clays Limited* (March 18) was the following paragraph:

"The Sub-contracting Department during the year procured the erection of 2,834 dwellings and secured orders for 3,138. In so doing, it made good progress in promoting its two main industrialized building systems, the XW (Crosswall) and the Rationalized Traditional. Both were shown to be popular with Local Authorities and economic to build. Substantial contracts were secured during the year and the order book is healthy. Design and development work continues on new types of dwelling and on construction methods. Introduction of the metric system to our designs is being studied."

Referring, in his statement (*The Times*, July 5) for *Higgs & Hill Limited*, to the formation in the previous year of Fram, Higgs & Hill (Camus) Limited in conjunction with The Fram Group Limited to exploit the Camus system of industrialized building in the Greater London area, SIR REX COHEN stated that the factory (which was built by the group's construction companies) had been in production for some months. Contracts worth nearly £14m. were now in progress.

241

In the industrialized building sector of *Sir Lindsay Parkinson & Co. Limited* (July 24), stated MR. A. E. PARKINSON, the Parkwall system had secured further substantial contracts aggregating some £4m. He added that traditional building contracts amounting to some £6m. had been obtained.

Among the points made by MR. H. V. HALLAM in his statement (*The Times*, May 29) for *Vic Hallam Limited* was the following:

"I have commented more than once on the effect that the lack of industrialized housing orders has had on our budgeted activity, but with orders now available this factor should be corrected to a considerable extent during 1968. Our two main timber building systems—Derwent and Type 6—continue to enjoy popularity on merit; their tender conversion factor points without doubt to our leadership position in this field."

MR. D. D. MORRELL included this paragraph in his review for *Mitchell Construction Holdings Limited* (July 18):

"We embarked upon the manufacture of industrialized housing units only after careful and prolonged consideration, and our Mitchell Camus factory, opened in July 1967 by Dr. Dickson Mabon, Minister of State, Scottish Office, is working exceptionally well. Over 250 dwellings have been erected on our first site in Airdrie and work is in progress on the first stage of the Gowkthrapple Development for the Burgh of Motherwell and Wishaw, involving 722 houses and associated works."

Commenting on the industrialized housing activities of *Concrete Limited* (August 2), MR. K. M. WOOD stated:

"It is of particular interest that of almost ten thousand dwellings for which we expect to complete the structures in Bison Wall Frame in the current year over half will be in low and medium rise schemes. We do not consider that the recent criticism of industrialised building is likely to affect us to any important extent. There are however signs in some parts of the country that the housing drive has passed its peak earlier than expected and we are carefully re-examining the prospects in this field for 1969/1970."

As regards the building division of *G. & J. Weir Holdings Limited* LORD WEIR in his annual review (*The Times*, May 7) said that the board would like to see more rapid acceptance of the group's Multicom system of industrialized housing. He found it frustrating that acceptance of such an obvious solution to the national housing problem should be so slow, "although our many years' experience in building should perhaps have conditioned us to the difficulties of introducing changes into this very conservative market."

242

The next quotation comes from MR. H. DARE'S review for *Dares Estates Limited* (June 6):

"Dare System Building Limited specialize in the provision of housing for Local Authorities. This company has been appointed sole licensee for eleven counties for Open System Buildings Limited. The system combines rationalized site construction with pre-planned components and our company has been awarded a contract of a value of £470,000 to construct the first phase of a project of a value of £2m. for a housing scheme for the City of Chester."

In the public sector the work of *John McLean & Sons Limited* (February 22) continued to grow, MR. J. G. McLEAN declared. Major new contracts had been obtained in the MACTRAD system, which he claimed was now one of the main timber-framed building systems in the United Kingdom.

MATERIALS

The year's trading experience of *The Associated Portland Cement Manufacturers Limited* (July 4) was summarized in the following extract from the statement by SIR JOHN REISS:

"Demand proved to be rather more buoyant last year than was generally expected and our deliveries at home increased by just under 5 per cent. This was indeed fortunate because it went some way towards mitigating the effects of the disappointingly small increase in price that we were allowed by the Prices and Incomes Board last August after nearly seven months of investigation into the Industry's affairs.

"The problem of over-production was with us throughout the year and we were only able to reactivate a small proportion of the old plant that was closed towards the end of 1966. However, our ability to supply a higher proportion of the total demand from the well sited works at which production had been increased resulted in a satisfactory rate of profit per ton after meeting the standing charges on plant not in use. Our products other than cement had a reasonably good year in difficult conditions with the exception of our Sand and Gravel Division whose rate of profit was unsatisfactory owing to intense competition in the area in which we operate. We continue to supply substantial quantities of Oil Well Cement to those companies engaged in oil and gas exploration in the North Sea."

For *Rugby Portland Cement Company Limited* (May 24) SIR HALFORD REDDISH referred in his usual uninhibited way to the Prices and Incomes Board:

"Our Group deliveries were again a record: our productivity

243

per man-hour was increased by 6·5 per cent over 1966: and the profit per employee by 7·7 per cent. Costs continued to rise and were only partially offset by a small and quite inadequate increase in the price of cement of two shillings a ton in August 1967. A temporary surcharge to cover the increased cost of fuel oil also came into force on the same date.

"I referred last year to the National Board for Prices and Incomes. After a much extended period of gestation this peculiar body produced a report which went far beyond its terms of reference. Some of us are still trying to understand it. Discussions between the industry and the Ministry of Public Building and Works have been proceeding at a leisurely pace ever since."

Although the return on capital of *The Tunnel Portland Cement Company Limited* (September 12), according to MR. C. HAGERUP, had increased steadily since the all-time low figure of 10·1 per cent was recorded for 1965–66, he thought the position was still unsatisfactory and one of the principal tasks facing the board and management was to improve the percentage return. He also stated:

"With the cost of money at its present level and the incidence of Corporation Tax which makes capital raising by rights issues almost as expensive, it will be difficult for the industry in this country, so long as the present price structure prevails, to justify the capital expenditure that will be necessary if home production is to keep pace with the forecasts of future home consumption. There are, of course, economies still to be made and this involves a good deal of reorganization and change. A great deal has been done in this direction and I firmly believe that future results will continue to record improvements in our operating efficiencies."

Profits from the cement and quarry interests of *Thos. W. Ward Limited* (November 29) should be maintained, but, MR. H. W. SECKER asserted, unless some reasonable increase in cement prices was permitted it would be impossible to show a sensible return on the capital employed, and particularly in relation to the capital expenditure recently incurred on extensions.

Commenting on the trading experience of the parent undertaking of *London Brick Company Limited* (May 30), SIR RONALD STEWART reported a strong recovery in the demand for bricks in 1967, primarily the result of an increase in house building. He continued:

"Nearly 70 per cent of fletton bricks are used in new housing and in 1967 there were more houses started, more completed, and more in construction than ever before. In fact, housing starts were some 18 per cent higher than in the previous year,

the greater increase being in the private enterprise sector where the popularity of brick construction remained undiminished. In the public sector the effect of the Government's renewed emphasis on cost meant an increase in the use of traditional and rationalized traditional methods of building in low rise housing. Both sectors therefore contributed to a heavy and sustained demand for bricks throughout the year."

The provision of new types of brick was alluded to by MR. A. J. R. COWARD of *Marston Valley Brick Company Limited* (April 25):

"We added to our range of facing bricks and each of the three new types has been well received by the trade. Additional presses and other plant were installed in 1967 and we are awaiting delivery of equipment in order to be in a still better position to satisfy customer demand. It is hoped that when the additional equipment is installed it will enable us to produce and offer in the coming autumn a yet further facing brick for which we expect there will be a good market."

The effect of changes in Government policy on the building industry in general and on *Baggeridge Brick Company Limited* (November 19) in particular was stressed by MR. P. A. WARD:

"The prosperity of the building industry is principally affected by the general economic climate in the United Kingdom. Inevitably changes in Government policy determine activity in the building trade and the company is affected like every other brickmaker. As the growth of profits and recent increase of turnover show, the company's management has succeeded in maintaining growth. There will no relaxation of effort in the company to continue to produce at high levels and to sell the outputs achieved, but the coming year may be a difficult one due to the existing large brick stocks in the country. In this respect I am glad to confirm that the stocks at our own works are relatively low. Such nation-wide stocking may inevitably result in an easing of prices which could affect the future profitability of this company."

Turnover of *Midhurst Whites Limited* for the current year, in common with general conditions of the trade, according to MR. E. MACARTNEY's statement (*The Times*, November 16), was so far showing a decline, possibly the result of non-availability of finance for building projects and of the unfavourable conditions prevailing during the summer months. However, it was hoped that the interim report when published would be favourable.

For *G. H. Downing & Company Limited* (September 18), MR. D. S. HARTLEY found it difficult to form a clear picture of the months ahead. He continued:

"Although our order book at the moment is better than at this time last year, present governmental financial restrictions are not conducive to forward planning by the construction industry except on a very short term basis. There is a continued pressure on profit margins and your directors are continually exploring ways and means of improving production methods to reduce costs. However, we have a group of efficient works and an energetic marketing force fully prepared to meet the challenging conditions facing both the brick industry and the construction industry as a whole today."

The better demand for bricks continued throughout 1967, stated MR. A. F. F. YOUNG of *Redland Limited* (September 17), and the company was able substantially to reduce stock levels and to restore full output at all works.

"Moreover," he went on to declare, "as the report of the Prices and Incomes Board inquiry gave us a degree of flexibility in prices, it was possible for us to go some way towards recovering the increases in cost which have unavoidably taken place over the last few years, and the profit of the Brick Division was thereby improved."

Trading to date in the current financial year for *H. & R. Johnson-Richards Tiles Limited* (August 28), MR. DEREK H. JOHNSON declared, had been good, with a continued high demand for the company's products in this country and overseas. He mentioned the "Do-it-Yourself" enthusiast in the home market as continuing to provide a substantial volume of business which, added to the high demand from trade outlets, was very satisfactory. He also had this to say on the various pressures on profit margins:

"We are of course confronted from time to time with increases in prices of some of our materials, and an increase in wages is pending. In addition to these increased costs, the premium on Selective Employment Tax granted to manufacturers has been withdrawn as also has the rebate on exports. All these items have their effect on profit margins which we do our best to counter by constant research and improved methods of production."

In general terms 1967 for *Clark & Fenn (Holdings) Limited* (July 11) was a year in which the company did well to maintain and improve slightly its position in the light of trading conditions rendered difficult by political influence. MR. V. W. HOSP thus summed up the year's experience, and went on to make these remarks on the outlook:

"The early months of the current year indicate a continuation of the conditions which obtained in the closing period of last year. Overall it must be recognized that the Building Industry

is running at an improved level of activity. This applies, however, more to the public sector than the private sector which embraces better class building work where there is a greater demand for our products and services. There are indications of an upturn in the private sector but we have yet to see fulfilment of this and we hope it will prove to be so as the year develops. The Group, however, is geared up and ready to take full advantage of any improved conditions in the industry and I feel confident that such improvement must come about."

Members of *BPB Industries Limited* (July 31) were informed by MR. R. S. JUKES that the output of gypsum and anhydrite from the group's mines and quarries in the United Kingdom exceeded 3m. tons, and that productivity improved as the result of further mechanization. He was also able to report a substantial reversal of the recent downward trend of profits, "fully justifying the heavy investment of recent years."

Announcing a 7·4 per cent increase in turnover of *Allied Iron-founders Limited* (July 25), as well as a 12·2 per cent growth in trading profits, MR. G. S. STEVEN made this analysis of the group's sales:

"The recovery in sales has been spread fairly evenly over the whole of our business, although prices of some goods have been reduced to maintain our position. Sales of both solid fuel and gas-fired room heaters have shown encouraging increases, as have cooking appliances, in particular the Aga Cooker. The decline which has persisted for some years in the sales of cast iron pipes and gutters, due to the introduction of plastic materials, has shown some signs of slowing down in recent months. It is also encouraging to note that there has been an improvement in the sales of catering equipment and boilers for industrial use, despite the difficult conditions in this market which prevailed over most of the year."

MR. CHAS. F. GOLTON made these comments on what he described as the deliberate policy of the Government in slowing up private house-building, in the course of his statement for *Pratt Standard Range Limited* (March 12):

"Since this Government came to power it has deliberately followed a policy of slowing up private housebuilding and stepping up Council housing including the scandalous and wasteful system of direct labour building work by Local Authorities. As a result there was a further decline in private housebuilding in 1967 and the recent decision to cut public sector building over the next two years means that the National Plan target of 500,000 houses a year by 1970 has been abandoned. It was very doubtful, however, even before the devaluation measures whether this objective would have been reached.

247

The outlook for housing in 1968 is far from encouraging and housing accounts for some 40 per cent of the total building output. However, your attention has previously been drawn to the fact that a substantial proportion of our business is in connection with repairs, maintenance and conversions on which a big section of the total building labour of the country is engaged."

Drawing attention to the size of the replacement demand for the products of *Twyfords Limited* (July 24), MR. J. R. T. HAY stated:

"In the Home Market our Sales force has been steadily strengthened with good results in the form of orders on the books, especially for delivery later in the year. I should perhaps remind you that although a great deal of publicity is given nowadays to the figures for new housing in the U.K., the replacement trade coupled with the opportunity which is usually taken during the expansion or alteration of existing buildings to provide for modernization and rising standards of hygiene, are really larger factors in our Home trade. As you know, there are many public schemes being accelerated for dealing with this aspect."

Over the last few years, *Armitage Ware Limited* had widened its manufacturing range, MR. C. KENNETH STOTT stated in his annual review (*The Times*, September 5), for the reason that the board foresaw advantages in being able to offer the building industry Armitage products which included vitreous china, heavy duty sanitary fireclay, brass fittings, and fixtures in plastic for all types of buildings in the public and private sectors. This comprehensive service he declared was now having its effect and was being further expanded.

The chairman of *John Sadd & Sons Limited* in his statement (*The Times*, August 30) gave the following breakdown of group profits, which incidentally were very substantially higher on the year: Manufacturing, 46 per cent (previous year, 53 per cent); timber importing, 34 per cent (21 per cent); builders' merchants, 20 per cent (26 per cent).

Significantly increased turnover in building products was recorded by *The Ruberoid Company Limited* (May 28), stated SIR RICHARD YEABSLEY, and the company, he claimed, was maintaining its lead in the field of bituminous building materials. Notable increases were achieved in sales of asbestos-based and glass-fibre-based roofings.

The rapidly developing building products division of the *Reed Paper Group Limited* was the subject of this extract from MR. S. T. RYDER's statement (*The Times*, July 5):

"Our Building Products Division has made considerable progress in establishing the Key Terrain plastics drainage

systems on a broad basis throughout the country, supported by a series of regional depots; rapidly growing sales indicate that these systems are now obtaining recognition for their outstanding quality. With increasing sales of pitch fibre pipe and a growing diversification in the plastics field, we have great hopes of this Division as one of the most promising in the Group.

"During the year we established a Merchant and Retail Division to take charge of our widespread interests in merchanting and retailing wallpaper and paint and the management of the new Division is proceeding energetically with the streamlining of our very extensive wholesale businesses.

"The whole of our activities in Decorative and Building Products is now organized under The Wall Paper Manufacturers Ltd. and the extensive re-organization which has taken place during the last three years has resulted in the promotion of young and vigorous executives to senior positions. I look forward to improved results from their efforts in the future."

The joint chairmen of *Bainbridge Bros.* (*Engineers*) *Limited*, MR. F. BAINBRIDGE and MR. H. BAINBRIDGE, announced in their annual review (*The Times*, June 27) that the company had started to market a new product for roofing garages and outside stores; this had had a "very encouraging" reception.

The main markets for *Magnet Joinery Limited* (August 19) were delineated in the following extract from MR. W. S. EMMOTT'S survey:

"Our main market is the U.K. building industry and all builders can only operate within the Government policy on housing. However, as suppliers of components (doors, windows, cupboards, &c.) I would remind you that in addition to the requirements for new housing there is the replacement trade arising out of the demand for improvement of existing houses."

An improvement of 30 per cent in net profits subject to tax of *Scaffolding Great Britain* (*Holdings*) *Limited* (March 28) was attributed by MR. E. C. BECK largely to the United Kingdom market, in spite of the problems which had faced the construction industry there. It should be remembered, he explained, that the establishing of overseas subsidiaries was always likely to be much slower in producing returns than the opening of a new branch in this country.

The next quotation comes from MR. S. G. MENELL'S review for *Anglo-Alpha Cement Limited* (Johannesburg, October 28):

"The present production capacity of the group, including kilns which were erected in 1934, is approximately 40m. pockets of cement per annum. Sales for the past financial year totalled

35m. pockets giving a utilization of 87·5 per cent and leaving current spare capacity of 12·5 per cent. It is considered essential to have at least 15 per cent spare capacity to meet peaks in demand and to operate at optimum profitability. Furthermore, profitability can be improved to some extent by the diversion of production from the older factories to the newer plants provided spare capacity is available. It is, therefore, planned to increase the rated capacity of the kiln at the Dudfield factory by approximately 48 per cent by the installation of a two-stage heater exchanger. This will represent approximately 4·75m. pockets per annum. The estimated cost of this expansion is R 1·5m., which will be met from retained earnings and existing overdraft facilities without prejudicing the existing dividend rate. Work will commence during the current financial year in order to have the additional capacity available by December, 1969."

PROVISION OF MORTGAGES

The dilemma with which the building societies were faced in 1968 with the decline of their net receipts in face of "an apparently inexhaustible demand for mortgages" is admirably summarized in the following extracts from the statement of MR. I. A. D. MAC-LEAN, the president of the *Halifax Building Society* (May 20):

"In the first quarter of this year we have lent £81,870,000, the largest sum ever lent by the Halifax in one quarter, while the amount of advances offered but not taken up has now increased to over £85 million. This record lending and the smaller inflow of funds experienced so far this year could lead to a reduction in liquidity to a point lower than the directors would be prepared to accept. These facts bring me logically to the question of interest rates which has been so much in prominence in recent weeks. It was only to be expected that devaluation and the 8 per cent Bank rate would affect the Society. At first, the impact was comparatively slight. Since the end of the year the situation has worsened and the net receipts in the first quarter of 1968 dropped to £26m. compared with £42m. in the first quarter of 1967. This was caused mainly by an increase in the withdrawals since gross receipts were maintained at a satisfactory high level, but there was mounting evidence, particularly after the Budget, that the rate being offered to investors was falling behind other forms of competition.

"It is naturally the wish of building societies that ample funds should continue to be available for home-ownership. Indeed it has been estimated that if the momentum in the private sector is to be maintained building societies will need to lend slightly more than the record amount which was lent last year. So the

Board fully supported the recommendation of the Building Societies Association that the rate should be increased. From the 1st May, therefore, the rate on Subscription Shares and Paid-up Shares Class I became 5 per cent, on Paid-up Shares Class 2 $4\frac{1}{2}$ per cent and on Deposits $4\frac{1}{4}$ per cent. The mortgage rate to new borrowers was increased to $7\frac{5}{8}$ per cent from 1st May 1968, and a similar increase will apply to existing borrowers from 1st October next. The resultant margin will, during the current year, produce a smaller surplus than the previous margin allowed. This is because the mortgage rate to existing borrowers is being increased five months after the increase in investors' rates. If, as is expected, the composite rate of tax is increased, the surplus will be further reduced by some £300,000 for every penny increase. In a full year, and on the assumption that there is no more than a modest increase in the composite rate, the new rate structure will allow a margin equivalent to the previous one."

Addressing the annual meeting of the *Abbey National Building Society* (April 2) SIR ROY MATTHEWS referred to the independent committee appointed by the Building Societies Association, in May, 1967, on the suggestion of the Prices and Incomes Board, to consider the question of minimum reserves, among other things. He said:

"This Committee, under the chairmanship of Mr. Charles Hardie, reported that, because the degree of risk of mortgage and other loss experience could be expected to move inversely with the size of a society, minimum reserve ratios for the conferment of trustee status should follow a sliding scale more closely than the requirement at present.

"The suggestions of the Hardie Committee have been considered by the Building Societies Association and by the Government. Regulations have now been laid before Parliament which, though they differ in detail from the Hardie Committee's proposals, do give effect to the sliding scale principle. The effect on the Abbey National is that, whereas with assets of over £1000m. the present minimum reserve ratio for trustee status is 2·05 per cent, under new regulations a minimum of only 1·8 per cent is required. This compares with our actual reserve ratio of 3·22 per cent."

During 1967 the *Co-operative Permanent Building Society* did more business than in any other year since it was formed, the directors' report (*The Times*, March 1) stated. For the first time in the Society's history lending on mortgage exceeded £100m., and in September another landmark was passed when total assets exceeded £500m.

Among the points made by SIR CYRIL BLACK, M.P., at the

annual meeting of the *Temperance Permanent Building Society* (March 8) was that the desire for home ownership was perhaps even stronger in times of uncertainty: it provided an investment almost certain to increase as the value of money fell.

The outlook for the current year is the subject of the following quotation, which comes from the speech of SIR THOMAS SPENCER at the annual meeting of the *Woolwich Equitable Building Society* (December 17):

"What then is the outlook for this financial year? There is a national shortage of capital and therefore high interest rates generally are likely to persist. I am pleased to tell you that since the beginning of October we have noticed some modest improvement in investment receipts accompanied by a slight but welcome reduction in the level of withdrawals. But as yet this improvement is only sufficient to permit a marginal increase in the amount of mortgage business which we are able currently to entertain. There remains a strong unsatisfied demand from would-be home-owners and undoubtedly the extent of our mortgage advances this year will be conditioned largely by the level of net receipts from investors. Thus the prospect of our matching last year's record total of advances completed is not encouraging because that level of lending was materially assisted by a deliberate, controlled reduction of over £14m. in the amount of our liquid funds."

Commenting on the possibility of a Government thrift plan at the meeting of *Leeds Permanent Building Society* (December 16), MR. RONALD COWLING said:

"It seems likely that a savings or Thrift Plan may be introduced by the Government in the not too distant future, and that it can take the form of Savings Funds into which tax-exempt deductions from wages or salaries will be paid but from which withdrawals will not be permitted for a period of years, perhaps five, save under the penalty of tax deduction. For genuine savers the yield will probably be extremely attractive. Building societies have, of course, been 'thrift plan' conscious for many years; our regular savings schemes in Subscription Shares are highly popular and the savings in them are channelled into equity interest in owner-occupation, itself a form of thrift which benefits both the nation and the individual. Building societies do, in fact, already operate contractual savings schemes for the benefit of members of the three Armed Services.

"We can readily adjust our own savings and investment facilities to any contractual savings plan which the Government may introduce and, indeed, would welcome the opportunity of using our tried and trusted service for the benefit of the national economy and the people."

The chairman of the *Burnley Building Society* (March 6) made these remarks (*inter alia*) on Government legislation affecting the movement:

"The year produced a considerable weight of legislation touching upon our business, the most momentous being the Housing Subsidies Act 1967. This provides for mortgage interest to be reduced by subsidy to qualifying borrowers who elect in exchange to forgo their tax relief on mortgage interest. The scheme is not without administrative complexities. We were obliged to circularize details to our 60,000 existing borrowers of whom 1,900 have exercised their option to take the subsidy. To date rather less than 8 per cent of new borrowers are exercising this option."

A number of mergers with other societies were reported to members of *Leek and Westbourne Building Society* by MR. HUBERT NEWTON (*The Times*, April 11). During 1967 the National Independent Permanent (of Manchester), the Acme and The Greater London Permanent (both of London) were amalgamated with the Leek, and on January 1, 1968, the Alliance Perpetual and the Globe were merged.

A revision of the upper limit on the size of normal housing advances was alluded to by MR. NORMAN D. ELLIS in his speech for the *Leicester Permanent Building Society* (April 2) in these terms:

"We have for some time held the view that the limit of £7,000, above which advances on normal owner occupied private dwelling houses are classified as Special Advances, was unrealistic. We were happy to grant larger mortgages on this type of security, especially in South East England, where house prices are so much higher. From January of this year the limit has been raised to £10,000 and we welcome this change."

While there were no restrictions on lending throughout the year until the exchange rate crisis in November, LORD HENDERSON said at the meeting of the ALLIANCE BUILDING SOCIETY, since then controlling action had been necessary. His speech was reported in *The Times* of May 2.

THE CHEMICAL INDUSTRIES

SALES of *Imperial Chemical Industries Limited* (*March* 28) for 1967 reached nearly £1,000m., the actual total for the group being £979m., £486m. in the home market and £493m. overseas. Giving these figures, SIR PETER ALLEN said that the total increase for the group was £94m., or 11 per cent over the previous year. These figures were swollen to some extent by the inclusion of new subsidiary companies, notably Ilford Limited and Wolverhampton Metals. Nevertheless, comparing like with like, the group sales increased by £56m. in value, or by over 6 per cent. And as selling prices were on average rather lower than in 1966. the increase in the volume of group sales was higher than in the value. "Taking it all round," said Sir Peter, "I think we can regard last year's sales with satisfaction at a time when trading conditions were far from easy." He hoped that group sales would show an advance of the order of £100m. in 1968, and that, after taking into account the additions to costs arising from both devaluation and the Budget proposals, group profits both before and after tax would be somewhat higher than in 1967, when they had risen sharply on 1966.

The annual report (*The Times*, November 1) of *Fisons Limited* showed that the group had fully achieved its trading budget for 1967–68: sales exceeded £100m. for the first time, making a 9 per cent increase on the year, and the pre-tax profit was almost doubled. All Divisions contributed to this achievement. Much of the benefit from the recently concluded £19¾m. investment in agricultural fertilizers was still to come, and it was expected that for a few years capital investment in the Fertilizer Division would be at a much reduced level. However, the fertilizer research effort would continue to be aimed at further cost reduction in existing plants as well as the development of improved products and processes. Among the other Divisions, a product which had shown remarkable promise in this country was Intal, a new drug for the treatment of allergic asthma and a product of Fisons' own research over the last eight years.

Another company whose sales exceeded £100m. for the first time was *Albright & Wilson Limited* (April 25), whose annual report indicated that the 1967 trading profit increased by 1·8 per cent, though pre-tax profit was nearly 10 per cent down because of a higher charge for interest on borrowed money, and the dividend was reduced. The directors forecast higher pre-tax profits for 1968 in spite of uncertainties concerning the United Kingdom economy, and they added:

"Better operating results are expected from our new plants, and further benefits from our internal reorganization. There should be some continuing gain from the beneficial effects of devaluation. It will not, however, be until 1969 as previously forecast, that the full benefits of our reorganization and massive capital expenditure programme will be obtained."

LORD HILL OF LUTON stated that *Laporte Industries Limited* (July 31) had decided to build a 40,000 tons per annum chloride process plant at Stallingborough, involving some £7m. of capital expenditure. For more than 35 years the company had made titanium dioxide pigments by the sulphate process, but the world market for these products was increasing and was now estimated to be $1\frac{1}{2}$m. tons per annum. Although Laporte was increasing its Stallingborough sulphate capacity to an annual 55,000 tons, he added, the group's European capacity could not be increased beyond this level without building a new plant. Laporte had been studying the alternative route to titanium oxide, the chloride process, for some 15 years, Lord Hill said, and he went on to declare:

"Our study has led us to the decision that we should build a 40,000 tons p.a. chloride process plant at Stallingborough to come on stream early in 1970. This decision will, we believe, bring great flexibility to our titanium dioxide business, extending the range of our products and enhancing our standing as an international supplier of high quality pigments."

During the period under review all companies in the *Reichhold Chemical Limited* group (June 18) encountered severe competition coupled with repetitive cost increases in basic raw materials, followed by further increases resulting from devaluation. In making this clear MR. G. S. BACHE added that the companies were obliged to absorb a substantial amount of these higher material costs, and as these were coupled with further unexpected advances in wages, salaries and national insurance contributions profit margins were reduced, resulting in some diminution of pre-tax profit.

As he had forecast a year previously, MR. C. H. TANNER was able to report a sharp recovery in the group profits of *Berk Limited* (May 2), and he made these remarks on prospects:

"Continuing recovery is confidently anticipated by the Directors as a result of the strenuous efforts of all management to rationalize the Group's activities. Energies are being directed to the expansion of sales and profitability, as well as to developing new products and improving traditional ones. A new department, Planning and Development, has been established to appraise projects and to promote plans for future development. Success in the future, however, does depend largely on

the level of national activity and relies on a reasonable degree of encouragement to private enterprise by the Government."

In his statement (*The Times*, February 20) for *Staveley Industries Limited* MR. DENIS HAVILAND said that profit in the Chemical Division as a whole was 7 per cent down. Both demand and production of salt were maintained, and greater efficiency had partly protected profits against rising costs. Plant and products at Staveley Lime Products were rationalized during the year, and, though manpower was reduced by some 30 per cent, output was raised. Competition in aggregates and increased costs, particularly of fuel oil, reduced profits. As to prospects, he stated that demand for salt, lime and lubricants was being maintained and profits should improve.

The British Oxygen Company Limited (February 28) also increased its sales to a total of almost £100m. MR. J. S. HUTCHISON stated that demand for oxygen and acetylene for general engineering purposes fell somewhat, but some recovery was perceptible towards the end of the year. Nitrogen sales continued to expand quickly. Demand for oxygen in tonnage quantities, mainly for steel-making, improved, and there were now 31 BOC tonnage plants operating in the United Kingdom with a total capacity of 2.1m. tons of oxygen a year. He also made these remarks about special gases and cryoproducts:

"These departments had a successful year with rapid growth in the supply of a great variety of gases and 'tailor-made' gas mixtures of a high degree of accuracy and purity. There is a notable increase in the sale of helium, the use of which in liquid form is a vital factor in the technology of extreme low temperatures. A new factory at South Shields, due on stream in a few weeks' time, will enable us to give improved service to the growing number of users requiring the sophisticated equipment necessary for handling and storing liquid hydrogen, liquid helium and other cryogenic liquids."

Referring to the Carbon Dioxide subsidiary of *The Distillers Company Limited* (September 19) MR. ALEX MCDONALD mentioned that although carbon dioxide sales to some industrial sectors were affected by the general recession in trade at the beginning of the year, sales generally continued to show substantial growth, evidence of the increasing use of this gas in a wide variety of industries; these included foundries, arc-welding, brewing and beer handling, mineral waters, fire-fighting and atomic energy. He added:

"Prices again came under pressure but profitability was maintained in the face of rising costs as a result of economies which derived partly from scale and partly from various productivity improvements."

256

The report of the directors of *British Glues & Chemicals Limited* (July 25) included this paragraph:

"The reorganization of our glue production units took longer than anticipated. The consequential obsolescence has been charged to Reserves, but the results for 1967–68 have borne the other costs of reorganization. While the world market for the higher grades of glue is encouraging and profitable, this cannot be said of other grades, and we are giving this aspect of our business especial attention."

MR. ALEX MCDONALD recalled that the total consideration for the sale of all the chemical and plastics interests (other than those concerned with carbon dioxide) of *The Distillers Company Limited* (September 19) to British Petroleum was to be 19m. fully-paid £1 Ordinary shares of BP and, subject to certain adjustments, £25m. in cash. However, he now stated that the exclusion of Bakelite Xylonite and of Distrene (because of objections to the transfer raised by the Distillers' partners in these businesses), together with certain adjustments required under the contract, had had the effect of reducing the total cash element of the consideration by £15·3m. The interest in Distrene Limited was later sold to the Dow company, Distillers' partner in Distrene.

As regards the effect of the purchase of the Distillers' chemical interests on *The British Petroleum Company Limited*, SIR MAURICE BRIDGEMAN had this to say in his statement (*The Times*, April 17):

"The additional chemical interests acquired last year have made BP the second largest chemical group in the United Kingdom. Financially, the results for 1967 were somewhat disappointing. This was primarily due to the increase in cost of chemical feedstocks due to political disturbances, but also to some extent to difficulties in commissioning and operating the acetylene plant at Barry. Devaluation of sterling could not immediately be covered by corresponding increases in prices, though it should in due course bring new opportunities for exports from this country. The process of fully integrating into our own organization the enterprises we have taken over will take some time, but the work of rationalization is well advanced. We are confident that the development of our chemical interests will be of great future benefit to the group, and results this year should show a definite improvement on those for 1967."

Among the points made by the directors of *The Petrofina Group* in their annual report (*The Times*, May 13) on the group's petro-chemical interests were the following:

"Petrochim's first steam cracking plant was commissioned early in 1968 and began commercial operation, with its entire output sold on long-term contracts. The second unit is due for

completion later in the year, raising total ethylene capacity to 500,000 metric tons a year. The aromatic compounds extraction plant, cyclohexane production plant and synthetic rubber plant came on stream early in 1968.

"A proposal initiated by Petrochim and involving the building of a large petrochemical complex in Belgium's Central Region, with pipelines linking the plant to Antwerp for raw materials supplies, is currently under negotiation."

PHARMACEUTICALS

Exports by the United Kingdom companies of the *Glaxo Group Limited*, declared SIR ALAN WILSON in his annual review (*The Times*, November 15), followed the pattern of previous years, and their exports of pharmaceuticals during the calendar year 1967 represented 20 per cent of the total pharmaceutical exports of this country. Glaxo increased its investment in the pharmaceutical and allied industries during the year by the acquisition of B.D.H. Group and of Farley's Infant Food. Sir Alan made these references to the industry's relations with the Government:

"The Committee on the Safety of Drugs under the Chairmanship of Sir Derrick Dunlop, which began its work in 1964, has operated extremely satisfactorily. However, the Government decided to introduce statutory safeguards to supersede the voluntary ones which had gradually been evolved, and accordingly the Medicines Act 1968 gave the Minister of Health, acting on professional advice, the power to secure the safety, efficacy and quality of medicines. The Act is a complicated piece of legislation, and its success will depend upon its application in a practical form.

"As a major exporter, we welcome the Minister's decision to postpone the licensing procedure under the Act in relation to the export of pharmaceutical products, which would have placed the British pharmaceutical industry in an adverse position as regards foreign competitors who do not have to fulfil similar obligations.

"Discussions have taken place between the Minister of Health and the pharmaceutical industry concerning the findings of the Sainsbury Committee. I am glad to report that the Minister has decided not to accept the recommendation to abolish brand names, a proposal which would have had profoundly adverse effects on our export trade. Discussions are continuing in an endeavour to establish an improved version of the Voluntary Price Regulation Scheme, and I am hopeful that solutions of the problems involved will be found which will be acceptable to the Minister and to the industry."

Both sales and profits of *The Wellcome Foundation Limited*

(January 31) reached new records, SIR MICHAEL PERRIN declared. He also referred in these terms to one of the group's new products which had an application to organ transplant operations:

"One product, 'Imuran' (azathioprine), which, with others of widely different application, had come from a long term research programme in the laboratories of the U.S. company, had attracted much public attention through its use in controlling the rejection mechanism in organ transplant operations. It was an interesting commentary on different national regulations that, while it had been approved for use and sale in the U.K. and many other countries, it was still not cleared by the Food and Drug Administration in the U.S.A. and in the thousands of cases in which it had been used there the drug had been supplied free on the understanding that it was only for clinical trial."

In his valedictory speech as chairman of *Beecham Group Limited* (July 24) MR. H. G. LAZELL pointed to "another step forward in the U.S.A.," where the public offer of 400,000 shares in Beecham Inc. had been successfully concluded. As a result, Beecham had obtained some $10·6m. to finance development in the Western hemisphere, while the group continued to hold 90 per cent of the equity in Beecham Inc. As showing that Beecham Group was now an established international company, he mentioned that 56 per cent of its profit was earned overseas; 10 years ago the figure was 24 per cent. Mr. Lazell referred to the company's attack on the European market in this paragraph:

"A long hard slog is ahead of us in the complex markets of Western Europe which at present provide 11 per cent of our profits. We are confident that we can find the products and the funds for European development and we are now giving the highest priority to building up our management teams in the main markets. I am very hopeful that we will create a substantial business in Europe within the next five years."

Research and development work on new products continued and covered a wide range of interests, declared MR. W. R. NORMAN of *Boots Pure Drug Company Limited* (July 11). For example, in the area of human medicines the company had continued to work on a series of compounds for the treatment of rheumatic diseases, and one potential product he mentioned had been undergoing long-term clinical trials in this country and abroad, with results to date that "look very promising."

The *Aspro-Nicholas Limited* Group (July 18), asserted the chairman in his annual statement, had been brought back on to its growth curve by the attainment of new high levels in profits, sales and dividend. Not only was the planned objective achieved in restoring greater profitability in the United Kingdom, but a major

contribution also arose from increases in sales and profits overseas.

Turnover of *Horlicks Limited* in pharmaceuticals, both ethical and standard drugs, increased, LORD COLERAINE stated in his survey (*The Times*, November 7). He added that over 10 per cent of group trading profits were devoted to research on pharmaceuticals and the development of specialized food products.

Trading losses of the pharmaceutical group belonging to *Arthur Guinness Son & Company* had been reduced, according to LORD IVEAGH'S statement (*The Times*, February 7). A number of new products were launched during the year, and several further important products were expected to be ready for marketing in the near future.

Court actions against *The Distillers Company Limited* (September 19) in connection with the thalidomide affair were mentioned by MR. ALEX MCDONALD in the following paragraph:

> "During the year a basis was agreed and approved by the High Court for the settlement of 65 actions brought against The Distillers Company (Biochemicals) Limited in the United Kingdom arising out of the sale of thalidomide products. A number of other actions in the U.K., based for the most part on the occurrence of what are alleged to be certain side effects of thalidomide in adults, are pending. The company is advised that the whole matter is still *sub judice*, and further comment is not appropriate at this time."

PLASTICS

The Distillers Company, Mr. McDonald also recalled, was an equal partner with Union Carbide Corporation (U.S.A.) in Bakelite Xylonite, which manufactured a wide range of plastics and resins, as well as fabricating finished articles for use by industry and the public. BX had recently undergone a considerable internal reorganization, and he found it encouraging that its profits in the calendar year 1967 showed a substantial improvement over those of 1966.

MR. KEITH D. ERSKINE made this reference to the plastics interests of *Metal Closures Group Limited* (June 26):

> "On the plastics side Coca-Cola and other soft drink manufacturers have now joined many leading brewers as users of the John Dale crate. Safe stacking, without distortion, and ease of handling are two important features.
>
> "Margins generally in the plastics business are narrow and specialization is the keyword."

Group trading profit of *Catalin Limited* (June 28) improved by just under 10 per cent on the previous year on a total value of sales only 5 per cent higher. However, MR. J. E. CURRIE declared that the

extra volume provided additional benefits from reduced overheads.

An arrangement for co-operation with I.C.I. in plastic films by *British Sidac Limited* (August 2) was mentioned by MR. S. H. MARECHAL:

"Certain of the newer plastic films make good progress and the company has exercised its option with Imperial Chemical Industries to form a joint company, Sidex Ltd., to manufacture biaxially oriented polypropylene film. An investigation of the available sites for the new plant by a joint I.C.I./B.S.L. team is nearing completion. The company has significantly increased its sales of polypropylene film, and other plastic films are under close study."

During 1967 Osma Plastics Limited, which falls within the *Power Securities Corporation Limited* group (October 28), was stated by LORD RENWICK to have achieved another record year with a turnover of nearly £3½m.; sales of all products increased, and he claimed that the company maintained its position as the leading supplier of plastics building products.

PAINT AND COLOURS, GLASS, PAPER AND LEATHER

The interests of *Courtaulds Limited* (July 10) in paints were the subject of this paragraph in SIR FRANK KEARTON's speech:

"You will recall that our interests in the UK, being largely associated with industrial end uses, and in particular with the motor trade, were quite badly hit in the year to March 31, 1967. Our overseas paint interests on the other hand maintained their performance. We once more had a far from easy time in the UK market, but profits overall showed some improvement. With the brisker industrial climate now developing, and the better outlook for the UK motor industry, the prospects for the coming year are distinctly more encouraging. We have also given a 'new look' to the organization of our paint business, and through a combination of retirements, both by reason of age and ill health, the top management team reflects this 'new look,' decisively."

A reduction of 4 per cent in trading profit of *Berger, Jenson & Nicholson Limited* (July 12) was attributed by LORD KINGS NORTON to operations in the United Kingdom, and particularly to the impact of U.K. conditions upon the industrial paint division, although sales of the group's well-known decorative brands had increased. Overseas profits again showed a small increase and, being augmented by devaluation, he stated, accounted for 56 per cent of the group total.

Orders for industrial paints received by *International Paints (Holdings) Limited* (May 30) also declined somewhat, stated MR.

CHARLES R. PETRIE, but marine and yacht paints turnover in the United Kingdom substantially improved. So also did decorative paints and painting contracts. Overseas companies contributed more than half of the group's profits.

For *Blundell-Permoglaze Holdings Limited* (March 6) MR. E. B. CALVERT had this to say about the progress of integration of the company's main business:

"In my last two statements I have endeavoured to keep shareholders informed with regard to the progress that has been made to integrate completely Blundell, Spence & Company Limited and Permoglaze Limited. Much has been done towards improving the profitability of the United Kingdom subsidiary. Some still remains to be done. Great economies have been effected but some further substantial savings will accrue during the current year and more particularly during the 1968–69 period. I am well satisfied with what has been achieved and by November 1, 1968, this subsidiary will be an efficient unit capable of holding its own in a highly competitive world.

"Almost throughout the whole of the trading period now under report, world conditions were not conducive to the profitable conduct of business. Nevertheless, the final trading result was slightly better than that recorded during the previous year."

Sissons Brothers, with Porter Paints and Ascol Products, were mainly concerned with paints and surface coatings and with sundry components supplied to the building industry, declared MR. B. N. RECKITT of *Reckitt & Colman Holdings Limited* (June 7), and he continued:

"Because of credit restrictions etc. this has been a sector of the economy which has had a difficult year; in the circumstances it is worth recording that their turnover was slightly increased though at the expense of margins which left their results virtually unchanged."

For *Horace Cory and Company Limited* 1967 was another year of significant and encouraging progress, MR. J. H. GRIMSHAW asserted, with sales, production and earnings as well as exports all reaching new high levels. In November, 1967, he added, work started on an extension to the factory to house a new project—the manufacture of cadmium colours; it was hoped to be in production later in the year. His statement appeared in *The Times* of May 14.

MR. IAN M. BAILEY informed members of *Rockware Group Limited* in his annual statement (*The Times*, April 19) that 1967 was the first full year of glass manufacturing operations since the acquisition of The Garston Bottle Company and of Forster's Glass Company. By the year end, he declared, marketing activities were fully integrated, and "we were able to obtain a growth rate in

unit sales of 8 per cent." He asserted that this increase, together with the 6 per cent rise in revenue from glass sales, compared extremely favourably with the performance of the industry. Another point in his review was the following:

"The acceptance of the one-trip no-deposit container for the soft drinks industry has been exceedingly encouraging. The market for this type of pack has moved ahead rapidly and, compared with 1966, sales have more than trebled. We are currently expecting a further substantial increase in demand and latest figures show that Rockware is now satisfying more than 50 per cent of this market."

Lower profits and dividend of *The Bowater Paper Corporation Limited* (April 24), in spite of some benefit from devaluation, were ascribed by SIR CHRISTOPHER CHANCELLOR to these causes:

"If I say that 1967 has been a year of trials and uncertainties I echo the words of many other chairmen of British companies who have had to contend with the continuing effect of major fiscal changes which have been introduced by the Government as well as increasing costs more often than not stemming directly from Government policies. The pulp and paper industry, more-over, has had some special problems because in many areas there has been a pause in the growth of demand for pulp and paper. This situation, combined with production coming on to the market in 1967 from newly installed capacity in the United States, Canada and Scandinavia, has resulted in increased com-petition in world markets. The Bowater Organisation has had to face similar situations in the past and they recur from time to time, being part of the pattern of the capital intensive industry in which we operate."

That 1967 would be remembered by the paper industry all over Europe and North America as the year in which supply exceeded demand more massively than at any time since the 1930s, so that prices fell and profit margins were seriously diminished, was declared by the directors of *Wiggins Teape Limited* (July 11). It was the more satisfactory, then, to them that they should be able to announce a significant advance in trading profit. And in his state-ment the chairman, MR. MARK NORMAN, revealed that for the first four months of 1968 sales and trading profit for the group as a whole were well up on 1967. He added:

"At home the order books at most of our mills and factories are satisfactorily full. But many profit margins are too slender and will remain so until all concerned in the EFTA countries achieve further rationalization of production and sales for the U.K. paper market, and the balance of supply and demand is restored.

"At Fort William our efficiency is slowly improving but we must have assurance for the years ahead about the cost of wood into the mill so that we can compete with imports, and thereafter develop the mill so as to provide a market for the rapidly maturing Scottish forests.

"Overseas, our manufacturing operations should have a better year in most countries, especially in Australia. Exports to many parts of the world are rising.

"Provided that Governments perform their primary economic responsibility for maintaining stable financial conditions and that present levels of trading do not deteriorate, then Group profits for 1968 should be higher than last year."

Recording the successful conclusion of negotiations with the Industrial Reorganisation Corporation to finance further de-inking projects by *Reed Paper Group Limited* MR. S. T. RYDER in his statement (*The Times*, July 5) mentioned that the group had for some time been operating and further developing the process for removing the ink from over-issue and used newspapers to produce pulp suitable again for newsprint manufacture. He continued:

"The case for the increased operations as an import saver is incontrovertible, so that the projects at Imperial and Aylesford Paper Mills for the extension of de-inking activity were most appropriate for a loan of £1½m. from IRC. These projects are to be spread over nearly two years and are expected to be completed by the end of 1969. I welcome the opportunity to pay tribute to the exhaustive manner in which IRC examined these projects which I am certain will fully justify their confidence in them."

A sharp setback in profits of *The Inveresk Paper Company Limited* (April 3) was reported by MR. A. L. HOOD. He explained that 1967 was an exceptionally difficult year for the United Kingdom paper industry, and many of the group's mills were not able to operate at optimum capacity during the period; moreover, an important proportion of sales was secured only by accepting smaller orders with shorter delivery times, resulting in reduced production efficiency. In particular, he remarked on the withdrawal on December 1, 1966, of the temporary import surcharge and the removal on January 1, 1967, of the last of the tariffs existing in the EFTA countries, which together resulted in severe intensification of competition from Scandinavian, Austrian and other foreign paper producers.

Another chairman to refer to the removal of EFTA duties was MR. JOHN W. RANDALL of *The Dickinson Robinson Group Limited*, from whose remarks (*The Times*, May 9) on the home market the following excerpt is taken:

"Our mills were again adversely affected by the final elimina-

tion of the EFTA tariff duties and the results shown by our Consumer Products Division were lower than for the previous year.

"The results of the Stationery and Packaging Divisions again showed increases in both turnover and profits. The latter was mainly achieved by economies in production. In our Packaging Division the re-organization arrangements carried out in previous years are now producing improved results, a trend which I expect to continue."

A reduction in the group trading surplus of *Portals Holdings Limited* (June 24) was ascribed by SIR FRANCIS PORTAL to cancellations and postponements of orders on the papermaking side in the later part of the year.

The mills of the *Associated Paper Mills Limited* group (April 1), it was claimed by MR. L. W. FARROW, were more efficient than they ever had been, and "given the right economic conditions they can produce greatly increased quantities of paper and board." In a plea for active help from the Government for the industry he declared that they should recognize its great potential in import saving.

Running-in difficulties in connection with the start of operations of a new machine in the paper mill of the *East Lancashire Paper Mill Company Limited* (April 25) were alluded to by MR. C. G. SEDDON, as the following quotation shows:

"The starting-up of the new No. 1 Machine which was officially declared 'on stream' in October by Mr. David Ensor, M.P., was followed by a running-in period, during which, due to this and also to new manufacturing procedures stemming from revised water and effluent legislation, the general efficiency of the whole of the 'fine' side of the mill became adversely affected resulting in an estimated loss of revenue of some £50,000. It is only fair to state that a major operation such as the installation of the new machine is bound to cause some disruption and, in fact, No. 1 and 2 were out of production for eight and three weeks respectively. All things considered this was an excellent achievement by all concerned. When all the teething troubles, however, have been eliminated, and we consistently achieve the results which it has now been proved are obtainable from this investment, I am confident that the figures for increased profit-earning, forecast in our viability study of this project, will be more than justified."

During an extremely difficult period for the paper industry as a whole the mills of *Brittains Limited* had been very well occupied, stated MR. S. HILL in his annual review (*The Times*, April 3). But he added that the full benefit of extended running hours had once again been eroded by inescapable increases in costs. Nevertheless,

S 265

pre-tax profit and turnover were respectively $8\frac{1}{2}$ per cent and $7\frac{1}{2}$ per cent higher than in 1966.

The export trade of *Barrow Hepburn & Gale Limited* (March 14), particularly in sole leather, received an immediate stimulus from devaluation, MR. GEORGE W. ODEY revealed, but it remained to be seen to what extent the benefits would continue to exceed the increased costs of production. He saw some lessening of over-capacity in tanning, and also hoped for greater stability in leather prices; the relevant passages from his statement follow:

"It is quite clear that there is still over-capacity in the tanning industry in this country, especially in sole leather, but to some extent this position has been improved by the closing of tanneries of considerable size in both the upper leather and the sole leather fields during the past year and the full effect of these closures has not yet been felt. Furthermore, there has not yet been time fully to appreciate to what extent the demand for leather will be stimulated by the fact that in a world of rising prices the price of leather has, broadly speaking, reverted to the level that was obtained in 1965 before the great fluctuation in price which occurred in 1966 and 1967. It appears that raw material prices are now at a low and stable level and signs of any collapse of prices on the scale that we have witnessed in the past two years simply do not exist.

"It will be appreciated, having regard to the very large turnover involved, which in the case of leather amounts to approximately £5m., and the very small margin of profit upon which this business is normally conducted, how cautious one must be in making a forecast for the next twelve months. Nevertheless, in view of the reasonable level of the price of our raw hide supplies and bearing in mind that the departments in heavy loss have been closed, it is anticipated that the trading profits of the Group should be substantially higher than those of the year under review."

It was not until the final quarter of the year of *Augustine Investments Limited* (June 12), stated MR. R. E. BROOK, that a substantial improvement began to make itself felt in the leather division; certainly, it came too late to make up fully for the adverse three quarters preceding, with the result that the division sustained a small loss for the year. In his additional remarks at the meeting Mr. Brook said that the late favourable trend had continued and even intensified; in particular, the tanneries had attained a striking increase in orders and output, which could not fail to have a favourable effect on profits for the year as a whole.

OVERSEAS COMPANIES

From the annual report of *Chas. Pfizer & Co. Inc.* (New York, April 29) the following extracts are taken:

"Pfizer's worldwide operations in 1967 achieved a record in sales for the 18th consecutive year. Earnings reached the second highest level in the company's 119-year history. Pfizer's worldwide sales in 1967 totalled $637·8m. This was an increase of $16m., or about three per cent over 1966 sales of $621m. Earnings of $58·3m. in 1967 were within about five per cent of the record $61·6m. level of 1966. Earnings per share for 1967 were $2·88 compared with $3·07 in 1966. Dividends of $29·3m. were paid to Pfizer shareholders in 1967. Payments were equivalent to $1·45 per share, the same as in 1966.

"Research and development expenditures, the majority of which reflected extensive studies in the medicinal products field, totalled $23·9m. This was an increase of about $1½m. over 1966. About $38m. was invested last year in capital improvements throughout the world.

"In the early part of 1967, some of the company's businesses operated behind the record profit base of the preceding year. However, the combined results of all businesses improved substantially as the year progressed. Sales and earnings for the fourth quarter of 1967 were higher than the same period in 1966 and represented the most successful quarter in Pfizer's history."

Among the interesting developments in the glass sector of the activities of the *Grängesberg Company* mentioned by MR. ERLAND WALDENSTRÖM in his speech (*The Times*, July 30) as President was that at Oxelösund of special windows for insulation against heat, noise and solar radiation. This, he said, was quite apart from the new and vastly improved production methods that would be employed at the company's new glassworks in Denmark.

In the annual statement (*The Times*, June 26) by the *CIBA Group* in Basle it was reported that world sales of group products increased by more than 10 per cent in the year, achieving a record £221·7m.; overall sales in the United Kingdom rose by 6·7 per cent to £22·3m. Pharmaceuticals were stated to be the group's most important branch with 42 per cent of total sales. CIBA products were now marketed in more than 100 countries; Europe was the main market, slightly more than half the group business being transacted there.

The motor car built from Bayer plastics was mentioned by PROF. DR. KURT HANSEN in this quotation from his address for *Farbenfabriken Bayer AG.* (Cologne, May 29):

"We have exhibited the largest reaction injection-moulded part yet made in the world at the Hanover Fair. It is made of the

267

novel Bayer material 'Polyurethane-Duromer', a rigid structural foam which makes it possible to produce economically, and without problems, complicated large mouldings with any kind of surface structure, both thick-walled and thin-walled. Examples of the use of these reaction injection-moulded parts can be found in motor manufacture, in the building industry and in making furniture and household appliances. The motor car built from Bayer plastics, which has been licensed for the roads by the authorities although the front and rear axles are not held by a metal frame but by a continuous plastic floor, has attracted considerable attention in Germany, France and the United States. This car has passed the test rigs of many world-famous motor manufacturers inside and outside Germany and has proved that our plastics are well suited for load-bearing and for heavily stressed parts."

Total world sales of *Farbwerke Hoechst AG.*, it appeared from the summary of the annual report published in *The Times* of July 9, increased from DM. 5,827m. to DM. 6,601m. on the year; foreign sales accounted for approximately 50 per cent of these, against about 46 per cent in 1966.

The next quotation comes from the annual report of the board of directors of *Montecatini Edison S.p.A.* (Milan, April 20) and briefly summarizes the experience of the Italian chemical industry in 1967:

"1967 was a year of further production development for the Italian chemical industry, but progress was less lively than in the past, with fresh cost increases and a drop in prices—in some cases quite considerable—as a result of the growing world competition on all markets. This situation did not fail, of course, to reflect upon the results attained by the company in this sector."

During the course of the year output of *ANIC S.p.A.* (Milan, April 27) increased appreciably and, as a whole, registered an average increase higher than that of overall chemical production in Italy. The annual report also showed that sales rose notably, both in quantity and in profit, even though prices moved unfavourably.

For the *Compagnie de Saint-Gobain* (Paris, June 10) M. A. DE VOGUÉ reported the decision by the Glaceries de Saint-Roch, a Belgian company in which Saint-Gobain holds substantial interests, to construct jointly with the Glacerie de Franière, the Belgian affiliate of Saint-Gobain, a production line utilizing the "Float Glass" process that will come on-line in 1970, when it will exceed in capacity any existing plant in Europe and perhaps in the world.

At the annual meeting of *L'Oreal* (May 10) it was reported that the consolidated turnover of the company and its direct French subsidiaries showed a rise of some $8\frac{1}{2}$ per cent compared with 1966.

ENGINEERING

HEAVY PLANT

THE continuing uncertainties in the United Kingdom power programme, declared LORD NELSON OF STAFFORD in his review for *The English Electric Company Limited* (March 27), had produced a situation in which manufacturers did not know when the next home order would be placed or the forward programme for which they were expected to provide manufacturing capacity. He continued:

"Our national life, expansion of existing industry and the establishment of new industry are to some extent dependent upon an economic and reliable supply of electricity. The time required to construct a large power station means that failure to provide for the country's need now can never be retrieved and could be a limitation to future expansion and prosperity.

"Success in selling large turbogenerator sets overseas has owed much to experience gained in building sets of advanced design for this country. Without a substantial programme of new UK power stations the difficulties of obtaining export orders will be increased."

After showing that the pre-tax profit of *Davy-Ashmore Limited* (September 24) improved on his forecast of a year previously, SIR MAURICE FIENNES warned members not to attach too much importance to the figures of group turnover which the company is now obliged to publish, for the reasons given in this extract from his statement:

"We are required this year to show a figure for turnover and a comparison with the previous year. The bare figures show an apparent drop from about £58m. to £50m., but the figure for 1966/67 was abnormally high due to an exceptional number of contracts being brought into account for a variety of reasons. In previous years I have avoided emphasis on turnover figures because their relevance to our profits in any given year is highly variable and they can be actively misleading. Although we observe consistent practices in bringing profit or loss into account in each financial year, the practices differ in the various group companies according to the nature of the respective business. Contract completion dates can affect annual turnover figures quite substantially, whilst the nature of the contracts (*e.g.* whether they comprise services only, or services plus equipment) can also render comparison of one year with another

largely irrelevant. Members should not, therefore, attach too much importance to the bare turnover figures which the Companies Act 1967 now requires us to show."

Whereas the financial results of *Babcock & Wilcox Limited* (May 30) might be regarded as satisfactory in difficult trading circumstances, SIR KENNETH HAGUE stated, the reduced order book was a cause of some anxiety for the future. He explained:

"To design and manufacture efficiently large steam-raising plant, conventional or nuclear—or indeed any process plant—a reasonably steady intake of orders is essential to balance the load on the engineering departments and the works. Many times during the last twenty years abrupt changes in the national programme have caused us major problems in dealing with the resulting imbalance in the company. It is essential that project, design and engineering skills be fully maintained to put forward competitive bids for export, but this is difficult to attain and also very costly when we have to contend with a violently fluctuating home demand. In spite of our constant endeavours to anticipate such changes this problem is at present more acute than ever before.

"Moreover, the present political and economic situation, both at home and abroad, adds to the difficulty of making reliable long-term, or short-term, predictions. Nevertheless, I would say that I am in no way despondent for the future of the company. The Management is fully alive to the implications in current trading conditions and all sections of the Group are well equipped in technical manpower and production facilities to meet the changing situations as they occur."

The steam generation and power plant division of *Clarke, Chapman & Company Limited*, according to MR. J. B. WOODESON's statement (*The Times*, March 11), had had an extremely busy year, and he claimed that the real benefits of the reorganized management structure were now apparent. He went on to state:

"It is particularly unfortunate that the economic crisis has resulted in yet a further reduction in the C.E.G.B. power station programme for 1973. This could cause a serious gap in the industry's workload in the next few years. I am pleased to report, however, that our associates, The Nuclear Power Group Ltd., last year negotiated a contract for an Advanced Gas Cooled Reactor Power Station for Hunterston. This Station is for the supply of energy to the South of Scotland Electricity Board and your company is responsible for the steam generation units. This contract is very similar to that received last year for Hinkley Point 'B'. Again, it will be shared with our partners, John Thompson (Design & Contracting) Ltd., of Wolverhampton, and these two contracts, together with three

270

2000Mw conventional stations on hand for the C.E.G.B. provide a reasonably satisfactory workload for 1968 and 1969. Despite this workload for the next two years there is ample capacity in all departments of this Division to handle further boiler and kindred plant."

SIR JOHN WRIGHTSON defined the areas to which the productive capacity of *Head Wrightson and Company* (July 11) was directed and made some remarks about the company's prospects in the subjoined extract from his review:

"Your company is involved in supplying plant and equipment to a wide range of industry, our principal markets being in the steel, mining, chemical and nuclear power industries. In addition we supply castings and forgings to the mechanical engineering industry and thus we have a wide range of customers. Almost everything that your company produces is dependent upon a decision by other people to sanction capital expenditure and almost everything we supply is custom built following the placing of an order and subsequent agreement on detailed design. This means that we are dependent first upon the world cycle of demand for capital goods and next, upon the consequent U.K. cycle of demand for similar goods.

"The present level of demand is depressed and accordingly there is relative over-capacity in the supplying industries. Our endeavour is to correct the company's position in relation to these market conditions. An improvement in the United Kingdom demand for capital plant and equipment would be reflected in our order position fairly quickly. The quality of the plant and equipment we supply and the repeat orders we receive are evidence of the confidence placed in us. Despite our present difficulties and the uncertainties with which the U.K. economy is beset our long term prospects are good."

Group turnover for the year of *International Combustion (Holdings) Limited* increased substantially to an all-time record, but SIR LAURENCE MENZIES (*The Times*, March 20) also had to admit that orders on hand had fallen by £18m. on the year, for which he also blamed the lack of available business from the nationalized electricity undertakings in the United Kingdom. It was much to be hoped that growth in the economy as a whole would before long re-assert itself, for this, he asserted, would inevitably lead to a revival in the rate of growth of demand for electrical power.

In his statement for *Yarrow and Company Limited* (December 30) SIR ERIC YARROW hinted at the possibility of future developments in two of the divisions remaining after the formation of Yarrow Shipbuilders Limited. He stated:

"Although within the Boiler and Engineering Divisions we are actively seeking new products, and indeed have had some

271

success in this, your Board is having a close look at the long term activities of both Divisions. It is our view that the Boiler Divisions, and possibly the Engineering Division with it, could be strengthened by development into a larger unit. With this in mind, we have had discussions with various organizations, and shareholders will be kept informed if we should propose any material change in either or both these Divisions."

Group products of *W. P. Butterfield Limited* (August 29) comprised capital equipment and components and consumer durables. Capital goods included road tankers and chemical and industrial plant, stated MR. R. M. DAVENPORT, but the markets for these were depressed and fiercely competitive, and he did not predict early inprovement. He continued:

"Orders for municipal refuse collection vehicles have shown an encouraging increase, but curtailment of local government expenditure could have immediate adverse effect.

"Components include pressings, drop forgings, hydraulic tipping gears and industrial hydraulics, all aligned to the motor vehicle, mobile and industrial plant manufactuers. They are largely dependent on activity in these industries, now somewhat uneven. Recent months have brought an increase in enquiries and we are striving to convert these to firm orders.

"Consumer durables, including dustbins, housewares and hollow-wares and rubber mouldings, have shown a very satisfactory increase in output and orders and determined efforts are being made to maintain our position despite growing competition."

It was the intention of the board of *Warne, Wright & Rowland Limited* to continue to develop a modern and sound operating basis to foster major expansion, GROUP-CAPTAIN J. P. CECIL-WRIGHT stated in his annual review (*The Times*, May 9). He added that this was to be achieved by further acquisitions, when the time was right, and by internal growth.

An increase of 16 per cent in turnover of *Wm. Park & Co. Forgemasters Limited* (March 18), unfortunately, was overtaken by increases in cost beyond the board's control, asserted MR. O. C. LACE, and in view of the price freeze the profit for the year inevitably was lower than that for 1966. And, with the national economic climate as it was, the new year's profit seemed likely to be down again.

The trading experience of *Horseley Bridge Limited* (September 26) was summarized by MR. JOHN V. SHEFFIELD as follows:

"In my statement a year ago I made the assertion that the expansion of the economy of this country will eventually have to be resumed and, while this must still hold true, the year under review remained one in which the cut-back in the capital goods

industry continued. This resulted in an acute shortage in the number and value of orders placed with your company and in some instances orders already received were cancelled or deferred. Thus, in general, the group operated considerably below its full capacity and consequently the profit for the year was almost 40 per cent less than the record figure obtained in the previous year."

Remarking that a characteristic of the operation of 400,000 volt air-blast circuit-breakers at high air pressure was to make a loud noise on the release of the air into the atmosphere, SIR HAROLD MULLENS of *A. Reyrolle and Company Limited* (May 17) stated that this had been found objectionable in or close to residential areas. Now, however, after much detailed research and development the company's engineers had successfully produced a silencer which effectively reduced the noise to an acceptable level. These silencers, he added, were being fitted to a large number of circuit-breakers already in service as well as to new ones to be delivered to sites where noise was of particular concern.

As regards the heavy equipment division of *Whessoe Limited* (July 30), MR. JOHN H. LORD included this paragraph in his statement:

"The order intake of this division, still the most important in the Group, increased by $22\frac{1}{2}\%$ over last year, the improvement in the early part of 1967 continuing throughout and also in 1968. The pattern of orders received was similar to that in the preceding year, the Oil and Nuclear Power Industries being outstanding with the Gas and Chemical Industries still reflecting the reduction in their capital expenditure programmes of the last two years."

In his statement (*The Times*, July 25) for *Ferranti Limited* MR. SEBASTIAN Z. DE FERRANTI reported that the company's output of transformers reached a new record figure in spite of the serious fire in the factory on September 1, 1967, which put the super test area out of action for three months. A considerable fall in the home input of transformers was more than made up by a substantial increase in export orders, to yield a higher total input.

At home profits in engineering of *The Low & Bonar Group Limited* (June 19) held up remarkably well in 1967, declared SIR HERBERT V. BONAR, but would be sharply reduced in 1968. He went on:

"Part of that prospective reduction stems from the recent high prices of copper, but that part should be covered by the use of Specific Reserves created in the past and increased in the 1967 Accounts for just such a situation. The rest of the fall stems from the current excess of capacity over demand in the transformer industry which has resulted in prices having to be

273

cut to the bone to ensure the continuance of a full work load in the factory. As I told you last year, the present over-capacity in the industry is the result of the sharp cutback in the planned electricity supply expansion programme which is controlled by Government policy, a cutback which has been in no way eased by the present economic state of the country and the need for reduced Government expenditure. This should be a temporary phase, but how long such a phase is likely to endure in present economic conditions is extremely difficult to predict."

As the Central Electricity Generating Board's power station programme appeared to be tailing off, MR. J. HARVEY HUMPHRYES stated, *Braithwaite & Co. Engineers Limited* (September 26) had been actively tendering for other work. In the year under review the company had succeeded in obtaining orders for nearly 20,000 tons of motorway and kindred bridgework. These orders had been obtained in the face of severe competition and consequently at bare prices, but would ensure full capacity at both works "and so maintain high efficiency and economic costs."

MR. G. C. D'ARCY BISS of *The Fairey Company Limited* (October 4) remarked that the future of the nuclear industry was at that time under discussion, and members would be aware that the Government had entrusted to the Industrial Reorganisation Corporation the task of recasting the industry and the companies in it in line with Government policy. "We have had many meetings with I.R.C. on the subject, but no finality has been achieved, and we have no clear picture of the future of Fairey Engineering Limited in relation to the industry."

For *H. M. Hobson Limited* (February 23) MR. T. SIMPSON included this paragraph in his speech:

"The company is entering upon a phase of increased activity in the nuclear field through the manufacture of fuel element containers which are required in large quantities for the new generation of Reactors of the advanced gas cooled type. I am pleased to report that valuable orders are already in hand and there is reason to believe that this activity will make an increasing contribution to our order book for some years to come."

ELECTRICAL, ELECTRONIC AND DOMESTIC APPLIANCES

In his statement (*The Times*, July 30) for *The General Electric Company Limited* LORD ALDINGTON said that the year to March 31, 1968, had seen the merger of AEI into GEC and the beginning of the construction of what would shortly become one of the great electrical companies of the world. He continued:

"It was also a year, as I forecast in my 1967 statement, of improved results for the pre-merged GEC and its then subsidiaries. The profit was £21,257,000, compared with £17,732,000 in 1966/67, and the turnover £197,500,000 compared with £180,000,000.

"In the course of our bid for AEI, we forecast profits for 1967/68 of the order of £21m. Although in total the actual result was better than this, the content of the final figure differed from the detailed forecasts. We made better profits from higher sales of consumer durables, and costs worked out slightly better than expected in switchgear and telecommunications. Several of our overseas companies fared worse than forecast. At home, neither Osram nor Woods of Colchester could maintain their profit margins. There were also some other less significant variations from predictions, but the figures were not enhanced by devaluation."

Profits of *British Insulated Callender's Cables Limited* (May 9) for 1967, as Lord McFadzean had forecast in his previous statement, did not achieve the record level of 1966, he now stated, but profits for the second six months, even before the effect of devaluation adjustments, improved on those for the first half-year. He went on to place these facts on record:

"In the United Kingdom, adverse conditions have applied to our non-ferrous metals products, particularly copper. For most of 1966 demand for these was at an exceptionally high level in a period of rising prices, whereas in 1967 the demand was at an abnormally low level and, for most of the year, prices were falling. Under the difficult conditions applying, business on our more important fabrication side was generally reasonably well maintained.

"On the other hand, although there have been difficulties in some areas, our Overseas Companies have in total had a successful year and their profits brought into the Group accounts have benefited substantially from devaluation. In accordance with our normal practice, the 1967 results of Overseas Subsidiaries have been converted into sterling at the rates of exchange ruling at the end of the year. As a result the sterling value of Sales by Overseas Companies has increased by £15·911m., Trading Profits by £1·663m. and Net Profit attributable to the Holding Company by £0·596m.

"In brief, the BICC Group has had a difficult year at home, but with the increased sterling contribution from our Overseas operations, our total Sales and Profits are the second highest in the history of the Group."

In the first half of the trading year which ended September 30, 1967, sales of the main subsidiary of *M. K. Electric Holdings*

Limited (July 25) were comparable with those for the same period of 1966, MR. F. D. O'BRIEN NEWMAN declared. However, in October, 1967, orders received increased very substantially, and this trend continued throughout the remainder of the trading year. He added:

"The heavy capital expenditure incurred in previous years to provide increased productive capacity, coupled with the facilities of a new centralized warehouse, enabled the company to execute promptly many of these substantially increased orders. A proportion of these orders was met from stocks of finished products built up in the previous year."

An interesting point in the statement (*The Times*, August 6) by MR. I. SCLAR for *James Scott* (*Electrical Holdings*) *Limited* was that the company's control panel manufacturing unit had been chosen to make the main control desks for the new Cunarder *Queen Elizabeth 2*.

Publication of a new edition of a valued electrical handbook was mentioned by MR. J. A. CRABTREE of *Crabtree Electrical Industries Limited* (December 19):

"In May, 1968, we published the fourth edition of 'The Crabtree Electrical Handbook'. This was first introduced in 1941 and rapidly established itself as a reliable book of reference in the Electrical Industry: reprints followed in 1947 and 1959. The present edition has been completely revised and extended and now runs to over 800 pages; the demand for this new edition has been most gratifying and clearly indicates that in producing such a publication we have met a real need."

Among the salient features of the statement (*The Times*, November 15) by LORD HARDING OF PETHERTON for *The Plessey Company Limited* were that turnover increased by 14·1 per cent and pre-tax profits increased by 15 per cent to a new record; that the profit forecast for 1969 was up by 21 per cent; that exports of the electronics group were doubled; that the company had taken a major stake in ICL, had made a major entry into the United States aerospace market, and that its telecommunications deliveries, home and overseas, were a record.

The formation of Holzer Controls Limited with Holzer Export G.m.b.H and *N.S.F. Limited* each holding half of the equity was mentioned by MR. G. E. LIARDET in his review (*The Times*, October 16) for the last named company. He stated that staff had been trained, and production of automatic time switches and controls was about to begin in the factory at Houghton-le-Spring, County Durham, which the Board of Trade had made available.

While the past year had brought with it many difficulties for *Painton and Company Limited* (October 7), MR. C. M. BENHAM declared none the less that the company had succeeded in improv-

276

ing its position. With the more optimistic sentiment and the greater business confidence which he felt was developing, shareholders could look forward to a period of more rapid progress.

Renewed difficulties faced by the plant and instrument division of the Vacwell subsidiary of the *Electronic Machine Company Limited* (August 15) were the subject of the following comment by MR. M. WELLING:

> "This Section, beginning to recover from the setback caused by the destruction of its Research Laboratories in 1966, was faced in May, 1967, with a Government Export Control order placing all its products on the strategic embargo list. This restriction destroyed overnight a multi-million pound export business and made it impossible for Vacwell to carry on developing and manufacturing its existing range of equipment as the home market was too small to carry the expenditures involved. However, quick surgery and the expansion of aviation activities made it possible to bring Vacwell and its subsidiaries into an overall profit position by March, 1968, in spite of the Plant and Instrument Division having made a net loss in excess of £60,000 for the year. It is this production unit which is slowly recovering from the blows it has received through circumstances outside the control of your Board."

Group sales of *George Kent Limited* increased by nearly £5m. on the year, and profit after tax exceeded £1m. for the first time, MR. RODNEY G. KENT showed in his statement (*The Times*, August 13). He declared the group was rigorously pursuing a policy of expansion both internally and externally, and added:

> "Continuing efforts are being made in rationalizing products and marketing and it is intended to maintain a judicious mixture of companies giving a high immediate return on capital employed, together with those having longer-term growth possibilities—also, to expand those areas of companies which are central and peripheral to the industry. It is noteworthy that following the acquisition of the Cambridge Instrument Company, the Group now employs more than 10,500 people and total capital exceeds £33m."

In the past year each of the companies in the *Concentric Limited* group (December 20) had made progress, asserted MR. S. G. MORGAN, but outstanding had been the greatly increased production of gas controls; it was planned and expected that the major progress would be made in this field. On Concentric Controls Limited he commented:

> "The high level of production reported last year has not only continued but has greatly increased so that output is now double that of a year ago and still increasing. Its share of the Gas

Domestic Appliance Controls market continues to expand and full advantage has been taken of conversion to North Sea Gas. We look to this company's growth continuing during the coming year."

The value of the group order book for *Drake & Gorham, Scull Limited* (September 24) carried into the new financial year reached a record figure of £41m., according to MR. R. H. M. DRAKE. Since the end of the old year, he added, certain large overseas contracts had been received, bringing the current value up to £45m., which was considered satisfactory in both quality and volume.

Commenting on the continued expansion of the electronics division of *Keelavite Hydraulics Limited* (November 5), MR. GEORGE V. KEELING declared that the continual improvement in electronic system components inevitably resulted in a continuous development programme in this field.

Group sales of *The Chloride Electric Storage Company Limited* increased to over £50m., it was stated in the annual report (*The Times*, April 10). Batteries and allied activities now accounted for 90 per cent of sales; but a developing source of income for the group was comprised of overseas contracts ranging from technical aid and consultancy services to complete factory installation.

The consumer products division of *The Ever Ready Company (Great Britain) Limited* did not achieve its profit target for the year, MR. L. W. ORCHARD declared in his statement (*The Times*, June 17), and the industrial division would not be making any worthwhile contribution to group profits until 1969–70. But, he added, the engineering and international divisions both returned satisfactory returns enabling the directors to show an overall increase in group profits before tax.

The year's figures for *Oldham & Son Limited* (September 12), MR. ORLANDO OLDHAM asserted, showed that some of the board's recent spadework was beginning to bear fruit. "We are a healthy company in a growing but changing industry," he added. Battery manufacture showed great vitality and versatility; new outlets were still opening up for the lead-acid battery; and the company retained its enthusiasm for Tomorrow without losing sight of immediate needs.

During the first half of 1967, declared MR. F. N. MANSAGER of *Hoover Limited* (April 2), the domestic appliance industry was severely handicapped by stringent credit restrictions; and turnover, especially for washing machines, was considerably lower than in the first half of 1966. He continued:

"The introduction of our new Keymatic De Luxe in April added some impetus to our sales and by the end of June we had recovered much of the ground we had lost. Profits were, however, squeezed by the persistent under-utilization of our production facilities and the initial run-up costs of the new Keymatic.

278

With the easing of hire-purchase restrictions in August, some improvement in sales was evident and the last quarter of the year provided the 30 per cent of the annual turnover which we normally expect.

"The policy of extending our product range also began to yield dividends, with the result that total group turnover for the year increased from £47,900,000 to £51,000,000—the highest figure since 1964."

The period since his previous statement, declared SIR JULES THORN of *Thorn Electrical Industries Limited* (August 30), had been one of unprecedented growth for the company: record profits had been achieved in 1967–68, and the group had been further strengthened by a number of important acquisitions, on which subject Sir Jules stated that the board had always been conscious of the necessity of competing on equal terms with major manufacturers in North America, Japan and Europe and realized that in many cases this could be achieved only by creating units of sufficient size.

In 1967 sales of *The Prestige Group Limited* (March 29) were slightly higher than in 1966, but profit before tax increased by 14 per cent, and MR. W. F. LAPORTE showed that considerable reductions in expense were obtained through improved efficiency in production and economics in all aspects of the business. He added that these had enabled the group to absorb higher costs in the United Kingdom.

Reporting a higher profit and an increased dividend for *Goblin* (*B. V. C.*) *Limited*, MR. O. D. ANGELL included this paragraph in his annual review (*The Times*, February 7):

"The Group is frequently thought of as being pre-eminently a consumer manufacturing organization. In fact, however, 50% of our production and 60% of our profit is represented by a diversified range of vacuum-cleaning, electrical and electronic equipment used in practically every industrial sector in Britain. Our growth in this sector has been strengthened by the steady progress we have made overseas with exports of industrial equipment. During the last five years exports have increased on an average by 30% each year. We confidently look forward to continued growth in exports."

The year 1967 presented many difficulties to *Midland Electric Manufacturing Company Limited* (April 2), but MR. W. J. BARBER declared that they were successful in achieving economies and improving efficiency, which had contributed to a small increase in the group net profit before taxation. Moreover, there was a definite improvement in demand towards the end of the year, which was continuing into the new year.

Another chairman who was able to report increased sales during

279

the final quarter of the year to March 30, 1968, was MR. J. C. WILKINS of *Wilkins & Mitchell Limited* (September 10), who stated:

> "Our range of SERVIS Washing Machines continues to receive wide acceptance, which has enabled us to maintain our share of an increased home market. The increased profit attributed to these sales was enhanced by reduced costs in distribution and a fuller and more efficient utilization of factory equipment helped by increased sales, especially during the last quarter of the year."

In his statement (*The Times*, November 22) for *Tube Investments Limited* LORD PLOWDEN said that demand for domestic electrical appliances was strong, and, though competition remained severe, both turnover and profits increased.

Although most of the overseas markets of *Dimplex Industries Limited* (July 19) showed increases in volume, MR. E. J. WADE stated that sales in the company's largest export market—Benelux —were "most disappointing"; and consequently for the first time in many years the company had not shown a substantial overall increase in export sales. As home market sales during the first half of the winter were well below forecast, thanks to the general economic situation and substantial electricity tariff increases, the board made an interim forecast that profits would be halved. However, orders for the last quarter were well above prediction because of the prolonged cold weather, low stocks in the trade pipeline, and, to a lesser extent, the pre-Budget boom. Accordingly, profits after all were down by only about one-seventh.

The *Kenwood Manufacturing Company Limited* (May 23), reported MR. IAN T. MORROW, had earned a satisfactory increase in profits through larger sales achieved in the second half of the year, the result of improved rationalization within the group on costs and profitability both at home and overseas.

AERONAUTICAL

In the British aircraft industry, stated SIR BERTRAM WARING of *Joseph Lucas (Industries) Limited* (December 16), the outstanding achievement of the year was the success of Rolls-Royce in winning the order for their RB.211 aero-engine for the American Lockheed airliner. He continued:

> "This is potentially the largest and most important overseas contract ever obtained by a British company and will secure their future for many years ahead. Elsewhere in the Industry however the future is uncertain. Although the Aircraft Manufacturers have made substantial sales to overseas countries, these represent the harvest from the design efforts of many

years ago and there is little now in the development stage to provide production work for the future. The only major new aircraft projects in which this country is participating are the consortium arrangements principally with France for the Concorde, the A-300 Airbus, the Jaguar strike-trainer and three helicopters. British airframe and equipment participation in these projects is insufficient to occupy their present capacity and facilities, and although Britain is contributing the biggest share of the total funds for these projects, airframe design leadership has in almost all cases been given to France. This country's future in the Aircraft Industry is being increasingly jeopardized by continuing Government indecision, and the time is rapidly running out in which a positive step can be taken."

The accounts for 1967 of *Rolls-Royce Limited*, LORD KINDERSLEY pointed out in his annual review (*The Times*, June 24), covered the first full year of operations following the merger with the Bristol Aeroplane Company and the acquisition of control of Bristol Siddeley Engines. Progress had been made, he added, in creating the organization designed to achieve the benefits of these acquisitions. All the activities previously carried on by Bristol Siddeley Engines had now been re-grouped as operating divisions of Rolls-Royce. Total turnover had exceeded the figure forecast in November, 1967, and gave good grounds for believing that all the measures which had been taken would yield the expected figure of £300m. in 1968. As regards prospects for 1968, Lord Kindersley stated:

"We commenced 1968 with outstanding orders amounting to £360m. and everything possible is being done to exploit all the advantage that can be obtained in export prices as a result of devaluation. Nevertheless, devaluation and the associated Government measures will have an adverse effect on costs. These must be matched by great productivity if we are to maintain our competitive position in the world. I am encouraged by the progress which is being made and in support of which there is a continuing programme of investment in new plant and the training of personnel at all levels. I believe that with the volume of business which we can foresee we can look forward to higher profits in 1968."

That the *British Aircraft Corporation* had made a remarkable recovery from the shattering blow it sustained in April, 1965, when the Government cancelled the contracts for the development and production of TSR-2, was stated by LORD PORTAL in his report (*The Times*, May 13). At that time, he wrote, BAC had become too dependent upon one key project, and its removal threatened the stability and even the viability of the whole corporation. He continued:

T 281

"Great efforts were needed to restore the situation and the success of the BAC sales teams, notably those engaged on the Lightning and the One-Eleven, played a major part in re-establishing a balanced position. By the end of last year the work load in the four Divisions of BAC was at a level which could hardly have been hoped for in mid 1965, and the Corporation was able to pay dividends of 6% in 1966 and $7\frac{1}{2}$% in 1967. Against this background, it is noteworthy that BAC has, in the three years ending June, 1967, exported products to a value of over £152m., and that the export order book then stood at another £113m., to which a number of subsequent orders have been added, including the recent big Libyan contract. At the time of writing this Report the orders for future exports stand at well over £200m. The Corporation gained a 1967 Queen's Award to Industry, having exported in the year ended June, 1966, equipment to a value of £58·9m. The Corporation has recently been honoured by a 1968 Award with a record export total in the year ended June, 1967, of over £68m. This trend is continuing and a further substantial increase in exports is expected in 1968. Since the Corporation's inception in 1960, it has delivered £250m. of equipment to export customers."

The next quotation comes from the annual report (*The Times*, June 19) of *Hawker Siddeley Group Limited*:

"For some time we have been in, and still are in, a period in which the state of the economy both at home and overseas, affects our activities adversely. Although the 'freeze' at home slowed down the upward trend of costs, it did not stop it, and we are now in the period in which many costs will increase following devaluation. War in the Middle East slowed our substantial export business in that area, although recovery is now becoming evident. There have been signs throughout the period of a tendency to contraction in the tempo of world trade in some of our products. The effect of the severe cancellations of military aerospace projects in 1965 continues to be felt and the more recent cuts in U.K. defence expenditure have inevitably affected our military business. The reduction of the rate of investment at home in electrical generating capacity has affected, and will continue to affect for some time, that part of our electrical business associated with generation and distribution."

Sir Walter Dawson's forecast a year previously that the new Jetstream aircraft could not begin to bring in substantial profits until 1969 remained unchanged, he declared in his annual review for *Handley Page Limited* (July 1), since the increased production planning was still geared to reach maximum rate at the end of 1969. He went on to state:

"The great improvement that had taken place in our sales

282

and sales prospects during the past year, together with our very satisfactory test and demonstration flying to date, results in a greatly increased potential for 1970 and the succeeding years. These facts justify the increased interim expenditure, without which we would fail to benefit from the great opportunities now open to us."

For *Westland Aircraft Limited*, SIR ERIC MENSFORTH in his statement (*The Times*, January 16) recalled that in October, 1967, the British and French Governments agreed to proceed jointly with the production of the SA.330 helicopter, and the design and development of the WG.13 and SA.340 helicopters. The company's share of the work on these three new types, together with the £24m. Sea King contract mentioned a year previously, assured the company—unless unexpected circumstances arose—of a great deal of work into the 1970s. He added:

"Joint production with Sud Aviation of the SA.330 tactical helicopter has begun; the design is proceeding to programme of the Westland WG.13 twin-engined helicopter. Discussions are nearing completion regarding the arrangements for sharing development and production of the SA.340 light observation helicopter. We are confident that this collaborative programme will increase our competitiveness."

The Government's cancellation of the F.111, whatever its justification on economic grounds, asserted LORD NELSON OF STAFFORD for *The English Electric Company Limited* (March 27), had meant the loss of equipment contracts by Marconi and Elliott-Automation and the possible loss of further offset business. He declared that the lack of a firm national policy to maintain the United Kingdom aircraft industry in the position it held until recently was a matter of grave concern.

For *Dowty Group Limited* (October 7) SIR GEORGE DOWTY mentioned that Dowty Rotol for many years had been a continuous supplier to the Fairchild Hiller Corporation in the United States and had recently received the Award of the Year presentation for 1967 as the most satisfactory of Fairchild's 400 suppliers, taking into account quality, deliveries on time and after-sales service. "We have retained a sales team in the United States," he stated, "in an effort to obtain orders to meet the increasing demands for airline equipment."

Referring to the capital investment which *H. M. Hobson Limited* (February 23) had undertaken in order to increase productive capacity, MR. T. SIMPSON said that a large part of the expenditure had been used to create a facility for machining larger components, thereby increasing the range of work available to the company. He continued:

"The increasing complexity of the demands on our machining

facilities and the need to maintain the company's position in the forefront of precision engineering calls for the most diligent attention to the maintenance of our workshop standards through the adoption of new techniques, using the finest and most advanced plant and machinery available. The effects of devaluation will add to the already high costs of capital replacement and expansion, but I am glad to report that the greater part of our capital needs in the immediate future has already been met."

Dealing with the Palmer Aero Products subsidiary of *BTR Industries Limited* (June 5), the late SIR WALTER WORBOYS stated that sales increased in spite of the difficulties of the aircraft industry. Products from the Palmer range of rigid and flexible pipes, harness and filters would be supplied to Concorde, Harrier and Jaguar aircraft, and further opportunities should arise in connection with the new generation of Rolls-Royce engines.

The aircraft division of *Electro-Hydraulics Limited* (March 13) had a good year in 1966–67, stated SIR ALFRED OWEN, but the current position was somewhat uncertain. However, it had a good percentage of commercial aircraft business which should build up in the future.

One of the points made by MR. C. J. FALK in his statement (*The Times*, October 16) for *Falks Limited* was that the company had supplied the instrumentation cables for the Concorde airliner.

CIVIL

The value of work carried out abroad by *George Wimpey & Co., Limited* (May 3), at £24·7m., SIR GODFREY MITCHELL claimed, was the highest the group had yet achieved, and represented a substantial contribution to the achievements of British contractors in the international field of building, civil, mechanical and electrical engineering.

In his statement (*The Times*, May 29) for *John Mowlem & Compamy Limited* MR. E. C. BECK remarked that Mowlem (Civil Engineering) Limited was undertaking many types of civil engineering works with a total value of £37m. Among a number of major projects which he mentioned were the Victoria Line tunnel and the reconstruction of London Bridge.

The following comment on the order book of *Mitchell Construction Holdings Limited* (July 18) is extracted from MR. D. D. MORRELL'S statement.:

"The overall position of the Order Book is again very satisfactory, the peak position during the year having again reached a record level. In general the work load is well distributed between the various companies in the Group, the one exception being that there is a shortage of heavy civil engineering work

out to tender in the United Kingdom at the present time. While this is redressed financially in other areas of our activity, we are naturally reluctant to see our resources in this field under-employed. We are accordingly increasing our efforts to secure appropriate overseas civil engineering projects, either acting on our own or in consort with other United Kingdom and overseas contractors.

"This does not, of course, alter our dependence upon our home operations to provide a satisfactory base from which to mount our overseas efforts and close attention is being paid to the balance of work load in the home market."

The next quotation comes from the annual review by COLONEL A. C. NEWMAN for *W. & C. French Limited* (May 31):

"During the past eighteen months the Ministry of Transport has afforded us opportunities to become one of the leading Con-tractors in the National Road Programme. We have taken the necessary steps to organize and equip ourselves accordingly and hope that this type of Civil Engineering work, in which we feel we have considerable experience extending over many years, will constitute an important part of our heavy engineering efforts of the future."

MR. A. J. MCALPINE informed members of *Marchwiel Holdings Limited* (April 4), controlling Sir Alfred McAlpine & Son Limited, that the company had a satisfactory volume of work in hand at least equal to that of a year previously, and he hoped that the year to October 31, 1968, given reasonable weather conditions, would be an improvement on the year under review, which itself had im-proved slightly on the previous year.

The policy of the directors of the *Staffordshire Public Works Company Limited* (March 29) in face of dwindling profit margins on certain types of civil engineering work was outlined by MR. F. MERCER PINFOLD in the following two paragraphs:

"The year under review has seen some benefit from the plans we made last year—firstly, to counteract the narrowing profit margins on certain sections of the civil engineering division, and, secondly, to develop the more profitable sections of mechanical engineering.

"The continuing shortage of major contracts in the Govern-ment, Municipal, and Industrial sectors has resulted in such an element of fierce competition that much of that work is currently being done at little or no profit to the contractors. With that in mind we have not actively pursued much of that trade, but have concentrated more on the smaller contracts of civil engineering in which our expertise can be put to better account."

With the full effects of the Budget still to be felt, MR. JAMES

ROBERTSON told members of *Whatlings Limited* (May 23), the long-term prospects for the construction industry remained uncertain. However, the company had an impressive volume of work on hand at slightly improved margins and was well placed to meet any problems that might arise. The results for the first six months, he added, indicated that a return to the practice of paying an interim dividend in September would be justified, but "with six months' trading still to be assessed and in view of the Government restrictions on dividends, this will not necessarily imply an increased total for the year."

Members of *F. C. Construction (Holdings) Limited* (June 18) were informed by MR. JOHN A. DRAKE that the civil engineering subsidiary had carried out a variety of contracts for private and nationalized industry, consulting engineers and architects. With a greater value of orders booked in the first four months of 1968 than in the corresponding period of 1967, prospects appeared satisfactory.

MACHINE AND OTHER TOOLS

The accounts for the past year, stated MR. R. D. YOUNG, related to an expanded *Alfred Herbert Limited* with total group sales of £44m. and profits before tax of £4,197,627. Lowered industrial confidence and cash flows had restricted the capital spending of many users, and the machine tool industry ended the year with order books at their lowest since 1964. However, a good start had been made with initiating the Herbert-Ingersoll project and in rationalizing products, plants and sales teams; and spending had been maintained on new designs and on the development of increased management and productive resources.

The next quotation, dealing mainly with the activities of Wickman Limited, comes from the statement by LORD ABERCONWAY for *John Brown and Company Limited* (September 6):

"The Wickman group has continued on its excellent way and has increased its profits. With the addition of machines of novel and advanced design to the already wide range of machines which Wickman can offer, the manufacturing load of the Group should be close to capacity. Whilst orders at home and abroad prove difficult to get and deliveries of machines exceed the volume of new orders, an order received since the end of the year from the U.S.S.R. for multi-spindle automatic lathes to the value of about £1,200,000 for the Togliatti motor car plant in the Soviet Union should ensure full production at Banner Lane during the current year. No less than 54 per cent of multi-spindle automatic lathes produced last year were exported.

"Wickham Wimet Ltd., which continues to enjoy a high reputation and a leading position in the tungsten carbide tool

field, secured a volume of orders not much less in total than in the previous year. Intense competition and increased costs, particularly of wolfram, led to a reduction in profits."

Machine tool companies in the *Staveley Industries Limited* group which were producing standard type machines had improved profits, while those making heavier and non-standard products had fared much worse than in the previous year. This was stated by MR. DENIS HAVILAND in his annual review (*The Times*, February 20). The net result had been a reduction of profit by one-third. Further steps were taken in rationalizing foundry capacity and products between factories, and the group continued to acquire other machine tool concerns.

LORD PLOWDEN in his survey (*The Times*, November 22) for *Tube Investments Limited* declared that a low level of demand affected the whole machine tool industry. He added, however, that new products had been introduced which, it was hoped, would lead to stronger demand in 1969.

The subjoined paragraph comes from MR. F. G. MORRIS'S statement for *A. A. Jones & Shipman Limited* (May 8):

"Preparation of machines for the International Machine Tool exhibition at Olympia in July of this year is well advanced. The equipment to be shown contains many technical improvements for our type of product. Moreover the company was pleased to be amongst those selected by the Ministry of Technology for orders placed under their Pre-production order scheme, whereby advanced Machine Tools are purchased by the Ministry for installation in selected customers' plants for a two year trial period. This scheme is designed to have the effect of speeding up acceptance by industry of the latest machine tool techniques available."

The slight setback which *The Newall Machine Tool Company Limited* (July 22) incurred in the previous year because of expansion and reorganization had now been more than made good, and the group profit before tax showed a solid increase. Thus stated MR. DENIS S. PLAYER, who went on to declare:

"Part of the results of the re-organization has made it necessary to revalue our stock and fixed assets to bring them into line with modern concepts of assessment of these assets and this has meant an addition to the net profit figure which has been transferred to reserve and has not been taken into account in arriving at any comparative figures.

"So far as our companies are concerned, Newall has been unaffected by 'cyclical dip' which is often talked about with regard to general machine tool business and I feel that the amount of effort which all members of our team have made over many years in the past, particularly in respect of export, has

helped us considerably to provide orders for our companies.

"Our policy of specialization which we have been practising for many years now has proved to be the correct approach to the world machine tool industry and I believe that in the future the number of manufacturing companies will be reduced and those left will have survived on technical achievement, efficiency and offering the customer equipment which he wishes to buy."

MR. A. OWEN, reporting a sharp setback in the results of the *Brooke Tool Manufacturing Company Limited* (March 29), stated that the parent company had been badly affected by a marked falling-off in demand for cutting tools and a corresponding reduction in sales which, combined with heavy pressures on margins, had produced a substantial fall in trading profit. The northern subsidiaries, however, had had an excellent year.

In a difficult year for the machine tool division of *Wilkins & Mitchell Limited* (September 10), turnover, both home and export, was lower than in the previous year. As regards the fall in home sales, there could be no question, in the view of MR. J. C. WILKINS that the uncertain political and economic climate that had existed in this country over the last two or three years had a detrimental effect on the sale of power presses.

"However," he continued, "our export orders for power presses have now increased considerably and we hope to more than restore the excellent export performance to which this Division is accustomed. Orders for our presses manufactured under licence in Australia have also increased. In addition we are currently increasing our facilities by extending our buildings and installing new plant."

In his statement (*The Times*, July 4) for *Whitecroft Industrial Holdings Limited* MR. E. G. GOOLD mentioned that the board had approved expenditure of £500,000 on buildings and plant to enable Thomas Ryder & Son Limited to handle demand for new products on show at the International Machine Tool Exhibition.

MECHANICAL, HYDRAULIC AND OTHER

With some commendable exceptions *Guest, Keen and Nettlefolds Limited* (May 2), MR. RAYMOND P. BROOKES stated, failed over a fairly wide front to achieve budgeted financial objectives, which when determined towards the end of 1966 did not and perhaps could not take into account the ensuing near-total collapse of United Kingdom Government policies and associated economic predictions culminating in devaluation. The lack of confidence thereby progressively generated, he added, affected all the major industries served by GKN, and in particular for the first time in many years the commercial vehicle, car and tractor industries were

simultaneously depressed and further hampered by a prolonged series of labour disputes. However, while rejecting complacency, he believed that under the stress of very difficult conditions the major internal reorganization initiated in recent years had demonstrated its practical worth and would continue so to do.

SIR LESLIE ROWAN remarked that during the present decade *Vickers Limited* (June 6) had had to carry through one of the biggest transformations ever made by a British industrial group. He went on to explain:

"Aircraft, armaments, shipbuilding and steel were the mainstays of the Group up to 1960. Steel has been nationalized, and aircraft is in BAC; shipbuilding has become concentrated on sophisticated vessels at one Yard and armaments, other than naval, have diminished greatly. An organization primarily engaged on armaments production has had to become an organization geared largely to commercial engineering, including commercial engineering in new fields, with the manufacturer directly concerned with a much wider spread of customers. This has meant different management structures, different methods, different attitudes. Inevitably change on this scale takes time; and progress has been slowed until recently by shortage of cash and restrictions on borrowing powers. Nor has the process been aided, to say the least, by frequent changes in Government defence policy which have made it difficult to plan how and when armament capacity should be reduced.

"It has been a phase of upheaval and disappointment but now, I believe, given a reasonably good economic environment, there are better things ahead. The planning and effort of those painful years should increasingly bring their rewards."

For *Tube Investments Limited* LORD PLOWDEN reported (*The Times*, November 22) that the efforts to reshape the group and to tackle its problem areas were taking effect. The principal objectives had been to obtain a better balance between capital and consumer goods and to improve profit potential in each field of activity. He added that the acquisition of Radiation and the sale of Loewy Robertson had brought the group to about the kind of balance it was seeking. The steps which had been taken should increasingly be reflected in profits in the future.

Turnover for the year of *Mather & Platt Limited* increased by over 20 per cent to a record figure, while group profits jumped by nearly 33 per cent, stated SIR WILLIAM L. MATHER in his review (*The Times*, April 4).

LORD EXETER was able to report a $3\frac{1}{2}$ per cent increase in trading surplus of *Birmid Qualcast Limited* (December 20) over the previous period, even though the latter included 13 months' and 16 months' trading respectively by Qualcast and by Wright Rain as a consequence of their joining the group. This result he con-

sidered satisfactory bearing in mind that it had been accomplished in a period of price restraint and against a background of unease and disruption in the motor car and component industries which provide one of the biggest outlets for the group's products.

The wide spread of the home business of *Associated Engineering Limited* produced a 1½ per cent increase in United Kingdom sales and a 7 per cent increase in profits, in spite of a substantial fall in sales to car manufacturers. Sales by the overseas subsidiaries rose by 14 per cent and profits by 22 per cent, and direct exports from the United Kingdom rose by 6 per cent. As to the outlook, Mr. H. R. Moore made this comment (*The Times*, January 26):

"Before devaluation we budgeted for a substantial profit increase for the current year. This is now probably unrealistic and we shall have a difficult but not impossible task to improve on the performance of last year. In spite of the present serious economic situation, we do not intend to cut back proposed expenditure on re-equipping our plants nor on research and development; both of these are vital for the future."

Group profits of *Glynwed Limited* (May 3) for 1967 picked up after an early setback, and Mr. W. G. A. Russell considered that on the whole the group should do at least as well in 1968 as in 1967, though as he stated no business man could then forecast the results of 1968 with any real confidence because of the uncertainty arising from Government economic policies on consumer demand, production costs and taxation burdens that could influence the cost of services and supplies which the group purchased. He continued:

"There seems little doubt that we shall have difficulty in exceeding our present share of the markets for most of our established products and if those markets contract we may suffer proportionately. On the other hand, some of our products which have, in recent years, been going through development difficulties, are now available in growing quantities. This will give new opportunities for profitable growth which may offset any contraction in other areas during 1968, giving greater opportunities for growth thereafter.

"Our figures for direct exports for 1967 look somewhat insignificant but they exclude several million pounds worth of 'indirect' exports. For example our sales of steel bar and sections and of bolts, nuts and studs include extensive sales to the motor vehicle industry which has itself achieved notable success in export sales. At the same time we are vigorously pursuing direct exports of such of our products as can find markets abroad and we look for a useful expansion of such sales in 1968."

Profits of *Peter Brotherhood Limited* (November 12) were the lowest for a number of years, but in the absence of events beyond

the directors' control MR. G. W. WILKS looked in the current year—to March 31, 1969—for a marked improvement in turnover invoiced and in profits before tax. "Our competitiveness could be further improved," he declared, "if we were not constantly being asked to absorb increases in taxation and in the charges of most public bodies. I referred to this last year, and the process is not only continuing but accelerating."

The next quotation comes from SIR THOMAS ROBSON'S statement for *Renold Limited* (August 1):

"The results for the year show the inevitable effect of restriction of demand in the home market at a time when world trade was also contracting because of similar deflationary action taken by foreign governments. Our fears on this score, which my predecessor expressed last year, were only too well founded and this was particularly true in Continental Europe. A recession in Continental Europe has a twofold effect on us: it affects our exports to that area and it restricts the activities of our subsidiaries which manufacture there."

Sir Thomas added that it seemed not to be altogether appreciated that the recession in Continental Europe in 1967 was even more severe than the one experienced in the United Kingdom. However, he was able to say that conditions in Europe were now very much improved.

The Hoffmann Manufacturing Company Limited (May 7) found competition at home and from abroad stronger than ever, while at the same time costs continued to increase, overtaking economies made in the first half of the year, MR. J. W. GARTON declared, and the price increase at the close of 1967 had not contributed significantly by way of relief to the results. As regards the outlook, he made these comments:

"Though we are taking every opportunity presented by devaluation to increase our export trade, if possible at improved prices, the switch from Home trade, which is the Government's aim, is bound to militate against any improvement in our profits. It is not possible to forecast what the company will achieve in 1968, and a recovery from the unfavourable trading conditions which we have been experiencing in recent years will be even more difficult, having regard to the impact on consumer spending and the effect on costs generally of the recent severe Budget measures. We shall continue our efforts to secure reductions in our costs and to cut down the degree of under-utilization of capacity in our factories."

Among the points made by MR. EDWARD SENIOR in his review (*The Times*, October 31) for *Ransome & Marles Bearing Company Limited* was the following:

"Orders received during the first three months of the current year are in excess of those of the same period of the previous year for both Home and Export markets. Although the Bearing Industry is a highly competitive one, the steps which we have taken and are constantly taking to improve our competitive position should ensure the future prosperity of your company, and the Board expects a further improvement for the current year."

There was a marked increase towards the end of the year in orders received by *Pollard Ball and Roller Bearing Company Limited*, and, according to MR. JOHN KING's statement (*The Times*, July 3), the group booked more new business during December than in any other month in its history.

MR. A. IVOR BAKER informed members of *Baker Perkins Holdings Limited* (June 28) that the large sums spent on the development of web offset magazine and newspaper printing presses were resulting in important orders and many inquiries.

With the constant interference in private enterprise by the Government it was difficult to be optimistic about the future, declared MR. N. P. NEWMAN of *Newman, Hender & Co. Limited* (August 23), but he nevertheless had great confidence in the ability of private enterprise in general and of the group in particular to overcome the many discouragements and difficulties with which they were faced. He added that in the light of somewhat improving export demand the board hoped to present more favourable accounts in a year's time.

Trading profits in the United Kingdom of *Westinghouse Brake and Signal Company Limited* (February 26) in 1966–67 had more than doubled, but with the Indian companies turning in a still larger loss, the total trading profit of the group was somewhat lower. This was shown by MR. P. EWEN, who added that the prospects in the United Kingdom were good, thanks to the increasing benefit from reorganization schemes, but that it was improbable that in the remaining months of their financial year to June 30, 1968, the Indian companies would be able to register a substantial improvement.

LORD ABERCONWAY included this reference to a change of product at Cravens Industries Limited in his statement for *John Brown and Company Limited* (September 6):

"Following completion of all outstanding railway rolling stock the factory in Sheffield was laid out and equipped to concentrate on the production of containers and trailers in light alloy and steel, for which substantial orders have been received."

After a good year, with increased productivity which enabled the company to contain rising costs, MR. C. W. HAWKINS took a

favourable view of the outlook for *The Dover Engineering Works Limited* (August 14):

"I can say that I view the future with confidence, that our management is now stronger than at any time in the company's history and well equipped to deal with whatever problems arise. These still include the problem of maintaining the labour force and of gradually extending the mechanized processes, coupled with the foreshadowed conversion to the metric system. Meantime, however, trade for the first quarter of the current year compares favourably with that for the same period last year and the forward order position remains satisfactory."

Thanks partly to an excellent last quarter, record results were achieved by *Ernest Scragg & Sons (Holdings) Limited* (March 19), stated MR. E. P. R. SCRAGG. With two new machines making an encouraging start, the order situation was most satisfactory, and output per month had averaged 50 per cent more than last year's rate. Factory extensions were now proceeding in order to cope with the demand, and he was confident that the results for 1967–68 would show a further very substantial improvement.

A Russian order for Constructors John Brown Limited, a subsidiary of *John Brown and Company Limited* (September 6), is the subject of this paragraph from LORD ABERCONWAY's statement:

"CJB has virtually completed the shipment to Russia of the materials, for which CJB itself is responsible, for the complex polyester fibres factory which, with Stone-Platt Industries Ltd., it is supplying to the U.S.S.R. The plant, which will fill an area almost the size of Hyde Park, will be erected by the Russians under the technical supervision of CJB, Stone-Platt and I.C.I."

The activities of the National Coal Board in mechanizing coal mining were praised by MR. F. BONSER in the following extract from his statement for *Bonser Engineering Limited* (June 27):

"Although 1967 sales constitute a record, the sales of mining equipment declined during the second half of the year. Despite the contraction of the coal mining industry, the National Coal Board is a most progressive thinking organization, especially in the field of mechanization, and much has been done in recent years in man-power saving techniques. There is still more to be done and I believe there is a great future for this company in the mechanization of the coal mining industry, both at home and abroad. Our development programme is at a higher level than ever before and for many years to come the National Coal Board will be one of the largest purchasers of mechanization equipment in this country."

During the past three years, stated MR. FRANK MORRIS of *Herbert Morris Limited* (March 15), the company had been busily

engaged designing and modernizing many of its product lines, including a complete range of new overhead electric cranes—the "Centre Lift 410," which had been very well received. In addition, it had developed a wide range of container handling equipment, for which an expanding world-wide market was envisaged. Other new developments included the setting up of a small electronics division for the purpose of developing its own electronic speed control systems.

Profit of *Stothert & Pitt Limited* (December 4), LORD BRECON reported, was adversely affected by the reduction in earnings of the crane division, which was the result in approximately equal measure of the development of container cranes and the short-fall in crane orders. He added that the number and type of crane inquiries being received at that time indicated some revival in the international market, but that competition was severe.

Following the shrinkage in coal and other traffic, stated MR. E. DUNCAN TAYLOR of *Wagon Repairs Limited* (September 26), the British Railways Board notified private repairing establishments that work would cease to be sent to certain of their works. As a result, the company was compelled to close 11 of its works in September and October, 1967. However, the group more than maintained its profit before taxation, thanks to increased work and improved mechanization in other directions.

The following information about the objects of *Transport and Chemical Engineering Limited* (December 20) was given by MR. J. H. M. MACKENZIE:

> "TACE was formed a year ago to invest mainly in progressive private and family controlled engineering companies, whose directors wish to make arrangements regarding succession or estate duty, or to remove their company from close company status. The Group's present interests are in the fields of transport and precision engineering and instrumentation. The first year's experience and progress indicate that there is considerable scope for further growth."

An entirely new and complete range of hydraulic valve and control gear was first shown to industry in 1968 at the International Machine Tool Exhibition by *Keelavite Hydraulics Limited* (November 5), MR. GEORGE V. KEELING mentioned; and he went on:

> "This range of valves complies with international standard mounting dimensions, which will enable us to attack certain markets—particularly export markets—which have previously been closed to the company. The knowledge gained in this development operation is now available to us for the purpose of producing similar valve ranges in other sizes with a minimum of effort and cost."

The new Supaheat central heating boiler was now in production by *William Sugg & Company Limited* (December 12), stated MR. R. W. YOUNG, and repeat orders indicated that considerable progress was being made. He also announced that the new range of air heaters was rapidly coming into production.

In view of the improvement in results of *Richard Crittall Holdings Limited* (June 7) the board were restoring the dividend to its 1965 level, stated SIR GEOFFREY ELEY. He added that orders received during the first quarter of the new year by the company's major contracting units were below those in the same period of the past year, but showed a slight improvement in profit margins. The volume of inquiries was also falling, but as soon as the country's massive building programme regained momentum the company, he asserted, should be well placed.

After a successful year, with sales and new orders received at record levels, for *The Walmsley (Bury) Group Limited* (November 8), MR. PERCY HOLLAND made these remarks on the outlook:

> "I have frequently pointed out that the level of profits in a company supplying large capital goods is greatly dependent in any one financial year on the delivery dates and terms of the contracts on which it is engaged. I cannot, therefore, give an assurance that, despite our excellent order book, profits in the current year will be maintained at last year's level. Present indications are that a reduced figure will be shown for 1969, with an up-swing in 1970, when profits will accrue on the more recently obtained contracts which I hope may prove to embody rather better margins. This is, inevitably, crystal gazing as much depends upon the efforts of all of us in containing costs."

CONTINENTAL COMPANIES

Generally speaking, the *Compagnie Générale de Télégraphie sans Fil* (Paris, June 5) had a share in most of the current great technical projects, it was stated in the report of the directors, and it gave the following examples:

> "The Concorde prototype, for instance, is fitted with C.S.F. controls. In space electronics there were a number of successful new ventures. In particular C.S.F. played a very important part in preparing the Franco-German 'Symphonic' programme of telecommunication satellites. . . .
> "In the field of colour television C.S.F. holds a third of the capital of Compagnie Française de Télévision, the other partners being Compagnie de Saint Gobain and the Floirat Group. Now that the French Government has injected fresh capital and acquired a holding in the company, the C.S.F. interest has shrunk to 25 per cent."

The board of the *S. A. des Engins Matra* (June 27) in their annual report drew attention to the considerable expansion of the 530 series of missiles and the development of the new Martel, Crotale and Masurca missiles; in the space division Matra formed part of national and international programmes (Diamant B launcher, TD heavy satellite and telecommunications satellite).

Among the features of the year for *Hoesch AG* (Dortmund, May 15) mentioned by Dr. WILLY OCHEL was that in November, 1967, Richard Thomas & Baldwins in the United Kingdom commissioned a spiral welding tube mill designed and equipped by subsidiaries of Hoesch.

In spite of a 14 per cent increase in turnover, *Waagner-Biro AG.* (Vienna, July 16) suffered a net loss in 1967, the result of fierce competition resulting from over-capacity of the capital goods industry and the increase in costs, as well as the Middle East crisis. However, the annual report stated that in view of the rationalization measures taken by the board and the safeguarding of annual turnover by current orders the management hoped for better results in 1968.

ENTERTAINMENT

TELEVISION AND RADIO

THE year 1967–68 was notable in the history of television for two main developments—the official start of colour television on the B.B.C. 2 channel and the inauguration of the new I.T.V. contracts under which some changes were made in the set up of companies responsible for the independent programmes. Officially, as MR. JOHN SPENCER WILLS recorded in his review for *Rediffusion Limited* (July 31), colour television on Channel 2 began in December, 1967, "after a protracted colour launching period which created a greater demand for colour receivers than the manufacturers could possibly meet."

"It was only towards the end of March," he continued, "that the trade managed to produce enough receivers to fulfil the waiting lists.

"The majority of our customers for colour television prefer rental to purchase. The initial demand has been split fairly evenly between reception off air and off wire, but we expect that the improved reception off wire, and the cheaper 'wired' colour receiver which is much simpler to operate, will increase the popularity of our wired services.

"We expect these trends to be accentuated after November 1969 when, in the greater part of the country, all three television services will be available on the new 625-line standard and all of them will give programmes in colour. Colour sets, which now have to accept two-line standards, should then be somewhat cheaper to produce for the single-line standard. The capital investment in colour television will be very large; costs are heavy and technicians are at a premium. But colour television offers a fine opportunity, which we intend to grasp."

All the relay networks of *British Relay Wireless and Television Limited* (September 27), LORD RENWICK revealed, were now carrying colour television, thereby extending it to many areas where satisfactory direct reception was not possible.

LORD THOMSON OF FLEET reported to shareholders of *Scottish Television Limited* (April 5) that the I.T.A. had renewed the company's contract for the six years beginning July, 1968, so that Scottish Television would again provide the independent television service for Central Scotland. But the renewal was subject to two major conditions, which he explained as follows:

"The first was that The Thomson Organisation should reduce its holding of voting and non-voting shares in the company from 55 per cent to a maximum of 25 per cent, and arrangements are now being made to enable this condition to take place in a manner satisfactory to both you and the company. The second major condition was that we should appoint at least three new Directors who would be representative of Scottish affairs and institutions and who would have no connection with The Thomson Organisation. We have taken this opportunity to approach three people to join the Board who will in their separate ways bring wisdom and distinction to the company, and we shall be announcing their names as soon as formalities are completed."

In the course of his review Lord Thomson also referred to "some very important policy decisions" on the future of broadcasting in the United Kingdom which the Government had made during 1967. He stated:

"In the middle of 1969 we shall originate all programmes on the 625-line standard which will be radiated in the Ultra High Frequency wavebands. During the years when the present generation of 405-line sets are still in use our 625-line pictures will be converted downwards and radiated in V.H.F. Virtually all of our technical equipment is capable of this 625-line origination and we shall be ready in good time for the changeover in mid-1969.

"It was also decided that colour would be broadcast on 625-lines in U.H.F. The changeover in 1969, which I have already mentioned, will also therefore open the door for I.T.V. and B.B.C. 1 to broadcast colour programmes. The present time-table is that London, Midlands and North of England will receive colour programmes from late 1969 with Central Scotland and the South of England next. We are therefore planning to start originating programmes in colour from the end of 1969."

On July 29, 1968, MR. JOHN SPENCER WILLS recalled in his statement for *The British Electric Traction Company Limited* (October 17), Rediffusion Television ceased to provide the weekday programmes from the I.T.A.'s London transmitter. It became instead an equal shareholder with Associated British Picture Corporation in the new London weekday programme contractor, Thames Television, although voting control rested with Associated British. He went on to make this comment (in part):

"During the 13 years from the beginning of Independent Television, Rediffusion Television and its predecessor, Associated-Rediffusion, won more national and international awards for their programmes than any other programme contractor. It is tragic that their record of great achievement should apparently

298

have counted for so little when the offer of new contracts came to be considered."

With the decision of the I.T.A. not to renew two-day licences in the Midlands, Lancashire and Yorkshire on their expiry in July, 1968, the *raison d'être* of ABC Television Limited disappeared, declared SIR PHILIP WARTER of *Associated British Picture Corporation Limited* (September 6). As a result, ABC Television had ceased to trade and would be wound up. He made this comment on the outlook for Thames Television Limited, which had effectively taken its place among the holdings of the Picture Corporation, whose interest in Thames was roughly equal to that of Rediffusion:

"Thames Television has established a strong team and with its modern facilities I believe that the prospects for that company are good provided the current labour problems can be satisfactorily resolved. However, it must be realized that the high costs involved in the initial stages of the new company's operations are bound to affect its profitability in the short term."

The annual report of the directors of *Associated Television Corporation Limited* (September 26), noting that ATV Network Limited was awarded the I.T.A. contract for the Midlands area, declared that this was the major contract under the current allocation of the Independent Television Authority. In his statement read at the annual meeting the chairman added:

"ATV Corporation is already one of the world's greatest producers of filmed television series for international distribution. Current production costs run at some £7m. a year and by 1970, when we will also be among the world's greatest producers of feature films for international distribution, ATV's annual expenditure will have been approximately doubled. Very large revenues indeed will by then be flowing in from overseas and these, of course, are in no way subject to the Turnover Levy which falls so heavily upon ATV Network."

That *The Bristol Evening Post Limited* (August 12) had sold its holding of shares in Westward Television Limited was among the points made by MR. W. A. HAWKINS. He added that a profit of £8,500 was made on the sale against which capital gains tax had been provided.

For *Pillar Holdings Limited* (March 29) MR. J. A. PATERSON mentioned that the company's television relay and rental group, which had the majority of its activities in Wales, had been one of the original financial sponsors and was now one of the most substantial shareholders of Harlech Television Limited; this was the company which obtained the independent television franchise for Wales and the West of England. He considered that this investment should prove attractive over the next few years and that it

would contribute to the profitability of Pillar's television group.

The next quotation comes from LORD TOWNSHEND's survey for *Anglia Television Limited* (April 24):

"This year I am in the happy position of being able to report an increase in our consolidated profit. The increase is primarily due to the enlargement of our area by the inclusion of the new transmitters at Sandy Heath and Belmont, and it is good news for the future of Anglia that the Independent Television Authority has allocated to us four UHF stations, which should effectively maintain the number of homes in our newly enlarged area when the changeover from VHF to UHF takes place. Ever since the Sandy Heath transmitter came on to the air in July 1965 we have been aware that the increase in our area involved an increase in our responsibilities. Viewers in the Sandy Heath and Belmont areas are being provided at considerable cost and effort with a service up to the same high standard that we have already achieved in our original area."

In the annual report of *Telefusion Limited* which was summarized in *The Times* of October 9 it was asserted that the creation of Yorkshire Television had been a wonderful new asset for Yorkshire. It added that Telefusion expected improved results over the next two years, during which the company should also receive the benefit of its investment in Yorkshire Television Limited.

CINEMAS AND THEATRES

The satisfactory profits of the cinemas belonging to the *Associated British Picture Corporation* group (September 6), stated SIR PHILIP WARTER, were mainly the result of the public reaction to the films which were available in the second half of the financial year; audiences, he remarked, were more responsive than ever to outstanding films. Dealing with the company's programme of building and modernizing of cinemas, and the delaying effects thereon of building controls, Sir Philip said:

"During the year new ABC Cinemas were opened at Doncaster and Glasgow, and the company purchased the Scala, Liverpool. Three small cinemas were disposed of. The number of cinemas operated by the company therefore remains unchanged at 269. This year we will complete a development in Newport, Mon., consisting of a modern stadium type cinema and seven shops. In the meantime we have continued our policy of modernization.

"The restriction on building imposed by the Control of Office & Industrial Development Act 1965 and by the Building Control Act 1966 has delayed our programme for building new cinemas and converting others. However, the licensing position seems to

be easing a little and the company hopes to open at least three new cinemas in each of the next three years."

In a comment on the theatres division of *Associated Television Corporation Limited* (September 26) the directors in their annual report stated that the Stoll Theatres Corporation group had enjoyed a record year. They found it particularly pleasing that one of their theatres, the London Coliseum, had now become the new Opera House for Sadler's Wells.

Commenting on the interests in cinemas and entertainments of *Union Property Holdings (London) Limited*, MR. MAXWELL JOSEPH in his statement (*The Times*, October 28) mentioned that the Cameo Group and 47 halls had been acquired during the year—a major expansion which had caused a disproportionately heavy burden of expenditure to be accommodated within the profits for the year.

Throughout the year, MR. PAUL ADORIAN informed shareholders in *Humphries Holdings Limited* (July 30), there was a steadily rising demand for the group's services from all the main sectors of the film industry, including feature, television, educational and industrial films, documentaries and commercials. All departments exceeded their sales targets, though profit margins were reduced by a substantial wage award and by an increase in the cost of film stock, both of which were absorbed during the year without raising selling prices. He added:

> "The company, through its London and Manchester laboratories, now handles a major share of the Independent Television processing market and is well equipped to maintain this position when the swing to colour starts next year."

OTHER FORMS

The following paragraph about the bingo activities of *Associated British Picture Corporation Limited* (September 6) is extracted from SIR PHILIP WARTER's annual survey:

> "In 1966 an Agreement was entered into with Mecca Limited under which Bingo and Prize Bingo is being operated in sixteen of our cinemas for the joint benefit of Mecca and the Corporation. The Corporation hopes to open and operate on its own account an average of ten Bingo and Prize Bingo establishments in each of the next three years. This activity will have a double advantage in that it should yield substantial profits and eliminate the losses which we have incurred in operating those properties as cinemas."

Ambassador Bowling, a subsidiary of *Associated Television Corporation Limited* (September 26), had continued to be profitable, stated the directors in their annual report. Indeed, they asserted, the general recession in the industry, which had led to

the closure of a number of competing bowling centres, had proved a direct benefit to Ambassador.

According to MR. J. MALCOLM BARR'S review for members of *Barr & Wallace Arnold Trust Limited* (June 7), the coaching division and holidays at home and abroad once again showed increased revenue. Unfortunately, increased costs reduced the contribution to the group profits from 68 per cent to 53 per cent in 1967.

The twenty-month period under review by *Associated Pleasure Parks Limited*, declared MR. PENTLAND HICK, had been one of steady growth with all the board's forecasts amply met; his statement appeared in *The Times* of April 25. Expressing his confidence in the future, he went on to state:

"Flamingo Park still remains our major pleasure park and has continued to go from strength to strength. We have acquired St. Asaph Zoo on the North Welsh coast and expect to establish further attractions to serve this rapidly developing holiday area. At Stanley Zoo in County Durham we hope to introduce artificial ski slopes this winter. The Winter Zoo in Newcastle has had another successful year, as did the zoo at Kelvin Hall, Glasgow. Our Winter Zoo in Leeds got off to an excellent start. Cricket St. Thomas Wild Life Park, of which we hold half the equity, opened during last summer and shows every sign of success. We hold an option on the Zoo at Cleethorpes and this is now developing well."

The Queens Hall, Leeds, continued to make excellent progress as, he claimed, the leading exhibition centre in the North of England.

It had been a difficult year in the exhibition business of *Olympia Limited* (September 30), MR. H. OLIVER-KING asserted, overheads as a result of inflation on occasions rising faster than the rent income. He continued:

"Subsequent to this we had the financial freeze followed by the epidemic of foot-and-mouth disease, both having the inevitable effect of restricting or cancelling exhibitions. Exhibitions reflect sharply national economics which, in this particular instance, had the effect of reducing profits."

A point of interest in the statement of MR. ROBERT F. BUTLIN, who had succeeded his father, Sir William E. Butlin, as chairman of *Butlin's Limited* (July 17), was the introduction of a completely new catering policy, with the objective, first, of satisfying the changing requirements of many regular campers and also of extending the company's activities by opening up the attractions of its camps to a new clientele. He explained:

"The traditional all-in tariff, on which our business has been

302

built, will continue, but as an alternative at all our Camps we now offer a one meal tariff for guests who prefer a bed and breakfast holiday arrangement, leaving themselves free to have other meals at the camp restaurants or elsewhere. To support this we have built a number of additional restaurants and snack bars which offer a wide choice of meals at reasonable prices.

"In addition we have introduced an entirely new scheme—the self-catering holiday. For this purpose, we have provided self-service holiday chalets inside five of our camps and adjoining Filey and Skegness Camps we have erected self-service holiday flatlets. We have also provided the necessary shopping facilities.

"A large variety of holiday will therefore be available and all our guests, whichever holiday plan they select, will continue to enjoy the vast range of Butlin Camp amenities and entertainments, which remain free of charge."

For *Phonographic Equipment Company Limited* MR. MAX FINE stated in his annual review (*The Times*, December 12) that "an exciting expansion programme" for the company's family leisure centres in cities and seaside resorts had been started side by side with the long-term modernization plans for Margate's Dreamland. Incidentally, he declared that the company was increasing its exports and had exhibited in Italy, France and Germany; its machines, moreover, had been sold behind the "Iron Curtain."

The new self-catering village at Camber, near Rye, Sussex, MR. F. W. PONTIN declared in his statement for *Pontin's Limited* (December 16), had operated to near capacity from beginning to end of the season: in his opinion the demand for this type of holiday would continue to increase in the years to come and would not necessarily be confined to this country.

Among the significant changes which had marked the year for *G. A. Robinson (Stoke-on-Trent) Limited* (September 16), the annual report of the directors recalled, were the purchase of Happy Days Holiday Camp at Towyn, North Wales; the purchase of Sandy Bay Country Club, Towyn; and the provision of a new banqueting suite at Plas Coch Camp, Anglesey.

The use of one of the reservoirs of the *South Essex Waterworks Company* (February 20) for birdwatching is the subject of the next quotation, which comes from the statement by MR. A. W. WHITE:

"The company's Abberton Reservoir has for many years been well renowned for its wild bird life and a very important Bird Ringing Station, sponsored by the Nature Conservancy through the Wildfowl Trust, has been established there. The company have sought to preserve this unique feature and, following application to the Home Office, the Wildbirds (Abberton Reservoir Sanctuary) Order, 1967 has been made and came into operation on the 1st April, 1967. Regulations have been made for the issue of bird-watching permits and following consultations with

303

Mr. Peter Scott, the well-known ornithologist and the Eastern Sports Council the company are arranging to provide facilities for public birdwatching to take place with the least disturbance to the bird life. This will make available to a wider public this unique aspect of the reservoir."

Another company that is allowing a reservoir—in this instance, the new Derwent reservoir—to be used for the diversion of the public is the *Sunderland and South Shields Water Company* (March 20). MR. H. F. RENNOLDSON mentioned the need to be selective in the types of recreation allowed, for obvious reasons.

"We believe," he stated, "we are proceeding on the right lines and we are working in cooperation with the [Durham County] Water Board and the Durham and Northumberland Planning Authorities. The first season's fishing was generally voted excellent; a successful sailing club has now been established; and at the Blanchland end of the lake an area of 155 acres is being treated as an experimental nature reserve."

Among the highlights of the 1968 review (*The Times*, November 13) by SIR JOSEPH LOCKWOOD for *Electric & Musical Industries Limited* were that total sales rose by 30 per cent to a record level while total profits before tax were 8 per cent up, also to a record figure; United Kingdom sales and profits before tax were higher by 33 per cent and 55 per cent respectively; a sharp reduction in profits of Capitol Industries Inc., the group's American company, was accounted for largely by factors of a non-recurring nature; several acquisitions during the year included the Blackpool Tower Company and 25 per cent of the equity of Associated British Picture Corporation; and the group's position as manufacturers of magnetic tape had been greatly strengthened by the merger of its American company with Audio Devices Inc. under the new name of Capitol Industries Inc., in which E.M.I. now owned 72 per cent of the equity.

FOOD, DRINK AND TOBACCO

EXTERNAL sales of *Ranks Hovis McDougall Limited* (January 25) for the year to September 2, 1967, increased by £23m. to £325m., a growth of 7 per cent over the previous year, LORD RANK announced. Sales within the group for further processing raised the total to £370m. Group profit before tax rose by 16 per cent to just over £13m. But he pointed out that during the previous year the result had been very severely affected by the Government's attitude towards flour and bread prices and by labour troubles in the bakeries. Indeed, the latest total was still some 9 per cent below the result for 1965 (a 53-week year), when a more reasonable level of profit was being earned. As a result of the restrictive Government policy the group was earning only 10·6 per cent on the funds employed, a return much below the average for British industry as a whole. He added that flour milling margins for the first four months of the year remained unsatisfactory, and throughout the year costs in all sections of the business continued to increase; devaluation would bring further cost increases, particularly of imported grain.

SIR ARCHIBALD FORBES reported that total turnover of *Spillers Limited* (June 7) for the financial year of 53 weeks at £160m. rose by 12 per cent, of which about one-third was attributable to new acquisitions. He also stated:

> "It is satisfactory that the ratio of trading profit to turnover has risen from 4·4% to 5·7% and that the rate of return on total funds employed at the year end has increased from 10·6% to 12·7%. The principal factors influencing this recovery were a restoration of bulk flour margins and increased volume of sales of most of our other manufactured products except bread. . . . It will, of course, be remembered that in the year 1966–67 flour margins were under severe pressure from rising wheat costs which the Government did not allow us to recoup in prices until the close of that financial year.
>
> "While I welcome the better trend in overall profit ratios I should make it clear that we do not regard these as wholly adequate and all possible effort is being directed to securing an improvement in those areas where the return is lower than we consider appropriate."

The United Kingdom biscuit and cake operations of *Associated Biscuit Manufacturers Limited* (May 21) showed an increase in profit of 24 per cent, stated MR. RUPERT E. CARR, but this was offset by reverses overseas, particularly in Australia; in any case,

there was no basis for true comparison because of the devaluation of the Indian rupee in 1966 and of sterling in 1967. As regards the outlook, he said the prospects for 1968 and 1969 were encouraging overseas, but in the United Kingdom Huntley, Boorne & Stevens was likely to return lower profits through reorganization of production facilities for expansion. He continued:

"The main biscuit and cake operations form the basis of the Group's prosperity, and this year there are factors which make forecasting difficult. However, in the past, biscuit sales have been remarkably unaffected by restrictions on the housewife's spending power and I have every confidence that in the longer term sales will continue to progress in spite of slightly higher price levels."

Reporting that group sales of *United Biscuits (Holdings) Limited* in 1967 were a record and the group profits the highest ever except for 1963, when sugar prices were exceptionally low, LORD CRAIGTON in his statement (*The Times*, April 26) forecast that the major reorganization now under way in all the group's functions would continue during the next two or three years.

"Because of substantial forward purchases, the benefits of which are being handed on to the housewife," he went on, "the full impact of devaluation will not be felt until towards the end of this year. The effect of increased Purchase Tax on chocolate lines will be felt at once and will adversely affect sales. Government controls add considerably to our difficulties, especially in orderly forward planning. However, I take the view that, though there are difficulties ahead, in the long term your group will go from strength to strength."

Scribbans-Kemp Limited (July 16), announced MR. G. C. D'ARCY BISS, had just acquired Fullers Kunzle in Birmingham; the name Fullers, he declared, was well known and well reputed. He remarked that the group's existing bakery had run into losses, but the directors believed that by this purchase, resulting in a turnover of the order of £5½m., the losses could be eliminated and profits restored by providing the public with products of special quality. "We are not budgeting for bakery profits in the current year," he stated, "but we do expect to minimise our losses."

During the year sales of cake by *Park Cake Bakeries Limited* (November 6), declared MR. H. D. LEETE, showed a creditable increase of 10 per cent, the total being £4,116,975. Net profits in a year fraught with difficulties also were materially higher.

For *Associated British Foods Limited* (October 24) MR. GARRY WESTON reported another year of record sales and profits: group sales to outside customers totalled £407·8m., an increase of £100m. on the year, and profits before depreciation rose from £20·2m. to £26·1m.

Trading profits of the Factory Division of *Allied Suppliers Limited* (June 7), MR. MALCOLM E. COOPER declared, were dominated for the second year in succession by the Richmond Sausage Company's disappointing result. He continued:

"A major reorganization of the administrative and selling structure of Richmond was undertaken at the half-year and the decline in sales was arrested by late Autumn. Additionally, considerable development expense has been borne in such fields as bakery plant modernization, machine packaging and computer techniques for the extensive van selling operation. The benefits of such expenditure will however take some time to achieve. Profitability was adversely affected during the closing weeks of 1967 due to the serious dislocation of the meat market caused by the foot and mouth epidemic and the effects continued to be felt in the early part of the current year.

"The cost of securing an economic share of the Irish sausage market has proved increasingly prohibitive and the joint venture undertaken in 1965 has been terminated with the full agreement of our partners."

In the course of several references to the individual food and soft drink activities of J. & J. Colman Limited and its subsidiaries in his statement for *Reckitt & Colman Holdings Limited* (June 7) MR. B. N. RECKITT declared that these subsidiaries had continued to trade successfully in a growth field, but were restricted by the various measures of control diligently exercised by the Government over the prices of foodstuffs.

The next quotation comes from the statement (*The Times*, June 24) by MR. E. B. KING for *Clover Dairies Limited*:

"The recommendations of the Prices and Incomes Board for a change in the method of remuneration of milk distributors, have not yet been finalized by the Ministry of Agriculture. However, the Directors are confident that subject to no major adverse changes, there should be a further increase in trading profits for the current year."

Among the activities of the food group belonging to *The Distillers Company Limited* (September 19) mentioned by MR. ALEX MCDONALD were the expansion of meat products facilities and of fruit and vegetable canning, about which he stated:

"As the expansion in sales of our meat products and canned fruits and vegetables to the catering trade has been restricted by insufficient productive capacity, a new meat products factory is being constructed at Skelmersdale, near Liverpool, and a substantial expansion of our canning facilities is being provided at Stratford-upon-Avon."

During the year, MR. H. J. HEINZ asserted in his annual review (*The Times*, August 16) the product research of the *H. J. Heinz Company Limited* directed much effort to the improvement of existing recipes and to the development of further packs suitable for the catering market. "Both our own products and those of Heinz-Erin Limited," he added, "are justifying our concentrated selling efforts in this growth market."

For *Fitch Lovell Limited* MR. R. E. BLANNING was pleased to report (*The Times*, September 27) that the company's long record of increasing trading profits had been maintained, especially in view of the many difficulties that were encountered—the dock strike, the disruption caused by the unfortunate foot and mouth epidemic, devaluation with some higher raw material costs, and also the additional burden of S.E.T. for a full year.

Referring to the fruit and vegetable side of the business of *Lockwoods Foods Limited* (November 19), MR. P. B. LOCKWOOD stated:

"Sales during the year have shown an increase and our forward contract position since June 1, 1968 also shows a further increase. The general outlook is healthy, although we are always to some extent at the mercy of the weather and our summer packs this year would have been larger had it not been for the exceptionally wet season. Production of carrots is being increased substantially this autumn at all our factories despite which we are still unlikely to be able to meet demand."

In the absence of the President, Sir Ian D. Lyle, the Chairman, MR. JOHN LYLE, addressed the annual meeting of *Tate & Lyle Limited* (March 20), and made this allusion to sugar refining:

"In Britain our major interest remains in sugar refining. It prospered in 1967 thanks to favourable conditions for trading in raw sugar and substantially increased export sales. However, despite devaluation, present indications are not very favourable for maintaining the volume of exports in 1968. Our cane refining operations compete with the beet surpluses of many countries and these surpluses are determined by factors other than those of price. Although devaluation is having the effect of forcing up the prices of many goods in the shops this will largely be avoided in the case of sugar because the Commonwealth Sugar Agreement fixes the price which Britain pays for a very large proportion of her import requirements in terms of sterling.

"There has been a welcome change from the recent downward trend of consumption of specialities such as Cubes, Caster and Golden Syrup. The initial successes of our new marketing methods encourage us to persevere and we intend increasingly to widen the choice we offer to consumers.

"One disturbing feature of recent years has been a reduction in our share of the total home market. We are meeting the com-

petition which has developed and this may have its effect on profits, but savings in cost through the closing of a refinery and working seven days a week at the others, with the resulting in-increase in productivity, will be a substantial balancing factor."

After recounting a number of factors which gave him confidence that they had reached the trough in the cyclical trend of the fishing industry, MR. MICHAEL NOBLE, M.P., told members of *Associated Fisheries Limited* (March 19) that if this was so and the Government took effective action, then by next year the company's profits should stand substantially higher. He was also looking for considerably better results in the current year from cold storage, catering, distribution and transport interests.

Having reported a severe drop in pre-tax profits of *Ross Group Limited*, MR. J. CARL ROSS in his speech (*The Times*, April 10) said that the setback was also a challenge for the future and provided a spur to look at things afresh. He went on to declare:

"From now on we intend to concentrate our activities on a more specialized front. We are taking active steps to dispose of some of our more diversified operations. The capital released by the disposals will be diverted into the expansion and develop-ment of our food production and distribution businesses as the focal points for the future.

"As our new policies take effect I am hopeful that there will be a recovery both in profits earned and dividends paid. Our food production activities, with the exception of fish catching, are all in growth sectors of the food industry and our record in these spheres is most progressive."

MR. K. M. STAINTON, M.P., informed members of *Burton, Son & Sanders Limited* (May 3) that the group's rationalization and re-equipment programme should now begin to yield benefits. The end-1967 acquisition of British Pepper & Spice would also contri-bute in 1968. But the outlook must be qualified in terms of the general economic situation.

In the general conditions of trading throughout the country MR. PHILIP RAKUSEN considered the results of *Lloyd Rakusen & Sons Limited* satisfactory, even though pre-tax profits showed a modest fall. His statement (*The Times*, November 28) included the following paragraph:

"Your directors are pleased to report an improved second half year's trading in spite of price control and rising costs of materials and services. We are also pleased to inform you that this trend has continued during the past three months and although it is difficult to make accurate forecasts it is hoped your company will be enabled to achieve further advancement."

For *Adams Butter Limited* (August 29) MR. F. ADAMS stated that

producing countries, such as Australia and Denmark, were going ahead with their plans for containerization, and more and more butter would be coming directly from these and other countries into the company's factory. He added:

"Our own transport organization is being geared to deal with this, and our deliveries are being done more and more from containers, which saves handling costs and reduces damage. Our plans for the project are well in hand."

At home, sales of Horlicks reached an all-time peak, which LORD COLERAINE stated in his annual review (*The Times*, November 7) for *Horlicks Limited* could well be attributable to the revised marketing policy over the past few years and the further widening of the product's appeal. Another point he made was that each of the four dairy subsidiaries in the West country—after rationalization and re-equipment of their milk bottling and cheese-making activities—produced higher profits.

Group trading results of *Bovril Limited* for 1967 showed improvement on those for 1966, partly the result of a turnround from loss to a small profit (before exchange differences) in the Argentine sector. In his statement (*The Times*, July 15) LORD LUKE forecast a further improvement during 1968, as shown below:

"In the first four months of 1968 our Argentine business continued to be affected by the ban on imports of beef into the United Kingdom, but on the other hand the peso exchange rate has been stable. At home, sterling devaluation will on balance involve the company in considerable extra costs, as will the effect of recent and proposed legislation. If the favourable trends continue for the remainder of this year, and subject to the usual proviso as to unforeseen circumstances, overall trading results for 1968 should show a marked improvement on those for 1967."

Lord Luke also reported an overall increase in sales of proprietary products of $8\frac{1}{2}$ per cent, Bovril itself showing a very encouraging upward trend, which was being maintained.

The main reason for the static profit of *Liebig's Extract of Meat Company Limited* (February 15), according to MR. K. R. M. CARLISLE, was that improvements in South America proved not so substantial as expected. Group sales of branded products, however, again increased in both volume and value, Oxo Limited achieving a record turnover in the United Kingdom.

J. Lyons & Company Limited (July 16) and the Union International Company Limited had agreed with The Nestlé Company Limited to merge their United Kingdom frozen food interests, declared MR. GEOFFREY SALMON.

"These interests," he went on, "consisted respectively of Fropax Limited (the 'Eskimo' and 'Frood' brands) and Findus

310

Limited (the 'Findus' brand) and a new combined operating company has been set up under the name Findus Eskimo Frood Limited; 50 per cent of the voting equity of Fropax Limited, the holding company for the combined business, is owned jointly by ourselves and Union International, the other 50 per cent being owned by Nestlé. As part of this arrangement, Nestlé bought the 21 per cent interest in Fropax formerly owned by Associated Fisheries Limited and about three-quarters of that company's former 21 per cent holding in Glacier Foods Limited, the ice cream company, which shares its distribution system with Fropax. We ourselves acquired the rest of Associated Fisheries' holding in Glacier Foods. This merger has afforded a larger, stronger and more economic basis for expansion in a quickly developing and highly competitive field."

For *Wright & Green (Holdings) Limited* (September 20) MR. CHARLES K. GREEN reported a gratifying increase in turnover, but declared that it was "no more than essential to keep pace with ever-increasing expenses." He particularly resented the imposition of S.E.T. on an essential service industry, as distinct from manufacturing.

CONFECTIONERY AND PRESERVES

Total sales of *Cadbury Group Limited* increased from £131m. in 1966 to £137m. in 1967, and MR. ADRIAN CADBURY stated (*The Times*, May 23) that if both figures were adjusted for non-recurring items and sterling devaluation, the real increase in total sales in a difficult trading year was 6 per cent. Group profits before tax were somewhat lower but after tax were a little higher, and he asserted that, looking ahead, there were good prospects of improving group profitability.

The combined United Kingdom sales organization set up by *Rowntree and Company Limited* (June 14) in April, 1967, with two field sales forces covering confectionery and grocery products respectively had settled down well and would produce increasing benefits in the group's highly competitive markets. Thus stated MR. D. J. BARRON, who also included the following paragraph in his survey:

"The existence of a Grocery Sales Force was an important factor in the smooth absorption into our Group of the Sun-Pat Nuts and Pan Yan Pickle businesses which we acquired during the year from the Receiver of H. S. Whiteside Ltd. The total consideration covering the buildings and plant at Hadfield in Derbyshire, the trading stocks and the trade marks, was some £1·1m. and a further payment may be made in due course when the past losses of the companies concerned are available to offset taxation on their future profits."

311

An increase in sales volume of the Mackintosh products of *John Mackintosh & Sons Limited* (May 8) necessitated a larger expenditure for marketing and selling, and with selling prices rigidly controlled by the Ministry profitability in the aggregate was lower, though good progress was made in several export markets. However, the fall in the profits on these products had been partially offset by increased profitability in certain subsidiary companies. These and other remarks by MR. ERIC D. MACKINTOSH made it clear how closely the group's actions were confined by Government regulations.

The factories of *Maynards Limited* (November 21), declared MR. J. DOUGLAS MAYNARD, had had a successful year, with substantially higher turnover and profits, resulting largely from improved manufacturing methods.

Having substantially maintained turnover and profit during 1967, *Waller & Hartley Limited* (May 24) had had "a very pleasing" increase in sales in the first three months of 1968, reported MR. R. L. CORSON.

The next quotation comes from the statement by MR. CHARLES J. ROBERTSON for *James Robertson and Sons, Preserve Manufacturers, Limited* (June 27):

"While the increase in group turnover was partly due to rises in some prices, there have been increases in the quantities sold, some of them substantial, in most sectors of the Group's operations. We have again been able to increase our share of the UK preserves market. The Group's tonnage sales of all types and packs of jams and marmalades increased by 5·5% during the year and now exceed one-third of the national total."

THE BREWERIES

Like a number of other brewery chairmen, the late SIR THOMAS BLAND referred to the first impact of the breathalyser on the trade; the relevant passage in his statement for *Tollemache & Cobbold Breweries Limited* (March 18) follows:

"As I have often emphasized, even at the best of times there are factors affecting our industry which make it extremely difficult to forecast a current year's profits; to these difficulties has now been added the Road Safety Act with its provisions relating to drinking and driving, which have adversely affected our trade during the first three months of the current year. It is quite impossible at this early stage, however, to judge the likely permanent effect of this legislation. Furthermore, if, as is possible, the forthcoming Budget includes provisions designed to reduce consumer spending, this will certainly not help our industry."

MR. D. P. CROSSMAN informed members of *Watney Mann*

Limited (January 26) that the immediate effect of the Road Safety Act on the company's sales was a "quite sharp drop." He added, however, that although the pattern of trade had altered and some houses were still badly affected, "the public are gradually adjusting themselves to these new circumstances, and the overall effect on our trade is not as great as might have been feared."

The views of COLONEL W. H. WHITBREAD on the same subject are given in the following quotation from his annual survey for *Whitbread and Company Limited* (September 6):

> "The new Drink and Driving laws initially had a serious effect on trade, especially in our many country houses, some of whose takings dropped drastically for a few weeks after the Act came into force. Furthermore, owing to the changing dates of Easter no trade for this period was included in this financial year. However, we have managed to hold our sales and since the end of the year they have been on the increase."

Home market sales of stout, lager and ale by *Arthur Guinness Son & Company Limited*, LORD IVEAGH reported, again established new records in spite of the stringent economic conditions, while sales overseas (including local production) continued to increase and, like the group profit, were likewise the highest yet recorded. There was some falling off in sales of bottled Guinness in the latter part of the year, but the distribution and sale of draught Guinness again advanced very substantially. His statement was summarized in the *The Times* of February 7.

In normal circumstances, stated SIR WILLIAM MCEWAN YOUNGER of *Scottish & Newcastle Breweries Limited* (September 5) it would be possible to say that real possibility of growth existed for the group.

> "The results for the year, before tax but after a large burden of increased charges, demonstrate this clearly enough," he continued. "As I said last year, there is now a substantially diminished return on investment in licensed properties, but by careful selection it is still possible to find trade investments of this and other kinds giving a return which is adequate even in existing circumstances. Sales over-all continue to show an increase."

Changing industrial conditions in the North, and the higher unemployment there, were alluded to by MR. DOUGLAS NICHOLSON of *Vaux and Associated Breweries Limited* (September 20), and he also contrasted the incomes of low-paid workers with social security benefits, as the following quotation from his speech shows:

> "Trading conditions throughout the North of England and Scotland which is our area continue to be difficult. Coal mines in Northumberland and Durham, at one time the main support of the area, are rapidly disappearing and in the last twelve

months no less than seventeen more mines have been closed. This makes a total of sixty mines which have been closed in Northumberland and Durham in the last three years.

"Unemployment figures in the North are consistently very much higher than the rest of the country. As an instance of this in Sunderland at the present time there are 9·7 per cent unemployed males. It is possibly fortunate for our industry that the rate for social security is so high that recipients can still afford to buy our products.

"As an illustration of the comparison of incomes, when working and not working, while a Brewery labourer earns a basic wage of £13 for a 40-hour week with a weekly average with overtime of about £15, if a man lives in a Council house at a rent of £3 per week and has a wife and three children he will be able to draw from Social Security £16 10s. per week. It does seem complete nonsense that while our lower paid workers can draw more on the dole than they earn working we are not allowed to raise their wages and to increase the price of beer to pay for it."

Increased profits of *Allied Breweries Limited* stemmed mainly from higher volume in sales of beer, notwithstanding the continued adverse effect of short-time working and unemployment in parts of the Midlands. This was stated in the directors' statement of preliminary results (*The Times*, January 5). Sales, they added, were well above the national average, with free trade sales of the group's national and regional brands remaining buoyant; they also announced the results of a revaluation of assets in these terms:

"The land and buildings which comprise our licensed estate, but excluding production centres, depots and offices have been revalued as at September 30, 1967, on the basis of a going concern as opposed to individual realizable market values. The resultant surplus of £64·3m. has been credited to Capital Reserve, and the opportunity has been taken of eliminating Goodwill amounting to £38·6m. by a deduction from Capital Reserve. The net assets attributable to the Ordinary shares now amount to £154·4m., giving a book value of 16/–½d. to each 5/– share."

Progress in the sales of canned beers was one of the topics which MR. R. H. COURAGE discussed in his annual statement for *Courage Barclay & Simonds Limited* (June 5):

"The application of modern marketing to our excellent range of canned beers has substantially increased sales through retail outlets for which the non-returnable container is essential. Further developments in quality control and improvements in methods of serving our draught beers have helped to maintain their high standard. Undoubtedly draught beer is today extraordinarily good value for money and increases in price of

314

draught beers to assist in recouping the heavy expenditure incurred in achieving their quality are overdue."

Sales of beer by *Truman Hanbury Buxton & Company Limited*, in a year which did not contain an Easter holiday, had slightly exceeded the previous year's figure, stated MR. M. A. PRYOR in his survey (*The Times*, July 16). However, the sales mix had altered somewhat, giving a small reduction in profit on some sales. He explained that there was a slight tendency for draught beers—bitter, in particular—to increase at the expense of the more profitable bottled beers, while it was difficult to keep up with the demand for keg and cellar tank beers.

High taxation, combined with the denial of freedom to put up beer prices and plough back a satisfactory amount into the business, caused the board of *Brickwoods Limited* (August 15) deep concern, MR. C. H. TIDBURY asserted, and he went on:

"In order to keep pace with the standards demanded by the public in this highly competitive industry today, it is essential that a company such as ours should be free to renovate and repair its properties in order to earn a satisfactory return on the capital employed. Our margins of profit are under very considerable pressure despite all we have done to make our business more productive. Nevertheless, we are determined that shareholders should have benefit from the increased pre-tax profit and are recommending the maximum increase in dividend allowed in one year."

At the meeting of *Hardy's Kimberley Brewery Limited* MR. W. G. HANSON said (*The Times*, February 21) that trading had been disappointing since the beginning of the new year. It was impossible to adduce any one reason for this but it could be a combination of the weather, the rise in the cost of living, the Breathalyser and, possibly most of all, a temporary increased spending upon durable consumer goods in anticipation of the Budget.

Among the factors contributing to the modest decrease in pre-tax profits of *Marston, Thompson and Evershed Limited* (September 27) were rising costs beyond the directors' control, the rigid Government control on selling prices, the effect of the breathalyser on the trade of licensed houses situated in rural areas, and the foot and mouth disease over a wide area which greatly restricted the social life of the countryside. These were all mentioned by SIR CLIFFORD GOTHARD in his review.

For *Samuel Webster & Sons Limited* (April 1) MR. J. R. G. MARCHETTI reported record sales of both draught and bottled beers, the increase being above the national average. The year's figures in the accounts, he admitted, were disappointing, but this was not unexpected in view of the additional non-recurring expenditure occasioned by the merger with J. Hey & Co. Limited.

MR. A. W. NIELSEN, managing director of the *Carlsberg Breweries* mentioned in his speech (*The Times*, April 16) the abolition of customs duties within the European Common Market, where the internal tariffs were to be practically liquidated as from July 1, 1968. The effects of this measure, which had already begun, he added, were that "countries outside the Common Market are being placed in a most unsatisfactory position." He continued:

"During the past year competition has been perceptible, especially from the Dutch, Belgian and German breweries, in fact Carlsberg is still saddled with a duty of about 30 per cent on its exports to the Common Market countries. All the same it is gratifying to note that Carlsberg's exports to the Common Market have increased."

WINES AND SPIRITS

MR. ALEX MCDONALD of *The Distillers Company Limited* (September 19) recalled that before the Budget the Scotch Whisky Association had made a strong plea to the Chancellor for a reduction in duty to assist the industry in export markets, as in recent years there were good grounds for believing that each successive increase in the British duty had been imitated by other Governments seeking additional revenue.

"At the same time," he went on, "the Association observed that, for the sake of the country's balance of payments position, there was an urgent need in the national interest to encourage the consumption of home-produced commodities and discourage imports. Despite these representations, the Industry was dealt another severe blow. This was the fourth increase since 1964, when the duty was 27/– per bottle. It is now 40/–. It is difficult to imagine any industry more harshly treated in its own country than this one, on which the nation depends so much for its earnings of foreign currency."

As regards gin, Mr. McDonald stated that following poor sales of the group's brands in the early part of the financial year sales were exceptionally high in the last four months of the year as a result of anticipation of the Budget. Sales in most countries where DCL manufactured gin made reasonable progress with the particular exception of New Zealand. There, he asserted, because of a "quite savage" increase in duty sales of all spirits suffered severely. This, he declared, was certainly a case where a Government would appear to have gone too far and to have crippled one of its major sources of revenue.

In his statement for *Teacher (Distillers) Limited* (July 10) MR. R. M. TEACHER replied to criticism of the Scotch whisky industry at the time of devaluation for putting up prices abroad, which some

people held largely to nullify the advantages of devaluation. He stated:

> "However, there are various factors to be borne in mind. The extent of devaluation was 14·3 per cent and the overall gross increase in the price of Scotch Whisky was 11·6 per cent. This increase will more than absorb the increased cost of preparing Scotch Whisky for export which arises from the effect of devaluation on the price of the imported element. Over and above this, in those overseas countries which have not devalued our Agents' increased costs in Sterling must be met by increased allowances and larger amounts for promotional support to stimulate export effort. We now have agency agreements in 128 countries abroad."

Trading of *Invergordon Distillers (Holdings) Limited* in the year under review suffered a further serious deterioration, according to the chairman's review (*The Times*, September 24), and the book values of the group's stock and assets had been drastically written down. Measures were being pursued which it was felt would accelerate the group's recovery, and though an immediate return to profitability could not be envisaged the company's prospects "may be regarded as greatly improved."

After reporting that home sales by *Arthur Bell & Sons Limited* (May 31) were up by 13 per cent on 1966 and export sales by 30 per cent, MR. W. G. FARQUHARSON referred to overproduction of whisky in these terms:

> "It is a well-known fact that the time has come when there must be some slowing down of distillation as, for the past year or two, there has undoubtedly been much overproduction of Grain Whisky, and these remarks can, in a lesser way, also apply to Malt Whisky distillation."

In his review (*The Times*, October 24) of the year for *R. Kemp, Macallan-Glenlivet Limited* MR. G. C. HARBINSON reported that the profit was in excess of the directors' forecast at the time of the public issue, and among other developments mentioned the following:

> "The company has entered into an Agreement with The Highland Distilleries Co. Ltd. to construct and operate a Feeds Recovery Plant to produce animal feeding stuffs from distillery by-products. The decision to proceed with a joint project with Highland was influenced by the substantial savings in capital and running costs to be obtained with an installation having double the size of the plant which would be required for Macallan alone. Your Company's net capital commitment in this project will be in the region of £100,000."

A feature of a successful year's trading by the *Highland Distilleries Company Limited* (November 22) was stated by MR. H. M. PENMAN to have again been the increased demand for the company's matured whiskies. While sales of new whiskies did not quite attain the previous year's peak, the level nevertheless was "very satisfactory."

The statement by MR. H. C. B. BERENS for *International Distillers and Vintners Limited* (December 19), extending to a full page, is, we believe, the first company chairman's statement to be printed in *The Times* in full colour. He remarked that the group's overall reorganization plans were now virtually completed and the new management structure was to become fully operative on January 1, 1969, and he continued:

"Much of the re-organization had to be held back pending the finalization of the negotiations for the purchase of Brown and Pank, because to a large extent, as I told you last year, the reorganization was planned to strengthen the home trade and obtain a better return on assets employed. The introduction of a new home trade element of the size and scope of Brown and Pank has obviously influenced some of the details of our original thinking, but not our basic concept of management by function within a divisional structure."

Mr. Berens also stated that sales of J. & B. Rare Scotch whisky, "a very major contributor" to the group profits, had again expanded, with an increase of $9\frac{1}{2}$ per cent in the United States and of 42·6 per cent in other world markets. Margins on shipments to most markets had materially improved as a result of devaluation, because IDV, in line with other exporters of Scotch whisky, were able to increase selling prices.

Announcing a significant rise in group consolidated profit for *Williams and Humbert Limited* (June 6), the result of increased sales, MR. H. ALAN WALKER sounded a warning note about rising costs. He stated:

"Increases in the cost of raw materials in Spain have markedly contributed to a rise in production costs. The effect of the devaluation of the peseta on the cost of casks, cartons and other materials bought in Spain from hard currency areas is becoming apparent as stocks are replenished. In my last report I mentioned wages in Spain and once again have to tell you that another official increase is operational as from the beginning of 1968. Increased costs during 1967 were offset by increased turnover, but conditions may not be propitious for a similar increase in sales in 1968. However, difficult as it is, every possible opportunity is being taken to reduce operational costs, and the yields from our vineyards, to which attention was drawn in 1965, enable us to stabilize in some measure the cost of mosto, or

318

young sherry. These vineyards are now coming into full production, and I am pleased to tell you that the quality is excellent and provides a sound basis for future shipments of our fine sherry.

"Increased sales call for increased stocks, and we have continually to forecast what the demand will be for some years ahead. This means most careful planning of stocks for sale after maturity in order to maintain our high quality. The storage of the produce from our own vineyards and wine-presses calls for considerable capital investment in the form not only of the stock itself, but also bodega space, casks, cooling plant, transport and all the other items essential for the efficient running of sherry bodegas."

Total sales of wines and spirits by the shipping and wholesale companies controlled by *Watney Mann Limited* (January 26), declared MR. D. P. CROSSMAN, reached the new record figure of £28½m. The brightest feature of the year's trading, he added, was the general increase in sales of table wines, with the cheaper wines faring best, which was hardly surprising in view of the "squeeze."

For *Whitbread and Company Limited* (September 6) COLONEL W. H. WHITBREAD made these remarks on the retail wine and spirit trade:

"So far as the retail side of our wine and spirit business is concerned, in spite of the severe competition of cut price trading after the abandonment of Resale Price Maintenance, it has more than held its own. This has been achieved by fairly drastic pruning of our least profitable outlets, a process which will have to continue. Our trade in wines has again increased and is one of the fastest growing parts of our entire business."

The *London Rubber Company Limited* (September 20), MR. A. R. REID thought, was first in the United Kingdom with supermarkets selling only wines, spirits and beers, all at heavily reduced prices. He considered this type of operation had an excellent future, and certainly consumption of table wines in the United Kingdom was increasing rapidly. As showing the scope for future expansion, he gave these comparative figures:

"It is expected that by the early '70's national demand will double, when it will amount to about eight bottles per annum per capita. A measure of the prospects of still further increase is that consumption in France on a comparable basis is 140 bottles, and in Italy 130 bottles."

The decrease in the trading profit of *Ellis & Co. (Richmond) Limited* (October 11) was caused by a number of reasons, among which MR. H. C. ELLIS listed severe price cutting affecting the company's off licences, the breathalyser scare affecting its wholesale and on licence trade, higher customs duties again reducing

margins, and general tax impositions such as S.E.T. and higher rate of corporation tax. He showed in the following extract that the company had entered the wine supermarket trade:

"Your Board, however, is confident about the future. It has been carrying through fundamental changes to the whole pattern of your company and opened experimentally last November a wine supermarket in Kingston under the name of Fairdeal Vintners. This experiment was successful and since March we are now operating 10 of these outlets and have a further seven in the pipeline for immediate opening."

To the improved results of *John Holt & Company* (*Liverpool*) *Limited* all sections of the business had contributed, MR. P. B. HUNTER declared in his preliminary statement (*The Times*, December 21); this included the wine interests, which, operating mainly in the United Kingdom and France, continued to progress and now provided approximately one-quarter of the group's profit before charging interest and group central administration expenses.

For *South African Distilleries and Wines Limited* (Cape Town, August 23) DR. M. L. ASHTON ascribed the lower pre-tax profits mainly to the increase in excise duty on brandy imposed in August, 1966, which had caused a 4 per cent fall in total demand for that spirit on the year. Another factor was the intensification of an already competitive situation in the retail liquor trade, which reduced the profits of the retail division and caused a substantial increase in the group's provision for bad debts.

SOFT DRINKS

MR. HANNING PHILIPPS made these remarks on the experience of the licensed and catering division of *Schweppes Limited* (May 9):

"This Division has had an extremely difficult year with excessively heavy tax burdens bearing down on the sales of mixed drinks and a forced change in drinking habits imposed by the breathalyser regulations. In these circumstances, the fact that the Division broke a new record for its pre-Christmas trade was more than creditable.

"In the latter part of 1967 a new soft drink made from malt and hops called 'Coaster' and a Vegetable Juice Cocktail were test marketed. We hope that both these tests, which will be supported by national scale advertising, will prove successful and that we can then go for full national distribution.

"In collaboration with the owners of Pimms, the Division will shortly be test marketing a canned Ready-to-Drink Pimms No. 1 Cup made, of course, with Schweppes' lemonade. We have high hopes of its eventual success, particularly in the important take-home market."

Sales in the trade of cider and soft drinks, produced by associated companies of *Courage Barclay & Simonds Limited* (June 5), had again increased, MR. R. H. COURAGE stated.

TOBACCO

In a keenly competitive but relatively static total market the tobacco division of *The Imperial Tobacco Company (of Great Britain and Ireland) Limited* (March 18) did well in 1967 to secure a further substantial increase in turnover and profit, declared MR. JOHN PARTRIDGE. He added that to date in 1968 all divisions reported increased turnover, but profitability per unit sold especially in tobacco products, was being adversely affected by higher costs. Incidentally, he said that the profits of the general trade division, assisted by the acquisition of H.P. Sauce Limited, were running at an appreciably higher level than a year before.

The sales picture of *British-American Tobacco Company Limited* (March 14) round the world is the subject of the next quotation, which comes from MR. D. R. N. CLARKE'S speech:

"Group sales of tobacco products continue at a rate higher than at this period last year, though the pattern is not uniform. In the United States Brown & Williamson continues to fight back against competition and even to make modest advances in a market of slow growth. Net profits in that country are of course threatened by the tax bill which the President has introduced. In Europe there is little change; the sales of our subsidiary in Germany are being maintained but there is some pressure on profit margins. In Latin America sales are still increasing in total, with our company in Brazil leading the way despite heavy increases in excise. In Africa the slight downturn appears to have been checked, at least temporarily, but the political instability of some parts of that Continent continues to cause concern. India suffered a drastic tax and price increase in February, 1967, and our companies are doing well to hold their volume there. There has, however, just been a further increase in taxation so the future must be a little uncertain. Sales in Pakistan continue to reach new record levels. With direct exports from this country and the USA continuing to do well I have reason to expect that Group sales of tobacco products for the whole of the current year will be above those for the year ended in September, 1967."

Total market sales of cigarettes were relatively static in 1967, stated MR. MARK NORMAN of *Gallaher Limited* (May 22), and he added that the growth section of the market continued to be filter cigarettes, with lower priced brands showing the most buoyancy. He continued:

"Although cigarette sales continued to decline in the first half of the year, marketing action succeeded in halting further loss in the second half. This progress has continued through to the first quarter of 1968 with sales running ahead of last year, although this may be partly due to pre-Budget buying. It is particularly encouraging to see that the main contribution to this improved position over the last nine months has come from sales of our filter brands."

Greatly improved results for *Godfrey Phillips Limited* (June 28) were reported by MR. P. A. GODFREY PHILLIPS. He pointed out that in 1966 the sterling value of the company's Indian profits had been reduced by devaluation of the Indian rupee, whereas in 1967 the group benefited substantially from the devaluation of sterling, which gave a higher sterling value to overseas earnings. In addition, there was a solid increase in other group profits not directly affected by devaluation.

During the year *Siemssen, Hunter Limited* (July 30) acquired the agency rights for a number of well-known foreign brands of cigarettes and tobaccos, and MR. ROBERT J. FREEMAN stated that turnover was most encouraging; although profits to date had not been significant, the directors were confident that this business within a year or two would be making a substantial contribution to group earnings.

HOTELS AND CATERING

WHILE hotel companies reporting in 1968 mostly announced moderately increased profits, they continued through their chairmen to complain of the disadvantages under which they laboured, among which the selective employment tax caused perhaps the greatest furore. There were, however, other handicaps on the industry which neither the proposals under the White Paper on Hotel Development Incentives nor the new statutory organization to promote British tourism and administer the incentive scheme entirely offset.

SIR WILLIAM MCEWAN YOUNGER of *Scottish & Newcastle Breweries Limited* (September 5) made these caustic comments on the White Paper:

"The actual proposals, though in some respects a substantial improvement, are, taken over-all, yet one more example of the practice of imposing very heavy additional burdens, and then claiming considerable credit for concessions and incentives which only offset them in part. For example, taking our hotels as a whole, the S.E.T. rebate in certain rural areas will amount, in cash, to only about half of the additional 50% and only about one sixth of the total S.E.T. charge to be borne by these hotels. The main effect of the proposals would seem likely to be to stimulate new construction outside the development areas. Investment in the Highlands is unlikely to receive any real impetus.

"It is worth noting, also, that a further substantial exaction results from the setting up of the Hotel and Catering Industry Training Board. This company has devoted much attention to training, with marked benefit to the standard of administration of our licensed premises. We now have imposed on us a levy amounting, in the year, to £66,000: our estimated reclaim amounts only to £16,000. I entirely fail to see why a company with satisfactory training provisions should be forced to subsidize others. Further, as things are, nothing is more likely than that this Board will follow the normal sequence of ever increasing staff and ever mounting expenses."

For the *Savoy Hotel Limited* (April 2) MR. HUGH WONTNER also devoted a considerable part of his speech to a critical examination of the particularly harsh way in which S.E.T. operated in the hotel industry. However, he continued:

"It is true that the President of the Board of Trade has lately

323

announced in Parliament a scheme of financial assistance designed to encourage the building of new hotels and the extension of bedroom accommodation to existing hotels, which, of course, is very welcome; but as far as can be seen from the bare outline of this scheme so far made available, this does not altogether replace the investment allowances that were withdrawn from existing hotels, at a cost in our case of over £50,000 a year.

"Primarily, the scheme offers a once for all grant if new bedroom accommodation can be made available, but it also does include a grant when certain fixed plant and machinery are installed in existing hotels. It is too early yet to say for certain what this will mean, but we are hopeful that the result will be of real benefit."

In lighter mood, Mr. Wontner told the following story of the missing kestrel:

"One Savoy visitor we have missed lately is the friendly kestrel, who made a home here at one time and brought up a family. He was treated with great respect by our pigeons, who made off to another habitat, for which we were devoutly thankful; and we were hoping that, like the starlings, who left these surroundings some time ago for Trafalgar Square, the pigeons would follow their excellent example. It is not often, ladies and gentlemen, that we wish to get rid of our visitors, but these we could gladly do without."

In October, 1967, according to MR. GEOFFREY SALMON, *J. Lyons & Company Limited* (July 16) made offers to acquire the shares it did not already own in the associated hotel companies, comprising The Strand Hotel Limited (with its 50 per cent interest in Cumberland Hotels Limited, the other 50 per cent of which was already owned by Lyons) and its subsidiary, The Palace Hotel Limited. All the companies concerned had now become wholly-owned subsidiaries of J. Lyons. The management of these hotel companies had always been closely interlocked with that of Lyons, and the board considered that it would be easier to develop both businesses if they were in common ownership; they also felt that common ownership would facilitate the provision of additional finance for developing the hotel business, which, he asserted, "had been somewhat inhibited by Strand's capital structure."

Mr. Salmon also stated that the group was continually seeking opportunities for expansion both in the United Kingdom and elsewhere in Europe, particularly in the field of high-standard hotels charging moderate prices. He continued:

"Progress has already been made on two such projects. One is in Amsterdam, where we are collaborating with Royal Dutch Airlines (KLM) in the planning and building of a 600-room

hotel in the Europa Boulevard, to be managed by us. The other is for a 250-room hotel in Glasgow, intended to form part of the Anderson Cross development.

"In the late spring of 1969 we plan to open the Albany Hotel in Nottingham, a city of growing importance in a prosperous and rapidly developing area. Meanwhile we are continuing the process of keeping our existing hotels up-to-date. The major modernization scheme at the Cumberland Hotel is nearly complete, and we shall now be spending some £750,000 on remodelling the restaurants and bars at the Strand Palace and the Regent Palace."

The chairman of *Trust Houses Limited*, in his annual statement (an extract from which appeared in *The Times* of March 6), declared that, because of the greatly increased burden of taxation, what was in fact a progressive and expanding company had been made to appear a stagnating or receding one. He gave these striking figures to illustrate his point:

"The total of all taxation borne by the company and its shareholders has increased, from 1965 to 1967, by 86 per cent. From taking 47 per cent of the profit, it has risen to 76 per cent. Nevertheless, if we can now hope for no new taxes and for no further increases in the rates of existing taxes, the momentum that has been built up by the development expenditures of recent years will continue and we shall reap the benefit in a steep rise of the post tax profit, two years late but none the less welcome for that."

Giving some details of the expansion programme of *Grand Metropolitan Hotels Limited* in the course of his review of the past year (*The Times*, February 16), the chairman reported the purchase of approximately 52 per cent of the capital of a quoted French company operating the Lotti and Scribe Hotels in Paris and the Carlton Hotel in Cannes; measures which had been introduced to improve the lettings and control the expenses of these hotels were already achieving better profitability. The share capital had also been acquired of The Bateman Catering Organization Limited which was a natural extension of the group's catering activities; Bateman was one of the leading firms in industrial catering. Another major new investment, in equal partnership with De Vere Hotels and Restaurants Limited, was the share capital of Connaught Rooms Limited. In addition, the Levy & Franks group had been completely reorganized, entailing heavy transitional and terminal expenses; the earnings of the reorganized group now were considerably greater than those at the date of acquisition. The chairman also gave some particulars of current and future development in the following terms:

"Our current programme of expansion and development in-

cludes three new hotels and two major schemes of improvement. The Kennedy Hotel, a 207 room hotel in Euston in which we have a half interest and which we are to operate is due to open in 1968, and The Britannia, our 460 room hotel in Grosvenor Square, is scheduled to open in the spring of next year. The construction of the proposed hotel in Belfast, which will have about 200 rooms with complementary facilities, is scheduled to start in April of this year. We are currently engaged in Phase III of the rebuilding of the Clifton Ford Hotel, which is the final stage of the demolition and rebuilding of this hotel which was one of the original cornerstones of the Grand Metropolitan Group. Finally a programme of major improvement at St. Ermin's Hotel is being carried out."

With its parent, Associated Hotels, *Kensington Palace Hotel Limited*, MR. KEITH ERSKINE claimed in his annual review (*The Times*, January 31), was one of the few companies which had taken advantage of the Government's "imaginative offer," as he termed it, to lend moneys for hotel development; the board had negotiated loans on terms which were fair and satisfactory to both parties. He continued:

"Looking to the future there is a growing need for government help, if orderly progress is to be maintained. Hotels must now reckon with other foreign countries, notably France, retaliating on America and Britain. When nations try to solve their currency problems by attacking symptoms instead of causes, there is bound to be trouble. What is needed in both America and Britain is a policy to stem wage-price inflation rather than hamper trade and tourism."

Incidentally, Mr. Erskine revealed that profits from Securicor now accounted for three-quarters of the company's total profits.

Although 1967 was not an easy year, the progress of *De Vere Hotels & Restaurants Limited* had been fully maintained and a new record of profitability had been achieved, while for the first four months of the current year trading showed a useful increase over the comparable period of 1967. This was stated in MR. LEOPOLD MULLER's survey (*The Times*, June 13).

MR. GEORGE R. GARDINER told shareholders in *Skyway Hotels Limited* (July 9) that probably one of the most significant factors affecting the possibility of future expansion in the hotel industry in the United Kingdom was the White Paper of May, 1968, on Hotel Development Incentives. He said:

"In the six years previous to 1967 overseas visitors increased from 2m. to 4m. By 1970 it is anticipated that this figure will increase to some 6m. Tourism represents some 10 per cent of the gross national product.

"The Government has seen fit to recommend incentives for

326

the development and extension of hotel facilities, to assist by direct grants as well as loans to those companies, such as ourselves, investing in this industry. As a result a number of marginal propositions studied in the past can now be re-evaluated. The return on your company's capital investment could obviously be greater with this proposed Government assistance.

"Acquisitions in hand; additional facilities at Skyway; the new expansion in the catering field in the United Kingdom; new hotel projects; all of these will give to your company a continuing growth pattern that will be exciting and rewarding to the shareholders."

While *Edger Investments Limited* (July 19) had spent just over £2m. on the Royal Lancaster Hotel in London, the total building cost was considerably greater because The Rank Organization, which had opened the hotel on August 1, 1967, had itself expended moneys in upgrading the hotel beyond the original specification. The hotel had already contributed to the rents receivable by Edger and had earned for itself, declared MR. DESMOND A. REID, a reputation as "one of London's leading hotels."

It was the intention of the board of *Court Line Limited* (June 27), MR. W. S. PHILIPPS announced, to build up a hotel division within the group which would be complementary to its aviation activities. Meanwhile, the acquisition of Durrant House which he reported would bring "useful knowledge of the hotel field into the group," since Durrant House owned directly or indirectly the freeholds of two hotels in Devon—Durrant House Hotel at Northam and Seagate Hotel at Appledore.

Anchor Hotels & Taverns were nearing completion of their modernization programme and had increased their turnover and profits, stated MR. R. H. COURAGE of *Courage Barclay & Simonds Limited* (June 5). He declared, however, that the impact of the breathalyser on banqueting business had been "quite severe."

The next quotation comes from MR. D. P. CROSSMAN's statement for *Watney Mann Limited* (January 26):

"In June our ninth Motel was opened in Stratford-upon-Avon by the Chairman of the British Hotels and Restaurants Association, Lord Shawcross, in the presence of the Mayor of Stratford-upon-Avon and the Chairman of the Warwickshire County Council. This Motel is a major extension to and development of the Falcon Hotel which was acquired in 1962. The alterations to this beautiful Tudor building have been acknowledged in the Press and elsewhere as a happy and most appropriate linking of the old and the new, and comprise 52 new bedrooms, each with its private bathroom, making over 70 bedrooms in all; a greatly extended restaurant and new kitchen; a new bar and improvements to existing bars. Large numbers of overseas tourists,

327

many of them from the United States, have already used the Motel and find the combination of the old and the new both interesting and agreeable. The early results suggest that the Falcon will be a successful project economically, and this in spite of the severe difficulties facing the Hotel industry at the present time."

Another chairman who reported that his company was entering the motel field was MR. M. A. PRYOR of *Truman Hanbury Buxton & Company Limited.* In his statement (*The Times,* July 16) he announced that, as a new trading venture, the company was currently building three motels adjacent to existing licensed houses. These were very strategically placed, two close to London and one in Devonshire. He added that the company's properties were being surveyed with a view to further developments of this nature. At the same time, considerable attention was being given to the improvement and enlargement of the company's hotel properties.

Among 11 new licensed premises which *Vaux and Associated Breweries Limited* (September 20) had built or purchased was a new 50-bedroom hotel The Bellahouston, Glasgow, said MR. DOUGLAS NICHOLSON; and in process of building was a new Swallow Hotel in the centre of Newcastle which would have 85 bedrooms and its own car park for 150 cars, and was expected to open in the spring of 1969.

Rowton Hotels Limited (May 30) was one of those companies which found that what would otherwise have been a record profit was transformed by S.E.T. into a slight decline. None the less, MR. WILLIAM B. HARRIS reported that nightly reservations by overseas guests rose from 87,000 to 99,000, the greater number coming from Northern Europe. As regards the company's hostels, the occupancy rate rose from 88·8 to 90·7 per cent, catering receipts improved and the policy of upgrading the accommodation and general amenities continued.

The catering division of *Associated Fisheries Limited* (March 19) had been expanding and its profits rose by 20 per cent, MR. MICHAEL NOBLE, M.P., revealed. Four new restaurants were opened during the year. The selective employment tax, he declared, "was a serious blow to this service industry."

A modest loss had been incurred by the Lombard Restaurant subsidiary of *The City Offices Company Limited* (April 4), and MR. G. S. PITT made this comment:

"During the year planning permission was obtained to change the use of the first floor to offices. The Restaurant has been re-decorated and there have been senior staff changes. With the prospect of a harsh Budget it is difficult to say with confidence that profitability will be restored."

IRON AND STEEL

WITH the major part of the British iron and steel industry having been nationalized in July, 1967, and no chairmen's statements for that section of the trade published, this chapter is perforce limited to quotations from the annual reviews of a few and mostly minor United Kingdom steel producers and fabricators, as well as steelworks plant manufacturers, refractory makers, steel stockholders and various foreign iron and steel firms.

After nationalization many problems needed to be dealt with or discussed between the Government-controlled British Steel Corporation and the private sector companies. On this subject MR. J. M. CLAY of *Thos. Firth & John Brown Limited* (March 7) stated:

> "The setting up of the British Independent Steel Producers' Association, following the dissolution of the British Iron and Steel Federation, will, it is hoped, provide a satisfactory means of communication with the British Steel Corporation. However, the major problem of selling prices is proving to be difficult and there would appear to be no alternative to the acceptance of price leadership from the B.S.C. for all those products which were previously controlled by the Iron and Steel Board. At the time of writing the B.S.C. have not yet announced when the prices of Alloy Steel will be increased to take note of the greatly increased costs of various raw materials and in particular Nickel and Ferro-Alloys. However, the indications are that the increases which are being discussed will not be sufficient to meet the increased costs which we have already incurred and that the major price review which is in hand will not be published until later in the year. This undoubtedly means that we shall be carrying increased costs for a number of months without being able to recover them in our selling prices. This delay in reflecting unavoidable increased costs in selling prices is unsatisfactory since it must exaggerate the final adjustments that have inevitably to be made. It is to be hoped that the British Steel Corporation will take steps to see that their selling prices are such as to give a satisfactory return on their invested capital and thus permit the Private Sector to compete on equal terms."

SIR G. WILTON LEE of *Arthur Lee & Sons Limited* (January 26) mentioned two matters which were of vital importance to the company in its dealings with British Steel Corporation. The first was the question of raw materials, for the major tonnage of which Arthur Lee was dependent on companies within the Corporation; he sincerely hoped that the excellent supplier–customer relation-

ships which had prevailed in the past would not be disturbed through the reorganization now taking place in the public sector. The second was the general matter of pricing policy, on which he expressed the following views:

"With regard to the Corporation selling policy, the private sector of the industry finds itself in a paradoxical position, due to the judgment of the Restrictive Practices Court on the Heavy Steel case in 1963, whereby any agreement between two or more suppliers regarding prices to be charged, was declared illegal. The 14 major companies now Government-owned constitute a corporate body and are able to agree a common price for a given product, without discrimination as between one consumer and another, whereas the companies in the private sector producing identical products are forbidden by law to enter into any agreement affecting prices, either by themselves or in co-operation with the public sector companies.

"If stability in prices, with competition only on quality and service, is desired, as is believed to be the wish of the Minister of Power, then surely this paradoxical position must be resolved, or the price structure of the industry as a whole will quickly become chaotic, with ultimate serious damage to the national economy."

No great hopes had been expressed for 1967, and the year did not develop well, declared LORD RIVERDALE of *Balfour & Darwins Limited* (June 13). Sales by comparison with 1966 were reduced by 9 per cent at home and $3\frac{1}{2}$ per cent for export, and, with departments working below capacity throughout the year, some orders were unprofitable. However, in the first three months of 1968 there had been a welcome rise in orders and sales. He made this statement about capital expenditure during the year under review:

"A number of re-equipment schemes and plant improvements, referred to last year, went ahead as planned, involving considerable expenditure from which benefit has been deferred by the low level of trade. We are now better placed to take advantage of the increase in demand predicted by recent economic forecasts."

MR. C. F. HURST informed members of *Samuel Osborn & Co. Limited* (December 30) that the Osborn-Hadfields merging of foundry interests had now completed its first year, and, as expected, had not yet fully integrated the main production units. He continued:

"The current year will benefit from the fact that it will not be burdened by many of the non-recurring costs associated with the merger and if the improved trend of the order book is maintained, will gain from a larger and more economic output. How-

330

ever, the full potential of our Foundry interests will only be achieved when integration is complete.

"The Wrought Steel Division has operated at a high level of capacity in the last nine months of the year and has a full order book. Subsequent to the interim report, the acquisitions of Hall & Pickles Alloy Steel Company and C. R. Denton Steel & Tool Co., Ltd., took place and the effect of the rationalization together with higher depreciation charges resulting from a realistic valuation of assets offset to some extent the profits brought into the Group by the two companies. This activity is prepared for considerable progress and development in the current year."

In the main products—wire and wire rope—of *Bruntons* (*Musselburgh*) *Limited* (May 2) competition had remained severe throughout 1967 and the industries making those products had suffered a recession, reported the late EARL OF BALFOUR. However, the consolidated profit before taxation was only a few thousands down and the dividend was maintained. One direction in which he discerned improvement was the group's export trade, about which he stated:

"One very pleasing factor in 1967 was an increase in our exports of some 13 per cent. We have thus helped our own position and made an increased contribution to the country's balance of payments. There are good reasons to hope that exports will continue to improve, and while it is difficult to speak of the home trade with any certainty, we believe we can at least maintain our share of the market."

Commenting on the trading of Brown Bayley Steels Limited, one of the subsidiaries of *Brown Bayley Limited* (May 9), MR. J. W. GARTON stated that the low level of demand continued throughout the financial year. As a result, sales turnover was considerably less than in 1966, and at the same time pressure on costs continued. Since the beginning of 1968 trading conditions had improved, but the steel company still suffered the effect of increased costs, many of which arose from devaluation.

The directors of *Duport Limited*, it was recorded in the Chairman's statement (*The Times*, November 18), had approved plans for the construction of a semi-continuous twin bar mill at London Works Steel Company Limited. Work had already begun, and the entire project, costing approximately £1,400,000, was scheduled for completion in mid-1970.

Announcing a moderate reduction in profits, the result of the general deterioration in trade, MR. S. J. L. MANN informed members of *Longmore Brothers Limited* (December 9) that the first signs of any improvement appeared in February, 1968, since when it had steadily developed. After the close of the company's year on

August 4, 1968, there had been a marked increase in the demand for its products over the same period of 1967, and, if that trend continued, an improvement in the trading results could be expected in the current financial year.

Apart from the impact of Government economic measures which reduced demand, more particularly for the hot rolled products of *Darlington & Simpson Rolling Mills Limited* (February 22), the value of business handled for overseas customers was reduced by 12 per cent compared with the high figure for the previous year. Placing these facts on record, MR. E. T. JUDGE went on to state:

> "Under the circumstances of the severe competition that prevails in the steel export market, even in the special light section market in which the company trades, there is no doubt that selling efforts overseas were assisted considerably by Export Rebate. The Government have now decided to withdraw this from the 1st April, 1968, and it is certainly not clear whether sterling devaluation will *in toto* be of greater or less benefit to Darlington & Simpson Rolling Mills' export performance."

That the offer by *Dunford and Elliott (Sheffield) Limited* (January 4) for Hadfields Limited had been accepted by holders of over 90 per cent of the share capital was announced by MR. G. P. CLARKE, who added that outstanding shares would be acquired in due course under Section 209 of the Companies Act 1948. He also stated that considerable progress had already been made towards reorganizing the group to take advantage of the opportunities for profitable integration.

Reporting a moderate decrease in trading profit, the President of *Neepsend Steel & Tool Corporation Limited* (November 14), SIR STUART C. GOODWIN, stated that while there had been a welcome improvement in orders the uplift came too late to allow sufficient time to retrieve the profit position in the past financial year. Now, however, the company was feeling the benefits of devaluation and the current year's trade figures should reflect an improvement in a number of sections of the group. After mentioning certain developments which should result in greater efficiency, he expressed confidence that trading conditions and financial results for 1968–69 should show reasonable improvement, and that there should be a marked advance in the succeeding year, in view of the higher efficiency of new plant installations and of the benefits of recent acquisitions.

Profits of *Thos. W. Ward Limited* (November 29) from activities within iron and steel and related industries had kept up remarkably well, said MR. H. W. SECKER—better in fact than he had expected in his forecast; and tonnage of ferrous and non-ferrous scrap metals delivered to the steel works and foundries had shown "a satisfactory increase." He also made these remarks on the outlook for this particular sector of the group's activities:

"The demand from the steel industry for scrap is likely to continue at a high level, but the market will become keener and more competitive so that, although I anticipate that our deliveries to the steel works will be maintained at least at the level of the previous year, it could well be that margins will be reduced and correspondingly profit from this source may show some decrease."

As regards nationalization of GKN Steel, MR. RAYMOND P. BROOKES informed members of *Guest, Keen and Nettlefolds Limited* (May 2) that negotiations concerning compensation and other related matters were complex and prolonged. Pending settlement, he declared, "there is inflicted upon us a situation in which we are paid an unreasonably low rate of interest upon a very low notional value."

STEELWORKS PLANT, REFRACTORIES AND STOCKHOLDERS

The medium term future of the iron and steel plant making companies belonging to *Davy-Ashmore Limited* (September 24), SIR MAURICE FIENNES asserted, must now depend to a large extent upon the development programmes of the British Steel Corporation. He continued:

"There have been few large scale capital developments in the British Steel industry since about 1960 and we have been having to live on export contracts, many of them unprofitable if only by reason of the costly marketing effort necessary to obtain them. Two years ago I gave reasons why your Directors believed that the British Steel Industry would need to proceed eventually to a new programme of development and nothing has occurred since then to suggest that we were wrong. To us, however, the time factor is crucial and the present indications are that it may be another 18 months to 2 years before the Corporation is able to proceed on a significant scale. Our problem is to fill the gap. We have, of course, represented the position ceaselessly to the Corporation itself and also to those organs of the British Government which we may reasonably expect to help us in filling the gap by further export contracts. However, with the world surplus of steel supply, even export contracts are fewer; and they are also harder to obtain, as our overseas competitors are in much the same position. This is the central problem in Davy-Ashmore at the present time. It is not new and in varying degree we have been facing it during the last five or six years of cyclical depression in demand. We have battled through before and, blessed as we are with a first class team of engineers and craftsmen, I do not doubt we shall do so again. The encouraging feature in the present situation is that there is now a glimmer of light at the end of the long tunnel."

Another chairman who stated that 1967–68 had been yet a further year of very limited demand for steelworks plant in the United Kingdom, the development plans of the British Steel Corporation not yet having been put into action, was SIR PETER G. ROBERTS of *The Wellman Engineering Corporation Limited* (October 3). The company, he pointed out, operated in a cyclical field, where new development and capital expenditure seemed to come in periods approximately seven years apart. He could only hope that "we are approaching a period of expansion in the British iron and steel industry." Meanwhile, the company was in a strong position to give modern and efficient service.

From SIR GEORGE BRIGGS's statement (*The Times*, March 28) for *General Refractories Group Limited* the following paragraphs are extracted:

"Shareholders may remember that last year in referring to the 1966 results I said we had experienced a difficult year. Unfortunately 1967 was no better, indeed worse, as trading conditions were very varied and costs continued to rise. The steel industry's output was 1·7 per cent down and there was reduced demand from the glass and foundry industries. As these three are our most important markets it was inevitable that we should suffer some setbacks. The current year has started better and there are indications of improvement in our activities but we cannot yet see the rate of expansion we should like.

"The merger with John G. Stein & Co. Ltd. has been completed. We now have a group able to offer products of every range with a technical backing and service unsurpassed in Europe or indeed the United States.

"The opportunity was taken during the year to widen our range of industrial sands and we purchased for cash the whole of the issued share capital of George Sheard (Congleton) Ltd. Congleton sand has unique properties which form the basis of foundry practice in some of the country's most important foundries."

After outlining some of the problems that had faced *Miles Druce & Co. Limited* in 1967—*e.g.*, price cutting at a time of falling demand and rising costs; S.E.T. and other increased costs; the cancellation by the British Steel Corporation of the quantity price concessions formerly received from the steel mills; heavy start up costs of the new Colnbrook warehouse and the central management and services complex, together with the computer, at High Wycombe—MR. G. P. PHILIPSON-STOW in his statement (*The Times*, April 24) reported slight indications in some directions of an upturn in demand; he was, however, not too optimistic about the immediate prospect. He added:

"We shall continue to try to keep down our costs wherever

334

possible and we shall naturally endeavour to speed up the attainment of the many benefits which we hope to reap from our computer and other improvements in our organization and methods."

Macready's Metal Company Limited (June 12), it was claimed by MR. R. E. J. MACREADY, was the largest stockholder in the United Kingdom of bright and hot rolled carbon, alloy and stainless steel bars, in which the company specialized. The total stocking capacity was now expanded to 15,000/16,000 tons of these products, which were supplied to industry throughout the country and abroad. He continued:

"I am able to report that a considerable increase for the company's products and services developed in the closing months of the year, but arrived too late to reverse the profit fall experienced in the first half of the year covered by this report. This increased demand has developed further during the opening months of the current year, permitting the company to take full advantage of the increased stock expansion. I will not, however, attempt to assess the future until the effects of the Budget are revealed on current trading conditions; certainly we have to face increased costs in respect of S.E.T., transport charges, corporation tax, etc. as legislated for in the Budget."

Recording expenditure on fixed assets during the year under review of almost £300,000, before investment and development grants, MR. NORMAN CASHMORE of *John Cashmore Limited* (June 27) revealed that this was largely incurred in completing the warehouses at Walsall and Risca, which he claimed were the best of their type in Europe and were now operating satisfactorily.

In future years the pattern of group trading of *Norton Industries Limited* (March 28), stated MR. J. D. NORTON, must be affected by nationalization of the major British steelmaking companies, since these were at once both the largest customers and suppliers of the company. However, he added, it was felt that the group was sufficiently flexible to adapt its activities to meet any changes in policy which might be introduced by the British Steel Corporation.

OVERSEAS COMPANIES

The recession which had first made itself felt in the Federal German Republic during 1966 affected the economy increasingly up to the middle of 1967. Then a gradual change took effect, and officially directed economic measures and others originating from the economy itself resulted in higher demand, production and turnover. The revival, however, did not fully offset the effects of the recession during the preceding months, so that during 1967, for the first time since the Republic was established, no economic growth was

recorded. This summary of the state of the German economy appeared in the report (*The Times*, September 27) of the board of directors of *Fried. Krupp Hüttenwerke AG.* While industrial output as a whole in Germany fell by $2\frac{1}{2}$ per cent from the preceding year's figure, they added, the iron and steel producing industry was able to increase its steel output, after a downward trend lasting two years. But reduced domestic demand and fewer orders from the other E.C.S.C. countries led to expanding business with third countries, exports of rolled steel products thereto rising by 34·3 per cent to $4\frac{1}{2}$m. tons. As prices in world markets hardly covered costs in view of worldwide overcapacity, the earnings position in the German steel industry further deteriorated during 1967 in spite of a slight consolidation of domestic prices. The four rolled steel sales organizations contributed to stabilizing the domestic market. The report included this reference to prospects:

"The revival in the iron and steel market which began towards the end of the period under review continued with greater impetus during the first few months of 1968. This development had a favourable effect on the company's business and on that of its associated companies. Since the beginning of 1968 capacity at all Krupp works has been almost fully utilized.

DR. EGON OVERBECK, chairman of the board of management of *Mannesmann AG.* (Düsseldorf, July 18), said that although crude steel production for the first time reached the 3m. metric ton mark during 1967, the group's external turnover at DM. 3,980m. was just over 4 per cent below the level of 1966. He found it the more encouraging therefore that the company had managed to maintain its profit, with the result that the board had been able to appropriate DM. 10m. to the free reserve and to distribute the same dividend as in the previous year. Dr. Overbeck made this brief reference to the Brazilian notes affair:

"There is little to report. In the pending court proceedings no final decisions have yet been given. Due to agreements with the bona fide bearers of notes about $4\frac{1}{2}$m. new Cruzeiros have meanwhile been paid in cash and about $1\frac{1}{2}$m. new Cruzeiros debentures have been issued at short notice."

In his address for *Hoesch AG.* (Dortmund, May 15) DR. WILLY OCHEL also pointed out that the German economic recession in 1967 hit in particular the main steel-consuming industries and thus adversely affected the group's business, a considerable decline in home sales being only in part offset by higher exports. He, too, was able to refer to better business in the current year in the following terms:

"The current business year shows an all-round improvement in capacity utilization. The order flow for the first six months was

15 per cent above the previous year's level, giving rise to hopes for better earnings. A long-term investment programme will help to continue concentration in all product sectors and to strengthen the Group's competitiveness under joint plans with Hoogovens."

The 1967 report (*The Times*, June 22) of *Italsider* noted that in 1967 Italian steel consumption increased by over 17 per cent to 16·3m. tons. Italsider itself contributed to total Italian production 94 per cent of pig iron, over 50 per cent of ingot steel, 48 per cent of hot-rolled sections, 54 per cent of cold-rolled sections and over 60 per cent of plated products. Fifty-four per cent of Italsider steel was produced by the LD process, and the ratio of pig iron to steel production rose to 86 per cent.

The following information on the steelworks interests of *Stora Kopparberg* (Falun, Sweden, May 10) was given in the report presented by the board of directors:

"At the Domnarvet steelworks production was at a high level throughout the year. Improvements in methods and processes led to higher yield from the raw materials and lower production costs. The equipment at Domnarvet is well suited for the production of special grades of steel designed to meet high quality demands and the proportion of such steel has increased. The new production lines for hot-dip galvanizing, plastic coating and profile shaping of sheet were assembled and will start up during the first half of 1968. The production of stainless steel has increased. The stainless ingots are rolled in the hot-strip mill at Domnarvet. Final processing is carried out at Söderfors. All speciality steel products are marketed under the 'Stora' name.

"Production and sales of all types of steel as well as research and development have been organized into a steel division."

The Highveld steel and vanadium complex, the most ambitious industrial project of the *Anglo American Corporation of South Africa Limited* (Johannesburg, June 14) and its partners, stated Mr. H. F. Oppenheimer, was then approaching completion.

"The first unit of the iron making plant was commissioned in February. It was not to be expected that in a plant of this magnitude all teething troubles would be avoided, and we are having our share and no doubt will have more. I can say, however, that on the whole the construction programme has gone well. Though world prices of vanadium have recently fallen they are in line with our estimates and we are satisfied with the long-term prospects for Highveld."

MINING AND METALS

GOLD AND URANIUM

THE non-monetary absorption of gold in the free world in 1967 was estimated by *Union Corporation Limited* (Johannesburg, June 6) at 81,800,000 ounces, stated MR. T. P. STRATTEN. By contrast, new production contributed 40,800,000 ounces, and the balance came from world official monetary stocks, which thus declined by 41m. ounces; the bulk of this reduction came from the United States, whose gold reserves declined by some 33,400,000 ounces, or rather more than the total gold production of South Africa in 1967. Mr. Stratten continued:

"Of this private absorption we estimate that consumption in industry and in the arts accounted for 17m. ounces, a figure which is in line with the steady increase in usage of gold in industry and the arts in recent years. But more than half of the private absorption, namely 44,800,000 ounces, represents purchases by companies, organizations and individuals who distrusted currencies—their own or others—who were convinced that at $35 per ounce, or near it, gold was cheap and was a safe store of value, and were willing to back their judgment to the extent of rather more than $1,568m."

Addressing members of *Rand Mines Limited* (Johannesburg, May 10), MR. P. H. ANDERSON reiterated the plea for a general revaluation of gold in terms of all currencies as a step in re-establishing a sound and disciplined economy in the western world, though he realized that he would be dubbed an interested party. He added:

"Rather than face up to unpalatable measures, political arguments against such a step are advanced and various ingenious devices are being evolved such as the two-tier gold price and special drawing rights. Cynics may find some comfort in the thought that the increase in the price of gold will have to be so much more if it has to be used eventually as a cure for economic disaster rather than as a preventive measure now, but it is to be hoped that such a train of events will not be allowed to develop."

He welcomed the new scheme for assistance to marginal gold mines announced by the South African Minister of Finance on March 27, 1968. The old scheme, he declared, did not in fact assist marginal mines but mines which had passed that stage and were rapidly dying. The new scheme, however, was different in

that it offered help at a much earlier and more effective stage. It took the form of tax credit payments calculated on a formula similar to that used for gold-mining taxation, but the amount of assistance granted would not exceed 25 per cent of working revenue. The plan could be used by mines which were within eight years of closure and would show a significant potential increase of life and gold production if granted assistance.

In a thoughtful examination of the problems facing the South African economy MR. D. A. B. WATSON of *Johannesburg Consolidated Investment Company Limited* (Johannesburg, November 26) dealt with—among other things—the imbalance between merchandise imports and exports. He said:

"Last year the total value of our merchandise imports exceeded the value of merchandise exports by over R500m. As usual this deficit was made up by the value of our gold exports. Gold remains the pillar which at present supports our economy and for this reason the scheme announced in the last Budget speech, enlarging the field of assistance towards needy gold mines, is very welcome. In the present atmosphere of doubt which surrounds the question of whether or when gold mining companies will in the future receive any additional revenue for their gold, any deferment of the curtailment of operations by individual gold mines may well prove to be of value to them and to the country. Furthermore, these short term subsidies will to some small degree extend the time available to us in which to replace future reductions in the value of our gold exports. While it is true that if the price received for gold *does* increase, our problems will to some extent be deferred, the Republic must ultimately free itself from its present complete dependence on gold exports. The sooner we can move towards this freedom, the better, and whether our problem continues to be urgent, or is deferred, it would seem prudent to treat it as urgent. We should therefore continue to borrow time by maintaining our gold production for as long as possible by means of a subsidy to producing mines and by measures designed to assist towards the opening up of new mines. Within this borrowed time we must then foster those other activities which will in due course enable us to maintain a balance on the foreign trade account."

For the first time for 16 years, reported MR. H. F. OPPENHEIMER to *Anglo American Corporation of South Africa Limited* (Johannesburg, June 14), there was a fall, albeit a small one, in the output of the South African gold-mining industry; and he added that though the output of the mines in the group itself was maintained at about the same level as in 1966, their working profit showed a small fall of just over $1\frac{1}{2}$ per cent. He went on to remark:

339

"In certain directions, however, plans for expansion are under way. The opening of Vaal Reefs South by our Group, and of the East Driefontein mine by Gold Fields of South Africa Limited, in which our Group will have a substantial participation, is going ahead satisfactorily, and in addition the industry is expanding in order to meet the increased demand for uranium. Nevertheless, even though gold production is likely to rise again slightly over the next few years, the fact remains that a long period of rapid gold mining expansion has come to an end and this is a matter of serious significance for South Africa and for our Group."

The year under review had been notable for *West Witwatersrand Areas Limited* (Johannesburg, November 15), Mr. A. Louw declared, in that it had seen yet another new mine, in this case East Driefontein, brought into existence on the West Wits line. There were today eight large gold mines on the now famous West Wits line, producing nearly 8m. ounces of gold and yielding revenue totalling some R200m. per annum.

Under the new monthly pay arrangements, Mr. C. B. Anderson informed shareholders in *St. Helena Gold Mines Limited* (Johannesburg, May 22), significant increases were awarded to union members, in return for which the unions agreed to abandon certain restrictive practices. Some benefits in this direction had accrued to the mine, but he asserted that continued co-operation was required if increased wages were to be matched by increased productivity.

After the temporary setback in 1966–67, group profits before tax of *Consolidated Gold Fields Limited* (November 19) in 1967–68 rose £5·1m. to a record £16·3m., but satisfaction at this achievement, Sir George Harvie-Watt showed, must be qualified by the disaster at the West Driefontein mine. He said:

"Our activities in South Africa and, indeed, the Group figures which I have just quoted, have inevitably been overshadowed by the news of the recent massive inflow of water at West Driefontein. This mine is the richest gold producer in the world. Its milling rate and working profits have been raised successively in each of the past five years and further increases were forecast. It is all the more calamitous, therefore, that its operations should have been interrupted. Recovery from a disaster of this magnitude will take time, but we have the greatest confidence in the direction of our South African Chairman, Mr. Adriaan Louw, and his highly experienced technical staff. They are to be congratulated on their magnificent work during the past weeks. Everything that is possible is being done to combat the problems which are facing West Driefontein."

Record production of *Ashanti Goldfields Limited* (April 4) led

to an increase in profit before tax and minerals duty of £77,700, but there was a material drop in the net figure, and MAJOR-GENERAL SIR EDWARD L. SPEARS showed that taxes and duty absorbed more than 76 per cent of the whole profit. This did not include an additional provision for 1966 resulting from the increase in tax rates and another sum for Ghana Social Security Levy. However, he was convinced that the Ghana Government realized that this was intolerable and that taxation would be reduced.

The revival in demand for uranium called forth these remarks (in part) from SIR KEITH ACUTT of *West Rand Investment Trust Limited* (May 24):

> "Last year I mentioned the revival in demand for uranium. This revival has continued over the last year and although much of the increased demand is for delivery in future years, there has been an encouraging demand for immediate supplies. The demand for future deliveries enables the gold mines to expand their uranium production with the long-term viability of the plants reasonably assured, but it may be some time before the full profit potential of these operations materializes."

COPPER, COBALT, ALUMINIUM AND NICKEL

During the early part of 1968 MR. H. F. OPPENHEIMER told members of *Zambian Anglo American Limited* (Lusaka, December 31), it was found possible to conclude a $70m. financing arrangement between Nchanga Consolidated Copper Mines Limited and the group's principal copper customers in Japan, Mitsui and Co. Limited and Mitsubishi Shoji Kaisha Limited. He continued:

> "The finance consists of loans totalling $42m. which will materially assist Nchanga to meet its heavy capital expenditure programme, and a credit facility up to the value of $28m. for purchases of Japanese plant and equipment. Repayment will be in the form of deliveries of copper over seven years which is included in an agreement for the supply to Mitsubishi and Mitsui by our group companies of 100,000 tons of copper a year over a period of ten years.
> "This is the largest loan raised for Zambia since independence and by any standards is a major commodity deal, reflecting the continued prosperity and growth of the Japanese economy and the increasing demand for copper in that country. The willingness of the two Japanese companies to assist the development of Zambia so substantially is propitious and I believe that both countries will benefit from the strengthened business relations."

Operations of *Rhokana Corporation Limited* (Lusaka, December

12) for the year ended June 30, 1968, were satisfactory, declared MR. OPPENHEIMER, a higher sales tonnage (resulting partly from a technical change) and an increased average price realized (partly a consequence of the prolonged strike in the United States copper mining industry) leading to a materially larger operating profit. However, with taxation heavier, the net profit after tax showed a less substantial increase. He had this to say about the corporation's cobalt interests:

"Cobalt production for the year dropped by 218 short tons to 1,499 tons, mainly because of the need to close the plant for two months for repairs and modifications. A weak market in the United Kingdom resulted in sales of only 1,032 short tons, compared with 1,702 tons for 1966/67."

High Zambian taxation and limitations on dividends payable outside Zambia were commented upon by SIR RONALD L. PRAIN in his annual statement (*The Times*, November 18) for the *R.S.T. Group of Companies.* He stated:

"We have pilot projects at Baluba and Chambishi which if proved viable will require further investment and will further increase the capacity of the group. The viability of such new projects however depends not only on technical considerations but also on fiscal conditions. The combined rate of taxes on copper mines in Zambia, high by almost any world mining standards, and based on formulae which lead to differential taxation, coupled now with dividend limitations, all serve to endanger the viability of new projects. When these constraints are viewed in the context of the high capital costs involved in modern mining, and the current high operating costs in Zambia . . . it becomes apparent that the viability of new mines in this country requires ore grades which may be several times greater than those now being worked in competitive countries. This is a problem which will require serious consideration by Government and the companies."

Addressing members of *Selection Trust Limited* (July 11), MR. A. CHESTER BEATTY mentioned that the company had entered Iran to carry out an examination of a copper deposit in a mountainous area in the south of that country. He added:

"The work carried out by our Iranian partners in establishing the existence of this deposit presented a mining opportunity at a rather unusually advanced and therefore more attractive stage than is normally the case with exploration targets. This is reflected in the terms to which we have agreed. A great deal of work lies ahead and we shall not know until next year whether the economics of the deposit are sufficiently attractive to justify our proceeding with the financing and equipment of the property."

That the copper-mining industry was apparently heading for some potential over-supply in the next few years was foreshadowed by COMMANDER H. F. P. GRENFELL of *Messina (Transvaal) Development Company Limited* (Johannesburg, February 8).

"Forecasts of new mining projects," he reported, "indicate that the cycle is moving towards a situation where the productive capacity of the copper mining industry during the next few years is likely to exceed the projected demand. However, much of the world's copper comes from countries where in the past there have been frequent and serious interruptions to production. Thus, although statistics at present indicate that the future trend may be towards a condition of over supply, in practice there is likely to be a considerable difference between productive capacity and actual production, and the problem may be minimized to that extent."

Pointing to the wide fluctuations in the price of copper, LORD McFADZEAN said that *British Insulated Callender's Cables Limited* (May 9) believed that it was the largest fabricator of the metal in the world, but he implied that aluminium was being increasingly substituted for copper. He continued:

"Virtually all low voltage mains cables up to 11 kV used by Area Electricity Boards in this country are now being supplied with aluminium conductors. Recently, following some major technical developments by the BICC Group, the British Post Office is specifying more aluminium cables. And in 1967 we have taken some important long-term decisions for the further use of aluminium involving greater research: a further substantial increase in our fabrication facilities: and steps to ensure regular supplies on beneficial terms.

"One matter of particular interest in the latter respect is our partnership with the Rio Tinto-Zinc Corporation as active contenders for a new aluminium smelter in Britain. This latter was an idea thought up by R.T.Z., to whose initiative full national credit should be given, and we were delighted to accept their invitation to become partners. Alas, the matter has now been in the hands of Government for months and whilst I can sympathize with them in their dilemma I deplore on wholly economic grounds the delay in decision, which is not only postponing an annual saving in imports of up to £18m. but deferring the further edge such a smelter would give us in international markets."

In his statement for *Sterling Cable Company Limited* (July 11) MR. J. D. CLARE also referred to the substitution of aluminium for copper. The changeover by the Electricity Boards to aluminium power cables continued during the year, he stated, "and has now become almost 100 per cent of their usage."

343

SIR VAL DUNCAN told members of *The Rio Tinto-Zinc Corporation Limited*—his speech was reported in *The Times* of May 17—that the group was now so broadly based that its prospects were more dependent on general world trading conditions than upon the results of any one particular commodity, but nevertheless Palabora in South Africa and Hamersley Iron in Western Australia played such an important part in the total picture at the present stage that he gave them special comment. From this comment there are extracted the following passages:

"The fortunes of Palabora must be closely bound up with the position of copper in the world. During 1967 copper prices were high—far too high, in my opinion, for the continued health of the copper industry. This was caused primarily by prolonged strikes in the United States, and had this situation continued any longer I think it would have done long-term damage to the copper industry as a whole. For many years now aluminium has provided a substitute for copper in the electrical industry, and I have no doubt that this process will continue and will further erode the use of copper. Nevertheless, the qualities of copper as a metal are such that it has a good and expanding future, provided that its price is not too high and it is in assured supply. Fortunately it is now moving to a more realistic level, and it is very much to be hoped that greater price stability of metal will be achieved in the near future. . . . As far as Palabora is concerned, it is one of the cheapest copper producers in the world, with operating costs of around £100 per ton. This means that there is no foreseeable price of copper which would make it an unremunerative operation. Nevertheless, the coincidence of falling copper prices (and with the ending of the U.S. strikes these have fallen even more quickly than was expected) and the end of the tax-free period for Palabora, will produce substantially lower profits this year.

"In contrast to Palabora which, notwithstanding its long life reserves, is already operating at near its optimum rate of production, Hamersley Iron not only contains the most tremendous reserves of iron ore which will enable it to go on expanding over many years, but its products are less susceptible to the fluctuation of market prices than has been the case with copper. Hamersley is a low-cost producer and though we do not expect iron ore prices in the world to increase in present value currencies, the favourable location and shipping facilities of Hamersley constitute a major world-base to serve the steel industry not only in Japan and Europe but also, we believe, in the United States. Thinking in the steel world is gradually changing, and though there is no question of the modern blast furnace capacity already installed being curtailed, it is likely that in the future part of the new production from Hamersley will

take the form of iron products of around 90 per cent ferrous content and also, in specialized instances, of semi-finished steel. We believe that as, for instance, South-East Asia develops, there will be great attractions in some of these areas in the provision of semi-finished products so that they can avoid the heavy capital costs of blast furnace installations and concentrate on rolling and finishing capacities. These developments are some years ahead, but no producer of high grade iron ore on a world scale can ignore this trend."

Contrary to expectations, 1967 witnessed a check to the continued growth of aluminium consumption, MR. NATHANAEL V. DAVIS showed in his annual report (*The Times*, February 28) as President of *Alcan Aluminium Limited*. There was a decline of 20 per cent from the company's record earnings of 1966, resulting from a slight reduction in sales volume, the impact of inflation on costs, lower fabricating profits, and increased non-operating charges in the fourth quarter. Among his references to the group's interests in the United Kingdom Mr. Davis wrote:

"A two-stage smelter is planned for the North of Scotland, the first stage of 60,000 long tons to come into production in 1970, and the second stage of a further 60,000 long tons due in 1971."

The next quotation comes from the 1967 report of *Alusuisse* (Swiss Aluminium Limited) which was summarized in *The Times* of May 2:

"All plants of the Alusuisse Group producing raw materials, electrical energy and primary aluminium operated at full capacity during the whole year. Contrary to this, our semis and foil plants had difficulty at times in obtaining sufficient orders at reasonable prices. In terms of tonnage our fabricating capacity was sufficiently occupied. Total production of primary aluminium in the Group was 342,000 metric tons which was 17 per cent more than in 1966. By the end of March 1968 the primary aluminium capacity of Alusuisse will be just short of 400,000 tons. Production of our rolling and extrusion plants increased slightly from 196,000 tons to 197,000 tons. The seven foil plants in Europe and U.S.A. produced a total of 52,000 tons, being 3 per cent less than in 1966. Our plastics and chemical plants with few exceptions operated at near capacity."

Among the points of interest in the report of the directors of *Elektrokemisk A/S* (Oslo, April 22) was the establishment of new aluminium production capacity at Mosjoen, about which the board stated:

"At Mosjoen Aluminiumverk an expansion programme comprising 84 new pots was completed. This increased the plant's

annual capacity from approximately 60,000 tons to almost 85,000 tons. As a result of an extensive rationalization programme the expansion entailed only a minor increase in the number of workers, a fact of considerable importance to the plant's economy."

Profits from aluminium of *Tube Investments Limited*, LORD PLOWDEN indicated in his annual statement (*The Times*, November 22), were much improved, but prices continued under pressure. He added that the construction of a United Kingdom smelter at Invergordon would lead to the full profits from an integrated aluminium operation being reflected in TI's consolidated accounts.

In his address for *Selection Trust Limited* (July 11) MR. A. CHESTER BEATTY commented on the group's Australian interests in these terms:

"The most exciting development affecting the company during the year has undoubtedly been the progress of Western Mining Corporation in Australia. We have a 10 per cent shareholding which was acquired over a period at a total cost of £4½m. At March 31, 1968 our holding had a market value of some £22·7m. and this has since appreciated further to a current value of almost £50m. The rights issue announced in February 1968 will increase the cost of our investment by £2·1m. This acquisition, bringing as it does a stake in nickel deposits of great promise, has provided an interesting adjustment in the spread of commodities represented by our assets and their geographical distribution.

"At this stage, as you will have seen from the analyses in the Annual Report, the income is not in line with the assets because of the time required to bring a new mineral deposit to profitable production. Consequently, although some 23 per cent of our total assets at March 31 related to Australia, only 1 per cent of our income is derived from there. The success of Western Mining in outlining ore deposits in its areas around Kambalda has understandably caused much interest in the possibilities of success in our own exploration activities close-by."

The report submitted by the board of directors to the annual meeting of *Le Nickel* (Paris, July 2), with M. LOUIS DEVAUX in the chair, recalled that 1967—in the course of which the imbalance between world nickel resources and the rising demand for its use was underlined—saw a new French policy of the company being initiated, which had been decided by the Government and indicates radical changes for the future not only of New Caledonia but also of the company itself.

TIN AND WOLFRAM

After outlining the effects of the change in the tin supply position on the buffer stock, SIR DOUGLAS WARING said at the annual meeting of the *Malayan Chamber of Mines* (June 19):

"The rapid change in the supply position was caused mainly by the conversion into metal of a large stock of concentrates in Thailand accumulated as a result of earlier operational difficulties at the Thaisarco smelter. Metal production in Thailand in 1967 was 26,551 tons compared with 16,990 tons in 1966. At the same time world mine production was on the increase with the result that world metal production in 1967 reached 173,900 tons compared with 156,300 tons in 1966. The availability of metal was increased in 1967 by imports from China of the order of 4,000 tons and U.S. stockpile disposals of some 6,100 tons making a total availability of about 184,000 tons. Against this, consumption is put at about 166,000 tons and exports to the communist bloc countries at about 9,000 tons, making a total of 175,000 tons. The difference of some 9,000 tons between these two totals compares closely with the increase (9,561 tons) in smelter production in Thailand during 1967 and explains why the buffer stock manager had to go into the market from time to time to support the price. It is perhaps reasonable to assume that most, if not all, of the back-log of concentrates in Thailand had been converted into metal and absorbed by the market by the end or 1967 and that consequently world metal production in 1968 should more closely reflect mine production than in 1967. After its meeting in La Paz in April this year the International Tin Council expressed the view that current mine production and metal consumption were roughly in balance."

As chairman of *Amalgamated Tin Mines of Nigeria Limited* (November 7) Sir Douglas made this reference to the company's Nigerian mining operations during the civil war:

"During the first half of the current year our estimates and calculations show that we are still working with a small margin of profit and one can only hope that hostilities can be brought to a speedy conclusion so that the inevitably slow return to normality can be started. As I have previously stated, your properties constitute a valuable mine and with a change in conditions your company should still be able to give a good account of itself in the future."

As chairman also of *London Tin Corporation Limited*, SIR DOUGLAS WARING mentioned in his annual review (*The Times*, July 9) that it had been decided to extend the group's activities by

347

enlarging its Australian organization to undertake mining investigations in that continent which would include tin potentialities and also other possible mineral discoveries.

MR. W. D. WILSON informed members of *Ayer Hitam Tin Dredging Limited* in his statement (*The Times*, December 13) that the company's provisional quota for the initial export control period under the International Tin Council's scheme was 9,033 piculs (537·7 tons). An increase in production for the current financial year had been forecast for the company, but its extent must depend on export quotas and other regulations. "If, however," he added, "the recent rise in tin prices is maintained and exports are not further restricted the company's profitability should continue to improve."

Hongkong Tin Limited (June 28) had applied to the United Kingdom Treasury for consent to change the residence of the company to Malaysia, stated MR. J. ADDINSELL, and stockholders would be kept informed of developments.

For the *Pahang Consolidated Company Limited* (December 12) MR. J. N. DAVIES summarized the year's results as follows:

"Production was slightly down on last year's results but the drop in pre-tax profit was largely due to lower tin prices and to a lesser extent rising costs. Every effort is still being exerted to contain costs and credit is due to all concerned for the way in which these have been controlled in the face of steadily rising prices of materials and labour."

Another company of which SIR DOUGLAS WARING is chairman is *Tongkah Harbour Tin Dredging Berhad* (December 30), for which he mentioned a technical development:

"The installation of a new bucket ladder on the Sea Dredge has for various reasons been deferred from time to time. In order to reach bedrock over portions of the property at present unbottomed, this work has to be carried out eventually though it will involve a close-down of the plant for some three to four months. An appropriate occasion is likely to arise about the middle of next year but a final decision will depend on how far our operating programme is affected by tin control at that time."

The strength of the wolfram market through 1967 had been exceptional, declared MR. G. W. FLINT of *Beralt Tin and Wolfram Limited* (May 22), and no doubt it had been substantially influenced by the conflict in the Far East. He continued:

"It was to be expected that the sterling price of tungsten concentrates would increase more or less proportionately with the devaluation of sterling and that the willingness of the U.S. General Services Administration to supply concentrates at the dollar equivalent to 401s. per long ton unit would create an

effective ceiling. The price has recently come back sharply from 427s. 6d. to 322s. 6d. due, it is believed, to sales of Chinese material at reduced prices. Although such an adjustment must have an adverse effect on profits, I believe prices in the region of 400s. to be too high to sustain a keen demand for tungsten."

LEAD, ZINC AND SILVER

At the beginning of 1967 world surpluses of both lead and zinc metal were forecast, stated SIR VAL DUNCAN of *New Broken Hill Consolidated Limited* (April 24). In the event, he added, supply and demand for lead and zinc were well balanced in 1967, though at lower levels than originally estimated. Reflecting the economic recession in many countries, consumption was more or less unchanged from 1966. In zinc several producers made voluntary cuts in metal production, and a major strike affected the output of both metals in the United States from July onwards. Prices, he showed, moved within a fairly narrow range until the devaluation of sterling, and then the prices were adjusted upwards by about the amount of devaluation. As to silver, Sir Val declared:

"1967 was a particularly interesting year for silver. During the early part of the year the price was around 111d. an ounce which was closely related to the United States price of 129 cents an ounce. However, on May 18, 1967, the United States Treasury announced that it was no longer a general seller at that price, and this factor combined with mine and smelter strikes in the United States and currency speculation caused violent fluctuations in the silver market during the second half of the year. Following devaluation the sterling price of silver rose further to touch 224d. an ounce and closed the year at the high level of 217d."

He also stated that the price levels of lead, zinc and silver then current were satisfactory for the operations of the company.

Reporting later in the year to members of *Consolidated Gold Fields Limited* (November 19), SIR GEORGE HARVIE-WATT declared that American Zinc had had another difficult period. Although the price of the metal was higher than expected and the company achieved a 14 per cent increase in sales, a loss of £585,000 was made. He claimed that the main reasons for the loss, which followed the previous year's strike, were high start-up costs and delays in achieving planned performance with new equipment, and he added that the outlook for American Zinc's operations in the near future must still be regarded as uncertain, but there were a number of hopeful indications.

349

PLATINUM

The statement by MR. T. P. STRATTEN for *U. C. Investments Limited* (Johannesburg, May 24) included this paragraph about a new platinum project:

"Union Corporation has for some time been engaged in prospecting for platinum in the Rustenburg area of the Transvaal. Last September it announced that the results of exploration had been sufficiently encouraging to warrant exploitation, that steps were being taken to apply for a mining lease for precious metals and that the longer term delivery items of plant had been ordered. We expect to be offered a 20 per cent. participation in Union Corporation's interest in this venture."

DIAMONDS

A large exchange loss of R3,607,000 was incurred by *De Beers Consolidated Mines Limited* (Kimberley, June 4) on the devaluation of sterling, but MR. H. F. OPPENHEIMER claimed that the maintenance of substantial funds in London was unavoidable for the purpose of the company's trading business; at the time of devaluation, unfortunately, these balances were at a high level. He gave these details of diamond sales and stocks:

"Diamond account, at R104,547,000, was R7,037,000 lower than in 1966. This reflects the decline in sales by the Central Selling Organisation from R355,692,000 in 1966 to R351,424,000 in 1967, in spite of a price increase of approximately $7\frac{1}{2}$ per cent, which was brought into effect in August, 1966. As the production of Group mines, particularly Finsch, rose considerably, and purchases by The Diamond Corporation from outside sources were also substantially higher than in 1966, stocks increased during the year by R32,514,000 to R67,729,000. In the present disturbed monetary conditions I do not regard this increase as altogether undesirable. After the first two months of 1967 the market was relatively quiet throughout the year. From January of this year, however, there has been a distinct improvement in demand and I am hopeful that our sales in 1968 will show a resumed upward trend."

As in previous years, MR. A. CHESTER BEATTY, of *Consolidated African Selection Trust Limited* (December 10) was critical of the marketing system in Ghana, but was rather more hopeful for the future in view of a possible overhaul of the system. He said:

"The company continued to experience difficulties in marketing its diamonds. The imperfections of the marketing system, to which I have drawn attention in previous years, coupled with

a decline in the demand for Ghana diamonds caused a serious drop in the price of our diamonds. I now understand that the marketing system is to be overhauled. I sincerely hope that the Marketing Corporation, in designing a new procedure, will take note of and incorporate some of the proposals we have made in various representations over the years both to the government and the Corporation."

Mr. Beatty, as chairman, of *Selection Trust Limited* (July 11), also declared that the security situation in the Sierra Leone Selection Trust licence areas continued to give grave cause for anxiety. Although successive Governments had recognized the urgent need to stamp out illicit mining and had entered into agreements with the company to introduce more effective security measures, he asserted, these measures had not yet been fully implemented, and the gangs of illicit diamond miners and their organizers continued to operate in defiance of law and order.

COAL, MANGANESE AND POTASH

MR. P. H. ANDERSON told members of *Rand Mines Limited* (Johannesburg, May 10) that the collieries of the group, in common with the coal-mining industry generally, again had a disappointing year and profits declined further as a result of rising costs of production, an unrealistic controlled price for coal and a decrease in sales.

A large new contract for the supply of coal in New South Wales is among the developments mentioned in the following paragraph extracted from MR. A. P. COSTAIN's statement for *Richard Costain Limited* (June 27):

"Work continues at the Westfield and Cudworth sites in Scotland and further open cast coal contracts for the National Coal Board have been obtained at Rushworth and Whiteside. We have been engaged in this type of work in Britain for the past 24 years in the course of which we have accumulated considerable expertise. With the doubts cast upon the future expansion of this activity by the publication in November of the Government White Paper on 'Fuel Policy' it was with considerable satisfaction that we were able to announce the award of a contract for the supply of 50m. tons of coal to the Electricity Supply Commission of New South Wales. Actual production will commence in 1972 and continue for 14 years. This contract, valued at approximately £44m. at current prices, is the largest of its type ever awarded and was won in the face of keen international competition."

Besides the intense competition in the manganese ore market and the consequent fall in prices of ore for metallurgical use, MR.

W. A. HARDY of *Central Provinces Manganese Ore Company Limited* (October 23) showed that Government-controlled handicaps on Indian ore were having a depressing effect:

"The increased railway freights in India combined with the Export Duty and heavy sea freights have now made all but the highest grades of Indian ore uncompetitive in the world market. The position of the Indian manganese ore industry is well before the Government of India, but it is not possible to state when any decision will be made to ease the burdens under which the industry is suffering at the present time."

A new company, jointly owned by Imperial Chemical Industries Limited and *Charter Consolidated Limited* (July 9), formed to run what MR. H. F. OPPENHEIMER claimed would be the largest underground mining operation ever undertaken in the United Kingdom outside the coal industry, is the subject of the next quotation, which comes from his statement for Charter:

"A new company called Cleveland Potash, in which Imperial Chemical Industries and Charter have equal shares, has been formed to establish a large potash mine near Staithes, in north Yorkshire. Extensive prospecting has proved sufficient reserves of high grade ore, most of which lies at a depth of between 3,500 and 4,000 feet, to support an annual output of one to one and a half million tons of potash products at a capital cost of approximately £25m. Provided planning permission is granted and the final feasibility study is satisfactory, work on the site should begin next year and production should start about four years later. This mine will be of considerable importance to the United Kingdom economy, as at present all potash products have to be imported. It is expected that at the time it comes to production Cleveland will have a substantial tonnage available for export and that in view of the grade it will be able to dispose of this tonnage at a satisfactory price."

MISCELLANEOUS METALS

Group income in 1967 of *Imperial Metal Industries Limited*, stated MR P. T. MENZIES in his report (*The Times*, March 1), was influenced by three special factors: (1) wide fluctuations in the price of copper led to exceptional losses on metal stocks; (2) a nominal dividend only was received from Yorkshire Imperial Metals Limited; (3) the appropriate part of the income of Wolverhampton Metal (Holdings) Limited for the nine months to December 31, 1967, was included. Excluding these factors, he revealed, group income before taxation was slightly higher than in 1966, thanks to improvements in efficiency and productivity and to increased dividends from associated companies in Europe. He added that

trading conditions in the United Kingdom, which continued to be difficult in the first half of 1967, showed some evidence of recovery in the third quarter and a distinct improvement in the fourth.

Group profit before tax of *Foseco Limited* was 14 per cent above the previous record in 1966 and sales were 19 per cent higher, according to MR. ERIC WEISS'S statement (*The Times*, May 30). He added that so far 1968 trading conditions had been favourable and the long-term outlook continued to be encouraging. Incidentally, he stated that although recent activities had intentionally broadened the company's base of operations, efforts to improve and broaden the range of products and service to the steelworks and foundry industries would continue.

Announcing an increase in profits and the distribution of higher dividends, MR. GUY DE ROTHSCHILD emphasized that the dividend distributed by *Société Minière et Métallurgique de Peñarroya* (Paris, June 26) for the financial year under review was supplied solely by the dividends received from the company's foreign subsidiaries, while the profits from the French exploitations were employed in the re-equipment of domestic installations.

The final quotation for this chapter comes from MR. L. WALLEF'S statement for *Union Minière S. A.* (Brussels, May 24):

"Work on reconverting the company, after the nationalization of its assets in the Congo, was begun in 1967. The necessary organization was set up and the corporate structure was adapted to the new situation at the Extraordinary General Meeting on February 15, 1968.

"Investigating missions were sent to different countries. Today Union Minière is established in two great countries, Canada and Australia, after following the same procedure: the setting up of an Investment company which will take shareholdings in the industry of the country and of an exploration and mining company the capital of which is wholly owned by the Investment company."

MOTOR INDUSTRY

FOR the vehicle industry the year to July 31, 1968, covered by the accounts of *Joseph Lucas (Industries) Limited* (December 16) opened in an atmosphere of cautious optimism, encouraged by the progressive easing of the credit restrictions imposed in July, 1966, but clouded by the underlying weakness of the economy. In these words SIR BERTRAM WARING began his comments on the experience of the motor trades, and he continued:

"The devaluation of sterling . . . in November, 1967, at once became the dominating event in the affairs of the Motor Industry, which has always been resilient and capable of rapid reaction to new conditions. This has never been better demonstrated than last year. Intensive efforts were made by the Manufacturers to exploit in overseas markets the competitive price advantage afforded by devaluation, and striking successes were achieved. Production for export fell to a low level towards the end of 1967, being seriously affected by the prolonged docks' strike, but from November, 1967 onwards, it steadily improved to finish no less than 12 per cent ahead of the previous year at 676,000—equivalent to 40 per cent of all cars produced.

"The experience in the home market, however, was almost the reverse of this. Home car business started the year at an encouraging level and developed, following the warnings of severe restrictions to come, into four months of boom sales. This in turn gave place to an abrupt collapse of the home market when the Budget, which took effect in April, 1968, imposed the greatest peacetime increase in taxation ever known in this country. In consequence the overall pattern for the greater part of the year was of the factories meeting a buoyant demand, first for the home market and later for exports, but never a firm and consistent total demand. Although car production for the year at nearly $1\frac{3}{4}$ million vehicles was some 12 per cent higher than the previous year, it fell far short of the Industry's capacity which is geared to a busy home market as well as rising exports and needs both to develop the full strength of its competitive abilities."

Overall, Sir Bertram stated, United Kingdom vehicle production increased over the previous year for the first time since 1963–64, the total being 5 per cent larger at $2\frac{1}{4}$m. units. With over 900,000 vehicles allocated for export, and with parts and acces-

sories, oversea earnings were equivalent to some £775m. for the year, and, he claimed, the motor industry thus retained its position as the country's leading exporter.

In his statement for *The Leyland Motor Corporation Limited* (February 20)—*i.e.*, before the merger with British Motor Holdings—LORD STOKES (he was then Sir Donald) stated that group net turnover was a new record at £305m., home sales being £161m. and overseas sales £144m., of which £94m. were direct exports from the United Kingdom. The year had been a particularly difficult one in the domestic market, which was sharply affected by the July, 1966, Government restrictive measures. In the circumstances he thought the results were very satisfactory. As regards technical progress, he declared:

"We are very conscious of the necessity for being technologically ahead and our research and development progamme for cars and commercial vehicles has been considerably expanded. We are certainly in advance in this country, and in the world, in the development of automotive diesel engines and automatic transmissions for heavy trucks and buses. Considerable progress has been made in the development of future generation of power units for trucks which may well be gas turbines."

LORD KINDERSLEY informed members of *Rolls-Royce Limited* in his annual statement (*The Times*, June 24) that the Rolls-Royce Silver Shadow and the T Series Bentley had continued in firm demand, and more than 50 per cent of output was being exported. They had successfully introduced in the United States new features required to meet the "very demanding" requirements of the Federal Safety standards.

Much attention was given by *Fodens Limited* (August 14) to customers' special requirements, asserted MR. ALBERT STUBBS, and after-sales service had been strengthened. Group turnover increased by 11½ per cent and pre-tax profit by 32½ per cent, and he added that the year ended with a large order book and an optimistic outlook.

Another company to announce records in both turnover and profits was *Atkinson Lorries (Holdings) Limited*, for which MR. A. W. ALLEN stated that the new production lines and the new service depot in Preston were completed during the year, and a great many problems relating to this expansion had been overcome. Extracts from his annual review were published in *The Times* of September 19. He also announced the company's intention to open up in Belgium in the belief that there were "reasonable opportunities for sales of our chassis in the Benelux market with possible extensions into the Common Market as a whole in years to come."

MR. E. P. FODEN expressed his confidence that in spite of the

355

difficulties in the United Kingdom economy and uncertainty in the future of private road transport *E.R.F. (Holdings) Limited* could expect a considerable rise in sales over the coming years. His annual survey (*The Times*, August 8) included the statement that the board expected the home market to remain fairly stable during the current year but anticipated that export sales would more than double.

In his review (*The Times*, January 16) for *Brook Motors Limited* MR. FRANK V. BROOK referred to Brook Victor Electric Vehicles Limited, which he stated had a full order book and should add a modest additional profit to the parent company this year; all designs were being modernized, and a three-wheel two-ton platform truck was to be launched.

The next quotation comes from MR. J. H. PITCHFORD's statement for *Ricardo & Co. Engineers (1927) Limited* (December 17):

"We have been given a Contract by General Motors (U.S.A.) to carry out a feasibility study of the application of a steam plant to road vehicle propulsion primarily with the objective of reduced emissions."

COMPONENTS AND ANCILLARY EQUIPMENT

Referring to the decline in profits of *Triplex Holdings Limited* (July 3), MR. T. E. PEPPERCORN said:

"I am glad to be able to say that the reasons for our lower profits are now largely behind us. I told you last year when Triplex Holdings bought British Indestructo Glass Limited that the initial expenses from the takeover would, for a period, outweigh the eventual benefits that would accrue to both Triplex and its customers. In the first half of the year it was our customers who enjoyed the benefit in the shape of substantial price reductions, while Triplex had to carry both the short term additional cost and increases in materials, services and wages of a more permanent nature. This was at a time when production in the motor industry was at a low level and, as you will know, loss of volume always hits us hard. The second half year saw a strong recovery. The volume that passed through Triplex safety glass factories increased by about one-third, and the expected benefits of concentration and rationalization of production began to materialize. During the final quarter group turnover at just under £5m. was the highest ever recorded. While this level is unlikely to be maintained throughout the current year, we may expect to enjoy for the full twelve months the additional business that previously went to Indestructo."

Profit of *The Dunlop Company Limited* (May 13) for the first half of 1967 was well down, but SIR REAY GEDDES said that trading

then improved, and the year ended strongly enough for the second half to make good the earlier shortfall. Thus the results for the whole year were much better than expected, but the directors were dissatisfied with the fall, slight as it was, to 11·1 per cent in the profit ratio to the funds employed. As regards the new year, he said:

"Our business, as you are aware, is normally seasonal, with the second half-year better than the first. For a number of special reasons—among them United Kingdom consumer demand before the Budget and the tyre safety regulations from 1st April—the early months of 1968 have been better than usual. How much they have borrowed from demand for the rest of the year is very hard to guess. It is important that the Budget and other measures to limit consumer demand, should succeed; so I think we must be prudent and assume they will do so and that trading in the latter part of the year will be affected by them. Furthermore, we shall also be carrying additional costs arising from devaluation. Overseas there are some encouraging signs, but these must be read with caution when the United States is being forced to limit its overseas spending on current and capital account.

"However, in spite of these uncertainties it will be disappointing if all our efforts directed to greater efficiency in the market places, as much as in the factories, do not result in an improvement in profit for the year as a whole."

Reporting a sizeable reduction in group profit of *Avon Rubber Company Limited* (January 22), MR. C. M. FLOYD declared that while the motor industry was restricted as in the past year it had been difficult for the company to reap the full benefit of its investments in the most modern heavy plant and machinery and supporting services, since for much of the financial year some of the factories had had to operate below capacity. Now, however, he could report, with a "very full" order book production was at a record level in nearly all the group's factories.

Tyre safety legislation and its effect on demand for tyres and tyre fabric was alluded to by some chairmen, including MR. I. M. L. D. FORDE, who stated in his review for *John Bright and Brothers Limited* (July 3):

"Demand for cord fabric was higher than ever before and at times it was indeed difficult to keep pace with the needs of our customers. The regulations introduced at the beginning of April covering the safety of tyres should have a beneficial effect on our sales of tyre cord fabric in that motorists will now have to fit replacements at an earlier stage than previously."

For *Albany Tyre Service Limited* (July 2) MR. W. A. STENSON declared that the new tyre safety regulations which came into

357

effect from April 1 had been reflected in an unprecedented rise in sales. Moreover, he added that it was estimated that these regulations should increase, on a continuing basis, the replacement tyre demand by approximately one-sixth—"and this growth is to be superimposed on a market which has been steadily growing at some 15–20 per cent each year."

From SIR FRANK KEARTON'S speech for *Courtaulds Limited* (July 10) is taken this excerpt about the company's interests in yarn for tyre reinforcement:

"Viscose industrial yarn, of which we make approximately 1,450,000 lbs/week, is used largely for tyre reinforcement, although numerous smaller outlets are being actively developed. It is a product which we have much improved in recent years. The newer radial passenger tyres are providing a growing market for our yarn. But the intense competition from nylon and steel now being added to by the emergence of polyester and glass for tyre reinforcement, has kept prices low and profits low. In fact, profits on industrial yarn are about one quarter of what they were only a few years ago. A small price rise seems inevitable here if profits are not to vanish altogether."

SIR WILLIAM FENTON referred to a licence agreement between *BBA Group Limited* (June 27) with the Borg-Warner Corporation of the United States under which Borg-Warner was to establish a plant for the manufacture of disc brake pads in the U.S. As the installation of this plant would take some time, licence fees from this source were not expected to be significant for the next year or two. He also stated that BBA was extending its licensing activities and that the negotiations were in progress with potential licensees in several countries.

More than 70,000 of the current design of the revolutionary A.P. automatic transmission had now been delivered, MR. W. EMMOTT informed members of *Automotive Products Associated Limited* (June 20). A new design with improved features and a much wider range of application was in the final stages of development and test, he added.

Stating that total group sales of *Joseph Lucas (Industries) Limited* (December 16) reached a new record of £213m., SIR BERTRAM WARING quantified the contribution made to this total by the newly acquired Simms Motor group, as shown below:

"During the year the company acquired the whole of the Issued Share Capital of Simms Motor & Electronics Corporation Limited, whose accounts are now incorporated in the Consolidated Balance Sheet and Profit and Loss Account. This is the main reason for the substantial increases shown in the Group assets and liabilities. Simms' trading for the period of approximately four months to July 31, 1968, contributed approximately £7m. to the Group sales and £½m. to Group profits before tax."

The following analysis of the sales by type of industry served of *Clayton Dewandre Holdings Limited* (May 9) was given by Mr. S. J. Barnes: Commercial vehicles, 83 per cent; passenger cars, 3½ per cent; tractor and agricultural vehicles, 3½ per cent; non-automotive, 10 per cent. Sales for the year advanced by 9 per cent and profits by 26 per cent, or very close to the company's record year of 1965.

Motor car components still provide the major share of the profits of *Wilmot-Breeden* (*Holdings*) *Limited* (May 29), though the company in its search for diversification now has important interests outside the motor industry. This was evident from figures given in the annual report, which stated that the problem of achieving satisfactory margins on car components was being successfully attacked. Growth in sales and earnings from this source was to be expected.

The next quotation comes from the statement (*The Times*, January 4) by Mr. S. B. Hainsworth for *J. H. Fenner & Co.* (*Holdings*) *Limited*:

"All large automobile manufacturers in this country now use the Pioneer design and development team on pre-production models. The new Vauxhall Victor has Pioneer seals on the rear crankshaft and the front wheels; the oilpan packings and the balanced water pump seal are also supplied by us."

Dealing with the affairs of Intalok Limited, one of the subsidiaries of *Slumberland Group Limited* (May 29), Mr. John C. Seccombe stated that it achieved record turnover and improved profitability. "The introduction of 'Posture Springing' to the motor trade has been highly successful, and this revolutionary and unique springing is now being incorporated in the products of a number of leading car manufacturers."

The automotive interests of *Adwest Group Limited* called forth these remarks in Mr. F. V. Waller's statement (*The Times*, November 2):

"Adwest Engineering had a successful year and benefited from the prosperity of the motor industry. The order book for this company is very healthy, and we anticipate another good year.

"Western Thomson Controls, which makes thermostats for the motor industry, also benefited from the buoyancy of this industry. We have also established a company in India in partnership with India Radiators, to manufacture our thermostats in that country."

Sales of safety belts and crash helmets by *Kangol Limited* (July 26) had more than doubled and profits from that source more than trebled, Mr. J. Spreiregen showed. He also stated that the new extension for the manufacture of safety belts had been completed,

which would enable the company to meet the increased demand for these belts.

Among the important recent developments for *Solar Industries Limited* (October 10) MR. R. K. CALDER mentioned the following:

"Agreement in principle has been reached with Kangol Limited for the establishment of joint manufacturing and marketing companies within the Common Market to handle production and selling of the well-known Kangol automotive seat belts and safety products under the aegis of Draftex in Europe. Orders from two German car manufacturers have already been obtained for fitting Kangol equipment to cars designed for export markets."

The *Excelsior Motor Company Limited* had been helped by legislation concerning safety belts for new cars, stated MR. O. A. PROCTOR in his annual review (*The Times*, January 11), and the proposed regulations covering cars registered in 1965 and 1966 would further increase demand. Factory extensions, then nearing completion, would enable the company to more than double the past year's output to meet the expected demand.

For *Cornercroft Limited* (December 20) MR. J. R. MEAD made this reference to the group's motor accessories activities:

"Sales of motor accessories, mainly comprising number plates of the conventional and reflective types, increased substantially and, despite some narrowing in the margin of profitability, the Motor Accessories Department increased its contribution to Group profits."

In his statement (*The Times*, January 15) for *Serck Limited* MR. S. F. BURMAN gave the break-down of Group turnover as 31 per cent to the petroleum, chemical and gas industries; 15 per cent to the manufacturers of Diesel engines including those used in the traction, power generation and marine industries; 18 per cent to other heavy industries, including steel, electrical and building; 8 per cent to the vehicle manufacturing industries; 17 per cent to the vehicle service and repair trades; 11 per cent to various other industries.

Lake and Elliot Jacks and Equipment Limited, one of the subsidiaries in the motor accessories division of *Lake & Elliot Limited* (November 19), was the subject of this comment by MR. C. J. LAKE:

"This company has again increased its output with a slightly improved margin of profit. The order position has remained very good and improvement in production and planning have enabled the company to keep pace with the increased demands from its original equipment customers, although there were again insufficient supplies of hydraulic jacks for other customers.

The rate of production of hydraulic and screw jacks and also of garage jacks is again being increased and further markets are being explored. The prospects of this company for the current year are promising."

MR. T. HARCOURT POWELL of *Revertex Holdings Limited* (March 28), referring to Aquaplas noise reduction materials, stated that the board were making great efforts to expand outside the motor industry, with which the main business then lay. So far in the new year profitability had increased because of the recovery of the motor industry together with the concentration of all production under one roof at Harlow.

In almost every area of activity of *Kirkstall Forge Engineering Limited* (November 14), MR. R. F. BUTLER declared, substantial improvement had been achieved, with total pre-tax profits up by 73 per cent. The group order book position was buoyant, he added, and the future looked most encouraging with demand increasing right across the company's product range. The axle division had shown an improvement in all sectors of its business.

After reporting an impressive recovery for the second half of the year in the profits of *Holt Products Limited* in his annual review (*The Times*, May 10) MR. MICHAEL R. HOLT went on to mention some of the activities which had contributed to the improvement, from which we extract the following:

"We have a substantial share of the aerosol spray and touch-in paint market. Our Cataloy range of car body repair compounds has shown excellent progress and sales of Anti-freeze were again a record for the Company. There has been a marked improvement in the turnover of Romac tyre repair materials. Sales of seat belts have been outstanding and represent a three-fold increase."

The next quotation, from MR. S. W. LIVESEY's statement for *Plantation Holdings Limited* (September 12), deals with the activities of Hills (Patents) Limited, a subsidiary:

"The vehicle number plates division had a reasonably successful year but the signs division operated at a loss. The company's management and methods of operation have been completely reorganized and adequate systems of credit and stock control introduced. The number plates division has gained from the pre-Budget rush to purchase motor cars and the new reflective number plates have proved popular. The road traffic signs division is suffering from the reduction in Government spending but an all-out assault is being made on the acquisition of orders for commercial signs and exports. Shareholders will be relieved to know that the first six months' trading have been profitable, the results for the year should be satisfactory and we have confidence in the future."

That *Pillar Holdings Limited* (March 29) had made considerable headway in designing and fabricating aluminium components for the automobile industry was among the points made by MR. J. A. PATERSON, who added that further expansion was planned, and the board expected a dramatic increase over the next few years.

Although not exactly a motor component, the safety barrier which is mentioned in the next quotation may possibly qualify for inclusion here as ancillary equipment. The remarks were among those made by MR. HARRY SMITH in his statement for *British Ropes Limited* (May 30):

"During 1967, a 32-mile length of wire rope safety barrier, using our latest design, was erected in Switzerland on the N.1 Berne–Oensingen motorway. The information we have is that in the first few months 57 accidents involving 68 vehicles occurred, many at high speed, and in one case a driver went into the barrier at approximately 80 miles an hour after falling asleep. In these accidents not one serious injury was suffered as a result of the vehicle striking the barrier. Trial sections of rope barrier have been erected in Denmark, and we are hopeful that it will be widely adopted in Europe in due course."

MOTOR CYCLES AND CYCLES

British motor cycle manufacturers continued to make a notable contribution to the export drive, declared SIR BERTRAM WARING of *Joseph Lucas (Industries) Limited* (December 16). Their heavy machines, he continued, were the best in the world, and although total production was slightly lower than in the previous year some two-thirds of the output was again sold overseas, mostly in the United States.

During the year the BSA and Triumph motor cycle companies directly exported more than half of their production, MR. ERIC TURNER revealed in his statement, (*The Times*, November 12) for the *Birmingham Small Arms Company Limited*. He added that the motor cycle division currently produced the majority of the company's profits, and that it was now much more favourably placed than in the past year.

LORD PLOWDEN had this to say of the cycle interests of *Tube Investments Limited* in the course of his statement (*The Times*, November 22):

"Profits were almost double those of the previous year. Cutting back cycle capacity has enabled the Division to make good profits on a lower level of demand. Devaluation was helpful to exports. The transfer of Cox of Watford's car seat business to Nottingham had taken the Cycle Division into a substantial new business with excellent growth prospects."

For *Halfords Limited* (May 3) MR. F. D. RUSHBROOKE stated that it had been decided to transfer the works of the subsidiary Birmingham Bicycle Company from Birmingham to Pontypool. He explained:

"The present factory is too small and is incapable of further economic expansion, and advantage is being taken of the grants available upon transfer to a development area. The availability of labour in the Pontypool area will enable the subsidiary company to build up a stable staff which has proved impossible in Birmingham. It is expected that the new factory will be completed by March 1969 and the improved physical conditions should enable the manufacturing costs to be reduced when the local labour has been trained in the necessary skills."

DISTRIBUTORS AND DEALERS

After reporting that turnover of *Henlys Limited* (February 29) for the year was almost in line with that of the previous year and that trading profit of the group (before taxation and exceptional credits) was slightly higher, MR. A. G. WHITE said that business to date in the new year had kept up very well indeed, and the buoyant conditions then being enjoyed would be reflected in the interim statement to be published about the end of May, 1968. "However," he added, "by that time we shall know details of the forthcoming Budget and be aware of any impact this may have upon us." He also expressed alarm about the new Transport Bill, which threatened to interfere seriously with commercial vehicle sales in the home market.

Although MR. S. M. CAFFYN was able to report record turnover and trading profit for *Caffyns Limited* (July 18), he asserted that the year had been particularly difficult for distributors who, like the company, had concentrated almost exclusively on the sale and service of B.M.C. cars and commercial vehicles, for it was well known that the share of the market held by B.M.C. had diminished. The future, he declared, was not entirely under the board's control: it depended in part on the state of the economy and on whether British Leyland could recapture the share of the home market lost by B.M.C. in the past year.

Another chairman who announced record turnover and profits was MR. ALAN JESSUP, who in his statement (*The Times*, December 23) for *Jessups (Holdings) Limited* included this paragraph:

"Success of the Vauxhall Motors range of products has brought direct advantage to the group. The acceptability of the Viva in all its model variants has enabled us to gain substantial inroads in the 'small car' market, particularly in fleet sales which we have developed to the fullest advantage. Both our parts business and Bedford sales have shown a significant improvement over last year."

363

Sales and profits of *Bristol Street Group Limited*, according to the annual report (*The Times*, May 23), also reached an all-time peak, and the demand for Ford and Vauxhall vehicles was increasing, with Ford now, it was claimed, the United Kingdom market leader.

Profits of *Lex Garages Limited*, too, were substantially in excess of any previous year in the company's history. In their statement (*The Times*, May 22) the joint chairmen, MR. NORMAN CHINN and MR. ROSSER CHINN, revealed that a total of 24,500 vehicles had been sold, 19,500 new—including more than 8,000 B.M.C., 5,400 Volvo and over 1,400 Renault—and 5,000 retail used cars. They claimed, also, that the company was now the second largest distributor of Rolls-Royce and Bentley cars in the United Kingdom.

Among the points made by the chairman of *Braid Group Limited* (March 17) was the following:

> "The subsidiary, Braids (Contract Hire) Ltd. had expanded its business in Leasing and Contract Hire, and it is anticipated that this expansion will continue in 1968."

Commenting on pre-Budget buying of cars, MR. R. P. HODGKINSON of *Hollingdrake Automobile Company Limited* (March 15) said:

> "From the beginning of our new financial year to date, sales of new cars in particular have been very good. There is little doubt there has been a great deal of pre-Budget buying, and it is reasonable to expect that the present very high rate of sales will decline after the Budget. During the past few weeks, however, we have taken a substantial number of orders for delivery if possible before the Budget, but not subject to cancellation automatically after the Budget. Whatever further restrictions are imposed, we do at least carry forward a reasonable order book."

The further expansion of *Oliver Rix Limited* into motor distribution by the acquisition of Amalgamated Garage Holdings Limited and W. Watson & Co. (Liverpool) Limited had placed the group in a strong position for the future, MR. J. F. NASH declared in his statement (*The Times*, May 21).

After reporting a generally satisfactory year for *Attwood Garages Limited* (July 5), though out of an increase of £18,957 in profit taxation had absorbed £15,790, MR. H. R. ATTWOOD made these remarks on the new year:

> "Coming to the current year, vehicle sales over the first four months are in excess of those for the corresponding period last year. Although some reduction in trading was anticipated after the Budget, this has not yet materialized, and to date turnover has continued at a satisfactory level. However, the effect of the

latest squeeze announced on May 24th will have to be taken into account."

In his review (*The Times*, March 29) for *Robert B. Massey and Co. Limited* MR. ROBERT B. MASSEY stated that successful negotiations with a major British manufacturer would enable the motor division to increase substantially its new and used-car turnover.

For *C. G. Skipper (Holdings) Limited* (March 6) MR. R. G. COOKE gave the following break-down of the pre-tax profit: 65 per cent from Ford main dealerships; 22 per cent from hire purchase and contract hire, and 13 per cent from the used vehicle outlet.

The next quotation comes from MR. F. C. DOBSON's statement for *Renwick Wilton & Dobson (Holdings) Limited* (September 30) and refers to the company's motor division:

"There has been a substantial increase in profits mainly attributable to a considerable improvement in the service facilities at our branches in various towns covering a wide area of the South West. We now hold franchises for Volkswagen, Vauxhall, Standard-Triumph and Austin. Satisfactory sales have been maintained from our Sidmouth factory which manufactures the Devon range of motorized caravan conversions on Volkswagen chassis."

As regards the B.M.H./Leyland merger, *H. A. Saunders Limited* as one of the larger distributors must find the forecast rationalization of the model range and streamlining of the distribution network to its advantage. This was one of the points made by MR. GORDON W. SAUNDERS in his statement (*The Times*, October 29).

Commenting on the possible effects of the increased purchase tax on the sale of new cars, MR. JACK B. PARKER told members of *P. J. Evans (Holdings) Limited* (March 22):

"Whilst it is obviously unwelcome in my view the raising of the purchase tax level to $33\frac{1}{3}\%$ will not have such a disastrous effect on the sale of new cars as may be imagined. It must be remembered that less than six years ago the rate was 45%. We do not expect new cars to continue to be sold at the pre-Budget level, when availability was the only limiting factor to the volume of sales, but I do not anticipate any great recession in demand for the very attractive range of cars that we handle."

The Ford Motor Company's recent introduction of the Escort, MR. R. E. HARVEY of *H. Young (Motors) Limited* (March 15) considered, had further improved its already popular range of vehicles and should command a greater market interest.

The improved results of *Mann & Overton Limited* (March 28) were attributed by MR. R. C. H. OVERTON to increased sales of the Austin taxicab, either for cash or financed by the hire purchase department.

OVERSEAS MANUFACTURERS

Looking back, Dr. Kurt Lotz told shareholders in *Volkswagenwerk AG.*—his speech was published in *The Times* of August 21— there were two clearly defined periods in the year, each of which made diametrically opposed demands on the company's short-term business policy. He continued:

"In the first of these periods—up to the works holidays— we had to throttle back production and work 33 days short time in all factories, so that we produced 312,000 cars between January and August 1967, that is to say 31·5 per cent less than in the same period in 1966.

"The second period was ushered in by the International Motor Show in Frankfurt. The technical developments we showed there, developments such as the new Commercial, the automatic transmission, the electronically controlled fuel injection engine and so on, were given such an outstanding reception by trade and public alike that, in autumn, demand came to life again almost with a bang. We could only keep up with this demand by working extra shifts and taking on new personnel.

"The result was that between September and December 1967 our factories produced just as many vehicles as in the same months of 1966. The Volkswagenwerk made a good recovery from the setbacks it had to face in the first half of 1967."

According to Dr. Joachim Zahn, spokesman of the board of directors, the policy of *Daimler-Benz AG.* is mainly directed at achieving the optimum increase in production in order to meet market requirements without undue delay and to reduce delivery times to their normal level. His speech, which was published in *The Times* of September 25, continued:

"We feel that the concept on which our production and investment planning has been based has proved its worth particularly during the period of recession. We shall adhere to this concept during the next few years and we envisage an increase in the average monthly rate of production to some 20,000 passenger cars during 1968/69. Moreover, the foundations for a further increase beyond this figure in subsequent years are being laid even now.

"With an output of some 103,000 passenger cars during the first half of 1968 Daimler-Benz AG, has shown that the delays due to model changes have been overcome."

In spite of the general economic downturn, 1967 was a successful year for *Bayerische Motoren Werke AG.* (Munich, August 14), and its production and sales continued to increase as in previous years. The annual report of the directors stated:

"The output of passenger cars including CKD vehicles was thus raised by 18·3 per cent. The production of two-cylinder motor cycles was increased from 6,617 to 7,896 units whilst the manufacture of single-cylinder machines was discontinued.

"Sales of passenger cars rose by 22 per cent to 88,501 vehicles in 1967. They included 49,803 vehicles (1966: 45,435) sold in the home market and 38,698 vehicles (1966: 27,120) sold abroad. Home market registrations increased by 5,308 or 12 per cent in 1967 whilst registrations as a whole in the Federal Republic of Germany were 10 per cent below the previous year's level.

"The BMW share of the market rose from 3·2 per cent to 4 per cent. It is felt that this trend confirms the correctness of the company's marketing policy and acknowledges the quality and efficiency of BMW vehicles."

The annual report of *Fiat S. p. A.* (Turin, April 24) stated that on the whole 1967 had been another year of positive development. Total value of sales increased by 12 per cent; 1,340,884 Fiat, OM and Auto Bianchi motor vehicles were produced, compared with 1,224,353 in 1966. Vehicle exports in 1967 numbered 398,259. In addition, about 240,000 cars were manufactured in several foreign countries under Fiat licence, compared with a 1966 figure of 200,000. Tractor production and sales were 45,339 units in 1967 (1966: 47,154) and showed an increase of 10 per cent in weight and value. Exports numbered 21,300 tractors.

NORTH SEA GAS

THE *British Petroleum Company Limited* began to deliver natural gas from under the North Sea to the Gas Council well in advance of the contract date of July 20, 1967, reported SIR MAURICE BRIDGEMAN in his annual statement (*The Times*, April 17). Since then, he added, the company had fully met its contract figure, which represented an average rate of 100m. cubic feet a day; indeed, during the winter of 1967–68, he disclosed, deliveries were maintained at 150m. cubic feet a day—a figure in excess of the maximum contract quantity. He continued:

"Our West Sole field is not as large as some of the subsequent discoveries, but it is fully adequate to sustain our earlier estimates of its potential. We have incurred heavy costs in burying the pipeline to prevent its being a hazard to shipping, and in the abnormally severe weather of last winter 'Sea Quest' broke adrift. Although, fortunately, there was no injury to the crew, the 'Sea Quest' had to be taken out of service for repairs. Such hazards, which cannot be calculated in advance, emphasize the need for an adequate return if any exploration venture is to be attractive, particularly in an area such as the North Sea in which there is little previous experience on which to draw, and where the climatic conditions are exceptionally severe.

"Our existing contract with the Gas Council extends for three years from July last, and we have not therefore been involved in the current price negotiations, though we have naturally followed these with great interest. With the high cost of borrowing and the need to conserve our financial resources it will be increasingly necessary to restrict ourselves to those projects which promise a return commensurate with the risks involved. Several of our best prospects have already been drilled, and the economics of continuing the search for structures of secondary importance will require careful evaluation."

Referring to the joint exploration venture with Esso in the United Kingdom part of the North Sea which had discovered substantial gas reserves in the Leman and Indefatigable fields, MR. D. H. BARRAN told members of The *"Shell" Transport and Trading Company Limited* (May 2) that in the expectation that a reasonable price would result from the negotiations with the Gas Council the group laid a 30-inch submarine pipeline connecting the Leman field with the shore in the summer of 1967 and went ahead with development drilling. On this question of price, he made the following comment:

"As a consequence, gas deliveries could begin in June, and it is therefore hoped that a price settlement will be reached shortly. Since no international group such as ours can afford to distribute its investment resources without regard to the long-term worth of each opportunity, it is to be hoped that any definite price agreement for North Sea gas will contain sufficient incentives to reinvigorate exploration."

For *Imperial Continental Gas Association* (July 1) LORD TANGLEY mentioned the hitherto unproductive investment in Century Power and Light Limited in connection with natural gas in the North Sea. He pointed out that an investment averaging £82,000 in 1965–66, £201,000 in 1966–67 and £402,000 in 1967–68 and bringing in no revenue represented for the moment a certain diminution of the association's earning capacity. Improvement must wait until gas was brought ashore and revenue began coming in. Meanwhile, he went on to say:

"You will have seen in the Press and in your directors' report that the Phillips consortium, of which we form part, has signed a contract with the Gas Council for the sale of the natural gas from the Hewett field. The negotiations leading up to this contract—and I speak with some feeling since I was one of the negotiators—were long and extremely intricate. The final result, I venture to think, was in the circumstances satisfactory to all parties so far as it relates to the Hewett field. Any finds in other fields will have to be separately negotiated. It is much to be hoped that the attitude of the Gas Council and the British Government will not, as I fear it may, slow down the exploitation of that great British asset, North Sea gas.

"It would be premature today to go into any detail concerning the effect of Century on our profits. We do not expect any of the gas to come ashore until well into 1969 and there is, of course, exploration and development expenditure to be written off. Nevertheless, as quantities build up, I am confident that this North Sea adventure will furnish us with a very welcome and substantial addition to our earnings."

One of the members of the Consortium that proved the Hewett field was the *Petrofina Group*, whose annual report (*The Times*, May 13) gave expression also to the hope that sales of gas from that concession would begin in 1969. It also stated that an initial drilling was carried out in the Norwegian zone of the North Sea and geophysical studies were continued in the Dutch zone.

Another company with a small stake in the Hewett field is *Tarmac Limited*, and SIR CHARLES BURMAN in his annual statement (*The Times*, May 24) mentioned the actual price agreed with the Gas Council for the supply of gas from the field—2·87d. per therm. He also gave these details:

"It is hoped that deliveries of gas will begin in the autumn of 1969 and, over a five-year period, build up to about 350m. cubic feet a day, more than 30% of the United Kingdom's present daily gas consumption. The contract lasts for 25 years and at the full estimated output will make an important contribution to earnings. Some contribution may be received in 1969."

As a result of an arrangement between British Petroleum and the group to which Selection Trust belonged, covering Blocks 42/12 and 13, MR. A. CHESTER BEATTY revealed, *Selection Trust Limited* (July 11) and Consolidated African Selection Trust between them would have an $8\frac{1}{3}$ per cent interest in both of these blocks. He added:

"A joint well by the two groups was started on 29th June in Block 42/13, a little more than 60 miles due east of the Tees Estuary, with British Petroleum as the operator, using its rig the 'Sea Quest'. Drilling is proceeding according to plan but it will be some time before any results can be expected."

However, later in the year, at the annual meeting of *Consolidated African Selection Trust Limited* (December 10), Mr. Beatty announced that the hole in Block 42/13, in which C.A.S.T. also had an interest, had unfortunately proved to be dry.

Another important development in the North Sea programme, it was stated in the annual report (*The Times*, June 20) of *Selection Trust*, was the recent award by the Netherlands Government to the Noordwinning Group, in which S.T. and C.A.S.T. together had an $18\frac{1}{2}$ per cent interest, of two licences covering seven blocks totalling just under 2,000 square kilometres for oil and gas exploration over the Dutch Continental shelf. The report also reported that in the current year it was expected that the consortia in which Selection Trust participated would materially increase their activities in the United Kingdom and Dutch sectors of the North Sea.

The coming of North Sea gas naturally has implications for British industry. For example, MR. J. M. CLAY informed members of *Thos. Firth & John Brown Limited* (March 7) that the coming year would see the start of the conversion to North Sea gas of all the existing town gas furnaces of the subsidiary Firth Brown Limited. This would make the company one of the largest consumers of natural gas in the country, he claimed.

The next quotation comes from the statement (*The Times*, October 3) of MR. W. J. A. PECK for *Calor Gas Holding Company Limited*:

"The Liquefied Petroleum Gas market in the United Kingdom, due to the advent of North Sea Gas, has entered a new era. Large tonnages of L.P. Gas previously taken by the Area Gas Boards will come on to the market at competitive prices. This

370

presents both a challenge and an opportunity which, with the support of our suppliers, we are making plans to meet."

The receipt by *Moler Products Limited* (October 4) of orders from the furnace and chemical engineering industries was very depressed in the first half of the year but recovered well subsequently even though the advent of natural gas had virtually eliminated the gas reformer plant industry which had provided a most useful outlet for the company's products. This was among the points made by MR. R. W. YOUNG in his annual statement.

Constructors John Brown Limited, a subsidiary of *John Brown and Company Limited* (September 6), had carried out a large amount of work on pipelines for the Gas Council and various area gas boards, stated LORD ABERCONWAY. He added that the contract for the 110-mile No. 3 Feeder Main to carry North Sea gas from Norfolk to Stevenage was believed to have been the largest pipeline contract ever awarded in the United Kingdom.

MR. K. M. STOBART, in his review for shareholders of *Charrington, Gardner, Locket & Co. Limited* (July 18), mentioned that delay in the settlement of the price negotiations for North Sea gas virtually held up the industrial conversion for which Anglo-Canadian (Industrial Pipework) Co. Limited had hoped to compete.

Turnover for the first two months of the current year for *William Press & Son Limited*, it appeared from MR. W. H. G. ROACH's statement (*The Times*, October 31), was affected by delays in the letting of major contracts, but was now running at the same rate as at the same time in the past year; and with the "welcome signs" of revival in the steel, process plant and other industries, he viewed the year as a whole with confidence. In addition, he declared, the company's gas conversion division continued to make excellent progress, and "should continue to benefit from further work as conversion of domestic and industrial appliances to natural gas gathers pace."

PETROLEUM

RECALLING that most of his annual statements for *The British Petroleum Company Limited* in recent years had indicated that for various reasons the preceding year had been one of unusual difficulty, SIR MAURICE BRIDGEMAN in his survey (*The Times*, April 17) for 1967 asserted that to describe that year in similar terms would be the extreme of understatement. He found little consolation in the fact that the difficulties arose from political disturbances over which BP and the oil industry in general had no control and for which they had no responsibility. These difficulties included closure for a time of the pipeline from Iraq to the Mediterranean by the Syrian Government which cost the group about £3m. in additional freight charges; the hostilities between Israel and the Arab countries, which necessitated very rapid alterations to shipping and refinery programmes and the switching of oil from other sources such as Iran and Venezuela to countries which had formerly been markets for Arab oil; and, far more serious, the closure of the Suez Canal.

"This," he declared, "meant that tankers carrying oil from the Gulf to Europe and the east coast of the U.S.A. and Canada had to go round the Cape of Good Hope. Not only did this require 40 per cent more shipping capacity but it caused considerable gaps in delivery as the process of rerouting was established. The combination of these factors triggered off a rise in voyage charter freight rates amounting to something like 400 per cent.

"To limit our freight requirements we took immediate steps to shed some of our less profitable business, particularly bulk sales of fuel oils and heating oils in north Europe. We also reduced our financial commitments by curtailing or postponing certain of the less vital items in our capital investment programme. Nevertheless, in order to fulfil our obligations to customers and avoid the necessity for rationing in parts of western Europe, we at once went into the charter market in a substantial way in the expectation—or at least the hope—that the additional freight costs would be recoverable from the consumer through surcharges on the selling price or through other means. Our problem would have been much easier had it not been for the outbreak of civil war in Nigeria in early July which brought about the cessation of production from this source. Nigeria had assumed added importance because of its geographical advantage by comparison with oil which had to be moved round the Cape. Certain quantities of oil were available

from the U.S.A., but only at a price higher than the average cost of bringing Middle Eastern oil round the Cape.

"The combination of these factors cost us £85m. principally in extra freight, and up to the end of 1967 only some £50m. was recovered through the operation of surcharges or other price increases. Although some governments adopted the system of a freight equalization fund, whereby the surcharge could be redistributed among the companies in proportion to the additional expenses they had been forced to incur, others, including the British government, did not see their way to adopting this principle. The result is that our shortfall in recoveries must necessarily fall on our stockholders, who are thus in effect bearing part of the cost of rescuing the consumer from the inconveniences of rationing."

Another chairman who referred to the closing of the Suez Canal and the cessation of the supplies of crude oil from Nigeria was MR. D. H. BARRAN of The "Shell" Transport and Trading Company Limited (May 2), who said that these problems involved most of the group companies in substantial additional costs, to meet which there were a number of increases in selling prices. No confident prediction could be made at that time of the possible date of reopening of the Canal or of the resumption of exports by Shell–BP Nigeria.

"In the meantime," he commented, "group companies will have to continue to purchase crude oil and oil products from alternative sources, and will have to charter additional tanker tonnage to cope with the shipment of oil from the Middle East to Europe by the Cape route. It is too early to assess what these exceptional measures will cost, although fortunately the additional charters which have been arranged so far this year are at rates below those ruling last July and August. They are, however, still considerably above the rates at which tanker tonnage could be obtained before the outbreak of hostilities last June.

"In view of the uncertainty about additional costs, it is impossible to make any reliable estimate of the adequacy of price levels to cover the exceptional costs which group companies are incurring, and will continue to incur. Last autumn and during the first quarter of this year there have been price reductions in Germany and Holland, and there has been an effective reduction in the United Kingdom, since half of the price increases obtained in mid-1967 are now, broadly speaking, to be regarded as offsetting increased costs of supplies to the United Kingdom resulting from devaluation.

"It is, of course, possible that the abnormal supply situation may continue beyond this year. In 1969, however, the position of group companies will benefit from the increasing number of

373

200,000-ton tankers coming into service, and there will be some resumption of exports of oil from Nigeria."

A record gross revenue of over £51m. was reported by LORD TANGLEY for the *Ultramar Company Limited* (May 29) in 1967, together with a cash flow from operations of £2,450,000 and a net profit of £1,240,000 after charging income taxes of nearly £800,000; the net profit was 82 per cent more than for 1966. He went on to make the following statement:

"I might remind you that up to 1959 the business of the group was concentrated entirely in the production side of the oil industry. In that year we made a major decision to establish facilities for refining and to create outlets for marketing oil products. Our first step was to acquire the Panama Company in 1960 which at that time had a project to build a refinery in Panama and owned Golden Eagle of California with its small refinery in Los Angeles and a marketing organization selling about 15,000 barrels per day of oil products along the west coast of the U.S.A. Shortly after we formed Golden Eagle of Canada and started to build the Newfoundland refinery and to create from scratch a marketing organization in Eastern Canada. For the first three years we had to take losses and incur considerable start-up expenses. The story since then has been one of growing profitability year by year and of expansion and diversification . . .

"In 1968 we are seeing a further growth in our operations and in our profitability. Sales of oil products for the first four months averaged about 70,000 barrels per day compared with 59,000 barrels per day for 1967. Financial results for that period indicate that we will have a very good first half. . . . The second half is more difficult to forecast. However, our expansion and momentum of progress is such that I shall be surprised if net profits for 1968 are not well above those for 1967."

The tonnages handled in and out of Thames Haven increased from 26,253,509 tons in 1966 to 26,416,625 in 1967, stated LORD LATYMER of *London and Thames Haven Oil Wharves Limited* (May 6), though the 1967 crisis in the Middle East naturally had some adverse effect on the company's trade, since the country's oil supplies were dislocated for a considerable period. He continued:

"During the year we have been successful in attracting some new customers. This should help to counteract any adverse effects that the coming into operation of new refineries in the United Kingdom might tend to have on the volume of business handled at Thames Haven."

Profits from oil and chemical storage were a record for *Powell Duffryn Limited*, according to the annual report (*The Times*, Sep-

tember 5) by Sir Henry Wilson Smith. Besides the installation of additional storage capacity at Purfleet and Barry and of facilities at Shoreham for handling fuel oil supplies arriving by sea, he mentioned that the closure of the Suez Canal had resulted in increased requirements by the oil companies at the group's installations at Las Palmas and St. Vincent, Cape Verde Islands, with a consequent improvement in profitability.

Stevinson, Hardy & Co. Limited (August 21) sustained a loss for the first half of the year in its United Kingdom oil products distributing subsidiary, stated Mr. V. G. Baker, but the position was rectified in the second half, and he was satisfied that the heavy losses on oil distribution would not recur. He then made the following comment:

"Competition between the integrated oil companies is intense and, with ever increasing administration and transport costs, margins available to an independent distributor are at present hardly sufficient to justify the substantial capital investment involved. We are keeping the rapidly changing conditions of the industry under constant review and I am hopeful that this part of our business will make a contribution to the profits in the current year. Our other fields of activity have started the year satisfactorily and we are seeking to improve and expand in several directions. I confidently expect that the recovery in the profitability of the group, which started in the latter half of last year, will continue and enable us to report a better return on our capital in 1968/69."

In his survey (*The Times*, April 10) for *Alexander Duckham and Co. Limited* Mr. Jack Duckham, after reporting a profit before taxation more than double that of the previous year, revealed that export turnover in 1967 was more than half as much again as in 1966. The motor oil department, he added, again made very striking advances in sales, and its share of the United Kingdom market was now 18 per cent. Further, he expected substantial growth during 1968 in sales, market share and profits.

Among the points made in the annual report (*The Times*, May 8) of *The Burmah Oil Company Limited* was that recent acquisitions of marketing companies in the United Kingdom and on the Continent would secure outlets for the increased refining capacity planned for Ellesmere Port. Motor spirit, kerosenes, gas oil and heavier fuel oils would increasingly be sold under the new Burmah mark, and lubricants and speciality products under the Castrol mark.

Included in Mr. C. H. Elliott's review for *Attock Oil Company Limited* (September 18) was the following paragraph:

"Production in 1967 was maintained but declining pressures in the older Fields are making it difficult fully to maintain pro-

375

duction at the 1967 level. These conditions are being offset to the extent possible by artificial means but a decrease in the quantities of oil and gas produced from these older Fields must be expected. The future of the company and of the subsidiary company depends, therefore, on success in the search for further reserves and much depends on the current drilling at Meyal."

Having reported a record consolidated net profit, 33·8 per cent above the previous year's figure, for *Ampol Petroleum Limited* (February 14), MR. L. J. THOMPSON made these remarks on the outlook for the company:

"The results of group operations for the first four months of the current trading year exceed budget which is based on achieving greater sales and profits than for 1967. While it is always difficult to forecast results for the full year, present indications are that, subject to a continuance of present conditions, the current year should be a good one for the company."

The British American Oil Company Limited in its 1967 annual report (*The Times*, April 2) claimed to be one of Canada's largest integrated petroleum companies, with over 6,000 service stations, agents and distributors marketing products in all 10 provinces; it operated nine refineries and five gas plants, and conducted an extensive exploration and production operation in Western Canada.

In his statement as Governor of the *Hudson's Bay Company* (May 24) LORD AMORY termed the recent success of Hudson's Bay Oil and Gas Company a development of "special importance and gratification." He went on to state:

"Hudson's Bay Company's original investment of $10m. made in the early 1950's has grown to a market value in excess of $150m. at 31st January, 1968. The four million shares owned by Hudson's Bay Company represent a 21·9 per cent equity interest in Hudson's Bay Oil and Gas Company. The growth of this asset is evidence of the soundness of the policy of regarding this venture as a long-term investment in the natural resources of Canada.

"For Hudson's Bay Oil and Gas, 1967 was an outstanding year. Record levels of production and sales produced new peaks in revenues, cash generation and net earnings; a successful exploration and development programme resulted in large net additions to reserves; the scope of activities was broadened to include the retail marketing of propane."

Among the highlights of the 1967 annual report (*The Times*, June 14) of *Trinidad Canadian Oils Limited* was the statement that the decline in Trinidad oil production had at last been arrested and a marginal increase achieved.

The figures included in the 1967 report (*The Times*, March 19) of

Texaco Inc. showed that the company's consolidated gross income was no less than $5,398,976,000; and that total worldwide gross production of crude oil averaged 2,534,000 barrels a day.

At the annual meeting of *Compagnie Française des Petroles* (Paris, June 21) M. VICTOR DE METZ said that during the first quarter of 1968 production increased by 22 per cent and provisional net profit figures by 12 per cent over those for the first quarter of 1967. He also mentioned that in the Persian Gulf area the company acquired a new source of supply in Oman; it had a 10 per cent interest in Petroleum Development (Oman), which would be producing at the rate of 15m. tons a year by the end of 1968.

The annual report (*The Times*, May 13) of *The Petrofina Group* contained a realistic summary of the difficulties faced by the oil industry in general; the relevant passages are as follows:

"In 1967 the world economic climate deteriorated seriously. The Middle East crisis and its repercussions; the British economic situation and subsequent sterling devaluation; the measures by both Britain and America to improve balance of payments; the recourse of American companies to European money markets—all presented complex problems. Reduced profit margins deprived investors of essential capital and restrained the advance of many projects.

"Thanks to the great flexibility with which our industry adapted itself, the shortage threatened by the Suez Canal closure did not materialize, but the additional heavy costs of bringing crude by the Cape route inevitably increased selling prices in most markets. Security was highlighted as an important factor in crude supply; intensive efforts to attain this through all possible sources therefore become most important.

"The trend towards dearer crude remains unchecked and this, together with increases in wages and taxes, and the necessity of finding capital for essential future investment, demand the earliest possible return to normal trading conditions, permitting the industry profit margins commensurate with the risks and commitments taken. Healthy competition is a source of progress—the present self-destructive spirit is not."

At the end of 1967 the *ENI* group of companies numbered 115, according to the annual report. In spite of a very sharp increase in Tunisian crude oil production, it stated, the occupation of Sinai, the Nigerian fighting and diminished production in Italy combined to limit overall average production to about 136,000 barrels a calendar day. Natural gas production in Italy rose by 5·3 per cent over 1966 to a total of 350,000m. cubic feet. Refinery crude runs were 9·1 per cent higher on the year, averaging for the 11 affiliated ENI refineries about 470,000 barrels per stream day; and the quantity of refined products manufactured rose 9·4 per cent above 1966.

PLANTATION INDUSTRIES

THIS chapter reproduces the views of chairmen of companies concerned either directly or indirectly with producing or trading in rubber, palm oil, tea, rice, sugar and cocoa.

RUBBER, OIL PALMS AND RICE

MR. M. D. FARROW told members of *The Rubber Growers' Association* (June 20) that the plantation industry in which they were engaged was of vital importance to the developing countries in which they operated. In many of these countries members had pioneered the natural rubber industry, and in more recent years they had been responsible for the introduction of oil palm cultivation. In both they had led the way in research and in the introduction of modern techniques, not only in planting, harvesting and collection but also in processing and presentation. The part they had played and were playing in the development of the countries where they operated was appreciated in those countries; and he assured the countries in question that they would do their best to continue to be as helpful as possible. Mr. Farrow went on to say:

"Most of our member companies are incorporated in the United Kingdom and we have asked the Chancellor of the Exchequer for some alleviation of the inequitable taxation which these companies have to bear. All that we ask for are certain changes in existing taxation arrangements which could be effected with little cost to the British Exchequer. It is to be hoped that the British Government, having set up a Ministry of Overseas Development, will appreciate the very important role which British private investment has played in such development and will take the necessary steps to permit it to continue to do so in the future."

At the annual meeting of *Chersonese (F.M.S.) Estates Limited* MR. T. B. BARLOW was a good deal blunter, asserting that every year companies worked more and more for a less and less share of the profit, and he said:

"The outlook is good from an agricultural point of view. Unfortunately the same can hardly be said of the economic outlook. Because of the complete volte-face on the part of our chancellors we are no longer encouraged to save and develop undeveloped land—just the opposite. The result of taxation on my dividend is that I shall not merely be penalized but fined for

holding shares. Perhaps it may be felt that this is an exceptional case amongst our 2,180 stockholders but we all suffer from the fact that because we pay corporation tax plus distribution tax, our estates are 20 per cent less profitable to us than they would be to an owner in Kuala Lumpur. The abolition of Overseas Trading relief is having its effect and some London companies are steadily selling their estates.

"For years I have asked stockholders to write to their M.P.s and to urge a policy which will encourage profit making—without profits what is there to tax?—and I've had unanimous approval from those with whom I've been in touch, so this year your board intend to give £100 to the Conservative Party Fund."

At the end of 1967, SIR ERIC GRIFFITH-JONES informed shareholders in *The Guthrie Corporation Limited* (July 31), the company's oil palm acreage was $17\frac{1}{2}$ per cent of its total. He continued:

"We have now finished a complete review of all our estates and have approved a programme of conversion to oil palms which will double our acreage by 1972, to give us over 60,000 acres of oil palms, and involve the construction of four new processing factories. Production forecasts for the next five years indicate a rise from the 1967 level of 30,700 tons to 48,000 tons in 1972. The major increase in production stemming from our replanting programme will, however, be seen beyond 1972 and we are thinking in terms of 100,000 tons per annum by 1977."

The programme, he added, provided for the reinvestment in Malaysia of £$6\frac{1}{2}$m., at the rate of exchange then current, over the next five years. This reflected both the continuing need to plough profits back into a plantation enterprise if it was to be maintained at competitive levels of production and efficiency, and also the board's confidence in Malaysia and in its Government's determination to preserve a climate for business investment which would attract overseas funds and enable expatriate enterprises to operate free from unreasonable political, economic or fiscal handicaps.

MR. J. F. E. GILCHRIST of *Harrisons & Crosfield Limited* (December 10) recalled that a year previously the rubber market was depressed and there was a considerable surplus of R.S.S.1, much of which was courageously bought by the Malaysian Government to stop the decline; there were also exceptionally high stocks of other grades. In spite of that Government's continued support, the price of R.S.S.1 in the Kuala Lumpur market reached a low point of $43\frac{1}{2}$ Malaysian cents in mid-February. Recovery followed, however, and by the end of May the price had risen to a peak of $58\frac{5}{8}$ cents, and it had since fluctuated quite narrowly in the 53–58 cent range. He also stated (in part):

"During the last few months there has been a general tightness

379

in supplies of nearby rubber which has extended to nearly all grades. Speciality rubbers such as concentrated latex, sole crepe, thin latex crepes and Superior Processing Rubbers have all been at worthwhile premia, while the discounts for lower grades have closed up. The Plantation Companies comprising the H. & C. Group are fortunately able to take advantage of favourable markets for these types of rubber. The H. & C. Latex Company increased production substantially and was able to sell at satisfactory prices not only its traditional standard grades of concentrate but also increasing quantities of special latices."

Palm oil, into the production of which many of the rubber plantations have been diversifying, had had a difficult year, continued Mr. Gilchrist. Twelve months previously the price had been around £80 a ton, c.i.f. United Kingdom, but it became evident, he declared, that, in spite of the virtual stoppage of palm oil shipments from Nigeria, there was a general surplus of vegetable oils and that the market must move lower. An unsuccessful attempt was made to raise the sterling quotation after devaluation, and the price declined persistently to the then current level of around £57, c.i.f. U.K. Palm kernels, on the other hand, enjoyed a good market, "although prices have fallen from the exceptionally high levels ruling at the beginning of the year." He also made the following reference to the question of quality:

"Buyers of palm oil are becoming steadily more quality-conscious, and in common with other growers we are doing our utmost to improve our product. To this end we have initiated a programme of intensive technical research geared closely to the requirements of refiners, which we hope may result in increases in consumption in the present applications and the development of new uses for palm oil."

The effects of the replanting programme of the estates owned by *Plantation Holdings Limited* (September 12) were now beginning to be felt, stated MR. S. W. LIVESEY: in 1965 the average yield per mature acre was 883 lb., and it rose to 932 lb. in 1966 and to 1,044 lb. in 1967, while the estimated figure for 1968 was 1,100 lb. As to the group's oil palm interests, he made this comment:

"Harvesting has commenced on the 786 acres of oil palms replanted in 1965. Next year a further 1,205 acres will come into bearing, so that, although the operations may not show a profit overall until 1970, from then on we shall benefit increasingly from revenue from this source. The Board has decided to bring forward the oil palms replanting programme for Brooklands Estate by planting up a further 2,462 acres during 1968, thus accelerating the ultimate profitability of that estate."

Oil palms now represented 43 per cent of the total planted

380

acreage of *Kulim Rubber Plantations Limited* (July 30), MR. P. B. L. COGHLAN revealed, and with the replanting of a further 2,000 acres of the older pedigree rubber areas which was planned to begin in 1970 there would be an almost equal division of the total planted area between the two types of cultivation.

As expected, SIR CHARLES MILES informed members of *R. G. Shaw & Company Limited* (October 22), the income from the company's tea and rubber investments had fallen, but this had been more than compensated from other sources, notably the improved results of the subsidiary Thames Rice Milling Company, about which he made the following statement:

"Trading results were very satisfactory. In international trade the company maintained a fair share of imports of eastern rice into the United Kingdom, although the aggregate tonnage from the east was not as high as in previous years, especially from Thailand. In consequence long-grain rice was nearly all purchased from the U.S.A.

"The Kennedy Round negotiations were concluded at the beginning of the year and the first reduction of the import duty on all white rice came into force on the 1st July, 1968. In the course of the next three years this duty will be reduced from £6 to £3 per ton thereby making the trade even more competitive.

"The modernization of the mill has proved a success and both quality and outturn have been enhanced."

Recalling that a year ago he had reported completed sales of all the properties of *Anglo Oriental Plantations Limited* (August 15) other than the Jugra estate, MR. R. S. ROWLAND now recorded the sale of Jugra for £1,358,281, representing an overall price of approximately £200 an acre. He added:

"Since members in general meeting resolved in September, 1966, that the Company's estates should be sold, over £3m. sterling has been realized from the sale of the Company's lands and assets in Malaysia. . . .

"It is the intention of your directors to arrange for the distribution to members of the funds now held in London at the earliest possible moment.

"I have stated that shareholders could expect a return of not less than 4s. 1d. per share on completion of the liquidation. This sum is in addition to the 1s. 11d. per share which was paid by means of a capital reduction in July, 1967. Various taxation matters, both here and in Malaysia, have to be resolved before a more precise figure can be announced."

Among the points made by MR. J. W. A. CALVER in his statement (*The Times*, March 16) for *Kuala Lumpur-Kepong Amalgamated Limited* were that land sales realized £35,000, that contracts awaiting completion would realize £75,000 and that sales

381

under negotiation, if realized, would result in a further £1,300,000. Of this amount, approximately £400,000 was dependent upon sub-division of title.

Announcing a "serious" fall in net profit before tax of *Seafield Amalgamated Rubber Company Limited* (April 24), MR. A. H. MARSHALL found consolation in the fact that substantial areas converted to palms were already producing such satisfactory results. "Although only a quarter of mature acreage is under palms," he disclosed, "42 per cent of the profit was derived from these areas and 47 per cent from rubber areas."

Referring to the New Guinea oil palm project, MR. J. F. E. GILCHRIST declared that relations between *Harrisons & Crosfield Limited* (December 10) and the Administration of the Territory, who were partners in this venture, continued excellent; and the Administration's separate commitment to settle indigenous farmers on adjacent land was ahead of schedule. He continued:

"It is inspiring to help pioneer a development where experienced management is contributing to a social experiment which will bring to hundreds of families benefits they would not otherwise enjoy, but to which most of us have become accustomed as part of our natural heritage.

"We have been handling commodities from Papua and New Guinea for many years. To consolidate our position and obtain a share of the business which the new development projects will generate, we have formed a new company, Harrisons & Crosfield (N.G.) Ltd., operating from Lae."

TEA

MR. J. F. E. GILCHRIST gave this account of the broad statistical position of tea to shareholders of *Harrisons & Crosfield Limited* (December 10):

"Tea production in the major exporting countries during the year to end June showed an increase of 97m. lb. over the previous 12 months. No reliable estimate of world absorption is yet available for the same period, but during the calendar year 1967 absorption exceeded the 1966 figure by about 80m. lb. It seems reasonable to assume that at present there is no excessive imbalance between supplies and absorption, but long-term estimates of increasing production reveal a serious potential problem of oversupply. For the welfare of this important industry it remains highly necessary to stimulate tea-drinking as widely and vigorously as possible. Promotion campaigns have had quite a marked success, but the biggest potential market is India herself with a population of over 500m.

"A rising trend in the consumption of tea would far outweigh any restrictive or other palliative method which could be

devised. In the meantime some progress is being made in developing Instant tea and various tea mixes and these are likely to tap new outlets apart from consumers of tea in its traditional form."

For *McLeod Russel & Co. Limited* (September 13) SIR GEORGE MACKINLAY referred to the constantly increasing costs of tea production, and asserted that, whether caused through taxation, obligations to labour or through a rise in the general price level, these higher costs could be met only by increased yields per acre and/or by increased prices obtained for tea.

"Unfortunately for us," he continued, "the supply and demand position secures that the British public, who provide our principal market, do not pay any more for their tea than they did ten years ago—a remarkable fact in this age of constantly increasing consumer prices, but a disturbing one for the Indian producer.

"Basically the situation which faces the tea industry in India today is one of potential over-supply. We are dealing with a commodity which is traded internationally and which is now produced in an increasing number of countries. In these circumstances, any question of restriction of overall production is probably not feasible although an agreement to regulate exports which took account of the reasonable aspirations of all the countries concerned and if accompanied by energetic efforts to promote consumption, particularly in Asia and Africa, would be most valuable. I accordingly welcome the recent initiative of the Governments of India and Ceylon in this direction. Meanwhile it is encouraging to note that, notwithstanding the huge increase in world production in recent years, it continues by and large to be absorbed, not only in India itself but elsewhere in the world. The reversal in 1967 of the trend to lower consumption in the United Kingdom may not be without significance, particularly as we now learn that this has continued into 1968."

Dealing with the tea agencies business of *Walter Duncan & Goodricke Limited* (May 30), MR. J. R. VERNÈDE stated that the merger with Alex. Lawrie and Co. Limited had added to the group's interests in the Assam district of India, in Malawi and in Tanzania. Production during 1967 from gardens within the enlarged agency was 106,200,000 lb., an increase of more than 4m. lb. over comparable figures for the previous season.

The next quotation comes from MR. L. W. PARKHOUSE'S review for *Longbourne Holdings Limited* (July 25):

"It was possible to report a year ago that season 1967 had got away to a good start and in the final result crop at 12,528,789 lb. exceeded that for the previous year by some 600,000lb. Indeed, but for the sudden cessation of rain in the latter part of October

which led to an unusually early close to the plucking season, the lead would almost certainly have been appreciably greater. By reason of the larger crop, the increase in unit cost at 45·11d. per lb. was not as great as it might have been, affected as it was by sterling devaluation, the usual run of wage increases and higher costs of all kinds covering materials for production and despatch. The price received for the commodity, although enhanced in terms of sterling by the U.K. devaluation, shows a considerable drop on the previous year, but by reason of the increased crop with its consequent salutary effect on production costs, the decline in profit is less than might have been expected. In all the circumstances the profit can be regarded as a reasonably satisfactory one."

Eastern Produce (Holdings) Limited (September 18), stated MR. R. MANN, had had a very bad year in Ceylon with a pre-tax loss for the first time since 1920. Ceylon tea producers generally, he added, had suffered from lower tea prices and rising costs. He also remarked:

"In Kenya we made good profits last year, but our accounts in future will show an increase in cost of production there as a result of the devaluation of sterling. This, we hope, will be more than compensated by higher yields as more of our tea matures.

"The profit from our trading and agency business was disappointing but would have been materially better if tea shipments and sales had not been delayed as they were by labour troubles.

"As to prospects, the figures we have at present indicates that unless the level of tea prices falls our group profits should be better than for last year."

While the new season had got away to a good start so far as crop was concerned, MR. J. R. VERNÈDE informed members of *Western Dooars Tea Holdings Limited* (October 29), the quality of the teas was not so well reported, and they had come on to a weak market so far. Unless the market firmed up in the fairly near future, of which there did not seem to be any immediate sign, it looked as though season 1968 would be a difficult one for producers.

"It is satisfactory," he went on, "to be able to report that thanks to the efforts of the promotion campaign sponsored by the Governments of India and Ceylon and the Industry in the United Kingdom, the decline in consumption in this country now seems to have been halted and efforts are being concentrated on expanding it, a very necessary object if the industry is to prosper. Stocks in London at the present time show little sign of falling and with new areas coming into bearing, not only in the traditional tea producing countries but in others where new planting with modern scientific aids is being undertaken, it

becomes essential to stimulate consumption if all are to remain on a profit-earning basis."

In his reference to the outlook for *Assam and African Investments Limited* (October 24), SIR HUGH MACKAY TALLACK mentioned that as a group they were now reaping the benefit of the considerable areas of young tea that had been put out in India, largely on virgin soil, over a number of years. This factor, among others, he declared, had resulted in the group's 1968 crops in India being the highest it had ever achieved by that stage of the season. In Tanzania, also, crops were ahead of the previous year. Unfortunately, world production was also running ahead of the previous year, and as a consequence prices in Calcutta, London and Nairobi were, and might continue to be, disappointing. Sir Hugh continued:

"However, there is possibly some hope to be drawn from an apparently growing awareness in New Delhi that the full potential of our industry as an earner of foreign exchange is not being realized, and that the industry's ability to maintain its position in the face of growing competition in the world markets will be jeopardized so long as existing financial pressures preclude adequate progress in modernization and rehabilitation. It is hoped that the Governments of India and Ceylon would be prepared to lend their support to consideration of some scheme for regulating exports from all producing countries to an extent necessary to avoid a situation, which I fear is already being reached, of world supply actually becoming excessive. I should, perhaps, stress that these hopes will inevitably take time to come to fruition and the prospects for the current year cannot be regarded at this stage with any great degree of optimism."

The tea gardens from which a greater part of the investment income of *Assam Trading (Holdings) Limited* (February 23) was derived, said SIR OWAIN T. JENKINS, were in excellent order and "must be among the finest properties in Assam." However, the tea industry in India was having a bad year; he was afraid that the then current fall in prices on the London market, the reduced proceeds after sterling devaluation and the continued high rate of export and excise duties levied by the India Government would reduce profits in spite of the increase in crop.

After strong representations to New Delhi by tea producer associations (which at first met with scant response), there had been a welcome if tardy recognition by Government that reasonable profits, far from being a sin, were an essential condition of survival for an industry which was an invaluable provider of revenue, a major earner of foreign exchange and a source of livelihood to some 800,000 employees. Thus wrote MR. J. R. VERNÈDE in his statement for *Assam-Dooars Holdings Limited* (November 27).

385

"Such recognition to date," he went on, "has assumed the form of a small reduction as from October 1, 1968, in excise and export duties which, taking 1967 as a hypothetical year, would have reduced the total paid out by your company from £495,927 to £428,996. Moreover, some modest but useful replanting subsidies have been introduced. These are by no means princely concessions and will not by themselves resolve our difficulties: still, they are a beginning and we must hope that the understanding of our problems will deepen although we can never aspire to the privileged position of exporters in other industries who not only enjoy freedom from excise but an export subsidy as well."

Apart from the continuance of unsatisfactory price levels over yet another year, the estates of *Jokai Tea Holdings Limited* (December 13), asserted MR. G. A. RAINEY, were again burdened under the double yoke of Indian excise and export duties, which in 1967–68 cost the group £833,690. He continued:

"The recent announcement of a more significant reduction in this duty, coupled with some measure of immediate relief as to excise duty, has therefore been welcomed.

"The Government of India announced a subsidy towards the cost of replanting, effective from October 1, 1968. Further progress is being made in Assam with the Group's tea extension programme. There has not yet been time for the new clonal tea to make its initial crop contribution, but from 1969 it should provide a useful boost to total annual production."

The two main factors which were responsible for the satisfactory results of *Imperial Tea Company Limited* (September 23), SIR GEORGE MACKINLAY declared, were the substantial increase in crop and a marked improvement in the quality of the teas produced, particularly in the Dooars.

The next quotation, on tea production in East Africa, is taken from the annual review of *Inchcape & Co. Limited* (October 30):

"But for the impact of sterling devaluation, the profits of both our tea producing subsidiaries in East Africa would have been appreciably better. The crop of Karirana Estates Ltd., which operates in Kenya, was also adversely affected by a severe drought early in the year. Quality on both estates was well maintained but the prices obtained in London were disappointing and proceeds suffered accordingly."

SUGAR

MR. T. P. NAYLOR reported better results from sugar in his statement (*The Times*, May 29) for *Demerara Company Holdings Limited*, and these were largely attributable to production higher than earlier forecasts; moreover, the board believed that the 1968

profits before tax would show some further improvement. He also stated:

"There is another attempt to reach an International Sugar Agreement and the results should be known this summer: we believe not only that such a commodity agreement would be good for sugar, but also heartening evidence that the developed countries are prepared to make practical commercial agreements to help, by trade, those which are less developed."

The raw sugar producing enterprises of *Tate & Lyle* (March 20) in the Caribbean all suffered losses, with world prices well below even the most efficient producer's costs, said MR. JOHN LYLE, the chairman, in the absence through ill-health of the president, Sir Ian Lyle. He also made the following reference (in part) to the outlook:

"Crops are promising for 1968, particularly in Trinidad and we hope for a significant increase in production in British Honduras. Mechanization of harvesting is proceeding steadily both in Trinidad and British Honduras and costs are successfully being reduced in both places, particularly in the latter where sugar can be produced at costs well below the average for the Caribbean. In Jamaica, the long awaited report of the Mordecai Commission has now been published. Assuming that the recommendations are implemented by the Government, we can at last look forward to the prospect of making a start on mechanical harvesting and of bulk loading of ships by modern methods. The removal of these restrictions is of vital importance to Jamaica whose economy depends on exporting sugar competitively with other countries of the world."

During 1967, reported SIR DENYS LOWSON to members of *Australian Estates Company Limited* (July 8), the Pleystowe sugar mill manufactured the first large quantity of cane invert (also known as high test molasses and molasses invert). He explained:

"Approximately 67,000 tons of invert were produced; this equals 49,000 tons of sugar and forms part of Pleystowe's total sugar production of 86,000 tons. Cane invert is used in Japan for fermentation in production of a Japanese whisky and in production of alcohol for the national Japanese drink of sake. The project necessitated fairly extensive modifications to plant at the mill and training of chemists in analytical techniques not usually required for raw sugar manufacture and the purchasers of the invert have expressed their complete satisfaction with the product."

The annual report of *Lonrho Limited* (June 20) stated that a provisional agreement had been reached with the Swaziland Sugar Milling Company Limited whereby the Lonrho sugar interests in

387

Malawi (Sugar Corporation of Malawi) and Mauritius (Anglo-Ceylon & General Estates) would be transferred to the Swaziland company in exchange for an issue of shares which would bring the operations of all three companies under Lonrho's control. It was expected that this extension and consolidation of the group's sugar interests would result in both increased efficiency and profitability.

COCOA

The advance in market prices of cocoa beans which took place during 1966 and which increased the 1967 usage price of *Rowntree and Company Limited* (June 14) by almost 30 per cent, remarked MR. D. J. BARRON, continued during 1967 on discouraging crop prospects. The devaluation of sterling in November, since the main producing countries did not follow sterling, raised United Kingdom prices still further; and by the end of 1967 the spot price of West African beans at 297s. 6d. per cwt. was at its highest level for eight years. He also stated:

"The year saw a further series of consultations aimed at concluding an international cocoa agreement. A number of considerations, some bearing only indirectly on cocoa, unfortunately prevented a successful conclusion but it is hoped that all the preparatory work which has now been done will in time lead to an agreement acceptable to all parties."

388

SHIPS AND SHIPPING

AFTER commenting on the extension of shipbuilding loans on favourable terms, previously reserved by Government to foreign shipowners, to British owners; on the Israeli–Arab conflict and consequent closing of the Suez Canal, which resulted in sharply higher freight rates for tankers and smaller rises in rates for bulk carriers, as well as some advance in the freight market generally; on the disastrous dock strike in September, 1967; on the devaluation of sterling in November which in the main benefited British shipping; and on the cessation of meat shipments from South America after the outbreak of foot and mouth disease in the United Kingdom, which particularly affected shipping engaged in the South American trades, MR. CYRIL W. WARWICK of *Houlder Brothers & Co. Limited* (July 15) made these remarks on the outlook:

"As for the future, the outlook is obscure, but that could well be the stock description of the future of the shipping industry at any time. Indeed it could never be otherwise. The only prediction on which I would venture would be that overseas movement of cargo and the need for ships to carry it will continue to expand. Although the rate of increase has slowed down in recent years, and official statistics for 1967 are not yet available, it seems likely that the figure of total traffic for that year, tanker and dry cargo combined, will emerge at about 1,850m. tons, which would represent an increase of about 6 per cent over 1966.

"But the merchant fleets of the world are also expanding rapidly. World tonnage increased by over 8 per cent last year, and a further large increase will occur during the current year, particularly in tankers and bulk carriers. The big question, therefore is whether the present spate of building will prove to have been overdone to an extent that will create a surplus with an uncomfortable time lag before demand for tonnage catches up with the greatly augmented supply. That will not necessarily be so, and the only reasonable certainty is what always happens —some ebb and flow between supply and demand with consequent fluctuations in rates from time to time.

"It is an impressive fact that deliveries of new bulk carriers last year plus estimated deliveries in the current year amount to the staggering total of about 20m. tons deadweight. It required some courage to join in this mass movement by ordering the two bulk carriers to which I have referred, and the decision to

389

enter the bulk carrier field on this limited scale represented a policy of endeavour to navigate safely between the Scylla of excessive optimism and the Charybdis of extreme caution. That could be a fair description of our policy generally, but with the important addition that we are consantly seeking opportunities for fresh enterprise, and are always ready to provide ships specially built for any requirement put to us with a reasonable prospect of steady employment."

The British shipping industry in 1967 was worth at least £300m. to Britain's balance of payments, claimed SIR DONALD ANDERSON of the *Peninsular and Oriental Steam Navigation Company* (March 20). This sum was earned mainly by "invisible exports," such as freight and passenger revenue. The importance of this major contribution was often overlooked, he declared, as public interest tended to be focused on visible exports. Sir Donald went on to say:

"Everyone who sees a tractor in a packing case going into a ship's hold can understand how exports earn us money. But it it is much harder to understand the processes by which the British ship which is carrying the tractor is earning us money too. Throughout the years the invisibles, of which shipping is one, have made a major contribution to our balance of payments. If at this time there were no British ships in overseas trades, our balance of payments would be worse off by some £300m. per annum. Yet there has been little national understanding of this, and correspondingly little effort to produce conditions in which this contribution could be increased."

Though recovery was a long process, *The Cunard Steam-Ship Company Limited* was now well on the way, declared SIR BASIL SMALLPEICE in his annual statement (*The Times*, May 31). Thus losses of over £2m. in the first half of 1967 were cut to £990,000 in the second half, and Cunard was budgeting for a small profit in 1968. He explained that the passenger fleet had been adjusted to meet modern market needs—sea travel as a holiday; the heavy losses on passenger ships had been stopped, and the reduced fleet should earn profits in 1969. Cargo services, he added, had been rationalized to increase productivity and cut overheads, and container ships owned by the group would go into service in 1969. Writing well before the fiasco of her trials, he stated that Queen Elizabeth 2 would make her maiden voyages from the United Kingdom and the United States early in 1969, and he described her as the newest and finest passenger ship in the world, designed to suit both cruising and Atlantic business.

For the *Danish Bacon Company Limited* (May 15) MR. F. HERBERT gave this account of the inauguration of container transport of Danish bacon to this country:

390

"The year 1967 saw the emergence of a new and advanced method of transporting Danish bacon, and in January the Container ferry 'Somerset' began bi-weekly sailings to Grimsby with the new roll-on, roll-off refrigerated 10-ton container, drawn by a prime-mover. It was soon obvious that bacon shipped in this way arrived in excellent condition and was easy to handle by those with the right facilities. Demand for bacon shipped in the new way grew apace and it was not long before the new liner 'Winston Churchill' was put into commission on regular sailing schedule to Harwich. This brought container supplies up to two-thirds of total shipments from Denmark.

"We encountered the problems of fractional loads and special 'intake' situations. To meet these our company has developed and put into service a flexible and highly manoeuvrable type of tail-lift vehicle."

Referring to the launch of the group's container ship for Overseas Containers Limited, SIR W. NICHOLAS CAYZER of *The British & Commonwealth Shipping Company Limited* (July 24) remarked that it would be unwise to expect profits initially as the benefit of changing from traditional ships to containers would not be achieved overnight, but he hoped that in due course this would be a worthwhile investment. He also said:

"During 1967 we sold six ships and one trawler, and so far this year we have sold three cargo ships. This is a shortening back of the Fleet in the face of rationalization and of possible further container development. We have also disposed of two tankers."

After citing the various reasons for what he described as "a most difficult trading year," MR. JOHN MACCONOCHIE included this paragraph in his statement (*The Times*, June 27) for *Furness Withy and Company Limited*:

"It is your board's intention by looking to other spheres, to broaden the base of our shipping operations and we are on the look-out for opportunities to invest in more diversified tonnage. It should not be forgotten that we have a large shareholding in Overseas Containers Ltd. As part of our general policy of diversification within the wider limits of the shipping industry, we are in the process of investing approximately one million dollars in a new terminal operation for our stevedoring organization in Vancouver, B.C. We have also recently expanded our agency business in the U.S.A. by taking over several agencies from Funch Edye & Co."

The two main features of the North American trade of *Manchester Liners Limited* (December 3) during the past year, declared MR. ROBERT B. STOKER, had been the build up in the number of

containers carried and the frustration in trying to run conventional services with long delays in United Kingdom ports because of labour shortages, resulting in longer periods for ships in port than at sea. He also asserted:

"Your company was the first to realize the potential of the total container concept in the Canadian trade where there is an expanding market. Two years ago we had six containers. At the beginning of 1967 we were using one thousand, and at present we are operating more than two thousand containers. This has been an essential build up for the start of a fully cellular weekly container service. In the meantime the carriage of containers on traditional ships is far from efficient."

The company, he added, had invested £10m. in three container ships, containers and a special container crane in Montreal.

SIR JOHN N. NICHOLSON mentioned that two ships belonging to *The Ocean Steam Ship Company Limited* (June 11) had been trapped in the Suez Canal when it was closed. The relevant passage in his statement follows:

"The ships have run without serious navigational or mechanical accident. But, unhappily, we can see no early prospect of recovering 'Agapenor' and 'Melampus' which have been trapped in the Suez Canal since June—a harsh penalty for maintaining schedules by allowing our average frequency of almost a daily transit to run unchecked before the Canal was closed."

Ocean steamship operations of the *Canadian Pacific Railway Company* (Montreal, May 1), said MR. I. D. SINCLAIR, the President, should benefit this season from the more settled labour situation. Canadian Pacific (Bermuda) had just taken delivery of the M.V. "J. V. Clyne", which brought the total tonnage operated by that subsidiary to 200,000; earnings from the subsidiary, he added, were expected to show excellent growth.

A return of capital and a change of name affecting *Moor Line Limited* (July 22) were announced by LORD RUNCIMAN in the following two paragraphs:

"The withdrawal of Anchor Line from owning and running liners on the North Atlantic together with the decision not to build ships for the general tramp market have reduced the amount of capital required by the Group for the purpose of its business. Accordingly we propose that the capital of the company be reduced by returning to the Stockholders ten shillings for each £1 of Stock held.

"With a decision to concentrate the Group's shipowning in Anchor Line and to move out of the general tramping trade associated with the name of Moor Line, that name as a title for

your company becomes inappropriate; we now therefore propose to you that the name of your company be changed to Walter Runciman & Co. Ltd."

An increase in operating profit of *Dene Shipping Company Limited* reflected among other things the addition of the *Sigsilver* and *Silvercove* to the vessels which the company had in service. High interest charges on borrowings to help finance these ships, however, had meant that net profit after taxation remained virtually unchanged. The higher trading profit was beginning to show the results of specialization. These points are taken from MR. L. C. GRAHAM-DIXON's statement (*The Times*, July 12).

Profits of *Shipping Industrial Holdings Limited* (June 25) in 1967 were almost doubled, MR. REGINALD MAUDLING, M.P., reported, and he made this reference to prospects for 1968:

"On results up to the present we look to the current year with confidence. Continued progress has been recorded in our Shipbroking, Insurance and Inclusive Tours Divisions. The Shipowning Groups are trading profitably and subject to the operation of individual ships should again provide encouraging results. Good progress is being made in the Transport companies and our Travel Agencies. On the assumption that there is no marked deterioration in world economic or monetary conditions and the state of the U.K. economy does not worsen, Group results for 1968 should be at least comparable with the past year."

An increase of approximately £100,000 in group profit before taxation of *Wm. France, Fenwick and Company Limited* (June 14) was attributed by the late SIR JULIAN PODE in the main to the recovery in earnings from the company's fleet. He made these comments (in part) on the coasting trade:

"The vessels engaged in the coasting trade operated well during the year but the demand for the 4,000 ton collier type, of which your company have only two remaining, is such that these ships by reason of their size became almost impossible to operate profitably. Since the end of the year one has been sold and unless satisfactory trade can be found for the other it will also be disposed of. As a tonnage replacement a secondhand bulk carrier of 7,500 tons has been purchased and it is confidently anticipated that this will prove to be a profitable unit."

That 1968 would be a year of wide reorganization of the shipping activities of *Coast Lines Limited* (September 26) was clear from SIR ARNET ROBINSON's statement, in which he mentioned some of the changes. At the meeting he added that other of the company's services were still under review, and stated:

"August and September are important months for the company. I am pleased to report that overall results are quite good, and, above all, the three new cross-channel ships have had satisfactory carryings both of passengers and vehicles. You will appreciate that radical changes in the methods of operation involve time and expense, and in some cases full benefits do not accrue immediately. I make this point because it is necessary to advise Stockholders that while they can expect some improvement in trading results in 1968 your Board is confident that in the absence of unforeseeable troubles substantial improvements will be achieved in 1969."

Although the aggregate profits of *Powell Duffryn Limited* from shipping and shipping services were substantially higher, the annual report of the board (*The Times*, September 5) declared that the decline in the coastwise movement of coal continued.

With regard to the shipping interests of *Tate & Lyle Limited* (March 20), MR. JOHN LYLE, the chairman (who spoke in the absence of Sir Ian Lyle, the president, through ill-health), said that the policy of maintaining up-to-date fleets in both Sugar Line and Athel Line had been continued.

"We have," he added, "taken delivery of two new ships and three more are following. Shipping profits rose sharply in 1967 due largely to the increase in tanker freights following the closure of the Suez Canal. In particular, both the 62,000 ton oil carriers of Athel Line were employed at high rates and, together with the other ships of the two fleets, should make another substantial contribution to the Group's results in 1968."

European Ferries Limited (December 30), the company formed to merge George Nott Industries Limited and Otto Thoresen Shipping Company A/S., of Oslo, was expected to operate nine ships in 1969 compared with only one in 1961; to carry 1,250,000 passengers (against 75,000); 300,000 tourist vehicles (against 25,000); and 65,000 commercial freight vehicles (against none). Stockholders are offered reductions ranging up to 50 per cent on normal fares on certain services. These details were given in the directors' report.

SIR DENYS LOWSON told members of the *Algoma Central Railway* (Sault Ste. Marie, April 3) that, following the opening of the St. Lawrence Seaway, the trend towards larger vessels on the Great Lakes has continued steadily. He continued:

"Because of more economical operation and greater productivity this trend has been accompanied by stable or declining rate levels for most major commodities. However, we now appear to be near the end of this process since the greater part of the Great Lakes fleet capacity is now in larger size vessels;

and there appear to be little further productivity gains on the average which can be achieved by the fleet in moving into larger vessels. On the other hand, within the past few years, the cost of new ship construction has been going up at a very rapid pace; for example, our new vessel, the 'Algorail', which was christened yesterday by my wife in a ceremony at Collingwood, Ontario, is a sister ship of the 'Roy A. Jodrey' which came into service in the spring of 1965, exactly three years ago. However, the cost of the 'Algorail' to the A.C.R. is almost 30 per cent higher than the cost of the 'Jodrey'. With the government subsidy to the shipyard declining, and construction costs for new capacity continuing to climb, we would expect this to be reflected in the general level of rates on the Grand Lakes in the near term future."

Severe competition in international commerce, industry and shipping persisted with undiminished strength, it was stated in the annual report presented by the board of *The East Asiatic Company Limited* (Copenhagen, April 5). In spite of the closing of the Suez Canal in June, 1967, and the consequent re-routing of shipping by way of the Cape, it had been possible, by rationalization and addition of further modern tonnage, to maintain the company's regular liner services. The report adds that it was once more especially through the company's overseas interests, which had been extended by an increasing number of local industries, that it was possible to present an improved result.

One of the points of interest in the annual report for 1967 of *Compagnie Maritime des Chargeurs Réunis* (June 26) was the statement that the French merchant navy had now entered a new era, that of freight containerization, which was going to imply for the shipowners not only purchases of new equipment but also increased activity in the field of transport and in their activities on dry land. It was in that light that an interest was acquired in Etablissements Walon, an important forwarding and land transport company.

The year under review had been probably the most difficult one for the fishing industry here and abroad this century, declared MR. MICHAEL NOBLE, M.P., of *Associated Fisheries Limited* (March 19); and he had this to say of the company's trawling interests:

"Last year I had to record the drop in profits which followed on a year where we had had 8 months good fishing and 4 months bad. This year we did not have a single month which came up to the results we were having before May, 1966. The large over supply of frozen fish in the world combined with the fact that Britain was the most open market for surplus fish meant that, while costs rose steadily, any inclination that the market had to rise was frustrated by the great tonnages of imports. Our new

freezer trawlers operated on the whole successfully but their profitability could not—at ruling prices—match up with our hopes."

TANKERS

The year 1967 would live in the memory of shipowners as the year of the Second Suez Crisis, declared Mr. BASIL M. MAVROLEON of *London & Overseas Freighters Limited* (July 29); and he went on to explain the repercussions of the closing of the Canal in this paragraph:

"The closing of the Suez Canal had tremendous repercussions on the oil companies' requirements for immediate tanker tonnage as their floating pipe-line was stretched an extra 5,000 miles round South Africa, but the situation was short-lived and the first wave of tanker chartering in June was not followed up. It is true, I am pleased to say, that there was an upsurge in demand for tankers last month and we made some very profitable fixtures for vessels which by chance were in the right position. Nevertheless, the closure of the Canal has come at a time when the oil companies are beginning to base their transport of oil by sea on the ever-increasing number of mammoth tankers which could not, in any event, use the Canal. It seems certain, therefore, that the movement of oil by sea in future will in no way depend upon the use of the Suez Canal. This change in the pattern of oil movement further limits the field of profitable operation of the small tanker which cannot compete with the giants on the ocean routes."

In August, MR. W. S. PHILIPPS informed members of *Court Line Limited* (June 27), the company purchased a 26,000 tons deadweight tanker and renamed her *Halcyon Wave*. When purchased, this vessel was fixed for one trans-Atlantic round voyage followed by two Persian Gulf round voyages at post Arab–Israeli war rates. She had made only a small contribution to profits in the year under review, he added, but would more than double the "surplus from shipping" for the half-year to March, 1968.

Large-scale chartering of tonnage resulting from the war in the Middle East was recorded in the report of the directors of *The Petrofina Group* which was summarized in *The Times* of May 13. The relevant passage is as follows:

"Because of the additional sailing distances occasioned by events in the Middle East, we had to supplement our fleet's own operation by chartering some 2m. tons at voyage rates. The 'Fina Norvège' has been increased in capacity from 36,000 to 62,000 metric tons, and was recommissioned towards the end of the year. Two 220,000 ton tankers have been chartered for

delivery in 1970, and other charters or projects for similar construction are programmed for the gradual replacement of our existing fleet with the aim of appreciably reducing costs."

SHIPBUILDING

LORD SHERFIELD referred to the activities of *Ship Mortgage Finance Company Limited* (October 8) in administering for the Government the guaranteed loan scheme for shipbuilding under the Shipbuilding Industry Act, and stated (in part):

"In my statement last year I reported that your company had been invited by the Government to act for them in operating the Guaranteed Loan Scheme under Section 7 of this Act for shipowners building in British yards. The Committee which deals with applications under this scheme has held twenty-three meetings and at the year's end had recommended the granting of guaranteed loans to the amount of £140 m. for the building of some ninety-six ships, with a total tonnage of over 1.4m. g.r.t. Seven ships have already been delivered under the scheme, and a number of loans under the scheme completed. More applications have been dealt with since the end of June, and more still are in the pipeline. It is evident that ship owners have taken advantage of the benefits and low rate of interest under the scheme, and that a number of new orders have been generated."

What he described as perhaps one of the most important events in the long history of shipbuilding on the Tyne was the emergence on January 1, 1968, of the new Tyne shipbuilding consortium, Swan Hunter & Tyne Shipbuilders Limited, declared SIR JOHN HUNTER of *Swan Hunter Group Limited* in his annual statement (*The Times*, May 6). The new company acquired in exchange for shares the Tyne shipbuilding interests of Swan Hunter, Vickers Limited, R. & W. Hawthorn Leslie & Co., and John Readhead and Sons. After giving details of the Capital of the new company and how that part of it which was issued was divided among the companies participating in the merger, Sir John stated:

"It was agreed that, when the new company came into being, it would complete on an agency basis the building contracts secured by the participating companies but not completed at 1st January, 1968. These contracts represented some £50m. of work. In addition to these, new contracts have been obtained by Swan Hunter & Tyne Shipbuilders Ltd. to the value of about £43m."

Dealing with the problems encountered in building supertankers, SIR JOHN F. MALLABAR of *Harland and Wolff Limited* (May 15) declared that entirely different techniques must be employed if

397

these large ships were to be built efficiently and economically and if worthwhile economies were to be achieved. He stated:

"The building dock system seemed most likely to give us these economies and accordingly plans were formulated for the construction of such a dock with its appropriate supporting facilities. These plans involved a great deal of work which was carried through in a surprisingly short time. The plans were submitted to the Shipbuilding Industry Board, who have agreed to support us in the construction of the dock, and its attendant facilities. Work has already started, and is being carried forward as a matter of extreme urgency. When it is completed it will leave us possessed of facilities for shipbuilding as good as anything existing anywhere in the world.

"The new building dock and its ancillary equipment will cost something of the order of £13½m. The Government and the Shipbuilding Industry Board have agreed that a substantial grant will be available towards this expenditure and that a long-term loan of up to £8m., which should cover the balance, will be advanced under the Shipbuilding Industry Act. The detailed arrangements are now being worked out. Before the decision to go ahead with the building dock was taken we had to ask ourselves whether it was wise to commit ourselves to spend so much capital, a large part of which would have to be borrowed. This decision was not a difficult one to take, for the advantages resulting from the construction of the dock were so obvious that there was little room for any argument.

"It would be wrong of me to minimize the task ahead of us in the construction of so large a project. The fact that it is being built adjacent to roads used every day by traffic on the Harbour Estate imposes considerable additional difficulties not only on our contractors but on the general activities of the estate and we are grateful to the Belfast Harbour Commissioners for their help, and tolerance, in this matter.

"By the same token it would be wrong to minimize the advantages which we can foresee accruing from the possession of the dock. Indeed, even though it is not yet built it has already begun to provide benefits, for because of our plans to build it we were able to submit a tender for two tankers of 240,000 dwt each required by Esso. We were successful in this tender. This order is tangible proof that our decision to create the building dock was the right one. I might add that we have already received inquiries for even larger ships which could not be built by us without such a facility.

"You will further be able to gauge the benefits likely to stem from the dock if I tell you that had it been available for the building of MYRINA I estimate the ship would have cost us some £500,000 less than she did."

398

John Brown and Company Limited (September 6) was another company involved in a large-scale merger. LORD ABERCONWAY declared that the most important event for the group during the year to March 31, 1968, was the merging of the Clydebank shipyard with the shipbuilding interests of other concerns on the upper Clyde to form Upper Clyde Shipbuilders Limited, in the equity of which John Brown had a stake of some 33 per cent. He described the launch on September 20, 1967, by the Queen, of the Cunarder *Queen Elizabeth 2* as marking the culmination of John Brown's shipbuilding activities.

The next quotation comes from SIR ERIC YARROW's statement for *Yarrow and Company Limited* (December 30):

"The most important event during the last year has been the sale to Upper Clyde Shipbuilders Ltd. of a 51 per cent interest in our subsidiary Yarrow (Shipbuilders) Ltd. The negotiations leading up to this arrangement were not easy, as your Board was determined to protect the interest of both shareholders and of employees of the company.

"Authority has been given by the Shipbuilding Industry Board for a loan to provide for major extensions to Yarrow (Shipbuilders) Ltd. These proposals include the erection of a large shop to build naval and specialist merchant ships under cover and will create shipbuilding working conditions possibly more advanced than anywhere else in the world. The ultimate economies likely to be achieved are expected to be considerable. When the accounts of Y(S)L are known a dividend will be declared in accordance with the terms of my statement of January 19, 1968."

For *Cammell Laird and Company Limited* (May 14) MR. PHILIP HUNTER mentioned, among the group activities, that Cammell Laird & Company (Shipbuilders & Engineers) Limited had increased their profit from £138,168 in 1966 to £852,573 in 1967. It was, he commented, good to see the results of the team building and modernization which he had described a year previously becoming thus apparent; there was in the shipyard now, he declared, "a young, highly qualified and enthusiastic team."

The possible merger of the three shipbuilding companies on the Wear into a single shipbuilding group was a subject of comment by SIR HENRY WILSON SMITH of *The Doxford and Sunderland Shipbuilding and Engineering Company Limited* (September 12). He had nothing specific to report at that time, but hoped that it would not be too long before he would have. He also mentioned the large increase in the company's orders.

The shipbuilding division of *Vosper Limited* (December 12) had had a busy year, declared SIR DAVID BROWN, and much progress had been made with the introduction of the new management techniques at Woolston. The board firmly believed that benefits

399

would now progressively emerge. He gave some information about work now in progress for foreign navies, and, on a smaller scale, made this announcement:

"In the last twelve months we have been developing a small and simple stabilizer for yachts of 40–50 feet, which we call the Mini-Fin; trials have been very succcessful and initial reactions from the market are most encouraging."

In a comment on the progress of Appledore Shipbuilders Limited, a 100 per cent subsidiary of *Court Line Limited* (June 27) MR. W. S. PHILIPPS stated:

"Appledore Shipbuilders had a very successful year during which fifteen vessels were completed, and it is particularly gratifying that all delivery dates were on or ahead of contract. The modernization programme for the Shipyard is now virtually completed, and Appledore will stand comparison with any other Shipyard of its type, as regards equipment and methods of production for small shipbuilding. The present order book is particularly satisfactory and although devaluation had an adverse effect on the cost of materials for existing contracts it has also made export prospects brighter and no time is being lost in attempting to exploit these opportunities. Although competition in this Industry is very severe it is considered that the Yard is fully able to continue on a profitable basis for the foreseeable future."

DOCKS AND PORTS

Traffic passing through the ports owned by *British Transport Docks Board* in 1967 totalled 50,873,000 tons, compared with 51,263,000 tons in 1966. General cargo increased by nearly 2m. tons mainly because of the rapid expansion of unit load services at a number of ports, but there was a decline of similar size in coal shipments, and a 492,000 tons drop in imported ores. These facts are extracted from the review by the chairman, MR. S. A. FINNIS, who also made these remarks on the future of the ports:

"Harbour reorganization schemes proposed by the National Ports Council have affected the Board's undertaking, with their docks on the Tees handed over to the new Tees & Hartlepools Port Authority at the beginning of 1967 and the ports of Grangemouth, Methil and Burntisland being transferred to the new Forth Ports Authority on January 1, 1968. Other schemes confirmed and due for implementation will make the Docks Board the sole estuarial authority for the Humber and for Southampton.

"An even more drastic re-shaping of the industry will result from the Government's proposal to nationalize the ports in

1971, but in the meantime the industry is facing a period of intense technological change. The British Transport Docks Board has achieved much in developing the already nationalized ports and during the next eighteen months will bring to fruition a number of major schemes at Southampton, in South Wales, and on the Humber, which will meet the needs of international commerce for many years to come."

SIR LESLIE ROBERTS made a strong case in opposition to the Government's proposed nationalization of the port of Manchester (among other ports) in his speech for the *Manchester Ship Canal Company* (February 29). It was too long to reproduce here, but his concluding paragraph is set out out below:

"As a comparatively large and enterprising organization—and we are placed number 145 in *The Times* list of major companies—we have always had proper regard for our national responsibilities. But the Government now propose to subject us—along with other independent ports—to political belief in state ownership regardless of the facts, regardless of the views of responsible commercial and industrial leaders and regardless also of the severely straitened economic circumstances of the country."

The development of Felixstowe as a port was commented upon by MR. H. GORDON PARKER in his statement for the *Felixstowe Dock and Railway Company* (October 31). He referred to the Freightliner connection with the port established by British Rail, and asserted that many container operators were taking advantage of the economies of this fast and regular service and the consolidation and groupage facilities available at the inland terminals which brought Felixstowe within the orbit of the small user. He added:

"Resulting from the decision to construct the container berth and second roll-on roll-off facility, your company now enjoys two North Atlantic container services and deriving from them 'feeder' services are being run from the Continent to Felixstowe—something I believe to be unique. A number of shippers and shipping companies are attracted to Felixstowe because of the services we offer, our geographical position, and as a result of the dredging of the main channel which provides 36 ft. at high water springs. Our traffic in paper of various kinds is a big feature and is some four times greater than obtained a year ago."

The development of the ports of Par and Fowey proposed by *English China Clays Limited* (March 18) was the subject of this comment by LORD ABERCONWAY:

"Record shipments of almost one million tons of china clay passed last year through our Port of Par which handles the major part of the continental and coastal traffic of the industry. We were glad to hear that the Minister of Transport had provisionally accepted the recommendations of the Rochdale and the Devlin Reports to omit single user ports from the scope of nationalization. On this basis, Par escapes a future which in our view would not lead to enhanced efficiency and thereby to the enhanced competitiveness in price of china clay delivered to the user.

"If the growth of the deep sea shipments of the industry is not to be curtailed, either the port of Fowey, owned by British Rail, must be extensively modernized, or deep sea facilities must be set up at Par. The latter course would spell the end of Fowey as a port, and the former is therefore preferable, and indeed would be less costly. Talks have been held with British Rail, and we await confirmation from British Rail and from the Ministry of Transport of the agreement reached whereby the company will take a long lease of the jetties and sidings at Fowey. We shall then seek planning consent so that we can construct a new jetty, establish buffer storage facilities, instal modern cargo handling and ship loading gear, and provide road access (the port is served at present only by rail). We have undertaken to offer employment to the workpeople employed on the jetties at Fowey. We will operate the port in conjunction with Par."

In his review for *The Proprietors of Hay's Wharf Limited* (March 28) SIR DAVID H. BURNETT stated that the group net profit before tax was 28 per cent down on the year, and he explained:

"This disappointing result has in the main been due to a heavy fall, for the second year running, in income from port transport operations in London, chiefly brought about by industrial disputes in which the company was not itself directly involved; and my warning given last year, of continuing adverse effects from the 1966 seamen's strike, has unhappily been justified. On the other hand, the greater part of the Group's interests outside port transport were expanded and produced substantially increased profits, after taking into account the cost of financing the capital work in progress."

As a tailpiece to this chapter there is given the comment on decasualization of dock labour which SIR JOHN N. NICHOLSON included in his statement for *The Ocean Steam Ship Company Limited* (June 11):

"For five years decasualization of dock work has been the subject of public enquiry and private wrangling and this seems to have largely distracted Trades Union officials from their

402

parallel task of expounding to their members the wider benefits that the great majority of dock workers would deservedly receive from the regularization of employment which they have sought for so long. Thus, when the related conditions were finally accepted by the Trades Union spokesmen they were at once rejected by the mass of dock workers at the instigation of men with a formidable record of strife on the docks and elsewhere of the type stigmatized by Lord Devlin as wreckers. The position of these men has been dangerously strengthened by their success in this episode. For this and similar tragedies flow inevitably from the destruction of internal discipline caused by the frequent insistence of successive Governments over a long period that industrial disputes should be settled on terms demanded by extremists in defiance of the Trades Union leadership. We reckon that, ignoring permanent loss in goodwill, the autumn stoppages in London and Liverpool cost us around £1.2m., two-thirds of which have been debited to the 1967 Accounts. And we calculate that the ultimate settlements, prompted by our present Government, may add one-third to our stevedoring costs in the United Kingdom—which already totalled £4.5m. a year—and will now be widely out of line with charges in competing ports. In the short run these disturbances which still persist have done considerable harm to our operations particularly in the port of Liverpool, while not surprisingly kindred activities such as ship towage have had to match the extravagant wage pattern set by the docks. We can only hope— so far without much confidence—that in the longer term this far-reaching scheme of reform will yield the improvement in working relations and in productivity which it was intended by its sponsors to achieve and so partly offset the aforementioned expenditure."

SHOPS AND SHOPPING

RETAIL distributors were hit specially hard by the Selective
Employment Tax and by the growing severity of corporation tax, as well as by the tightening of hire purchase terms.
However, in many branches of the retail trade turnover expanded
under the influence of the buying spree, and the result was that
profits on balance were for many companies actually higher than
for the previous year.

DEPARTMENTAL STORES

In his annual statement (*The Times*, July 26) for *House of Fraser
Limited*, which among its interests controls Harrods and the John
Barker group, SIR HUGH FRASER reported a record group turnover, exceeding £100m. for the first time. Moreover, as a result of
better merchandising and more economical administration, the
rate of profitability was slightly higher than in recent years. As to
the outlook, he made these remarks:

> "The current year has made a good start. Turnover shows a
> satisfactory improvement, and we have meantime been success-
> ful in containing the increase in costs to a level which leaves our
> profit margin unimpaired. To do this in the face of such diffi-
> culties as the increase in Selective Employment Tax and the
> increase in the financial burden of carrying stocks inflated by
> additional purchase tax, makes increasing demands on the
> merchandising skills of our management."

Besides its footwear, manufacturing and retail, and its jewelry
and silverware interests, *Sears Holdings Limited* owns the departmental stores businesses of the Selfridges and Lewis's groups, to
say nothing of other important commercial and industrial subsidiaries. In his annual review (*The Times*, June 6) MR. CHARLES
CLORE announced that total sales were £251m., of which exports
accounted for £30m. Every section of the group, he added, secured
an increase in trading profits during 1967. He expected that retail
trade would be maintained, and said the group was ready to take
advantage of any expansion of trade as the economy of the country
improved.

SIR BERNARD MILLER reported that sales of the *John Lewis
Partnership* rose by £8·6m. to £77·6m. Of this, his statement (*The
Times*, May 24) showed that £61·3m. came from department
stores, &c., £13·5m. from supermarkets, and £2·8m. from whole-

sale and manufacturing, &c. He went on to make this forecast of the current year's trading:

"Sales for the first twelve weeks of 1968/69 were up by 23 per cent. We must reckon however that much of this additional trade anticipated expenditure that would otherwise have been made in the remainder of this trading year. Nevertheless we expect to make some increase in turnover in the department stores in the remainder of the first half of the trading year and to do at least level sales in the second half. So far as the Waitrose supermarkets are concerned we feel that there is unlikely to be any material slowing down in the rate of growth."

The increase in sales of *United Drapery Stores Limited* during the first half-year was insufficient to offset additional operating expenses, including S.E.T., so that the profit for that period was lower, MR. J. A. SAMPSON reported in his annual statement (*The Times*, July 10). But he noted that a marked improvement occurred in the second half of the year, with the result that the profit for the complete period of 12 months was slightly higher than for the previous year. He made these remarks on the current year's trading:

"The current year has moved off to a most encouraging start. The volume of pre-Budget buying was abnormally high, especially in consumer durables, the main impact of the exceptional demand being felt in our Department Stores. Sales and profits generally have since continued at a higher level than the corresponding period last year. Prospects for the rest of our trading year depend to some extent on the effect of the Government's economic policy. Nevertheless, having regard to the buoyancy of this year's sales performance to date, progress should be made in turnover and profits."

A. W. Gamage Limited was another store company whose sales declined during the first six months but improved sufficiently in the second half of the year to convert the deficit into an increase for the whole period. MR. OLIVER FROST placed this fact on record in his annual review (*The Times*, May 10). He also reported the board's decision to open a branch at Romford, Essex; the new store of about 60,000 sq. ft. would be in a shopping precinct in the centre of the town, and its opening was planned for the early spring of 1970.

MR. W. GARFIELD WESTON'S statement indicated that *Fortnum & Mason Limited* (June 25) also had a disappointing first half-year, but the buying spree before Christmas (which continued through and beyond the end of the financial year) lifted turnover above that for the preceding year. He also gave these details of the board's development policy:

"We have continued our policy of progressive improvement to the store during the past year. The renovation and overhaul of the second customer lift was duly completed and the engineers recently finished work on the third and final customer lift. The complete re-carpeting of the First Floor was put in hand towards the end of January this year and completed with the minimum of inconvenience to our customers. Air conditioning was installed in the Soda Fountain Restaurant which has added to the comfort of our patrons. Similar equipment has been installed in the Gift Department on the Lower Ground Floor and will shortly be put into service. The Patio Bar was further enlarged taking in the area vacated by the Travel Bureau and the kitchen facilities have been improved enabling a more comprehensive menu to be introduced. Plans have been made for the refurbishing of the Toy Department and the Children's Department on the Second Floor and the Cigar and Cigarette Department on the Ground Floor to be carried out this year."

For *Chiesmans Limited* (May 31) the late MR. C. S. CHIESMAN was pleased to record a return to increased annual profits—a record of 11 years' continued increase in profits marred only by the previous year's loss at Leonards (Rochester) Limited, which the board had decided to place in voluntary liquidation. The parent company had been granted an off licence for the Lewisham store. He added that after many teething troubles, the computer delivered some 12 months previously was now paying its way and must result in increased profitability and efficiency.

After announcing higher sales and profits for *Frederick Lawrence Limited* (June 11), SIR FREDERICK LAWRENCE stated that they had had a full year's benefit from the extensions to the Bristol showrooms, and that the public response had been excellent, as he had expected, since the showrooms provided the largest and most comprehensive furniture display in the West of England.

MR. J. A. H. NORMAN in his statement (*The Times*, April 11) for *Owen Owen Limited* declared that there had been a marked improvement in the operating efficiency of the Owen Owen (Stores) group, and he specially commended the performance in Coventry, Southampton and Chester. While contracts for capital expenditure already entered into for 1968 amounted to £165,000, mainly for completion and fixturing of the Doncaster branch, the directors had authorized additional expenditure of £950,000, which covered certain costs at the Burlington (Canada) shopping centre, as well as the complete equipment for the store in the Bootle Strand shopping centre and the Wolverhampton branch.

A moderate reduction in profits of *Combined English Stores Group Limited* (September 4) was more than accounted for, declared MR. JACK RUBIN, by the loss of £174,000 (including terminal losses of approximately £90,000) in the B. B. Evans

London Store Group. The pruning and reorganization of this group was now well advanced.

After a record year for turnover and profits, MR. CYRIL CANTOR mentioned that the results of *Cantors Limited* (November 5) for the current year so far showed an increase over the preceding year, but added that in considering the future the new restrictions on the hire purchase of furniture must be taken into account. The dividend of 10 per cent for the year was at the same rate as for the previous year, but was payable on the capital increased by the free scrip issue of one for four made during the year. However, the total distribution was still within the Government's policy "as the managing directors and their wives had waived the necessary proportion of the final dividend."

On October 10, 1967, stated MR. F. L. CHAPLIN, a new phase of the operations of *F. W. Woolworth and Co. Limited* (March 8) began with the opening of the first Woolco department store at Oadby, on the A.6 motorway, three miles from the centre of Leicester. He continued:

> "The range of merchandise, comparable to that carried by a conventional department store, is displayed on the air-conditioned ground floor area of 91,000 square feet. Free parking space for 800 cars is provided. The store is organized as a mass display central checkout unit and incorporates the most up-to-date developments in retailing. Various forms of credit facilities are offered and a Woolco Credit Card reduces formalities to a minimum. A first-class restaurant service is available, and when customers have finished shopping they can take their purchases through the checkouts in the light-weight trolley baskets provided and transfer them to their cars in the pick-up area in front of the store. The build-up in regular credit customers proves that this out-of-town shopping meets a need stemming from the severe traffic congestion in town centres."

CHAIN STORES

Operating costs of the Woolworth group as a whole in 1967, Mr. Chaplin asserted, exceeded those of 1966 by over £2m., the greater part of which related to Selective Employment Tax, though the increase in local rates was also a material amount. The board's policy had been to minimize price increases arising from the higher cost of goods and to reduce prices wherever possible. The combined effect of these factors, he declared, had reduced profit margins in a year when, over the country as a whole, there had not been a normal rate of sales expansion. The results had also been affected by delayed deliveries of goods through industrial disputes at the docks and on the railways, which had caused a loss of sales both at home and overseas and had involved additional transport costs.

Sales and profits of *Marks and Spencer Limited* had reached new records, stated MR. J. EDWARD SIEFF in his annual review (*The Times*, June 6), and the year's results showed once again the effectiveness of the M. & S. system of retailing. With a belief in private enterprise, he claimed, "it was possible for the company to satisfy its customers, benefit its suppliers, look after its staff and make adequate profit for its shareholders." He also made these remarks on store development:

"Within the last three years selling space in stores had been extended by 600,000 sq. ft. The Company now had nearly 4,000,000 sq. ft. Thirty stores had been enlarged; two new ones opened in Belfast and Solihull. The policy of enlarging existing stores would continue. New stores were planned for the peripheral districts of major cities and new towns. Stores enlarged had been modernized to provide high standards for customers and staff, and had contributed to the increases in turnover and profits."

After a somewhat disappointing first half-year, according to SIR MARK TURNER's survey (*The Times*, May 31), a sales increase of 11·6 per cent was achieved in the second half by *British Home Stores Limited*.

"Autumn sales were a little below our expectations," he continued, "and bad weather in the early part of December meant that the Christmas trade was late in starting. But we began to do excellent figures a fortnight prior to Christmas, and this very good trend was maintained into the New Year and continues to the present time. During this period we do not believe that devaluation played an important part in the trend of sales, but consider that the very good results achieved in the last quarter were largely attributable to more dynamic merchandising techniques and the running of a number of very successful promotions in the stores."

Retail business of *Boots Pure Drug Company Limited* (July 11) was slow in the first quarter, stated MR. W. R. NORMAN, but sales quickened in the second and third quarters, and in November were being influenced by devaluation and the approach of Christmas. He went on:

"Sales over the Christmas period were excellent and brought an increase of $7\frac{1}{2}$ per cent with more than £1m. going into our tills on each of four days. In the New Year we benefited to the full from the increased spending in the period leading up to the Budget. Our policy was still to emphasize value at Boots and this we did by holding the prices of all goods of our own manufacture and those that carry the Boots brand name, in all covering some 4,000 items. Then when Purchase Tax was increased

by the Budget we announced that prices would not be increased until after Easter. The outcome of all these events was a sales increase for the final quarter of 12½ per cent.

"Dispensing, which we have always regarded as the cornerstone of our service to the community, increased substantially. At times during the winter dispensing was exceptionally heavy and at the height of the influenza epidemic we dispensed more than a million prescriptions in a single week."

Although sales of *Timothy Whites & Taylors Limited* (May 2) were larger on the year, MR. G. I. RUSHTON had to report a moderate decrease in profits because competition from a variety of sources was keener and in order to meet it profit margins had to be reduced. Another reason for the decrease in profit margins, he added, was that there were further reductions in "on cost" in connection with goods used in the dispensing of prescriptions under the National Health Serivce.

MULTIPLE AND SUPERMARKETS

For *Tesco Stores (Holdings) Limited* SIR JACK COHEN declared in his annual report (*The Times*, July 26) that the board's aim was to bring genuine "one-stop" shopping to every major town in the country to make shopping speedier, more comfortable, more convenient and more exciting. Sales in the food division had reached new high levels, and during the year the emphasis on the fresh food departments had been increased. And with the Home 'N' Wear division now firmly established, he added, "we feel we shall be able to extend our range to include every commodity that the housewife should need."

Twelve new branches were opened by *Pricerite Limited* in 1967, and all these stores were making satisfactory progress, MR. GEOFFREY KAYE revealed in his statement (*The Times*, June 7), adding that during 1968 it was hoped to open a minimum of 20 new stores.

Turnover in the retail shops of *Allied Suppliers Limited* (June 7) on a comparable basis increased moderately over 1966, MR. MALCOLM E. COOPER showed, but with severe competition and mounting expenses profit margins were under pressure. He also made this complaint about heavier expenses "which continue to be imposed upon us":

"I would like to refer briefly to these mounting expenses, some of which appear to arise from deliberate discrimination against the retail trade. In 1967 the iniquitous Selective Employment Tax cost the retail companies in the Group £970,000 and the withdrawal of Investment Allowances adversely affected our profits to the extent of £250,000. The continued refusal of successive Governments to bring commercial buildings into line

DD　　　　　　　　　　409

with industrial buildings in the matter of depreciation allowances for taxation purposes constitutes a grave injustice to the distributive trades. It seems to me that there is a lack of understanding by Government of the role of the retailer. An efficient retailer is an essential to obtain the full benefit of increased productivity of the manufacturer."

An increase in trading profits of *International Stores Limited* (September 25), more than accounted for by the improvement in the second half of the year, was partly attributed by MR. FRANK E. HAWKINS to the high proportion of the company's branches which sold wines, spirits and beer. He stated:

> "One of the main factors which contributed to the improvement in the results of the second half of the year was that our turnover during this period was more buoyant than in the first half—we enjoyed a very good pre-Christmas trade and derived considerable benefits from the large number of our branches which are licensed for the sale of wines, spirits and beer. Out of a total of 1103 branches within the group, 243 have licences, 34 having been obtained in the past year. We shall continue to apply for further licences in respect of our branches where we consider this added facility will bring benefit to our customers and to our trade."

Among the highlights of MR. E. K. ROBARTS's statement (*The Times*, July 10) for *Express Dairy Company Limited* was that expansion of the dairy products business on a nation-wide scale, channelling of resources into more profitable directions and greater efficiency had led to a record turnover and higher profits, in spite of a slight decline in per capita milk sales. However, devaluation of the £ and the 1968 Budget measures would bring extra costs in the current year, which the company would endeavour to contain.

In his additional remarks (*The Times*, July 3) at the annual meeting of *Redman Limited* MR. A. H. REDMAN said that in addition to the new supermarket in York, two further supermarkets were then being planned to open later in the year. He added that these three units would increase the company's total retail sales areas by about 12 per cent to 112,000 sq. ft. Further supermarket developments in addition to the eight already trading or planned were being investigated.

For *Cullen's Stores Limited* MR. J. D. CULLEN remarked in the course of his annual statement (*The Times*, August 30) that the alterations to some shops, and the method of trading in them, had been carefully adjudged in each particular case. He explained:

> "In some, we have provided an area of self-selection, a few we have converted to self-service, others we have made into cheap cash wine shops, and one we have even established as a

410

washeteria. We have plans for the conversion of many others but on the other hand this does not mean that the traditional Cullen's shop will disappear because, in our opinion, they are second to none in certain areas."

Commenting on the ever increasing expenses of *Milletts Stores (1928) Limited*, of which he mentioned particularly the "iniquitous" Selective Employment Tax and the "fantastic" overall increase in rates and rents, MR. A. D. MILLETT in his annual report (*The Times*, August 26) remarked:

"The days when England was a nation of shopkeepers have been replaced when the shopkeepers of England are a nation of tax gatherers."

Under the Government squeeze retail trade up to August, 1967, was exceedingly difficult for the group of stores controlled by *Maple & Company Limited* (May 24), but in that month, stated MR. GERALD R. HOLMAN, the President, some relaxations were announced in hire purchase controls, and immediately trade began to pick up—so much so that the group recovered the loss of turnover and ended the year with an important increase. The net profit increased by an apparent 39 per cent, but adjusting for the extra gross profit which had been thrown up a year earlier by a change of accounting system, the real increase in the year under review was in reality much greater proportionately.

During the year under review, stated MR. BARRY BAKER in his annual review (*The Times*, February 1), *Bakers Household Stores (Leeds) Limited* opened two new branches, which were trading satisfactorily; a new branch had been acquired in Bradford, and negotiations for two further branches were almost complete. He also announced an important policy change by the board: it had been decided to reduce the company's furniture interests in order to concentrate on the expansion of its self-service business.

The chairman's statement (*The Times*, November 13) for *New Day Holdings Limited* referred to a special surplus of £61,479 (after tax) which had arisen from the disposal of the remaining rental contracts in the furniture division, from the closing down of the associated television service company and from a re-appraisal of the provision for outstanding debts.

The pilot scheme run by *Hardy & Co. (Furnishers) Limited* for computerization of hire purchase accounts had proved successful and was now being expanded, declared DR. M. LEONARD SLOTOVER in his annual survey (*The Times*, July 23). He also revealed that additional ranges of furniture would be introduced shortly and these should add to the profitability of the company.

Highlights from MR. DAVID HYMAN's statement (*The Times*, August 9) for *Henderson-Kenton (Holdings) Limited* were that sales and profits alike reached new records, four new branches were

411

opened and the Ilford branch would transfer soon to a much-improved trading position, and premises had been acquired in six other centres.

In his survey (*The Times*, May 10) for *Times Furnishing-Willerby Tailoring Limited* MR. LAWRENCE JACOBS showed that a higher trading profit in tailoring was not quite sufficient to offset a smaller one in furnishing, which showed a modest increase in turnover, but not enough to compensate for higher expenses. Thanks to heavy pre-Budget buying, however, turnover in furnishing in the first quarter of 1968 was considerably higher than that of the corresponding quarter of 1967, and turnover in tailoring also increased.

An eventful year for *Montague Burton Limited* (February 20) was notable not only for record group trading and profit figures in spite of adverse economic conditions, but also for the proposed merger with United Drapery Stores, which, however, was turned down by the Board of Trade after reference to the Monopolies Commission which recommended against it. MR. LIONEL JACOBSON put these facts on record, and cited the Commission's report as showing that the men's tailoring division had reached a high level of efficiency. He also referred to the stores division in the following terms:

"The Stores Division, to which all the 'Shop within Shop' sales . . . refer, increased their turnover from £7,253,000 to £7,452,000. The Board of Directors is concerned to improve the profitability of this division, and in particular that of Peter Robinson, which has suffered most from the impact of S.E.T. The rebuilding of the main Peter Robinson Store in Oxford Circus was completed during the year. After the anticipated removal at Easter 1968 of obstructions to vehicular and pedestrian traffic occasioned by the reconstruction of the Oxford Circus Underground Station, it is hoped that the Peter Robinson Store will reap the full benefits of this rebuilding on what is an outstanding trading position."

Reporting a decrease in trading profit of *Bradleys (Chester) Limited* in his statement (*The Times*, May 31) MR. H. D. LEETE referred to the outlook in these terms:

"Your Directors are expressing their confidence in the future by recommending that the dividend be maintained at 17 per cent for the year. Sales during the year under review are slightly down as compared with those of the previous year and it is imperative, if the company is to show the growth in profits which has been absent for many years that sales are promoted with even more vigour and effectiveness than that shown heretofore. Your directors are now pursuing a multiple trading policy which they are confident will show growth and I am very happy

412

to tell you that the sales figures for the first 11 weeks of this year are up by over 9 per cent."

Though the dividend of *Evans (Outsizes) Limited* (June 12) was maintained pre-tax profits declined moderately, and MR. J. GREEN in his annual review made this plea for a respite from Government measures affecting retail traders:

"The much publicised post-devaluation boom in consumer durables did not help our section of the trade and I do not need to elaborate on the heavy additional expenses with which we have been faced once again. It is to be hoped that the Government will now allow the retail trade some respite from their attentions and permit us to proceed with our function, which is to supply the public with the finest selection of merchandise at the lowest possible prices."

That *Polly Peck (Holdings) Limited* (July 2) had a total of 48 Boutiques which formed a very important part of the group's trading was among the statements made by MR. RAYMOND ZELKER; the directors were adding to these as the opportunity arose.

The efforts of the board of *A. Lewis and Co. (Westminster) Limited* (January 4) to improve the profitability of the business are illustrated in the following quotation from MR. P. L. FLEMING'S statement:

"During the year we closed 13 branches which were not doing well and replaced them with 11 more newspaper shops, which show a better margin of profit. We therefore finished with 277 branches against 279 and with a stock reduced by about £130,000. Further improvements in the cash position have taken place since the end of the year.

"All this suggests that our efforts to get into more profitable lines of merchandise have begun to pay off, thanks to the strenuous efforts of our management and staff. But a good deal, under the conditions prevailing for our type of business, remains to be done. The abolition of Resale Price Maintenance on confectionery does not appear to have had any effect on our turnover but the same may not be true of tobacco and cigarettes; and there are other pressures to which the small shop is more vulnerable than the supermarket.

"We therefore decided to take a critical look at ourselves through the eyes of a firm of Management Consultants. Some of their proposals will take time to implement, but there are others which we are already putting into practice and which seem likely to result in appreciably higher profits during the current year."

Record turnover and profit were announced by MR. O. C. STRICKLAND for *Forbuoys Limited* in his review (*The Times*,

413

December 6). The improved figures, he declared, had resulted mainly from increased sales both at previously existing branches and at new branches either purchased or opened. At the year end the company was trading from 234 branches, a net increase of 19.

Sales of *Allied Retail Trades (London) Limited* were a record, 12 per cent up at over £10m., and the pre-tax profit was also the highest yet attained. With 13 more retail branches in the year, the company now had 245 branches. These facts were mentioned in the annual report, summarized in *The Times* of February 1.

While the profit of *Maynards Limited* (November 21) from the business as a whole was a record, MR. J. DOUGLAS MAYNARD hinted that the same was not true for the net earnings of the retail shops, as will be seen from the following excerpt:

"Although retail sales were again a record, the increase was not sufficient to cover the continually rising costs of this operation. Nevertheless having regard to the curb on consumer spending and increased operational expenses, the results achieved do credit to the quality of our merchandise and the standard of service that we endeavour to provide in our shops."

In view of the improvement in turnover of *Halfords Limited* (May 3) MR. F. D. RUSHBROOKE was disappointed to have to report a reduction in profit, for which he blamed Selective Employment Tax and other increases in expenses beyond the board's control. "There has," he maintained, "been a continual pressure to reduce the margins between cost and retail prices, and there seems no sign of any relaxation of this pressure."

While *Plushpile (Wharf Mill) Limited* (July 29) benefited from the pre-Budget buying spree, stated MR. A. F. LOMAS, the effect of this was not wholly reflected in profit figures, as a fair proportion of the trade was on credit, and it had therefore been necessary to make increased reserves for deferred profit.

In the short term the effect of the 1968 Budget on the business of *Johnson Group Cleaners Limited* (May 16), MR. T. B. S. JOHNSON asserted, was to make it more difficult to maintain even their much reduced profits. However, the added burdens would not alter the purpose or form of the directors' reorganization plans, though the necessary action now became more urgent and more drastic. He gave this information about the trading policy of the board:

"Ever since 1960, when we opened our first successful group of Shop Units, we have pursued the policy of changing our public appeal to one of On the Spot Dry Cleaning gradually moving away from the traditional cleaning service. Our efforts so far have resulted in the Group, as at 31st December last, operating 340 Shop Units (now increased to 450 with the acquisition of Martins). Further important developments have been and are taking place which will benefit our future prospects."

Although retail trade improved sharply at the end of the year, and business in the retail shops of *Lotus Limited* was buoyant at the start of 1968, MR. JAMES BOSTOCK in his speech (*The Times*, April 5) said that 1967 was by no means an easy year for shoe manufacturers. However, with the help of substantial exports to the Soviet Union and other countries and a vigorous home sales policy the company kept its factories operating at capacity throughout the year, with consequent benefit to profits. As to the current year, they had obtained another large Russian order, and the home trade orders were "highly satisfactory."

For *Harry H. Payne Limited* MR. J. E. Payne stated in his survey (*The Times*, July 23) that the decline in shoe repairs continued, but substantial growth in footwear retailing had been achieved. The policy of closing less profitable outlets and exploiting better trading positions was being pursued. The directors expected a substantial increase in profits this year.

MR EDWARD RAYNE in his review (*The Times*, June 12) for *H. & M. Rayne Limited* declared that further benefits were expected from the rationalization of the retail organization in the United Kingdom; the Bruton Street shop had been successfully integrated with Bond Street. The turnover and profit of the American subsidiary, Rayne-Delman Shoes Inc., were the best ever recorded, and a policy of extending retail outlets in the United States was being pursued. The shoe department of Gidding-Jenny in Cincinatti, owned by Genesco Inc., had been taken over from June 1, 1968.

For *Morris and Blakey Wall Papers Limited* (July 3) MR. ARNOLD G. MORRIS declared it to be the intention of the group to concentrate mainly on the retailing of wallpaper, paint and other decorating lines "with a particular eye on the ever-growing do-it-yourself market."

In the current year *Dixons Photographic Limited*, according to the chairman's statement, expected to open its 100th branch.

The new branches of *Moss Bros. Limited* (August 5) in the City, Croydon and Kingston-upon-Thames had started very well and should contribute to the company's profitability in the current year. MR. HARRY MOSS gave this information.

The policy of *Windsors* (*Sporting Investments*) *Limited* (October 24) of acquiring additional betting shops and improving existing ones had been continued, stated MR. JIM WINDSOR, and had resulted in the group having in operation at that time 137 offices, compared with 109 at the date of the balance-sheet and 97 at that time in 1967.

JEWELLERS

The main reason for the marked improvement in the results of *H. Samuel Limited*, declared MR. GILBERT H. EDGAR in his annual

review (*The Times*, August 16), was that, while sales were merely maintained during the first and second quarters of the year, an improvement occurred in the third quarter, and the effect of devaluation and the approach of Christmas created a more than usually buoyant last quarter.

After reporting a substantial increase in the group profit before taxation of *Asprey & Company Limited*, MR. P. R. ASPREY in his statement (*The Times*, December 17) made this comment on the company's interior decoration department:

> "Our Interior Decoration Department has had a very successful year and is responsible for the major part of direct exports. Antique silver and period furniture form a very important part of our trade and the collection of Georgian jewellery and objets d'art is always of interest. During the last few years, the antique side of the business has been extended to include a collection of carriage clocks, bracket clocks and long case clocks."

MAIL ORDER

SIR ISAAC WOLFSON'S report for the *Great Universal Stores Limited* showed that the company operated over 2,500 mail order and retail establishments in the United Kingdom and overseas. The directors' desire to expand had again shown results, and "we intend to continue our policy of expansion by acquisition whenever suitable opportunities occur." The company's trading activities were being supplemented by the development of the investment, property and finance division, which was now an important section of the business.

A record turnover, bringing a record profit, was reported by MR. R. H. OWTHWAITE for *Grattan Warehouses Limited* (May 17). He referred to the company's purchasing policy in these terms:

> "In these days of 'Back Britain' and 'Buy British', it is the policy of your company to do so when and wherever possible. Whilst raw materials must come from abroad, foreign-made goods are bought by us only when it is necessary to have them in order to make or complete a suitable range. However, our buyers do go abroad to seek out new ideas and fashions and trends, bringing them back and arranging for their manufacture in this country. We work very closely and, I am glad to say, amicably with our suppliers and we are appreciative of the enthusiastic support they give us in solving the variety of stocking problems which invariably crop up in this type of trading. It is not often that we feel some of them might be a little more helpful."

Substantially increased turnover and profits for *Empire Stores (Bradford) Limited* during the year under review, MR. JOSEPH

FATTORINI showed in his annual statement (*The Times*, May 22), had been followed by an increase of more than 23 per cent in sales for the first two months of the new year. He added:

"It is the opinion of your Managing Director that some part of this increase must obviously have arisen from pre-Budget buying although probably the percentage of increase which we received from the buying spree is much less than the increases reported by the larger departmental stores and luxury shops. I therefore believe that when I come to give my half year statement for 1968 I shall be able to confirm the progress we are making, although probably at a slightly lower rate than for the first two months."

The mail order division of *S. & U. Stores Limited* continued to develop rapidly, turnover having increased substantially, necessitating some 40,000 sq. ft. of additional floorspace. This was stated by MR. C. COOMBS in his survey (*The Times*, September 6), and he declared that "we can now compete with anyone in the mail order world." Incidentally, he mentioned that the company had acquired for cash from the Tesco Group their 18 credit stores trading as Harrow Stores."

The mail order project of *Montague Burton Limited* (February 20) reached its turnover target for the year, stated MR. LIONEL JACOBSON, who added:

"Burton-by-Post increased its turnover figures by 41 per cent to reach £2,987,000. Reducing costs as new computer applications streamline the administration will further lower the break-even level of this division, but it is necessary to comment that in the current financial year sales have so far been disappointing. It may be that in present economic conditions the Group must be satisfied with slower progress in the immediate future."

Turnover of *John Myers and Company Limited* (November 8) reached £14,866,424, having grown from a figure of some £50,000 in the year 1957, a record of which MR. STANLEY G. COOKE declared "we can all be justly proud."

MR. F. N. HEARNSHAW regretted that the mail order division of *Henry Wigfall and Son Limited* (October 7) was still operating at a considerable loss. However, he stated that they were now co-operating with another mail order company in an experimental venture centred on joint merchandising and joint catalogue production in an attempt to reduce costs substantially.

OVERSEAS

Commenting on the progress of the department stores owned by the *Hudson's Bay Company* (May 24), the Governor, LORD AMORY, included these three paragraphs in his statement:

"Retail sales followed the same pattern as the previous year—slightly more buoyant in the first half, then levelling off to give an increase for the year on a comparable basis of 7.3 per cent. A reduction in housing completions in 1967 led to a decline in demand on the part of consumers for furniture and major appliances.

"For the second year running wage rates increased at a faster pace than sales. The resulting pressure on profit margins was partially, but not entirely, offset by higher productivity and very close control over expenses.

"Sales of Morgan's, Montreal, grew at a faster rate than the average for the company. This was mainly due to the public appreciation of improved and expanded facilities. The immensely successful World's Fair, Expo '67, was also a factor, though to a lesser extent than expected. The final stages in the modernization of the Morgan Main Store will be taking place during 1968 and 1969, when resetting of the two most important fashion floors, postponed until after Expo, will be carried out."

Sales of *Harrods (Buenos Aires) Limited* (January 25), according to MR. O. R. GUARD, increased by just under 10 per cent. However, in spite of the strictest control of expense, there was a reduction in the rate of operating profit. He continued:

"The largest factor in our costs, payroll and the accompanying social law provisions, was affected by two general increases during the year. We also had to meet increases in tariffs for public services and naturally other types of expense reflect the general upward trend.

"Devaluation of the peso has a twofold effect on the accounts. First the sterling value of the peso profits is calculated at a lower rate and then we have to provide for the fall in sterling value of our net current assets in Argentina."

Notwithstanding intense competition, sales for 1968 of *O. K. Bazaars* (1929) *Limited* (November 8), the annual report of the directors showed, amounted to R157m., exceeding the 1967 figure by some R15m. The report included the following paragraph on development:

"Since the date of the last report new branches were opened at Bonaero Park (East Rand), Walmer (Port Elizabeth), Southdale (Johannesburg) and a furniture and household appliance store in Pretoria. Building control had an inhibiting effect on our expansion programme, but now that there has been a partial relaxation our store development division is busily engaged in planning expansion for the next five years and the modernization and extension of existing branches."

The first supermarket built for *Felix Potin* (Paris, November 22)

418

on the sites already acquired would be opened to the public in the spring of 1969, and would raise the number of establishments in service to 13. This was stated in the report submitted to the annual general meeting under the chairmanship of COMTE G. CAHEN D'ANVERS.

While the turnover of department stores grew at a rate of only 3.3 per cent and that of mail order houses in general at some 15 per cent, *La Redoute* (July 11), it was claimed at the annual meeting with M. HENRI POLLET in the chair, "has consolidated its position as the leading French mail order company."

THE TEXTILE TRADES

THE general picture of the textile trades was one of continuing difficulties and fierce competition until well on into 1967, followed by a good recovery, only partly the result of devaluation, gathering strength as 1968 progressed. SIR FRANK KEARTON told shareholders of *Courtaulds Limited* (July 10) that the 1967–68 financial year was a time of tough competitive conditions both at home and overseas. He continued:

> "We did get some benefit in the Accounts from devaluation, since the sterling equivalent of profits made by our overseas companies was increased. But in our all-important home market, devaluation brought us increased costs, and less than half of these were recovered by increased prices. We kept our post devaluation prices down to give greater opportunities for import saving. This will benefit the balance of payments, and in both the medium and longer term will benefit the company."

On the other hand, he mentioned a few "sharpish blows," including a prolonged strike at the Alabama factory, a fierce attack on the United Kingdom market for acrylic fibres launched by a large American company and which hit Courtaulds' profits on Courtelle very hard, and the virtual collapse of the French textile market in those areas where the group operated in the second half of 1967. However, he added:

> "But on the bright side we had, working in our favour, the steady integration of the various parts of what is now a very substantial and broadly based textile company. We had the progressive improvement in the management skills of the company. We had some real success in our efforts to get more efficient production, and more market orientated in our outlook. And we did have, particularly after devaluation, better demand at home, and better opportunities for our export effort."

At that time Sir Frank felt justified in taking a soberly optimistic view of prospects, and if there were no major economic setbacks in the United Kingdom or the world at large he thought they could look forward to a full year's profit for 1968–69 of over £40m. The group's target profit figure for the early seventies was £50m.

For *Viyella International Limited* (June 12), too, MR. JOE HYMAN stated, there was every reason to expect that 1968 would produce a substantial increase in trading profits and a higher net profit after tax (and special items). Already, for the first quarter,

he was able to state that profits were 30 per cent in excess of 1967 and sales approximately 10 per cent in advance.

"The improved profitability," he declared, "can be attributed to the relief from the heavy costs of rationalization, the continuing elimination of business with unsatisfactory margins and their substitution by our new products and constantly increasing use of synthetics and improved productivity. The last three years have been devoted to integrating and streamlining acquisitions totalling £40m. comprising over 200 manufacturing units, investments and businesses in Great Britain and overseas, and this has involved millions of pounds in direct costs and loss of profits. We are now in the fourth year of our 5 year programme and have no reason to believe that we shall not be able to repeat the organic growth of profitability which took place in the original founder companies."

MR. CHARLES RIDING of *Carrington and Dewhurst Group Limited* (July 18) was in the happy position of being able to report that his expectation of a year previously that 1966–67 would prove to be low-water mark had been justified by the event. The tide, he declared, did indeed turn during 1967–68. The decisive change did not occur until the second half of the year, but sales then rose significantly as the stores and shops, against a background of strong consumer demand, started re-stocking. Without including Jersey-Kapwood Limited (acquired in January, 1968), turnover rose in the year to March 30, 1968, by 12 per cent and pre-tax profits by 19½ per cent. He went on to state:

"The steeper rise in the profits curve as compared with the sales curve owes a lot to the trading climate, which as the year progressed, gave us the benefits of scale and the full utilization of plant. In large measure, however, it reflects the advantages we won for ourselves by realigning and concentrating production. We took the opportunity presented by the phase of dull trading to accelerate factory reorganization, even though this meant absorbing the costs of physical dislocation at a time when profits were especially hard to earn. As soon as the tide turned we started to reap our reward in much enhanced productivity."

Among the points made by MR. I. E. KORNBERG in his statement for *Lister & Co. Limited* (December 17) was that the simulation mink fabric marketed under the brand name Minquilla was enjoying a highly successful market acceptance and had been particularly outstanding in its export achievements. Another was that the maximum development in production and sales of the company's Crimplene products had enabled it to maintain a leading position in this important field, embracing both yarns and knitted fabric. And a third was that the household textile products which the company offered had been extended by the introduction of acrylic

furnishing velvets in modern colours. "These fabrics," he asserted, "are easily cleaned, moth proofed, and extremely hard wearing."

The next quotation comes from MR. A. J. PENTECOST's survey for *Hicking Pentecost & Co. Limited* (October 3):

> "The Knitwear Division of the company has made steady progress throughout the year but certain sections of the Dyeing and Finishing Division had a period of extremely difficult trading up to the beginning of January. However, since then there has been a substantial improvement in this section. The general policy of diversification to reduce the company's dependence on commission dyeing and finishing has continued and now approximately one third of the capital employed by the company is invested in the Knitwear Division. I am glad to be able to report that our Long Eaton factory which was closed approximately a year ago has now been sold at a satisfactory price and we are taking further steps to concentrate our dyeing and finishing production units."

In his annual statement (*The Times*, December 10) for the *Lancashire and Yorkshire Tulketh Group Limited* MR. S. M. ROSS announced that the directors proposed shortening the name of the company to Tulketh Group Limited.

The new extensions at the Barnstaple works of *John C. Small and Tidmas Limited* (April 30) had been completed, stated MR. L. E. FOLMAN, and the warp knitting plant was now installed in one of the air-conditioned bays so that the machines worked in ideal conditions of temperature and humidity. He added that the dyeing and finishing plant, which was started in 1966, was now fully operative, and the company was beginning to expand this department. One-third of the company's turnover was sold overseas.

Among the subsidiaries of *Parker-Knoll Limited* (October 31) which were mentioned by MR. C. H. JOURDAN were Parker-Knoll Textiles and C. P. & J. Baker, both textile designers and convertors; they had done very well indeed by increasing their turnover and profit, their increases in exports being especially notable.

A new design of textile machinery was the subject of the following quotation, which comes from the review by LORD ECCLES for *West Cumberland Silk Mills Limited* (September 24):

> "After satisfactory tests we have ordered a number of looms of a new design which are capable of substantially increasing our production. The increase will be modest this financial year but large in the following year."

Seafield Gentex Limited (Youghal, County Cork, December 19), MR. RICHARD D. LORD said, had started production of fitted warp knitted nylon sheets, production of which was now an urgent priority, both for home and export sales; and the company was then setting up a completely new and separate unit in Athlone for

the purpose. The current rate of production he expected to be more than doubled by early 1969.

MR. CHARLES W. BELL informed members of *Coats Patons Limited* through his annual statement (*The Times*, May 30) that both turnover and profits of J. & P. Coats Limited increased during the year, though trading had been variable as between markets, the United Kingdom market being affected by the overall depression in the textile industry. He also stated:

> "On the manufacturing side the steady grind for improved efficiency continues. Activity in manufacturing re-organization was again geographically fairly widespread. This involved continuing modernization not only for cost efficiency and for quality improvement, but also to an increasing degree for additional capacity to meet demand for synthetic threads. These threads in their differing constructions account each succeeding year for a greater proportion of our total business."

For *John Bright and Brothers Limited* (July 3), MR. I. M. L. D. FORDE remarked that there had been a pronounced trend towards the use of man-made fibres in industrial fabrics, particularly belting duck, and the board had decided to order a fabric dipping and heat setting machine designed to the company's own special requirements. He also made these comments on the outlook:

> "It was disappointing that the improvement in profits for last year should have been more than swallowed up by the increase in Corporation Tax, but the outlook for the current year gives reason for some optimism. With business generally likely to remain buoyant and export prospects favourable, the demand for our chief products should remain firm, and our investment in increased capacity and new machinery should be reflected in greater profitability."

WOOL, WORSTED AND MOHAIR

The year 1967 was a bad year for the worsted spinning industry, declared MR. CHARLES W. BELL, dealing with the trading experience of Patons & Baldwins Limited in the course of his statement (*The Times*, May 30) for *Coats Patons Limited*. In hand-knittings, where he claimed Patons were brand leaders, deliveries of yarn by the trade as a whole were at the lowest level of the past 10 years. On the industrial side, he declared, the knitwear industry also suffered from the economic climate, and total deliveries of worsted spun yarns were the lowest since 1952. In these conditions the need to keep spindles running engendered severe price cutting with consequent erosion of profit margins. Conditions were not much better in the export markets, especially Europe. He continued:

"For the reasons outlined above, the profits from Patons' U.K. operations have fallen well below those for 1966. An improvement is expected in 1968, for which year figures so far available are more encouraging. There are substantial industrial yarn contracts on hand, and deliveries of hand-knittings for the first quarter are well up on the levels of a year ago. Exports should receive some stimulus at least in the short term from devaluation of sterling, and there are already some signs of an improvement."

Commenting on the recent "storms and vicissitudes" of the industry, MR. M. W. SHELTON of *West Riding Worsted and Woollen Mills Limited* (February 21) declared that a particularly serious feature was the almost complete cessation of the import market in America for high-grade and expensive cloths. However, this market had improved recently, and generally he had felt more optimistic in the autumn of 1967 than a year previously. Since then had come devaluation, which should help some export markets, particularly for the company's specialized weaving section, though this was accompanied by other measures which would have the opposite effect. In his additional remarks at the meeting Mr. Shelton said:

"As the Budget statement by the Chancellor will not be available until March 19, forecasting is largely crystal gazing. However, I am pleased to inform you that for the first four months of the current financial year internal figures show our profits some 30 per cent up on the same period last year and providing the Government does not upset too greatly our trading this trend could be expected to continue."

The board of *Yorkshire Fine Woollen Spinners Limited* (May 10). MR. K. R. DYSON announced, had exercised their option to take the remainder of the share capital of the Greenwood Group, the profits of which had been well maintained. He stated:

"The Knitted Jersey Fabric trade has developed considerably during the period under review and in order to meet the growing demands, the capacity of the group is being increased by extension of buildings and installation of new machinery which should be in operation in the latter part of the year."

One of the difficulties which beset the industry in 1967 was shown by MR. W. R. B. FOSTER in his statement (*The Times*, May 29) for *John Foster & Son Limited* to have been the fall in wool prices which continued during the year and even became worse in the early autumn until the devaluation of sterling and of the New Zealand pound in November had the effect of raising some wool prices in the United Kingdom. He stated:

"While botany wool in this country finished the year at levels

higher than those ruling on January 1, the prices of lower qualities were between 10 per cent and 20 per cent less. In these circumstances, once again it was inevitable that we should incur losses on stock in the course of the year. Business in the early months of 1967 was very slow. However, in the second half of the year the tempo improved and turnover was better than in the second half of 1966."

After asserting that 1967–68 was "probably the most difficult of the post-war period," MR. MAURICE OSTRER went on to state that the last few months had witnessed a considerable revival of trade for *Illingworth, Morris & Company Limited* (October 10). Order books, both for home and for export, were very much healthier than at the same time in 1967, and full-time production with some overtime was now operative throughout the group. Addressing the meeting, he said that the improvement in profits to which he had referred in his statement—according to which trading results before finance charges for the first four months of the new financial year were running approximately 60 per cent above the comparative results of the past year—was continuing.

In his valedictory statement as chairman of *Bulmer & Lumb (Holdings) Limited* (August 29) SIR IAN STEWART-RICHARDSON also reported improvement in demand in the last three months of the financial year, as shown by the following extract:

"The last three months of the financial year covered by the accounts saw an improvement in demand for both our oil and dry spun yarns, coloured tops and commission dyeing. The current order book is very satisfactory as to volume, and profit margins have improved. The group's products and therefore its markets are broadly based, upon wool, mohair, the branded polyesters and acrylics. Whilst direct yarn exports are only 7 per cent of yarn production, approximately two-thirds of the group's turnover goes indirectly or directly to markets overseas. If the progress evidenced over the last few months can be maintained, the current year will show an improvement in trading results compared with the year under review."

Although short-time working had continued throughout the year for *C. F. Taylor & Co. Limited* (March 27), MR. J. C. INGRAM was able to record recently a marked improvement in demand for the company's products: the order book currently stood 40 per cent higher than a year previously; production was increasing; and trading was now profitable.

The export trade of *H. F. Hartley Limited* (June 11) was steadily expanding, declared the late MR. H. F. HARTLEY, and the company's new ranges, composed of wool and a variety of man-made fibres, had been well received in many overseas markets.

Robert Clough (Keighley) Holdings Limited (March 21), with a

pre-tax profit more than halved, had not escaped the impact of the exceptionally difficult conditions throughout the wool textile industry, declared MR. HAROLD P. CLOUGH. However, he concluded his annual review with these remarks:

"The situation of our spinning subsidiaries has greatly improved in the last few months and since September demand for our yarns has grown and production as a result was increased. Taking a view of present market conditions and, subject to unforeseen adverse factors, I can anticipate an improved financial result in October, 1968."

Corporation tax had been increased, the export rebate had been cancelled, and now the Selective Employment Tax had been increased by 50 per cent, reported MR. E. KEIGHLEY of *Keith & Henderson Limited* (October 21), and he added:

"In what way this senseless legislation is going to help Exporters in our type of business can only be left to your imagination. Certainly, had it not been for these changes, there would have been no question of any reduction in the rate of our dividend this year."

MAN-MADE FIBRES

The share of *Courtaulds Limited* (July 10) in the man-made fibres business in the United Kingdom, which SIR FRANK KEARTON a year previously had mentioned was rather more than 60 per cent by weight, he now remarked was still at about the same figure, more than 60 per cent by weight "in today's stiffly competitive conditions."

During the first half of the year the world-wide recession in the textile industry, together with the period of severe restraint called for by the Government, affected the growth of the sales by *British Enkalon Limited* (May 17), and, according to COLONEL F. T. DAVIES, prices were also depressed. It was only in the latter half of the year that more normal trading conditions were resumed. Nevertheless, trading profit was higher by 12 per cent; and he was happy to state that in the first months of 1968 volumes and profits were "considerably up" on the corresponding period of 1967. "We anticipate," he declared, "a good demand for synthetic fibres during this year, provided there is no substantial change in the trading conditions in the textile industry in this country."

Widening of the range of activity in synthetics of *Klinger Manufacturing Company Limited* was alluded to by MR. W. G. CASTELL in the following extract from his statement (*The Times*, June 17):

"Much work and investment has taken place, especially in the past two years, in preparing opportunities which will enable us

426

to operate a wider range of activity within the synthetic yarn business. By these means it is hoped to establish ourselves on a broader basis for the future. We have had to act in extreme discomfort at times during the recent difficult period, but it is felt that the company's staff and workpeople have benefited from this experience, which will stand us in good stead in future years."

Group profits of *William Baird & Company Limited* in 1968. MR. S. A. FIELD forecast in his annual survey (*The Times*, May 16) should show a material improvement, and it was reasonable to expect this trend to continue into 1969–70. In the company's textile interests, an improving return was expected in 1968 and 1969 on the £4½m. investment in the synthetic fibre grouping. He also asserted that vigorous marketing, world-wide, should also improve the return on the £3·9m. then employed on the natural fibre side.

Reiterating his confidence in the long-term growth of demand for synthetic fibres and in the increasing use of textured yarns at home and overseas in his statement (*The Times*, September 30), MR. A. LIKIERMAN declared that *Qualitex Yarns Limited* was well placed to meet the challenge of any change that took place in trading conditions.

The investment programme of *Snia Viscosa* (Milan, April 30) continued in the year under review, according to the annual report submitted by ING. LUIGI CROSTI. In Sardinia two plants were brought into service for the production of lilion and velicren; the expansion of plants in Naples and Cesano Maderno resulted in increased production of wistel; contracts were concluded in Spain and Argentina for plants producing polyamidic fibres and in Bulgaria for the production of methane carbon disulphide.

HOSIERY, KNITWEAR, CLOTHING

Group profits of *Contour Hosiery Limited* (February 21), though substantially higher, were rather less than might have been expected since the increase, MR. R. A. PALFREYMAN explained, had come from the subsidiaries acquired during the year, the combined earnings of the "old" group being more or less the same as for the previous year. A decline in profits of the main stocking manufacturing subsidiary was caused by the fact that it had no Christmas trade within the year. "This simply means," he added, "that some of the profits which would normally have been reflected in 1967 will fall into the current year."

The chairman of the *Nottingham Manufacturing Company Limited* in his statement (*The Times*, April 25) covering the nine months to December 30, 1967, pointed out that home and overseas sales as well as the profit for the shorter period exceeded those for the whole of the preceding 12 months.

Among the points made by the chairman of *Sunbeam Wolsey Limited* (Millfield, Cork, April 17) was the following:

"The Sales of Nylons and Half-hose of Sunbeam Limited showed little change from last year, but there was a considerable increase in our Knitwear Sales. In spite of keen competition, the Sales of both Nylons and Knitwear for the Export Market show a substantial improvement, which we feel must indicate that our merchandise meets international standards. To satisfy this increased demand for our Knitwear, we have ordered two additional machines."

The knitwear division of *Klinger Manufacturing Company Limited*, MR. W. G. CASTELL declared in his statement (*The Times*, June 17), was operating at a high level of activity, although competition remained extremely keen. This department, he asserted, was most useful to the group's operations as a whole, "in evaluating latest developments in the yarn field associated with new machinery developments."

An increase in profit of *Joseph Dawson* (*Holdings*) *Limited* was explained by MR. ALAN SMITH in his statement (*The Times*, April 3) as primarily following the acquisition of Pringle of Scotland Limited during 1967. With other acquisitions he mentioned the group now included "three fine knitwear companies in the high class end of the industry."

The buoyant optimism expressed by MR. BEN RAVEN of *Raybeck Manufacturing Company Limited* (December 9) a year previously had been borne out by the increase in profits now reported. Turnover with home retail groups, stores and shops was at a very satisfactory level; the new rainwear division had already exceeded expectations. Mail order sales continued upward.

Wilson, Smith & Sutcliffe Limited (October 25), the chairman announced, had made contractual arrangements with Marks and Spencer—one of the group's major customers—for production of approximately £600,000 during 1969, with prospects of even higher production in 1970.

Points made by MRS. J. A. KAYE in her statement (*The Times*, March 13) for *W. L. Pawson & Son Limited* included the fact that the company was opening up an export market. She forecast a steady increase in overseas sales, and stated that agents had been appointed in several Scandinavian, African and North American areas.

The outstanding success of Simpson (Piccadilly) Limited, claimed DR. S. L. SIMPSON of *S. Simpson Limited* (December 17), was closely linked with the increasing popularity of Daks clothes for men and women, especially with overseas visitors.

The demand for the specialized garments and textiles imported by *I. D. & S. Rivlin Holdings Limited* (July 24) from Hongkong and other parts of the Far East continued to expand. A new company trading under the old-established name of Star Frocks (Regent Street) Limited had been incorporated to develop the company's

428

Hongkong fashion trade. These statements were made by MR. I. D. RIVLIN.

The next quotation comes from the annual report (*The Times* June 18) of *Pasolds Limited*:

"In 1967 Pasolds took the economic squeeze and the need for restraint seriously, deferred the leap forward for which they were geared and concentrated instead on good housekeeping— reducing stock levels, cutting back production and slowing down expansion. This resulted in higher profits and increased liquidity. Contrary to expectation, the public continued to spend. Sterling devaluation caused a buying spree leaving he company short of merchandise. Only eighteen months ago Pasolds congratulated themselves on having overcome delivery problems, but now, because of our over-correction, another £500,000 worth of Ladybird garments are needed to fill open orders.

"Expansion is again going ahead rapidly and in spite of the temporary slow-down Pasolds are still ahead of programme with their 7-year plan designed to increase production to £25m. Exports remain a challenge. Group total in 1967 was £1,320,150, supplied to 81 different markets."

Lower trading profits of the clothing division caused a decrease in the pre-tax profit of *Steinberg & Sons* (*London & South Wales*) *Limited* (October 10), MR. JACK STEINBERG stated. In the current year, he added, home sales were being maintained, while export sales were higher, with particular advances in North America.

Sales of umbrellas by *Lawtex Limited*, which declined sharply after April because of high retail stocks and unusually large imports from low labour cost countries, showed a return to the normal trading pattern after the beginning of the new financial year, it appeared from MR. H. E. SALOMON's report (*The Times*, December 13). Demand for polyester cotton work clothing had improved satisfactorily over the past few months, he added, and production facilities had been increased.

Referring to the expansion policy of the board of *J. Collett Limited* (July 16), MR. MAURICE HARRIS said:

"In the current year, no effort is being spared to expand wherever possible in the Home and Export fields by catering for a wider section of the public than heretofore. We are gradually building up a strong enough team to deal with the growth of the business which, we believe, lies ahead of us, and, by wise planning, I am hoping we shall secure an even larger share of the market by offering a greater variety of merchandise. We are now actively engaged in the search for the possible acquisition of established businesses."

CARPETS

Having alluded to the company's record sales and profits for the year under review, MR. KENNETH M. HAMILTON gave this account of the course of carpet sales in his statement for *Blackwood Morton & Sons Limited* (October 28):

"In the twelve months to June 30, 1968, sales of carpets in the U.K. were running at record levels. In the first six months to the end of December, there was an improvement after the relaxation of the severe restrictions introduced in July 1966. The early months of 1968 saw massive pre-Budget consumer spending and carpet sales benefited along with sales of other consumer goods. Somewhat surprisingly, demand did not fall off as expected after the Budget. The very substantial improvement in profits was of course partly due to the higher volume of sales but, in addition, increased production resulted in a lowering of the rate of overheads. Advantage was also taken of lower levels of raw material prices in the early part of the year and as a result we had, for most of the year, the benefit of stocks of raw materials purchased at pre-devaluation prices."

Among the highlights of COLONEL H. H. AYKROYD's statement (*The Times*, July 23) for *T. F. Firth & Sons Limited* were that while group turnover increased by $11\frac{1}{2}$ per cent pre-tax profits jumped by 38 per cent; that both home and export sales were a record; and that besides an increase in productive capacity through rationalization and capital expenditure of £570,000, new plant was to be installed for tufted carpet production.

After reporting a highly successful year for *A. F. Stoddard & Company Limited* (September 26), SIR ROBERT A. MACLEAN mentioned a new product of which he evidently has high hopes; the relevant passage in his statement follows:

"During the year the first Telsax product was successfully introduced to the trade. This is a plain carpet of fine texture similar to Plain Wilton, although made by a much faster process. Thus the price of Telsax is relatively low and as its appearance and wearing qualities are exceptionally good, it is equally suitable for both domestic and contract use. Sales of this quality are steadily increasing at home and overseas. It is something of a technical breakthrough and experience to date suggests that Telsax type carpets have a promising future."

In his annual review (*The Times*, April 9) for *Lancaster Carpets & Engineering Limited* MR. E. S. HAMMETT claimed that Lancaster Carpets Limited maintained its commanding position as one of the largest manufacturers of tufted carpet in the United Kingdom. He continued:

430

"Sales by quantity were 14·6 per cent and by value 11·0 per cent of total U.K. sales. Whilst maintaining a large volume of sales in the lower price range of the market, Lancaster Carpets Ltd. has during the last two years adopted a trading up policy and is now successfully competing with the higher priced ranges of traditional Axminster and Wilton carpets. The growth of sales of tufted carpet has been extremely rapid and in 1967 accounted for 51 per cent by quantity of total carpet sales in the U.K."

In his annual review for *The Guthrie Corporation Limited* (July 31) SIR ERIC GRIFFITH-JONES made the following reference to the new London carpet centre:

"The new Kingsmead Carpet Centre opposite Oxford Circus Underground Station, which we established a year ago and in which leading manufacturers of fabrics, paints, wallpapers and laminates participated to provide "mix and match" facilities, has proved extremely popular with the trade and with the public. In its first year the Centre received more than 15,000 visitors."

The pre-tax profit of *James Templeton & Company Limited* (March 25), stated SIR WILLIAM GORELL BARNES, had increased by 59 per cent in spite of lower sales, and he explained that the improved margin was the result of discontinuance of unprofitable lines, the benefits then beginning to flow from production re-organization and from cost reduction measures, and lower raw material costs.

The year's trading of *Hugh Mackay and Company Limited* was referred to in these terms by MR. JOHN MACKAY in the course of his report (*The Times*, February 15):

"In the unstable climate of this financial year, it is perhaps not surprising that turnover suffered as a result of the general lack of commercial confidence and of domestic purchasing power. Fortunately raw material costs eased and these tended to counter-balance other increased costs; in consequence, the trading profit shows only a marginal decrease from that of the previous year."

The chairman of *Thomas Bond Worth and Sons Limited* (September 19) remarked that they had continued to press on with the planned expansion programme, and group sales in the first quarter of the new financial year (exclusive of sales of Rivington Carpets Limited) were up by 25½ per cent on the same period of the past year. The company, he claimed, probably now had the largest and most versatile complement of tufting and ancillary machinery in the country.

MR. H. W. HARTLEY in his annual statement (*The Times*, July 24) for *Shaw Carpet Company Limited* informed shareholders that

431

during 1967 the company's sales represented 14 per cent of total United Kingdom tufted carpet manufacturers' sales and 9 per cent of their export sales.

HARD FIBRES

Included in Sir William Walker's address for *Jute Industries (Holdings) Limited* (February 12) was the following appraisal of the jute markets following devaluation:

"With the devaluation of sterling, the raw jute situation was radically changed. Neither Pakistan nor Thailand devalued and, in consequence, at the end of November, we had to raise our prices of yarn and cloth, but those of our customers covered by forward contracts will not feel the effects of this until the spring or early summer of this year: on the other hand, in so far as your Group is concerned, these forward contracts are covered by raw jute acquired at pre-devaluation prices.

"Imported manufactured goods have also risen in price. Users within the United Kingdom will, therefore, find themselves paying more for jute goods as a result of devaluation at a time when users in other countries, which did not devalue, are probably paying slightly less in terms of their own currencies."

TIMBER

ALTHOUGH costs continued to rise—and in this respect devaluation was not a helpful factor—the majority of timber importers and merchants reporting in 1968 showed a good recovery in earnings from the setback of the preceding year, when the first impact of the Government's restrictive measures of July, 1966, had been inevitably to reduce demand for timber.

That the structure of the timber trade was changing radically was the opinion of MR. ANTHONY BENN of *Price & Pierce* (*Holding Company*) *Limited*, but in his statement (*The Times*, April 19) he expressed the view that timber agents still had an important part to play since they were able to provide many essential services. It was because they firmly believed this that Price & Pierce, Hallam Ramsay, and Foy Morgan had consolidated their interests, had widened their range of activities, and were in a position to continue to offer significant service in the future. Meanwhile, during the year under review trading continued successful in timber and sheet material, but woodpulp presented various problems. With a temporary over-supply of woodpulp in some areas, and no lasting solution then in sight for world dollar problems, Mr. Benn thought the current year was bound to have its uncertainties. However, the board looked forward to the maintenance of earnings for Ordinary shareholders at the 1967 level, bearing in mind the general prospects for both timber and woodpulp.

MR. ROBERT LAW of *J. Gliksten & Son Limited* was another chairman who in his statement (*The Times*, December 31) took a distinctly hopeful view of the outlook, though, as will be seen from the following quotation, subject to one important qualification:

> "As far as can be seen at the present time turnover and profitability are in excess of the position at this time last year. Our budgets indicate that we should achieve profits in excess of those for 1967/68 and with full and healthy order books it would seem that our expectations should be achieved. However, I must sound a note of caution by repeating that our business relies to a great extent on the building and consuming industries and these are always affected by the fiscal policies of the present Government so that any extension of the 'credit squeeze' cannot fail to affect us in some way."

Earlier in his review Mr. Law remarked that during the year there had been a considerable increase in the interest taken by investors in the prospects of the timber trade. This interest, he added, had been heightened by a number of mergers and take-overs

which, coupled with other developments in the structure of the trade—particularly in importation and distribution of raw materials—was bound to have far-reaching effects on the future of those engaged in the timber trade. Much had already been said about the necessity for larger units and the likely composition of those units. The board, he asserted, intended to continue to prove that their slogan "Gliksten—Foremost in Timber" was the right one for the group. Incidentally, he had already mentioned the acquisition by the company of the old-established Manchester timber distributors, John Ashworth & Co. (Timber) Limited, and of Graham & Wylie Limited, an old-established and profitable company dealing in sheet materials and specialized products in Scotland. These acquisitions, he stated, opened up areas for sales and distribution new to the group.

Three main reasons for the excellent results of *Bambergers Limited*—the profit before tax was a record and the dividend was restored to its 1965–66 level—were enumerated by MR. CECIL D. WOODBURN-BAMBERGER in his annual review (*The Times*, September 3), as follows:

"Firstly, the comparison with the previous year is so pronounced because in that year we suffered the disastrous fire which caused some disruption to our business. Secondly, devaluation of sterling had the effect of up-valuing our forward book. Thirdly, the cargo discharge and handling at our Port on the River Crouch are much more efficient."

He added that softwood consumption had been very good for the first half of the calendar year, but thought the trade's forward commitments were now on the high side. While hardwood trading had increased, the whole tempo was much less than a few years ago. He also mentioned that the company had acquired the entire share capital of John Webb (Swindon) Limited, a timber and builders' merchant with annual sales of over £1m.

In a generally difficult year the devaluation of the pound caused considerable confusion for a time, said MR. J. C. C. SIM, and resulted in a number of contracts held by *Churchill & Sim Limited* (June 12) having to be either cancelled or renegotiated. However, the level of consumption of timber and sheet materials was surprisingly well maintained, and the year's results were not very different from those of the preceding year. Business for the current year having begun exceptionally well, he forecast "considerably improved" results for the year as a whole.

Considerably higher profits and an increased dividend by *Montague L. Meyer Limited* (September 10) were announced by MR. JOHN M. MEYER, who went on to state:

"The main reasons for the increase in profits are some improvement in softwood margins, the continued development of

434

our trading in plywood and board materials, and the total elimination of losses in Blacknell Buildings Ltd. Last year I informed you that this company had earned a profit in the first three months. There was further expansion during the year and a modest return on the capital employed was achieved. The business is now consolidated on a firm basis and in the future I anticipate further progress. On the debit side, Blacknell Buildings (Scandinavia) A/S continued to make losses and we decided therefore to put it into liquidation. Full provision for the losses and the cost of liquidation has been made in the year's trading results."

He went on to declare that, after three disappointing years, profit margins on softwood had risen during the current year "to a figure more in line with what we have been accustomed to in the past."

After reporting record net profits before tax for *Parker Timber Group Limited* (October 15) in the past year, MR. K. WHITBY disclosed that turnover and profits for the first five months of the current year were "very encouraging," and, subject to unforeseen events, the board looked forward to another successful year. While the past year had been mainly one of consolidation of existing activities, the directors were now actively pursuing further outlets to increase the company's national coverage. In fact, at the annual meeting Mr. Whitby announced that negotiations were then taking place for the acquisition of further companies, and it was hoped to make a Press announcement in the very near future.

The plywood and board department of *James Latham Limited* had again increased both turnover and profits, MR. BRYAN LATHAM reported in his annual review (*The Times*, October 4), and the directors, with further expansion in view, were planning increased storage and handling facilities. The hardwood department and mill had enlarged turnover and profits alike, in spite of a national fall in hardwood consumption influenced by Government restrictions. Likewise, building restrictions had failed to prevent the softwood department from largely increasing both turnover and profts. He referred in the following terms to the experience of the Nigerian Hardwood Co., a subsidiary of James Latham:

"Owing to the disturbances in Nigeria the company's operations had to be closed down from August to November. The result has been that the Nigerian Hardwood Co. Ltd. was unable to make its usual satisfactory contribution to the Group profits. However the sawmill was reopened and forest operations resumed by the end of the year. The Board report that production and sales are now normal and that the company is now working at a profitable level."

Trading conditions during 1967–68 were more favourable for

435

Horsley Smith Group Limited (September 6) than in any year since 1965, stated MR. MARK HORSLEY, and a substantial advance in profits showed that past expenditure on development had not been in vain. The development programme embarked upon in the year under review was of unprecedented extent for the group, with a total cost exceeding £2m., including the acquisition of the Sherry companies. Incidentally, the company was one of those whose dividends were held down by Treasury restriction below the level which the directors wished to declare, and Mr. Horsley declared that it was the board's intention to raise the dividend to 17½ per cent as soon as the Government restriction had been lifted.

Another company with timber interests which was in the same boat as regards dividends was *Southerns Limited*, whose annual report (*The Times*, October 8) also recorded that since the end of the financial year the William Evans group of companies had joined the Southerns group. Among the benefits expected to accrue in the future from this union were better use of stocks and improved productivity of plant. Together the two groups now operated over 50 branches or subsidiary companies throughout Britain, and further expansion would follow by the acquisition of other well-established timber merchants.

Dealing with the timber interests of *Powell Duffryn Limited* in his annual survey SIR HENRY WILSON SMITH stated (September 5):

"The reorganization which began last year has continued and, in spite of problems in national trading conditions, profits improved so that the group timber division almost maintained its percentage of the much higher group profit. Everything is being done to keep stocks at reasonable levels, to operate with maximum efficiency and to keep abreast of trade developments."

A considerable addition to the profits of *Olympia Limited* (September 30) was made by the timber importers and builders' merchants enterprise during the year, declared MR. H. OLIVER-KING; this interest of the company was developing and further expansion was expected.

In his statement for *Liden* (*Holdings*) *Limited* (March 11) MR. D. OLLMAN made the following reference to the subsidiary Arnhem Timber Company Limited:

"Profits have again reached a satisfactory level and the acquisition of the wharf at West Ferry Road, London, E.14, has been fully justified. Both automated Band Saws and all kilns are fully occupied. A further battery of kilns is now nearing completion. We have recently purchased the wharf adjoining, and the large warehouse facilities are proving to be of immense value."

Both the timber and the chemical divisions of *Burt, Boulton and Haywood Limited* had shown a substantial improvement, according

436

to the annual report (*The Times*, September 20), with consequent record profits. The softwood business had benefited from increased sales and improved margins, and sales of plywood and wallboard were up both in volume and profitability.

A record year was also announced by MR. MAXWELL STERN for *Hahn Holdings Limited* in his statement (*The Times*, April 25). It was then too early to forecast what the full effects of the Budget measures would be, but the group had had a very profitable first quarter's trading, with sales on the timber side 15 per cent higher in the first three months of 1968.

The next quotation comes from the statement of the chairman of *Aaronson Bros. Limited* (March 19):

> "Notwithstanding short-term trading fluctuations, the results for the full year reflect the steady and consistent demand for the parent company's products. On the production side we are now beginning to reap the benefits of installing the latest and most efficient type of machinery available. Returns for the first few months of the current year indicate a substantial improvement over the same period last year. Nevertheless your board must emphasize how difficult it is at present to make firm forecasts for the future, but provided reasonable trading conditions continue, we consider that 1967/68 should be a successful year for the group."

As timber was used exclusively in the manufacture of doors by *Leaderflush (Doors) Limited*, MR. R. A. BROUGH declared in his survey (*The Times*, March 29), the impact of devaluation on material costs was heavy; it was indeed fortunate, he added, that benefits accruing from the company's production developments to a large extent had offset these additional material costs and improved the company's relative competitive position.

Dealing with activities other than the match industry, the annual report (*The Times*, August 15) of *British Match Corporation Limited* contained the following two paragraphs:

> "In the U.K. Airscrew-Weyroc increased its sales of wood chipboard by 18%, in spite of heavy competition from imports. The Thetford plant was reopened in February, 1968, and all five plants are expected to be in full production during the current year.
>
> "In Canada, the profits of Eddy Match were severely affected by a strike which shut down the logging, sawmilling and plywood division for over seven months."

The statement for 1967 of the directors of *Millars' Timber and Trading Company Limited* (July 11) revealed that in Australia the labour content in production costs was contained, and a new mill which recently began operating would also help to keep down costs. Turnover and profits improved not only as a result of large

437

orders for the iron ore railways but also from expansion in the company's business as general timber and builders' merchants. They also had this to say of the outlook for the future:

"The values of the company's fixed assets are constantly under review and the board have concluded that some of them should be sold and the proceeds reinvested in other parts of the business. The board are confident that the redeployment of this money will continue to increase profits, especially from Australia."

In his review (*The Times*, December 18) for *Tanganyika Concessions Limited* LORD COLYTON declared that trading conditions for Commonwealth Timber Industries Limited became even more difficult during the year, and increased competition was encountered in selling timber and the range of Novobord products. In addition severe drought conditions resulted in a reduced citrus crop and the consequent cancellation of orders for citrus boxes which had been placed with the Port Elizabeth wirebound box factory. He continued:

"Large scale investigations are being undertaken with a view to seeking improvements in the company's timber and board manufacturing activities. Meanwhile constant research is being undertaken to develop new methods and products in order to increase profitability.

"The plans for the improvement of sawmilling activities to which I referred last year were completed by the merging of the company's Witelsbos mill with the Kleinbos mill of Boskor Sawmills (Cape) Limited, a subsidiary of Bonus Investment Corporation of South Africa, an important South African financial group. As consideration for the assets transferred the company was allotted 49 per cent of the equity of Boskor for R 359,560 and credited with a long term loan of R 491,440."

Production in the timber division of *Assam Trading (Holdings) Limited* (February 23), stated SIR OWAIN T. JENKINS, continued to be restricted up to the end of the year by the shortage of glue; and, with the selling prices of tea chests already low, the rise in costs resulting from this limitation led to a trading loss for the year. Supplies of glue became normal again from August, 1967, and he declared that since then production levels had been brought up to the break-even figure, while since November the division had shown a small profit. In his additional remarks at the meeting he said that production and sales of all products in the timber division continued to show "a useful upward trend," but warned that margins on sales of tea chests would have to be raised further.

In the annual review of *Inchape & Co. Limited* (October 30) it was stated that the group's timber interests were part of the Borneo Berhad companies, and of these Austral Sendirian Berhad

traded profitably, but was still suffering from a reduction in the permissible extraction rate. While the associated company, The Borneo Timber Company Sendirian Berhad also operated profitably, results were lower than expected because of the effects of sterling devaluation on sales towards the end of the year in the United Kingdom market and of increased competition in the United States. The review also gave these details of new timber acquisitions:

"During the year the group acquired, with Malaysian and local partners, an interest in an extensive swamp forest of nearly half a million acres in West Kalimantan, Indonesia, containing excellent stands of timber, and extraction is expected to begin towards the end of the current year. An interest in a smaller forest in West Malaysia was also acquired."

That 1967 was a record year for *Sabah Timber Company Limited* (July 18) in almost every respect was asserted by Mr. H. G. C. Townsend. Log production exceeded 17m. cubic feet, 20 per cent above the previous record (in 1966). The group profit before taxation increased by more than 50 per cent, and the figure after tax by 40 per cent. He continued:

"These improved results, even after meeting heavier royalties and taxation, are attributable to increased production, good log prices and a high level of efficiency in the forest, coupled with a larger contribution from our U.K. subsidiaries."

Log sales to date in 1968, he added, had been satisfactory, but some markets were less firm and buyers were becoming increasingly selective. Current world liquidity problems, he suggested, made it more difficult than usual to judge the future trend of prices.

In his report (*The Times,* May 10) to shareholders in *MacMillan Bloedel Limited* Mr. J. V. Clyne claimed that the group was Canada's largest forest products company, besides which it had manufacturing operations in Britain, Canada and the United States and had interests in paper mills in Holland and Spain. He also made this statement (in part) about operations in the United Kingdom:

"New distribution methods in the United Kingdom, based on the delivery of packaged lumber by bulk carriers from British Columbia, came into effect with the opening of central distribution terminals at Newport and Tilbury in July. Ports of discharge in Britain have been reduced to two, and deep draft facilities have enabled the use of larger ships."

The following paragraph dealing with the forestry interests of *Stora Kopparberg* (Falun, Sweden, May 10) is extracted from the annual report of the directors:

439

"Timber deliveries were larger than scheduled, both from the company's forests and from outside suppliers. Stocks of wood built up accordingly. Advantageous weather and thorough rationalization measures made possible a reduction in the number of people employed in logging and hauling as well as a lowering of costs per wood unit."

The forest department of *Oy Tampella AB*. (Tampere, Finland, April 19), it was stated in the board's report, provided the different production units with a total of 1,404,600 cubic metres of piled wood and 5,682,900 cubic feet of saw logs. Also included in the report was the following paragraph:

"To cut supply costs for raw timber, four companies—A. Ahlström Oy, Oy Kaukas AB, Kymmene AB and the Company —agreed to contribute one-quarter each towards a new joint company named Tehdaspuu Oy. This company is to supply the four contracting parties, rationally and economically, with the quantities of timber required for their forest products factories. Logging in the companies' own forests is, however, subject to special stipulations. The first supply season of the new organization will begin on July 1, 1968."

440

TRANSPORT

THE *Transport Holding Company* in an earlier report had described itself as a new experiment in the constitution and working of public ownership, and it had earned about £74m. in five years. However, the annual report (*The Times*, June 13) for 1967 pointed out that under the Transport Bill then before Parliament the company would probably cease to exist in its present form at the end of 1968, though the report expressed the hope that the philosophies and policies which had inspired the holding company would be inherited by its successor bodies.

In a hard year the profit for 1967 before tax of *Transport Development Group Limited* fell only a little short of the record figure for 1966, the directors stated in their annual report (*The Times*, March 27) among the highlights of which were the statements that container delivery services were extended; that trade flourished at the inland stores, but the port warehouses were affected by strikes in London and Liverpool; that in almost every one of its activities the group was providing vital services to export trade; and that 1968 had started well with profits running ahead of those for the corresponding period of 1967.

THE TRANSPORT BILL

The subject of paramount interest to companies which engaged substantially in road haulage, whether as public carriers or to shift their own goods, was the controversial Transport Bill, and numerous chairmen gave utterance to the concern with which that legislation was regarded. Few company chiefs had any quarrel with those provisions of the Bill which were designed to foster road safety, although these were bound to raise costs, but most of them severely criticized the so-called quantity licence. Typical of their views was the following excerpt from MR. R. R. KEARSLEY'S statement (*The Times*, June 20) for *United Carriers Limited*:

"For a considerable time our engineers have been implementing programmes to maintain our fleet to the standards necessary to qualify for the quality licence, and we have no misgivings on this point. The problems arising from the shorter working hours for drivers will, we anticipate, be eliminated by the re-organization which will follow the completion of several new depots later this year.

"The most controversial section of the Bill is, of course, the quantity licence. This means that a vehicle of over 16 tons gross weight cannot operate over routes exceeding 100 miles without a

special permit. That permit will only be granted if a Freightliner service is not operating on that particular route. Fortunately the majority of our vehicles do not come into this category, and are therefore not affected. We do, however, have a limited number of routes exceeding 100 miles on which we operate heavier vehicles, and where a Freightliner service is in existence on such routes it is our intention to use it. We have already started a pilot scheme on our Leeds to Glasgow trunk route which has been operating for several months and has proved to be an economic proposition."

The directors of *United Transport Company Limited* (August 29), declared MR. D. LLOYD JONES, agreed with much of the criticism of the Bill and had fully supported the Road Haulage Association in the considered objections that they had raised against it and in the sensible amendments which they had sought to bring about in its provisions. However, the Bill did contain, he asserted, much that was good, and the directors were largely in agreement with its provisions for improving road safety and the general standard of the industry.

The seriousness with which *English China Clays Limited* (March 18) regarded the Bill is clear from the extended reference made by LORD ABERCONWAY to the subject in his statement part of which is reproduced below:

"It is the Government's expressed intention to divert traffic from roads to rail, and it appears that one method of accomplishing this is to impose upon road transport grievously heavy taxes in addition to the heavy tax burden which it already bears.

"The Government's proposals affect adversely all the operating divisions of the company, as the bulk of their products are carried by road and, in the majority of cases, there is absolutely no alternative. The fact is, however, that wherever we can satisfactorily, and more cheaply, use rail transport we do, as of course does every other sensible commercial enterprise in the country. Indeed, our daily liner trains to the Potteries are evidence of this.

"No distinction whatsoever is to be made between the transport of those goods where consignment by rail is feasible and that where it is not. The latter includes all those cases where the source or the destination is not rail-connected and where, therefore, at least one transhipment will in future be necessary. In the case of your company's products, the increase in taxes on road vehicles will result in the transfer to rail of only a very small tonnage of goods; the remainder must continue to go by road, because it can go no other way, and it will go at a heavily increased cost. The licensing system proposed by the Government is complex and inflexible, and will involve much administrative work by both industry and by licensing authorities which, on

442

grounds of national efficiency and productivity, should be eliminated not augmented. The exercise is thus grossly inflationary and can do nothing to promote the greater competitiveness of our products.

"The solution of the problem lies in the Government recognizing the reasons why the road haulage industry has won traffic from rail; because service, economy, speed, reliability and flexibility are factors which command a ready market. It is emphatically not the answer to compel the customers of the transport industry to forsake road for rail by the pressures of laws and taxes. The road haulage industry is already bearing a vast burden in road and fuel taxes, whereas the railways are not now paying, and nor is it intended that they shall pay, the very heavy fuel tax of 3s. 7d. per gallon suffered by road haulage."

As an example of how essential it was to keep down transport costs for new bricks SIR RONALD STEWART informed members of *London Brick Company Limited* (May 30) that at points over 120 radial miles from the works more than half the ultimate cost of the bricks lay in the expense of their haulage. He continued:

"At the present time we have freedom to send bricks to these distant points either direct by road or rail and, indeed, in the case of facing bricks it is essential, if they are to escape damage in transit, that they are despatched direct by road. I very much hope, therefore, that under the new Government proposals for the transport of freight this freedom will be fully retained. In our case we have worked closely with British Rail in developing the use of 'liner' trains, but it would be quite wrong to infer from this that it would be either practical or economic to send all long distance deliveries by rail. The Government proposals in their present form must increase the distribution cost of bricks and could adversely affect service to the customer."

Asserting that the main effect of the new Transport Bill was to increase costs without the benefit of any additional revenue, MR. A. F. F. YOUNG revealed that the transport directors and executives of *Redland Limited* (September 17) were concentrating on increasing efficiency by introducing mechanical handling of loads and by greater co-ordination of traffic movement through two group clearance houses. By these means it was hoped to offset at least part of the rising costs.

The following uninhibited quotation is from SIR HALFORD REDDISH's statement for *Rugby Portland Cement Company Limited* (May 24):

"Bulk deliveries now account for about 70 per cent of our trade in the home market. These are effected in the main by quite expensive pressurized vehicles. In this country we have a fleet of some 375 lorries, so we are bound to view the additional

costs imposed at the time of the Budget with concern and dismay; and if the Transport Bill reaches the Statute Book in anything like its present form it will mean a further heavy addition to our costs of delivery, and of course to the cost of everything we buy. Transport enters cumulatively into the ultimate price of all manufactured goods. Yet time and again its cost is increased by Government action. *Mit der Dummheit kämpfen Götter selbst vergebens*—with stupidity the gods themselves struggle in vain."

Dealing with the Government's proposals, included in the Transport Bill, for reorganizing road and rail freight traffic, MR. GEOFFREY SALMON asserted that *J. Lyons & Company Limited* (July 16) used rail transport whenever it was found to be more efficient, but the vast bulk of the group's goods was delivered by road. While welcoming some aspects of the Bill—in particular those designed to promote road safety—the board were "seriously worried" about other aspects. He went on to give some details of the company's problems in the transport of perishable foodstuffs, as shown in the next quotation:

"Many of our products are perishable foodstuffs, and in this section of the food industry the means of distribution are as vital as the means of production. In order to ensure that our products reach consumers in proper condition, we have developed a number of specialized road transport fleets which provide an exceptionally prompt and flexible factory-to-depot-to-shop delivery system throughout the country. It is vital, in our view, that businesses should be left free to choose the means of transport best suited to their individual needs. We regard as misconceived a restrictive licensing system for heavy vehicles on journeys of over 100 miles, because it would deny to businesses the right to manage this key area of their own affairs. In planning to divert traffic from road to rail, the Government should recognize the reasons why the railways have lost traffic to road haulage; official effort should be concentrated on rendering rail more efficient and competitive instead of taxing road into a less competitive position and giving rail a right of pre-emption over much traffic which it cannot secure on its merits.

"We are equally concerned at the heavy extra costs which will be imposed on us by the Bill. Our estimate is that its provisions will add at least another £100,000 to the cost pressure upon the Group, and this can only increase the likelihood of yet more food price increases."

Another chairman who protested at the threatened loss of control by the board over the method of transportation of perishable goods in particular was MR. MALCOLM E. COOPER of *Allied Suppliers Limited* (June 7). From an extended but reasoned attack

444

on the Bill there is room here only to reproduce his reference to the increase in the cost of distribution that it will entail:

"Let there be no doubt about it, if the Bill becomes law, distribution costs will be increased. It can be stated with firm assurance that the additional costs arising from the Bill will materially increase the operating costs of our group fleet of vehicles. There is no doubt that it is the public who will have to pay for the increased costs arising and this will be at a time when there is to be restriction on both incomes and spending."

Opposition of a similar kind to the Bill was expressed by MR. FRANK E. HAWKINS of *International Stores Limited* (September 25). He protested especially at clauses "which might deprive a company such as ours of the right to carry its own goods in its own vehicles to its own depots and branches."

The Transport Bill also alarmed *Maynards Limited* (November 21), declared MR. J. DOUGLAS MAYNARD, for these reasons:

"If we should be unable freely to control our transport as between factories, customers, warehouses and shops, the results would be chaotic. At present we operate a closely integrated system of regular deliveries to our branches, and it is important that we plan the arrival of goods on a precise day and often at a precise time. Furthermore, we must be able to handle a considerable quantity of returnable empties and to transfer goods from one branch to another. If this Bill becomes law in its present form, distribution costs will increase steeply and the vicious spiral of rising prices will be sharply accelerated."

Besides the Transport Bill other Government measures which must involve the *Danish Bacon Company Limited* (May 15) (and other concerns) in heavier costs, MR. F. HERBERT declared, included the Budget increases in fuel tax and road fund tax and the higher selective employment tax, in addition to further cost increases to meet the demands of existing and proposed legislation of a technical and administrative nature.

SIR ARCHIBALD FORBES revealed his natural chagrin at the way in which Government measures were threatening to annul the praiseworthy efforts of the board of *Spillers Limited* (June 7) to reduce costs of distribution. He stated (in part):

"Considerable progress has been made in the rationalization of our commercial vehicle fleets and the establishment of new distribution warehouses. . . . These steps have been taken with a view to increasing efficiency and reducing costs, and it is not encouraging to find that recent legislation places an even greater burden on transport. Those sections of the Transport Bill which relate to annual rates of licence duty for commercial vehicles have been included in the recent Budget, and the effect of this

445

has already shown itself in increased operating costs of our own vehicles and also in the rates quoted by outside hauliers and contractors. These costs fall particularly heavily on the distribution of bread."

The board of *The Metal Box Company Limited* (July 25) were anxious to put as much of their traffic on the railways as they could, asserted MR. DAVID DUCAT—provided that the service to customers did not suffer. To Government statements that the Transport Bill would not compel companies to put traffic on rail unless it could be proved that the service would not suffer thereby he made the natural rejoinder that if this was so there was no need whatever for the licensing provisions in the Bill "as we would not choose to use other than the best service available."

An estimate of the cost of the Bill to multiple shops is included in the next quotation, which comes from MR. W. R. NORMAN's survey for *Boots Pure Drug Company Limited* (July 11):

"The Multiple Shops Federation, which represents some 450 multiple retailers operating approximately 40,000 shops with names that are familiar in every High Street, calculate that the Bill will increase the distribution costs of its members by between $6\frac{1}{2}$ per cent and $8\frac{1}{2}$ per cent, while increases in the Budget affecting transport will bring this rise up to between $9\frac{1}{2}$ per cent and $11\frac{1}{2}$ per cent. This addition to cost is bound to come through to customers in higher prices and could amount to between 3d. and $3\frac{1}{2}$d. in the £. Let it be remembered also that this is only one of a dozen measures enacted during the last six months alone to cause higher prices in every shop in this country. In my view the customer will be really appalled at the result when all these measures have worked through into the price of goods and services."

During the year under review the transport division of *Associated Fisheries Limited* (March 19), MR. MICHAEL NOBLE, M.P., revealed, completed a new maintenance and servicing depot at Grimsby. He continued:

"In the present uncertain state of the haulage industry it is clear that only the most efficient fleets can survive and make profits. Your fleets suffered at the beginning of the year from the run down in general business activity, but by hard work managed to turn in satisfactory profits at the year end. In the first quarter of the current year profits have more than regained last year's setback."

Disappointing results of the road transport interests of *Hargreaves Group Limited* (July 9) were attributed by MR. KENNETH HARGREAVES partly to increases in wages and repair costs and to considerable competition. However, the business was being reorganized and he believed it would progress and develop.

446

An excerpt about the road transport holdings of *Coast Lines Limited* (September 26) from the address of SIR ARNET ROBINSON follows:

"Our road transport companies continued to expand, concentrating on business of a specialized nature in accordance with our policy. We were involved in a considerable expenditure both in respect of new vehicles and depot improvements but all of this was judged to be worthwhile and fully justified in terms of return on capital."

In his statement for *United Transport Company Limited* (August 29) MR. D. LLOYD JONES mentioned the serious accident in which a heavy transporter owned by a subsidiary was involved in January when it was hit by an express train while passing over a continental type crossing at Hixon in Staffordshire. He stated:

"The report of a Public Enquiry has only just been issued and is being carefully studied by the Management of the Wynn Group, in whom your Board has complete confidence. I would like to pay tribute, as the report does, to the crew of the Wynn vehicle for their courage in trying to get the enormous vehicle out of the way of the train. At great risk to themselves, they stayed at their posts right up to the moment of impact."

PASSENGER ROAD SERVICES

That the year under review had probably been the most significant in the history of *The British Electric Traction Company* (October 17) since its formation in 1896 was asserted by MR. JOHN SPENCER WILLS. The company had started as pioneers in electrically operated road passenger transport in the United Kingdom, and in 1968 it ceased to be operators of road passenger transport there. He stated:

"On behalf of our Railway partners and ourselves, we continued to operate 12,000 public service vehicles employing approximately 50,000 people and producing an annual gross revenue of nearly £70m. From the proceeds of the sales of our other public utility interests we invested in public services of various kinds, such as laundries, piped radio and television.
"In recent years, the continued growth in the number of private vehicles on the roads resulted in a general decline in the numbers of passengers carried by public transport and this, together with rising costs, has made it increasingly difficult for bus operators to earn satisfactory profits. In my review last year, I referred to the uncertainty which existed about the future of the private enterprise sector of the bus industry in consequence of the Government's plans for reorganizing public transport and

setting up passenger transport authorities in major conurbations outside London.

"It was with these two considerations in mind that your Board, when approached by the Transport Holding Company in November 1967, decided to negotiate the sale of the B.E.T. Group's United Kingdom bus interests, and a basic price of £35m. was agreed for the purchase of our equity interests in the companies."

SIR ROBERT CARY, M.P., devoted a large section of his annual review for *Lancashire United Transport Limited* (May 3) to an examination—it might well be termed a denunciation—of that part of the Transport Bill which provided for fundamental changes in the organization of road passenger transport. He found it regrettable that the "guillotine" which prevented adequate discussion and examination should be applied to such complex legislation.

THE ROADS SITUATION

Writing for shareholders in *Man-Abell Holdings Limited* (July 16), MR. B. S. BARLOW expressed the hope that the Government would see fit to devote as much energy and zeal to the road programme as it did to the recently much publicized Transport Bill. He went on to declare:

"Although strict laws on drinking, vehicle maintenance and the like must reduce accidents, a properly built roadway system shows the most dramatic results of all—the proof of which may be seen by comparing density of traffic to accidents on the actual motorways themselves. As more and more motor vehicles pour on to our roads it is getting harder and harder to provide a 'just adequate' road system."

The road surfacing and civil engineering division of *William Briggs & Sons Limited* (March 28), which had suffered in the preceding year a diminution in the general business available and had therefore been unable to maintain the very high turnover and profit of the year before that, in the past year had produced a record overturn and profit. This was stated by MR. N. W. BRIGGS. The result, he added, came from the efficient handling of a larger number of contracts, perhaps the most interesting of which concerned considerable road works on the Isle of Skye; the group had recently been awarded a second large contract there.

From SIR CHARLES BURMAN'S annual review (*The Times*, May 24) for *Tarmac Limited* the following passage is extracted:

"Tarmac Roadstone Holdings have in the past provided about 70% of the Group's overall profit before tax and their further growth this year may be inhibited by the effect of Government expenditure cuts in road maintenance. However, Government

expenditure on major road schemes is still rising and we can benefit from this, provided we increase our plant mobility in order to exploit the considerable but local fluctuations in demand entailed by the new construction programme. While, therefore, the Roadstone Group should more than hold its own, I am also looking to the Construction Group for an increased contribution and to the Industrial Group for continuing progress to provide an improvement in overall profits for 1968. Subject to the usual reservations, the year shows promise."

Recording the success of the bid by *Redland Limited* (September 17) for Universal Highways Limited, MR. A. F. F. YOUNG gave this description of the new member of the Redland group:

"Universal Highways Ltd are engaged in the manufacture and laying of all forms of road-marking and have a major share in the application of white lines to roads throughout the country. Their Spray-plastic material, for which they have designed their own laying machines, is being used in increasing quantities, and their licensees in the United States have secured the marking contract for the City of New York with this material. We are confident that there is great scope for profitable expansion in this business both in the United Kingdom and overseas."

At the annual meeting of *Galliford Brindley Limited* (November 5) MR. DOUGLAS H. BRINDLEY said that some months previously the board had been approached by a large Midland quarrying company which had decided to start surfacing work itself to sell Road Surfacing Company Limited. By coincidence, he declared, two main suppliers of raw materials to Road Surfacing Company had recently merged, and it was clear to the board that that subsidiary would be very vulnerable to changed circumstances. A figure fair to both parties having been agreed, he expected that contract for the sale of Road Surfacing Company would be signed in the very near future.

RAILWAYS AND OVERSEAS TRANSPORT

During 1967 further progress was made by the *Canadian Pacific Railway Company*, according to the annual report (*The Times*, April 3). In transportation, the country and the company entered upon a period of adjustment to fundamental changes wrought by the National Transportation Act which was passed in February, 1967. The report stated:

"Among other things now permitted is the offering of unit train and multiple car rates. Canadian Pacific took advantage of this new opportunity and is now handling unit trains of sulphuric acid from Copper Cliff, Ontario, to south-western Ontario. This is the first movement of its kind in North

America for liquids in tank cars. In the environment of intense competition in which we live and which the new Act recognizes, the company's planned marketing approach is a most useful tool. Marketing projects were carried out during the year at the system, region and division levels to increase volume in specific transportation markets."

The most important event in 1967 for the *Antofagasta (Chili) and Bolivia Railway Company Limited* (October 8), according to MR. W. T. CAULFIELD, was the conclusion of the agreement with the Bolivian Government on the compensation payable for the company's properties and investments in Bolivia. While not enthusiastic about the terms, he considered them to be the best that could be obtained, as the following extract from his speech indicates:

"It was a considerable surprise and disappointment to your Board that, when the terms recommended by the Mixed Commission were on the point of acceptance, the Bolivian Government decided that it could not commit the country to annual payments extending over a period of 25 years. Instead, the Government offered the whole of the proceeds of the Trust Fund held in London, and included a number of houses and some land in the City of La Paz which the company was authorized to sell and for which the Government undertook to provide American dollars for remittance.

"If this offer had been refused the negotiations might well have dragged on indefinitely and your Board decided, therefore, after most careful consideration and in consultation with the company's representatives and lawyers in Bolivia that it should be accepted as the best settlement obtainable."

In view of its now preponderant shareholding in *Trans-Zambesia Railway Company Limited* (Lisbon, December 12) and of the fact that the railway's activities were wholly in Portuguese territory, stated MR. VIVIAN L. OURY, the Portuguese Government expressed the wish that the company's head office should be transferred to Lisbon. The necessary consent of the British Treasury having been obtained, he added, all board meetings were now held in Lisbon; and the physical transfer of the company's office from London to the Portuguese capital was nearing completion.

Questions at issue now that the *Lisbon Electric Tramways Limited* (June 26) was entering the last 20 years of its concession were dealt with by MR. ALASTAIR F. ROGER when he stated:

"It is our earnest desire that when we come to the end of the concession there should be handed over to the municipality a surface transport system of which we can all be proud and which one hopes the Municipality will be pleased to take over. We are now at a stage when we must be considering the phased replace-

450

ment of the older buses and also the method by which we are going to expand the bus fleet in the future in order to meet the growing demand of an ever increasing population.

"It is six years since we were asked by the Municipality to revise the existing Contract and agreement on this revision has not yet been reached. It grows increasingly important that we should enter into negotiations with the Authorities concerning the Contract in order that this future expansion and replacement of our older vehicles may be made possible. Continued representation is being made to the Authorities by myself and the General Manager in Portugal, Mr. Richard Wyatt. I have every hope that talks will commence soon which will embrace all the difficulties which we are facing at the present time and which I am sure our eventual successors have no wish to inherit from us. I am confident that, with the goodwill of the Authorities, solutions to the benefit of both the City of Lisbon and the company can be found and agreed."

AIRLINES AND AIRPORTS

At the annual meeting of *Alitalia* (Rome, May 22) DR. NICOLO CARANDINI presided for the last time. He had intimated that he did not wish to seek re-election as chairman, a post which he had held for exactly 20 years. In a tribute to Dr. Carandini the representative of IRI, the majority shareholder, said:

"In twenty years of uninterrupted work at the service of Alitalia, concrete proofs of Dr. Carandini's abilities were abundantly evident. Under his guidance Alitalia rose from a modest domestic airline to the 7th ranking worldwide carrier. This was due in great part to the men of courageous vision and ability who followed the example that he set; and who worked with him in a spirit of self-sacrifice and dedication to the company."

Dr. Carandini was, however, unanimously appointed Honorary Chairman as a mark of recognition of his high abilities, his dedicated honesty and his great personal standing.

The air lines subsidiary of *Canadian Pacific Railway Company* (Montreal, May 1), according to the President, MR. I. D. SINCLAIR, did not have a good first quarter for the current year, for while operating revenues increased, they did not rise sufficiently to counteract the effects of escalating costs. Even with the benefit of rate adjustments, he added, net earnings would probably dip below their 1967 level.

Since the close of the year, stated SIR W. NICHOLAS CAYZER, *The British & Commonwealth Shipping Company Limited* (July 24) had acquired the air transport activities of the Air Holdings Group, in which it had and continued to have a 46 per cent interest. He

added that it was hoped that as a result of the Edwards Committee of Inquiry into Civil Aviation it would be recognized that the well-managed independent air line could be complementary to the national corporations. Although B.U.A. was expected to make a loss in 1968, he took a more hopeful view of 1969, and with the interest in helicopters he thought they had a balance which over the years would make a contribution to the future of the group.

MR. W. S. PHILIPPS disclosed in his review for *Court Line Limited* (June 27) that the subsidiary Autair International Airways Limited had much reduced its loss for the year, even although the modernization of its fleet had not been completed. The swing round in results was now being achieved; the company was now equipped with its planned fleet of aircraft; and the board expected a substantial growth in profits from this member of the group.

After revealing that *The Thomson Organisation Limited* now held 20 per cent of the market for inclusive air holidays and was in fact the largest operator in the field, LORD THOMSON OF FLEET made these comments (*The Times*, May 1):

"In our 1967 activities we decided to continue with our growth programme even at the cost of some reduction in profitability: this policy trims margins in the short run, but strengthens our position for future development.

"Britannia Airways' fleet of Bristol Britannia 102s operated at a high level of utilization throughout the summer. Following devaluation we reviewed the decision to augment the fleet by the acquisition of four Boeing 737 short-haul jets, but it was clear that this aircraft would still be more efficient and economical than any alternative. Two of these new aircraft are being delivered this summer, and the next two in the spring of 1969: they are expected to make a marked increase in the profitability of the line."

The report (*The Times*, September 11) by MR. PETER G. MASE-FIELD for the *British Airports Authority* recorded solid progress in the development of its business, and gave figures to show that its second year had been a period of expansion and of sound commercial advance. He went on to comment on the problems of growth and of noise which were common to most airports all over the world and which had run like a thread through all the activities of the Authority during the year. He also made these statements about the projected third airport to serve London and about the expected rapid growth of air cargo traffic:

"They [the problems above mentioned] have underlined the need for a further major airport to serve London and to relieve congestion and noise—and, later, saturation—at Heathrow and Gatwick, and they have led to the Government's decision to hold a new Inquiry. The Authority welcomes the work of the

Commission under Mr Justice Roskill on the Third London Airport and it will offer every assistance to it.

"In the current year—1968/69—the, undoubtedly temporary, reduction in the rate of growth of air traffic into and out of the United Kingdom continues, as a result, primarily, of restrictions on travel currency. This drop in the rate of increase does not apply, however, to air cargo traffic which continues to increase at a rate which is doubling the traffic every four years. The new Cargo Area of 160 acres at Heathrow, to be completed in 1969, will become one of the World's great centres for international trade. Estimates show that it will be handling more than £2,000m. value of airborne goods per annum by the early 1970's. On this, as in other ways, the Authority is working closely with the 80 airlines which operate through its airports."

In his statement (*The Times*, January 16) for *Westland Aircraft Limited* SIR ERIC MENSFORTH referred to the activities of British Hovercraft Corporation, saying that hovercraft had not yet reached the profit-earning stage; this was because of the need to incur and write off substantial private venture expenditure. As to the future, results from hovercraft sales were difficult to forecast as they would be greatly influenced by the then forthcoming trials of the SR.N4. He did state, however, that any new orders for such craft could well result in sizeable recoveries of past private venture expenditure at an early date.

PERSONAL INDEX

A

Aberconway, Lord, 91, 110, 118, 241, 286, 292, 293, 371, 399, 401, 442
Acutt, Sir K., 341
Adams, F., 309
Addinsell, J., 348
Adeane, Sir R., 9, 148
Adorian, P., 301
Aldington, Lord, 37, 126, 141, 169, 201, 274
Allen, A. W., 355
Allen, Sir P., 103, 115, 254
Amory, Lord, 110, 209, 376, 417
Anderson, C. B., 191, 340
Anderson, Sir D., 390
Anderson, J., 89, 130
Anderson, P. H., 158, 220, 338, 351
Andrews, A. E., 173
Angell, O. D., 279
Annetts, J., 100
Ashenheim, Sir N., 211
Ashton, M. L., 320
Asprey, P. R., 416
Atherton, T., 108
Attwood, H. R., 364
Aykroyd, H. H., 430

B

Bache, G. S., 255
Backhouse, J., 68
Bacon, Sir E., 228
Bailey, I. M., 262
Bainbridge, F. & H., 249
Baker, A. I., 292
Baker, B., 411
Baker, V. G., 375
Balfour, Earl of, 184, 331
Banks, Sir J. G., 144
Barber, W. J., 279
Barber-Lomax, J. G., 186
Barclay, T. D., 53, 64, 199
Barker, H. P., 149
Barlow, B. S., 448
Barlow, C. S., 191
Barlow, Sir J. D., 76
Barlow, T. B., 378
Barnes, S. J., 359
Barnes, Sir W. G., 431
Barnetson, W. D., 177
Barnett, Sir G., 173
Barr, J. M., 302
Barran, D. H., 18, 86, 115, 368, 373
Barrett-Lennard, Sir R., 29
Barron, D. J., 1, 83, 124, 210, 212, 311, 388
Beatty, A. C., 208, 209, 342, 346, 350, 351, 370
Beck, E. C., 138, 193, 239, 249, 284
Bell, C. W., 15, 128, 423
Bell, H. P., 30
Bell, J., 240
Bell, Sir S., 49
Benham, C. M., 276
Benn, A., 433
Benn, G., 79
Benn, Sir J., 59, 112
Berens, H. C. B., 318
Berisford, A., 16
Bibby, H. M., 101
Biggart, W. G., 135, 162
Biggs, G., 70
Binny, J. A. F., 13
Biss, G. C. d'A., 187, 274, 306
Black, Sir C., 251
Blair, A. C., 9, 11
Blair-Cunynghame, J. O., 26
Bland, Sir T., 83, 312
Blanning, R. E., 308
Bolding, J. F., 100
Bolton, Sir G., 36, 195
Bonar, Sir H. V., 273
Bonser, F., 293
Booth, J. F., 153
Bostock, J., 415
Bowthorpe, J., 161
Brangwin, K. C., 88
Brecon, Lord, 99, 294
Bridgeman, Sir M., 75, 257, 368, 372
Brierley, P. R., 102
Briggs, Sir G., 17, 87, 334
Briggs, N. W., 91, 448
Brindley, D. H., 449
Brockhouse, J., 4
Brook, F. V., 356
Brook, R. E., 34, 98, 239, 266
Brookes, R. P., 288, 333
Brooks, R. C., 61, 143
Brough, R. A., 437
Broughton, W., 138
Brown, Sir D., 399
Brown, Sir J., 16
Brown, M. G. H., 41
Browne, G. R., 135
Buchanan, J. J., 35
Buckton, Lord, 177, 190
Buist, C., 118, 171
Bullock, Sir C., 132
Burman, Sir C., 369, 448
Burman, S. F., 360
Burnett, Sir D. H., 402
Bussell, D., 4
Butler, A. C., 43
Butler, R. F., 106, 361
Butlin, R. F., 302

C

Cadbury, A., 311
Caffyn, S. M., 363
Cahen d'Anvers, Comte G., 419
Calder, R. K., 360
Calver, J. W. A., 381
Calvert, E. B., 262
Cann, D. C., 63, 65, 67
Cantor, C., 407
Capper, W. P., 88
Carandini, N., 451
Carlisle, K. R. M., 310
Carnwath, A. H., 235
Carr, R. E., 91, 124, 305
Carr, Sir W., 93
Carrington, Lord, 40
Cary, Sir R., 448
Cashmore, N., 335
Castell, W. G., 101, 107, 219, 426, 428
Caulfield, W. T., 450
Cayzer, Sir W. N., 391, 451
Cecil-Wright, J. P., 272
Chamberlain, W. R. F., 194
Chancellor, Sir C., 17, 108, 218, 263
Channing, H. J. T., 240
Chaplin, F. L., 14, 116, 137, 407
Chester, R. P., 88
Chiesman, C. S., 406
Chinn, N. & R., 364
Clague, J. D., 204
Clare, J. D., 343
Clarfelt, J. G., 225
Clarke, D. R. N., 12, 224, 321
Clarke, G. P., 332
Clarke, J. D., 172
Clarke, L. H., 69
Clay, J. M., 182, 329, 370
Clayson, Sir E., 5
Cleary, F. E., 236
Clegg, Sir C. B., 24
Clifford, Sir M., 207
Clitheroe, Lord, 1
Clore, C., 404
Clough, A. J., 135
Clough, H. P., 426
Clyne, J. V., 439
Coghlan, P. B. L., 381
Cohen, Sir J., 409
Cohen, J. S., 232

456

COMPANY MEETING REPORTS

published in THE TIMES during the year

1968

Figures in parentheses are page references to the companies.

461

462

466

COMPANY MEETING REPORTS

COMPANY MEETING REPORTS

	Date of publication		*Date of publication*

United British Securities Trust Ltd. .. Sept. 20
United Builders Merchants Ltd. .. May 20
United Carriers Ltd. (441) .. .. .. June 20
United City Merchants Ltd... .. Dec. 21
United Dominions Trust Group (48) .. Sept. 5
United Drapery Stores Ltd. (117, 151, 405).. July 10
United Kingdom Property Co. Ltd. .. Oct. 18
United Kingdom Provident Institution (59, 112) .. .. Apr. 25
United Merchants & Manufacturers Inc., New York .. .. Nov. 19
United Newspapers Ltd. (177) .. .. May 6
United Real Property Trust Ltd. .. .. Nov. 28
United Spring Co. Ltd. (100) .. .. Feb. 26
United States & General Trust Corpn. Ltd. Mar. 14
United States Debenture Corpn. Ltd. .. Mar. 12
United Transport Co. Ltd. (206, 210, 442, 447) .. .. Aug. 8
Universal Grinding Wheel Group Holdings Ltd. (156) .. .. Dec. 18
Universal Printers Ltd. .. .. .. May 31
Utilico N.V. .. .. Aug. 29

V

Vaal Reefs Exploration & Mining Co. Ltd... Apr. 10
Vale & Sons Ltd., Thomas (164) .. .. Sept. 27
Valor Co. Ltd... .. .. .. Apr. 5
Van Dyk Consolidated Mines Ltd. .. May 17
Van Moppes & Sons Ltd., L. M. (111, 150) Aug. 9
Vantona Ltd. .. .. Oct. 7
Vaux & Associated Breweries Ltd. (178, 313, 328) .. .. Sept. 23
Venner Ltd. .. .. Jan. 8
Vereeniging Estates Ltd. .. .. May 2
Vereeniging Refractories Ltd. .. .. Mar. 28
Vickers Ltd. (167, 289) .. .. May 16
Victory Insurance Co. Ltd. .. .. June 24
Viyella International Ltd. (127, 420) .. June 13
Vokes Group Ltd. .. .. .. Sept. 20
Volkswagenwerk AG. (366) .. .. Aug. 21
Voltas Ltd. (201) .. .. .. Feb. 22
Vosper Ltd. (399) .. .. .. Dec. 13

W

W.G.I. Ltd. .. .. July 5
Waagner-Biro AG. (296) .. .. Sept. 5
Wadkin Ltd. .. .. .. May 22
Wagon Repairs Ltd. (294) .. .. Sept. 27
Walker & Martin Ltd. (50) .. .. June 27
Walker Crossweller & Co. Ltd. (136) .. July 5
Walker Goldsmith & Silversmith Ltd., James Jan. 18
Walker Holdings Ltd., C. & W. (122) .. July 12
Wallace & Sons Ltd., John .. .. Sept. 3
Waller & Hartley Ltd. (312).. .. May 27
Walmsley (Bury) Group Ltd. (295) .. Oct. 16
Ward & Goldstone Ltd. .. .. Aug. 30
Ward Holdings Ltd., George (83, 178, 186) Oct. 9
Ward Ltd., Thos. W. (244, 332) .. Nov. 30
Wardle & Co. Ltd., Bernard.. .. Apr. 2
Wardle Group, Arthur (240).. .. Mar. 29
Warne (Holdings) Ltd., William .. June 12
Warne, Wright & Rowland Ltd. (272) .. May 9
Warnford Investments Ltd. .. .. Sept. 27
Warrington & Sons Ltd., Thomas (239) May 27
Warwick Engineering Investments Ltd. .. Sept. 30
Waterfall Holdings Ltd. .. .. Nov. 19
Watney Mann Ltd. (131, 312, 319, 327) .. {Jan. 4 / Dec. 5
Watney Mann Property Co. Ltd. .. Nov. 21
Webster & Sons Ltd., Samuel (315) .. Apr. 2
Weir Holdings Ltd., G. & J. (242) .. May 7
Welkom Gold Mining Co. Ltd. .. Jan. 3
Wellcome Foundation Ltd. (258) .. Feb. 1
Wellman Engineering Corpn. Ltd. (334) Oct. 4
Wesleyan & General Insurance Society .. Apr. 11

West Cumberland Silk Mills Ltd. (422) .. Sept. 25
West Rand Investment Trust Ltd. (341) .. May 3
West Riding Worsted & Woollen Mills Ltd. (123, 182, 424) .. .. .. Feb. 22
West Witwatersrand Areas Ltd. (340) .. Oct. 18
Western Areas Gold Mining Co. Ltd. .. Apr. 3
Western Credit Ltd. (50) .. .. Oct. 31
Western Deep Levels Ltd. .. .. Apr. 10
Western Dooars Tea Holdings Ltd. (80, 384) Oct. 7
Western Ground Rents Ltd. (235) .. .. June 26
Western Holdings Ltd. .. .. Jan. 3
Western Reefs Exploration & Development Co. Ltd. .. .. Apr. 10
Westinghouse Brake & Signal Co. Ltd. (292) Feb. 27
Westland Aircraft Ltd. (283, 453) .. .. Jan. 16
Westminster Bank Ltd. (24) .. .. {Jan. 22 / Feb. 15
Weston-Evans (Holdings) Ltd. .. Aug. 16
Weyburn Engineering Co. Ltd. .. Feb. 5
Wharf Holdings Ltd... .. .. May 24
Whatlings Ltd. (286) .. .. May 24
Wheelock Marden & Co. Ltd. (204) .. Nov. 8
Whessoe Ltd. (132, 170, 273) .. July 5
Wheway Watson Ltd. (135, 162) .. Sept. 6
Whitbread & Co. Ltd. (82, 130, 146, 192, 222, 313, 319) .. .. .. Aug. 13
Whitecroft Industrial Holdings Ltd. (288) July 4
Whites & Taylors Ltd., Timothy (409) .. May 3
Whittingham (Holdings) Ltd., William .. Mar. 22
Wigfall & Son Ltd., Henry (190, 417) .. Oct. 8
Wiggins & Sons Ltd., C. S. (240) .. Oct. 14
Wiggins Teape Ltd. (263) .. .. June 19
Wiles Group Ltd. .. .. .. Oct. 31
Wilkins & Mitchell Ltd. (280, 288) .. Sept. 11
Wilkinson Sword Ltd. .. .. Apr. 24
Williams & Humbert Ltd. (318) .. May 16
Williams Deacon's Bank Ltd. (25) .. {Jan. 24 / Dec. 2
Williams Hudson Ltd. (98) .. .. July 9
Williamson Tea Holdings Ltd. .. Sept. 13
Wilmot-Breeden (Holdings) Ltd. (359) .. May 30
Wilson Bros. Ltd. .. .. .. Aug. 21
Wilson Lovatt & Sons Ltd. (150) .. June 18
Wilson, Smith & Sutcliffe Ltd. (428) .. Oct. 26
Wimpey & Co. Ltd., George (171, 236, 284) Apr. 11
Windsors (Sporting Investments) Ltd. (415) Oct. 25
Wingate Investments Ltd. .. .. Oct. 3
Winkelhaak Mines Ltd. .. .. May 18
Winn Industries Group (124) .. .. May 13
Winterbotham, Strachan & Playne Ltd. (128) July 26
Witan Investments Co. Ltd. .. .. July 23
Wolseley-Hughes Ltd. .. .. Dec. 12
Wolstenholme Bronze Powders Ltd. (110) .. May 7
Wombwell Foundry & Engineering Co. Ltd. Nov. 28
Woodall-Duckham Group Ltd. .. Apr. 19
Woodhead & Sons Ltd., Jonas (122) .. July 29
Woolwich Equitable Building Society (252) Dec. 18
Woolworth & Co. Ltd., F. W. (14, 116, 137, 407) .. .. Feb. 15
Worth & Sons Ltd., Thomas Bond (431) .. Sept. 17
Worthington-Simpson Ltd. .. .. May 30
Wright & Green (Holdings) Ltd. (311) .. Sept. 21
Wrighton & Sons (Associated Co.s) Ltd., F. (108) .. .. Aug. 29
Wykes (Leicester) Ltd., E. .. .. Feb. 27

Y

Yarrow & Co. Ltd. (271, 399) .. .. Dec. 6
Yatton Furniture Ltd. (4) .. .. Sept. 26
York County Savings Bank (30) .. Jan. 11
Yorkshire Fine Woollen Spinners Ltd. (424) May 13
Young (Motors) Ltd., H. (365) .. .. Mar. 18

Z

Zambian Anglo American Ltd. (341) .. Dec. 18

471

Printed in Great Britain
by Richard Clay (The Chaucer Press), Ltd.,
Bungay, Suffolk.